Technology and Capital Formation

Technology and Capital Formation

edited by Dale W. Jorgenson
and Ralph Landau

The MIT Press
Cambridge, Massachusetts
London, England

This book was set in Palatino by Chiron Inc., Cambridge, Massachusetts, and printed and bound by Halliday Lithograph in the United States of America.

Library of Congress Cataloging-in-Publication Data

Technology and capital formation / edited by Dale W. Jorgenson and Ralph Landau

   p.   cm.
   Includes bibliographies and index.
   ISBN 0–262–10039–8
   1. Technological innovations—Economic aspects—Congresses.
2. Saving and investment—Congresses.   3. Capital—Congresses.
I. Jorgenson, Dale Weldeau, 1933–.   II. Landau, Ralph.
HC79.T4T4377 1989   88–12954
338′.06—dc19   CIP

Contents

Preface   vii

1   Capital as a Factor of Production   1
    Dale W. Jorgenson

2   The Application of a Hedonic Model to a Quality-Adjusted Price
    Index for Computer Processors   37
    Ellen R. Dulberger

3   The Postwar Evolution of Computer Prices   77
    Robert J. Gordon

4   Price and Technological Change in a Capital Good: A Survey of
    Research on Computers   127
    Jack E. Triplett

    Comments on Chapter 3 (Gordon)   215
    Rosanne Cole, Ellen R. Dulberger, and Jack E. Triplett

    Comment on Chapter 4 (Triplett) and Rejoinder to the Cole-
    Dulberger-Triplett Comments   221
    Robert J. Gordon

5   Energy, Obsolescence, and the Productivity Slowdown   225
    Charles R. Hulten, James W. Robertson, and Frank C. Wykoff

6   Economic Depreciation and the User Cost of Business-Leased Automobiles   259
Frank C. Wykoff

7   Construction Price Statistics Revisited   293
Paul Pieper

8   Rates of Return and Capital Aggregation Using Alternative Rental Prices   331
Michael J. Harper, Ernst R. Berndt, and David O. Wood

9   The Market Valuation of Credit Market Debt   373
John S. Strong

10 Capital in the U.S. Postal Service   409
Dianne C. Christensen, Laurits R. Christensen, Carl G. Degen, and Philip E. Schoech

11 New Estimates of Federal Government Tangible Capital and Net Investment   451
Michael J. Boskin, Marc S. Robinson, and John M. Roberts

12 Technology and Capital Formation   485
Ralph Landau

List of Contributors   506

Author Index   509

Subject Index   513

Preface

This book reports the proceedings of the Conference on Technology and Capital Formation held at the John F. Kennedy School of Government, Harvard University, on November 7–9, 1986. The conference was sponsored by the Program on Technology and Economic Policy at the Kennedy School and had the objectives of reviewing current research and developing an agenda for future research on the interrelationships of technology and capital formation. The participants included policy analysts from universities, business, and government and reflected an unusually broad range of perspectives on the issues.

The primary focus of the conference was on assessment of the role of capital in the production process. An overview of previous research on this problem is presented by Dale Jorgenson in his introductory essay to the volume. The existence of a perpetual inventory of capital goods of different "vintages," corresponding to investments at different points of time, provides the framework for research on capital formation and its economic impact. For example, this inventory provides the empirical basis for assessing the role of investment in the national product and measuring the impact of capital on the growth of the national output.

The practical problem that arises in implementing the perpetual inventory approach is to combine data for the different types of capital goods and different vintages of each type into summary measures that reflect the economically relevant aspects of capital formation. The solution to this problem involves characterizing the relative efficiencies of the different capital goods in terms of observable characteristics like age, size, and performance. Implementation of this solution requires a detailed representation of the technology for using each type of capital. The results are embodied in a rapidly expanding body of empirical research that has greatly increased the economic understanding of technology.

A dramatic illustration of the power of the relative efficiency approach is provided by recent research on the evolution of computer prices. This volume presents two important studies of the very extensive body of empirical evidence on computer prices by Robert Gordon and by Ellen Dulberger. The volume also contains an unusually detailed and comprehensive review of the economic literature on the problem by Jack Triplett. Triplett also discusses the important issues that arise in applying the results of this research to the measurement of capital formation in the U.S. national product accounts.

Computer prices have declined very rapidly since the introduction of commercial computers in the 1950s. This decline has resulted in a steady increase in the proportion of capital formation devoted to computers and associated peripheral equipment. Both engineers and economists have attempted to assess the decline in computer prices. Dulberger reports on her own research as part of an interdisciplinary team at IBM. An unusual private-public sector collaboration between IBM and the Bureau of Economic Analysis at the U.S. Department of Commerce has led to new measures of capital formation through investment in computers in the official U.S. national product accounts.

Robert Gordon presents an investigation of computer prices that has many of the same objectives as Dulberger's research. As in any extensive empirical research program, a wide range of alternative approaches can be considered. Comparisons between the results of Dulberger and Gordon, the detailed and perspicacious review of the literature by Triplett, and the exchange of views among Rosanne Cole, Dulberger, Triplett, and Gordon over the unresolved issues provide an unusual glimpse of the internal workings of the process of empirical research in economics. Important progress takes place through the interchange of ideas among proponents of competing viewpoints.

Research on computer prices requires the comparison of new and old computer models in order to assess their relative efficiencies. However, existing models of capital goods decline in efficiency with age. A very important issue in capital measurement is the assessment of the relative efficiencies of old and new vintages of capital goods. Charles Hulten, James Robertson, and Frank Wykoff discuss the latest results in an ongoing research program, initiated more than a decade ago by Hulten and Wykoff.

The energy crisis of the 1970s was associated with a slowdown in the growth of productivity. An explanation of the slowdown advanced by many investigators is that old capital goods have deteriorated in terms of efficiency relative to new capital goods, as a consequence of higher energy prices. Hulten, Robertson, and Wykoff test this hypothesis empirically and find no evidence of this deterioration in a very substantial body of empirical evidence on the prices of assets of different ages. Accordingly, they reject deterioration in the efficiency of older capital goods as an important explanation of the slowdown in productivity growth.

The work of Hulten, Robertson, and Wykoff substantiates the approach to capital measurement based on stable relative efficiencies of new and older vintages of capital. Their results provide additional evidence on these relative efficiencies for a wide range of assets. Wykoff, by himself, presents an analysis of an unusually rich data base on business-leased automobiles, which comprise an important part of capital formation and make up a substantial proportion of the U.S. capital stock.

The research on the evolution of computer prices by Gordon, Dulberger, and Triplett and the studies of relative efficiencies of new and old capital goods by Hulten, Robertson, and Wykoff focus on technologies involving the use of producers' durable equipment. Paul Pieper reviews the available measures of the prices of structures, which are a product of the construction industry and an input in the form of capital services into virtually all industrial sectors of the economy. Pieper shows that the relative efficiency approach, which has proved so successful in representing technologies for different types of equipment, can also be applied to technologies involving structures.

The rate of return is a critical element in linking capital formation to expansion of productive capacity. The rate of return is essential in converting the price of an asset, like a computer or a building, into the price of a capital service, like the use of a computer or a building for a given period of time. The rate of return represents the time value of the use of capital assets. Michael Harper, Ernst, Berndt, and David Wood review alternative approaches to measuring the rate of return and assess these approaches as solutions to the problem of converting asset prices into service prices in the measurement of capital.

Many measurements of the rate of return involve comparisons of a flow of property income with the value of a stock of assets. Assets can be assessed in terms of the values of capital goods of different ages. An alternative approach is to use the value of debt and equity claims on the assets of an enterprise or an industrial sector to value these assets. These claims can be "priced out" in the financial markets, just as assets can be evaluated in the markets for new capital goods. The resulting asset values can be used in measuring rates of return.

John Strong presents a comprehensive new data set on the value of debt claims in U.S. financial markets, including all of the types of claims that are compiled as part of the national balance sheets. These balance sheets are regularly reported as part of the U.S. flow of funds accounts. Much of the available data on the value of debt claims reflects book values rather than market values. With rapid changes in interest rates, the book values diverge sharply from market values, resulting in serious distortions on measures of the rate of return based on the value of financial claims.

While much of the interest in capital formation is focused on the private sector, recent research has increasingly recognized the important role of capital formation in the public sector. Dianne and Laurits Christensen, Carl Degen, and Philip Schoech report on the application of new methods for capital measurement to detailed accounting data for the largest government enterprise in the United States, namely, the U.S. Postal Service.

Michael Boskin, Marc Robinson, and John Roberts provide comprehensive estimates of federal government capital formation and capital stock in the form of tangible assets. These data are fully comparable with the estimates for the private sector produced by the perpetual inventory method. An important feature of the estimates of Boskin, Robinson, and Roberts is that they successfully exploit the latest available information on the relative efficiencies of capital goods of different vintages.

The extensive body of empirical research reported in this volume provides overwhelming evidence of the fruitfulness of the perpetual inventory method for capital measurement. This evidence strongly supports the focus of recent research on the determination of relative efficiencies of different capital goods. These relative efficiencies make it possible to summarize the economically relevant features of the vast and heterogeneous collection of capital goods that make up the inventory of capital in an advanced industrial economy like the United States.

The efforts of many investigators, including the contributors to this volume, have produced a wealth of empirical data on capital goods prices. These data have been analyzed by increasingly rigorous methods that make it possible to represent technologies in a more detailed and more satisfactory way. The successful implementation of these methods requires the understanding of technology from both engineering and economic points of view. These viewpoints have been successfully combined, most strikingly in the analysis of the evolution of computer prices. A new and powerful approach to generating economic knowledge about technology has come into existence.

The research reported in this volume has generated important new findings on technology and capital formation. These findings are often surprising, differing sharply from ideas that have achieved acceptance among policy analysts in the absence of careful analysis of the empirical evidence. Important gaps in our understanding of the role of capital in the U.S. economy are rapidly being overcome. The results of recent research are now finding their way into the official statistics that provide quantitative measures of performance used in the analysis of alternative economic policies.

New knowledge generates controversy as older perspectives give way to better understanding. Ralph Landau documents the vigorous debate that took place at the conference itself, both at the sessions reporting original research and at a series of roundtable discussions on the implications of the new research on technology and capital formation. Landau emphasizes the close interrelationship between the introduction of new technology and the formation of capital. Comprehension of the implications of this interrelationship is crucial to successful policy applications of the research reported in this volume.

While recognizing that a great deal has been accomplished in improving our understanding of the role of capital in the U.S. economy, Landau identifies important new issues for future research. Substantial progress in the measurement of capital suggests that the time is ripe for a reassessment of the role of capital formation in U.S. economic growth. The new assessment will undoubtedly have important implications for the formulation of economic policies to revive economic growth and enhance the living standard of all Americans.

Technology and Capital Formation

1 Capital as a Factor of Production

Dale W. Jorgenson

In the intertemporal theory of production the outputs and inputs are distinguished by point of time in the production process. For example, an hour of labor today and an hour of labor tomorrow are treated as different inputs. Given this interpretation, the intertemporal theory of production is formally analogous to the atemporal theory, as demonstrated by Fisher (1961), Hicks (1946), Lindahl (1939), and Malinvaud (1961). However, the number of outputs and inputs required for the intertemporal theory may be very large.

The special character of the intertemporal theory of production arises from a more detailed specification of technology. The most important specialization arises from the introduction of capital as a factor of production. Although the central concepts of capital theory—capital assets, capital services, and investment—are not essential to the theory of production, they provide additional structure that permits a more precise characterization of producer behavior at different points of time.

1.1 Aggregation over Vintages

The distinguishing feature of capital as a factor of production is that durable goods contribute services to production at different points of time. The capital services provided by a given durable good are proportional to the initial investment. We can refer to durable goods acquired at different points of time as different *vintages* of capital. The services provided by different vintages at the same point of time are perfect substitutes.[1]

1.1.1   Relative Efficiency

The flow of capital services is a quantity index of capital inputs from durable goods of different vintages. Under perfect substitutability among the services of durable goods of different vintages, the flow of capital services is a weighted sum of past investments. The weights correspond to the relative efficiencies of the different vintages of capital.

The durable goods model of production is characterized by price-quantity duality. The rental price of capital input is a price index corresponding to the quantity index given by the flow of capital services. The rental prices for all vintages of capital are proportional to the price index for capital input. The constants of proportionality are given by the relative efficiencies of the different vintages of capital.[2]

In the durable goods model of production the relative efficiency of a capital good depends on the age of the good and not on the time it is acquired. Replacement requirements are determined by losses in efficiency of existing capital goods as well as by actual physical disappearance or retirement of capital goods. When a capital good is retired its relative efficiency drops to zero.

The relative efficiencies of capital goods of different ages can be described by a sequence of nonnegative numbers:[3]

$$d_0, d_1, \dots. \tag{1}$$

We normalize the relative efficiency of a new capital good at unity and we assume that relative efficiency is nonincreasing, so that:

$$d_0 = 1, \qquad d_\tau - d_{\tau-1} \geqq 0 \qquad (\tau = 0, 1, \dots).$$

We also assume that every capital good is eventually retired or scrapped so that relative efficiency eventually drops to zero:

$$\lim_{\tau \to \infty} d_\tau = 0.$$

As illustrations of patterns decline in relative efficiency, we can consider "one-hoss shay," straight-line, and declining balance patterns. In the one-hoss shay pattern, efficiency is constant over the lifetime of the capital good. Where T is the lifetime, relative efficiency is given by

$$d_\tau = \begin{cases} 1 & (\tau = 0, 1, \dots, T-1) \\ 0 & \text{otherwise.} \end{cases}$$

In the straight-line pattern efficiency declines linearly over the lifetime of the capital good:

$$d_\tau = \begin{cases} 1 - \dfrac{\tau}{T} & (\tau = 0,\ 1,...,\ T-1) \\[2mm] 0 & \text{otherwise.} \end{cases}$$

In the declining balance pattern efficiency declines geometrically:

$$d_\tau = (1-\delta)^\tau \qquad (\tau = 0,\ 1,\ ...\ ).$$

These patterns of decline in efficiency represent alternative specifications of technology in the durable goods model of production.

1.1.2   Investment and Capital Services

Investment represents the acquisition of capital goods at a given point of time. The quantity of investment is measured in the same way as the durable goods themselves. For example, investment in equipment is the number of machines of a given specification and investment in structures is the number of buildings of a particular description. The price of acquisition of a durable good is the unit cost of acquiring a piece of equipment or a structure.

By contrast with investment, capital services are measured in terms of the use of a durable good for a stipulated period of time. For example, a building can be leased for a period of years, an automobile can be rented for a number of days or weeks, and computer time can be purchased in seconds or minutes. The price of the services of a durable good is the unit cost of using the good for a specified period. In the durable goods model of production, capital input plays a role that is analogous to that of any other input.

We can develop notation appropriate for the intertemporal theory of production by denoting the quantity of output at time t by y_t and the quantities of J inputs at time t by x_{jt} ($j = 1,\ 2\ ...\ J$). Similarly, we can denote the price of output at time t by q_t and the prices of the J inputs at time t by p_{jt} ($j = 1,\ 2\ ...\ J$). In order to characterize capital as a factor of production, we require the following additional notation:

A_t: quantity of capital goods acquired at time t,

$K_{t,\tau}$: quantity of capital services from capital goods of age τ at time t.

$p_{A,t}$: price of acquisition of new capital goods at time t,

$p_{K,t,\tau}$: rental price of capital services from capital goods of age τ at time t.

To present the durable goods model of production we first represent technology by means of a production function, say F. We assume that the production function is homothetically separable in the services of different vintages of capital:[4]

$$y_t = F[G(K_{t,0}, K_{t,1},..., K_{t,\tau} \, ... \,), x_{2t},..., x_{Jt}, t].$$ (2)

Where K_t is the flow of capital services, we can represent this quantity index of capital input as follows:

$$K_t = G \, ,$$

where the function G is homogeneous of degree one in the services from capital goods of different ages.

If we assume that the quantity index of capital input K_t is characterized by perfect substitutability among the services of different vintages of capital, we can write this index as the sum of these services:

$$K_t = \sum_{\tau=0}^{\infty} K_{t,\tau} \, .$$

Under the additional assumption that the services provided by a durable good are proportional to initial investment in this good, we can express the quantity index of capital input in the form

$$K_t = \sum_{\tau=0}^{\infty} d_\tau A_{t-\tau} \, .$$ (3)

The flow of capital services is a weighted sum of past investments with weights given by the relative efficiencies $\{d_\tau\}$ of capital goods of different ages.

1.1.3 Duality

Under constant returns to scale, we can express the price of output as a function, say Q, of the prices of all inputs. We can refer to this as the price function for the producing unit. The price function is homothetically separable in the rental prices of different vintages of capital:[5]

$$q_t = Q[P(p_{K,t,0}, p_{K,t,1},..., p_{K,t,\tau,} \, ... \,), p_{2t},..., p_{Jt}, t].$$ (4)

Where $p_{K,t}$ is a price index of capital services, we can represent this index as follows:

$$p_{K,t} = P,$$

where the function P is homogeneous of degree one in the rental prices of capital goods of different ages.

Under perfect substitutability among the services of different vintages of capital, we can write the price index of capital input P as the price of the services of a new capital good:

$$p_{K,t} = p_{K,t,0}.$$

Under the additional assumption that the services provided by a durable good are proportional to the initial investment, we can express the rental prices of capital goods of different ages in the form

$$p_{K,t,\tau} = d_\tau \, p_{K,t} \qquad (\tau = 0, 1, \dots). \tag{5}$$

The rental prices are proportional to the rental price of capital input with constants of proportionality given by the relative efficiencies $\{d_\tau\}$ of capital goods of different ages.

Given the quantity of capital input K_t, representing the flow of capital services, and the price of capital input $p_{K,t}$, representing the rental price, capital input plays the same role in production as any other input. In section 1.2 we outline a vintage accounting system for deriving the prices and quantities of capital inputs from the prices and quantities for acquisition of durable goods $p_{A,t}$ and A_t. In section 1.3 we present econometric methods for describing the durable goods model of technology in terms of relative efficiencies $\{d_\tau\}$. In section 1.4 we compare alternative measures of capital input employed in recent studies of productivity.

1.2   Replacement and Depreciation

In this section we present the theory of replacement and depreciation and its application to the measurement of the price and quantity of capital input. At each point of time durable goods decline in efficiency, giving rise to needs for *replacement* in order to maintain productivity capacity. Similarly, the price of a durable good declines with age. The *depreciation* reflects both the current decline in efficiency and the present value of future declines in efficiency.

The measurement of replacement is required in order to determine the quantity of capital input. The measurement of depreciation is required in order to determine the price of capital input. In the full price-quantity duality that characterizes the theory of replacement and depreciation, capital stock corresponds to the acquisition price of durable goods and investment corresponds to rental price of capital services.

1.2.1 Mortality

Capital goods decline in efficiency at each point of time, giving rise to needs for replacement to maintain productive capacity. The proportion of an investment to be replaced during the τth period after its acquisition is equal to the decline in efficiency during that period. We refer to the decline in relative efficiency as the mortality distribution of a capital good, say m_τ, where

$$m_\tau = -(d_\tau - d_{\tau-1}) \qquad (\tau = 1, 2, \ldots) .$$ (6)

By our assumption that relative efficiency is nonincreasing, the mortality distribution may be represented by a sequence of nonnegative numbers:

$m_1, m_2, \ldots ,$

where

$$\sum_{\tau=1}^{\infty} m_\tau = \sum_{\tau=1}^{\infty} (d_{\tau-1} - d_t) = d_0 = 1 .$$

For the patterns of decline in efficiency considered in section 1.1.1, above, we can derive the corresponding mortality distributions. If efficiency is constant over the lifetime of the capital good, the mortality distribution is zero except for period T:

$$m_T = 1 .$$

For linear decline in efficiency the mortality distribution is constant throughout the lifetime of the capital good:

$$m_\tau = \frac{1}{T} \qquad (\tau = 1, 2, \ldots, T) .$$

For geometric decline in efficiency the mortality distribution declines geometrically:

$$m_\tau = \delta(1-\delta)^{\tau-1} \qquad (\tau = 0,\ 1,\ \dots)\ .$$

1.2.2 Replacement

Replacement requirements can be expressed in terms of the mortality distribution for capital goods. Requirements can also be expressed in terms of the proportion of an initial investment replaced τ periods after the initial acquisition. This proportion includes replacement of the initial investment and subsequent replacements of each succeeding replacement. We refer to the sequence of these proportions as the replacement distribution of a capital good; each coefficient, say δ_τ, is the rate of replacement of an investment replaced τ periods after initial acquisition.

The sequence of replacement rates $\{\delta_\tau\}$ can be computed recursively for the sequence of mortality rates $\{m_\tau\}$. The proportion of an initial investment replaced at time v and again at time $\tau > v$ is $m_v\,\delta_{\tau-v}$. The proportion of the stock replaced in the τth period is the sum of proportions replaced first in periods $1, 2, \dots$, and later at period τ; hence,

$$\delta_\tau = m_1\delta_{\tau-1} + m_2\delta_{\tau-2} + \cdots + m_\tau\delta_0 \qquad (\tau = 1,\ 2,\ \dots)\ . \tag{7}$$

This equation is referred to as the renewal equation.[6]

For constant relative efficiency over the lifetime of a capital good, the replacement distribution is periodic with period equal to the lifetime of the capital good:

$$\delta_\tau = 1 \qquad (\tau = T,\ 2T,\ \dots)\ .$$

For linear decline in efficiency, the replacement distribution may be represented in the form

$$\delta_1 = \frac{1}{T}\ ,$$

$$\delta_2 = \frac{1}{T}\left[1 + \frac{1}{T}\right]\ ,$$

.

.

.

For geometric decline in efficiency, the replacement distribution is constant:

$$\delta_\tau = \delta \qquad (\tau = 1,\ 2,\ \dots)\ .$$

1.2.3 Quantity of Capital Input

The relative efficiency of capital goods of different ages and the derived mortality and replacement distributions are useful in measuring the price and quantity of capital input. We begin our description of the measurement of capital input with the quantities estimated by the perpetual inventory method. First, capital stock at the end of each period, say K_t, is the sum of past investments, say $A_{t-\tau}$, each weighted by its relative efficiency:

$$K_t = \sum_{\tau=0}^{\infty} d_\tau A_{t-\tau} .$$

For a complete system of accounts both capital stock and investments in every preceding period are required. For this purpose a system of vintage accounts containing data on investments of every age in every period is essential.

Taking the first difference of the expression for capital stock in terms of past investments, we obtain

$$K_t - K_{t-1} = A_t + \sum_{\tau=1}^{\infty} (d_\tau - d_{\tau-1}) A_{t-\tau'}$$

$$= A_t - \sum_{\tau=1}^{\infty} m_\tau A_{t-\tau'}$$

$$= A_t - R_t ,$$

where

$$R_t = \sum_{\tau=1}^{\infty} m_\tau A_{t-\tau} \tag{8}$$

is the level of replacement requirements in period t. The change in capital stock from period to period is equal to the acquisition of investment goods less replacement requirements.

Replacement requirements may also be expressed in terms of present and past changes in capital stock, using the replacement distribution:

$$R_t = \sum_{\tau=1}^{\infty} \delta_\tau [K_{t-\tau} - K_{t-\tau-1}] .$$

The average replacement rate for capital stock at the beginning of the period,

$$\hat{\delta}_t = \frac{R_t}{K_{t-1}} = \sum_{\tau=1}^{\infty} \delta_\tau \frac{[K_{t-\tau} - K_{t-\tau-1}]}{K_{t-1}} , \qquad (9)$$

is a weighted average of replacement rates with weights given by the relative proportions of changes in capital stock of each vintage in beginning of period capital stock.

1.2.4 Price of Capital Input

We turn next to a description of the price data required for the measurement of the price of capital input. For this purpose a system of vintage accounts containing data on prices of capital goods of every age in every period is needed. This system of vintage accounts is dual to the perpetual inventory method in the sense that there is a one-to-one correspondence between the vintage quantities that appear in the perpetual inventory method and the prices that appear in our vintage price accounts.[7] To bring out this correspondence and to simplify the notation we use a system of present or discounted prices.

Taking the present as time zero, the discounted price of a commodity, say q_t, is multiplied by a discount factor:

$$q_t = \prod_{s=1}^{t} \frac{1}{1+r_s} p_t .$$

The notational convenience of present or discounted prices results from dispensing with explicit discount factors in expressing prices for different time periods.

In the correspondence between the perpetual inventory method and its dual or price counterpart the price of acquisition of a capital good is analogous to capital stock. The price of acquisition, say $q_{A,t}$, is the sum of future rental prices of capital services, say $q_{K,t}$, weighted by the relative efficiency of the capital good in each future period:

$$q_{A,t} = \sum_{\tau=0}^{\infty} d_\tau q_{K,t+\tau+1} . \qquad (10)$$

This expression can be compared with the corresponding expression giving capital stock as a weighted sum of past investments. The acquisition price of capital goods enters the production account through the price of investment goods output. This price also appears as the price component of capital formation in the accumulation account. Vintage accounts, containing data on the acquisition prices of capital goods of every age at every point of time, are required for a complete system of accounts.

Taking the first difference of the expression for the acquisition price of capital goods in terms of future rentals, we obtain

$$q_{A,t} - q_{A,t-1} = -q_{K,t} - \sum_{\tau=1}^{\infty} (d_\tau - d_{\tau-1}) q_{K,t+\tau}$$

$$= -q_{K,t} + \sum_{\tau=1}^{\infty} m_\tau q_{K,t+\tau}$$

$$= -q_{K,t} + q_{D,t},$$

where

$$q_{D,t} = \sum_{\tau=1}^{\infty} m_\tau q_{K,t+\tau} \tag{11}$$

is depreciation on a capital good in period t. The period-to-period change in the price of acquisition of a capital good is equal to depreciation less the rental price of capital. Postponing the purchase of a capital good makes it necessary to forgo one period's rental and makes it possible to avoid one period's depreciation. In the correspondence between the perpetual inventory method and its price counterpart, investment corresponds to the rental price of capital and replacement corresponds to depreciation.

We can rewrite the expression for the first difference of the acquisition price of capital goods in terms of undiscounted prices and the period-to-period discount rate:

$$p_{K,t} = p_{A,t-1} r_t + p_{D,t} - (p_{A,t} - p_{A,t-1}), \tag{12}$$

where $p_{A,t}$ is the undiscounted price of acquisition of capital goods, $p_{K,t}$ the price of capital services, $p_{D,t}$ depreciation, and r_t the rate of return, all in period t. The price of capital services $p_{K,t}$ is the sum of return per unit of capital $p_{A,t-1} r_t$, depreciation $p_{D,t}$, and the negative of revaluation, $p_{A,t} - p_{A,t-1}$.

Depreciation may also be expressed in terms of present and future changes in the price of acquisition of investment goods, using the replacement distribution:

$$q_{D,t} = \sum_{\tau=1}^{\infty} \delta_{\tau} [q_{A,t+\tau} - q_{A,t+\tau-1}] \cdot$$

The average depreciation rate on the acquisition price of a capital good,

$$\bar{\delta}_t = \frac{q_{D,t}}{q_{A,t}} = -\sum_{\tau=1}^{\infty} \delta_{\tau} \frac{[q_{A,t+\tau} - q_{A,t+\tau-1}]}{q_{A,t}}, \tag{13}$$

is a weighted average of replacement rates with weights given by the relative proportions of changes in futures prices in the acquisition price of investment goods in the current period. This expression may be compared with that for the average replacement rate $\hat{\delta}_t$ given above. For a complete system of accounts vintage data on the depreciation of capital goods of every age at every point of time are required.

1.3   Vintage Price Functions

In the perpetual inventory method data on the quantity of investment goods of every vintage are used to estimate capital formation, replacement requirements, and capital stock. In the price counterpart of the perpetual inventory method data on the acquisition prices of investment goods of every vintage are required. The price of acquisition of an investment good of age v at time t, say $q_{A,t,v}$, is the weighted sum of future rental prices of capital prices. The weights are relative efficiencies of the capital good in each future period, beginning with age v:

$$q_{A,t,v} = \sum_{\tau=0}^{\infty} d_{\tau+v} q_{K,t+\tau+1} \cdot \tag{14}$$

A new investment good has age zero, so that

$$q_{A,t,0} = q_{A,t} \cdot$$

Given the acquisition prices, we require estimates of depreciation and the rental price for goods of each vintage.

1.3.1   Measuring Capital Input

To calculate depreciation on capital goods of each vintage we take the first difference of the acquisition prices across vintages at a given point in time:

$$= \sum_{\tau=1}^{\infty} m_{\tau+v} q_{K,t+v+\tau}$$

$$= q_{D,t,v} , \tag{15}$$

where $q_{D,t,v}$ is depreciation on a capital good of age v at time t. Again, a new investment good has age zero, so that

$$q_{D,t,0} = q_{D,t} .$$

To obtain depreciation in terms of future prices or undiscounted prices, we observe that acquisition prices across vintages at a given point in time and the corresponding depreciation are associated with the same discount factor, so that

$$p_{A,t,v} - p_{A,t,v+1} = p_{D,t,v} .$$

To calculate the capital service price for goods of each vintage we first observe that the rental of a capital good of age v at time t, say $p_{K,t,v}$, is proportional to the rental of a new capital good,

$$p_{K,t,v} = d_v p_{K,t} , \tag{16}$$

with the constant of proportionality given by the efficiency of a capital good of age v relative to that of a new capital good. New and used capital goods are perfect substitutes in production. To calculate the service price for new capital goods we use the formula derived above:

$$p_{K,t} = p_{A,t-1} r_t + p_{D,t} - (p_{A,t} - p_{A,t-1}) .$$

To apply this formula we require a series of undiscounted acquisition prices for capital goods $p_{A,t}$, rates of return r_t, depreciation on new capital goods $p_{D,t}$, and revaluation of existing capital goods $p_{A,t} - p_{A,t-1}$.

To calculate the rate of return in each period we set the formula for the rental price $p_{K,t}$ times the quantity of capital K_{t-1} equal to property compensation. All of the variables entering this equation—current and past acquisition prices for capital goods, depreciation, revaluation, capital stock, and property compensation—except for the rate of return, are known. Replacing these variables by the corresponding data we solve this equation for the rate of return. To obtain the capital service price itself we substitute the rate of return into the original formula along with the other data. This completes the calculation of the service price.

We conclude that acquisition prices for capital goods of each vintage at each point of time provide sufficient information to enable us to calculate depreciation and rental value for capital goods of each vintage. These data together with current investment, capital stock, replacement, and investments of all vintages at each point of time constitute the basic data on quantities and prices required for a complete vintage accounting system. Price and quantity data that we have described for a single durable good are required for each durable good in the system. These data are used to derive price and quantity indexes for each durable good that play the role of prices and quantities of individual inputs in the theory of production.

1.3.2 Geometric Decline in Efficiency

For each durable good with a full set of data for every time period, price and quantity indexes for capital input can be constructed at each point of time. For durable goods with a less complete set of data a simplified set of price and quantity indexes can be constructed in the basis of the assumption that the decline in efficiency is geometric.[8] Under this assumption the rate of replacement and the rate of depreciation are constant and equal to the rate of decline in efficiency:

$$\hat{\delta}_t = \bar{\delta}_t = \delta . \qquad (17)$$

Vintage accounts can be dispensed with since replacement is proportional to capital stock and depreciation is proportional to the current acquisition price of investment goods.

In the construction of a simplified accounting system we estimate capital stock at the end of each period as a weighted sum of past investments:

$$K_t = \sum_{\tau = 0}^{\infty} (1 - \delta)^{\tau} A_{t - \tau} . \qquad (18)$$

With a constant rate of replacement, replacement becomes

$$R_t = \delta K_{t-1} . \qquad (19)$$

The price of acquisition of new investment goods is a weighted sum of future rentals:

$$q_{A,t} = \sum_{\tau=0}^{\infty} (1-\delta)^{\tau} q_{K,t+\tau+1} \, . \tag{20}$$

With a constant rate of depreciation, depreciation becomes

$$p_{D,t} = \delta p_{A,t} \, . \tag{21}$$

The acquisition price of investment goods of age v at time t is

$$p_{A,t,v} = (1-\delta)^v p_{A,t} \, . \tag{22}$$

The service price for new capital goods becomes

$$p_{K,t} = p_{A,t-1} r_t + \delta p_{A,t} - (p_{A,t} - p_{A,t-1}) \, . \tag{23}$$

1.3.3 Econometric Models

Under the assumption that the pattern of decline in efficiency of a durable good is geometric, the vintage price system required for construction of price and quantity indexes for capital input depends on the price for acquisition of new capital goods $p_{A,t}$. At each point of time the prices for acquisition $\{p_{A,t,v}\}$ of capital goods of age v are proportional to the price for new goods. The constants of proportionality decline geometrically at the rate of decline in efficiency δ. The rate of decline can be treated as an unknown parameter in an econometric model and can be estimated from a sample of prices for acquisition of capital goods of different vintages.

To formulate an econometric model of the technology that characterizes the durable goods model of production we add a stochastic component to the equation for the prices of acquisition of capital goods of different vintages. We associate this component with unobservable characteristics of the durable goods. We assume that the equation for the prices for acquisition has two additive components. The first is a nonrandom function of the age v of the capital good and the price for acquisition of new capital goods $p_{A,t}$. The second is an unobservable random disturbance that is independent of these variables.

We obtain an econometric model for vintage price functions by taking logarithms of the prices for acquisition $\{p_{A,t,v}\}$ and adding a random disturbance term:

$$\ln p_{A,t,v} = \ln p_{A,0} + \ln(1-\delta) v + \ln(1+\gamma) t + \varepsilon_{t,v'}$$
$$= \alpha_0 + \beta_v v + \beta_t t + \varepsilon_{t,v'} \qquad (t=1,2,...,T; \ v=0,1,...), \tag{24}$$

where $\varepsilon_{t,v}$ is an unobservable random disturbance for the price for acquisition of a capital good of age v at time t.

We assume that the disturbance has expected value equal to zero for all observations, that the variance, say σ^2, is constant, and that disturbances corresponding to distinct observations are uncorrelated:

$$E(\varepsilon_{t,v}) = 0,$$
$$V(\varepsilon_{t,v}) = \sigma^2 \qquad (t = 1, 2 \dots T; \quad v = 0, 1, \dots), \qquad (25)$$
$$C(\varepsilon_{t,v}, \varepsilon_{t',v'}) = 0 \qquad (t = t'; v = v').$$

Under these assumptions, the rate of decline in efficiency of a durable good δ and the rate of inflation in the prices for acquisition of new durable goods γ can be estimated by linear regression methods.

1.3.4 Generalizations

The econometric model for vintage price functions can be generalized in several ways. First, the age of the durable good v and the time period t can enter nonlinearly into the vintage price function. Hall (1971) has proposed an analysis of variance model for vintage price function. In this model each age can be represented by a dummy variable that is equal to one for the price for acquisition of a durable good of that age and equal to zero otherwise. Similarly, each time period can be represented by a dummy variable equal to one for that time period and zero otherwise.

The analysis of variance model for vintage price functions can be written

$$\ln p_{A,t,v} = \alpha_0 + \beta'_v D_v + \beta'_t D_t + \varepsilon_{t,v} \qquad (t = 1, 2, \dots T; \quad v = 0, 1, \dots), \qquad (26)$$

where D_v is a vector of dummy variables for age v and D_t is a vector of dummy variables for time t; β_v and β_t are the corresponding vectors of parameters. In the estimation of this model dummy variables for one vintage and one time period can be dropped in order to obtain a matrix of observations on the independent variables of full rank.

An alternative approach to nonlinearity in an econometric model for vintage price functions has been proposed by Hulten and Wykoff (1981b). They propose to transform the prices of acquisition $\{p_{A,t,v}\}$, age v, and time t by means of the Box-Cox transformation, obtaining

$$p^*_{A,t,v} = (p_{A,t,v}^{\Theta_p} - 1) / \Theta_p, v^* = (v^{\Theta_v} - 1) \Theta_v, t^* = (t^{\Theta_t} - 1) / \Theta_t,$$

where the parameters Θ_p, Θ_v, and Θ_t can be estimated by nonlinear regression methods from the nonlinear model for vintage price functions:

$$p^*_{A,t,v} = \alpha_0 + \beta_v v^* + \beta_t t^* + \varepsilon_{t,v} \qquad (t = 1, 2, \dots ; \quad v = 0, 1, \dots). \qquad (27)$$

The econometric model of vintage price functions giving the logarithm of prices for acquisition as a linear function of age v and time period t is a limiting case of the Hulten-Wykoff model with parameter values:

$$\Theta_p = 1, \qquad \Theta_v = 0, \qquad \Theta_t = 0.$$

A further generalization of the econometric model of vintage price functions has been proposed by Hall (1971). This generalization is appropriate for durable goods with a number of varieties that are perfect substitutes in production. Each variety is characterized by a number of characteristics that affect relative efficiency.[9] As an illustration, Hall analyzes a sample of prices for half-ton pickup trucks with characteristics such as wheelbase, shipping weight, displacement, ratio of bore to stroke, horsepower, torque, and tire width. Observations of these characteristics are analyzed for pickup trucks produced by Ford and Chevrolet in the United States for the period 1955–1966.

We can express the price for acquisition of new capital goods at time zero as a function of the characteristics:

$$\ln p_{A,0} = \alpha_0 + \beta'_c C,$$

where C is a vector of characteristics, such as those employed for pickup trucks in Hall's study, and β_c is the corresponding vector of parameters. The econometric model of vintage price functions becomes

$$\ln p_{A,t,v} = \alpha_0 + \beta'_v D_v + \beta'_t D_t + \beta'_c C + \varepsilon_{t,v}$$
$$(t = 1, 2, \dots T; \quad v = 0, 1, \dots). \qquad (28)$$

The unknown parameters of this model can be estimated by linear regression methods.

Hall's (1971) methodology provides a means for determining both a quality-corrected price index for new capital goods and relative efficiencies for different vintages of capital goods. Hall (1971) and Jorgenson and Griliches (1967) have identified Solow's (1960) concept of embodied technical change with changes in the quality of capital goods. The line of research suggested by this concept involves substituting quality-corrected price indexes for existing price indexes of capital goods. Changes in quality can be incorporated into price indexes for capital goods by means of the "hedonic technique" employed by Griliches (1961) and studies in the volume edited by Griliches (1971). For example, Cole, Chen, Barquin-Stolleman, Dulberger, Helvacian, and Hodge (1986) have developed quality corrections for computer price indexes employed in the U.S. national product accounts.

1.3.5 Applications

To illustrate the econometric modeling of capital as a factor of production, we present a model that has been implemented by Hulten and Wykoff (1981b) for eight categories of assets in the United States: tractors, construction machinery, metalworking machinery, general industrial equipment, trucks, autos, industrial buildings, and commercial buildings. In 1977 these categories included 55% of investment expenditures on producers' durable equipment and 42% of expenditures on nonresidential structures.

With perfect substitutability among durable goods of different ages market equilibrium implies the existence of a vintage price function for each durable good. This function gives the price of acquisition as a function of age and the price of a new durable good of the same type, expressed as a function of time. Vintage price functions for each category of assets can be estimated from annual observations on used asset prices.

In the estimation of econometric models based on vintage price functions, the sample of used asset prices is "censored" by the retirement of assets from service. The price of acquisition for assets that have been retired from service is equal to zero. If only surviving assets are included in a sample of used asset prices, the sample is censored by excluding assets that have been retired. In order to correct the resulting bias in estimates of vintage price functions, Hulten and Wykoff (1981b) multiply the prices of surviving assets of each vintage by the probability of survival, expressed as a function of age.[10]

Vintage price functions for commercial and industrial buildings are summarized in table 1.1. For each class of assets the rate of economic depreciation is tabulated as a function of the age of the asset. The natural logarithm of the price is regressed on age and time to obtain an average rate of depreciation, which Hulten and Wykoff refer to as the best geometric rate (BGA). The square of the multiple correlation coefficient (R^2) is given as a measure of the goodness of fit of the

Table 1.1
Rates of economic depreciation

	With censored sample correction		Without censored sample correction	
Age	Commercial	Industrial	Commercial	Industrial
5	2.85	2.99	2.66	2.02
10	2.64	3.01	1.84	1.68
15	2.43	3.04	1.48	1.50
20	2.30	3.07	1.27	1.39
30	2.15	3.15	1.02	1.25
40	2.08	3.24	0.88	1.17
50	2.04	3.34	0.79	1.11
60	2.02	3.45	0.72	1.06
70	2.02	3.57	0.66	1.03
BGA	2.47	3.61	1.05	1.28
R^2	0.985	0.997	0.971	0.995

Source: Hulten and Wykoff (1981a), Table 5, page 387; commercial corresponds to office and industrial corresponds to factory.

geometric approximation to the fitted vintage price function for each asset. Vintage price functions are estimated with and without the correction for censored sample bias described above.

The first conclusion that emerges from the data presented in table 1.1 is that a correction for censored sample bias is extremely important in the estimation of vintage price functions. The Hulten-Wykoff study is the first to employ such a correction. The second conclusion reached by Hulten and Wykoff (1981b) is that "... *a constant rate of depreciation can serve as a reasonable statistical approximation to the underlying Box-Cox rates even though the latter are not geometric.* [Their italics.] This result, in turn, supports those who use the single parameter depreciation approach in calculating capital stocks using the perpetual inventory method."

In table 1.2 we present rates of economic depreciation derived from the best geometric approximation approach of Hulten and Wykoff for all assets employed in the U.S. National Income and Product Accounts (1977). Hulten and Wykoff have compared the best geometric depreciation rates presented in table 1.1 with depreciation rates employed by the Bureau of Economic Analysis in perpetual inventory estimates of capital stock. The Hulten-Wykoff rate for equipment averages 0.133, while the BEA rate averages 0.141, so that the two

Table 1.2
Asset classes and rates of economic depreciation (annual percentage rates of decline)

Producers durable equipment	
1. Furniture and fixtures	.1100
2. Fabricated metal products	.0917
3. Engines and turbines	.0786
4. Tractors	.1633
5. Agricultural machinery (except tractors)	.0971
6. Construction machinery (except tractors)	.1722
7. Mining and oilfield machinery	.1650
8. Metalworking machinery	.1225
9. Special industry machinery (not elsewhere classified)	.1031
10. General industrial equipment	.1225
11. Office, computing, and accounting machinery	.2729
12. Service industry machinery	.1650
13. Electrical transmission, distribution, and industrial apparatus	.1179
14. Communications equipment	.1179
15. Electrical equipment (not elsewhere classified)	.1179
16. Trucks, buses, and truck trailers	.2537
17. Autos	.3333
18. Aircraft	.1833
19. Ships and boats	.0750
20. Railroad equipment	.0660
21. Instruments	.1473
22. Other	.1473
Private nonresidential structures	
1. Industrial	.0361
2. Commercial	.0247
3. Religious	.0188
4. Educational	.0188
5. Hospital and institutional	.0233
6. Other	.0454
7. Public utilities	.0316
8. Farm	.0237
9. Mining exploration, shafts, and wells	.0563
10. Other	.0290

Source: Hulten and Wykoff (1981b, table 1, p. 95).

rates are very similar. The Hulten-Wykoff rate for structures is 0.037, while the BEA rate is 0.060; these rates are substantially different.

Hulten and Wykoff (1981b) have summarized studies of economic depreciation completed prior to their own study. The most common methodology for such studies is based on vintage price functions. This methodology was first employed by Terborgh (1954) and has been used for studies of automobiles by Ackerman (1973), Cagan (1965), Chow (1957, 1960), Ohta and Griliches (1975), Ramm (1970), and Wykoff (1970). The vintage price approach is used in studies of prices of tractors by Griliches (1960), pickup trucks by Hall (1971), machine tools by Beidleman (1976), ships by Lee (1978), and residential housing by Chinloy (1977). Unfortunately, none of these studies correct for censored sample bias; the results presented in table 5 in Hulten and Wykoff (1981a) demonstrate the importance of such a correction.

An alternative to the vintage price approach is to employ rental prices rather than prices of acquisition to estimate the pattern of decline in efficiency. This approach has been employed by Malpezzi, Ozanne, and Thibodeau (1987) to analyze rental price data on residential structures and by Taubman and Rasche (1969) to study rental price data on commercial structures. While leases on residential property are very frequently one year or less in duration, leases on commercial property are typically for much longer periods of time. Since the rental prices are constant over the period of the lease, estimates based on annual rental prices for commercial property are biased toward the one-hoss shay pattern found by Taubman and Rasche; Malpezzi, Ozanne, and Thibodeau find rental price profiles for residential property that decline geometrically.

A second alternative to the vintage price approach is to analyze investment for replacement purposes. This approach was originated by Meyer and Kuh (1957) and has been employed by Eisner (1972), Feldstein and Foot (1974), and Coen (1975, 1980). Coen (1980) compares the explanatory power of alternative patterns of decline in efficiency in a model of investment behavior that also includes the price of capital services. For equipment he finds that 11 of 21 two-digit manufacturing industries are characterized by geometric decline in efficiency, 3 by sum of the years' digits, and 7 by straight-line. For structures he finds that 14 industries are characterized by geometric decline, 5 by straight-line, and 2 by one-hoss-shay patterns. Hulten and Wykoff (1981b) conclude that "the weight of Coen's study is evidently on the side of the geometric and near-geometric forms of depreciation."

1.4   Alternative Measures of Capital Input

To provide additional perspective on capital as a factor of production we find it useful to compare the measurement of capital input in recent studies of productivity by the Bureau of Labor Statistics (1983), Denison (1985), Jorgenson, Gollop and Fraumeni (1987), and Kendrick (1983). Measures of capital input are index numbers constructed from data on services of capital stocks and rental prices of capital services. For each type of capital input capital stock is a weighted sum of past investments with weights given by the relative efficiencies of capital goods of different ages. The corresponding rental price is based on the relationship of the price of investment goods to future prices of capital services. The price of investment goods is a weighted sum of future rental prices with weights given by the relative efficiencies.

The estimates of capital stock in the form of equipment and structures employed by Jorgenson, Gollop, and Fraumeni (1987) are derived by the perpetual inventory method. This method is applied to investment data by industry that are reconciled to control totals for the economy as a whole from the U.S. national product accounts. Denison and Kendrick employ estimates of capital stock for equipment and structures from the Bureau of Economic Analysis capital stock study. These estimates are also derived by the perpetual inventory method using investment data from the U.S. national product accounts. The Bureau of Labor Statistics utilizes the perpetual inventory method to derive estimates of capital stock for equipment and structures, based on investment data from the U.S. national product accounts.

The perpetual inventory method is employed by all four studies we have considered. In addition, all four studies utilize investment data from the U.S. national product accounts. However, the studies differ substantially in the treatment of relative efficiencies of capital goods of different ages. In *Accounting for United States Economic Growth, 1929–1969* (1974), Denison employs Bureau of Economic analysis estimates of capital stocks, gross and net of depreciation, based on Bulletin F service lives and straight-line depreciation. In *Accounting for Slower Economic Growth* (1979), Denison utilizes Bureau of Economic Analysis estimates based on Bulletin F service lives less 15%. This same set of estimates is employed in his book *Trends in American Economic Growth, 1929–1982* (1985).[11]

Kendrick (1973) uses Bureau of Economic Analysis estimates of capital stock, gross and net of depreciation, based on Bulletin F lives less 15% and straight-line depreciation. Kendrick (1976) and Kendrick and Grossman (1980) employ Bureau of Economic Analysis estimates based on Bulletin F lives less 15% and double-declining balance depreciation. This same set of estimates is utilized by Kendrick (1983).[12] The Bureau of Labor Statistics (1983) employs relative efficiencies of capital goods of different ages obtained by fitting hyperbolic functions to the Box-Cox functions estimated by Hulten and Wykoff (1981a, b, c).[13] Jorgenson, Gollop, and Fraumeni (1987) use the best geometric average (BGA) rates fitted by Hulten and Wykoff, as described in section 1.3.5.

This completes our comparison of methods and sources for estimating capital stock among the four studies of productivity. An internally consistent measure of capital input must employ the same pattern of relative efficiencies of capital goods of different ages for both capital stocks and rental prices. The requirement that estimates of rental prices of capital services must be consistent the corresponding estimates of capital stocks is very stringent. Only two of the studies of productivity we have considered satisfy this requirement. These are the studies by the Bureau of Labor Statistics (1983) and by Jorgenson, Gollop, and Fraumeni (1987). By contrast, the studies by Denison (1985) and by Kendrick (1983) are internally inconsistent. Denison has employed no less than three different internally contradictory approaches to measuring capital input in successive studies of productivity dating back to 1962, while Kendrick has used two different internally contradictory approaches in studies dating back to 1961.

Jorgenson, Gollop, and Fraumeni (1987) employ geometric relative efficiency functions estimated by Hulten and Wykoff (1981a, b, c). Hulten and Wykoff have shown that the best geometric average (BGA) rates of depreciation provide an accurate description of the decline in the price of acquisition of capital goods with age. The geometric relative efficiency functions are also consistent with evidence from studies of rental prices of capital goods and patterns of replacement investment. Jorgenson, Gollop, and Fraumeni (1987) utilize the same geometric rates for estimates of capital stock and estimates of rental prices.

The Bureau of Labor Statistics (1983) employs relative efficiency functions estimated by Hulten and Wykoff. However, BLS does not utilize the geometric relative efficiency functions fitted by Hulten and Wykoff. Instead, BLS has fitted a set of hyperbolic functions to the Box-Cox relative efficiency functions estimated by Hulten and Wykoff. Consistency is preserved between the resulting estimates of capital stocks and rental prices by implementing a complete system of vintage accounts for each class of assets. Implicitly, this set of accounts includes prices of acquisition and quantities of investment goods of all ages at each point of time. Measures of capital input based on hyperbolic and geometric relative efficiency functions are very similar.[14]

For each class of assets Denison's estimates of capital stock are based on a linearly declining pattern of relative efficiency. In *Sources of Economic Growth* (1962) Denison employs a measure of capital input for equipment and structures with relative efficiency constant over the lifetime of the capital good, the one-hoss shay pattern of relative efficiency we have described above. In *Why Growth Rates Differ* (1967) Denison uses a measure of capital input with relative efficiency given by an unweighted average of the one-hoss shay and straight-line patterns:

$$d_\tau = \begin{cases} 1 - \dfrac{\tau}{2T} & (\tau = 0, 1, ..., T - 1) \\ 0 & \text{otherwise.} \end{cases}$$

In *Accounting for United States Economic Growth 1929–1969* (1974) Denison introduces a measure of capital input based on a weight of one-fourth for straight-line and three-fourths for one-hoss shay patterns:

$$d_\tau = \begin{cases} 1 - \dfrac{\tau}{4T} & (\tau = 0, 1, ..., T - 1) \\ 0 & \text{otherwise.} \end{cases}$$

This measure of capital input is employed by Denison in *Accounting for Slower Economic Growth* (1979) and *Trends in American Economic Growth, 1929–1982* (1985).[15]

For a linearly declining pattern of relative efficiency the mortality distribution can be represented in the form

$$
m_\tau =
\begin{cases}
\dfrac{1}{\theta} T & (\tau = 1, 2, ..., T-1) \\[2ex]
1 - \dfrac{1}{\theta}(1 - \dfrac{1}{T}) & (\tau = T) \\[2ex]
0 & \text{otherwise.}
\end{cases}
$$

where θ is unity for straight-line replacement, positive infinity for one-hoss shay replacement, and two and four, respectively, for Denison's two averages of straight-line and one-hoss shay. To derive the method of depreciation appropriate for linearly declining relative efficiency, we first express depreciation for an asset of age v at time t, say $p_{D,t,v}$, in the form

$$
p_{D,t,v} = \sum_{\tau=1}^{\infty} m_{\tau+v} \prod_{s=1}^{\tau} \frac{1}{1+r_{t+s}} p_{K,t+\tau}
$$

$$
= \frac{1}{\theta T} \sum_{\tau=1}^{T-v-l} \prod_{s=1}^{\tau} \frac{1}{1+r_{t+s}} p_{K,t+\tau}
$$

$$
+ \left[1 - \frac{1}{\theta}\left(1 - \frac{1}{T} \right) \right] \prod_{s=1}^{T-v} p_{K,t+T-v}.
$$

Assuming that the rates of return $\{r_{t+s}\}$ and the prices of capital services $\{p_{K,t+\tau}\}$ are constant, we obtain the following expression for depreciation on an asset of age v:

$$
p_{D,v} = \frac{1}{r\theta T} - \left[\frac{1}{r\theta T} - 1 + \frac{1}{\theta} \right] \left(\frac{1}{1+r} \right)^{T-v} p_K \qquad (v = 0, 1, ..., T-1).
$$

Similarly, the value of a new asset is equal to the sum of depreciation over all ages:

$$
p_A = \sum_{v=0}^{T-1} p_{D,v}
$$

$$
= \frac{1}{r} \left[\frac{1}{\theta} - \left[\frac{1}{r\theta T} - 1 + \frac{1}{\theta} \right] \left[1 - \left(\frac{1}{1+r} \right)^{T} \right] \right] p_K,
$$

so that depreciation allowances appropriate for a linearly declining relative efficiency are given for each age by the formula

$$\frac{p_{D,v}}{p_A} = \frac{\dfrac{1}{\theta T} - r\left[\dfrac{1}{r\theta T} - 1 + \dfrac{1}{\theta}\right]\left(\dfrac{1}{1+r}\right)^{T-v}}{\dfrac{1}{\theta} - \left[\dfrac{1}{r\theta T} - 1 + \dfrac{1}{\theta}\right]\left[1 - \left(\dfrac{1}{1+r}\right)^{T}\right]} \qquad (v = 0,\ 1,...,\ T-1).$$

The value of depreciation at time t for linearly declining relative efficiency is the sum over assets of all ages:

$$\sum_{v=0}^{T-1} p_{D,t,v} A_{t-v-1} = p_{A,t} \sum_{v=0}^{T-1} \frac{\dfrac{1}{\theta T} - r\left[\dfrac{1}{r\theta T} - 1 + \dfrac{1}{\theta}\right]\left(\dfrac{1}{1+r}\right)^{T-v}}{\dfrac{1}{\theta} - \left[\dfrac{1}{r\theta T} - 1 + \dfrac{1}{\theta}\right]\left[1 - \left(\dfrac{1}{1+r}\right)^{T}\right]} A_{t-v-1}.$$

Denison employs linearly declining relative efficiency in measuring capital stock; in his three studies he employs three different weighted averages of the straight-line and one-hoss shay patterns. In all three studies Denison employs the straight-line method of depreciation. The straight-line method of depreciation is not appropriate for any of his methods of measuring capital stock, so that the resulting measures of capital input are internally inconsistent.

For linearly declining patterns of relative efficiency, depreciation allowances are increasing, constant, or decreasing with age for values of the parameter θ greater than, equal to, or less than $1 + (1/rT)$, respectively. For the straight-line pattern depreciation allowances are decreasing with age; for the one-hoss shay pattern depreciation allowances are increasing with age. There is no value of the parameter θ for which depreciation is independent of age as Denison assumes.

Kendrick (1961, 1973) employs capital stock estimates based on linearly declining relative efficiency in allocating property compensation among assets on the basis of "net earnings." Kendrick's measure of "net earnings" is based on capital consumption allowances from the U.S. national income accounts as an estimate of depreciation. These estimates are based in turn on depreciation allowances for tax purposes and do not reflect a consistent valuation of assets over time or a consistent method of depreciation.

The method of depreciation appropriate for Kendrick's estimates of capital stock is the same as that we have given above for Denison with the parameter θ equal to unity:

$$\frac{p_{D,v}}{p_A} = \frac{\frac{1}{T}\left[1 - \left(\frac{1}{1+r}\right)^{T-v}\right]}{1 - \frac{1}{rT}\left[1 - \left(\frac{1}{1+r}\right)^{T}\right]} \qquad (v = 0, 1, ..., T-1).$$

The value of depreciation at time t for linearly declining relative efficiency is the sum over assets of all ages:

$$\sum_{v=0}^{T-1} p_{D,t,v}\, A_{t-v-1} = p_{At} \sum_{v=0}^{T-1} \frac{\frac{1}{T}\left[1 - \left(\frac{1}{1+r}\right)^{T-v}\right]}{1 - \frac{1}{rT}\left[1 - \left(\frac{1}{1+r}\right)^{T}\right]} A_{t-v-1}.$$

Kendrick (1973) also employs alternative capital stock estimates based on constant relative efficiency in allocating property compensation among assets on the basis of "gross earnings." This is the one-hoss shay pattern described above. Constant relative efficiency is also utilized by Kendrick and Grossman (1980) and Kendrick (1983).[16] For constant relative efficiency, the appropriate method of depreciation is given not by the declining balance pattern as assumed by Kendrick but by the formula described above with θ equal to positive infinity:

$$\frac{P_{D,v}}{p_A} = \frac{r\left(\frac{1}{1+r}\right)^{T-v}}{1 - \left(\frac{1}{1+r}\right)^{T}} \qquad (v = 0, 1 ... T-1).$$

The value of depreciation at time t for constant relative efficiency is the sum:

$$\sum_{v=0}^{T-1} p_{D,t,v} A_{t-v-1} = p_{A,t} \sum_{v=0}^{T-1} \frac{r\left(\frac{1}{1+r}\right)^{T-v}}{1 - \left(\frac{1}{1+r}\right)^{T}} A_{t-v-1}.$$

Our overall conclusion is that none of Denison's measures of capital input satisfies the criterion that the same pattern of relative efficiency must be employed in estimates of capital stock and of the rental price of capital services. In allocating property compensation among assets Denison uses the straight-line method of depreciation, so that his estimates of rental prices of capital services are based on this method of depreciation. In estimating capital stocks Denison uses three alternative linearly declining patterns of relative efficiency. None of these patterns results in straight-line depreciation method, as Denison assumes.

Similarly, neither of Kendrick's two measures of capital input is based on an internally consistent treatment of capital stock and rental prices. In estimating capital stocks Kendrick uses straight-line and one-hoss shay patterns of relative efficiency. His weights based on "gross earnings" ignore differences among assets in rates of depreciation; his weights based on "net earnings" employ depreciation as calculated for tax purposes, so that neither the method for depreciation nor the valuation of assets is consistent over time.

The internal contradictions in Denison's measures of capital input were first analyzed in detail by Jorgenson and Griliches (1972a, especially pp. 81–87). Denison (1972, especially pp. 101–109) has defended the use of straight-line depreciation in his studies of productivity. However, he has failed to respond to the criticism that straight-line depreciation is inconsistent with the assumptions about the relative efficiencies of capital goods of different ages that he has used in measuring capital stock.

From Denison's point of view the problem apparently arises from the definition of depreciation itself. His defense of the straight-line formula is based on a concept of "depreciation" that he originally introduced in 1957. This concept was subsequently adopted in the U.S. national income and product accounts.[17] The definition is given in the following form by Young and Musgrave (1980, p. 32): "Depreciation is the cost of the asset allocated over its service life in proportion to its estimated service at each date." Denison (1972, pp. 104–105) refers to this method of allocation as the "capital input method."

Within the framework for the measurement of capital input presented above, Denison's concept of "depreciation" is based on the notion of allocating the cost of an asset over its lifetime in proportion to the relative efficiencies $\{d_\tau\}$ of capital goods of different ages. Jorgenson and Griliches (1972b, p. 11) have pointed out that this is consistent with the economic concept of depreciation only if the relative efficiencies decline geometrically. In this case and only in this case, depreciation, replacement, and "depreciation" in the sense of Denison and the U.S. national income and product accounts coincide.

Young and Musgrave (1980, pp. 33–37) contrast the Denison definition with the "discounted value definition" employed in the economic theory of depreciation outlined above. Among the advantages for the "capital input" definition claimed by Denison (1957, p. 240) and by Young and Musgrave (1980, p. 33) is that this definition avoids discounting of future capital services. In fact, discounting can be avoided in the measurement of depreciation if and only if the decline in the efficiency of capital goods is geometric. In this case the replacement rates $\{\delta_\tau\}$ are constant and equal to the average depreciation rate (13).

The Bureau of Labor Statistics (1983) provides an illustration of an internally consistent framework for the measurement of capital input. This framework does not employ geometrically declining efficiencies of capital goods. Within the Bureau of Labor Statistics framework the quantity of capital input from each vintage of capital goods is proportional to an efficiency function based on the estimates of Hulten and Wykoff. Replacement plays a role in the measurement of the quantity of capital input, while depreciation appears as a component of the rental price of capital services.

Jorgenson, Gollop, and Fraumeni (1987) have provided a second illustration of an internally consistent framework for the measurement of capital input. They employ the simplified accounting system for capital input originated by Christensen and Jorgenson (1969, 1970, 1973). This simplified accounting system is based on the best geometric average (BGA) efficiency functions fitted by Hulten and Wykoff. The studies by the Bureau of Labor Statistics and by Jorgenson, Gollop, and Fraumeni employ the Hulten-Wykoff estimates of efficiency functions for different classes of assets distinguished in the U.S. national income and product accounts.

Straight-line depreciation has been employed in the measurement of national income in the U.S. national income and product accounts. Concepts of gross and net capital stocks have been utilized in the underlying capital stock study by Musgrave (1986). However, this study contains a measure of capital input that is identical in concept to that employed in the Bureau of Labor Statistics (1983) study of productivity. Unfortunately this measure is inconsistent with the measures of depreciation utilized in the national accounts and with the measures of gross and net stocks presented in the capital stock study.

The U.S. national income and product accounts provide much useful raw material for productivity studies like those carried out by the Bureau of Labor Statistics (1983), Denison (1985), Jorgenson, Gollop, and Fraumeni (1987), and Kendrick (1983). However, the national accounts fail to provide an internally consistent set of measures of capital stock, capital input, and depreciation. This is regrettable, since studies of productivity like those of Denison and Kendrick will continue to rely on national accounting data.

The steps required to make the U.S. national income and product accounts more useful in future productivity studies can be outlined briefly. First, the "capital input definition" of depreciation originated by Denison (1957) can be replaced by the "discounted value definition." The Denison definition has been firmly rejected by economists outside the Bureau of Economic Analysis.[18] Second, the available empirical evidence on efficiency functions for different classes of assets, growing out of the work of Hulten and Wykoff (1981a, b, c), can be utilized in measuring capital stock, capital input, and depreciation with the U.S. national income and product accounts.

The economic theory of capital can provide a consistent framework for measures of both capital stock and capital services. Measures of capital stock and asset prices can be employed in the national wealth accounts, while measures of capital input and rental prices can be utilized in national production accounts. Depreciation is best regarded as a component of the rental price of capital services. Capital input, labor input, and productivity can be combined to form the input side of the national production account in constant prices, as in the accounting system outlined by Jorgenson (1980) and implemented by Fraumeni and Jorgenson (1980, 1986). Discounting can be avoided in the measurement of depreciation if the simplified accounting system originated by Christensen and Jorgenson (1969, 1970, 1973) is adopted.

Notes

1. The durable goods model of production was originated by Walras (1954). Capital as a factor of production has been discussed by Diewert (1980) and by Jorgenson (1973, 1980).

2. The dual to the durable goods model of production was originated by Hotelling (1925) and Haavelmo (1960). The dual to this model has been further developed by Arrow (1964) and Hall (1968).

3. We assume that the sequence of relative efficiencies is nonrandom. For a treatment of the economic theory of replacement with random deterioration in efficiency, see Jorgenson, McCall, and Radner (1967).

4. The concept of homothetic separability was introduced by Shephard (1953, 1970).

5. A proof of this proposition is given by Lau (1978).

6. The renewal equation is discussed by Feller (1968, pp. 311–313, 329–331).

7. The system of vintage accounts described below was originated by Christensen and Jorgenson (1973). This system is discussed by Jorgenson (1980).

8. The simplified system of vintage accounts was originated by Christensen and Jorgenson (1969, 1970, 1973) and has been employed by Fraumeni and Jorgenson (1980).

9. The "hedonic technique" for price measurement originated by Court (1939) and employed, for example, by Griliches (1961) is based on a number of varieties that are perfect substitutes. The hedonic technique is analyzed by Muellbauer (1975) and surveys of the literature have been given by Griliches (1971) and by Triplett (1975).

10. Hulten and Wykoff have estimated vintage price functions for structures from a sample of 8,066 observations on market transactions in used structures. These data were collected by the Office of Industrial Economics of the U.S. Department of the Treasury in 1972 and were published in *Business Building Statistics* (1975). They have estimated vintage price functions for equipment from prices of machine tools collected by Beidleman (1976) and prices of other types of equipment collected from used equipment dealers and from auction reports of the U.S. General Services Administration.

11. See Denison (1974, p. 53), Denison (1979, p. 50), Denison (1985, p. 65).

12. See Kendrick (1973, p. 29), Kendrick (1976, p. 20), Kendrick and Grossman (1980, p. 26), and Kendrick (1983, p. 56).

13. Bureau of Labor Statistics (1983, pp. 41–45).

14. Bureau of Labor Statistics (1983, pp. 57–59).

15. See Denison (1962, pp. 97–98), Denison (1967, pp. 140–141), Denison (1974, pp. 54–55), Denison (1979, pp. 50–52), Denison (1985, p. 65).

16. Kendrick (1973, pp. 27–29), Kendrick and Grossman (1980, p. 26), Kendrick (1983, pp. 56–57).

17. See Denison (1957, especially pp. 238–255); the role of this concept in the U.S. national income and product accounts is described by Young and Musgrave (1980). The role of Denison's concept in the underlying capital stock study is described by the Bureau of Economic Analysis (1987), p. viii.

18. See the comments on Denison (1957) by Copeland (1957), Kuznets (1957), and Schiff (1957), the comments on Denison (1972) by Jorgenson and Griliches (1972b), and the comments on Young and Musgrave (1980) by Faucett (1980) and Rymes (1980). The measurement of capital input in productivity studies has also been discussed by Diewert (1980, especially pp. 470–486), and by Norsworthy (1984a, b).

References

Ackerman, S. R. (1973), "Used Cars as a Depreciating Asset," *Western Economic Journal*, Vol. 11, No. 4, December, pp. 463–474.

Arrow, K. J. (1964), "Optimal Capital Policy, the Cost of Capital, and Myopic Decision Rules," *Annals of the Institute of Statistical Mathematics*, Vol. 16, Nos. 1/2, pp. 16–30.

Beidleman, C. R. (1976), "Economic Depreciation in a Capital Goods Industry," *National Tax Journal*, Vol. 29, No. 4, December, pp. 379–390.

Bureau of Economic Analysis (1977), *The National Income and Product Accounts of the United States, 1929–1974: Statistical Tables, a Supplement to the Survey of Current Business*, Washington, U.S. Department of Commerce.

_____ (1987), *Fixed Reproducible Tangible Wealth in the United States*, Washington, U.S. Department of Commerce.

Bureau of Labor Statistics (1983), *Trends in Multifactor Productivity, 1948–81.* Bulletin 2178, Washington, U.S. Department of Labor.

Cagan, P. (1965), "Measuring Quality Changes and the Purchasing Power of Money: An Exploratory Study of Automobiles," *National Banking Review*, Vol. 3, No. 2, December, pp. 217–236.

Chinloy, P. (1977), "Hedonic Price and Depreciation Indexes for Residential Housing: A Longitudinal Approach," *Journal of Urban Economics*, Vol. 4, No. 4, October, pp. 469–482.

Chow, G. C. (1957), *The Demand for Automobiles in the United States*, Amsterdam, North-Holland.

_____ (1960), "Statistical Demand Functions for Automobiles and Their Use for Forecasting," in A. C. Harberger, ed., *The Demand for Durable Goods*, Chicago, University of Chicago Press, pp. 149–180.

Christensen, L. R. and D. W. Jorgenson (1969), "The Measurement of Real Capital Input, 1929–1967," *Review of Income and Wealth*, Series 15, No. 4, December; pp. 293–320.

_____ (1970), "U.S. Real Product and Real Factor Input, 1929–1967," *Review of Income and Wealth*, Series 16, No. 1, March, pp. 19–50.

_____ (1973), "Measuring the Performance of the Private Sector of the U.S. Economy, 1929–1969," in M. Moss, ed., *Measuring Economic and Social Performance*, New York, Columbia University Press, pp. 233–351.

Coen, R. (1975), "Investment Behavior, the Measurement of Depreciation, and Tax Policy," *American Economic Review*, Vol. 65, No. 1, March, pp. 59–74.

_____ (1980), "Depreciation, Profits, and Rates of Return in Manufacturing Industries," in D. Usher, ed., *The Measurement of Capital*, Chicago, University of Chicago Press, pp. 121–152.

Cole, R., Y. C. Chen, J. A. Barquin-Stolleman, E. Dulberger, N. Helvacian, and J. H. Hodge (1986), "Quality-Adjusted Price Indexes for Computer Processors and Selected Peripheral Equipment," *Survey of Current Business*, Vol. 66, No. 1, January, pp. 41–50.

Copeland, M. A. (1957), "Comment," in Conference on Research in Income and Wealth, *Problems of Capital Formation*, Princeton, Princeton University Press, pp. 280–281.

Court, A. T. (1939), "Hedonic Price Indexes with Automotive Examples," in *The Dynamics of Automobile Demand*, New York, General Motors Corporation, pp. 99–117.

Denison, Edward F. (1957), "Theoretical Aspects of Quality Change, Capital Consumption, and Net Capital Formation," in Conference on Research in Income and Wealth, *Problems of Capital Formation*, Princeton, Princeton University Press.

———— (1962), *Sources of Economic Growth in the United States and the Alternatives before Us*, New York, Committee for Economic Development.

———— (1967), *Why Growth Rates Differ*, Washington, The Brookings Institution.

———— (1972), "Final Comments," *Survey of Current Business*, Vol. 52, No. 5, Part II, May, pp. 95–110.

———— (1974), *Accounting for United States Economic Growth, 1929–1969*, Washington, The Brookings Institution.

———— (1979), *Accounting for Slower Economic Growth*, Washington, The Brookings Institution.

———— (1985), *Trends in American Economic Growth, 1929–1982*, Washington, The Brookings Institution.

Diewert, W. E. (1980), "Aggregation Problems in the Measurement of Capital," in D. Usher, ed., *The Measurement of Capital*, Chicago, University of Chicago Press, pp. 433–528.

Eisner, R. (1972), "Components of Capital Expenditures: Replacement and Modernization," *Review of Economics and Statistics*, Vol. 54, No. 3, August, pp. 297–305.

Faucett, J. G. (1980), "Comment," in D. Usher, ed., *The Measurement of Capital*, Chicago, University of Chicago Press, pp. 68–81.

Feldstein, M. S., and D. K. Foot (1974), "The Other Half of Gross Investment: Replacement and Modernization Expenditures, *Review of Economics and Statistics*, Vol. 56, No. 1, February, pp. 49–58.

Feller, W. (1968), *An Introduction to Probability Theory and Its Applications*, 3rd ed. (1st ed. 1950), New York, Wiley.

Fisher, Irving (1961), *The Theory of Interest*, New York, A. M. Kelley.

Fraumeni, B. M., and D. W. Jorgenson (1980), "The Role of Capital in U.S. Economic Growth, 1948–1976," in G. von Furstenberg, ed., *Capital Efficiency and Growth*, Cambridge, MA, Ballinger, pp. 9–250.

_____ (1986), "The Role of Capital in U.S. Economic Growth, 1948–1979," in A. Dogramaci, ed., *Measurement Issues and Behavior of Productivity Variables*, Boston, Martinus Nijhoff, pp. 161–244.

Griliches, Z. (1960), "The Demand for a Durable Input: U.S. Farm Tractors, 1921–57," in A. C. Harberger, ed., *The Demand for Durable Goods*, Chicago, University of Chicago Press, pp. 181–210.

_____ (1961), "Hedonic Price Indexes for Automobiles: An Econometric Analysis of Quality Change," in *The Price Statistics of the Federal Government*, New York, National Bureau of Economic Research, pp. 137–196.

_____ (1971), "Hedonic Price Indexes Revisited," in Z. Griliches, ed., *Price Indexes and Quality Change*, Cambridge, MA, Harvard University Press, pp. 3–15.

Haavelmo, T. (1960), *A Study in the Theory of Investment*, Chicago, University of Chicago Press.

Hall, R. E. (1968), "Technical Change and Capital from the Point of View of the Dual," *Review of Economic Studies*, Vol. 35(1), No. 101, January, pp. 35–46.

_____ (1971), "The Measurement of Quality Changes from Vintage Price Data," in Z. Griliches, ed., *Price Indexes and Quality Change*, Cambridge, MA, Harvard University Press, pp. 240–271.

Hicks, J. R. (1946), *Value and Capital*, Oxford, Oxford University Press.

Hotelling, H. S. (1925), "A General Mathematical Theory of Depreciation," *Journal of the American Statistical Association*, Vol. 20, No. 151, September, pp. 340–353.

Hulten, C. R., and F. C. Wykoff (1981a), "Economic Depreciation and the Taxation of Structures in United States Manufacturing Industries: An Empirical Analysis," in D. Usher, ed., *The Measurement of Capital*, Chicago, University of Chicago Press, pp. 83–120.

_____ (1981b), "The Estimation of Economic Depreciation Using Vintage Asset Prices: An Application of the Box-Cox Power Transformation," *Journal of Econometrics*, Vol. 15, No. 3, April, pp. 367–396.

_____ (1981c), "The Measurement of Economic Depreciation," in C. R. Hulten, ed., *Depreciation, Inflation, and the Taxation of Income from Capital*, Washington, The Urban Institute Press, pp. 81–125.

Jorgenson, D. W. (1973), "The Economic Theory of Replacement and Depreciation," in W. Sellekaerts, ed., *Econometrics and Economic Theory*, New York, Macmillan, pp. 189–221.

_____ (1980), "Accounting for Capital," in G. von Furstenberg, ed., *Capital Efficiency and Growth*, Cambridge, MA, Ballinger, pp. 251–319.

Jorgenson, D. W., and Z. Griliches (1967), "The Explanation of Productivity Change," *Review of Economic Studies*, Vol. 34(2), No. 99, July, pp. 249–280.

_____ (1972a), "Issues in Growth Accounting: A Reply to Edward F. Denison," *Survey of Current Business* Vol. 52, No. 4, Part II, May, pp. 65–94.

_____ (1972b), "Issues in Growth Accounting: Final Reply," *Survey of Current Business* Vol. 52, No. 5, Part II, May, p. 111.

Jorgenson, D. W., F. M. Gollop, and B. M. Fraumeni (1987), *Productivity and U.S. Economic Growth*, Cambridge, MA, Harvard University Press.

Jorgenson, D. W., J. J. McCall, and R. Radner (1967), *Optimal Replacement Policy*, Amsterdam, North-Holland.

Kendrick, J. W. (1961), *Productivity Trends in the United States*, Princeton, Princeton University Press.

_____ (1973), *Postwar Productivity Trends in the United States, 1948–1969*, New York, National Bureau of Economic Research.

_____ (1976), *The National Wealth of the United States*, New York, Conference Board.

_____ (1983), *Interindustry Differences in Productivity Growth*, Washington, American Enterprise Institute.

Kendrick, J. W., and E. S. Grossman (1980), *Productivity in the United States: Trends and Cycles*, Baltimore, Johns Hopkins University Press.

Kuznets, S. (1957), "Comment," in Conference on Research in Income and Wealth, *Problems of Capital Formation*, Princeton, Princeton University Press, pp. 271–280.

Lau, L. J. (1978), "Applications of Profit Functions," in M. Fuss and D. McFadden, eds., *Production Economics*, Amsterdam, North-Holland, Vol. 1, pp. 133–216.

Lee, B. S. (1978), "Measurement of Capital Depreciation within the Japanese Fishing Fleet," *Review of Economics and Statistics*, Vol. 60, No. 2, May, pp. 225–237.

Lindahl, E. (1939), "The Place of Capital in the Theory of Price," in E. Lindahl, *Studies in the Theory of Money and Capital*, London, Allen and Unwin.

Malinvaud, E. (1961), "The Analogy between Atemporal and Intertemporal Theories of Resource Allocation," *Review of Economic Studies*, Vol. 28(1), No. 82, June, pp. 143–160.

Malpezzi, S., L. Ozanne, and T. Thibodeau (1987), "Microeconomic Estimates of Housing Depreciation," *Land Economics*, Vol. 63, No. 4, November pp. 372–385.

Meyer, J., and E. Kuh (1957), *The Investment Decision*, Cambridge, MA, Harvard University Press.

Muellbauer, J. (1975), "The Cost of Living and Taste and Quality Change," *Journal of Economic Theory*, Vol. 10, No. 3, June, pp. 269–283.

Musgrave, J. C. (1986), "Fixed Reproducible Tangible Wealth in the United States: Revised Estimates," *Survey of Current Business*, Vol. 66, No. 1, January, pp. 51–75.

Norsworthy, J. R. (1984a), "Capital Input Measurement: Options and Inaccuracies," in Japan Productivity Center, Measuring Productivity, New York, UNIPUB, pp. 73–94.

———— (1984b), "Growth Accounting and Productivity Measurement," Review of Income and Wealth, Series 30, No. 3, September, pp. 309–329.

Office of Industrial Economics (1975), Business Building Statistics, Washington, U.S. Department of the Treasury.

Ohta, M., and Z. Griliches (1975), "Automobile Prices Revisited: Extensions of the Hedonic Price Hypothesis," in N. Terleckj, ed., Household Production and Consumption, New York, Columbia University Press, pp. 325–390.

Ramm, W. (1970), "Measuring the Services of Household Durables: The Case of Automobiles," Proceedings of the Business and Economics Section, Washington, American Statistical Association, pp. 149–158.

Rymes, T. K. (1980), "Comment," in D. Usher, ed., The Measurement of Capital, Chicago, University of Chicago Press, pp. 58–68.

Schiff, E. (1957), "Comment," in Conference on Research in Income and Wealth, Problems of Capital Formation, Princeton, Princeton University Press, pp. 261–271.

Shephard, R.W. (1953), Cost and Production Functions, Princeton, Princeton University Press.

———— (1970), Theory of Cost and Production Functions, Princeton, Princeton University Press.

Solow, R. M. (1960), "Investment and Technical Progress," in K. Arrow, S. Karlin, and P. Suppes, eds., Mathematical Methods in the Social Sciences, 1959, Stanford, Stanford University Press, pp. 89–104.

Taubman, P. and R. Rasche (1969), "Economic and Tax Depreciation of Office Buildings," National Tax Journal, Vol. 22, No. 3, September, pp. 334–346.

Terborgh, G. (1954), Realistic Depreciation Policy, Washington, Machinery and Allied Products Institute.

Triplett, J. E. (1975), "The Measurement of Inflation: A Survey of Research on the Accuracy of Price Indexes," in P. H. Earl, ed., Analysis of Inflation, Lexington, MA, Heath, pp. 19–82.

Walras, L. (1954), Elements of Pure Economics, trans. W. Jaffe, Homewood, IL, Irwin.

Wykoff, F. C. (1970), "Capital Depreciation in the Postwar Period: Automobiles," Review of Economics and Statistics, Vol. 52, No. 2, May, pp. 168–176.

Young, A., and J. C. Musgrave (1980), "Estimation of Capital Stock in the United States," in D. Usher, ed., The Measurement of Capital, Chicago, University of Chicago Press, pp. 23–58.

2

The Application of a Hedonic Model to a Quality-Adjusted Price Index for Computer Processors

Ellen R. Dulberger

2.1 Introduction

Quality change presents difficult problems for economic measurement. The computing equipment industry is a case in point. Technological improvements have successively led to the introduction of new models of equipment with greater capabilities than existing ones. In the rapidly changing environment in which these products compete, price comparisons of equipment with the same quality required to construct meaningful price indexes are often not observed. Quality change prevents direct comparison of observed prices. In order for meaningful price comparisons to be made, quality must be held constant. This is a study of quality adjustment in prices of newly manufactured computer processors, one component of computing systems.[1]

Hedonic models, which have been used for many years and applied to many different products, provide one way to deal with the problem. The basic premise therein is that price differences across different units of transaction are due mainly to quality differences that can be measured in terms of common attributes, also called characteristics. A hedonic function, in effect, disaggregates transaction units into common characteristics.[2] Estimates of implicit (because they are not observed) characteristics' prices are derived from estimates of characteristics' coefficients. These implicit characteristics' prices are then used to estimate the price of an unobserved model by valuing its embodied characteristics.[3] In constructing a quality-adjusted price

This study has benefited from the generous and valuable help of many colleagues. I especially wish to thank Jack Triplett of the BEA, who posed thoughtful, focused questions. Most of all, I am indebted to Rosanne Cole of IBM, whose knowledge, wisdom, energy, and endless generosity of spirit made it all happen.

index such estimates are then used for prices of models not transacted in the reference period.

The issues to be addressed in the application of a hedonic model to a quality-adjusted price index for output of the computing equipment industry are as follows: (1) selection of the appropriate level of aggregation, (2) specification of the characteristics, and (3) expansion of the hedonic model to deal with technologically induced price disequilibrium that occurs when models embodying new technology are sold at lower prices than existing ones because full market adjustment is not instantaneous.

Earlier studies have often shown the underlying theme of technologically induced price equilibrium, though none have explicitly dealt with its presence. In addition, all have suffered from the specification of characteristics that were either inadequate or redundant, or both, and in some cases there has been a mismatch between included equipment and price.

This study will show that with the selection of appropriate performance characteristics, for which the equipment was designed and used, a hedonic model expanded to deal with this phenomenon of technologically induced disequilibrium can be useful in estimating a quality-adjusted price index for the output of computer processors.

Once estimated, such an index is useful in estimating real output. The Paasche-like index constructed in this paper declines at an average annual rate of 17.8% over the period 1972–1984. When this index was combined with analogous indexes estimated for storage devices, printers, and displays, and used in the recent revisions by the BEA of the GNP accounts, it showed that an estimated 22.5% average annual growth in current dollar purchases of computing equipment represented a 42.5% average growth rate for constant dollar purchases.

The equipment under study and specification of characteristics as well as the meaning and role of technology as it affects market prices will be described. Then the framework for the empirical work will be developed. In so doing, the traditional approach will be expanded to allow for the presence of technologically induced disequilibrium. This will be followed by a description of the sample and discussion of the empirical results. The presence of technologically induced disequilibrium and the path of ensuing price adjustment will then be examined. The best equation will be used to estimate the alternative quality-adjusted price indexes explored next.

The object of analysis of this study is the computer processor, one component of a computing system. It is part of SIC 35731 and more narrowly defined as large and intermediate general purpose digital processors, at the seven-digit SIC level, 3573106–3573109.

2.1.1   The Role of a Computer Processor in a Computing System

In order to gain perspective on the focus of the study and the characteristics selection, it is helpful to understand the components of a computing system in terms of their contribution to the system. A computing system is comprised of many component parts custom configured to meet a user's needs. Each component, also known as a box, provides a specialized service to the system. The activities of a computing system can be described briefly as follows: information is entered, instructions are executed, results are stored, and reports are generated. The computer processor, also called the CEC, houses the central processing unit (CPU), and main memory. The CPU executes instructions, and the main memory stores the essential and most frequently used information so that it is available to the CPU.

2.1.2   Focus

The selection of system components rather than whole systems was based on two considerations. Keeping in mind that the goal is an output price index for newly manufactured products, the selected unit of study should be such that the valued sum of the units shipped equals the current value of industry shipments.

Newly manufactured computing equipment, SIC 3573, during the time period studied here, 1972–1984, is comprised of components, not systems. Although data-processing services are provided by the stock of computing systems, changes to that stock are often in the form of components that are used to modify existing configurations rather than to configure new whole systems. Hence, total shipments of newly manufactured computing system components do not map into newly manufactured whole systems. This alone is sufficient reason to base a study today on components rather than systems.

The second consideration is a practical one concerning the tractability of measurement of performance characteristics and the feasibility of measuring performance with the hedonic technique. At the component level, performance characteristics, of value to both producer and purchaser, are based on each component's role in the system. System performance, however, though driven to a large extent by the performance of individual hardware components, has the added dimension of component interactions (and nonhardware elements such as system and application software). Information-processing systems get the work done through a network of component queues. Research, thus far, indicates that such analysis requires a more complicated technique than the hedonic one.[4]

2.1.3   Specification of Characteristics

Effective disaggregation of any unit of output into its embodied characteristics requires that the selected characteristics provide a good representation of the unit in terms of what is valued by buyer and seller. The selected characteristics must provide a complete representation of the product's capabilities.

The capabilities of a processor can be described in terms of speed with which instructions are executed and the capacity of main memory. Measurement of main memory capacity is straightforward and easily obtained (and uncontroversial). Megabytes, units of 1,024 x 8, binary digits (0s or 1s) that can reside in main memory, are a readily acceptable measure of capacity.[5]

Speed, however, is an attribute more difficult to measure. Previous studies of computing equipment, some of which focused on processors and others on configured systems, have generally failed to include an adequate measure of processor speed.

A weighted composite of all the instruction execution rates for a typical job mix (or benchmark) is a better representation than any single one. A widely used measure of this kind is MIPS—millions of instruction executions per second, in which each instruction is weighted by its frequency of use in the job mix. However, two types of problems arise with the use of this measure. The first is comparability. If two processors have different instruction formats or different logic designs, their MIPS ratings will not be comparable. They can be made comparable as follows: Assume the MIPS rating of a given processor equals $MIPS_1$ and that N_1 equals the number of instruction executions in processing the job mix. If some other processor has a rating of $MIPS_2$ and its number of instruction executions equals N_2 for the same job mix, then the "equivalent MIPS" rating equals $MIPS_2(N_1/N_2)$.[6] The second problem relates to the choice of the job mix. It arises because of the difficulty of defining a truly representative benchmark. The advantage of equivalent MIPS as a measure of processor speed is realized only if the specified job mix is representative of the jobs expected to be performed by the processors being compared.[7]

To be assured of a comparable measure of processor speed, this study included IBM and plug-compatible processors for which equivalent MIPS are publicly available.

2.1.4   The Role of Technology

Technological improvements permit greater outputs to be produced with the same inputs. This has certainly been true for computer processors. The manufacture of processors with greater capabilities has been directly attributable to improvements in semiconductor technology. These improvements take the form of increased density, that is, packing more information (circuits) in the same physical space. Increased densities lead to greater capabilities because they shorten the distance electrons travel, which means that more information can be stored, and instruction execution time is reduced. The impact of changes in technology over time has been to reduce quality-adjusted prices. This time series phenomenon, by itself, however, need not require explicit treatment of technology in the hedonic framework. The need arises in individual cross-sections that are in a state of technologically induced price disequilibrium. When existing products are leapfrogged by products embodying a newer technology at a lower quality-adjusted price, initially the marketplace is in a state of disequilibrium. This means that there is a period of time when two sets of prices for processors with the same characteristics coexist—one for products based on the old technology and one for those based on the new.

Explicit treatment of technology-induced disequilibrium is required in a hedonic function of prices in a dynamic environment because failure to do so risks producing biased estimates of characteristics' coefficients. The potential for bias occurs because the forces causing the disequilibrium are likely to be correlated with the characteristics.

Fisher, McGowan, and Greenwood (1983) recognized this problem and dealt with it by selecting only new models of one manufacturer (IBM) for inclusion in their analysis. It was assumed that such models embody the same level of technology and thus will be on the same hedonic surface. This made sense in their view because technological "leapfrogging" made each new announcement likely to move out the production possibility frontier (lowering the supply function), creating a new hedonic surface to be identified. Stoneman (1976) attempted to deal with the problem in another way. Generation dummies whose values were based on dates of introduction were intended to sort models by technology, that is, hold technology constant, while estimating the relationship between price and characteristics. Michael (1979) noted the underlying theme in his own and other studies—lower prices for newly introduced models—and it was suggested that the presence of multiple prices is related to the unavailability of new models. The BEA (1985), in its study, similarly found evidence of multiple frontiers producing multiple quality-adjusted prices. Statistical significance of the estimated coefficients on the "new" dummy in regressions of consecutive year pairs indicated that "new" models were sold at lower quality-adjusted prices than those that sold in the prior year as well.

No other study that included models embodying different technologies directly used information on those technologies to examine the presence of technologically induced disequilibrium, and the path of ensuing market adjustment using characteristics' coefficients estimated without risk of associated bias.

2.2   Empirical Framework

A hedonic equation can be specified for a single cross-section in double-log form as

$$\ln P_i = a + \sum b_k \ln X_{ki} + u_i \tag{1}$$

where

P_i = price of the ith box,

X_{ki} = price of the quantity of the kth characteristic in the ith box,

a = intercept,

u_i = error associated with the ith box.

The equation can then be expanded (as it often has been) to incorporate pooled time series and cross-sections where changes in the intercept, that is, parallel shifts in the hedonic surface, are estimated over time by adding a dummy variable D_t for each year in the sample except one:

$$\ln P_{it} = a + \sum_{t}^{t-1} d_t D_t + \sum b_k \ln X_{ki} + u_i. \tag{1a}$$

The estimate of a represents the intercept for the year in which the time dummy was omitted, that is, the reference period. The estimates of d_t represent the difference (or shift) between the surface in each base year t and the reference period.

Generally, to ease exposition, the omitted time dummy is that of the first sample year, so that estimates of d_t permit convenient comparisons of the shift in the hedonic surface through time. Other studies of computing equipment have produced estimates of d_t that are negative and generally increase in magnitude over time. These negative price changes, holding quality constant, have been attributed sensibly to technological change.

In order for the time dummies of (1a) to capture technology-driven price reductions successfully, and to avoid the possibility of technology-associated bias in the estimated characteristics coefficients, one of two conditions must hold within any time period t: all products transacted in the same time period embody the same level of technology, or, in the absence of immediate (total) diffusion of new technology, prices of products embodying older technologies adjust fully and instantaneously, resulting in one prevailing quality-adjusted price for all products (regardless of differences in embodied technologies). To test directly for the failure of either condition, (1a) will be expanded to allow for nonquality-associated price differences to be present. This requires grouping the processors in the sample into classes according to their embodied technologies within each period. These technology classes enter the equation as follows:

$$\ln P_{it} = a + \sum^{t-1} d_t D_t + \sum^{m-1} c_{mt} T_m D_t + \sum b_k \ln X_{ki} + u_i, \tag{2}$$

where T_m denotes a dummy variable for the mth technology class and $T_m D_t$ denotes a dummy variable for the mth technology class in the tth period. There will be $(m-1)t$ such variables.

In the event that only one technology class is present ($m = 1$) the technology class by time dummies will not enter the equation ($m - 1 = 0$). If $m - 1$ classes are present in period t but are embodied in products that compete at the same quality-adjusted price, then the dummies will enter the equation but their coefficients c_{mt} will not differ from zero, indicating that all m classes have quality-adjusted prices not different from that of the omitted class in the same year.[8]

The empirical work will be conducted as follows: Equations (1a) and (2) will be estimated and compared to assess the contribution of technological stratification. Intrayear comparisons of coefficients across technology classes each year will be tested for statistical difference with each other. Equation (2'), a simplified version of (2) with two kinds of restrictions, will be estimated. First, technology class coefficients not different from zero (that is, not priced differently from the omitted class) are restricted to be zero by dropping them out of the equation. Second, technology class coefficients not different from one another are restricted to be equal by collapsing those technology class dummies into one variable. Equations (2') and (2) will be compared to test the validity of the restrictions as a group. Corresponding equations will be estimated for each cross-section underlying (2') and the set of single-year regressions compared with pooled equation (2') to confirm the constancy of b_k over time. Box-Cox transformations will be used on pooled (2') to compare and select the best functional form.

2.3   Empirical Work

2.3.1   Sample

Characteristics and purchase prices covering the years 1972–1984 were collected for a total of 67 boxes sold by 4 vendors. Characteristics were obtained for compilations published in *Computerworld* and *Datamation*. The data were augmented by reports of new product announcements in the general and trade press. Estimates of 370 equivalent MIPS are publicly available for processors produced by IBM and plug-compatible manufacturers. MIPS ratings published for the processors of other manufacturers may not be equivalent. The published data are unclear on this matter. This problem imposed a constraint on sample size. A reduced sample was accepted to enable the use of a comparable, and, in principle, superior measure of speed in order to avoid the bias created by measurement error.

This study included large and intermediate general purpose processors. It also excludes small processors because they are typically packaged with auxiliary storage devices (disk drives or cassettes) under the covers. Estimates of their performance must account for component queues.

Typically, manufacturers make each CPU available with a choice of main memory capacities that are available in increments. Since there was no means by which to determine a typical main memory capacity, two models of each processor were included in the sample. Prices were obtained for two main memory capacities: (a) one increment greater than the minimum offered (b) and the maximum.

Implementing these memory size rules often meant changes in memory size over time for the same CPU, and the values for the characteristic were changed accordingly in the data set in the next calendar year. Prices for IBM products were taken from historical sales manuals. Other manufacturers' prices were derived from price information in press articles. Base prices for processors with minimum memory, memory increment size and price, and maximum capacity available were used to calculate values for included main memory capacity and corresponding prices. Annual prices were created by weighting together different prices within a year by their respective duration. No reports of price change were treated as no price change.

In principle, a model should remain in the sample as long as it was in new production. However, volume of shipments data for each processor model is unavailable. Quantities shipped in each sample year were estimated from the year-to-year changes in IDC's annual tabulation of installed general purpose computing systems in the United States, published in EDP reports.[9]

A model was included in the sample for each year that the stock of its installed equipment increased. It was assumed to be in new production during those years because an increase means that new shipments exceeded the sum of customer returns of leased equipment and retirements. A decrease indicates that the converse was true and it was more likely that shipments, if any, were comprised of recycled equipment manufactured in a prior year.[10] A model entered the sample the first year it appeared in the stock and was deleted the year after its stock peaked.

Small sample size and poor quality shipments data present serious limitations to the data set. Neither, however, in the author's view could have been avoided. As noted earlier, when faced with the choice of a large sample or adequate measure of speed, better measurement was selected.

The year 1972 was chosen to begin the sample period for two reasons. The introduction of semiconductor main memory in 1971 made it practical for the first time to house logic and main memory under the same cover, and henceforth was called the processor or the CEC (central electronic complex). The CEC together with minimum required gear from then on comprised a basic transaction unit.

By 1972, outright purchase overtook lease arrangements as the dominant mode of equipment acquisition. Purchase prices are preferred to lease prices for the purpose of this study because when

Table 2.1
Regression coefficients: 1972–1984 pooled regressions[a]

	1		2		2′	
Characteristics	Coeffi-cient	t value	Coeffi-cient	t value	Coeffi-cient	t value
Speed	.798	(35.1)	.780	(39.0)	.783	(41.4)
Capacity	.173	(6.6)	.219	(10.0)	.215	(10.1)
Intercept	7.578	(94.1)	7.945	(79.1)	7.944	(79.5)
Year dummies	*		*		*	
Technology class by year			*		*	
R^2		.953		.953		.973
Mean square error		.062		.039		.038
Sample size	296		296		296	

a. Dependent and independent variables, except dummies, are in natural logarithms. An asterisk denotes set of dummies included in regressions.

multiplied by the number of units shipped they yield the current value of shipments, the series for which a quality-adjusted price index is desired. Though transaction prices would be preferred, they were not available, imposing the use of manufacturer's list prices. The severity of this problem depends on the degree to which transactions occur at unpublished discounted prices.

2.3.2 Empirical Results

Equation (1a), the traditional hedonic equation with price as a function of characteristics and time dummy variables for each but one year, was estimated for the full sample period, denoted 1 in table 2.1. The results indicate that, in accord with prior expectations, MIPS and main memory both contribute directly and significantly to the price of processors. Speed is shown to be by far the dominant characteristic. It should be. After all, the role of processors is to execute instructions.

To investigate the matter of technologically induced disequilibrium, dummy variables were defined for models in each technology class each year as detailed in table 2.2. The density of magnetic core memories (which are not chip-based), which were present in the sample only in 1972, required approximation. One additional distinction was made in 1973, the only sample year in which two different types of semiconductors memory with the same density

Table 2.2
Processor main memory technologies 1972–1984

Class code	Material	Type	Memory chip density (kilobits) per chip)	Years in sample	Years "best"
1	Magnetic core		.0025[a]	1972	
2	Semiconductor	Bipolar	.125	1972	
3	Semiconductor	Bipolar	1	1973–1974	
4	Semiconductor	FET	1	1973, 1976–1979	1973
5	Semiconductor	FET	2	1974–1983	1974
6	Semiconductor	FET	4	1975–1982	1975–1978
7	Semiconductor	FET	16	1981–1984	
8	Semiconductor	FET	64	1979–1984	1979–1984

a. Estimated using relative volume/megabyte from Pugh et al. (1981, table 1).

were both present. This final sort was made because the two types of semiconductors, bipolar and FET, differ greatly in price and circuit speed.

An explicit test of technology-induced disequilibrium was made with the introduction of these technology class-by-year dummy variables (for each but one technology class), for each but one year in the sample. For example, one such dummy for technology class 8 in 1980 is assigned a value of one for all processors embodying 64k memory chips in the year 1980 and zeros for all other processors and all other years. For convenience of exposition, the omitted technology class was that of the "best," defined as the densest. The omitted year was 1972. This means that, for any given year, estimated coefficients on the technology class dummies for that year represent (in log form) price differences between each of those classes and the "best." Furthermore, the combined effect of omitting the 1972 time dummy and the best technology class in each year means that the estimated coefficient of each time dummy represents the price difference between the "best" technology in that year as compared with the "best" in 1972.

Comparison of (nested) equation (2) with equation (1a) in table 2.1 indicates that technological stratification reduces the mean square error substantially. An F ratio of 7.9 as compared with a value of 2.21 at the 1% level of significance indicates the improvement made by the addition of the technology by year dummies.

Table 2.3A
Regression coefficients on technology class by year dummies for processors

Year	"Best"	Equation (2) Technology class 1	2	3	4	5	6	7	8
1972		−.554 (−4.4)	*						
1973	−.239 (−1.8)			.295 (2.3)	*				
1974	−.195 (−1.6)			.284 (2.3)		*			
1975	−.746 (−4.3)					.524 (3.3)	*		
1976	−.798 (−4.6)				.160 (.8)	.557 (3.5)	*		
1977	−1.003 (−7.5)				.318 (2.4)	.383 (3.0)	*		
1978	−1.245 (−9.3)				.379 (2.9)	−.084 (−.7)	*		
1979	−2.283 (−13.1)				1.181 (6.0)	.877 (5.4)	.833 (5.3)		*
1980	−2.257 (−16.7)					.537 (4.6)	.544 (5.3)		*
1981	−2.167 (−17.7)					.262 (2.7)	−.038 (−.4)	.327 (3.7)	*
1982	2.293 (−19.0)					.147 (1.0)	.142 (1.6)	.281 (3.7)	*
1983	−2.392 (−20.3)					.173 (1.2)		.032 (.4)	*
1984	−2.554 (−21.0)							−.050 (−.8)	*

Table 2.3B
Regression coefficients on technology class by year dummies for processors

Year	"Best"	Equation (2') Technology class							
		1	2	3	4	5	6	7	8
1972		−.554 (−4.4)	*						
1973	−.235 (−1.8)			.293 (2.3)	*				
1974	−.192 (−1.6)			.282 (2.3)		*			
1975	−.743 (−4.3)					.524 (3.3)	*		
1976	−.715 (−5.1)				0	.477 (4.0)	*		
1977	−.997 (−7.5)				.318 (2.5)	.383 (3.0)	*		
1978	−1.282 (−10.7)				.420 (3.6)	0	*		
1979	−2.276 913.1)				1.179 (6.0)	.877 (5.5)	.833 (5.3)		*
1980	−2.250 (−16.8)					.539 (5.7)	.539 (5.7)		*
1981	−2.172 (−18.5)					.273 (3.0)	0	.338 (4.1)	*
1982	2.248 (−19.3)					0	0	.243 (3.4)	*
1983	−2.273 (−20.5)					0		0	*
1984	−2.564 (−21.8)							0	*

Table 2.3A displays the estimated technology and time differences of equation (2). Upon examination by row of these coefficients and their t statistics it appears that in 7 cases the prices of nonbest technology classes may not be significantly different from the best (zero) within the same year. Furthermore, there are 4 cases where nonbest technology classes, though different from the "best," do not appear to be different from one another.

A formal test for statistical difference between two coefficients is

$$t_{n-k} \sim \frac{\hat{B}_i - \hat{B}_j}{S_{Bi}^2 + S_{Bj}^2 - 2 \, (\text{est cov } \hat{B}_i \hat{B}_j)}$$

and yields, as shown in table 2.4, the following results for computing "nonbest" technologies.

In 1980, two nonbest technologies are embodied in processors not priced differently from one another (holding characteristics constant). Equation (2′), a simplified form of equation (2), in which the coefficients on technology classes not statistically different from zero were restricted. The estimated time and technology class coefficients are displayed in table 2.3B. An alternative expanded specification that includes direct measures of embodied technology is considered in the author's dissertation (Dulberger, 1986).

Although the restrictions were indicated as the result of individual t tests, it is necessary in addition to test the validity of the restrictions as a group. An F test comparing equation (2) with nested equation (2′) yields a value of 0.7 with a critical value of the 1% level equal to 3.6, enabling one to reject the null hypothesis that they are different. In other words, we are entitled to implement the restrictions and proceed to examine equation (2′) with direct focus on significant technology-associated price differences appearing in the lower left panels of table 2.3A and 2.3B.

Inspection by row reveals that in all cases but one, that is, class code 1 in 1972, products embodying nonbest technologies have quality-adjusted prices higher than or equal to those competing products embodying the best in current production. The odd case occurring in 1972 concerns memories made from magnetic core, a material that had been in production at least since 1955. Although core memory, over its production life, experienced great improvements in densities and cost reductions by 1972, further improvements in density and cost were unlikely, even though it was relatively inexpensive to continue production. The future belonged to semiconductors. In all other cases, newer technology meant lower quality-adjusted prices.

The estimated time and technology class dummy coefficients from (2′) are used to derive price indexes for each technology class as shown in table 2.3C. Arbitrarily setting the value for technology class 2 in 1972 to 100, all values in this panel are relative to this class. Equal index numbers within a year represent technology classes priced alike. Intrayear differences indicate multiple-price regimes.

As the estimated 1972 price difference indicates, semiconductors were initially expensive. It may be that the enormous reduction in size permitted consumer tolerance of such a premium. By 1975, however, 4k FET chips enabled processor prices to be 15% lower than those embodying core in 1972.[11] Furthermore, the manufacture of processors with empty slots to permit future insertion of additional memory (and logic) indicated that once in the world of semiconductors, floorspace reductions were not considered important.

Inspection by column reveals that over time, with one exception—technology class 4—the estimated price differentials between "non-best" and each prevailing "best" technology continually erode. The introduction of a new "best" initially shows high estimated price differentials, which again erode with time. Prices of products embodying older technologies are cut or production ceases; that is, the technology class drops out of the sample.

Technology class code 5, representing the 2k FET chip, has the longest life—10 years. It is "best" only in its year of introduction, 1974, and over the next 4 years becomes fully competitive in price with the "new best," the denser 4k FET technology (class code 6).[12] In 1979, yet another "best" is introduced, and once again, with successive price reductions, technology class 5 becomes fully competitive and remains so through 1983, its last year in production.

The prices of technology classes 6 and 7 become fully competitive and remain so until further price reductions of the best drive them from production.

Technology class 4 is peculiar. First introduced in 1973, it is "best" only in that year, and is substantially less expensive than its only competitor. However, after just one year it is no longer in production and is replaced by a new "best," in 1974 shipments of the same models. It is reintroduced in 1976, this time embodied in new processors at prices fully competitive with the current best, class 6. Subsequently, although this class did sustain price cuts, it continually lost ground (that is, its price differential with "best" increased) through

Table 2.3C
Price indexes by technology class (1972 "best" = 100)

Year	"Best"	1	2	3	4	5	6	7	8
			Technology class						
1972	100.0	57.5	100.0						
1973	79.0		106.0	79.0					
1974	82.5		109.4		82.5				
1975	47.6				80.3	47.6			
1976	48.9				48.9	78.8	48.9		
1977	36.9				50.7	54.1	36.9		
1978	27.7				42.4	27.7	27.7		
1979	10.2				33.3	24.6	23.6		10.2
1980	10.5					18.1	18.1		10.5
1981	11.4					15.0	11.4	16.0	11.4
1982	10.6					10.6	10.6	13.5	10.6
1983	10.3					10.3		10.3	10.3
1984	7.7							7.7	7.7

Table 2.4
Test for intrayear differences across technology classes

Year	Class codes	$\dfrac{\hat{B}_i - \hat{B}_j}{S_{\hat{B}i} + S_{\hat{B}j} - 2(\text{est cov } \hat{B}_i \hat{B}_j)}$	t	Result
1977	4,5	$\dfrac{.318 - .383}{(.127)^2 + (.127)^2 - 2(.006)}$	$= -3.1$	Different
1979	4,5	$\dfrac{1.182 - .876}{(.197)^2 + (.161)^2 - 2(.010)}$	$= 6.8$	Different
	5,6	$\dfrac{.876 - .831}{(.161)^2 + (.156)^2 - 2(.020)}$	$= -4.4$	Different
1980	5,6	$\dfrac{.535 - .541}{(.115)^2 + (.101)^2 - 2(.007)}$	$= -.6$	Not different
1981	5,7	$\dfrac{.260 - .326}{(.097)^2 + (.088)^2 - 2(.003)}$	$= -5.9$	Different
1982	6,7	$\dfrac{.142 - .282}{(.091)^2 + (.075)^2 - 2(.002)}$	$= -14.1$	Different

1979, its last year in manufacture. As expected, though, shipments declined because prices did not, reflecting reduced demand for models with reduced price competitiveness.

Equation (2′) interestingly reveals that although 8 of the 13 sample years contain products embodying at least 3 different technologies, 5 of those years indicate the presence of only 2 price regimes. This means that for the most part, products embodying "nonbest" technologies are priced alike or priced like the "best." Two years, 1983 and 1984, are found to be in equilibrium. In 1977, 1979, and 1981, there are more than 2 coexistent quality-adjusted prices—a finding to be investigated.

In 1977, although processors embodying each of the 2 classes of nonbest technologies did sustain competitive price cuts, the regression results indicate that they are not quite priced alike. The less dense class code 4 lost competitiveness vis-à-vis the best (class 6) while technology class 5 gained. The estimated price differential is a small 6.8% (though statistically significant). Though not alike, the two nonbest classes are priced closely, and both are expensive relative to the best.

In 1979, the findings indicate the presence of four price regimes. This was the last year of production of products embodying the FET 1k chip (technology class 4). Few transactions took place that year which is not surprising, because quantity should adjust (due to reduced demand) when prices do not.[13] The other competing nonbest technologies are priced very much alike, with an estimated 4.5% difference, which is not very meaningful though statistically significant. Again, though processors in all classes underwent price reductions from their prior levels, those embodying nonbest technologies were not able immediately to match the prices of the spanking new best.

The finding that three different quality adjusted prices were present in 1981 may be related to a sample phenomenon. This is the only example of a first-time introduction of a new technology that is not the "best" technology, technology class 7. Furthermore, stratification indicated that the difference in its quality-adjusted price relative to another FET 2k, "nonbest" was small, 6.7%, although, significant. Successive price cuts did improve the 16k chip's product competitiveness and by 1983 this class had met fully the 64k challenge (class 8).

The last two years in the sample, 1983 and 1984 are found to be in equilibrium. In the movement to full equilibrium from 1982 to 1983, only three of the four classes present in 1982 continued in production the following year. In 1984 equilibrium was maintained, but only two technology classes survived.

The results support the view that technological improvements induce disequilibrium, the market does adjust, and the period of adjustment is longer than one year.[14]

It should be emphasized that technological improvements need not have resulted in transactions at more than one quality-adjusted price. Transactions in multiple-price regimes (reflecting technologically associated cost differences) could only occur when matched by consumers' tolerance of the differences. Consumer intolerance of the inability of producers to offer fully competitive prices on models embodying older technologies would result in a full adjustment in quantity (disappearance of higher-priced models embodying older technologies) and transactions would be observed at only one quality adjusted-price—the "best."

A puzzle that still remains is why manufacturers do not do one of the following: raise the quality-adjusted prices of the new models in limited supply to equal those of models widely available or make the new models widely available right away. One possibility is that offering new models at low prices is a way of disseminating information about the impact of the new technology.

2.3.3   Further Testing

Pooling of Cross-Sections

Thus far, the results presented have been estimated using pooled time series and cross-section data. While pooling provides an obvious convenience, it is necessary to test whether it is appropriate.

Selecting equation (2') for further testing, individual cross section equations were estimated for each of the 13 sample years that when combined yield the full regression. These equations are shown in the appendix.

The results indicate that for all 13 cross-sections MIPS and main memory are significant and furthermore, t statistics on technology dummies support all of the restrictions in the full pooled equation. An F value equal to .04 supports the null hypothesis that the errors in the single equations come from same population as the full multiyear equation. This means that the characteristics coefficients are constant over time. The contour of the hedonic surface does not change over time; it experiences parallel shifts resulting from technological change. (It should be noted that constant characteristics coefficients do not imply constant characteristics prices.) Continued use of the pooled sample is based on this finding.

Functional Form

Comparison of the frequently used semilog functional form with the alternative double-log form, which is made with the use of the Box-Cox transformation.[15]

$$y = \begin{cases} \dfrac{y^{\lambda} - 1}{\lambda} & (\neq 0) \\ \\ \log y & (= 0). \end{cases}$$

This transformation is advantageous because it permits direct comparison of the residual sum of squares, and hence mean square error (MSE). A semilog equation, where $\lambda = 1$ for price and 0 for characteristics, was estimated and yielded an MSE = .198, proving to be inferior to the double-log form, whose MSE = .038.[16]

Linear Homogeneity

It is interesting to note that equations (2) and (2′) appear to be linear homogeneous functions of price with respect to characteristics. A formal test of linear homogeneity of equation (2′) in the form of a restriction yields coefficients of .783 on ln MIPS and .217 on ln memory, with an insignificant $t = -0.2$ on the restriction (see appendix). The implication of this finding is intuitively pleasing; that is, a doubling of characteristics leads to a doubling of price, so that for any given technology, at any point in time, doubling processors characteristics will double its price. Moreover, a valuation of the characteristics yields the box price.

Memory Size Rule

Since the sample includes CECs with two different memory sizes for each CPU, it is necessary to test whether the characteristics coefficients are affected by included main memory capacity rules. Adding two additional variables to equation (2′) permits such a test. A dummy

variable is defined representing those CECs with minimum plus one
increment of memory with a value of 1 for all CECs with minimum
plus one increment of memory and a value of 0 for those with maximum. Then two variables are defined representing ln(MIPS) and
ln(memory) of CECs with minimum plus one increment of memory,
by multiplying this dummy variable by ln MIPS and ln main memory
previously used. Adding these two variables to equation (2') and
reestimating will provide estimates of the difference between (a) each
characteristic's coefficient for those CECs that include minimum plus
one increment of memory and (b) the entire sample. The coefficients
(t statistics) on these differences are .019 (0.5) on ln(MIPS) and −.012
(−0.4) on ln(main memory), indicating no significant difference in the
estimated characteristic coefficients between the one memory size and
the entire sample.[17]

Technologically Associated Coefficient Bias

To address the question of biased estimates of characteristics
coefficients when failing to account for the presence of technologically
induced price disequilibrium, a standard *t* test is used to compare
each characteristic's estimated coefficient between the traditional
equation (1) and the fully expanded equation (2). For ln(MIPS) and
ln(Memory), the *t* statistics equal 20.0 and 39.4, respectively. These
results indicate a significant difference at the 1% level. We can conclude from this that failure to account for this phenomenon does
result in biased characteristics coefficients estimates.

Plausibility of Findings

The willingness of sellers to offer products embodying older technologies at higher quality-adjusted prices than those embodying newer
ones (as production costs dictate) makes sense. However, in order for
transactions to occur at more than one quality-adjusted price, buyers
must be willing to pay such a price difference. Why would they, and
why would their willingness be related to memory chip density or any
measure of technology?[18]

   At the time of their introduction, the supply of processors embodying new technology is limited.[19] Over the life cycle of a product (also
called product cycle), availability increases in subsequent years and
then declines as manufacturers gear up production of the successors.
To the extent that the newer products are not widely available, one

can view the premium on older products with the same capabilities as the price of immediate delivery. It has also been suggested that there is uncertainty or a lack of information regarding how "good" the new products really are. Until information on what they can really do is available, it is possible that the older products, which are "known," could command a premium.

In answer to the second part of the question, embodied technology need not be directly related to all consumers' willingness to pay a price differential, and yet it might be to some. If we assume a competitive marketplace in which producers offer the lowest price possible, then transactions will occur at those supply prices or not at all. If buyers consider the premiums too high and the manufacturers cannot lower them, then transactions will not occur and buyers who cannot get the newer products now will wait for them to become available. In this sense, the premiums only indicate the behavior of some buyers. Others have effected a quantity adjustment when it failed to occur sufficiently in price.

Characteristics Prices

Estimated characteristics prices for processors as shown in table 2.5 are calculated as follows. The price of the kth characteristic in year t, denoted P_{kt}, is estimated as

$$\hat{P}_{kt} = \frac{\partial P_t}{\partial x_k} = b_k \sum_m \left(\frac{\overline{P}_{imt}}{x_{ki}} \right) v_{mt},$$

where the overbar denotes the arithmetic mean; P_{imt} denotes the price of the ith model of the mth technology class in year t; x_{ki} denotes the quantity of the kth characteristic in the ith model; v_{mt} denotes the share of characteristics from the mth technology class shipped in year t; and b_k denotes the regression coefficient for the kth characteristic.

The characteristics prices, as estimated from equation (2′) are shown in table 2.6. These estimates are partial derivatives; they are stated as the price of speed, *ceteris paribus* (including memory) and the price of memory, *ceteris paribus* (including speed).

The prices of both characteristics have fallen dramatically over the period 1972–1984. As table 2.5 indicates, the price of speed in 1984 is approximately 1/8 of its price in 1972. The price of memory is approximately 1/20.

Table 2.5
Estimated characteristics' prices (thousand dollars per unit)

Year	Speed, in MIPS	Capacity, in megabytes
1972	1801	497
1973	2293	404
1974	1906	332
1975	1827	283
1976	1821	285
1977	1385	154
1978	771	97
1979	661	80
1980	419	41
1981	394	24
1982	288	26
1983	264	25
1984	220	25

Table 2.6
Price indexes (1982 = 100)

	Matched models	Regression	Composite pooled TS/CS[a]	Composite single years	Composite characteristics TS/CS[a]
1972	214.1	989.5	834.3	934.5	787.5
1973	214.6	1047.5	865.8	998.5	924.5
1974	219.9	814.2	788.6	847.4	780.0
1975	228.9	792.5	703.7	743.4	721.0
1976	223.6	777.6	665.3	681.6	711.8
1977	183.5	499.3	473.6	527.1	505.3
1978	147.5	262.0	242.0	271.3	283.3
1979	136.4	242.5	204.9	215.9	242.8
1980	115.4	177.0	147.2	146.8	148.0
1981	111.1	113.3	118.6	119.8	125.4
1982	100.0	100.0	100.0	100.0	100.0
1983	89.7	90.6	93.9	86.5	92.7
1984	73.7	77.0	80.8	69.6	80.6
1972–1977	−3.0	−12.8	−11.2	−10.8	−8.5
1977–1984	−12.2	−23.4	−22.3	−25.1	−23.1
1972–1984	−8.5	−19.2	−17.8	−19.5	−17.3

a. TS/CS = time series/cross section.

2.4 The Price Indexes

The price index used as a deflator to convert current-dollar values to constant-dollar values is a Paasche formula index,

$$I_{o,t} = \frac{\sum P_{it} Q_{it}}{\sum P_{io} Q_{it}}, \tag{3}$$

where, for model i, P_{it} and P_{io} denote prices in the current and base periods, respectively, and Q_{it} denotes the quantity purchased in the current period. The problem encountered in constructing such an index for products experiencing rapid change is that models purchased in the current period may not have existed in the base period.

2.4.1 Matched-Model Index

The most frequently used approach for dealing with these problems uses observations only for the models that exist in both period t and in period 0. Models that exist only in the current period are ignored. Such an index may be referred to as a "matched-model" index.

Because models of computing equipment change so rapidly from one time period to another, it was not possible to calculate a matched-model index as such. Instead, matched models for 2 adjacent years were used to calculate an index where the base period is the first of the 2 years (that is, $t - 1$):

$$I_{t-1,t} = \frac{\sum P_{it} Q_{it}}{\sum P_{i,t-1} Q_{it}}. \tag{4}$$

An index for the entire period is calculated as a multiplicative "chain" of the adjacent-year indexes:

$$I_{o,t} = I_{o1} \times I_{12} \times \cdots \times I_{t-1,t}. \tag{5}$$

The index is referred to as a "chain index of matched models."

The assumption underlying the matched-model procedure is that the mean price change associated with the introduction of new models (or the discontinuance of old ones) equals the mean price change observed for models that are common to both periods. In other words, use of the matched-model procedure assumes that prices of models embodying old technology adjust instantaneously, so that their quality-adjusted prices are equal to those of the models embodying improved technology. If the assumption holds, the price change in the matched models equals the unobserved price change implicit in the introduction of new models (or the discontinuance of old ones). When there is price disequilibrium, as in the case where newly introduced models are sold at lower quality adjusted prices than existing ones, this assumption is invalid; the matched-model index will understate the magnitude of changes in quality adjusted prices.

2.4.2   The Composite Index

The "composite" index uses the matched-model approach whenever models exist in both current and base periods and estimates hypothetical prices for the models that did not exist in the base period from hedonic equations. If an "overlap" model (one that exists in both periods) is designated i and a model present in period t but not in period o is designated j, then the composite index is

$$I_{ot} = \frac{\sum P_{it}Q_{it} + \sum P_{jt}Q_{jt}}{\sum P_{io}Q_{it} + \sum P_{jo}Q_{jt}}. \tag{6}$$

In this formula, P_{jo} denotes the estimate, taken from the hedonic equation, or the hypothetical price that the "missing" model would have commanded in the base period. Note that when 1982 is the base (as it is for all the present calculations) and a year subsequent to 1982 is "year t," then P_{jo} is the hypothetical price for a new model. When a year earlier than 1982 (such as 1977) is "year t," then P_{jo} is the hypothetical price for a discontinued model.

When the base period is in a state of technological disequilibrium and multiple-price regimes are present, some convention must be adopted in estimating P_{jo} because there is more than one price prevailing for any set of model characteristics. In this study, the dominant technology—that is, the technology class with the greatest value share of shipments in the base period (1982)—was used to determine the hypothetical price P_{jo}. In 1982, for processors, the majority of models shipped were from technology class 8, embodying 64k memory chips.

Two composite indexes are presented in table 2.6. The first, called composite pooled TS/CS uses estimates of missing 1982 values from the pooled time series (TS), cross-section (CS) equation (2′). The composite single-years index uses estimates of the unobserved 1982 values from the 1982 cross-section equation.

2.4.3   The Characteristics Price Index

In hedonic studies, one can identify more than one kind of price. The conventional concept is that of the price of the model. A second concept is that of the prices of the "characteristics." One can use the estimated characteristics prices—shown in table 2.5—to construct a price index.

Given the formulation of the hedonic functions, the implicit dollar price of the kth characteristic possessed by the ith model of the mth technology class would be

$$\hat{P}_{kimt} = \hat{b}_k \frac{P_{imt}}{x_{kim}}. \tag{7}$$

where b_k is the regression coefficient for the kth characteristic—estimated as constant in equation 2′ for all years of the study—x_{kim} denotes the quantity of the kth characteristic possessed by model i, and P_{imt} is the price for model i, of technology class m, at time t.

The characteristics price index is

$$I_{ot} = \frac{\sum_k \sum_m \sum_i \left[\hat{b}_k \dfrac{P_{lmt}}{X_{kim}} \right] \left[x_{kim} Q_{imt} \right]}{\sum_k \sum_m \sum_i \left[\hat{b}_k P_{lmo} \right] \left[x_{kim} Q_{imt} \right]}, \tag{8}$$

where $x_{kim} Q_{imt}$ denotes the quantity of the kth characteristic possessed by model i of the mth technology class in period t. If the technology classes and models within them exist in both period t and in the base period, the characteristics price index would equal the matched-model index in equation (1).

The composite characteristics index shown in table 2.6 uses estimates of unobserved processor prices in 1982 derived from estimates of the embodied characteristics prices.

2.4.4   The Regression Index

The regression index uses no actual prices. It is frequently shown in other studies and is presented here for purposes of comparison. It is created directly from the year dummies in the regressions. The price index number for the regression index in table 2.6 is based on the combined expression for the regression coefficients for the year dummies and the dominant technology class. Dominant is defined as the technology class whose value share of shipments was highest in each year. It will be truer than an index of "best" (which could be constructed directly from the year dummies) because it represents products that are widely available.[20] Regression indexes may produce indexes that differ from alternative indexes that use hedonic methods.[21] Regression indexes assume that all observations lie on the regression line; that is, there are no box specific errors.

2.4.5   Index Comparisons

With the exception of the matched-model index, all of the indexes show dramatic 17–20% average annual price declines over the period. As expected, the matched-model index understated the magnitude of price reductions in periods of technological innovation and diffusion. During 1982–1984, a period characterized by no new technological introduction, it is comforting to see that changes in the matched-model index are close to those in the other indexes.

2.4.6   Use in Estimating the Computer Component of the Office, Computing and Accounting Machinery Component of PDE

The composite index, estimated from equation (2') was combined by the BEA with analogous indexes estimated for storage devices, printers, and displays and used in the latest revision of the GNP accounts. Using revised estimates of current dollar purchases of computing equipment and the new deflator, the growth in the constant dollar value of computing equipment for the period 1972–1984 averaged 42.5% per year. This compares with a 22.4% growth rate it would have shown, had the previously published deflator been used.[22]

2.5   Summary

An expanded version of the traditional hedonic model to allow for the presence of technologically induced disequilibrium was developed and estimated. Empirical results in the case of computer processors indicate that the introduction of new models of computer processors embodying technological improvements initially creates price disequilibrium. The market for computer processors is rarely observed in equilibrium over the period 1972–1984 and full market adjustment takes longer than one year. The marketplace reacts with the reduction in prices of models embodying older technologies as they continue to be sold until age-associated price reductions of the new technology make them unable to maintain their price competitiveness, driving them out of production. With rare exception, disequilibrium was characterized by two price regimes—one for models priced like those embodying "best" technology available and another, higher one priced like those embodying a "nonbest."

Plausibility of the findings is based on the explanation of consumer tolerances of non-quality-associated price differences, that is, multiple-price regimes, which must be present for transactions to occur at technology-driven different supply prices. The path of adjustment is most often observed in the form of continued price reductions of models embodying older technologies as the new one becomes diffused (widely available), tracing out the workings of a dynamic and competitive marketplace.

Limitations of the study include small sample size directly resulting from the requirement that the measure of processor speed must be adequate and comparable. The use of list prices rather than transactions prices is a second limitation. It could result in an upward bias in the magnitude of technology class estimated price differentials if models embodying aged "nonbest" technologies are sold at unpublished discounted prices.

This study represents an improvement over other hedonic studies of computing equipment in three ways. The selection of processors, rather than configured systems, provides the basis for estimating quality-adjusted price indexes that more closely match the industry's output. The specification of characteristics that more completely account for the capabilities of the equipment enables increased likelihood of full quality adjustment. The expansion of a traditional hedonic model to account for technologically induced disequilibrium (which is shown to be necessary) provides the means to derive useful estimates of prices of unobserved models for the purpose of constructing quality-adjusted price indexes without risk of technology-induced bias on characteristics' coefficients.

2.6   Conclusion

A hedonic model can be useful in estimating quality-adjusted price indexes for output of complex products manufactured in an industry characterized by rapid technological change. Three ingredients contributed to its successful application in the case of computer processors: (1) the unit of study closely matches the industry's output, (2) the selected characteristics provide adequate means to measure overall quality in a comparable way, and (3) the model is expanded to allow for the presence of technologically induced disequilibrium, which avoids the risk of biased estimates of characteristics' coefficients.

The expanded hedonic model is used to derive estimates for missing reference period prices in a quality-adjusted price index. This represents an improvement to the alternative matched-model approach, which requires market equilibrium in prices—an assumption that in the case of computer processors is rarely valid. Furthermore, the expanded model also permits, for the first time, direct examination of the path of market adjustment back to equilibrium and, in the case of processors, revealed the workings of a marketplace characterized by rapid change and intense competition.

Appendix

		Equation (1)		
		SSE	17.290600	F ratio 413.77
		DFE	281	
Dependent variable: ln(price)		MSE	0.061532	R^2 0.9537
		parameter	standard	
Variable	DF	estimate	error	T ratio
INTERCEPT	1	7.577679	0.080545	94.0802
LMIPS	1	0.797566	0.022699	35.1365
LMEM	1	0.172742	0.026348	6.5561
DUM73	1	0.247558	0.112419	2.2021
DUM74	1	0.263217	0.107741	2.4431
DUM75	1	0.053405	0.113390	0.4710
DUM76	1	−0.019843	0.108893	−0.1822
DUM77	1	−0.388725	0.109503	−3.5499
DUM78	1	−0.761353	0.108027	−7.0478
DUM79	1	−1.062589	0.107190	−9.9132
DUM80	1	−1.410951	0.106002	−13.3106
DUM81	1	−1.601752	0.104905	−15.2686
DUM82	1	−1.737711	0.104821	−16.5779
DUM83	1	−1.913002	0.106613	−17.9435
DUM84	1	−2.094333	0.109289	−19.1633

Dependent variable: ln(price)		Equation (2)		
		SSE	9.958698	F ratio 247.05
		DFE	257	
		MSE	0.038750	R^2 0.9734
		parameter	standard	
Variable	DF	estimate	error	T ratio
INTERCEPT	1	7.945483	0.100405	79.1347
LMIPS	1	0.780404	0.020006	39.0090
LMEM	1	0.218943	0.021791	10.0475
DUM73	1	−0.238623	0.129157	−1.8475
DUM74	1	−0.195011	0.122238	−1.5953
DUM75	1	−0.746222	0.174610	−4.2737
DUM76	1	−0.797988	0.174610	−4.5701
DUM77	1	−1.002879	0.134351	−7.4646
DUM78	1	−1.244792	0.134351	−9.2652
DUM79	1	−2.283200	0.174798	−13.0619
DUM80	1	−2.257239	0.135341	−16.6782
DUM81	1	−2.167541	0.122725	−17.6618
DUM82	1	−2.292601	0.120431	−19.0366
DUM83	1	−2.391602	0.117703	−20.3190
DUM84	1	−2.554427	0.121670	−20.9948
CORE72	1	−0.554157	0.127186	−4.3571
BP1K73	1	0.294874	0.128023	2.3033
BP1K74	1	0.283982	0.121088	2.3453
FET2K75	1	0.523900	0.158340	3.3087
FET1K76	1	0.159619	0.199764	0.7990
FET2K76	1	0.557116	0.158340	3.5185
FET1K77	1	0.318507	0.130192	2.4464
FET2K77	1	0.382654	0.127528	3.0006
FET1K78	1	0.378800	0.130192	2.9096
FET2K78	1	−0.084079	0.113689	−0.7396
FET2K79	1	0.877286	0.161463	5.4334
FET4K79	1	0.833202	0.157017	5.3065
FET2K80	1	0.537243	0.115726	4.6424
FET4K80	1	0.543794	0.102056	5.3284
FET2K81	1	0.261775	0.097510	2.6846
FET4K81	1	−0.037550	0.098922	−0.3796
F16K81	1	0.326954	0.087536	3.7351
FET2K82	1	0.147398	0.145683	1.0118
FET4K82	1	0.142178	0.090941	1.5634
F16K82	1	0.281465	0.075935	3.7066
FET2K83	1	0.176058	0.142916	1.2319
F16K83	1	0.032037	0.086229	0.3715
F16K84	1	−0.049791	0.061379	−0.8112

		Equation (2′)		
		SSE	10.219432	F ratio 326.27
		DFE	266	
Dependent variable: ln(price)		MSE	0.038419	R^2 0.9727
Variable	DF	parameter estimate	standard error	T ratio
INTERCEPT	1	7.943541	0.099875	79.5351
LMIPS	1	0.782893	0.018910	41.4017
LMEM	1	0.215084	0.021232	10.1304
DUM73	1	−0.234675	0.128565	−1.8253
DUM74	1	−0.191375	0.121667	−1.5729
DUM75	1	−0.742013	0.173687	−4.2721
DUM76	1	−0.713853	0.141169	−5.0567
DUM77	1	−0.996704	0.133588	−7.4610
DUM78	1	−1.280713	0.120635	−10.6165
DUM79	1	−2.276428	0.173962	−13.0857
DUM80	1	−2.248901	0.134552	−16.7140
DUM81	1	−2.170567	0.117730	−18.4369
DUM82	1	−2.246169	0.116959	−19.2048
DUM83	1	−2.371737	0.116153	−20.4191
DUM84	1	−2.562078	0.118104	−21.6934
CORE72	1	−0.553615	0.126636	−4.3717
BP1K73	1	0.292540	0.127453	2.2953
BP1K74	1	0.281960	0.120558	2.3388
FET2K75	1	0.523327	0.157411	3.3246
FET2K76	1	0.476617	0.120637	3.9508
FET1K77	1	0.317258	0.129382	2.4521
FET2K77	1	0.381630	0.126958	3.0060
FET1K78	1	0.419647	0.116036	3.6165
FET1K79	1	1.178943	0.196806	5.9904
FET2K79	1	0.877021	0.160694	5.4577
FET4K79	1	0.832551	0.156193	5.3303
FET24K80	1	0.540045	0.095372	5.6625
FET2K81	1	0.272866	0.091740	2.9743
FET16K81	1	0.337813	0.082057	4.1168
FET16K82	1	0.242539	0.072299	3.3547

Dependent variable: ln(price)		Equation (2′) Restriction: coefficients on LMIPS and LMEM sum to 1		
		SSE DFE MSE	10.220373 267 0.038279	F ratio 339.16 R^2 0.9727
Variable	DF	parameter estimate	standard error	T ratio
INTERCEPT	1	7.946551	0.097827	81.2309
LMIPS	1	0.783340	0.018659	41.9820
LMEM	1	0.216660	0.018659	11.6116
DUM73	1	−0.237588	0.126980	−1.8711
DUM74	1	−0.193328	0.120804	−1.6003
DUM75	1	−0.747761	0.169450	−4.4129
DUM76	1	−0.717615	0.138855	−5.1681
DUM77	1	−1.003138	0.126874	−7.9066
DUM78	1	−1.286944	0.113668	−11.3219
DUM79	1	−2.280930	0.171255	−13.3189
DUM80	1	−2.253646	0.130853	−17.2227
DUM81	1	−2.176893	0.110374	−19.7229
DUM82	1	−2.253829	0.106033	−21.2560
DUM83	1	−2.379826	0.103835	−22.9192
DUM84	1	−2.570846	0.103785	−24.7709
CORE72	1	−0.554453	0.126291	−4.3903
BP1K73	1	0.294793	0.126406	2.3321
BP1K74	1	0.283254	0.120055	2.3594
FET2K75	1	0.527121	0.155249	3.3953
FET2K76	1	0.478425	0.119864	3.9914
FET1K77	1	0.321218	0.126653	2.5362
FET2K77	1	0.383272	0.126292	3.0348
FET1K78	1	0.423404	0.113319	3.7364
FET1K79	1	1.181669	0.195676	6.0389
FET2K79	1	0.875313	0.160029	5.4697
FET4K79	1	0.830412	0.155309	5.3468
FET24K80	1	0.538008	0.094307	5.7048
FET2K81	1	0.271733	0.091287	2.9767
FET16K81	1	0.338303	0.081847	4.1333
FET16K82	1	0.244088	0.071487	3.4144
RESTRICTION	−1	−0.465425	2.967945	−0.1568

		Equation (2′) Test of memory size rule		
Dependent variable: ln(price)		SSE DFE MSE	10.206962 264 0.038663	F ratio 303.31 R^2 0.9727
Variable	DF	parameter estimate	standard error	T ratio
INTERCEPT	1	7.937632	0.101661	78.0791
LMIPS	1	0.778486	0.021989	35.4036
LMEM	1	0.214175	0.023522	9.1054
LMINMIPS	1	0.018961	0.036081	0.5255
LMINMEM	1	−0.012370	0.030808	−0.4015
DUM73	1	−0.228340	0.130858	−1.7449
DUM74	1	−0.185508	0.123795	−1.4985
DUM75	1	−0.736839	0.175263	−4.2042
DUM76	1	−0.706702	0.143732	−4.9168
DUM77	1	−0.985042	0.139365	−7.0681
DUM78	1	−1.269083	0.126883	−10.0020
DUM79	1	−2.263620	0.179688	−12.5975
DUM80	1	−2.234509	0.143814	−15.5374
DUM81	1	−2.156646	0.127406	−16.9273
DUM82	1	−2.231971	0.126729	−17.6121
DUM83	1	−2.356720	0.126969	−18.5614
DUM84	1	−2.546587	0.129465	−19.6700
CORE72	1	−0.552890	0.127063	−4.3513
BP1K73	1	0.287839	0.128761	2.2355
BP1K74	1	0.277728	0.121724	2.2816
FET2K75	1	0.524020	0.157920	3.3183
FET2K76	1	0.475333	0.121082	3.9257
FET1K77	1	0.315443	0.129912	2.4281
FET2K77	1	0.377330	0.127924	2.9496
FET1K78	1	0.417864	0.116531	3.5859
FET1K79	1	1.175264	0.197831	5.9407
FET2K79	1	0.875917	0.161246	5.4322
FET4K79	1	0.830691	0.156821	5.2971
FET24K80	1	0.537233	0.096253	5.5815
FET2K81	1	0.272591	0.092041	2.9616
FET16K81	1	0.338214	0.082320	4.1085
FET16K82	1	0.241659	0.072587	3.3292

Single-year regressions results

Year	Constant	ln(MIPS)	ln(MEM)	Technology class								R^2	F	SSE	DF
				1	2	3	4	5	6	7	8				
1972	8.074 (37.7)	.764 (3.8)	.322 (2.0)	-.590 (-2.6)	*							.9689	62.4	.696	6
1973	7.559 (82.6)	.553 (6.3)	.266 (3.4)			.149 (1.3)						.9831	116.3	.159	6
1974	7.614 (79.8)	.668 (8.6)	.212 (2.8)			.243 (2.1)		*				.9837	160.8	.248	8
1975	7.293 (61.6)	.726 (9.8)	.200 (2.7)					.358 (2.4)	*			.9934	299.2	.141	6
1976	7.250 (66.1)	.749 (11.1)	.173 (2.6)				-.007 (0.0)	.402 (2.9)	*			.9938	279.3	.141	7
1977	7.176 (38.8)	.698 (5.0)	.145 (1.5)				-.014 (0.0)	.254 (1.7)	*			.9782	101.2	.255	9
1978	6.710 (41.5)	.557 (7.3)	.322 (3.1)				.101 (0.5)	**	*			.9822	220.5	.193	12
1979	5.626 (59.1)	.560 (10.4)	.185 (3.2)				.867 (7.5)	1.176 (12.5)	1.225 (11.7)		*	.9944	423.6	.008	12

Single-year regressions results

Year	Constant	ln(MIPS)	ln(MEM)	Technology class								R^2	F	SSE	DF
				1	2	3	4	5	6	7	8				
1980	5.636	.593	.170					.922	.922		*	.9859	465.3	.326	20
	(57.7)	(9.6)	(3.4)					(7.4)	(7.4)						
1981	5.656	.801	.270					.232	**	.355	*	.9730	261.6	.767	28
	(61.9)	(20.2)	(5.6)					(2.9)		(5.2)					
1982	5.629	.852	.203					**		.294	*	.9600	287.8	1.925	36
	(42.2)	(14.2)	(2.8)							(3.2)					
1983	5.520	.834	.204					**		**	*	.9689	1692.0	.887	45
	(65.9)	(24.1)	(4.6)												
1984	5.261	.813	.235							**	*	.9524	450.0	2.182	45
	(35.5)	(15.0)	(3.4)												

* Class present in sample but coefficient omitted from regression to avoid singular matrix.

** Present in sample but omitted because not statistically different from zero.

Notes

1. This study is part of a larger one at IBM in which hedonic equations were developed for three other types of computing equipment as well: auxiliary storage, printers, and displays. The quality-adjusted price indexes estimated from these equations were used by the BEA in the recent revisions of the GNP accounts as described in Cartwright (1986).

2. For a more complete discussion of hedonic functions as a disaggregator, see Triplett (1976).

3. The formula for deriving the characteristics' prices from the estimated coefficients depends on the functional form of the estimated equation.

4. When two or more components are packaged together, other approaches — such as analytic models (which are designed to cope with the queueing aspects of the interactions among the components) — may be more efficient. See Bard and Sauer (1981) for a general description of analytic models as well as other types of computing system performance modeling at IBM.

5. For a discussion of the conversion of information into binary digits and how computers work see Goldstine (1980).

6. Discussion on this topic with Y. C. Chen has been most helpful.

7. Fisher, McGowan, and Greenwood (1983) do make comparisons of price/MIP. It appears that lack of comparability prevented its further use in their study. Knight (1966) developed a measure similar in design to native or own, MIPS (millions of own instructions per second), which were not comparable.

8. An alternative expanded equation for processors where direct measures of technology are used in place of the dummies is explored in the author's dissertation and for auxiliary storage devices in Chen and Hodge (1985).

9. CECs could be identified because systems are known by their CEC model name (or number).

10. Even if IDC stocks were accurate, returns of leased equipment will cause a downward bias in the shipments estimates derived this way. There is no publicly available alternative.

11. The estimated price difference between processors embodying FET 2k chips in 1975 and those with core memories in 1972 is taken as the antilog of the difference between the estimated coefficients, $e^{-.715-(-.554)} = .850$.

12. The continued ability of the FET 2k technology class to incur price reductions may stem in part from the fact that in the sample, only IBM processors embody this technology and IBM's packaging is said to have enabled the 2k chip to be as effective as a 16k chip. For a discussion of packaging at IBM, see Seraphim and Feinberg (1981).

13. The only processor still shipped in 1979 with FET 1k technology was 3138 manufactured by IBM. While it may be suggested that the premium is likely to be overstated because it reflects the 3138's list price premium relative to the best that year and that transaction prices would surely have been lower, this is not the case; IBM did not discount 3138s.

14. It has been suggested that the finding that products embodying new technologies are initially cheaper may be due in part to unbundling—the pricing of fewer different characteristics together as a unit, especially likely with the introduction of the 4341 by IBM in 1979, which was the first processor to embody 64-kilobit memory chips. If this were the case, one would expect the estimated premiums of competing "nonbest" technologies to persist and never be driven to zero. The finding that in most cases, prices of products embodying older technologies do become fully competitive is evidence that unbundling does not refute the interpretation of the finding given here.

15. For a description of Box-Cox transformations see Maddala (1977, pp. 315–317).

16. A range of alternatives were examined where λ was varied from 0 to 1 in increments of .1 for the dependent variable independently of both characteristics. (λ was not varied independently for each characteristic.) The lowest standard error of estimate was .027, which resulted from $\lambda = 0$ for price $\lambda = .3$ for characteristics. This is so close to double-log that my preference for simplicity combined with my a priori expectation that the function would be double-log led me to choose from the three alternatives shown in table 2.5.

17. It has been suggested that the smallness of the sample, which contributes to the finding that the individual cross-sections can be pooled, is in part due to the failure to include a model for every main memory size available with a CPU. Whether or not such additional observations would contribute in a meaningful way is answered, at least, in part, by this test. The arbitrary selection of the memory sizes included in the sample differ in range by model, and over time. The finding that the characteristics' coefficients do not differ suggests that additional observations would not alter the results and would be an artificial way to increase sample size.

18. Discussion on the topic with Zvi Griliches has been most helpful.

19. This limited supply of new models phenomenon was noted in Michael (1979).

20. The regression could have been reestimated omitting the dominant class in each year rather than "best." The resulting time dummy coefficients are linear transformations of those estimated with "best" omitted and would yield the same result.

21. See Triplett and McDonald (1977).

22. The previously published deflator had a value of 1 in every period. It had been assumed that price changes were exactly offset by quality changes. This practice had long been recognized as poor, but a replacement was not easily devised.

Bibliography

Archibald, Robert B., and Reece, William S. (1979). "Partial Subindexes of Input Prices: The Case of Computer Services," *Southern Economic Journal* 46 (October): 528–540.

Bard, Yonathan and Sauer, Charles H. (1981). "IBM Contribution's to Computer Performance Modeling," *IBM Journal of Research and Development* 25 (September): 562–570.

Barquin-Stolleman, Joan A. "Quality Adjusted Price Indexes for Printers: A Hedonic Approach," report in preparation.

Bloch, Erich and Galage, Dom (1978). "Component Progress: Its Effect on High Speed Architecture and Machine Organization," *IEEE Computer* (April): 64–75.

(U.S. Department of Commerce) Bureau of Economic Analysis (1985). *Improved Deflation of Computers in the Gross National Product of the United States.* Working Paper Series WP-4. Washington, D.C.

Cartwright, David W. (1986). "Improved Deflation of Purchases of Computer," *Survey of Current Business* (March): 7–9.

Chen, Yung C. and Hodge, James H (1985). "Using Hedonics to Measure Performance: A Study of Computer Disk Drives," report.

Chow, Gregory C. (1967). "Technological Change and the Demand for Computers," *American Economic Review* 57 (December): 117–130.

Cole, Rosanne, Chen, Y. C., Barquin-Stolleman, Joan A., Dulberger, Ellen R., Helvacian, Nurhan, and Hodge, James H. (1986). "Quality-Adjusted Price Indexes for Computer Processors and Selected Peripheral Equipment," *Survey of Current Business* (January): 41–50.

Dulberger, Ellen R. (1986). "The Application of an Hedonic Model to a Quality Adjusted Price Index for Computer Processors," CUNY dissertation.

Fisher, Franklin M., McGowan, John J., and Greenwood, Joen E. (1983). *Folded, Spindled, and Mutilated,* Cambridge, MA: MIT Press.

Fisher, Franklin M., McKie, James W., and Mancke, Richard B. (1983). *IBM and the U.S. Data Processing Industry: An Economic History,* New York: Praeger.

Goldstine, Herman (1980). *The Computer from Pascal to Von Neumann,* Princeton: Princeton University Press.

Griliches, Zvi, ed. (1971). *Price Indexes and Quality Change,* Cambridge, MA: Harvard University Press.

Knight, Kenneth E. (1966). "Changes in Computer Performance: A Historical View," *Datamation* (September): 40–54.

Maddala, G. S., (1977). *Econometrics,* New York: McGraw-Hill.

Michael, Robert J. (1979). "Hedonic Prices and the Structure of the Digital Computer Industry," *Journal of Industrial Economics* 27 (March): 263–274.

Pugh, Emerson W., Critchlow, Dale L., Henle, R. A., and Russell, Louis A. (1981) "Solid State Memory Development in IBM," *IBM Journal of Research and Development* 25 (September): 585–602.

Ratchford, Brian T., and Ford, Gerald (1976). "A Study of Prices and Market Shares in the Computer Mainframe Industry," *Journal of Business* 49 (April): 194–218.

Rosen, Sherwin (1974). "Hedonic Prices and Implicit Markets: Product Differentiation in Price Competition," *Journal of Political Economy* 82 (January/February): 34–55.

Rymaszewski, E. J., Walsh, J. L., and Leehan, G. W. (1981). "Semiconductor Logic Technology at IBM," *IBM Journal of Research and Development* 25 (September): 603–616.

Seraphim, Donald P., and Feinberg, Irving (1981). "Electronic Packaging Evaluation in IBM," *IBM Journal of Research and Development* 25 (September): 617–629.

Stoneman, Peter (1976). *Technological Diffusion and the Computer Revolution*, Cambridge: Cambridge University Press.

Triplett, Jack E. (1976). "Consumer Demand and Characteristics of Consumption Goods." In *Household Production and Consumption*, pp. 305–324. Edited by Nestor E. Terlecky; Conference on Research in Income and Wealth, Studies in Income and Wealth, Vol. 40. New York: National Bureau of Economic Research.

Triplett, Jack E., and McDonald, Richard J. (1977). "Assessing the Quality Error in Output Measures: The Case of Refrigerators," *Review of Income and Wealth* 23 (June): 137–156.

Data Sources

"General Purpose Computer Census," *IDC Industry Report*: 3/30/72.

"General Purpose Computer Census," *IDC Industry Report*: 3/30/73.

"General Purpose Computer Census," *IDC Industry Report*: 4/19/74.

"General Purpose Computer Census," *IDC Industry Report*: 4/30/75.

"General Purpose Computer Census," *IDC Industry Report*: 4/30/76.

"General Purpose Computer Census," *IDC Industry Report*: 4/22/77.

"General Purpose Computer Census," *IDC Industry Report*: 5/19/78.

"General Purpose Computer Census," *IDC Industry Report*: 6/30/79.

"General Purpose Computer Census," *IDC Industry Report*: 5/28/80.

"General Purpose Computer Census," *IDC Industry Report*: 6/29/81.

"General Purpose Computer Census," *IDC Industry Report*: 9/22/82.

"General Purpose Computer Census," *IDC Industry Report*: 9/30/83.

"Large Scale Computer Census as of Jan. 1, 1984," *IDC Industry Report*: 10/25/84.

"Medium Scale Computer Census," *IDC Industry Report*: 12/12/84.

"1984 Preliminary Census Report for Selected Vendors," *IDC Corporate Planning Service Market Data*: 1/85.

Henkel, Tom (1981). "Hardware Roundup," *Computerworld* (7/13):11–14.

Henkel, Tom (1982). "Hardware Roundup," *Computerworld* (8/2):23–26.

Henkel, Tom (1983). "Hardware Roundup," *Computerworld* (8/8):29–32.

Henkel, Tom (1984). "Hardware Roundup," *Computerworld* (8/20):23–23.

Lias, Edward J. (1980). "Tracking Those Elusive KOPS," *Datamation* (Norway):99–105.

3   The Postwar Evolution of Computer Prices

Robert J. Gordon

"Economics is a one or two digit science." [1]

"If the auto industry had done what the computer industry has done in the last 30 years, a Rolls-Royce would cost $2.50 and get 2,000,000 miles to the gallon." [2]

3.1   Introduction

It is now 35 years since the first delivery of the UNIVAC I electronic computer, and 32 years since the introduction of IBM's first electronic computer model. It is well-known that price of mainframe computers per unit of performance has fallen radically since those early days, by a factor of hundreds or even thousands, and that a modern personal computer costing a few thousand dollars has more memory and a faster speed than mainframes costing a million dollars or more as recently as the mid-1970s. Yet to this day, the Bureau of Labor Statistics (BLS) in its Producer Price Index (PPI) includes no price index for computers (either mainframe or personal), despite its inclusion of many hundreds of commodity indexes for less important types of mechanical and electrical machinery. And only in its December, 1985,

An earlier version of this chapter was prepared for the Conference on Technology and Capital Formation, Kennedy School of Government, Harvard University, Cambridge, MA, November 8–9, 1985.

    This research is supported by the National Science Foundation. I am exceedingly grateful to Peter Fisher for locating data sources and creating our data file, and to Gabriel Sensenbrenner both for carrying out the econometric estimation and for making numerous suggestions that improved the results that appear here. Helpful comments on the first draft of this chapter were contributed by Ellen Dulberger, Franklin M. Fisher, and Matthew Gilfix. Special thanks go to Jack Triplett for his acute comments on each succeeding draft.

benchmark revision did the Bureau of Economic Analysis (BEA) introduce a deflator for the computer component of producers' durable
equipment (PDE) dating back to 1969, after more than two decades of
publishing national income and product accounts (NIPA) based on the
assumption that the prices of electronic computers remained fixed
year after year.[3]

This chapter attempts to construct a single price deflator for electronic computers for the full period 1951–1984, based on an application of the hedonic regression technique to two different data sets.
The source of one of these data sets (Phister, 1979) also forms the basis
of a recent study by Flamm (1987), although this chapter is the first to
estimate hedonic regression equations for the Phister data, which
cover the period 1951–1979.[4] The other data source, *Computerworld*
magazine, covers 1977–1984 and is studied here for the first time.[5]
While the "final" price index developed in the chapter is based
entirely on the Phister and *Computerworld* data sets, we also reestimate
our equations for the new-model portion of two other data sets used
previously by Chow (1967) and Dulberger (1988). This allows us to
explore the sensitivity of the implied hedonic price indexes to alternative data sources, while holding constant other aspects of the analysis.

The coverage of the study includes mainframe computer processors
for the full 1951–84 period, minis from 1965 to 1984, and personal
computers for 1982–1987. This is the first study of computers to cover
such a long sample period and to provide separate treatment of mini
and micro computers.[6] The final price index for mainframe and mini
computer processors exhibits a 1951 index number, on a base 1984 =
100, of 133,666, implying an annual rate of change over the 33 years of
−21.8%.

The chapter begins with three sections providing background
material. Section 3.2 provides a brief overview of the postwar
development of the computer industry and exhibits data on value and
numbers of computers sold by major type (the same data are subsequently used to supply weights for the separate mainframe and minicomputer price indexes). Section 3.3 examines aspects of the hedonic
regression methodology that are relevant to this study, including data
availability and definitions, specification, functional forms, structural
stability, and make effects. Section 3.4 provides an introduction to our
data, while section 3.5 discusses the hedonic regression estimates and
section 3.6 the issues involved in choosing one equation in preference
to another, including equations covering the same time interval
yielded by alternative data sets. To remain within the strict length and

scope guidelines set down by the editors, this chapter provides only new research results and does not present any comparison of our results with the previous literature. Results of other studies are cited in Triplett's companion chapter in this volume (1988).[7]

3.2   The Postwar Development of the Computer Industry

This study develops price indexes for computer processors displaying enormous changes over time; a price index that shrinks from 100,000 to 100 over a span of 33 years is probably unprecedented in economic history (although changes in the opposite direction from 100 to 100,000 over shorter periods have occurred in hyperinflations). A bit of intuition to support these startling numbers is provided by a few details on the first electronic computer, the ENIAC, which was developed during World War II. The ENIAC had a trifling computational capacity in comparison with today's PCs yet was gigantic in size, measuring 100 feet long, 10 feet high, and 3 feet wide, and containing about 18,000 vacuum tubes. This machine was programmed by setting thousands of switches, all of which had to be reset by hand in order to run a different program. It is reported to have broken down "only" about once per day.[8]

The first major successor to the ENIAC was the UNIVAC I, originally built on contract with the U.S. government for use in the 1950 census. All the UNIVACs built through 1953 were purchased by the government, and an initial commercial purchase occurred in 1954. Unlike the ENIAC, the UNIVAC operated with stored programs rather than hand-set switches, and is the first machine in our hedonic regression sample from the Phister (1979) data source.[9]

The development of computer technology is often described with a terminology of technical "generations." Early first-generation machines through the late 1950s operated with vacuum tubes, followed by the second-generation machines based on transistors, starting with the IBM 7000 series introduced in 1959. The first IBM third-generation machines with integrated circuits were the series 360 models, first installed in 1965. Since the introduction of semiconductor chips, continuous improvements have been achieved by packaging increased numbers of circuits closer together, both lowering the marginal cost of additional memory and reducing instruction execution time.

The evolution of the computer industry is quantified in table 3.1, which displays domestic purchases (i.e., including imports and

Table 3.1
U.S. domestic purchases of electronic computers, 1955–1984 (value in millions of dollars)

Year	Mainframes Units	Value	Minis Units	Value	Micros Units	Value	Total Units	Value
1955	150	63					150	63
1956	500	152					500	152
1957	660	235					660	235
1958	970	381					970	381
1959	1150	475					1150	475
1960	1790	590					1790	590
1961	2700	880					2700	880
1962	3470	1090					3470	1090
1963	4200	1300					4200	1300
1964	5600	1670					5600	1670
1965	5350	1770	250	29			5610	1799
1966	7250	2640	385	40			7635	2680
1967	11200	3900	720	69			11920	3968
1968	9100	4800	1080	100			10180	4900
1969	6000	4150	1770	152			7770	4302
1970	5700	3600	2620	210			8320	3810
1971	7600	3900	2800	218			10400	4118
1972	10700	5000	3610	271			14310	5271
1973	14000	5400	5270	369			19270	5769
1974	8600	6200	8880	577			17480	6777
1975	6700	5410	11670	642	5100	77	23470	6128
1976	6750	5580	17000	816	25800	374	49550	6770
1977	8900	6600	24550	1203	58500	761	91950	8563
1978	7500	7590	29550	1596	115600	1098	152650	10284
1979	7200	7330	35130	2038	160000	1488	202330	10856
1980	9900	8840	41450	2487	250500	2104	301850	13431
1981	10700	9540	44100	2699	385100	2503	439900	14842
1982	10600	10300	47820	2821	735000	4190	793420	17311
1983	9985	10480	45420	3330	1260000	5300	1315405	19110
1984	10700	10360	72130	4185	2100000	7750	2182005	22295

Source: 1960–1984: Einstein and Franklin (1986, table 1); 1955–1959: Phister (1979, table II.1.21).

excluding exports) for mainframes, mini-computers, and micros (mainly PCs in the 1980s). Both numbers of units and the value of shipments are exhibited for each group.[10] Unit values are not shown to save space but can be calculated. These range for mainframes from $420,000 in 1955 to $968,000 in 1984; for minis from $110,000 in 1965 to $58,000 in 1984; and for micros from $15,000 in 1975 to $3,690 in 1984. Prior to 1965 virtually all computers were mainframes, and unit sales grew at a 50 percent annual rate while the value of shipments grew at a 44% rate (1955–1964). In subsequent decades the annual growth rate of mainframe units tapered off to 4% (1964–1974) and 2% (1974–1984), while the value of shipments grew at annual rates of 14% and 5% in these two decades, respectively. For these two decades growth rates were much faster for minis (48% and 23% for units versus 40% and 22% for values for 1965–1974 and 1974–1984, respectively). The annual growth rate for micro units during 1975–1984 was 95% and for value was 67%.

In assessing the data in table 3.1, we stress the importance of the shift from mainframes to minis and micros; the value share of mainframes declined from 97% in 1969 to 46% in 1984. Since this is the period covered by the new BEA deflator for computers, which excludes both minis and micros, that deflator becomes less representative of the total computer industry as the years go on.

3.3   The Hedonic Regression Model

3.3.1   "Matched Model" versus Hedonic Regression Indexes

Several years ago a paper on the development of computer price indexes for use in the NIPA would have required a substantial conceptual section. This would have addressed the stated opposition of the BEA to the inclusion in the NIPA of computer price indexes based on the hedonic regression methodology. In the last few years, however, the BEA has dropped its previous conceptual objections to regression-based price indexes. Convergence has occurred to such an extent that there are no conceptual issues that separate the three chapters on computers in this volume, nor the indexes developed here from those that are now included in the NIPA for the period since 1969. Any differences involve choices made in empirical implementation.

Triplett (1986) has provided a concise introduction to the interpretation of hedonic price indexes. These indexes can be distinguished from the "conventional method" used by the BLS to construct the Consumer Price Index (CPI) and the Producers Price Index (PPI). In the recent literature on computer price indexes, the conventional method has been called the "matched-model" method, since it involves comparing prices only for models that are identical in quality from one year to the next.

The most important potential defect in a matched-model index is the omission of price changes implicit in the introduction of new or "unmatched" models. A matched-model index assumes that the price change implicit in the introduction of new models is identical to the price change of the matched models over the same time interval. While this might be a valid assumption for some products, it is clearly invalid for electronic computers, as has been demonstrated recently by Cole et al. (1986) in their comparison of matched model and hedonic price indexes for the same sample of computers. The effect of the introduction of new technology that reduces the price of quality characteristics (e.g., computer speed and memory) is to cause the price of old models to be bid down. The prices of old models included in the matched-model price indexes may fail to duplicate the price reductions on new models either because (a) firms may sell old models at a discounted price but report list prices to the compiler of the price index or (b) firms may fail to reduce the transaction price of old models, thus causing their sales to disappear at a speed that depends on lags in information, lags in consumer reaction (due perhaps to employee training costs for switching to new models), and supply bottlenecks or backlogs on new models.

3.3.2   Basic Features of the Hedonic Method

The hedonic regression approach can be viewed as one of several methods to estimate the slope of the function relating the cost of a product to its quantity of characteristics. It assumes that the price of a product observed at a given time is a function of its quality characteristics, and it estimates the imputed prices of such characteristics by regressing the prices of different models of the product on their differing embodied quantities of characteristics. Thus the hedonic price approach does not represent a new concept in the measurement of quality change, but is an alternative to the manufacturers' cost estimates used for quality adjustment in most of the "matched-model" commodity price indexes compiled by the BLS for the PPI and CPI, to be used when practical factors make it more suitable.

A common approach to the estimation of quality-adjusted price change is to include time dummy variables (D_t) in cross-section regressions explaining price (p_{it}) for two or more years:

$$\log p_{it} = \alpha_0 + \sum_{t=1}^{N} \delta_t D_t + \sum_{j=1}^{m} \beta_j \log y_{ijt} + u_{it'} \tag{1}$$

$$(i = 1, \ldots, n; t = 0, \ldots, N).$$

Here y is the quality characteristic. In equation (1) we choose a log-linear (or "double-log") specification, following the majority of hedonic regression studies of computers. An alternative would be a semilog specification, with the log of price of the left and the unlogged values of the y variables on the right. Whatever the functional form, as long as the log of price is related to linear time dummy variables like the D_t in (1), a hedonic price index with a base of 1.0 in year $t = 0$ can be calculated from the antilogs of the δ_t coefficients. This has been the most common procedure in hedonic regression studies and is what Triplett (1988) calls the "dummy variable method."

The leading alternative is the "imputation method," in which an imputed base-year price for each model is calculated as the fitted value of (1), with the time coefficient for year t (δ_t) replaced by the time coefficient for the base year ($\delta_0 = 0$). If, for instance, the regression equation covers 1954–1965 and 1954 is the base year, the imputed 1954 price of a 1965 model can be calculated as the fitted value with the time coefficient set to zero. Since computer prices fell rapidly from 1954 to 1965, the imputed 1954 price of a 1965 model will be much higher than the actual price charged in 1965.

Triplett (1988) compares the dummy variable and imputation methods and on balance prefers the latter. In this chapter we compute price indexes using both methods. To his list of advantages of the imputation technique we can add the extremely useful role of imputed prices in providing a straightforward measure of base-year quality that can be used to edit a data set. If the ratio of the actual to the imputed price for a given model is much higher than the average of all models for a given year, that model is "overpriced," i.e., its actual price in year t is much higher relative to base-year quality than the average model. Below we adopt this criterion to omit selected models from our Phister data set, following the precedent set by Knight (1966).[11]

Returning to equation (1), there remains the problem of determining the optimal sample period for the regression. At one extreme we can obtain an aggregate index of price change from the series of δ_t coefficients obtained in a single regression for an entire data set, and at the other extreme an index can be calculated by linking together a string of δ_t coefficients obtained from a series of "adjacent year" regressions on data for successive pairs of years. To the extent that the prices of quality characteristics are changing through time, the adjacent-year technique allows the regression coefficients on the y_{ijt} to change every year. The disadvantage of the adjacent-year technique is that sample sizes are sometimes too small to yield efficient estimates, and estimated coefficients on the quality characteristics jump erratically from year to year and may even change sign.

Clearly there is no reason to choose either the extreme of running a single regression or N separate adjacent-year regressions. Instead, we can begin with numerous equations estimated for overlapping short periods and successively pool the data into longer periods, checking for structural change with the conventional "Chow test" for aggregation. This chapter tests for aggregation not only over time but also across different types of computer models.

3.3.3   Interpreting Residuals in Hedonic Regression Equations

No hedonic regression equation will fit the data perfectly. The estimated residuals (u_{it}) represent the effects of excluded attributes, incorrect specification of functional form, marketing practices unrelated to production costs, demand discontinuities, and time lags due to the fact that a new model may have a lower price than an older model containing the same quantity of characteristics. Some variables are omitted because they are highly correlated with other variables that are included. The coefficient on an included variable thus represents not just its own effect on price, but also that of the omitted variable(s). Thus the estimated β coefficients cannot necessarily be interpreted as representing the value that users place on a particular attribute.

Omitted attributes afflict all hedonic regression studies but may be particularly important in research on computer prices, since no study, including this one, has been able to quantify software maintenance, engineering support, or manufacturer's reputation. If these omitted variables differ systematically across manufacturers, then their effect on prices can be captured by manufacturer dummy variables or "make effects." Since our major emphasis is on changes in computer price indexes over time, our investigation of make effects is limited to the inclusion of IBM make-effect dummy variables in all those regression equations that include IBM models.

Related to make effects is the question of commodity boundaries. In a sense our study does not extend back far enough in time, since the first electronic computer may have represented a decline in the price-performance ratio of the previous "computer," some mixture of a punched card sorting machine and a clerk with a calculator.[12] The same issue arises in a cross-section, since one can ask whether mainframe, mini, and micro computers are all the same product. Below we find that pooling tests reject the aggregation of minis and mainframes into a single equation.

3.4   The Data

3.4.1   The Four Data Sources

The results in this study are based on two overlapping data sources. For the years 1951–1979 we have the compilation by Phister (1979), which provides for roughly 100 mainframe models a long list of quality characteristics, as well as a variety of sales prices and rental rates. For many but not all of the models, the Phister tables list 95 separate quality characteristics, including a wide variety of different performance measures (e.g., included memory, several dimensions of speed, and the Knight commercial and scientific indexes) as well as a number of attributes of more dubious importance (e.g., floor space, weight, and price per pound of both central processor and memory), and 20 lines of information on prices and rental rates.

For the period 1977–1984 our data source is *Computerworld* magazine, published by the International Data Corporation (IDC), which also publishes the bimonthly *EDP Industry Report*, the source of data in several earlier studies. We were attracted to *Computerworld* because of its annual hardware issue, which makes available all the required information in a single place for each year of the sample period. Later we discovered that the annual hardware issue began only in 1981, making an issue-by-issue search necessary for earlier years. It was possible to search only back to 1977 by the time the deadline for this chapter approached.

Two other data sources are used to check the sensitivity of our results to data sources. Gregory Chow provided the data used in his original 1967 article, and the BEA provided the data used by Ellen

Dulberger (1988) and Cole et al. (1986) for computer processors. In the following sections we describe the Phister and *Computerworld* data in some detail, since these are used here for the first time, and devote less attention to the Chow and Dulberger data, since these are described by those authors.

3.4.2 The Phister Data

Phister's data on speed and memory mainly come from *Auerbach Computer Technology Reports*, a comprehensive guide published since the early 1960s by Auerbach Information, Inc. His sources for system prices include General Service Administration catalogs, price lists published by various manufacturers, and Auerbach. Phister dates his prices as pertaining to "roughly two years after a model was introduced," where the introduction dates come from IDC.[13] The Phister data include, for most computer models, two types of prices. First, there is a system price accompanied by information on the amount of memory included in that price. Second, there is information on the price of incremental memory. A pitfall in working the Phister data is that the prices of several machines are listed with zero memory included. For most (but not all machines) information is given on the incremental price of memory, and for each such machine we created three observations, corresponding to the price and characteristics of models configured with minimum, maximum, and mean memory sizes. This procedure is identical to that carried out by Dulberger in creating her sample, except that she creates two observations corresponding to minimum and maximum memory. In short, in our Phister data set each model is entered three times if data on the price of incremental memory are provided, but only once if only a single price at a fixed memory configuration is provided without any supplemental information on the price of incremental memory.[14]

Seven indexes of speed are provided by Phister, including memory cycle time and several different measures of addition and multiplication speed. Initially we included memory cycle time and multiplication speed, as did Chow (1967), but soon found that they are highly collinear in the Phister sample. We omitted multiplication speed from the results presented in section 3.5, which include only memory and memory cycle time for the regressions estimated for the Phister data.

Also available from Phister are the Knight commercial and scientific performance indexes, which use a formula to weight together memory, processor time, and input-output time factors, and these are calculated from more basic specifications of each computer. Because the Knight indexes are composite blends of memory and speed based on "the opinions of 43 senior computer engineers and programmers"[15] in the early 1960s, the weighting factors may be obsolete, and so we prefer to let the weights on memory and speed be freely estimated and do not include the Knight indexes as explanatory variables. In the last part of the chapter we do use the Knight indexes as part of a comparison of the quality of particular IBM models over time. It is interesting that, as an example of the extent of reduction in the price-performance ratio in the industry, the Knight commercial index increases from 119 for the 1954 IBM model 650 to 564,000 for the 1979 IBM model 4331, yet the nominal price of the 4331 was less than half that of the 650.[16] This comparison is even more impressive when we note that the general price level as measured by the GNP deflator increased by a factor of 3.0 between 1954 and 1979.

3.4.3   The *Computerworld* Data

The *Computerworld* data set for 1977–1984 includes several quality attributes not available from Phister, including minimum and maximum number of input-output channels, cache buffer size, and, most important, millions of instructions per second (MIPS) beginning in 1981. Additional input-output channels allow a computer to use its central processor and memory more efficiently by loading instructions and data from several devices at the same time, and a cache buffer memory allows a powerful processor to use a low-cost, relatively slow integrated circuit memory.[17] Triplett (1988) discusses the advantages of MIPS over machine cycle time as a quality attribute, and for the 1981–1984 period we estimate equations that contain both MIPS and cycle time. Because these additional variables are available in the *Computerworld* sample but not in the Phister sample, we estimated separate equations for each sample and did not pool them.

3.4.4   Other Data Sources

In addition to our new data from Phister and *Computerworld*, we have also obtained two other data sets, the original Chow (1967) data covering 1954–1965, and the Dulberger (1988) data set covering IBM and compatible machines for 1972–1984. The Chow data set is considerably larger than the Phister sample for the years of overlap but yields similar results. The main defect of the Chow data set, as we discuss in section 3.6, is its underrepresentation of IBM mainframes and over-representation of minicomputers. The Dulberger data set includes information on the technological class of computers not available in either the Phister or *Computerworld* samples.[18] The main limitation of the Dulberger data set is its relatively small size, particularly when it is limited to new models only. During 1972–1979 the Dulberger data set includes just 19 new models (all IBM except for 4 plug-compatibles), as contrasted to 41 new models in the Phister data set. In the 1981–1984 period the Dulberger data set includes 42 new models (11 IBM and 31 plug-compatible), in contrast to the 266 new models in the *Computerworld* data set (34 IBM and 232 others, including 68 minis and superminis).[19]

There are several differences among these data sets that we need to keep in mind. Chow (with a few exceptions) and Phister include only computers in their first year of production (new models), while Dulberger and *Computerworld* cover all models in production. Dulberger's data cover a narrower range of manufacturers (IBM and three plug-compatible manufacturers) but is the most carefully developed for the consistency of price and quality characteristics. We deal with the first aspect of noncomparability by editing the Chow, Dulberger, and *Computerworld* data sets to include only new models. We check for the importance of the data consistency issue by comparing the estimate of performance improvements on specific IBM models implied by the estimated coefficients from the Phister, Dulberger, and *Computerworld* data sets (see pp. 111–117).

3.4.5 Data Issues

New Models versus All Models

Numerous pitfalls in applying the hedonic regression technique have surfaced in the literature, but one seems to apply with particular force in the computer industry. The Rosen (1974) equilibrium interpretation of a hedonic surface may not apply in the computer case, because the computer market has "never been close to long-run equilibrium in its entire existence."[20] Old inferior models do not just disappear when a new superior model is introduced, nor are they repriced at a lower price-performance ratio equal to that of the new model. This suggests that new and old models may lie on different hedonic surfaces.

When new models are introduced, they tend to offer a lower ratio of price to performance than existing models. Instead of falling until price-performance ratios are equalized across machines, older models that remain in production tend to be overpriced. This phenomenon suggests two possible arguments for excluding old models in hedonic regressions. First, mixing old and new models having different price-to-performance ratios together in the same hedonic regression equation may lead to biased estimates of the rate of price change. Second, the rate of price change will be sensitive to the changing fraction of the sample consisting of old models in a given year. For these reasons, Fisher, McGowan, and Greenwood (1983) argue forcefully that a hedonic regression study should include only new models.

By including only new models, the hedonic price index traces out the technological "frontier" as successively more powerful new models are introduced. The main limitation of such a price index is that the total production of computers includes both new and old models, and so for deflation of current dollar computer sales the price index should take into account existing models as well as new models. Thus a case can be made for producing two hedonic price indexes, one including and one excluding old models. To be consistent over time, a hedonic price index should be of one form or another, rather than mixing forms. If a data source included both old and new models, there would be no problem, since separate indexes could be developed based on all and new-only models.

Unfortunately, the Phister data source used in this chapter contains only new models, and thus to be consistent the resulting Phister-data price index should be compared to price indexes for the other data sets based only on new models. To maintain consistency, our basic results for the *Computerworld* data set include new models only. Our results for both the Chow and Dulberger data sets estimate hedonic indexes only for the subset of new models in those data sources; *hence our hedonic price indexes for the Chow and Dulberger data do not constitute a replication of those authors' results and would not be expected to be identical to the results published by those authors.*[21]

Weighting by Market Shares

Ideally it would be desirable to weight each observation by market share in each year. However, the requisite market share data are not available from our data sources. Phister presents an inventory of the installed number of computers for some but not all models, and

Computerworld does not provide numbers produced or installed. Our regression equations weight each observation equally, which results in an underweighting of IBM machines, which had a share ranging from 60% to 75% in the total revenue of the data processing industry, but represent only about half of the observations in the Phister sample and only about 18% of the observations in the *Computerworld* sample. We deal with the weighting issue by estimating separate price indexes for mainframe and mini computer processors over 1965–1979 and weighting the separate rates of price change by market shares in each year. Yearly market share weights are also applied to separate indexes over 1979–1984 for (1) IBM and plug-compatible mainframes, (2) other mainframes, and (3) minis and superminis. We also present a linked imputed price index over our entire sample period for major IBM mainframe models, in order to assess the plausibility of our final price index for those models that had the dominant market share.

Rental Rates versus Purchase Prices

The dependent variable in all our regressions is the log of purchase price. How different would be the results if the log of the rental rate were instead taken as the dependent variable? Phister provides data for all models on the rental rate, purchase price, and price-rental ratios. A scan of this ratio of purchase price to monthly rental indicates that it falls within the range of 40–60 for almost all models in the Phister sample, with no evident time trend. The variance of this ratio over time is trivial compared to the variance of the price-performance ratio over time, suggesting that alternative regressions using the rental rate would yield similar results to those exhibited in section 3.5. Further evidence that this distinction is not important comes from the similarity of the price indexes yielded by the Phister and Chow data sets over 1954–1965 (see table 3.3), where the Phister results are based on prices and the Chow results are based on rental rates.

Peripherals

While price-performance ratios for peripheral equipment (tape and disk drives, printers, etc.) fell over time by substantial amounts, the available evidence, especially that presented by Cole et al. (1986) and Flamm (1987), suggests that the rate of price decline was less than that for mainframe processing systems. Sufficient data exist in Phister's book to provide a price index for each major type of peripheral, but this exercise is beyond the feasible research scope of the present chapter. In one sense, the omission of peripherals implies that our final price index for computer *processors* will overstate the rate of price decline for computer *systems* that include peripherals, in light of evidence summarized by Triplett (1988) showing that peripheral prices declined somewhat more slowly than processor prices. However, as Franklin M. Fisher has pointed out to me in correspondence, the improvement in computer performance involves the way in which processors interface with peripherals and with operating systems. While Fisher does not think that it is possible to handle this problem with available methods and data, he suggests that the failure of this and other studies to quantify the benefits of improved interaction between processors and peripherals causes the true rate of improvement in the performance of computer systems to be understated.

Software

Our regressions cover only hardware prices, not the full operating cost of performing "computations," which would also include costs of software, maintenance, electricity, and rent on floorspace. However, our hardware prices include the basic system software that a manufacturer supplies with each machine. This has increased manyfold in quality and quantity, along with the increase in system performance. For instance, in 1954 IBM supplied only about 6,000 lines of code as programming support for the model 650 computer. The company provided an assembler and a few basic utility routines, but that was all. But as new models were introduced, the software provided grew exponentially. By the late 1960s the operating system for the IBM 360 series, designed to improve system performance and to provide a wide variety of useful operating features, included over 5 million lines of code. From 1965 to 1975, software was a constant share (roughly 35%) of the total developmental cost of computer manufacturers.[22]

Then in 1969 IBM announced its "unbundling" decision, that separate charges would be made for systems engineering services and education and for new program products, "as distinct from system control programming." IBM also reduced its prices by 3%, an amount that represented its estimate of the value of the excluded services. No adjustment is made in this study for unbundling, partly on the ground that 3% is a small number, and partly because software developments had led to increasingly sophisticated operating systems that have relieved customer programmers of various complex tasks and made them more self-sufficient of the manufacturers' systems-engineering personnel.[23]

3.5   Regression Results

3.5.1   Phister Data: General Procedures

All regressions estimated for the Phister data include two basic quality characteristics, memory and speed ("memory cycle time"). In addition, two types of dummy variables were included. First, an intercept dummy, equal to unity for an IBM machine and zero for a non-IBM machine, was included to test for an "IBM effect." Second, the data source listed the type of memory, and we were able to test for the effect of memory types other than the standard core or integrated circuit types.

Perhaps the most important difference in memory type occurred in the early years of our sample period, when "drum" memory was supplanted by "core" memory. Although we would have preferred to include a dummy for drum memory, we were precluded from doing so by the unfortunate fact that all our 1954 observations but none of our 1955 observations have drum memory. Hence, the drum memory coefficient is collinear with the 1954–1955 price change and prevents us from estimating plausible price coefficients in 1954–1955. However, in the 1969–1972 period we were able to identify several isolated machines with unusual memory types ("wire" memory and "rod" memory). Because only a few machines had these memory types, inclusion of a memory-type dummy in this period did not preclude estimating the time coefficients. The form of the memory-type dummy was left to the computer, which selected an interactive memory-type and memory slope dummy in preference to a shift in the intercept or in the speed coefficient.[24]

Since we did not know a priori whether coefficients on quality characteristics could be assumed to remain constant over long periods, our estimation procedure began with short periods. In developing the estimates presented here, we began with overlapping "triplets" of years, extending from 1951–1954–1955 through 1977–1978–1979.[25] Subsequently groups of triplets were joined together and subjected to aggregation (or "pooling") tests to determine whether coefficients were stable across three-year periods. In the tables below, the triplet results are not presented, and the estimates shown are for the longer sample periods, which accept aggregation over time.

For each of these longer sample periods, we then inspected the ratio of the actual price to imputed base-year price for "overpriced" models—see the discussion of the imputation method above following equation (1). Models selected for exclusion were those that had a log ratio of actual price to imputed price greater than 1.5 times the standard error of the estimated regression equation (in most equations this criterion translates into the statement that the excluded models had an actual price double or greater the imputed price). Then the equations were reestimated with the overpriced models excluded. We can cite as a precedent for excluding observations Knight (1966, p. 49), who excluded overpriced models lying more than one-half of a standard error above an initially fitted regression line.[26] It should be noted that less than 10% of our observations are excluded by this procedure, in contrast to Knight, who appears to have discarded about half of his observations.[27]

3.5.2   The Phister Sample: Regression Results

The regression results are presented beginning in table 3.2 for the 1951–1969 period. The specification is double-log, as in equation (1), with asterisks used to designate the significance levels of the coefficients so as to avoid an excessive clutter of numbers in the tables. The base year for each equation is indicated by the word "base." The implied price index in each other year can be calculated by taking the antilog of the coefficient shown opposite each year.

In successive aggregation tests we found that we were able to pool over the entire decade 1960–1969 but not beyond. There is a decisive break in 1969 revealed by the failure of 1960–1969 to pool with 1969–1972, 1969–1975, and 1969–1979. The break in 1960 is less decisive. One can test for such a break in two ways, by asking (1) whether the addition of, say, 1951–1959 to 1960–1969 passes an aggregation test but also (2) whether the addition of 1960–1969 to 1951–1959 passes an aggregation test. These are two separate questions, and there is no statistical reason why the answer to them should be the same. We find that aggregation test (1) is accepted at the 5% level but (2) is rejected at the 1% level. In light of this mixed finding, our final price index for 1951–1965 is based on the *average* of the price changes

Table 3.2
Hedonic regressions, Phister sample, 1951–1969

	1951–1960 (1)	1960–1969 (2)	1951–1969 (3)
Memory	0.64**	0.65**	0.70**
Memory cycle time	−0.17**	−0.55**	−0.22**
IBM dummy	−0.25	0.11	0.08
Other memory[a]	—	0.16*	0.20**
1951	1.32*	—	1.46**
1954	Base	—	Base
1955	−0.01	—	−0.45
1956	No data	—	No data
1957	Excluded	—	Excluded
1958	−0.29	—	−0.42
1959	−0.62	—	−0.88*
1960	−0.72	Base	−1.02**
1961	—	−0.40**	−1.30**
1962	—	−0.49**	−1.33**
1963	—	−0.54**	−1.26**
1964	—	−1.04**	−1.67**
1965	—	−1.81**	−2.33**
1966	—	−2.06**	−2.64**
1967	—	−2.28**	−2.58**
1968	—	Excluded	Excluded
1969	—	−3.07**	−3.52**
R^2	0.808	0.894	0.872
SEE	0.427	0.431	0.451
Observations	39	110	133

* indicates significance at 5%; ** indicates significance at 1%.

a. "Other memory" is a dummy that allows for a shift in the coefficient on memory for models having wire or rod memory.

shown in columns (1) and (2) and those shown in column (3). For the years after 1965 we have sufficient data to split our sample into two separate segments for minis and mainframes, as shown below in table 3.5.

In table 3.2 the coefficients on memory and speed ("memory cycle time") are highly significant. That on memory is stable across the 1960 break, as shown in a comparison of columns (1) and (2), while that on speed increases in absolute value after 1960. The "other memory" dummy variable is significant in both columns (2) and (3); the IBM dummy is not significant but is included to remain consistent with results displayed below that extend after 1969. The other point of interest in table 3.2 is that the time coefficients imply a relatively smooth rate of price decline. There are no price increases registered in any year in columns (1) and (2), while in column (3) there are small increases of 7% and 6%, respectively, in 1963 and 1967.

Data source effects are explored in table 3.3, which compares results for the Phister and Chow data sources. The sample period ends in 1965, which is the last year in the Chow data set. The "other memory" dummy is excluded, since it is not defined over 1951–1965, and the IBM dummy is excluded in light of its insignificance in table 3.2. The only difference in the specification of the Chow equations is in the differing speed variables included in the data, "access time" and "multiplication time" as contrasted with the single Phister speed variable, "memory cycle time."

The Chow data used in table 3.3 refer only to new models, not to both new and old models as in the original Chow (1967) article. Editing the Chow data in this way is necessary to achieve consistency with the Phister data set. While the overall rate of price decline over 1954–1965 is not affected by excluding old models, one aspect of Chow's original research is altered. When all models are included, an aggregation test to add 1954–1959 to 1960–1965 is rejected at the 5% level, but this is not true for new models only. The new-only data set easily passes an aggregation test over 1954–1965 by either method (1) or (2) listed above.

Thus the basic Chow result is that presented in column (6). Because of the ambiguous results in aggregating the Phister data over 1954–1965, we can compare the Chow estimates in column (6) with either columns (1) plus (2), or (3) alone. The most interesting similarity is in the overall rate of price decline: on a base 1965 = 100 the implied Chow index number for 1954 is 987, while the implied Phister index number for 1954 in column (3) is 1,028—columns (1) and

Table 3.3
Comparison of hedonic regressions, Phister vs. Chow (new models only),
1951–1965

	Phister			Chow (new models only)		
	1951–1960 (1)	1960–1965 (2)	1951–1965 (3)	1954–1960 (4)	1960–1965 (5)	1954–1965 (6)
Memory	0.67**	0.66**	0.71**	0.38**	0.58**	0.54**
Memory cycle time	−0.21**	−0.57**	−0.21**	—	—	—
Access time	—	—	—	−0.16**	−0.14**	−0.15**
Multiplication time	—	—	—	−0.13**	−0.06**	−0.07**
1951	1.59**	—	1.43**	—	—	—
1954	Base	—	Base	Base	—	Base
1955	0.03	—	−0.42	−0.02	—	−0.03
1956	No data	—	No data	−0.17	—	−0.33
1957	Excluded	—	Excluded	−0.18	—	−0.22
1958	−0.11	—	−0.45	−0.60**	—	−0.56**
1959	−0.40	—	−0.92*	−0.63**	—	−0.74**
1960	−0.54	Base	−1.01*	−1.20**	Base	−1.14**
1961	—	−0.42**	−1.31**	—	0.13	−1.24**
1962	—	−0.56**	−1.37**	—	−0.47**	−1.62**
1963	—	−0.56**	−1.24**	—	−0.58**	−1.72**
1964	—	−1.15**	−1.73**	—	−0.91**	−2.03**
1965	—	−1.86**	−2.33**	—	−1.15**	−2.29**
R^2	0.801	0.887	0.856	0.932	0.896	0.902
SEE	0.435	0.433	0.456	0.340	0.387	0.380
Observations	39	86	109	43	81	115

* indicates significance at 5%; ** indicates significance at 1%.

(2) together imply 1,102. A further similarity between columns (3) and (6) is the roughly similar rate of price decline over the 1954–1960 and 1960–1965 subperiods; columns (1) and (2) differ in this regard in exhibiting a much slower price decline over 1954–1960 and a much faster price decline over 1960–1965. The other notable differences in table 3.3 are in the pattern of coefficients: both sets of results indicate a shift in coefficients after 1960, but for the Phister data in columns (1) and (2) this takes the form of a jump in the absolute value of the speed coefficient, whereas for the Chow data in columns (4) and (5) the jump is in the coefficient on memory.

We turn now to the Phister results covering the remainder of the sample period through 1979, as displayed in table 3.4. The sample periods shown are 1960–1969, 1969–1979, and 1960–1979. We arrived at these periods as the outcome of a set of aggregation tests. We found that 1960–1965 could be extended to 1960–1969 but not beyond 1969. We also found that 1969–1972 could be pooled with 1973–1979. But pooling any period before 1969 with any period after 1969 is rejected, usually at the 1% level.

It is evident from a comparison of columns (1) and (2) in table 3.4 that the large coefficient shifts are not in memory and speed, but in the dummy variables for IBM. The IBM dummy has an enormous coefficient of 1.25 during 1969–1979, which implies that IBM charged more than triple the price per unit of quality during this interval as other manufacturers. It seems puzzling that IBM would pursue such an extreme price policy during the decade of the famous antitrust case. However, as we shall see in the next table, this result results from an aggregation error, the inclusion of mini and mainframe computers in the same equation.

We have already examined the coefficients on the time dummies for the 1960–1969 equation in table 3.2. The time dummies for 1969–1979 in column (2) of table 3.4 exhibit more of a tendency to zigzag around a declining trend. We should view these results as more useful for indicating the magnitude of price changes for periods of several years than for annual changes between successive pairs of years.

It is important to note that this tendency to zigzag can occur in any data set consisting of new models. Note in table 3.3 that the Chow data display a price increase of 10% in 1957. Columns (3) and (4) in table 3.5 indicate that the Dulberger data for new-only models display price increases of 10% in 1973, 21% in 1974, and 23% in 1976 (this occurs when her technological class variables are omitted; price

Table 3.4
Hedonic regressions, Phister sample, 1960–1979

	1960–1969 (1)	1969–1979 (2)	1960–1979 (3)
Memory	0.65**	0.73**	0.71**
Memory cycle time	−0.55**	−0.43**	−0.51**
IBM dummy	0.11	1.25**	−0.70**
Other memory[a]	0.16*	0.20	0.19
1960	Base	—	Base
1961	−0.40**	—	−0.34
1962	−0.49*	—	−0.23
1963	−0.54**	—	−0.57
1964	−1.04**	—	−0.70*
1965	−1.81**	—	−1.82**
1966	−2.06**	—	−2.05**
1967	−2.28**	—	−1.83**
1968	Excluded	Excluded	Excluded
1969	−3.07**	Base	−2.84**
1970	—	−0.19	−3.07**
1971	—	−0.60	Excluded
1972	—	−0.81	−3.43**
1973	—	−0.80	−3.41**
1974	—	−1.37**	−3.96**
1975	—	−1.28**	−3.95**
1976	—	−2.12**	−4.54**
1977	—	−1.52**	−4.05**
1978	—	−2.04**	−4.44**
1979	—	−3.04**	−5.32**
R^2	0.894	0.896	0.885
SEE	0.431	0.626	0.604
Observations	110	139	243

* indicates significance at 5%; ** indicates significance at 1%.

a. "Other memory" is a dummy that allows for a shift in the coefficient on memory for models having wire or rod memory.

Table 3.5
Hedonic regressions for mini and mainframe models, Phister sample, 1965–1979, and for new-only portion of Dulberger sample, 1972–1984

	Phister data		Dulberger data	
			Technology variables	
	Minis (1)	Mainframes (2)	Excluded (3)	Included[a] (4)
Memory	0.59**	0.47**	0.19**	0.24**
Memory cycle time	−0.31**	−0.45**	—	—
IBM dummy	0.75**	0.30**	−0.01	0.02
Other memory[b]	—	0.06	—	—
MIPS	—	—	0.84**	0.80**
Core 72	—	—	—	−0.60**
FET1K77	—	—	—	0.33
FET4K77	—	—	—	0.59**
FET24K80	—	—	—	0.40**
FET2K81	—	—	—	0.33
F16K81	—	—	—	0.36**
F16K82	—	—	—	0.40*
1965	1.17**	0.95**	—	—
1966	1.48**	−0.13	—	—
1967	1.44**	0.77*	—	—
1968	Excluded	No data	—	—
1969	No data	−0.07	—	—
1970	0.37	No data	—	—
1971	No data	No data	—	—
1972	Base	Base	Base	Base
1973	0.07	−0.52	0.11	0.29
1974	−0.16	No data	0.41	−0.01
1975	−0.40	−0.05	−0.49	−0.84**
1976	−1.13**	−0.52	−0.23	−0.65**
1977	−1.01**	−0.48	−0.57	−1.07**
1978	No data	−0.83*	−1.03**	−1.44**
1979	−1.41**	−2.08**	−1.66**	−2.36**
1980	—	—	−1.65**	−2.33**
1981	—	—	−1.65**	−2.28**
1980	—	—	−1.94**	−2.40**
1983	—	—	−2.12**	−2.52**
1984	—	—	−2.35**	−2.76**
R^2	0.599	0.953	0.951	0.965
SEE	0.637	0.220	0.256	0.217
Observations	111	68	133	133

* indicates significance at 5%; ** indicates significance at 1%.

a. Because only new models are excluded, there are too few observations to permit the following technology variables from the original Dulberger specification to be entered: BP1K73, BP1K74, FET2K75, FET2K76, FET2K77, FET1K78, FET1K79, FET2K79.

b. see note from table 3.4.

increases still remain in 1974 and 1976 when those variables are included).

In the process of checking for aggregation over time, we also checked for aggregation over minis and mainframes. This test is carried out for 1965–1979, since this is the first year when we have substantial data on minis, and for various subperiods. In each period the test rejects the aggregation of minis and mainframes at a 1% significance level or better, confirming a similar result reported below for the *Computerworld* data. However, a combined test of time and type aggregation indicates that both mini and mainframe equations accept aggregation over the full 1965–1979 period.

These results are shown in the first two columns of table 3.5. We note that minis tend to have a higher coefficient for memory and mainframes have a higher speed coefficient. This suggests one source of the aggregation problem. The pooled equation for 1969–1979—table 3.4, column (2)—has a coefficient of 0.73 on memory, higher than for either minis or mainframes separately in table 3.5. This implies that the marginal price of memory is greater when a purchaser shifts from a mini to a mainframe than when a purchaser shifts to a larger machine within each category. A sensible interpretation is that minis and mainframes are different products, and mainframes provide extra services, e.g., more channels and input-output ports, that justify their high relative prices.

Another interesting result is that the IBM dummy, which was implausibly high in the 1969–1979 regression in table 3.4, declines substantially in table 3.5. The mainframe IBM coefficient of 0.30 seems consistent with the range of 0.24–0.34 in our results for IBM and plug-compatible mainframes for 1977–1984 in the *Computerworld* data set (table 3.6). The coefficient of 0.75 for minis still seems high; an inspection of imputed prices traces this mainly to two particular 1970 models (S3/6 and S3/10).

Time dummy coefficients are missing for some years where we are missing an observation on minis, mainframes, or both. Hence price indexes cannot be constructed for every year. Also, partly because of smaller sample sizes, the separate mini and mainframe time coefficients display more of a tendency to "jump" than the pooled results in table 3.4. For minis there are three periods when the overall price decline is interrupted, 1966–1967 and by lesser amounts in 1973 and 1977. These jumps clearly result from the small sample size, just two mini models in 1966, two in 1967, one in 1973, and one in 1977. For mainframes there are substantial jumps in 1967 (one model) and

Table 3.6
Hedonic regressions by type of machines, *Computerworld* sample, 1977–1984 and 1981–1984

	IBM and plug compatible machines			Other mainframes			Minis (including superminis)		
	(1)	(2)	(3)	(4)	(5)	(6)	(7)	(8)	(9)
Memory	0.43**	0.43**	0.31**	0.21**	0.20*	0.18**	0.44**	0.43**	0.44**
Machine cycle time	-0.23**	-0.16	-0.08	-0.93**	-0.93**	-0.20*	-0.31	-0.05	-0.09
MIPS	—	—	0.43**	—	—	0.79**	—	—	-0.06
Minimum number of channels	0.58**	0.28*	0.20*	0.36*	0.36*	0.10	—	-0.04	-0.02
Maximum number of channels	0.16*	0.50**	0.27**	0.16	0.17	-0.05	—	0.27**	0.26*
Cache buffer size[a]	0.003**	0.003**	0.001	0.002	0.002	0.000	—	0.005	0.005*
IBM dummy	0.24**	0.34**	0.28**	—	—	—	—	—	—
1977	1.43**	—	—	—	—	—	—	—	—
1978	1.30**	—	—	—	—	—	—	—	—
1979	1.06**	—	—	1.94**	—	—	1.33**	—	—
1980	0.84**	—	—	No data	—	—	0.84**	—	—
1981	0.50**	0.55**	0.67**	0.53	0.52	0.99**	0.62**	0.81**	0.83**
1982	0.32**	0.44**	0.43**	0.43	0.43	0.54**	0.42	-0.05	-0.09
1983	0.17	0.26	0.34**	0.75**	0.74**	0.85**	0.06	0.17	0.15
1984	Base	Base	Base	Base	Base	Base	Base	Base	Base
R^2	0.866	0.890	0.928	0.776	0.780	0.920	0.398	0.508	0.502
SEE	0.472	0.470	0.380	0.759	0.761	0.457	0.660	0.664	0.669
Observations	191	110	112	94	92	92	111	68	68

* indicates significance at 5%; ** indicates significance at 1%.

a. This variable is not in log levels because it often takes a zero value.

1975 (two models). Below in constructing our final price index we smooth the estimated time dummy coefficients for mainframes over the 1966–1976 period, but this does not prove to be necessary for minis.

Columns (3) and (4) of table 3.5 display equations for the new model component of the Dulberger data set (which includes only mainframes, not minis) over the 1972–1984 period. These results do not correspond to the equations estimated in Dulberger (1988), which covers both new and old models (consisting of 132 new models and 164 old models). Column (3) omits Dulberger's technology-type variables for purposes of comparison with our Phister results, and column (4) reestimates the equation with the technology variables included. While the standard errors are not comparable, since the sample periods are different, they are of the same order of magnitude in our mainframe results (column 2)—and the two Dulberger equations. On a base 1972 = 100, the implied price index for 1979 in columns (2)–(4) are 12.6, 19.0, and 10.6, respectively.

3.5.3   The *Computerworld* Sample: Regression Results

The *Computerworld* sample is very large in comparison with the other data sets studied in this chapter. The number of new model observations is 50 per year, as contrasted with 9.6 for Chow, 5.1 for Dulberger, and 3.8 for Phister (all these calculations refer to individual models, not observations created by doubling and tripling as in the Dulberger and Phister data sets). Compared with the Dulberger data set that overlaps its 1977–1984 time period, it not only covers minis, superminis, and mainframes of noncompatible manufacturers, which are excluded from Dulberger's data set, but also it provides a much greater coverage of IBM and plug-compatible mainframes (191 new models over 1977–1984 as contrasted with 55 for Dulberger), hereafter abbreviated I/PC. It also makes available additional variables (minimum and maximum channels and cache buffer size). Its main limitation, in addition to lacking the Dulberger technology variables, is that coverage of non-I/PC mainframes begins only in 1981 (plus two 1979 models), mini and supermini coverage begins only in 1979, and the "MIPS" measure of quality is available only beginning in 1981.

In table 3.6 the results are presented in three groups: I/PC mainframes, other mainframes, and minis. We do not present a pooled regression equation for the entire *Computerworld* data set, since aggregation tests indicate that these three subsets cannot be merged. Because the MIPS variable is not available before 1981, for each group we display the results for an equation that omits MIPS from 1977–1984, then one that omits MIPS for 1981–1984, and finally an equation that includes MIPS from 1981–1984. In every case the third equation that includes MIPS indicates a more rapid rate of price decline between 1981 and 1984 than either equation omitting MIPS. The third equation also indicates a faster 1981–1984 rate of price decline for other mainframes and minis than for I/PC mainframes. The other main difference in the three groups is that the price decline for I/PC mainframes is smooth, while the other mainframes have a price jump in 1983. Columns (8) and (9) also display a·smaller and statistically insignificant price jump for minis in 1983.

There are several interesting features of the estimated coefficients for the various quality characteristics. For I/PC mainframes, almost all the estimated coefficients are significant. The inclusion of MIPS in column (3) greatly improves the fit and reduces the coefficient on memory but still leaves room for a significant contribution of the minimum and maximum channels variables. Cache buffer size is significant when MIPS is omitted but insignificant in conjunction with MIPS. The IBM dummy is quite stable in the range of 0.24–0.34 and highly significant. The elasticity on MIPS is considerably lower than in the Dulberger data set results—table 3.5, columns (3) and (4)— probably because those results do not include any variables for the number of channels.

For other mainframes the results including MIPS—column (6)— yield memory and MIPS coefficients very similar to the Dulberger data set results, and it is interesting that the inclusion of MIPS still leaves a signficant role for cycle time. Interestingly, MIPS is not significant for minis. In light of the high standard error in this equation, it would appear that mini prices are largely explained by variables omitted from the data set.

3.6   The Final Price Index and Its Interpretation

3.6.1   Linking the Component Indexes

With the hedonic regression equations now estimated, there are only a few decisions required to develop a final index of computer processors. We present our basic results for indexes constructed from tables 3.2, 3.5, and 3.6 using the dummy variable technique. We have

Table 3.7
The final price index for computer processors, 1951–1984, 1984 = 100 (all indexes shown are based on the dummy variable method)

| | Phister data set (1965=100) | | | | | Computerworld (1984=100) | | | |
| | All models | | | 1965–1979 | | | | | |
Year	1951–1960 (1)	1960–1969 (2)	1951–1969 (3)	Minis (4)	Main-frames (5)	IPC main-frames (6)	Other main-frames (7)	Minis (including supermini) (8)	Final price index (9)
1951	4699	—	4426	—	—	—	—	—	133666
1954	1255	—	1028	—	—	—	—	—	33293
1955	1243	—	655	—	—	—	—	—	26452
1956	No data	—	No data	—	—	—	—	—	25373
1957	Excluded	—	Excluded	—	—	—	—	—	24337
1958	939	—	675	—	—	—	—	—	23344
1959	675	—	426	—	—	—	—	—	15726
1960	611	611	371	—	—	—	—	—	13948
1961	—	410	280	—	—	—	—	—	9928
1962	—	374	272	—	—	—	—	—	9349
1963	—	356	292	—	—	—	—	—	9444
1964	—	246	193	—	—	—	—	—	5992
1965	—	100	100	100	100	—	—	—	2931
1966	—	57	73	136	34	—	—	—	1583
1967	—	90	78	131	84	—	—	—	1582
1968	—	Excluded	Excluded	Excluded	No data	—	—	—	1296
1969	—	28	30	No data	36	—	—	—	1058

Year	(1)	(2)	(3)	(4)	(5)	(6)	(7)	(8)	(9)
1970	—	—	—	45	No data	—	—	—	1065
1971	—	—	—	Excluded	No data	—	—	—	1084
1972	—	—	—	31	39	—	—	—	1099
1973	—	—	—	33	23	—	—	—	846
1974	—	—	—	26	No data	—	—	—	831
1975	—	—	—	21	37	—	—	—	813
1976	—	—	—	10	23	—	—	—	606
1977	—	—	—	11	24	495	—	—	638
1978	—	—	—	No data	17	435	—	—	554
1979	—	—	—	7.6	4.8	342	1102	466	439
1980	—	—	—	—	—	275	No data	286	307
1981	—	—	—	—	—	195	269	229	211
1982	—	—	—	—	—	154	58	91	138
1983	—	—	—	—	—	140	234	116	145
1984	—	—	—	—	—	100	100	100	100

Sources by column:

(1)–(3) Table 2, columns (1)–(3).

(4)–(5) Table 5, columns (1)–(2).

(6)–(8) Table 6, columns (1), (4), and (7), linked in 1981 to columns (3), (6), and (9).

(9) 1977–1984: Tornquist index of columns (6)–(8).
    1965–1977: Tornquist index of columns (4)–(5), with the the mainframe index smoothed by taking an average of 1966–1967 as the value for both years; an average of 1972–1973 as the value for both years; and by omitting 1975.
    1951–1965: A geometric average of Tornquist indexes of column (1) linked to column (2), and of column (3).

Geometric interpolation is used to span any year where an index value is missing because of no data or excluded observations.

Source of weights for value share of mainframes and minis, table 3.1. Source of weights for value share of IPC mainframes and other mainframes, *Computerworld*, various issues.

also constructed indexes for the same equations using the imputation technique. Because the year-to-year changes are extremely similar when the two different methods are used, we save space by presenting only the dummy variable indexes in year-to-year detail, and subsequently present growth rates over multiyear intervals for the imputation indexes.

The final price index and its ingredients are displayed in table 3.7. The first eight columns of table 3.7 exhibit the components. Because the aggregation test yielded an ambiguous conclusion regarding the feasibility of pooling the 1951–1960 and 1960–1969 regressions on the Phister data set, we include both the separate 1951–1960 and 1960–1969 results in columns (1)–(2) with the pooled 1951–1969 results in column (3). Since aggregation tests reject the pooling of minis and mainframes in the post-1965 period, separate indexes are shown for these two components over 1965–1979. This aggregation test result leads us to make no use at all of the equation estimated for the full Phister data set over 1969–1979, as displayed in table 3.4. Columns (6)–(8) exhibit the *Computerworld* results. In each case the indexes displayed for 1981–1984 use the results with the significant MIPS variable included, and these are linked at 1981 to the 1977–1984 equations that omit the MIPS variable.

The separate components are aggregated using the Tornquist approximation to an ideal index number. This simply weights the logarithmic changes between year t and year $t+1$ of each component index by the *average* in t and $t+1$ of the value shares of the components being combined. Then the string of weighted changes is cumulated starting with zero in the base year and converted into a price index by taking antilogs. In table 3.7 the final price index is presented with a base of 1984 = 100. For instance, with hypothetical 1983 index values for components A and B of 98 and 150, and a value share for A in 1983 of .44 and in 1984 of .56, the weighted change would be

$$(0.44)(\log(100/98)) + (0.56)(\log(100/150)) = -0.218,$$

and the resulting 1983 index value would be $100(\exp(0.218)) = 124.4$.

Working backward from 1984, for 1979–1984 the index combines the *Computerworld* indexes from columns (6)-(8) with value shares for I/PC mainframes, other mainframes, and minis (see source notes to table 3.7). For 1977–1979 only the *Computerworld* I/PC mainframe index—column (6)—is used. An alternative would have been to weight this index with the Phister index for minis—column (4)—interpolated through the missing year 1978. By coincidence, the

1977/1979 ratio for these two indexes is identical (1.45), indicating that the alternative would have made no difference. More important is the fact that the choice of the *Computerworld* indexes after 1977 implies that no use is made of the Phister mainframe index for 1977–1979, which has a drastically different 1977/1979 ratio of 5.0. This large discrepancy implies that the decision to omit the 1977–1979 decline in the Phister mainframe index has an important effect on our final results. At first we had planned to use an average of these two conflicting indexes for mainframes, but further examination of actual and imputed prices for individual models convinced us that the *Computerworld* results are more reliable because of their larger sample size and lesser dependence on particular unusual models. Below we will argue that the excessive reliance of both the Phister and Dulberger samples on a particular atypical model in 1979 causes both resulting indexes to overstate the rate of price decline during 1977/1979 and to understate it during 1979–1984.

The aggregation test results suggest that the separate Phister mini and mainframe indexes should be used as far back as possible, i.e., from 1977 back to 1965. Note that our choice of the component indexes makes no use of the 1960–1969 or 1951–1969 results for *all* Phister models during the years 1966–1969. Over the period 1951–1965, the ambiguity of the aggregation test results leads us to use an unweighted geometric average of separate Tornquist indexes of the 1951–1960 linked to the 1960–1969 equation—columns (1) and (2)—and the pooled 1951–1969 equation—column (3).

3.6.2   The Price and Performance History of IBM Mainframes

In the next section we shall inspect the annual percentage growth rates of our final price index over several basic multi-year intervals, e.g., 1954–1960, 1960–1965. While the overall growth rate of our final price index is in the same general range as other research, −19.4% per year, the pace of its decline is irregular, with rates of −22.1% in 1954–1965, −12.7% in 1965–1977, and −26.5% in 1977–1984. The relatively slow rate of price decline observed between 1965 and 1977 conflicts with some other research, including some of that surveyed by Triplett (1988).

What would seem a hopeless task of reconciling conflicting results becomes a bit more feasible when one considers the dominant market share of IBM.[28] By comparing major IBM models of succeeding computer "generations," we can determine whether the evolution of

Table 3.8
The history of price and performance for selected IBM computer processors

Year	IBM model (1)	Memory (Kbytes) (2)	Memory cycle time (ms) (3)	Knight commercial index (4)	MIPS (5)	Actual system price ($000) (6)	Imputed 1965 price ($000) (7)	Actual/imputed (1965= 100) (8)	Actual/imputed (1984= 100) (9)	Regression (10)
1946	[ENIAC]	—	—	0.04	—	—	—	47753	1095252	A
1951	[UNIVAC I]	8	220	0.29	—	750	17	4406	101055	B,D
1954	650	10	2400	0.27	—	174	19	998	22890	B,D
1955	704	108	12	3.79	—	1054	153	588	13486	B,D
	705	30	17	2.09	—	608	62	864	19817	B,D
1958	709	108	12	10.23	—	1108	149	642	14725	B,D
1959	7090	197	2.2	45.47	—	1652	282	465	10615	B,D
1960	7070	37	6.0	5.14	—	488	81	506	11606	B,D
1961	1410	45	4.5	4.7	—	424	91	380	8716	C,D
	7074	88	4.0	31.7	—	1012	196	473	10849	C,D
	7080	100	2.2	30.9	—	1366	244	508	11651	C,D
1962	7094	197	2.0	95.9	—	1274	435	278	6376	C,D
1963	7010	70	2.4	11.5	—	578	201	272	6238	C,D
	7044	122	2.0	23.4	—	963	318	290	6651	C,D
1965	360–20	10	3.6	4.5	—	41	49	81	1858	E
	360–30	36	1.5	17.1	—	132	138	90	2064	E
	360–40	136	2.5	50.1	—	340	500	82	1881	F
	360–50	288	2.0	149	—	721	784	103	2362	F
	360–65	1088	0.75	810	—	2458	2255	115	2638	F
1966	360–44	144	1.0	858	—	252	813	33	757	F

1972	370–135	304	0.94	172	0.16	472	1123	42	963	F
	370–145	1184	0.61	446	0.30	798	2574	31	711	F
	370–155	1152	0.12	1203	0.55	1553	5355	29	665	F
	370–165	1792	0.08	3515	1.90	2647	7785	34	780	F
1973	370–125	176	0.48	70	0.08	266	1209	22	505	F
1974	370–115	165	0.48	39	0.05	147	474	31	711	E
1975	370–158–3	3328	0.12	2423	0.83	2593	8643	30	688	F
1976	370–138	768	0.94	496	0.21	395	1717	23	528	F
1977	370–148	1000	0.23	1014	0.42	687	3440	20	459	G
1978	3031	2000	0.12	2317	1.05	831	6812	12	280	G
	3032	2000	0.08	6921	2.50	1905	13004	15	336	G
	3033	6000	0.06	19019	5.90	3613	15757	23	526	G
1979	4341	2000	0.12	1863	0.72	247	3555	6.9	160	G
1980	3081	16000	0.03	—	10.40	3723	56927	6.5	150	G
1981	8140	1000	0.80	—	0.36	81	780	9.2	211	G
	3033–M	16000	0.06	—	9.10	2678	2880	4.1	93	G
1982	4321	1000	0.90	—	0.19	85	1284	6.7	153	G
1984	4361–5	2000	0.10	—	1.14	201	4518	4.4	102	G
	4381–2	4000	0.07	—	2.70	499	11560	4.4	99	G

Sources by column:

(2)(3)(6) Phister data set 1951–1976, *Computerworld* data set, 1977–1984. Cycle time linked by dividing *Computerworld* machine cycle time by 1000; by this method cycle times coincide exactly on five models that overlap the Phister and *Computerworld* data sets in 1977–1979.

(4) Phister data set.

(5) Dulbergér data set, 1972–1980, *Computerworld* data set, 1981–1984.

(7) Obtained from predicted value of regression indicated in column 10. Regressions C, D, E and F all have 1965 base year. B is linked at 1960, G by the average of the five overlapping observations in 1977–1979.

Table 3.8 (continued)

(8) 100 times column (6) divided by column (7), except for 1954–1965, for which is reported the average of imputed indexes from the regressions indicated in column (10).

(9) Column (8) divided by 0.0436, which is the 1984 index number of a 1965 base implied by the average of the five overlapping observations in regressions E and F.

(10) A: ENIAC linked to UNIVAC I with Knight's performance/price ratio (1966, table 1, column (4) divided by column (5)).

B: Phister 1951–1960, table 2, column (1).

C: Phister 1960–1969, table 2, column (2).

D: Phister 1951–1969, table 2, column (3).

E: Phister minis 1965–1979, table 5, column (1).

F: Phister mainframes 1965–1979, table 5, column (2).

G: *Computerworld* IBM and plug-compatibles, 1977–1984, table 6, column (1).

the price-performance history of IBM models is consistent with the behavior of our final price index. This history is displayed in table 3.8. For each of 35 different IBM models, plus the early ENIAC and UNIVAC I machines, data are shown on memory, speed, the Knight "commercial index" of computation power, MIPS (since 1972), the actual system price with the memory configuration shown, and the imputed system price in the 1965 base year. The latter is calculated separately for each of the regression equations that serves as a component of our final index, and, if 1965 is not part of the sample period of that equation, the resulting imputed price is linked to 1965 at some common overlap period (see notes to table 3.8). The ratio of the actual to the imputed 1965 price is shown in column (8) as an index number (1965 = 100) and again in column (9) on the basis 1984 = 100.

3.6.3   Using the IBM History to Evaluate Index Discrepancies

We need to examine table 3.8 in conjunction with table 3.9, which converts all of the relevant price indexes discussed thus far into annual percentage growth rates over key intervals divided in 1960, 1965, 1972, 1977, 1979, and 1981. The year 1960 was a dividing point within Chow's study, 1965 marks the end of Chow's study, 1972 the beginning of Dulberger's data, 1977 the beginning of our *Computerworld* data; and 1981 the year when the MIPS variable becomes available in our *Computerworld* data. 1979 is also included, since this is the introduction date of the IBM 4300 series which plays such an important role in explaining the divergent behavior of alternative indexes in the 1977–1981 period.

The IBM price index in column (8) or (9) can be interpreted as an imputation index for a subset of the available data. In order to isolate the effects of the selection of particular IBM models as opposed to the effect of using the imputation technique itself, most of the indexes in table 3.9 are displayed as pairs; the index constructed by the dummy variable technique is shown as the top member of the pair, with the corresponding imputation index directly below. Comparing the growth rates of the IBM index in line 10 of table 3.9 with the mainframe component of our final price index in line 9 and with the results for the Chow and Dulberger new-only (N-O) samples in lines 4, 6, and 7, we can isolate four main discrepancies that warrant discussion. These are (1) the differing growth rates for the Chow and Phister samples within the 1954–1965 period, (2) the slow price decline

Table 3.9
Comparison of alternative indexes for computer processors, annual percentage growth rates, various intervals, 1954–1984

	1954–1960 (1)	1960–1965 (2)	1965–1972 (3)	1972–1977 (4)	1977–1979 (5)	1979–1981 (6)	1981–1984 (7)	1954–1965 (8)	1972–1984 (9)	1977–1984 (10)	1954–1984 (11)
Mainframes[a]											
1. Ph. (51–60) (imputation)	−12.0 −7.2	—	—	—	—	—	—	—	—	—	—
2. Ph. (60–69) (imputation)	—	−36.2 −32.6	—	—	—	—	—	—	—	—	—
3. Ph. (51–69) (imputation)	−17.0 −15.1	−26.2 −26.8	—	—	—	—	—	−21.2 −20.4	—	—	—
4. Ch. N–O (54–65) (imputation)	−19.0 −18.8	−23.0 −22.7	—	—	—	—	—	−20.8 −20.6	—	—	—
5. Ph. mainframe (imputation)	—	—	−13.6 −13.5	−9.2 −9.7	−80.5 −81.1	—	—	—	—	—	—
6. N–O "index A" (imputation)	—	—	—	−11.4 −12.7	−54.5 −54.2	+0.5 +0.4	−23.3 −23.1	—	−19.6 −20.0	−25.4 −25.3	—
7. N–O "index B" (imputation)	—	—	—	−21.4 −22.1	−64.5 −64.7	+4.0 +4.9	−16.0 −15.5	—	−24.1 −23.7	−23.0 −23.1	—
8. CW IBM/PC (imputation)	—	—	—	—	−18.5 −12.9	−28.0 27.1	−22.3 −22.8	—	—	−22.9 −20.3	—
9. Linked mainframe (imputation)	−14.5 −11.2	−31.2 −29.7	−13.6 −13.5	−9.2 −9.7	−18.5 −12.9	−28.0 −27.1	−22.3 −22.8	−22.1 −19.6	−17.2 −15.9	−22.9 −20.3	−18.2 −16.7

10. IBM mainframe (imputation)	-11.3	-33.6	-13.8	-10.6	-53.2	-2.6	-14.0	-21.4	-17.2	-21.9	-17.9
Minis											
11. Combined Ph. and CW	—	—	-16.7	-20.2	-20.0	-35.5	-27.6	—	-24.5	-27.7	—
Mainframes and minis											
12. Final price index	-14.5	-31.2	-14.0	-10.9	-18.7	-36.6	-24.9	-22.1	-20.0	-26.5	-19.4

Sources by line:

(1)–(3) Table 3.2, columns (1)–(3).

(4) Table 3.3, column (6).

(5) Table 3.5, column (2).

(6)–(7) Table 3.5, columns (3)–(4).

(8) Table 3.7, column (6).

(9) 1954–1977 this table, lines 1–3 and 5; 1977–1984 this table, line 8.

(10) Table 3.8.

(11) Table 3.5, column (1), and table 3.7, column (8).

(12) Table 3.7, column (9).

of the final index during 1965–1972, which differs from some of the results surveyed by Triplett, (3) the slow price decline of the final index during 1972–1977, and (4) the differing time path of the price decline of the final index from the Dulberger results during 1977–1984. (See note to table 3.9 explaining abbreviations used.)

1. *1954–1965: Chow versus Phister.* All of the indexes for 1954–1965 summarized in column (8) agree on a rate of price decline in the range of 20–22% per annum. Particularly remarkable is the close agreement over 1954–1965 of the pooled Phister equation with the new-only component of the Chow sample (lines 3 and 4). A greater discrepancy occurs in the timing of price changes before and after 1960. The Phister sample registers a smaller price decrease before 1960 and a faster price decrease between 1960 and 1965. This is particularly pronounced in 1963–1965, and more so for the separate regressions split at 1960 (lines 1 and 2) than the pooled regression (line 3).

The IBM history provides a clue as to the source of this phenomenon; for the IBM subset the imputed price index shows a tendency to decline slowly during 1954–1960 and more rapidly during 1960–1965. Some intuition about this is provided by the Knight commercial index, which is not used in our regressions. Taking pairs of machines with roughly equivalent Knight indexes, we get an annual rate of decline of the price/performance ratio from 1955 (model 704) to 1961 (model 1410) of 19%, from 1959 (model 7090) to 1965 (model 360–40) of 28%, and from 1961 (model 1410) to 1965 (model 360–20) of 57%.

We interpret the differing pattern for the Phister and Chow samples as largely due to the greater IBM share of the observations in the Phister sample (49%) than in the Chow sample (21%). Another indication that the Chow sample is less representative comes from its higher proportion of mini computers, which, as is evident in table 3.1, had negligible sales before 1965.[29] Particularly worth noting is the much higher representation in the Phister sample of the third-generation IBM 360 series in 1965 (15 of 24 observations) than in the Chow sample (5 of 16 observations, of which 12 are minis). This helps explain why the Phister indexes drop so fast between 1963 and 1965. Although the agreement between the two samples over 1954–1965 is reassuring, an index weighted by market shares would show more similarity to the slow-fast pattern over the 1954–1960 and 1960–1965 subperiods evident in the Phister data than the more evenly paced tempo of Chow's price decline.

2. *1965–1972: comparing the 360 and 370 series.* Timing of new-model introductions is uniform across data sets: the same five 360-series IBM models are introduced in the Chow and Phister data in 1965, and the same four 370 series models in the Dulberger and Phister data in 1972. Given the dominant market share of IBM and the miniscule value share of minis during this period, the price history of 1965 to 1972 boils down to a single question: How much did the quality-corrected price of 370s decline relative to 360s? The imputed base-year prices (1965 = 100) for the 1972 370s in table 3.8 indicate an average 1972 price index of 34. This is a far more modest price decline than in the the evidence for 1965–1972 surveyed by Triplett, which leads him to a 1972 index number of 15 (1988, table 3.6A).

It seems inconceivable that anyone could compare the 1972 370 models and the 1965 360 models and conclude that a quality-corrected price index had declined from 100 to 15. In fact, it is hard to justify an index of 34. Note, for instance, that the average Knight performance index for the 370–145 and 370–155 is 825, close to the 360–65 value of 810. Yet the ratio of the average 1972 price of the two 370 models to the 360–65 price in 1965 is 0.48. To use the information contained in the Knight index more systematically, we estimate an additional regression equation only for our 36 Phister model 360 and model 370 observations over 1965–1974 with our speed variable replaced by the Knight index.[30] Because we are comparing like with like, the standard error is just 0.139, far lower than in any other equation estimated in this paper. Both the memory and Knight index variables are highly significant, with respective coefficients of 0.44 and 0.40, and the price indexes (1965 = 100) are as follows:

	1966	1972	1973	1974
Dummy variable method	23	52	60	47
Imputation method	23	48	61	44

Thus the use of the Knight index yields an even slower rate of price decline over 1965–1972 than our basic Phister index for mainframes. The underpricing of the single 1966 model (360–44) stands out as well.[31] These results suggest that, far from understating the rate of price decline over 1965–1972, we may have overstated it.

3. *1972–1977: the second-generation 370s.* The next discrepancy in table 3.9 occurs during 1972–1977. The Phister mainframe index on line 5 agrees fairly well with price index (A) from the Dulberger new-only sample, registering a 9.2% annual rate of decline, compared with 11.4.

But both indexes decline far more slowly than the 21.4% rate registered for price index (B), which is based on the same sample but adds the Dulberger technology variables. On the basis 1972 = 100, in 1977 the Phister price index is at 61, index (A) at 57, and index (B) at 34. Which rate of change is more plausible? Once again, turning to the IBM data in table 3.8, we note that the only new 1977 model is the model 370–148. This is the only new IBM model introduced in 1977 in either the Dulberger or Phister sample.

To assess the rate of price change over 1972–1977 we can compare the price performance characteristics of the 370–148 with the similar-sized 370–155 in 1972. The Phister 1977/1972 ratio of actual prices for these two models is 0.48; the equivalent ratio in Dulberger's data is an identical 0.48. The imputed quality ratio is 0.58 for Phister, 0.69 for index (A), and 2.56 for index (B).[32] The implied imputed price index, expressed as the actual ratio over the imputed quality ratio, is 83 for Phister, 70 for index (A), and 19 for index (B). The index (B) result seems implausible. By every measure of quality listed in table 3.8, the 1977 vintage 370–148 is inferior to the 1972 vintage 370–155: it has 87% of the memory, operates at half the speed, has 84% of the Knight performance index, and 76% of the MIPS performance measure. The only reason the (B) result attributes such high quality to the 370–148 is the contribution of the technology variables—these alone imply that the 370–148 has 255% of the quality of the 370–155 simply because of the different materials used in the memories of the two machines (magnetic core versus semiconductor). However useful the technology variables may be in explaining price differences of particular machines within a given year, they seem misleading in evaluating quality across a span of years. Viewed from the standpoint of the user, who neither knows nor cares about chip technology but values quality characteristics like memory, cycle time, and MIPS, it seems implausible to argue that the 370–148 had a higher quality than the 370–155, much less 2.5 times the quality! Fully 2/3 of the contribution of the technology variables to the implausible imputation of the 1972–1977 price increase comes from the 1972 coefficient, which rates the 370–165 as having 7 times the quality of the 370–135, as contrasted to 12 times the quality when the technology variable is omitted. Rather than concluding that the 370–165 and 370–155 were of low "quality" relative to their content of memory and MIPS, we prefer the alternative conclusion that the price-to-MIPS gradient was unusually flat in 1972, and that the technology variable is standing as a proxy for an equally plausible MIPS-slope dummy in that year.[33] As is evident from the growth rates displayed in table 3.9, the implausible discrepancy between the (A) and (B) results for the Dulberger new-only data applies only to 1972–1977, and for 1977–1984 both the (A) and (B) indexes decline at about the same rate as our *Computerworld* index for mainframes.

4. *1977–1984: the influence of the IBM 4341.* Recall that our final price index is based on the *Computerworld* results from 1977 to 1984 and ignores the rapid rate of price decline exhibited by the Phister mainframe results in the overlapping years 1977–1979. Overall, from 1977 to 1984, there is no conflict between the rate of change of the *Computerworld* and price indexes (A) and (B). The big difference is in timing within that interval: the (A) and (B) indexes fall at a 55–65 annual rate in 1977–1979 and then rise in 1979–1981 before resuming their decline. In complete contrast, the *Computerworld* mainframe index declines at a relatively constant rate over 1977–1984, with if anything an acceleration after 1979.

This discrepancy is explained entirely by the small sample size of the Dulberger data set for new models, which contains only two new models in 1979. One of these is the IBM 4341, which is famous in the history of the computer industry for its low price in relation to performance, which suggested at the time to observers that IBM was adopting a newly aggressive marketing strategy.[34] The other model is a plug-compatible; both it and the IBM 4341 have an actual-to-imputed price ratio on a 1984=100 base of about 150, quite similar to the imputed ratio for the IBM 4341 in our *Computerworld* regression of 160. Quite simply, these two models introduced the price level of 1982–1983 about three years early. But an index based only on these two models is misleading if other new models sold in 1979 were not similarly underpriced. The *Computerworld* sample contains not 2 but 42 observations on new IBM and plug-compatible models introduced in 1979, having actual-to-imputed ratios on a 1984 base ranging from 111 to 644. The IBM models alone range from 160 to 474. Since the model 4341 was a relatively small mainframe, it is likely that other larger new machines with much less favorable prices had a substantial market share in 1979, suggesting that the *Computerworld* index is more reliable than the (A) and (B) indexes. Gradually in the years after 1979 lower-priced machines are introduced into the *Computerworld* sample, so that over the entire period 1977–1984 its rate of price decline is roughly the same as in the Dulberger new-only data. The heavy reliance of the Dulberger new-only data on the two unusual 1979 models explains the starkly different timing of price decline evident in table 3.9.

3.7   Conclusion

This chapter has developed a single price index for mainframe and mini computer processors over the entire history of the computer industry, extending from 1951 to 1984. The chapter shares with others the conclusion that computer prices have declined rapidly, at roughly a 20% annual rate. The unique contribution of this chapter is its consistency: the price index is based only on new models in their year of introduction. In contrast, other studies are based on a mixture of only new models (Knight, 1966), mainly new models (Chow, 1967), or a mixture with old models in the majority (Dulberger, 1988). One would expect *ex ante* that the behavior of new-only and all-model indexes would be different: a new-only price index can exhibit a sharp decline when new technology is introduced, as in our index during 1963–1966. An all-model index will introduce the effect of new technology more gradually, reflecting the influence of old models that remain in production. Both types of indexes are useful, a new-only index for indicating changes in the pace of technological change, and an all-model index for the purpose of deflating the nominal value of current computer production. But it is clear that the two types of indexes measure two different concepts, and they should not be compared or mixed across historical eras. This can easily lead to double-counting a technological improvement if, for instance, an index for new-only models that incorporates a new generation of computers in year t is linked to an all-model index that incorporates the effect of the growing share of new-generation models in year "t+1."

The resulting "final" price index for new-only models in this chapter has the additional advantage that it is based on only two data sources, and the overlap between the two in 1977–1979 has been handled to avoid double-counting the technological improvement that occurred at that time. The plausibility of the final index has been checked against the price-performance history of major IBM mainframe models. Given the dominant market share of IBM in mainframe sales, this cross-check is extremely important to avoid placing undue weight on models having a low market share. Our final index tracks an imputation index for IBM mainframes very closely except in the final interval, 1981–1984, when the growing share of minis and the rapidly falling prices of minis lead to a somewhat faster decline for our final index than for IBM mainframe prices.

We have considered at length several discrepancies between our final results and the results implied by estimating similar equations on the new-only subset of the observations compiled by Chow for 1954–1965 and Dulberger for 1972–1984. We have shown for 1954–1965 that our results and Chow's are similar for the period as a whole but differ in the timing of price decline before and after 1960, and that our timing corresponds more closely to the evolution of IBM mainframe models, reflecting the greater share of IBM mainframes and smaller share of mini-computers in our sample than in Chow's. For 1972–1977 our results accord with the two indexes (A) and (B) developed from Dulberger's new-only subsample as long as the technology variables are omitted; we have argued that the technology variables yield an implausible relation between the quality of the major 1972 and 1977 IBM models and should be excluded in the calculation of price and quality indexes. For 1977–1984 our results are similar to those for indexes (A) and (B) but differ radically as to the pace within the period, a discrepancy we attribute to the overweighting of two underpriced machines in the Dulberger sample in 1979. Finally, for the "mystery period" 1965–1972 that spans the gap between the Chow and Dulberger studies, our final index produces a result of relatively slow price decline that is confirmed by a detailed quality comparison of IBM 360 and 370 series models.

3.7.1   Future Research: The Impact of Personal Computers

As shown in table 3.1, the share of microcomputers, i.e., PCs, has grown rapidly in the 1980s and by 1987 came close to exceeding mainframe sales, with the mini category running third.[35] For the 1980s an adequate price index of computer processors will need to consider the price-performance behavior of PCs. In an earlier version of this chapter, we developed (but omitted here to save space) a matched-model price index for PC processors that declined at an average annual rate of 26.3% over 1981–1987, or 32.7% when a shift to PC "clones" was included. More important than the decline of prices within the PC category, however, is the extremely rapid price decline implied by the shift from mainframes to PCs. If the relevant computer characteristic being priced is MIPS, then the transition from mainframes with 1984 prices in the range of $100,000–$200,000 per MIPS to PCs with 1984 prices of $8,000 per MIPS and 1987 prices of

$2,000 per MIPS is relevant, weighted by value shares.[36] For instance, if half of the calculations performed during the 1984–1987 period were shifted over that interval from mainframes to PCs, the implied annual rate of price decline for that half is about 100% per year, and when weighted with the half that did not shift is in the range of 50–60% per year. The next task in this line of research is to extend the index for mainframes and minis after 1984 and to aggregate it properly with an index for PCs, allowing for the effect of the shift by mainframe users to PCs.

Appendix

1. Data Sources

Phister (1979), table 2.11, pp. 338–357, continued pp. 630ff.

Computerworld:

1977: October 10 and 17, and two other issues.

1978: January 16, June 5, and one other issue.

1979: January 8, February 5 and 12, July 16, Nov. 5.

1980: January 21, March 17, May 12, July 28, September 22, October 20, November 17, November 24, and one other issue.

1981: July 13.

1982: August 2.

1983: `August 8.

1984: August 20 and 27, September 3.

2. Omitted Observations in Phister Data Set

The following observations were omitted after the discovery that on the first round of the research they yielded actual to imputed prices more than 1.5 times the standard error of the relevant regression equation. Note that only a single IBM model is excluded. Numbers in parentheses are the ratios of actual to imputed prices for the mean memory configuration from the regressions listed in table 3.8, column (10).

1957: IBM 305 (2.11) UNIVAC II (2.43).

1968: Burroughs 500 (2.66).

1969: UNIVAC 1106 (1.93).

1971: NCR 50 (7.69).

1973: Cyber 76 (3.23), UNIVAC 1110 (3.35).

1978: DEC VAX 780 (3.74).

Notes

1. This was a remark of Norbert Wiener, apparently quoted with approval by Oskar Morgenstern in his work on the accuracy of economic statistics (Phister, 1979, p. 4).

2. *Forbes*, December 22, 1980, p. 24, attributed to *Computerworld* magazine.

3. The BEA's deflation procedures are described by Cartwright (1986) and are based on hedonic price indexes for computer processors and peripherals developed in Cole et al. (1986). The NIPA still assume that computer prices remained fixed before 1969.

4. Also, Flamm's index is based on the price-performance ratio of the installed stock of computers, not on the flow of newly produced models as in this study.

5. The BEA also uses *Computerworld* data to update its computer price index for years after 1984.

6. The only other hedonic price index that covers both the 1950s and the late 1970s is the Knight (1983) index, as quoted by Alexander and Mitchell (1984, table 9, p. 48). Triplett's (1988) survey summarizes results of other studies over our period but does not present new research results.

7. Triplett's chapter cannot be used to compare other studies with the results of this chapter, however, since his chapter refers to an earlier and obsolete version of this research. See my comment, which follows his chapter 4.

8. This section is based on Cole et al. (1986), the conference draft of Dulberger (1988), Einstein and Franklin (1986), and Fisher, McKie, and Mancke (1983).

9. The vintages associated with each observation in the Phister sample are those listed in the source. Thus the UNIVAC I is attributed to the 1951 vintage, the year that the first unit was delivered to the Census Bureau. Those that may be interested in extending our price index further back in time should note that the price/performance ratio of the ENIAC to UNIVAC I is 10.9, according to Knight's commercial index (1966, p. 45).

10. The source for table 3.1 defines the breakpoint between micros and minis at $20,000 per units and between minis and mainframes at $250,000. The $250,000 figure corresponds precisely with Phister (1979, figure 1.21.5, p. 13), which shows that $250,000 remains a consistent borderline between mainframes and mini computers over the 1955–1974 period. Correspondingly, we classify all machines in our Phister data set with prices below $250,000 as "minis." When the minimum, mean, and maximum memory configurations of a model straddle the $250,000 boundary, the classification is decided by whether the mean configuration lies below or above $250,000.

11. This discussion omits the third type of price index described by Triplett (1988), the "characteristics price index," since this technique is not used here.

12. Fisher, McKie, and Mancke (1983, p. 3) report that the first electronic computer, the ENIAC, carried out calculations between 100 and 500 times faster than punched card machines with electromagnetic relays.

13. This two-year-lag criterion is not consistently applied, however, since Phister presents prices for the IBM 4331 and 4341 models that were introduced in 1979, the same year as his book was published.

14. 89 models are entered as triplets and 8 as single observations, for a total of 287 total observations. Dulberger's data set includes 66 new models (27 IBM and 39 plug-compatible), for a total of 132 observations on new models.

15. Phister (1979, p. 358).

16. This implies an annual rate of change of the performance/price ratio of 36.9 percent, when we use the price of the 4331 with the mean memory configuration. Price and performance data come from Phister (1979, pp. 339, 359, and 631).

17. Phister (1979), p. 524.

18. The Dulberger data set includes a technological class variable for each mainframe processor (those produced by IBM and three other "plug-compatible" manufacturers), including two classes of "bipolar" semiconductors and five classes of field effect transistor (FET) semiconductors, which gradually increased from 1 to 64 kilobits per chip.

19. Each of these comparisons refers to separately numbered models. In the Dulberger data set each model appears twice, priced at minimum and maximum memories. In the Phister data set most but not all models appear three times, priced at minimum, mean, and maximum memories. The *Computerworld* data set is unduplicated.

20. Fisher, McGowan, Greenwood (1983, p. 149).

21. Readers can find price indexes based on the full Chow and Dulberger samples in the original papers by those authors and in Triplett (1988).

22. Facts in this paragraph come from Phister (1979, pp. 26–27).

23. Facts in this paragraph come from Fisher, McKie, and Mancke (1983, pp. 173–179).

24. Thus the "other memory" dummy is equal to the value of memory for those machines with wire or rod memory and zero otherwise. The estimated coefficient on this dummy in table 3.4 is positive, indicating that extra memory raises price more for these other memory types than for standard memory types. We also tested for a difference between integrated circuit and core memory but did not obtain any significant coefficients.

25. In some previous versions of this chapter regressions for pairs of adjacent years were presented. Since sample sizes in some of those regressions were so small, in this version we began with triplets of years.

26. This sentence translates Knight's actual procedure into the language of this chapter. As shown by Triplett's (1988) equations (9) and (10), Knight's

procedure amounts to a regression of performance on price, rather than the usual regression of price on performance, and a price index can be calculated from the antilogs of the *negatives* of the estimated time dummy coefficients. Hence when Knight states that he eliminates observations lying more than half a standard deviation below the regression line, he means that he eliminated overpriced observations, i.e., those that had a low ratio of performance to price. I was guided to this precedent for omitting observations by Triplett (1988, section 4.2.2.3).

27. Our procedure led to the exclusion of 9 of the 97 models in the Phister data set (21 observations of 287). The list of overpriced models and their ratios of actual to imputed prices is presented in the appendix. Knight (1966) does not report how many observations were omitted, but the number must have been substantial, since he began with 225 observations (pp. 45–46) but reports "over 120 observations were used [in the final regressions] . . ." (p. 49).

28. IBM's 360 line accounted for about 70% of mainframe revenue in the last half of the 1960s; IBM's overall share of world mainframe revenues in 1987 was 76%. See *Business Week*, November 30, 1987, p. 121.

29. Chow's data provides monthly rentals and Phister's provides both monthly rental and purchase prices. As noted above, price tends to equal 40–60 times monthly rental. Corresponding to our $250,000 dividing line between minis and mainframes would be about a $10,000 monthly rental. 57% of Chow's new-only observations are minis by this definition, versus 36% of our Phister sample.

30. This use of the Knight index in preference to speed is an afterthought. If we were beginning this research again we would have tested each equation to learn if the Knight index was superior to speed as an explanatory variable, or whether it and speed should enter together along with memory.

31. The very low value of our mainframe index in 1966 is no accident. It is due entirely to the underpriced IBM model 360-44, which in corresondence Franklin M. Fisher describes as "deliberately stripped down." According to Fisher, "Any study that didn't show the 360-44 as underpriced wouldn't be doing its job." Because Fisher observes that this model did not sell very well, he assesses it as being off the pricing surface and believes that it should have been excluded from our regression equations.

32. Using the substitute equation that employs the Knight commercial index instead of speed, the Phister quality ratio is 0.87.

33. The same evaluation applies to Dulberger's own results (1988), which differ from those here by including both old and new models. However, the Dulberger (1988) sample consists entirely of new models in 1972, and her estimate of the 1972 techology dummy of –0.55 is close to the estimate of –0.60 shown in table 3.5. It should be noted that the Dulberger sample for 1972, in addition to the four 370 models shown in table 3.8, also includes a model 2022. However, as a minicomputer priced at just $46,000 with maximum memory, our Phister results suggest that it should not be pooled with the much larger mainframes in her sample.

34. See "IBM's New Models Jolt the Industry," *Business Week*, February 12, 1979, p. 42.

35. "Computers: The New Look," *Business Week*, November 30, 1987, p. 115.

36. The 1984 mainframe figures are from our *Computerworld* sample. For PCs we establish the MIPS of the IBM PS/2 model 80 at 2.3, based on a report that IBM "has boasted that its fastest 80386–based Personal System/2 has the raw processing speed of a 1975 370/168 mainframe ..." from *Business Week*, November 30, 1987, p. 114. We then establish rough MIPS estimates for the 1984 IBM AT 6mhz unit at 0.8 and the original IBM-PC at 0.25, using benchmark speed tests from *PC* magazine, January 26, 1988, p. 96 and September 6, 1986, p. 164. Prices include monitors, hard disks, and at least 512K of memory.

References

Alexander, Arthur J., and Mitchell, Bridger M. (1984). *Measuring Technological Change of Heterogeneous Products*. Rand Report R-3107–NSF. Santa Monica: Rand, May.

Cartwright, David W. (1986). "Improved Deflation of Purchases of Computers," *Survey of Current Business*, 66 (March), 7–10.

Chow, Gregory C. (1967). "Technological Change and the Demand for Computers," *American Economic Review*, 57 (December), 1117–1130.

Cole, Rosanne, et al. (1986). "Quality-Adjusted Price Indexes for Computer Processors and Selected Peripheral Equipment," *Survey of Current Business*, 66 (January), 41–50.

Dulberger, Ellen R. (1988). "The Application of an Hedonic Model to a Quality-Adjusted Price Index for Computer Processors," this volume (chapter 2).

Einstein, Marcus E., and Franklin, James C. (1986). "Computer Manufacturing Enters a New Era of Growth," *Monthly Labor Review*, 109 (September), 9–16.

Fisher, Franklin M., McGowan, John J., and Greenwood, Joen E. (1983). *Folded, Spindled, and Mutilated: Economic Analysis and U.S. vs. IBM*. Cambridge, MA: MIT Press.

Fisher, Franklin M., McKie, James W., and Mancke, Richard B. (1983). *IBM and the U.S. Data Processing Industry*. New York: Praeger.

Flamm, Kenneth (1987). *Targeting the Computer: Government Support and International Competition*. Washington, D.C.: Brookings.

Knight, K. E. (1966). "Changes in Computer Performance," *Datamation*, 12, 40–54.

_____ (1983). "A Functional and Structural Measurement of Technology," paper prepared for Workshop on Technology Measurement, Dayton, Ohio, October.

Phister, Montgomery (1979). *Data Processing Technology and Economics,* 2nd ed. Santa Monica: DEC Press.

Rosen, Sherwin (1974). "Hedonic Prices and Implicit Markets: Product Differentiation in Pure Competition," *Journal of Political Economy,* 82 (January/February), 34–49.

Triplett, Jack E. (1986). "The Economic Interpretation of Hedonic Methods," *Survey of Current Business,* 66 (January), 36–40.

_____ (1988). "Price and Technological Change in a Capital Good: A Survey of Research on Computers," this volume (chapter 4).

4

Price and Technological Change in a Capital Good: A Survey of Research on Computers

Jack E. Triplett

The first commercial computers appeared in the early 1950s. Over the subsequent three decades, rapid rates of technological change in computer equipment, and consequent declines in performance-corrected computer prices, have been evident to computer professionals and computer users and captured the attentions of numerous researchers.

Economic researchers, who were interested in measuring the computer's price movement, and engineering technologists, who desired to quantify advances in the computer's technological capabilities, both employed some form of hedonic function as a research tool. A substantial number of hedonic estimates of technological change and "quality-adjusted" price indexes have accumulated, covering the whole period of the computer's history. This survey combines the best of those estimates: By 1984, computer processor prices had fallen to *one-tenth of one percent* of their introductory level in 1953, and rates of price decline for peripheral equipment—though somewhat slower over the full period—are still prodigious by any standard.

Hedonic price indexes for computer processors and peripheral equipment constructed by Cole et al. (1986) and Dulberger (chapter 2, this volume) are now used for deflation in the National Income and Product Accounts (Cartwright, 1986). One objective of this survey is to provide perspective on the new NIPA indexes, by comparing them

Research for this chapter began as part of the process that resulted in the incorporation of hedonic price indexes for computer equipment into the National Income and Product Accounts. I am indebted to my colleagues in BEA, especially David Cartwright, to Rosanne Cole and Ellen Dulberger of IBM, and to Kenneth Flamm for stimulating discussions, and to Zvi Griliches, Franklin M. Fisher, Frank de Leeuw, Gerald Donahoe, Ernst R. Berndt, B. K. Atrostic, W. Erwin Diewert, Arthur Goldberger, Dan Usher and the editors for insightful and helpful comments on earlier drafts. Views expressed are my own and do not represent an official position of the Bureau of Economic Analysis or of the U. S. Department of Commerce.

with alternative research estimates and by reviewing the robustness of hedonic methods. The nearly 30 separate hedonic or quasi-hedonic studies on computer equipment, conducted over nearly 25 years, using a variety of different data bases, and covering various periods, offer a unique opportunity to assess robustness.

In the empirical portions of this survey, I first review the hedonic *functions* that were estimated by researchers. The assessment combines the economic theory of hedonic functions (summarized in section 4.1.2) with a rudimentary technological model of the production and use of computers; the empirical review itself occupies section 4.2. I present in section 4.3 hedonic price indexes covering 1953–1984 and subperiods for computer processors, for peripheral equipment, and for computer "systems." These indexes are interpreted in the light of the theory of hedonic price indexes, as summarized in section 4.1.2.

4.1 Conceptual Considerations: Hedonic Functions and Hedonic Indexes for Computers

The validity of any economic measurement depends both on the data that go into it and on its conformance to the appropriate economic theory of measurement. Its interpretation rests even more vitally on theory. The theory of hedonic functions and of "constant quality" price indexes is therefore a prerequisite to this survey. This section presents a summary of relevant theoretical results.

4.1.1 Definitions

A *hedonic function* is a relation between prices of varieties or models of heterogeneous goods—or services—and the quantities of characteristics contained in them:

$$P = h(c),   \tag{1}$$

where P is an n-element vector of prices of varieties, and (c) is a $k \times n$ matrix of characteristics. For computers, *characteristics* are specifications, such as speed, memory size, and so forth, that are outputs for producers and productive inputs for buyers (as explained in the next section). A *variety* is particular machine, such as an IBM 370/168–3 or a CDC 6600, which is identified uniquely by the vector of its characteristics. The theory providing the hedonic function's economic interpretation rests on the *hedonic hypothesis*—heterogeneous goods are aggregations of characteristics.

A *characteristics price index* is an index that is defined on the characteristics of goods or on behavioral functions in which characteristics are arguments. The characteristics price index may be *exact* or an approximation (see below). A *hedonic price index* is one that makes use of information from a hedonic function. Because characteristics serve as independent variables in hedonic functions, a hedonic price index can thus be thought of as a particular implementation of a characteristics price index.

4.1.2 Summary of the Theory

1. *Theory of Hedonic Functions*

The major contribution to the theory of hedonic functions is Rosen (1974). A recent statement in Triplett (1987) builds on Rosen's work and on other contributions. The following summary is based mainly on these two articles.

The hedonic hypothesis implies that a computer transaction is a tied sale of a bundle of characteristics. The price of a particular computer is the seller's revenue from the sale of a characteristics bundle; from the buyer's perspective, it is the outlay or expenditure on computer characteristics occasioned by the purchase of that computer. If the computer is rented, rather than purchased, each rental is interpretable as an aggregate monthly revenue/outlay for a bundle of monthly characteristics service flows.

A behavioral implication of the hedonic hypothesis is that computer characteristics (or characteristics service flows) are the true inputs to the production process. Hence, for a production process that *uses* a computer:

$$Q = Q(c, Z), \tag{2}$$

where Q is scalar output, Z is a vector of other, homogeneous productive inputs, and for expositional simplicity we specify only one heterogeneous good in the system, the computer, with characteristics (c). It is convenient to suppose that (2) can be written

$$Q = Q(q(c), Z), \tag{2a}$$

where $q(\cdot)$ is an aggregator over the characteristics (c) that are embodied in computers.

Under the hedonic hypothesis, the *production* of computers can be represented as the joint output of a bundle of computer characteristics.

The usual *KLM* (capital, labor, materials) production function becomes

$$t(c, K, L, M) = 0,\tag{3}$$

where (c) represents a vector of computer characteristics, and t denotes a transformation relation. The output of the computer manufacturer is the joint production of units of speed, memory, and so forth, rather than the number of machines produced. This view of production accords with computer vernacular: It is common within the computer industry to speak of output in terms such as "number of MIPS (a measure of speed) shipped." One assumption necessary to validate (3) is the absence of joint production with some other product—that is, characteristics of computer processors are jointly produced, but computer processors and, say, auxiliary storage devices (which augment the storage capacity of main memory) are not.

The economic behavior of buyers and sellers of computers can be described by sets of demand and supply functions for computer characteristics. These demand and supply functions are derived from the optimization of buyers' and sellers' objective functions, in which $q(\cdot)$ and $t(\cdot)$, above, carry information about using and supplying technologies and the hedonic function—$h(\cdot)$—provides information about the characteristics price surface.

Major results of the theory of hedonic functions are summarized in the following statements (for exposition and proofs, refer to Rosen, 1974, or Triplett, 1987).

1. If there are n competitive buyers, with dispersion in using technologies, the hedonic function, $h(\cdot)$, will trace out an envelope to the set of using technologies, $q_1(\cdot), \ldots, q_n(\cdot)$. As with any envelope, the form of $h(\cdot)$ is independent of the form of $q(\cdot)$—except for special cases—and is determined on the demand side by the distribution of buyers across characteristics space.

2. If there are m competitive sellers, with dispersion in producing technologies, the hedonic function, $h(\cdot)$, will trace out an envelope to the set of producing technologies, $t_1(\cdot), \ldots, t_m(\cdot)$. In parallel with the user case, the form of $h(\cdot)$ is influenced on the supply side by the distribution of sellers across characteristics space, but the form of $h(\cdot)$ cannot in general be derived from the form of $t(\cdot)$.

3. As a consequence of results (1) and (2), the form of the hedonic function, $h(\cdot)$, is in the general case purely an empirical matter. In particular, and despite many statements to the contrary that have appeared over many years, nothing in the theory rules out the semi-

logarithmic form, which has frequently emerged as "best" in functional form tests in the hedonic literature (Griliches, 1971).

4. Special cases exist in which $h(\cdot)$ can be "identified," in the econometric sense, either by seller or buyer technologies. If the using technology, $q(\cdot)$, is identical for all users, the form of $h(\cdot)$ is determined by the form of $q(\cdot)$, and should conform to the principles of classical utility or production theory. If the producing technology, $t(\cdot)$, is identical for all sellers, the form of $h(\cdot)$ is determined by the form of $t(\cdot)$, and the usual reasons apply for assuming convexity of production output sets.

2.   Theory of Hedonic Price Indexes

The economic theory of price indexes distinguishes the exact indexes from empirical indexes that are approximations and/or bounds to the exact indexes. The conventional theory of index numbers and of approximating indexes is developed in goods space (homogeneous goods are implicitly assumed); to confront the empirical results of hedonic functions, conventional index number theory must be extended to characteristics space, and the extension must cover both the exact indexes and their approximations (the main reference for this extension is Triplett, 1983; Zieschang, 1985, presents a restatement for the output measurement side).

The following paragraphs summarize results of price index theory that are relevant for this survey (for convenience in reference in the rest of the paper, the numbering of results continues from section 4.1.2.1).

5. An *input-cost index* (ICI) is an exact index that shows the minimum change in cost between two periods that leaves output unchanged— i.e., the ratio of costs of optimal points on the same production isoquant under two input price regimes. It is the production-side analog to the more familiar notion of the cost-of-living index, on which the literature is voluminous (see Pollak, 1983).

6. When extended to characteristics space, the full ICI depends on all the inputs in equation (2)—the homogeneous inputs, Z, and the characteristics, c, of heterogeneous inputs; it also depends on the form of the hedonic function, $h(\cdot)$, and on the form of the production function, $Q(\cdot)$—Triplett (1983). On the definition given in section 4.1.1, the full ICI is an exact characteristics price index.

7. Generally, the full ICI is intractable. For the separable production

function (2a) an exact "subindex" (Pollak, 1975; Blackorby and Russell, 1978) can be computed that involves only computer characteristics.[1] This "computer price index" is the ratio of the costs, under two characteristics price regimes, of two constant-output collections of computer characteristics (Triplett, 1983, 1987). The subindex is also an exact characteristics price index, and it is a "constant quality" or "equivalent quality" price index because the two collections of computer characteristics implied by it are equivalent in production. It is a price index for the capital services provided by computers when they are used as the inputs in the production of something else (or, indeed, in the production of other computers).

8. The hedonic price index for computers—a calculation based solely on $h(\cdot)$—can be thought of as an approximation to the exact characteristics subindex, provided conditions necessary for the exact subindex are met—that is, the production function can be written as (2a).

9. An exact *output price index* is an index composed from the ratio of costs of optimal points on a single production possibility curve under two price regimes (Fisher and Shell, 1972).

10. The characteristics-space form of the *exact* output price index for computers is the ratio of two points taken from a particular value of the transformation function, $t(\cdot)$, in equation (3)—that is, it is a price index constructed from collections of computer characteristics that can be produced with the same resource cost. It is an exact characteristics price index and is a "constant quality" price index in the sense defined in Triplett (1983, pp. 298–299).

11. A hedonic price index for computers—that is, a price index derived solely from the hedonic function, $h(\cdot)$—can be thought of as an approximation to the exact output price index for computer characteristics. This result is parallel to result (8).

12. In view of some confusion that exists in the hedonic literature, one should note that in the general case the hedonic index is *neither* of the exact (characteristics) indexes. The hedonic index depends solely on the hedonic function; the functional form of the hedonic index thus depends on the form of the hedonic function, which is in general independent of the form of both using and producing technologies—see result (3). The exact index, on the other hand, requires information on the technology on the relevant side (e.g., using technology for the ICI) *and* the hedonic function (Triplett, 1987). For the special cases noted in result (4), the hedonic index will coincide with one of the exact indexes, but will differ from the other exact index. For example,

if producing technologies, $t(\cdot)$, are identical across producers, the hedonic function will map the producing technology; in this case the hedonic index is the exact output price index for characteristics, but it is *not* the computer user's exact input-cost index.

13. Because a long, and sometimes acrimonious, debate over "resource-cost" and "user-value" approaches to quality change has taken place over many years, a brief summary of the current understanding of this matter may be helpful.

The *output* characteristics price index—result 10—is defined on a fixed value of the transformation function, $t(\cdot)$, the position of which, technology constant, depends on resources employed in production; accordingly, "constant quality" for this index implies a *resource-cost* criterion. On the other hand, the *input-cost* index described in result (7) is defined on a fixed (user) production isoquant; for the ICI, "constant quality" implies a *user-value* criterion (an extended discussion is contained in Triplett, 1983).

Fisher and Shell (1972) were the first to show that different index number measurements (they considered output price indexes and consumer cost-of-living indexes) imply alternative theoretical treatments of quality change, and that the theoretically-appropriate treatments of quality change for these two indexes correspond to "resource-cost" and "user-value" measures. Triplett (1983) derives this same result for cases where "quality change" is identified with characteristics of goods—and therefore with empirical hedonic methods; the conclusions are that the resource cost of a characteristic is the appropriate quality adjustment for the output price index, and its user value is the quality adjustment for the input cost index. Since Rosen (1974) had already shown that in the competitive case the hedonic function, $h(\cdot)$, provides estimates of the incremental acquisition cost of, and revenue from, characteristics, hedonic "prices" can serve as approximations to either user-value or resource-cost quality adjustments.

The debate on this subject sometimes generated more heat than light because (a) it was not recognized that there were, in effect, two different questions and accordingly two correct answers, not one, and (b) there was an inappropriate linking, on *both* sides of the debate, of hedonic indexes with the user-value criterion. It was thus thought, incorrectly, that use of hedonic methods in an economic measurement implied accepting one of the two theoretical positions over the other one (for further discussion, see Triplett, 1983).

4.1.3   Application of Hedonic Models to Computers

A hedonic price index can be taken as an approximation to either of the exact indexes, if the assumptions necessary to construct the exact indexes are met—results (8) and (11). Normally, therefore, the distinction between input and output price measures, though of considerable theoretical interest, is of minor practical importance in interpreting hedonic indexes.

Certain aspects of computer technology suggest, however, that most existing hedonic studies of computer equipment are more nearly approximations to output price indexes than to input price indexes. That is, they are better interpreted as deflators for the outputs of computer equipment producers than as price measures for computers as investment goods.

Input and output price indexes might differ because of the capital goods-capital services distinction. The services of a capital good are the proper inputs for any production function. In characteristics space, this principle means that the (c) variables in (2a) should represent flows of characteristics services generated by the computer. On the other hand, the total stock of characteristics embodied in the computer must appear in (3), and presumably in (1), if the machine price is the dependent variable in the hedonic regression.

If the computer's capability for yielding characteristics service flows decays at a uniform rate across characteristics, stocks and flows of characteristics will be proportional. There is at least anecdotal evidence of this (Archibald and Reece, 1979, report no decay at all in the productive capabilities of computer equipment). It should not matter, then, whether the hedonic regression uses monthly rentals or machine sales prices, or whether the variables in (c) are interpreted as flows or stocks, since in most hedonic functional forms the stock-flow distinction will be impounded in the constant term.

There is, however, a more serious problem with the way computer characteristics are entered into (2a). In (2a), the production function is written as separable on the characteristics of the computer (or peripheral equipment), which condition justifies construction of an input price index for "computers" (or peripheral equipment).

Separability of the characteristics of individual pieces of computer equipment may not be an appropriate specification. A common view, expressed in both economics and computer systems literatures, holds that capturing the full impact of technological change on the cost of computing requires that modeling be done at the level of the computer system. A computer executes instructions when used in concert with peripherals, with software, and with computer labor, energy, and other inputs. Computer characteristics are combined with the other inputs (properly, with their characteristics, all of them being heterogeneous) used by the computer center to minimize the cost of executing computer center tasks. This view can be expressed by modifying the model in section 4.1.2.

Suppose a computer system is composed of r pieces of equipment, or "boxes," and the characteristics of each box are the inputs to production, according to the hedonic hypothesis. Equation (2) becomes

$$Q = Q\ (c_1, c_2, \ldots, c_r, Z_1, Z_2), \tag{4}$$

where each c_i represents the vector of characteristics in the ith piece of equipment, Z_1 is the vector of other computer center inputs (computer software, labor, supplies, and so forth), and Z_2 is the vector of non-computer center inputs. The "systems" view for modeling the computer as a productive input amounts to the specification

$$Q = Q\ (q^*[c_1, c_2, \ldots, c_r, Z_1], Z_2), \tag{4a}$$

or alternatively

$$Q = Q\ (q^*[q_1(c_1), q_2(c_2), \ldots, q_r(c_r), Z_1], Z_2). \tag{4b}$$

In both cases, $q^*[\,\cdot\,]$ is the computer center, whose output (which is typically a vector) provides an input or inputs in $Q(\,\cdot\,)$.

In equation (4a), it is not possible to form an exact input price index for individual pieces of computer equipment, because the production function is only separable on the computer center, not on the individual boxes—refer to result (7). The computer center is first optimized with respect to the characteristics of all the boxes (and labor, energy, and other inputs as well), and then the outputs of the center serve as inputs into the production process. The input price index that is appropriate to production is the cost of processing jobs, or executing instructions—that is, the cost of $q^*[\,\cdot\,]$—not the separate costs of the boxes.[2]

Equation (4b) is a stronger assumption, with a similar result. It may be possible to form price indexes for computers and for the other boxes—the costs of $q_1(\,\cdot\,)$, $q_2(\,\cdot\,)$, and so forth. But additional efficiency gains can be achieved by optimization among the boxes and in the software and so forth, so that price indexes for the various boxes can only be aggregated by a method that takes account of gains in efficiency from an optimized computer system. Again, one wants the cost of executing or processing computer tasks as the appropriate input cost index, and this is represented by the cost of $q^*[\ \cdot\ ]$.

One would expect, under either of these alternatives, that research at the box level would understate the total fall in prices, or (what is the same thing) understate the degree of technological improvement from the user's perspective. Fairly primitive approaches to capturing efficiency gains at the systems level are considered in section 4.3.4; these estimates make use of specification (4b).

Since output price indexes require only the assumption of non-jointness in production of the boxes, individual hedonic price indexes may be appropriate for deflating the outputs of the separate manufacturing processes for computers and for peripheral equipment (even if designers of the boxes must consider their interaction in use in the design process). Accordingly, because most of the hedonic studies reviewed here have concentrated on measuring the characteristics content of the computer "box," we shall interpret them as approximations to output price indexes.

One additional aspect of computer markets has influenced the specification of computer hedonic functions: Though technical innovation in computers makes the hedonic function an attractive research vehicle, Fisher, McGowan, and Greenwood (1983) note that hedonic functions are in principle equilibrium relations. Rapid technological change implies that the computer market may not be in equilibrium. Further discussion is deferred to section 4.2.2.3.

4.2 Empirical Hedonic Functions for Computers

4.2.1 Choice of Variables

In the theory of hedonic functions, characteristics are interpreted as joint outputs on the supply side—equation (3)—and inputs to a production (or consumption) process on the demand side—equation (2) or (2a). The theory implies, therefore, that independent variables chosen for the hedonic function—characteristics—should reflect technical information about both the use and the production of the product. In practice, there are always data and conceptual problems,[3] so there is room for statistical hypothesis testing. Nevertheless, whether a particular computer specification is an appropriate variable for the computer hedonic function is in principle an engineering or technological question.

The hedonic literature for computers has a firmer technical base than does the parallel hedonic literature for, say, automobiles. The earliest relevant research for this survey grew out of, or was influenced by, the computer systems literature, and so reflected the concerns and orientations that were present in that literature. Some technological investigators wanted to measure technical progress in computers, primarily from pure intellectual curiosity. Alternatively, performance measures were devised as a practical aid to equipment selection. Economists carrying out hedonic studies on computers have more or less followed the lead of technologists. Even so, hedonic studies on computers are still not completely devoid of interpretive difficulties that surround the choice of variables.

1.   Characteristics of Computer Processors: Memory

From the earliest empirical work, the hedonic specification of computer processors has consisted primarily of the speed with which the computer carries out instructions and its memory size (main memory storage capacity). Phister (1979), Sharpe (1969), and Flamm (1987) contain good statements of the rationale for the specification, and Fisher, McGowan, and Greenwood (1983, at pp. 140–141) emphasize its limitations.

The measurement of main memory size has posed few problems. Standard measures exist in the industry, and have been employed in similar forms in all existing hedonic studies on computers (see table 4.1). Variations in treatment among individual researchers are largely related to idiosyncracies of the data sets they employed: Specifying both maximum and minimum memory sizes for the same computer, for example, as done in a number of studies, either reflected the researcher's lack of information about which of a range of optional memory sizes was supplied for the price that was recorded in the data set, or—when a separate price was recorded for each memory size, as in Dulberger (chapter 2, this volume)—was adopted to avoid undue influence on the estimates of pricing pecularities for bottom-end models.

2.   Characteristics of Computer Processors: Speed

It has been difficult to obtain a publicly available measure of processor speed that is both sufficient and at the same time comparable across processors.

Table 4.1
Comparison of variables in hedonic functions for computers

Author	Data sources	Dependent variable'	Explanatory variables
Schneidewind (Sharpe, 1969)	Not specified	Monthly rental	1. Memory size (thousands of characters) 2. Memory cycles per second (words)
Skattum (Sharpe, 1969)	Not specified	Monthly rental	Same as *Schneidewind*
Early, Barro, and Margolis (Sharpe, 1969)	Not specified	Monthly rental	1. Memory size (in bits) 2. Memory cycles per second (presumably in bits) 3. Several others (including additions per second), which were not significant
Patrick (Sharpe, 1969)	*Computer Characteristics Quarterly; Computers and Automation*	Monthly rental for "typical" configuration, 2nd-generation computers	1. Space occupied (in square feet) 2. Additions per second (in thousands) 3. Minimum memory (in bits) 4. Maximum memory (in bits) 5. IBM dummy 6. Number of months since first installation 7. Number of machines installed since introduction
Jacob (Sharpe, 1969)	As Patrick	As Patrick, 3rd-generation computers	1. Additions per second (in thousands) 2. Minimum memory (in thousands of bits) 3. Maximum memory (in thousands of bits) 4. Memory cycles per second (thousands of bits) 5. Number of operations codes 6. IBM dummy 7. Number of months since first installation 8. Number of machines installed since introduction

Knight (1966, 1970, 1985)

Price: "published" rental prices

Independent variables: own, plus "published" specifications

Monthly rental for "most typical" configuration

1. Computing "power" (operations per second)

$$C = \frac{10^{12}\,(M\,(L-7)\,Wk)^a}{t_1 + t_2} = \frac{10^{12}}{t_1 + t_2} \times (\text{"memory factor"})$$

2. s = monthly seconds per dollar of monthly rental

Definitions:

M = memory size (in words)
L = word length (in bits)
W = "word factor" (dummy variable for memory types)
k = scaling constant
t_1 = time to perform one million operations (in microseconds)
t_2 = I/O or other idle time for one million operations (in microseconds)
a = .05 for scientific, .33 for commercial

NB: t_1 and t_2 were calculated (from computer specifications and computer center operations data) as weighted average of five categories of computations.

Chow (1967)

Special government survey; *Computers and Automation*; and IBM

Average monthly rental for specific configurations of computers newly introduced in year t

1. Multiplication time (in microseconds)
2. Memory size (words × word length)
3. Memory access time ("average time required to retrieve information from the memory"

NB: Also tried addition time, rejected for multicollinearity with multiplication time ("a slightly inferior variable"). Notes other omitted hardware characteristics, which he assumes correlated with included characteristics.

Table 4.1 (continued)

Author	Data sources	Dependent variable	Explanatory variables
Ratchford and Ford (1976, 1979)	Auerbach Corp.; (two sources), cross sections for 1964, 1967, and 1971	Average monthly rental, computer systems (CPU plus peripherals)	1. Memory size (maximum words in storage available with particular CPU) 2. Add time (in microseconds) 3. Dummies for age of machine and manufacturer NB: 36 variables tested with factor analysis; however, regression based on 4 variables mentioned by Chow, with 2 retained.
Archibald and Reece (1979)	*Computer Price Guide*; characteristics from various published sources	Asking price for used IBM machines of specified configuration	1. Add time (in microseconds) 2. Memory size (bits) in configuration 3. Cycle (read) time (in microseconds) 4. Access time (in millisecons) 5. Number of time share features 6. Number of CPU "intensiveness" features 7. Printer speed (hundreds of lines per minute) 8. Card reader speed (hundreds of cards per minute) 9. Several other characteristics of peripherals NB: Got "incorrect" signs for major variables, which often happens with multicollinearity and many variables.
Michaels (1979)	Auerbach Corp. (same as Ratchford and Ford: 264 "configurations" of CPU and peripherals, as of July 1971)	"Basic" monthly rental for specified configuration	1. Add time (in microseconds) 2. Index, memory core size (thousands of bytes) and transfer speed within core (in kilobytes per second) 3. Index, card reader speed and card punch speed 4. Index, number of tape drives and maximum read-write speed 5. Storage capacity (millions of bytes) in configuration

Study	Data source	Price variable	Characteristics
Stoneman (1976)	British Commercial Computer Digest; Computers and Automation; other	Published average price, all installations, all years machine is sold	1. Cycle time in microseconds 2. Maximum storage in thousands of bits 3. Floor area in square feet 4. Year and "generation" dummies 5. (not shown) 6. Dummies for manufacturer and introduction year (gives price index, relative to earliest machines) NB: Final set of variables selected from a much larger original set by comparing adjusted R^2 for groupings of the original variables. Author comments that owing to multicollinearity floor area proxies for speed. NB: Justification for forming indexes based on technical assumptions—e.g., number of tape drives substitutes for speed in achieving same results.
Stoneman (1978)	British Commercial Computer Digest; Computers and Automation; other	Prices of newly introduced machines	1. Cycle time in microseconds 2. Maximum storage in thousands of bits 3. Dummies for year of introduction
Cale, Gremillion, and McKenney (1978)	Datapro	Price at introduction for a "balanced" system (processor plus peripherals)	1. Memory size in bytes 2. Size (in megabytes) of on-line direct access storage NB: Addition time and other unspecified speed measures insignificant, partly owing to multicollinearity.
Fisher, McGowan and Greenwood (1983)	Government lease price lists	Lease prices to federal government	1. Memory size in thousands of bits 2. Addition time (including access time) 3. Transfer rate (bytes per second)

Table 4.1 (continued)

Author	Data sources	Dependent variable	Explanatory variables
Gordon (1987) *1954–1979 regressions*	Phister (1979)	Prices of newly introduced machines	1. Memory cycle time (in microseconds) 2. Memory size (in megabytes) 3. IBM dummy
1977–1984 regressions	*Computerworld*	Prices of all machines	1. Machine cycle time (in nanoseconds) 2. Memory size (in megabytes) 3. Minimum Number of channels 4. Maximum Number of channels 5. Cache buffer size (units not given)
Wallace (1985)	GML Corp.; International Data Corp; Phister (1979)	List prices of all machines	1. Linear combination of MIPS and KOPS 2. Memory size included, or minimum memory size (units not given) 3. Dummy variables for computer size class 4. Dummy variables for manufacturers
Cartwright, Donohoe, and Parker (1985)	Auerbach Corp.; Datapro Corp.; and *Computerworld*	List prices, all machines available	1. Speed (memory cycle time, machine cycle time, or MIPS, depending on period) 2. Memory size (in megabytes) 3. Maximum number of channels
Dulberger (this volume)	*Datamation; Computerworld*; IBM	List price, IBM and "plug-compatible" machines	1. MIPS 2. Memory size (in megabytes)—maximum and minimum 3. "Technology class' dummy variables

NB: Each machine entered twice in the data set, once with maximum memory size available, once with minimum memory size, with the appropriate price for each.

Flamm (1987)	Phister (1979)	List price, all machines in source	1. KOPS × 10^{-3} 2. Memory size in megabytes
Levy and Welzer (1985)	*Computerworld*	Published (list) prices, all machines from major producers	1. MIPS 2. Average memory size 3. Dummy variables for manufacturer, and for newly introduced models
Kelejian and Nicoletti (1971)	*Computers and Automation; Computer Characteristics Quarterly*	Minimum monthly rental	1. Add time (in microseconds) 2. Storage cycle time (in microseconds) 3. Minimum memory size (thousands of bits)
Ein-Dor (1985)	*Computerworld;* other sources	List price, selection of 106 machines	1. MIPS (a number of other performance measures were related to MIPS and to "average computational cost")

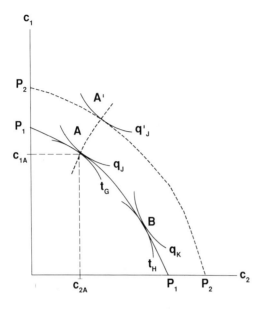

Figure 4.1

A computer executes a variety of instructions, and applications require them in different proportions or amounts. Consider figure 4.1, where two "users" or applications (we might think of them as "commercial" and "scientific"), *given* the hedonic contour $P_1 P_1$, demand different proportions of instructions c_1 and c_2 (which might be, say, file-sort and matrix inversion instructions). User J buys machine A, where user K buys machine B, because of differences in using technologies, $q_J(\,\cdot\,)$ and $q_K(\,\cdot\,)$—see result 1 in section 4.1.2.1 and also equation (2a). Producing the "specialized" computers A and B might also imply alternative technologies, architectures or designs, $t_G(\,\cdot\,)$ and $t_H(\,\cdot\,)$—refer to result (2), and equation (3).

The foregoing implies that, from both production and user considerations, the execution rate of each instruction is properly a computer characteristic. Computer "speed" is accordingly a vector, not a scalar.

High correlation among instruction execution rates precludes entering all, or even very many, of them in hedonic functions, so that some scalar summary of the speed vector must be developed. Three approaches have been employed in hedonic studies, and others exist in the computer literature.

a. *Single-instruction speed measures.* In this approach, the speed of one instruction is chosen (addition time or multiplication time), which then serves as a proxy for the rest. Examples are Patrick (1969), Chow (1967), Ratchford and Ford (1976), and Michaels (1979).

Neither additions nor multiplications is a very representative instruction. In analyses of instruction mix frequencies cited in Sharpe (1969, pp. 301–302), and Serlin (1986), additions accounted for only between 13% and 25% of total instructions, and multiplications around 5–6%. "Logic" or "other" or "miscellaneous" instructions, not easily measured, were the largest category. In another instruction mix cited by Serlin, neither additions nor multiplications were among the "10 most frequent instructions," which in total accounted for 67% of all operations.

Use of addition or multiplication times to represent computer speeds thus requires that their correlations with the execution rates of other instructions are high and stable. The stability requirement, especially, is doubtful, since logic design and internal architecture of the computer can be chosen to optimize specific applications.[4] Thus, a single-instruction speed measure will not adequately characterize a cross-section of computers, and may produce a biased hedonic price index.

b. *Intermediate-stage proxy measures.* Some variable that is an intermediate step in the execution of many instructions may serve as a proxy for the vector of execution times. One example is memory cycle speed—memory cycles per second, or its inverse, defined as the time (in microseconds) to read a word from the main memory and replace it.[5]

Memory cycle speed has been the most popular speed measure for computer hedonic studies, and its employment actually predates experiments with single-instruction speed measures. Memory cycle time has also sometimes been combined with the speed of some single instruction, such as addition (table 4.1). Closely related measures also appear in the regressions of Chow (1967—memory access time), Michaels (1979), and Fisher, McGowan, and Greenwood (1983—transfer rate).

The execution of one or more memory cycles is required for most computer instructions, so memory cycle speed is a common element contributing to speeds of executing instructions (Sippl, 1985, p. 110). As a perhaps more compelling argument, memory cycle time will be highly correlated with the speed of other processor operations, and therefore acts as a proxy for those other determinants of speed.

Despite these arguments in favor of the measure, it has always been clear that memory cycle time is an unreliable proxy (Sharpe, 1969, p. 298). The use on modern computers of high-speed intermediate "Cache" memories (which are intended to reduce the proportion of accesses to the relatively slower main memory) suggests that the conventional measure of memory cycle time is obsolete as a proxy for the speeds at which instructions are executed (see note 10). Bell (1986) reports that memory access speeds have increased relative to the speeds of logical operations, again serving to bring into question the stability over time of the proxy relation between memory cycle or access time and the speeds of executing instructions.

Another intermediate-stage proxy measure is machine cycle time. The execution time of the logical portion of any instruction equals machine cycle time multiplied by the number of machine cycles required for that instruction. Bloch and Galage (1978) present an equation for machine cycle time that relates it to the type and numbers of circuits required, and the time to complete each type of circuit. Minimum machine cycle time occurs for circuits that are wholly contained on a single chip (which is an element of machine design).

Though every instruction requires one or more machine cycles, the relation between machine cycle time and the execution speeds of instructions depends on the number of cycles per instruction. Serlin (1986) contains a table showing machine cycles for different instructions for an unnamed computer, with a range from 0 to 18 and a mean of 2.2. Even for a single machine, therefore, the proxy relation between machine cycle time and instruction execution speed will shift with the instruction mix. Across machines, moreover, the relation varies with machine design. Thus, machine cycle time contains the potential for substantial proxy error, both from machine to machine in the cross-section and over time.

In some computer studies, it is unclear which of the two "cycle times" the investigator selected. Alternatively, inconsistent measures may have been gathered for the various machines in the sample.

c. *Benchmarks*. Single-variable proxies for a multivariate vector of instruction speeds will always present the problem that the particular proxy chosen may represent very poorly the speed at which a computer performs actual jobs. It is thus natural to measure computer speed by presenting the same job or mix of jobs to various computers and measuring the time actually taken to perform them. Such an exercise is called a "benchmark" or a "benchmark test." Computer users have often performed benchmarks for machine selection, and benchmark results for standardized or stylized data processing problems have been published for many years (Phister, 1979, p. 100, presents examples that include filing and sorting problems, matrix inversion problems, and so forth).

An advantage of a benchmark measure is that it measures directly the speed, or cost, of jobs or applications, rather than of the instructions that are required for the job. However, benchmarks usually reflect system speed, not solely the speed of the processor. A second problem with benchmark data stems from a trade-off between cost and representativeness. Representativeness requires selecting a group (possibly a large group) of alternative computer uses and running each benchmark test on each machine in the sample. If problems are realistic, the test may be expensive. A third problem arises when results of multiple benchmark tests are highly, but not perfectly, correlated (as they generally will be): The researcher must either select one benchmark as a proxy for all the rest or find some way to combine them—a problem exactly parallel to the use of single-instruction speed measures and discussed above.

Despite these problems, it is a bit surprising that no researcher has yet collected benchmark data for use in a hedonic regression on computers.

d. *Weighted instruction mix measures.* A weighted instruction measure combines speeds of many instructions. It provides a practical alternative that achieves much the same ends as a benchmark, but with far less expense.

To form a weighted instruction measure of computer speed, a large number of computer jobs are examined—records of actual computer centers, or analysis either of "test packages" or of a sample of widely used programs. An internal "instruction trace" is carried out, which provides counts of the frequency of each machine instruction encountered in the programs. Execution speeds for each instruction are then timed (or obtained from published machine specifications). The scalar speed measure is formed by weighting the speeds of the various instructions by the relative frequencies recorded in the instruction trace.

An early example of a weighted instruction mix is the "Gibson mix," which Serlin (1986) dates around 1960.[6] Serlin presents an example of the use of the Gibson mix to estimate processor speed.

The first published use of a weighted instruction mix speed measure for scientific purposes was Kenneth Knight (1966, 1970, 1985). Knight's set of instructions included fixed-point addition, floating-point addition, multiplication, division, and finally, logic operations,[7] each of which receives an instructional weight for scientific applications and another for commercial ones. Instruction frequencies for the scientific speed measure were derived from traces at a scientific computer center, with some arbitrary adjustments for aspects of the architecture of certain machines (for details, see Knight, 1985, table 3, p. 117). For commercial uses, Knight collected the mix of instructions that were executed in a sample of commercial programs. Knight's speed measure also contains an estimate of processor idle time, for input-output or other operational reasons, which varied substantially among processors at the time Knight first carried out his investigation.[8]

Knight's second innovation, for which there are precursors (mentioned in Sharpe, 1969), was to combine the characteristics of speed and memory size into an index of processor "computing power." Knight's computing power formula is displayed in table 4.1.[9] Some of the parameter values that were assumed in combining memory size with speed are arbitrary.

Knight's computer processor performance measure remains controversial among computer professionals—largely, one gathers, for the arbitary nature of some of its assumed parameter values. Yet there can be no question that when it was devised in 1963, Knight's approach was a substantial step forward over the alternatives (such as using only addition or multiplication time as a proxy for other instruction speeds), and it did build into the speed measure a great many of the variables that determine processor speed. Much time has passed since 1963, and no post-1963 update of the weights was ever done (Knight's updated indexes, which extend through 1979, retain the original 1963 weights).

In the interim, other weighted instruction mix measures of processor speed have been developed, and used in hedonic functions for computers. Studies using either KOPS (thousands of operations per second) or MIPS (millions of instructions per second), which are similar, include Cartwright, Donahoe, and Parker (1985), Wallace (1985), Flamm (1987), Levy and Welzer (1985), and Dulberger (chapter 2, this volume).

Bloch and Galage (1978), and also Serlin (1986) and Lias (1980), present formulas as approximations to MIPS.[10] The MIPS formula includes both intermediate-stage proxy measures that have appeared in computer hedonic functions (machine cycle time and memory access time). Morever, additions and multiplications are among the instructions whose speeds are incorporated into MIPS. MIPS is thus clearly superior as a processor speed measure to alternatives employed in hedonic studies on computers, and because of its superiority, hedonic studies that use it are preferred to those that use single-speed or intermediate-stage proxies, other things being equal. MIPS is, however, not without problems of its own.

All applications or jobs reduce to frequencies of commands to execute the instructions in a processor's instruction set. These are sometimes referred to as "native MIPS," a measure that is not necessarily comparable across different manufacturers. Though MIPS can be made comparable or equivalent (see Dulberger's discussion in chapter 2 of this point), published MIPS ratings for some machines are noncomparable, or reflect informed guess work. "MIPS figures are useful for comparisons among members of the same architectural family; they cannot be relied upon to compare systems that have substantially different architectures" (Serlin, 1986, p. 114; see also Bell, 1986; Lias, 1980, p. 101; *Wall Street Journal*, April 4, 1986, p. 23; and note 10).

For the foregoing reasons, Dulberger (chapter 2, this volume) restricts the sample to machines (IBM and "plug-compatibles") for which "equivalent MIPS" are published (see her discussion of this point); introduction of other machines in the sample was eschewed on the grounds that the noncomparable measurement of MIPS could introduce a bias in the price indexes.[11] However, a noncomparability that may be disastrous for machine selection purposes may yet be acceptable for an economic measurement, in that the measurement error (which Lias, 1980, p. 105 puts at 10–30%) may be randomly distributed around the true hedonic regression line.

e. *Synthetic benchmarks.* MIPS is sometimes termed a "synthetic benchmark." There are others. The "Whetstone" reflects primarily scientific and engineering problems; the "Dhrystone" (obviously a reaction) is based on systems-programming work, rather than numerical calculations. The "Linpack" measures solution speeds for systems of linear equations. Other special benchmarks exist for, e.g., banking transactions (Serlin, 1986, gives some representative results).

None of these synthetic benchmarks has yet been used in hedonic functions for computer processors. Since finding a satisfactory speed measure is the biggest challenge to measuring price and technological change in computer processors, future work will no doubt explore the usefulness of synthetic benchmarks.

f. *Interpreting the hedonic coefficient on computer speed.* A number of the preceding methods for forming scalar measures of speed can be viewed as economic aggregations. They aggregate over a subset of the characteristics in equation (2a) or (3). That is, if there are (say) k speed characteristics in (2a), then a MIPS measure can be interpreted as a *quantity* index of speed characteristics.[12]

MIPS is, however, a quantity index that is formed without price "weights" (because we have no hedonic prices for the separate characteristics). Implicitly, therefore, each speed is assumed to have the *same* hedonic price, which is the justification for simply summing them to form MIPS.

When the quantity index of speed characteristics (MIPS) is introduced as a variable in the hedonic regression, the hedonic coefficient on "speed" is interpretable as a price *index* over the k speed characteristics. By its construction, this price index of "speed" involves the implicit assumption that the prices of individual speeds, such as addition time and file/sort time, move together over time— there is no relative price change among the various computer speed characteristics.

The fact that these two price and quantity subindexes are aggregations from the user, rather than the production, side is probably of minor empirical importance. That the aggregations imply that speeds of different instructions all have the same price, and therefore move together over time, is an assumption that economists will find difficult to accept. It is, however, an inherent liability that grows out of the inability, so far, to model the full vector of computer speeds in the hedonic function.

3.   Other Variables in Computer Hedonic Functions

A variety of computer processor specifications have been entered into hedonic functions, largely reflecting the empiricist hedonic tradition of stepwise regression and other "hunts" for maximum R^2. Ratchford and Ford (1976), for example, report trying 36 different computer specifications before settling on the variables of Chow (1967). Archibald and Reece (1979), who entered a string of specifications for processors and peripheral equipment into a single regression, got "wrong" signs on important variables, a probable indication of multicollinearity.

Two studies (Patrick, 1969, and Stoneman, 1976) used floor area occupied by the machine. Though for any state of technology, bigger (in performance) machines take more space, the steady thrust of miniaturization invalidates the floor space proxy as a hedonic function variable for any purpose (see also the discussion in section 4.3.2).

Of the studies in table 4.1 that used an instructional mix measure of speed, only Cartwright, Donahoe, and Parker (1985) report a variable in the hedonic function other than speed and memory size. This evidence suggests that where other hardware attributes have been employed as variables in hedonic functions for computers, they were correcting in some sense for an inadequate measure of processor speed.

It seems plausible that processor characteristics other than speed and memory size should have some role in a computer hedonic function. Archibald and Reece used several measures of time-sharing capability and of "intensiveness" built into the processor, but multicollinearity makes the result indeterminant. Reliability is important to the user and costly to produce, and moreover has improved over time, so its exclusion produces potential upward bias in the price indexes. Phister (1979, pp. 437–442) presents fragmentary data showing that "availability" increased from around 65% to over 90% of total time between the early 1950s and 1965. However, except for the "seconds" variable in Knight's formula, no availability variables appear in the computer studies that have so far been carried out. "User friendly" attributes are more prominent in today's computer environment, though much of the improvement comes from the system's software; again, measures of such attributes do not appear in computer hedonic functions, and their omission probably biases price indexes.

4. Peripheral Equipment Variables

Space precludes comparable attention to independent variables in hedonic functions for peripheral equipment, though their definition and measurement are nonetheless of equal importance. Most of the variables that have been used are, like those in the processor hedonic functions, some form of speed or capacity measure. As has been true of the processor studies, variables relating to reliability and ease of use have not played a prominent role in these studies, though it is clear that intangible characteristics of peripherals have also improved over time. For the best discussion, see the several sections on peripherals in Cole et al. (1986).

Table 4.2
Functional forms for computer hedonic functions

Author	Functional form adopted	Other functional forms tested	Test method and/or comments
Schneidewind (Sharpe, 1969)	Double-log	None	—
Skattum (Sharpe, 1969)	Double-log	None	—
Early, Barrow and Margolis (Sharpe, 1969)	Linear	Double-log	Goodness of fit
Patrick (Sharpe, 1969)	Double-log	None	—
Jacob (Sharpe, 1969)	Double-log	None	—
Knight (1966, 1970, 1985)	Double-log	None	Uses primitive method of frontier estimation
Chow (1967)	Double-log	None	—
Ratchford and Ford (1976, 1979)	Double-log	None	—
Archibald and Reece (1979)	Semilog	None	—
Michaels (1979)	Semilog	Not explicitly specified	Significance of coefficients; goodness of fit
Stoneman (1976)	Double-log	None mentioned	—
Stoneman (1978)	Double-log	Not explicitly specified	Goodness of fit
Cale, Gremillion and McKenney (1978)	Double-log	None	—

Fisher, McGowan, and Greenwood (1983)	Double-log	None	—
Gordon (1987)	Double-log	Semilog	Goodness of fit
Wallace (1985)	Translog	Double-log Semilog	Goodness of fit and prediction test
Cartwright, Donahoe, and Parker (1985)	Double-log	Linear	Goodness of fit
Dulberger (1988)	Double-log	Linear Semilog	Box-Cox
Flamm (1987)	C/P (see text)	None	—
Levy and Welzer (1985)	Double-log	"Standard functional forms"	Goodness of fit
Kelejian and Nicoletti (1971)	Linear	None	—
Horsley and Swann (1983)	Double-log	None	Fitted convex hull
Ein Dor (1985)	Double-log	None	—

Table 4.3
Test results, hedonic functional forms for computers

"Winner"	Test calculated by	Functional forms "defeated"
Linear	Early, Barro, and Margolis	Double-log
Semilog	Michaels	Not recorded
Double-log	Stoneman	Not recorded
	Cartwright, Donahoe, and Parker	Linear
	Dulberger	Linear, semilog
	Levy and Welzer	Not recorded
	Gordon	Semilog
Translog	Wallace	Double-log
		Semilog

4.2.2   Choice of Functional Form

1.   Research Results

The theory of hedonic functions states that the hedonic function, $h(\cdot)$, is an envelope of the many $q(\cdot)$ functions on the buyer side and the many $t(\cdot)$ functions on the seller side—results (1) and (2), section 4.1.2. Apart from special cases, functional form is thus an empirical matter and is appropriately determined in the usual statistical way, as has been the practice in the hedonic literature (Griliches, 1971).

Four functional forms appear as computer processor hedonic functions: linear, semilog, double-log, and translog (table 4.2). Most computer researchers have chosen the double-log functional form out of a priori conviction, rather than by testing alternatives.[13]

In the seven tests that were conducted with computer processor data, each of the four functional forms came out on top at least once (table 4.3). The double-log was reported the contest "winner" more times (five) than any other functional form—but then it also played in the most games! And though the semilog was "defeated" the most (three times), it is not clear whether the double-log was present in the one situation (Michaels) where the semilog won a contest, nor is it clear whether or not the semilog participated in the match for some of the cases where the double-log came out on top. It is instructive that both semilog and double-log were defeated in the only case (Wallace, 1985) where a more flexible functional form (the translog) was on the field.

Of the studies on peripheral equipment, only Cole et al. (1986), considered alternative functional forms. All researchers eventually settled on the double log, save for Flamm (1987), discussed below, and Randolph (1985), who adopted the semilog form.

This empirical work is unsatisfactory for three reasons: (1) The number of functional forms considered was limited, and excluded a class of functional forms that the theory of hedonic functions shows is plausible—namely, those with contours shaped like P_1P_1 and P_2P_2 in figure 4.1 (see section 4.2.2.2). (2) Even among the functional forms that were tried, no researcher has tested the entire panoply; many of the tests involved only two alternatives. (3) Finally, and perhaps most seriously, researchers who have looked at the functional form question have been content to carry out minimal goodness of fit tests, and then proceed to the empirical work using a chosen functional form. No one has worried very much about the sensitivity of estimated hedonic price indexes to what is essentially an arbitrary specification of functional form.

2. What Functional Forms Should Be Considered?[14]

The theory of hedonic functions suggests special cases—result (4), section 4.1.2—where the hedonic function may be identified econometrically. Assuming that the true characteristics are known and are measured correctly, when production transformation functions, $t(\cdot)$, are identical for all producers—that is, producers all have access to common technology—then $h(\cdot)$ coincides with the common technology surface, $t(\cdot)$. We refer to this as the production, or "t-identification" case. Alternatively, when all users have identical use technologies—$q(\cdot)$ from equation (2a)—$h(\cdot)$ coincides with $q(\cdot)$. We refer to this as the use, or "q-identification" case (the basic reference for these results is Rosen, 1974, as noted in section 4.1.2).

Each of the two special cases implies a particular form for the hedonic function. Consider

$$P^* = h(c_1, \ldots, c_k), \tag{5}$$

where P^* is any *fixed* value of P from equation (1). We refer to equation (5) as a "hedonic contour." A hedonic contour connects all bundles of computer characteristics selling for the same price (examples of hedonic contours are P_1P_1 and P_2P_2 in figure 4.1).

The two special cases can be stated compactly in terms of the second derivative of the hedonic contours:

q–identification implies: $dc_i^2 / d^2c_j > 0$ (6a)

(example: $\ln P = \ln c_o + a_1 \ln c_1 + a_2 \ln c_2$);

t–identification implies: $dc_i^2 / d^2c_j < 0$ (6b)

(example: $\ln P = a_o + a_1 c_1^r + a_2 c_2^s$ $(a_1, a_2, r, s, > 0)$).

If q-identification obtains, hedonic contours bow *in* toward the origin, in the manner of normal production isoquants—for that is what they are in this case. A hedonic function that exhibits this "bowed-in" property is the double-log function—the example in (6a)—which has been employed in many hedonic studies of computer equipment.

With t-identification, on the other hand, hedonic contours bow *out* from the origin (as drawn in figure 4.1), in the normal form for production transformation curves for multiple-output production processes—which indeed in the t-identification case they are. An example (not the only one) of a hedonic function with this "bowed-out" property is the semilog exponential function (6b).

To make empirical use of the theoretical results, two approaches are possible. (1) A priori knowledge of the computer industry could be utilized to justify an assumption that *either* use or production technologies were identical; the hedonic function could then be constrained to a form that is consistent with the assumption, and the hedonic price index would then be exact for the case corresponding to the assumption. The computer industry is technologically dynamic, so that the hypothesis that $h(\cdot)$ coincides with $t(\cdot)$ is worth considering. On the other hand, identical use technologies, $q(\cdot)$, does not seem probable; Flamm (1987), for example, notes that one hardly ever observes two computer centers configured in exactly the same way. Accordingly, a priori knowledge suggests specification of a computer hedonic function with bowed-*out* contours (like figure 4.1), a functional form with the property of (6b).

(2) An alternative empirical approach is to note that the sign of the second derivative of empirical hedonic contours is a necessary—though not sufficient—condition for one or the other of the two identifications. If the hedonic function were estimated with a flexible functional form,[15] the normal statistical tests for convexity are equivalent to testing the necessary condition for one of the special cases against the other.[16] One could take acceptance of the necessary

condition as grounds for maintaining that the function is approximately identified, and interpret empirical results accordingly.

The t-identification case has a great amount of economic appeal as a description of the computer industry; regrettably, none of the computer studies, even those that make use of flexible functional forms to choose among nested functions (Wallace, 1985; Dulberger, chapter 2, this volume), test for a functional form consistent with t-identification. The hedonic functions considered were those with linear hedonic contours (linear and semilog hedonic functions) or those with bowed-in toward the origin contours (double-log hedonic function). None of the functional forms so far employed permits hedonic contours of bowed-out form, which leaves a considerable gap in our knowledge.[17]

3.   Curve-Fitting Methods: "Technological Leapfrogging"

When new innovations continually supplant older ones (a process Fisher, McGowan, and Greenwood, 1983, call "technological leapfrogging"), observations that represent obsolescent machines lie inside the technological frontier. They may also be systematically dominated by superior machines in the price/performance plane represented in the hedonic function.

Consider figure 4.1, where the contour $P_1 P_1$ maps the set of points

$$P_1 = h(c). \tag{7}$$

In the long run, there can be no computers selling for price P_1 that lie inside the hedonic contour $P_1 P_1$; but if $P_1 P_1$ is composed of computers that embody the latest technology, older machines priced at P_1 but with performance interior to $P_1 P_1$ may continue to be sold for a time owing to inertia, availability, the cost of changing existing systems to new technologies, and so forth. For example, price reductions on existing models of IBM personal computers were reported in early 1986; but even after the price cuts on existing models, new IBM models with faster speed or increased storage were available at the same (list) price.[18]

What appear to be premiums for older machines when *list* prices appear on the left-hand side of equation (1) may instead be indications of differential discounting on machines that embody older technology or lower performance levels. Thus, if researchers had cross-sections of transactions prices to work with, the observed premiums for older machines would no doubt be greatly reduced—though perhaps not eliminated entirely. This, however, affects our *interpretation* of "premiums" on older machines, not the necessity to allow for the phenomenon—whether technological leapfrogging or differential discounting—in empirical work.

There are two concerns here, one we might call "technical" and the other "substantive." The points that are dominated could bias the estimated hedonic function (for example, if machines containing the newest technology are larger or faster), producing unreliable estimates of coefficients. Dulberger (chapter 2, this volume) notes that estimated implicit hedonic prices for computer characteristics were sensitive to the inclusion of the "technology variables" that were introduced into her equations to model "multiple price regimes." Regardless of the substantive use of the hedonic estimates, and regardless of whether the dominated points are technological slow runners or list price-transaction price errors, one must choose an estimator for the hedonic function that takes account of points systematically interior to the frontier.

On the other hand, what one *does* with estimates incorporating multiple price regimes depends on one's interpretation of them and on the use of the data. If the objective requires an estimate of the position of the technological frontier (estimating the rate of technical progress, for example, as in Knight, 1966, or comparing price/ performance positions of different manufacturers, as in Fisher, McGowan, and Greenwood, 1983), then obviously the frontiers, and only the frontiers, are wanted.

If the objective is to compute a price index for computers, the situation is more complicated. If the older machines really sell for more, relative to their performance, then a price index taken solely from the frontier is biased, because it does not incorporate the price behavior of older computers. Alternatively, if apparent multiple price regimes reflect differential discounting from list, then the frontier estimate is again the proper one, since discounting moves prices of older machines from the interior of $P_1 P_1$ to a point on the $P_1 P_1$ contour.

Estimating hedonic functions in the presence of "technological leapfrogging" is a form of the frontier-regression problem. One approach, followed by several researchers (listed in table 4.1) is to restrict the observations included in the regression to newly introduced machines. Provided new machines were on the technological frontier and older ones within it, this would insure that the hedonic function estimates the frontier. Chow (1967) is perhaps the best-known example of this approach.[19] Knight (1966), starting from an observation set of new machines, discarded those that lay more than one-half of a standard error below the initially fitted least-squares line, thus eliminating newly introduced machines that were not on the frontier. Knight's final results were taken from a regression estimated from the remaining points. As already noted, restricting the observations to newly introduced machines produces a biased price index because the index does not reflect the price behavior of older computers.[20]

An alternative approach is to combine observations for all machines currently marketed in a single regression, but to introduce explicit econometric frontier-fitting techniques to the estimation. The most extensive analysis so far is in Horsley and Swann (1983), who fit convex hulls to Knight's data to determine the undominated points, and therefore the movement through time of the technological frontier. The exercise was not entirely successful, however, partly because so few data points were left for curve-fitting.

Dulberger's work (chapter 2 in this volume) has already been referred to. She estimates the frontier by introducing into her regressions a set of technology variables (based on the density of the chips used in the computer), which were allowed to shift the hedonic function. Usually, the older technology was associated with a premium—that is, the newer technology dominated in price-performance space. Note, however, that Dulberger's price indexes are not constructed solely from points on the technological frontier (see section 4.3).

4.3   Price Indexes for Computers

Twelve studies of computer processors and seven of peripheral equipment estimate "quality-adjusted" price indexes using hedonic methods. Not all of them are explicit in using the "hedonic" nomenclature; yet their methodologies are nonetheless hedonic and their results fit the definition of a hedonic price index (section 4.1).

Hedonic price indexes for specific items of computer equipment ("box" price indexes) can be viewed as approximations to output price indexes—section 4.1.2.2 and results (8) and (11). For the reasons discussed in section 4.1.3, we adopt the output price index interpretation for hedonic price indexes for computer processors and peripheral equipment. The computer processor price indexes are reviewed in section 4.3.2; studies on peripheral equipment are considered in section 4.3.3. The final section, 4.3.4, contains estimates of price indexes for computer systems, indexes that are interpretable as input price indexes—i.e., as price indexes for investment.

4.3.1   Computational Procedures for Hedonic Price Indexes

Three methods for calculating hedonic price indexes from hedonic functions have appeared in the computer literature. The examples presented in the following paragraphs presume the double-log functional form—the dominant functional form in empirical studies on computers (section 4.2.2).

1.   The Dummy Variable Method

In the most common technique for computing hedonic price indexes, a series of time dummy variables is entered in a multiyear pooled cross-section hedonic function. In the double-log formulation, we have (suppressing notation for the regression residual)

$$\ln P_{it} = \sum_j a_j \ln c_{ijt} + \sum a_t D_t, \tag{8}$$

where when $t = 0$, a_t is the normal regression intercept. The coefficients a_t capture the residual price change between periods that is not accounted for by changes in the characteristics.

The price index is computed by taking the antilogs of the estimated a_t coefficients from equation (8). A number of the computer studies reviewed in this survey omit this latter step, and take the regression coefficients a_t themselves as the index numbers.[21] In those cases, indicated in source notes to the tables, I have computed price indexes from antilogs of the author's published coefficients. Some unavoidable round-off error is thereby introduced.

It is well-known that the antilog of the OLS estimate of a_t is not an unbiased estimate of antilog a_t, which means that price indexes estimated by the dummy variable method are biased. A standard bias correction (Goldberger, 1968; also Teekens and Koerts, 1972) is to add one-half the coefficient's squared standard error to the estimated coefficient.

A variation on the dummy-variable method appears in Knight (1966, 1970, 1985). Knight estimated the rate of technical change for computers, rather than "constant quality" price indexes. However, his estimating equation is similar to the multiyear hedonic regressions used by other researchers:

$$\ln (s/P)_{it} = a_o + a_c \ln (\text{computing power})_{it} + \sum a_t D_t, \tag{9}$$

where s is the number of seconds the user obtained from a computer per month (Knight's computing power variable, discussed in section 4.2.1, measured computations per second). Hence, it is only necessary to move the "seconds" variable over to the right-hand side, obtaining

$$-ln\ P_{it} = (a_o - a_s\ ln\ s_{it}) + a_c\ ln\ (computing\ power)_{it} + \sum a_t\ D_t, \tag{10}$$

and the price index can be computed by taking the antilogs of *negatives* of the a_t coefficients that Knight published. Note that in this formulation, when $s_{t+n} > s_t$ (which implies decreasing monthly "down time") without an increase in monthly rental, the coefficient a_{t+n} falls relative to a_t; thus Knight's measure correctly records improvement in computer reliability as a price decrease.

2. The Imputation Method

Consider arrays of prices for computer "models" for two periods, r and s:

$$P_r = (P_{1r}, \ldots, P_{gr}; P_{hr}, \ldots, P_{h+n,r}),$$
$$P_s = (P_{1s}, \ldots, P_{gs}; P_{ks}, \ldots, P_{k+m,s}). \tag{11}$$

The first g models are common to both periods, but the rest are "new models" or "discontinued models," observed in one of the two periods but not the other.

The hedonic function can be used to estimate one of these "missing" prices.[22] With the double-log hedonic function, one has

$$\hat{P}_{it} = exp(a_t + \sum_j a_{jt}\ ln\ c_{ijt}). \tag{12}$$

These estimated, or "imputed," prices can then be used in a price index formula defined in the conventional way on goods prices and quantities. The imputed price $\hat{P}_{it}$ incorporates the bias to the estimate of a_t that was discussed in the preceding section, plus what Teekens and Koerts (1972) refer to as a "transformation bias," though the estimated a_{jt} coefficients are unbiased.

Two variants of the imputation method occur in the computer processor studies. Chow (1967) computed unweighted price indexes for which prices for 1960 were imputed for all the models present in each comparison year (1954–1965), regardless of whether an observed price existed for any of these same models in 1960. Letting $r = t$ and $s = 1960$ (in array 11), each yearly index, including the index for 1960, has the form

$$I_{t,\ 1960} = \sum_i (P_{it}/\hat{P}_{i,\ 1960})\ (1/(h+n)) \qquad (13a)$$
$$i = 1, \ldots, h+n \qquad \text{(for all } t \neq 1960\text{)},$$
$$i = 1, \ldots, g \qquad \text{(for } t = 1960\text{)},$$

where $\hat{P}_{i,\ 1960}$ is defined by equation (12).[23] Note that models $k, \ldots,$ $k+m$, which were observed in 1960 but were not available in year t, do not enter Chow's index.

In Dulberger's (chapter 2 in this volume) imputation indexes, (a) imputation is carried out only for models whose prices were "missing" (that is, both years' observed prices were used for models $1, \ldots, g$);[24] (b) the observations are weighted by market shares; and (c) the decision about which models to impute is tied to the weighting formula selected for the index. Letting $r = t$ and $s = 1982$, in array (11), Dulberger's imputation index is

$$I_{t,\ 1982} = \sum P_{it}\ Q_{it} / \sum \hat{P}_{i,\ 1982}\ Q_{it} \qquad (13b)$$
$$i = 1, \ldots, h+n,$$

where

$$\hat{P}_{i,\ 1982} = \hat{P}_{i,\ 1982} \qquad \text{when } i = 1, \ldots, g,$$
$$\hat{P}_{i,\ 1982} = P_{i,\ 1982} \qquad \text{when } i = h, \ldots, h+n,$$

and $\hat{P}_{i,\ 1982}$ is defined by equation (12). Imputation methods for three peripheral equipment indexes summarized in Cole et al. (1986) are similar to Dulberger's.

As with Chow's imputation, models $k, \ldots, k+m$, available in 1982 but not in year t, do not enter Dulberger's index. The weighting pattern, however, determines the prices to be imputed. Models $k, \ldots,$ $k+m$ have zero weight in year t, so cannot affect the "Paasche" form of the price index chosen by Dulberger (to match the system used for deflation in the NIPAs).

One could also compute the "Laspeyres" version of an imputation index:

$$I_{t,\ 1982} = \sum \hat{P}_{it}\ Q_{i,\ 1982} / \sum P_{i,1982}\ Q_{i,\ 1982} \qquad (13c)$$
$$i = 1, \ldots, k+m,$$

where

$$\hat{P}_{it} = P_{it} \qquad \text{when } i = 1, \ldots, g,$$
$$\hat{P}_{it} = \hat{P}_{it} \qquad \text{when } 1 = k, \ldots, k+m,$$

and $\hat{P}_{it}$ is defined by equation (12). In the Laspeyres case, imputation is performed for the models omitted from the Paasche version; conversely, the imputations performed in (13b) have no weight in 1982, and do not enter into (13c). We thus have the somewhat odd result that "Laspeyres" and "Paasche" forms of the imputation index differ in the *prices* included in them, and not only in the weights, as in conventional cases.[25]

3. The Characteristics Price Method

Hedonic functions estimate prices for characteristics. In the double-log case, we have

$$r_j = \hat{a}_j (P/c_j)^*, \tag{14}$$

where $\hat{a}_j$ is the estimated regression coefficient for characteristic j, and the characteristic price, r_j, is valued for a particular point $(P/c_j)^*$ on the hedonic surface.

It is natural to construct an index from the characteristics prices, using the quantities of characteristics as weights. Such calculations relate directly to the theory of hedonic functions and of characteristics-space index numbers, summarized in section 4.1. Characteristics price indexes apparently were first calculated by Griliches (1964).

To construct index numbers from characteristics prices, one needs (whenever the hedonic function is nonlinear) to determine which characteristics prices from the domain are appropriate. Two "natural" choices are (1) evaluate (14) at the mean quantities of characteristics— that is, set c and P equal to their mean values for some period (obviously, for a two-period index there are two possible means); (2) evaluate (14) for each point in the domain where a computer is actually observed, and form an index from these prices. In the latter case, index weights are the quantities of characteristics sold:

$$q_{ij} = c_{ij} S_i. \tag{15}$$

That is, the quantity of characteristic j contributed by variety i is the amount of characteristic j embodied in variety i (c_{ij}) times the sales of variety i (S_i). A unique quantity weight exists for characteristic j for each variety i, and thus an index weight is associated with each observed value of r_j in (14), and similarly for all j.

The second procedure for implementing the characteristics price method was followed by Dulberger (chapter 2 in this volume), and also, in modified form, in the peripheral equipment studies in Cole et al. (1986).

Though they were not estimated as hedonic functions, Flamm's (1987) "box" indexes for computer processors and peripheral equipment can be interpreted as characteristics price indexes, and his estimating procedure as implying a linear hedonic function through the origin. Flamm obtains an average price for, e.g., processor speed by removing the value of peripheral equipment from Phister's (1979) value of installed U.S. computer systems, and then calculating a measure he calls "effective bandwidth" (the term comes from the computer literature). The values of speed and of memory are isolated from the value of the installed bandwidth, and the price of, e.g., speed is calculated by dividing the value of the "stock" of speed by average speed (this terse description is regrettably inadequate; Flamm's appendix A provides the details). He then computes an index from the price changes for processor speed and memory size, which is the processor index reported in section 4.3.2. Except for the 1965–1972 period, I use Flamm's box processor indexes mainly as a check on other hedonic studies, or as inputs to his computer systems estimates.

4. Properties of the Three Methods

Of the three methods for computing hedonic price indexes, the dummy variable method is the simplest to implement in normal research contexts. For this reason, it is the method most frequently utilized in the empirical studies on computers (and on other products as well).

Against its simplicity is the fact that the dummy variable method holds constant the slopes of the P^* contours of figure 4.1 for any ratio c_i/c_j, thus imposing the restriction that the hedonic contours shrink toward the origin in a homogeneous fashion; the price index measures the rate of shrinkage. Alternatively, an estimated contour can be thought of as the average hedonic contour across the y years included in the pooled regressions; the price index measures the average rate of shrinkage.

Neither the imputation method nor the characteristics price method imposes restrictions on the slopes of the hedonic contours. With either method, the hedonic function is free to take on a unique value for any period.[26]

Because hedonic regressions usually are not weighted, price indexes produced with the dummy variable method are an unweighted mean of all of the price changes observed across the hedonic surface. With the imputation method or the characteristics price method, it is easier to introduce market-share weights into the index number, without necessarily estimating a weighted regression. The absence of weights, then, is a potential bias in the dummy variable method.

Compared with the other two, the imputation method permits maximum utilization of *observed* prices, thereby minimizing measurement error from misspecification of the hedonic function, mismeasured characteristics, and so forth. Set against this is the potential bias that results because either new or discontinued models must be excluded from the comparison, at least when a fixed weight index is computed.

The characteristics price method results in an index number that corresponds more closely to the theory—see results (7) and (10) from section 4.1.2.2. It also explicitly incorporates both new and discontinued models. On the other hand, it can be cumbersome to compute, and because it represents a less-familiar index number concept, it is less appealing to some users.

On balance, price indexes produced by the imputation or characteristics price methods are preferable to dummy variable indexes. The empirical section notes evidence on the robustness of hedonic price indexes to the calculation method.

4.3.2   Empirical Estimates: Hedonic Price Indexes for Computer Processors

It is convenient to divide the history of the computer into three epochs, and to consider separately price index estimates for each epoch. In each epoch, substantial dispersion is observed among the price indexes estimated in different studies.

Dispersion in estimated price indexes can be attributed to the following components: (1) the hedonic function (with separate contributions from choice of independent variables, from specification of the dependent variable, and from functional form), (2) computational methods for forming hedonic price indexes out of hedonic functions, (3) data source effects, and (4) investigator effects. To determine the robustness of hedonic methods, one would like to decompose the total dispersion in hedonic indexes into these separate sources.

Data source effects deserve particular emphasis. Most hedonic investigations employ specifications and/or prices from some published source (trade journals and the like). The prices are usually manufacturers' list or suggested retail prices, or nominal monthly rentals; information on applicable discounts is seldom available, so the price indexes are subject to an unknown bias.

Less obviously, perhaps, error in the price indexes can also enter from inaccuracies in published specifications data used as independent variables. Data from different sources may not agree, or when they agree may still contain a variety of compilation or editing errors. Because of multicollinearity in most hedonic functions, estimated coefficients are often quite sensitive to perturbations in the data.[27] Careful "cleaning" of the data—cross-checking published specifications with other data and against direct knowledge of the product—often yields more stable (and believable) hedonic functions, and may affect the indexes as well. Thus, there is a sense in which data source effects and investigator effects intermingle, since a careful investigator will invest substantial effort "cleaning" the data. A study that shows the usual evidence of "dirty" data—instability in coefficient estimates, implausible implicit prices for characteristics, erratic movements in hedonic price indexes—may, conversely, simply reflect investigator effects.

In the following sections, I review the substantive evidence presented by the price index estimates in each epoch. I also consider the importance, influence, or probable size of price index dispersion originating from the hedonic function (drawing on section 4.2), the index computation method, and data sources and investigator effects. For several reasons, the order of the discussion varies with the period being discussed.

1. From the Beginning to the Introduction of the Third Generation

The first epoch of computer history begins with the earliest models that were sold commercially and extends to 1964–1965. By the end of this period, "second-generation" computers (transistors) began to be replaced by "third-generation" machines (integrated circuit technology). The price indexes presented in table 4.4A thus encompass first- and second-generation computers.[28]

The four studies in table 4.4A exhibit two computational methods for using hedonic functions to construct price indexes, three different data sets, and four definitions of the speed variable. Index computa-

Table 4.4A
Alternative research price indexes for computers, 1953–1965 (1965 = 100)

	Chow (1967)		Knight (1966, 1970)		Gordon (1987)		New models only[d] (6b)	Flamm (1987)
	Imputation[a] (1)	Dummy variable[b] (2)	Scientific[c] (3)	Commercial[c] (4)	"Augmented" sample[d] (5)	New models only[d] (6a)		(See text)[e] (7)
1953	NA		1657.5	1401.3	1243	NA	NA	NA
1954	953.0				466	1038	2154	NA
1955	866.8		1201.2	1072.9	289	570	1182	NA
1956	741.7				289	NA	NA	NA
1957	678.2		837.1	806.1	342	1799	NA	1427
1958	595.5				313	1038	1206	1086
1959	465.0		664.8	770.1	275	371	876	844
1960	313.7	319.5	500.0	614.2	236	378	500	539
1961	264.7	280.8	327.7	471.5	201	349	414	428
1962	201.2	196.5	227.5	327.4	175	175	285	379
1963	167.2	176.4	173.4	222.8	172	303	289	252
1964	122.5	126.8	150.2	158.9	154	163	152	148
1965	100.0	100.0	100.0	100.0	100	100	100	100

a. $\sum (P_t/\hat{P}_{1960})/n$, where $\hat{P}_{1960}$ is imputed from regression for 1960; taken from Chow (1967, table 2), rebased to 1965.

b. Computed from antilogs of coefficients in Chow (1967, table 1).

c. Dummy variable. Index numbers computed from antilogs of coefficients on time dummies (with signs reversed) presented in Knight (1966, 1970). Coefficients for 1962–1965 are from Knight (1970), equations 11 and 12, pp. 218, 222. Coefficients for 1953–1962 are from Knight (1966), equations 3 and 4, p. 49.

d. Dummy variable. From Gordon (1987, table 8), columns (4), (5), and (7).

e. From Flamm (1987, table A–5), column headed "box only," rebased to 1965.

Table 4.4B
Year-to-year percent changes: alternative estimates for computer prices

	Chow		Knight		Gordon			Flamm
	(1)	(2)	(3)	(4)	(5)	(6a)	(6b)	(7)
1953–1954	NA	NA			−62.5	NA	NA	NA
1954–1955	−9.0	NA	−27.5[b]	−23.4[b]	−38.0	−45.1	−45.1	NA
1955–1956	−14.4	NA			0	NA	NA	NA
1956–1957	−8.6	NA	−30.3[b]	−24.9[b]	+18.3	+215.6[a]	NA	NA
1957–1958	−12.2	NA			−8.5	−42.3	+2.0[a]	−23.9
1958–1959	−21.9	NA	−20.6[b]	−4.5[b]	−12.1	−64.3	−27.4	−22.3
1959–1960	−32.5	NA	−24.8	−20.2	−14.2	+1.9	−42.9	−36.2
1960–1961	−15.6	−12.1	−34.5	−23.2	−14.8	−7.7	−17.2	−20.6
1961–1962	−24.0	−30.0	−30.5	−30.6	−12.9	−49.9	−31.2	−11.3
1962–1963	−16.9	−10.2	−23.8	−31.9	−1.7	+73.1	+1.4	−33.6
1963–1964	−26.7	−28.1	−13.4	−28.7	−10.5	−46.2	−47.4	−41.2
1964–1965	−18.4	−21.1	−33.4	−37.1	−35.1	−38.7	−34.2	−32.4
(a) Average* rate of decline, period studied	18.2	20.3	19.9	18.1	—	—	—	27.7
(b) Average* rate of decline, 1960–1965	20.3	20.3	27.1	30.3	−15.0	—	—	27.8

Source: Calculated from table 4.4A, or the original sources cited there (for Flamm, 1987, changes are from his table A–5).

* Computed as the simple average of yearly percent changes.

a. Percent change computed from the last available index number (so it is the percent change over two or three years, whichever is the case).

b. Two-year period change (see text).

tional methodologies (dummy variable or imputation, as explained in section 4.3.1) for each of the four studies in table 4.4A are designated in the table. Variables and functional form have already been considered in section 4.2. Yearly changes for each of these indexes are presented in table 4.4B.

a. *Effect of alternative index computational methods.* One direct estimate of computational method effect comes from comparing Chow's published imputation and dummy variable estimates for the period 1960–1965—columns (1) and (2). The two hedonic indexes move fairly closely together, with no discernible pattern in yearly percentage changes (tabulated in table 4.4B), and no differences at all in the average yearly rate of decline (last line of table 4.4B).

However, in the 1960–1965 interval, which corresponds approximately to the reign of the second-generation computer, Chow could not reject the hypothesis that the computer hedonic function was homogeneous across all years. For the longer 1954–1965 period, Chow reported rejection of homogeneity across first- and second-generation computers; accordingly, over the longer interval one might expect greater differences between price indexes computed by dummy variable and imputation methods.

Insight on this question can be gained from Gordon, who obtained Chow's data and reestimated his model. These regressions are displayed in the three columns headed "Chow sample" in Gordon (1987, table 6), and the associated price indexes appear in his table 8. Gordon maintained the homogeneity hypothesis (across first- and second-generation computers) that Chow reports was rejected, and also explored minor specification changes to Chow's original model. None of the three dummy variable indexes Gordon produced in his verification of Chow's research differs significantly from the 1954–1965 imputation index Chow published. Though the imputation index is the superior approach, since it imposes no constraints on characteristics prices, hedonic indexes appear quite robust to calculation method, at least with Chow's data.

b. *Effects of data sources and variables.* With respect to data, Knight's was a painstaking effort that supplemented standard published sources with a good amount of useful data generated through his own devices. Chow relied primarily on an early government survey on computer installations. Gordon and Flamm obtained their data from the same secondary source (Phister, 1979), though they used different aspects of the Phister data base.

Unfortunately, none of the four authors estimated the others' specifications on his own data, so we have no direct estimate of data source effects. I infer, from considerations discussed below, that much of the rather substantial range of estimates shown in table 4.4A stems from procedures, rather than data sets, and also that the Phister data used by Flamm and Gordon are inferior to the data of Chow and of Knight.

With respect to independent variables, Knight's speed measure, described in section 4.2.1, is clearly superior to the speed measures employed in the other three studies, even if one has reservations about the arbitrary way that Knight combines speed with memory size. His variable measurement, therefore, gives his indexes a substantial claim on our attention. However, one needs to know whether improving the description of the computer in the hedonic function makes a difference in the hedonic price index, and not merely what variables are "best" in a descriptive sense. None of the studies presents data that show the sensitivity of the indexes to the measurement and choice of independent variables.

c. *Evaluation of the studies.* In view of the above, evaluations must rest on judgments based on the behavior of the estimated hedonic indexes and on what we know about the quality of the studies. Note first that despite differences in index computation method (Knight's is exclusively a dummy variable approach), definition of independent variables, and also data sources, Chow's imputation index—column (1)—and Knight's scientific[29] index—column (3)—show almost exactly the same overall total decline up to 1960 (69.8% and 67.1%, respectively.[30] This robustness is gratifying—of the indexes of table 4–A, the ones with the best data, variable measurement, and index computation procedure are all found among Chow's and Knight's results. Consistency does not extend to the second-generation computer, where Knight records a more rapid decline (see last line, table 4.4B).

Flamm's indexes show steady downward movement in computer prices throughout the whole period of the first- and second-generation computers (as do Chow's and Knight's). Overall, Flamm estimates a larger rate of decline than do the other two—line (a), table 4.4B— though his indexes for 1960–1965 are close to Knight's. The Phister value-of-the-stock data used by Flamm have conceptual shortcomings, particularly, as noted by Phister himself, in the method of valuation of machines in the stock that were not in current production; on the other hand, the data cannot completely be dismissed, because in the 1950s

Table 4.4C
Estimates of average annual rates of change: computer prices, various dates

Author	Period	Estimate
Schneidewind (1969)	1954–1965	−48%
Skattum (1969)	1950?–1966	−50%

Source: Sharpe (1969).

and early 1960s, increments were large relative to the size of the stock, and the increments were of course machines for which current or introductory prices were available. Flamm's hedonic function (in effect, linear through the origin), with separate functions for speed and memory, has disadvantages relative to the less-constrained functions used by other researchers. I judge Flamm's estimates to be dominated by those of Chow and Knight.

Gordon employed Phister's data on newly introduced processors, and produced a number of price indexes from them.

Taken in isolation, Gordon's results might suggest there is little robustness to hedonic methods. Columns (5)–(6) of Table 4.4A indicate that the computer processor price index lies somewhere between 466 and 2,154 for 1954, between 313 and 1,206 for 1958, between 175 and 285 for 1962, and so forth. This range of estimates on the same data reflects relatively minor and arbitrary research decisions. On the other hand, the greater degree of robustness across studies by other researchers suggests that, for whatever reason, Gordon's results are not representative of the robustness that can be achieved from hedonic indexes.[31]

Putting together the previous discussion, I judge Chow's and Knight's indexes to provide the most valid measures of price change for first- and second-generation computers.

d. *Behavior of the indexes.* The preferred indexes of Chow and Knight show a steady decrease in the quality-corrected price of computers over the entire 1953–1965 period, which is perhaps no great surprise to those familiar with this industry. Both researchers suggest a quickening of the rate of price decrease during the second-generation computer's production span, with Knight recording a greater acceleration.

The estimates in table 4.4A are lower than those of earlier studies reported in Sharpe (1969)—refer to table 4.4C. Too little information

Table 4.5A
Alternative research price indexes for computers, 1965–1972 (1965 = 100)

Year	Knight (1)	(1a)	Gordon "Augmented" sample (2)	New models only (3a)	New models only (3b)	Cartwright, Donahue, and Parker (4)	Flamm (5)
1965	100.0		100	100	100	NA	100
1966	33.0		94	92	76	NA	44
1967	27.8		58	68	65	27.8[a]	25
1968	25.5		54	94	66	28.4	19
1969	7.2	(25.5)	40	49	61	28.1	19
1970	6.5	(23.0)	33	18	28	30.0	17
1971	5.4	(19.1)	33	68	27	23.2	12
1972	NA	NA	29	22	10	21.6	8

Sources:

Column (1): Knight (1985). Computed from antilogs of (negative) of numbers labeled "% changes" tabulated in figure 4, p. 125.

Columns (2)–(3): Gordon (1987), table 11, columns (1), (4), and (7), rebased to 1965.

Column (4): Cartwright, Donahoe, and Parker (1985), table 4 (index labeled "hedonic"), rebased by setting their index value for 1967 equal to the value for that year from column (1).

Column (5): Flamm (1987, table A–5), column headed "Box only," rebased to 1965.

a. See explanation in "column 4" under "Sources."

was published to permit evaluation of these studies. They add to the evidence that prices have been falling rapidly over the entire history of the computer, but have been supplanted by the studies recorded in table 4.4A.

2. The Third Generation through 1972

Third-generation computers came onto the scene at the beginning of this interval (1965), and they were a substantial technological advance (see Fisher, McGowan, and Greenwood, 1983, for discussion of the price/performance ratio of IBM third-generation computers relative to their predecessors). For the period after 1972, more studies exist;

Table 4.5B
Year-to-year percent changes: alternative estimates for computer prices, 1965–1972

	Knight	Gordon			Cartwright et al.	Flamm	Archibald and Reece
	(1)	(2)	(3a)	(3b)	(4)	(5)	(6)
1965–1966	−67.0	−5.7	−7.8	−24.4	NA	−56	—
1966–1967	−15.7	−38.3	−26.5	−14.0	NA	−43	—
1967–1968	−8.2	−6.9	+39.0	+2.1	+2.3	−24	—
1968–1969	−71.9	−27.0	−47.8	−7.7	−1.3	−1	—
1969–1970	−9.2	−15.9	−64.3	−53.7	+6.9	−9	—
1970–1971	−17.0	−0.9	+290.1	−5.9	−22.8	−30	−7.6
1971–1972	NA	−13.0	−68.4	−60.9	−6.7	−37	−6.1

Sources: Calculated from indexes in table 4.5A, or the original sources cited there, except for column (6), which was computed by multiplying together quarterly changes for third-generation machines, from Archibald and Reece (1979, table 1, p. 534).

moreover, the various studies show greater agreement after 1972. Thus, even though it lacks particular significance in the history of the computer, 1972 provides a convenient point at which to divide the review of research.

Price indexes for the major studies are arrayed in tables 4.5A and 4.5B.[32] Except for Flamm's study, all employ the dummy variable method for estimating hedonic price indexes (with the minor variations for Knight's, already noted in section 4.3.1.1). To facilitate comparison, I have linked in the index computed by Cartwright, Donahoe, and Parker (1985), by setting its 1967 value equal to that of Knight—column (1)—for the same year. Archibald and Reece (1978) present only quarterly percent changes in their study, which begins with the fourth quarter of 1969; these changes are chained together and presented in table 4.5B.[33]

a. *Evaluation of the studies.* Though all of the studies in table 4.5A agree that computer prices fell rapidly between 1965 and 1972, the range of estimates is astounding; Knight's index for 1971 (the last year of his study) stands under 6; one of Gordon's indexes—column (3a)— records 68 for the same year. The range of these estimates is not at all easy to rationalize. Because these studies provide even less opportunity for determining the sources of dispersion than did the studies for the 1953–1965 epoch, we fall back on judgments about the quality of individual studies and on the plausibility and consistency of the hedonic price indexes they produce.

Knight's study has the virtues that were described in the preceding section. However, the odd behavior of this index in 1969, and the fact that the researcher published no index value for 1972 that could link this part of his work with the post-1972 indexes published in the same place, makes me less confident in the Knight time series for the 1965–1972 interval.[34]

As before, Gordon produces a range of price indexes from the same Phister (1979) data. Both Gordon's "new models" indexes show a larger price drop for computers *after* 1968, and very little initial impact of the new third-generation technology—column (3) of tables 4.5A and 4.5B. Gordon's results thus contradict industry folklore, as well as findings of other researchers.[35]

Flamm's indexes, though one expects some downward bias from their estimation procedure, record a similar story to those of Cartwright, Donahoe, and Parker, and also to those of Knight, if one excludes Knight's index value for 1969.

b. *A synthesis of the estimates.* Between 1965 and 1967, Knight and Flamm agree that a very steep drop in computer prices occurred, more than 70% in two years. The first of the third-generation machines (the IBM 360 series, announced in 1964) was first delivered in 1965. Other machines embodying the new technology followed those introduced by IBM and affected market prices well into 1967, as Knight's and Flamm's price indexes show.

From 1967 on, Flamm, and also Cartwright, Donahoe, and Parker, who only pick up the picture in 1967, suggest a slowing in the rate of decline—as does Knight, if one ignores the sudden and inexplicable drop in his index between 1968 and 1969. However, if that one index change were omitted, and the "pause" suggested by Flamm and by Cartwright, Donahoe, and Parker substituted in its place, Knight's indexes, post 1968, would appear very close to theirs, with an index level at roughly 19 in 1971—see values in parentheses, column (1a) of table 4.5A. Thus, linking in Cartwright, Donahoe, and Parker at 1967, and factoring out Knight's change for 1968–1969, gives three indexes for 1969 that range from 19 (Flamm) to 28.1 (Cartwright, Donahoe, and Parker). That presents a picture of substantial slowing of price decrease over the 1967–69 interval, which seems plausible since the initial impact of the third generation would have been spent by that time. The studies then suggest a reacceleration of price decline in 1971 and further decreases in 1972. However, the 1971–1972 index change estimates are not robust across investigators, and reference to Archibald and Reece's estimates for that period (table 4.5B) does not help very much to bring the picture into clearer focus.

The 1965–1972 period poses great difficulties in interpreting research price indexes for computers. In addition to the problems noted above, "unbundling" of computer processors from associated software and maintenance began in the late 1960s, and continued to an extent well into the 1970s. With any computation method, prices for computers need to be adjusted for ancillary services deleted from the transaction. None of the researchers who produced indexes for this period, however, reports an adjustment for unbundling, or consideration of the problem. The effect, of course, is to bias the indexes downward. It is conceivable that computer prices actually rose slightly in the late 1960s, or early 1970s.

This is an important period in computer history that deserves some additional price index research.[36]

3. A "Best-Practice" Research Price Index for Computers, 1953–1972

The discussion in the previous two sections provides the basis for a price index for computer processors that combines results of the best studies. This section presents the calculation.

The procedure for combining research estimates is entirely judgmental. Results judged significantly below "best practice," as noted in the preceding two sections, are discarded. The remaining indexes are then arbitrarily assigned weights, and used to construct the "best-practice" index number displayed in table 4.6A. The source studies and the weights assigned for each year are documented in table 4.6B.

The computations are straightforward, except for years in the 1950s when Knight computed an index spanning two-year intervals.[37] The changes in Knight's two-year indexes (from table 4.4B) were first converted to annual changes. For these years only, the index number in the left-hand column of table 4.6A is constructed by linking *backward* the annual changes in the right-hand column, where each change is in turn a weighted average of the three annual percentage changes computed from Chow and Knight (see entry for 1954–1958 in table 4.6B).[38]

There is no question that the procedure is arbitrary and judgmental. The results, however, are intriguing.

Table 4.6A
A "best-practice" research price index for computers,
1953–1972

Year	Index (1965 = 100)	Percentage change from preceding year
1953	1320	
1954	1139	−13.7
1955	1010	−11.3
1956	862	−14.7
1957	761	−11.8
1958	689	−9.4
1959	591	−14.2
1960	435	−26.4
1961	332	−23.7
1962	239	−27.9
1963	183	−23.6
1964	139	−24.2
1965	100	−27.8
1966	38.0	−61.5
1967	26.9	−30.1
1968	24.3	−9.7
1969	24.3	−0.4
1970	23.3	−3.7
1971	18.1	−22.3
1972	14.8	−18.2

Sources: See text and table 4.6B.

First, note that the quality-adjusted price of computers (monthly
rental for much of the period) dropped every single year for two
decades. At the end, a computer's price was roughly 1% *percent* of
what it cost when computers first came on the market!

Looking at subperiods is even more instructive. During the first
generation, the best-practice index tells us that computer prices fell
steadily, but at most about 15% in a single year. Second-generation
(transistor) computers appeared in 1958–1959, touching off a
substantial acceleration in the rate of decline, in the neighborhood of
25% per year, a rate that was sustained through the entire period of
the second generation's dominance. The advent of the third
generation (1965–1966) was marked by a further acceleration in the
rate of price decline, so that in the first three years of the third

Table 4.6B
Indexes and weights used for constructing the "best-practice" price index

Period	Investigator	Table and column	Weight
1953	Knight	4.4B, (3)*	0.50
		4.4B, (4)*	0.50
1954–1958	Chow	4.4B, (1)	0.50
	Knight	4.4b, (3)*	0.25
		4.4B, (4)*	0.25
1959–1965	Chow	4.4A, (1)	0.50
	Knight	4.4A, (3)	0.25
		4.4A, (4)	0.25
1966	Knight	4.5A, (1)	0.50
	Flamm	4.5A, (5)	0.50
1967–1971	Knight	4.5A, (1)	0.33
	Cartwright, Donahoe, and Parker	4.5A, (4)	0.33
	Flamm	4.5A, (5)	0.33
1972	Cartwright, Donahoe, and Parker	5A, (4)	0.50
	Flamm	5A, (5)	0.50

* Annual index change for these entries taken as the square root of the two-year indexes underlying table 4.4B (see text).

generation (through 1967) prices fell to *under a fifth* of the cost of a second-generation computer in 1964.

These price movements appear consistent with industry folklore, and with the pattern and timing of technical innovations. Moreover, the regularity of the series and absence of implausible yearly movement gives confidence in the index—in this respect, especially, the best-practice index appears more reasonable than any of the individual components from which it was derived. Smoothness was to an extent imposed on the best-practice index by the process by which its components were selected, and by averaging of its component series. Nevertheless, the result has plausibility, and represents the best information we have about the price history of the computer during its first two decades.

The index of table 4.6A is probably biased downward in its last two years or so because of the unbundling problem. It should be noted that the computer price series now in the NIPA shows less decline over the 1969–1972 interval than does the best-practice index. But since the NIPA index for this interval was based exclusively on Cartwright, Donahoe, and Parker (1985), whose estimates were also biased because of unbundling, unbundling does not acount for the difference between the NIPA deflator and the best-practice index between 1969 and 1972.

4. Computer Prices in the United Kingdom, 1954–1974

Comparison with another market, covering the two decades explored above for the United States, can be obtained from the work of Stoneman (1976, 1978).

The left-hand column in table 4.7 is Stoneman's preferred index from his earlier work. As noted in section 4.2.1, Stoneman in his first study used the floorspace occupied by a computer as a proxy for its speed. With miniaturization of components, floorspace shrinks over time relative to speed, biasing the hedonic indexes—a well-known problem with the use of proxy variables in hedonic functions (see Triplett, 1969, pp. 414–416).

The two right-hand columns of table 4.7 were taken from a subsequent study of price premiums for non-IBM machines in the United Kingdom. Because the non-IBM premiums were found to have no time trend, an index for all computers in the United Kingdom (which could be formed from Stoneman's second study by combining his IBM intertemporal index with the premiums for other machines) would presumably follow the trends for IBM machines, as shown in the right-hand columns of table 4.7.

Index (a) shows highly erratic movements that appear implausibly large, even after allowing for exchange rate revaluations on IBM machines imported (from Europe) into the United Kingdom. Stoneman reports a test of the significance of the coefficients of time dummy variables from this equation; the hypothesis that prices were constant after 1964 (roughly, introduction of the third-generation computers) failed of rejection. Accordingly, Stoneman prefers index (b), which index replaces one puzzle with another: Could prices of computers in the United Kingdom really have been stable in face of the enormous declines in the United States? If so, one would expect a consequent difference between the two countries in the utilization of computers and therefore in the pattern of investment and of productivity change.

Table 4.7
Indexes of computer prices in the United Kingdom (1965 = 100)

| Year | Stoneman (1976, 1978) | | |
| | 1976: all machines, imputation | 1978: IBM only, dummy variable | |
		(a)	(b)
1954	243.5	—	
1955	296.4	—	
1956	291.9	—	
1957	262.5	—	
1958	284.5	—	
1959	267.2	—	
1960	190.7	—	
1961	163.6	1096.5	223
1962	149.5	645.7	223
1963	151.4	691.8	223
1964	119.8	645.7	223
1965	100.0	100.0	100
1966	72.5	134.9	100
1967	63.5	83.2	100
1968	74.9	14.1	100
1969	73.5	245.5	100
1970	72.5	177.8	100
1971	—	63.1	100
1972	—	61.7	100
1973	—	81.3	100
1974	—	52.5	100

Sources:

Stoneman (1976, p. 42, table 3.2), column (e), rebased to 1965 = 100.

Stoneman (1978), equations (4) and (5): Published coefficients were first converted to base e, then antilogs were taken to yield the index tabulated above (same regressions are reported as equations (iv) and (v) in Stoneman, 1980).

Table 4.8A
Alternative research price indexes for computers, 1972–1984 (1972 = 100)

Year	Dulberger Imputation (1)	Dulberger Characteristics price (2)	Dulberger Dummy variable (3)	Cartwright, Donahoe, and Parker (4)	Gordon / Phister Augmented (5a)	Gordon / Phister New (5b)	Computerworld (6)	Knight (7)	Cale, Gremillion, and McKenney General purpose (8)	Cale, Gremillion, and McKenney Small business (9)	Flamm (10)	Archibald and Reece (11)	Levy and Welzer (12)
1972	100.0	100.0	100.0	100.0	100	100	—	100.0	NA	NA	100	100.0[b]	—
1973	103.8	117.4	105.9	99.2	89	231	—	NA	100.0[a]	100.0[a]	85	75.0	—
1974	94.5	99.0	82.3	96.5	55	146	—	90.1	NA	NA	79	70.9	—
1975	84.3	91.6	80.1	65.8	47	123	—	73.3	86.9[a]	74.8[a]	79	43.4	—
1976	79.7	90.4	78.6	53.6	30	67	—	66.0	NA	NA	78	—	—
1977	56.8	64.2	50.5	46.4	29	29	50.5	64.7	65.0[a]	67.0[a]	73	—	—
1978	29.0	36.0	26.5	39.9	—	41	45.7	52.8	—	—	43	—	—
1979	24.6	30.8	24.5	25.1	—	23	38.9	40.8	—	—	—	—	—
1980	17.6	18.8	17.9	11.9	—	20	35.5	—	—	—	—	—	—
1981	14.2	15.9	11.5	10.4	—	16	22.0	—	—	—	—	—	11.5[c]
1982	12.0	12.7	10.1	10.4	—	12	17.3	—	—	—	—	—	11.7
1983	11.3	11.8	9.2	6.3	—	12	19.5	—	—	—	—	—	8.7
1984	9.7	10.2	7.8	—	—	6	10.9	—	—	—	—	—	—

Sources:

Columns (1)–(3): Dulberger (this volume) table 2.6 (three indexes labeled "composite pooled, composite characteristics, and regression"), rebased to 1972.

Column (4): Cartwright, Donahoe, and Parker (1985), table 4 (index labeled "hedonic").

Columns (5)–(6): Gordon (1987): (5a)—table 12, column (4); (5b)—unpublished; (6)—table 15, column (6), rebased by setting the 1977 level of the index (first year available) equal to column (3), for comparison of price indexes for IBM—column (3)—and non-IBM—column (6)—machines, estimated with common computation method.

Column (7): Knight (1985): Constructed from antilogs of the (negative) values of "% change" tabulated in figure 4, p. 125 (see section 4.3.1 for explanation).

Columns (8)–(9): Cale, Gremillion, and McKenney (1979): Indexes computed from antilogs of "effects" displayed in table II, p. 230.

Column (10): Flamm (1987, table A–5), column headed "Box only."

Column (11): Archibald and Reece (1979): Calculated by chaining the quarterly percent changes for third generation computers presented in table II.

Column (12): Levy and Welzer (1985): Calculated by taking antilogs of the time dummy coefficients in table 1, and expressing the resulting figures as an index number with its 1981 value set equal to column (3)—judged the closest comparable study.

a. For this study, 1972–1973 = 100 and values are reported for two year intervals. The value tabulated for, e.g., 1975 is actually the average 1974–1975 level, relative to the average two years before.

b. 1972 I = 100, and index records over the year changes (value for, e.g., 1974 refers to 1974 I).

c. Index value for 1981 set equal to column (3), for comparison purposes.

5.   From 1972 to 1984

Studies providing price indexes for computers are more numerous for the recent period than for earlier epochs of computer history. Table 4.8A shows price indexes for 1972–1984, or for part of that period, produced by eight separate studies.[39]

a. *Behavior of the indexes.* It is evident from table 4.8A that there is considerably more robustness to the 1972–1984 estimates than was true for studies covering the earlier periods. Leaving aside Gordon's Phister-data indexes—columns (5a) and (5b)—most of the rest suggest that prices dropped by roughly half, or perhaps somewhat less than half, between 1972 and 1977. Archibald and Reece (1979) show the most rapid rate of price decline, at least through the end of their study in 1975, Flamm (1987) the slowest rate.

For the subsequent five-year period (1977–1982), studies suggest an even more rapid rate of price decline. Indexes from Dulberger (chapter 2, this volume), Cartwright, Donahoe, and Parker (1985), and Gordon (1987, the *Computerworld* index) stand in 1982 somewhere around 1/5, or less, of their values in 1977 (refer to table 4.8B). Where researchers have produced indexes that cover only a short period (Levy and Welzer, 1985, or Cale, Gremillion, and McKenney, 1979), results are compatible with those of researchers who estimated longer time series.

Gordon's (1987) index for non-IBM mainframe computers from *Computerworld* data—column (6)—is a useful complement to the work of Dulberger, since her data include only IBM and "plug-compatible" machines. To facilitate comparison of IBM and non-IBM price indexes, Gordon's index value for 1977—in column (6)—has been set equal to the level of Dulberger's dummy variable index for the same year (thus holding constant the index computation method in comparison of the two studies). Dulberger's and Gordon's studies differ in data source and, to some extent, in the measurement of speed.[40] Nevertheless, except for the first year the results are similar. Prices of non-IBM machines declined somewhat more slowly than did IBM prices, though the differences may not be significant. Both show declines of about 60% between 1978 and 1982, and in the vicinity of 80%, overall (refer to table 4.8B).

Gordon (1987) uses a selection of his results different from what is presented in tables 4.8A and 4.8B, and argues from it that the BEA index used in the NIPAs, which is Dulberger's column (1), falls too

Table 4.8B
Percent changes, selected price indexes for computers, selected periods, 1972–1984

Interval	Dulberger			Cartwright, Donahoe, and Parker	Gordon			Knight	Flamm
	(1)	(2)	(3)	(4)	(5a)	(5b)	(6)	(7)	(10)
1972–1977	−43.2	−35.8	−49.5	−53.6	−71	−71	NA	−35.3	−27
1977–1982	−78.9	−80.2	−80.0	−77.6	NA	−59	−65.7	NA	NA
1977–1984	−82.9	−84.1	−84.6	NA	NA	−79	−78.4	NA	NA

Sources: Computed from the corresponding columns of table 4.8A.

slowly.[41] In assessing Gordon's position, it is important to note the high degree of agreement in the indexes of the other seven researchers represented in tables 4.8A and 4.8B.

Over the full interval covered in table 4.8A, the studies suggest that by 1984 quality-corrected computer prices were in the neighborhood of 1/10 of their values in 1972, or even less—a price decrease approaching 90% or more.

b. *Effect of alternative index computational methods.* Only Dulberger's study computes hedonic price indexes by alternative methods—table 4.8A, columns (1)–(3). Though year-to-year differences in the alternative indexes are sometimes fairly large, the medium and longer-term trends are quite similar: All Dulberger's indexes rose in 1973, fell from this peak at a moderate rate until 1976, fell at an accelerated pace between 1976–1978 (after Amdahl introduced a new technology), and then continued falling at a more moderate pace until the end of the study. Moreover, none of Dulberger's indexes exhibits erratic or anomalous movements.

The characteristics price method yields the greatest "bulge" in the early 1970s (mainly because it rose more in 1973), so that it falls the least over the first five years (1972–1977). After 1976 or 1977 this index declines at a rate close to that of the imputation index. The dummy variable method produces an index that declines slightly more rapidly than the other two over the whole period.[42]

Two of Dulberger's three indexes—columns (1) and (2)—are explicitly weighted by market shares. Although the unweighted dummy variable index shows the greatest overall decline, it is not clear that weighting—as opposed to calculation method—is the reason.

Index computation methods do matter, especially for shorter-term comparisons. Computation method has too often been ignored in computing hedonic indexes; most researchers have been content with reporting dummy variable indexes, without considering alternatives.

c. *Effects of hedonic function specification and data sources.* I first consider Dulberger's introduction of technology variables into the hedonic function. Dulberger, arguing that multiple price regimes exist because of technologically induced disequilibria, introduces variables that measure chip technology used in the computer, and retains them in her regression whenever they are statistically significant. The sign patterns in her results show that the newer (and better) are cheaper per unit of capability. Dulberger's approach can be interpreted as responsive to Fisher, McGowan, and Greenwood (1983), discussed in section 4.2.2.3.

Even if one does not accept the "technological disequilibrium" argument or its relevance—on the grounds that a general purpose price index ought to represent the prices of all varieties that are for sale at time t, or that competition ought to bid down the quality-adjusted prices of the less advanced machines (so there should be only a single hedonic price regime)[43]—there is another possible interpretation of the "multiple price regimes" reported in Dulberger's study. The prices in her data set are list, not transactions, prices (true also of all the other studies included in table 4.8A): if older machines were discounted more heavily than the latest technology, then technology variables could be acting as proxies for differential degrees of discounting on older machines. In this case, then, one would certainly want to control for differential discounting, and Dulberger's technology variables might be so interpreted.[44]

How sensitive are the price indexes to the inclusion of technology variables? Unless they are sensitive, the methodological issue might be sidestepped, until we have a better understanding of what multiple price regimes are telling us.

Information is contained in regressions in Dulberger's study, as well as some unpublished regressions performed by David Cartwright as part of the internal BEA review prior to acceptance of the IBM computer indexes in the NIPAs. Table 4.9 presents the relevant results.

All the indexes in table 4.9 use the same hedonic function and the same independent variables, and all are constructed with the dummy variable method, thus holding constant the computational method. Column (1) reproduces Dulberger's index from a regression containing technology dummies—same as table 4.8A, column (3).

Moving from column (1) to column (2) in table 4.9 shows the effect of the inclusion of technology dummies on the price indexes. The column (2) index rises substantially more in the early 1970s; but oddly enough, the fall from 1974–1984 is exactly 90.5% in both indexes! Thus, the path of the price index differs somewhat when technology variables are included, but whether the information conveyed differs depends on the period; the largest effect from including technology variables occurs in the early 1970s and for this period the index that includes them seems more plausible.

Columns (3) and (4) extend the sensitivity exercise to consider data and samples. The data on which these two indexes are based were

Table 4.9
Price indexes showing effects of alternative procedures, 1972–1984 (1972 = 100)

| Year | Dulberger IBM + plug-compatible | | Cartwright | |
	With technology dummies (1)	Without technology dummies (2)	IBM + plug compatible (3)	All manufacturers (4)
1972	100.0	100.0	100.0	100.0
1973	105.9	128.1	121.3	95.8
1974	82.3	130.1	135.3	83.1
1975	80.1	105.5	94.6	57.5
1976	78.6	98.0	86.3	53.3
1977	50.5	67.8	59.0	48.1
1978	26.5	46.7	42.3	41.9
1979	24.5	34.6	27.2	30.3
1980	17.9	24.4	23.8	22.4
1981	11.5	20.2	19.2	16.8
1982	10.1	17.6	16.3	13.0
1983	9.2	14.8	13.7	12.0
1984	7.8	12.3	—	—

Sources:

Column (1): Dulberger (this volume) — same as table 4.8A, column 3, this chapter.

Column (2): Computed from antilogs of time dummy variables in Dulberger (this volume), appendix table headed "Equation (1)."

Columns (3)–(4): Unpublished regressions supplied by David Cartwright, Bureau of Economic Analysis.

originally compiled for the study by Cartwright, Donahoe, and Parker (1925), but were subsequently "cleaned" additionally through IBM cooperation. The regression that produced column (3), like those producing columns (1) and (2), is restricted to observations on IBM machines and those made by "plug-compatible" producers. The data are not exactly the same as Dulberger's, however, and represent what a careful researcher might have put together from alternative sources, procedures, and sample selection. Comparison of columns (2) and (3) is thus an estimate of the size of data source and sample selection effects on hedonic price indexes.

In this experiment, data source effects appear considerably smaller than the effect of the procedural comparison contained in columns (1) and (2). Cartwright's replication of Dulberger's "without technology dummies" index reproduces her result. I emphasize, however, that the experiment was performed on two data sets that were carefully "cleaned"; it therefore does not represent the effects that would occur had one or both of the researchers accepted all the errors in the original *published* data.

Finally, one might ask, How sensitive are the indexes to their restriction to IBM (and plug-compatible) machines? After all, if the computer market has never been close to equilibrium, as Fisher, McGowan, and Greenwood (1983) assert, prices of IBM and non-IBM machines may not move in concert, at least in the short run. Accordingly, we need indexes that include non-IBM computers.

Broadening the sample, however, changes it in two ways, not just one. It is not entirely clear whether MIPS, the speed variable in the regressions, is measured consistently among the non-IBM producers (see Dulberger's discussion of this point, and also section 4.2.1).

Two relevant comparisons exist. Cartwright's unpublished regressions—columns (3) and (4), table 4.9—compare *all* manufacturers with a regression restricted to IBM and plug compatible machines. The more broadly inclusive sample produces an index that falls continuously—it falls, rather than rising in 1973–1974, as do the IBM indexes in table 4.9. Note that most of the indexes of table 4.8A that are based on more-inclusive samples also show this monotonic falling pattern; thus, either sample selection or measurement of speed (which, we cannot be sure) appears associated with the early 1970s rise in computer prices recorded in samples restricted to IBM and plug compatibles. Otherwise, however, the column (4) index—Cartwright's data, all machines, no technology variables—shows a pattern of computer price movements broadly

Table 4.10
Annual rates of price change, selected items of computer peripheral equipment

Product	Schneidewind (1969) dates: 1954–1965	Skattum (1969) dates: 1950–1965
Tape drives	−27%	−14%
Card readers	−22%	−17%
Card punches	—	−12%
Line printers	−8%	−12%

Sources:

Schneidewind (1969): Taken directly from Sharpe (1969, table 9–12, p. 329, "Form 2").

Skattum (1969): Calculated from regression coefficients in Sharpe (1969, table 9–13, p. 330), by converting monthly rates of *price* change (negatives of the rates tabulated) to an average annual rate.

similar to those of the column (1) index—Dulberger's data, IBM computers, technology variables included in the regression.

The second comparison has already been mentioned above: Gordon estimated a non-IBM mainframe index for the years 1977–1984 that agrees closely with Dulberger's IBM index over the same span of years (tables 4.8A and 4.8B). Thus, both Cartwright's and Gordon's evidence suggests that prices of non-IBM and IBM computers were moving in tandem, and provides little reason to suspect that Dulberger's results are sensitive to her restricting her sample to machines of similar architectures (except possibly, as already noted, for 1972–1973).

One should note, for balance, that the index dispersion among studies in tables 4.8A and 4.9 is far smaller than what has been noted in studies for early years. Nearly all the indexes of tables 4.8A and 4.9 lie in the plausible region. However, one would always like even more robustness.[45]

4.3.3   Price Indexes for Peripheral Equipment, 1950s to 1984

Peripheral equipment accounts for about half the value of U.S. computer equipment shipments, so there is great interest in price indexes for these capital goods.

Early studies by Schneidewind (1969) and Skattum (1969) estimated only average annual rates of change (table 4.10). These rates do not agree very closely; Sharpe (1969) concludes that Skattum's is the better study (it was based on a far larger sample, for one thing). Skattum measured "effectiveness" of each peripheral with only a single characteristic (as did Flamm).

Flamm (1987), produced price indexes for several peripheral equipment "boxes," extending back into the decade of the 1950s (table 4.11). Flamm's objective was a price index for a computer system, defined as an optimal combination of equipment. In pursing that objective, he sacrificed more detailed specification of the hedonic indexes for specific items of computer equipment in favor of modeling an aggregator function that is derived from the theory of production (discussed in section 4.3.4).

As a simplification, Flamm assumed that each item of computer equipment had but a single characteristic. As already noted in the discussion of computer processors, above, Flamm's hedonic indexes are computed by dividing the value of installed stocks of equipment by the "stocks" of installed characteristics, from Phister (1979). They are thus equivalent to linear hedonic functions without intercepts.

Obviously, errors in the price indexes may arise from the simplified specification of hedonic functions for the individual boxes. We can use hedonic price indexes from other studies to evaluate the less complex versions estimated by Flamm. The processor case has already been discussed; the "best-practice" box index of table 4.6A declines considerably less than Flamm's computer box index for 1957–1972.[46] After 1972, the opposite result obtains: Flamm's computer index falls less rapidly than Dulberger's (chapter 2 in this volume)—see table 4.8A.

A test of Flamm's peripheral equipment indexes is to compare them with the three IBM studies for the post-1972 period summarized in Cole et al. (1986). The comparisons are contained in table 4.12. In each case, the measures are quite similar, exceptionally so if one considers mainly the final year (1978) of Flamm's series—the two disk drive indexes stand at 40 and 41, printers at 73 and 75 (even though the IBM index covers more varieties of printer), and even indexes in the category labeled "input-output devices" (which actually are not closely related pieces of equipment) are not far apart. Moreover, Flamm's tape drives index shows, as does the more sophisticated one by Randolph (1985), little or no price change from 1976 through 1978, after falling earlier. The degree of robustness between Flamm's peripheral equipment price indexes and the four by IBM researchers

Table 4.11
Price indexes for computer peripheral equipment, 1957–1972 (1965 = 100)

Year	Flamm (1987)			
	Disk drives (mean) (1)	Tape drives (mean) (2)	Printers (3)	Card reader / punchers (4)
1957	529	1607	609	561
1958	466	791	591	350
1959	390	530	565	255
1960	310	367	527	190
1961	222	291	340	149
1962	132	155	209	116
1963	122	104	139	107
1964	112	103	117	102
1965	100	100	100	100
1966	87	94	100	98
1967	60	88	99	97
1968	41	68	95	96
1969	31	56	89	94
1970	24	47	85	92
1971	18	30	76	88
1972	13	21	71	84

Sources: Flamm (1987, table A–3).
Column (1): Column headed "Moving Head Files, Geometric Mean."
Column (2): Column headed "Magnetic Tape Units, Geometric Mean."
Column (3): Column headed "Line Printers."
Column (4): Column headed "Card Readers and Punches."
All indexes are rebased to 1965 = 100.

Table 4.12
Price indexes for computer peripheral equipment, 1972–1984 (1972 = 100)

Year	Disk drives Flamm	Cole et al.	Tape drives Flamm	Randolph	Printers Flamm (line)	Cole et al. (all)	Input-output devices Flamm (card reader)	Cole et al. (displays)
1972	100	100	100		100	100	100	100
1973	86	97	72		94	96	92	100
1974	72	73	55		91	99	83	97
1975	60	69	44	44	87	90	80	90
1976	52	55	38	42	83	78	76	82
1977	46	45	38	42	79	73	76	81
1978	40	41	38	42	74	75	76	72
1979		33		39		69		63
1980		29		—		65		56
1981		29		38		65		54
1982		31		42		63		57
1983		23		36		21		49
1984		20		—		17		40

Sources:

Flamm (1987): Same as analogous columns in table 4.11.

Cole et al. (1986): table 7, p. 49, columns headed "Composite" for the equipment specified, rebased to 1972 = 100.

Randolph (1985): table 5, part (a), column headed "Laspeyres Index"; index linked in by setting its value for 1975 equal to Flamm's index for the same year, to facilitate comparison.

and by Randolph—each of which I judge substantially more sophisticated (and superior)—is considerably greater than what is observed in many of the processor hedonic studies discussed in earlier sections.

Thus, if Flamm's peripheral equipment price indexes are as adequate in the 1957–1971 period as they seem to be post-1972, they can be taken as appropriate measures of price trends for peripherals.

Prices for most peripherals have declined somewhat more slowly than the rates recorded for processors over comparable periods, but they are still prodigous by any standard (table 4.11). Moreover, indexes for all the peripherals show the same steady rates of decline apparent in the best of the processor studies. Tape drives show the greatest drop over the whole 1957–1972 period (greater than for processors), disk drives the largest drop from 1965–1972. Input-output equipment, including printers, lags, especially after 1965, as this portion of the system became a technological bottleneck.

Turning to the post-1972 interval, table 4.12 shows us that the broad trends continue. Disk drives, as in the 1965–1972 period, fell in price relative to tape drives—and disks have increasingly supplanted tapes as the primary auxiliary storage medium. Printers and input-output devices lag the other peripherals, except that a surge in imported printers affects that price index late in the period.

4.3.4 Price Indexes for Computer Systems

A "computer system" is an optimal combination of computer equipment—processors and peripherals—for a specified employment.

Equation (4b) incorporated a separability assumption on the computer user's production function that, under the theory of price indexes, permits forming an input cost subindex—result (7), section 4.1.2—over the inputs employed by the computer center—that is, the inputs contained in $q^*[\cdot]$. However, those inputs include software, programming labor, and so forth, which cannot be considered here.[47] Accordingly, we impose additional assumptions that can be used to justify constructing price indexes for computer systems out of the computer equipment price indexes presented in previous sections of this chapter.

Suppose first that the computer center's output of jobs or tasks, which is normally a vector, can be written as a scalar, say J' (this assumption was made by Flamm, 1987), so that the computer center portion—$q^*[\cdot]$—of equation (4b) can be written

$$J' = q^*[q_1(c_1), q_2(c_2), \ldots, q_r(c_r), Z_1]. \tag{16}$$

Next, assume that $q^*[\cdot]$ is itself weakly separable on the r pieces of computer equipment; under this assumption, the theory of price indexes permits forming a price index for capital inputs to the computer center, neglecting Z_1—see result (7) of section 4.1.2 and the references cited there.

The assumption that one can write, in equation (16), expressions such as $q_1(c_1)$ means that it is possible to form scalar measures of "quality" for each item of computer equipment (Triplett, 1987), which in turn permits constructing the computer systems price index out of (quality-adjusted) price indexes and quantities for the r individual computer equipment "boxes." If $q^*[\,\cdot\,]$ is *known*, these assumptions permit an input cost index for investment in computer equipment, which index depends on the form of $q^*[\,\cdot\,]$, or its dual cost function.[48]

Unfortunately, neither $q^*[\,\cdot\,]$, nor its dual cost function, are known. Diewert (1976) has shown that a certain class of index numbers, which he termed "superlative," provide good approximations to the *exact* input cost index when $q^*[\,\cdot\,]$ is not known. One member of the superlative class of index numbers is the well-known Fisher Ideal index, or

$$FI_{t,s} = [(\textstyle\sum P_t Q_s / \sum P_s Q_s) \cdot (\sum P_t Q_t / \sum P_s Q_t)]^{1/2}$$
$$= [_s I_{t,s} \cdot {}_t I_{t,s}]^{1/2}, \tag{17}$$

where in the bottom expression the first subscript on each index number indicates the period from which weights are taken and the second two subscripts indicate the index number comparison and reference periods.

For binary comparisons, it is well-known that the *FI* index is the geometric mean of Paasche and Laspeyres formulas, which are staples of statistical agencies, in the United States and abroad. It is also well-known that Paasche and Laspeyres formulas contain a "substitution" bias whenever relative prices change; Diewert's result thus shows that their geometric mean is approximately free from substitution bias, and can be used to judge the extent of the bias in fixed weight price index formulas.

Index number theory pertains to binary comparisons. Price indexes are published as time series, not merely as binary comparisons. There are a number of ways to form time series out of binary index number comparisons.

One convenient property for a time series price index number is

$$I_{t,r} = I_{t,s} / I_{r,s} \tag{18}$$

for all r lying between s and t. This property was designated "circularity" by Irving Fisher. Circularity implies that one can compute the *change* in the index number between *any* two periods from the time series. A time series of the usual Laspeyres price index number (which is designated the "fixed weight" price index in BEA publications) has the desired property of circularity. Paasche price indexes, as they are usually prepared, lack circularity.

The *FI* index can be generalized to obtain a time series form with circularity. Consider any year between s and t, say r. Then the "Time-series Generalized Fisher Ideal" index (*TGFI*) is defined by

Table 4.13A
Price indexes for computer systems, 1957–1972 (1965 = 100)

Year	1958 fixed-weights	1965 fixed-weights	1972 fixed-weights	TGFI	Flamm
	(1)	(2)	(3)	(4)	(5)
1957	729	880	800	801	994
1958	623	651	644	637	769
1959	534	531	534	533	616
1960	415	404	399	410	437
1961	305	301	301	303	331
1962	210	198	203	204	248
1963	159	149	158	154	172
1964	128	123	128	125	126
1965	100	100	100	100	100
1966	62	68	58	63	67
1967	53	58	44	51	48
1968	48	50	36	42	38
1969	46	46	32	38	35
1970	43	42	29	35	31
1971	37	37	22	27	22
1972	33	29	17	22	15

Sources:

Columns (1)–(4)—computed by the author, from indexes for processors (table 4.6A) and peripheral equipment (table 4.11), using weights from Flamm (1987).

Column (5)—Flamm (1987), table A–5, column headed "Index using geometric mean for components," rebased to 1965.

Table 4.13B
Summary, three computer processor and computer systems indexes (1965 = 100)

Year	Flamm		This survey	
	Processor	System	Best-practice processor	TGFI
1957	1427	994	761	801
1965	100	100	100	100
1972	8	15	15	22

Sources:

Flamm: Processor — tables 4.4A and 4.5A, this survey. System — table 4.13A, this survey.

Best-practice processor — table 4.6A. TGFI — table 4.13A.

$$TGFI_{t,r} = [{}_sI_{t,r} \cdot {}_tI_{t,r}]^{1/2}. \tag{19}$$

Suppose we have two fixed weight price indexes covering the interval $s,..., r,..., t$, the first index with beginning period (s) weights, the second with end period (t) weights; the TGFI for each period in the interval is the geometric mean of the two fixed weight indexes for that period. For a comparison involving the two end points, the TGFI reduces to the usual FI index. The TGFI is one form of superlative, or quasi-superlative, index number being considered for alternative price and output measures in the national income and product accounts (NIPAs); more detailed discussion of the TGFI's properties, and the rationale for choosing an index of this form, is contained in a forthcoming study.

In this survey, the TGFI is applied to various computer equipment price indexes discussed in earlier sections. The TGFI computer systems price index thus accounts, approximately, for substitution among the various computer equipment "boxes," under the assumptions listed above. Such an index is an appropriate measure of the price of investment in computer equipment.

Table 4.13A presents TGFI indexes for computer systems for 1957–1972; table 4.14 brings the measures up to 1984. Each table contains ordinary fixed weight price indexes constructed from the same data, to facilitate comparison of fixed weight and superlative index number forms. Each table also includes a somewhat similar computer systems index from Flamm (1987).

Table 4.14
Price indexes for computer "systems" 1972–1984 (1972 = 100)

Year	NIPA data 1972 fixed-weights (1)	1977 fixed-weights (2)	1982 fixed-weights[a] (3)	TGFI[b] (4)	Flamm (5)
1972	100.0	100.0	100.0	100.0	100
1973	98.8	98.5	100.3	98.6	85
1974	80.7	79.8	88.7	80.3	75
1975	73.5	73.0	79.7	73.2	70
1976	66.4	64.9	74.0	65.7	67
1977	51.8	50.9	54.3	51.4	63
1978	37.7	38.9	32.1	34.5	44
1979	32.8	33.6	27.3	29.6	—
1980	27.8	28.6	21.0	23.9	—
1981	25.9	27.1	18.3	21.8	—
1982	24.5	26.2	16.6	20.4	—
1983	18.7	19.9	14.1	16.4	—
1984	16.3	17.2	12.1	14.1	—

Sources:

NIPA Data — index numbers for processors and peripherals, aggregated from component price indexes used for deflation in the NIPAs, using shipments weights from the NIPAs for the periods indicated.

Flamm — Flamm (1987), table A–5, column headed "index using geometric mean for components."

a. See note 50.

b. Time-series Generalized Fisher Ideal index number formula, calculated by the author from the same component price indexes used for columns (1)–(3). See also note 52.

For the period before 1972, the processor index for the *TGFI* computer systems price index is the Best-Practice composite index in table 4.6A; price indexes for peripherals are Flamm's (table 4.11). Weights are value of installed stock, from Phister, as tabulated in Flamm (1987, table A-4), which seems to be only information available for this period.[49] I choose Economic Census years 1958 and 1972, plus 1965 (midway between 1963 and 1967 censuses) as weight years, for compatibility with other parts of the larger project on alternative NIPA price and output measures, in progress. This means there are really two *TGFI* indexes—1958–1965 and 1965–1972—which are linked together to cover the whole period.

Flamm's "complete systems" index—column (5)—is similar to the *TGFI*: Flamm's peripheral price indexes appear in each, and I have also adopted Flamm's weight information. Flamm also uses a variation on the *FI* formula. The major data difference is my employment in the *TGFI* of the "best-practice" price index, which is a composite of several research studies, over Flamm's processor index.

I now turn to the results (table 4.13A). For the 1957–1965 interval, relevant weights are 1958 or 1965. One would expect, if input substitution takes place among components of computer systems in response to relative price changes, that 1965 weights would produce an index that declines more than 1958 weights. This expectation is born out for the earliest years (1958–1961), though not for 1962–1965—table 13–A, columns (1) and (2)—and the differences are in any case slight.

For the 1965–1972 portion of table 4.13A, relevant weighting choices are 1965 and 1972—columns (2) and (3). As expected, the 1972–weight index declines more, standing about 40% lower for the last year tabulated.

The *TGFI* index has the properties of a superlative index *only* for the "links" 1958–1965 and 1965–1972. For the first link, the two fixed weight indexes for 1958 stand only about 4% apart—623 compared with 651; the *TGFI* measure for 1958 (637) allocates substitution bias equally (14 index points) to each of the fixed-weight indexes.

For the 1965–1972 period, the *TGFI* suggests that each fixed weight index contains a proportionately larger substitution bias. The value of the *TGFI* for 1972 (22) lies between the "bounds" of Laspeyres (29) and Paasche (17) formulas, indicating a substitution bias of 5–7 index points on a total price decline exceeding 75%.

For years other than the weighting years, the *TGFI* does not, strictly, have the properties of a superlative index number. In all cases, however, the *TGFI* lies between the two fixed weight indexes, as one would expect in this case the superlative index to do. The *TGFI* appears to be a reasonable time series approximation to binary-comparison superlative index number formulas.

Note that Flamm's systems index—column (5) of table 4.13A—drops more than the *TGFI*. That is attributable largely to the fact that his processor index drops substantially more than the best-practice processor price index used in the *TGFI*. Table 4.13B provides a summary showing relations between computer processor and computer systems indexes estimated by Flamm and compiled by myself from research reviewed in this survey.

For 1972–1984, the three Economic Census years 1972, 1977, and 1982 serve as weight years for the *TGFI*. Shipments weights employed in the NIPAs (see Cartwright, 1986) were used to create three fixed weight indexes and the *TGFI* shown in table 4.14. The first four columns of table 4.14 use price indexes from the "computer" category of the NIPAs—which include the processor index of Dulberger (this volume) and the peripheral indexes in Cole et al. (1986).[50] Because the better of the alternative studies presented in tables 4.8A and 4.12 show nearly the same price movements as the indexes of the group of IBM researchers, it does not seem fruitful to synthesize research results for this period in any formal way (as was done for processors for 1953–1972).[51]

The *TGFI* between 1972 and 1977 provides an estimate of substitution bias in the 1972 and 1977 fixed weight indexes; the *TGFI* between 1977 and 1982 gives a comparable measure for the 1977 and 1982 fixed weight indexes.[52] The substitution biases are modest, relative to the drop in indexes, yet for some purposes (obtaining measures of real investment in computer equipment, say) they could affect conclusions.

The information in table 4.14 can be related to price information in the NIPAs. Currently, base year for the NIPAs is 1982. Three alternative price measures are routinely prepared. Of the indexes in table 4.14, the change between 1977 and 1982 in the *1977 weight* price index corresponds to the NIPA *implicit deflator* for purchases of computer equipment (in the implicit deflator the reference year, 1982, always remains constant, and weights are taken from the comparison year). The same 1977–1982 change in the *1982 weight* price index is termed (in BEA publications) the "fixed weight" price index (the fixed weight price index always takes its weights from the fixed reference year, which has been 1982 since the last benchmark revision). From table 4.14, the former declines *less* than the latter (the 1977 weight index, or implicit deflator, drops 49% between 1977 and 1982, the 1982 weight index declines 70%). The *TGIF* suggests that the true economic change is instead a decline of 61%.

In the 1972–1984 interval, all the component indexes in the TGIF differ from those in Flamm's systems calculation—column (5) of table 4.14. The *TGFI* drops more rapidly over the common years (1972–1978), mainly because Dulberger's processor index declines more than Flamm's.

Even superlative index number formulas, however, do not capture all of the decline in the costs of executing computer center tasks. In the first place, the form of equation (16), which embodied assumptions necessary for aggregating "box" price indexes into a price index for computer systems, is unduly restrictive: The *scalar* quality measures it implies for each piece of computer equipment exclude substitution possibilities among *characteristics* of different boxes, and thus ignore much technical change that has taken place in computer equipment.

Second, equation (16) neglects the possibility of technical change in the computer center itself, either pure learning by doing or in the form of substitution among computer center inputs other than the hardware. The superlative index number calculation allows for technological change that takes the form of straightforward factor substitution among equipment boxes, and/or (in the hedonic "quality" adjustments) is embodied in the boxes in the form of increased quantities of characteristics per box. It misses other technological change. Ein-Dor (1985, p. 150), for example, remarks, "Powerful software . . . requires powerful hardware to run it. Thus, it may in fact be optimal to buy powerful computers even if the computational speed is not required, just so as to take advantage of the powerful software than can render a whole system more cost effective."

To bound price indexes of the kind reviewed for this chapter, we need cost estimates for the *output* of the computer center, not just estimates of the cost function for computer center inputs under the *maintained hypothesis* of constant (quality) output.

Figure 4.2, which was supplied by Victor L. Peterson, Ames Research Center, National Aeronautics and Space Administration, is taken from a study of the costs of solving a set of partial differential equations that arise in an aerodynamic problem encountered in aircraft design.[53] The equations, which relate lift and drag to shapes

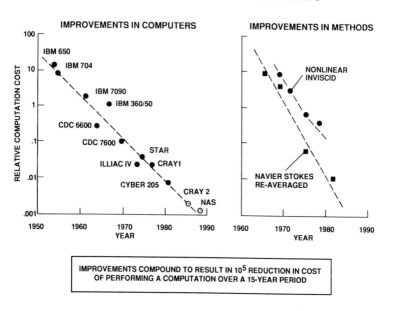

Figure 4.2

and attitude of the aircraft, cannot be given a closed-form solution even with today's largest computers, and so have been simulated through various approximation methods.

The left-hand panel in Figure 4.2 shows the decline in computational costs, algorithm constant. That graph declines a bit faster than the computer processor price indexes in this survey (linking Dulberger's index on to the best-practice index gives a 1984 index about one-tenth of one percent of its 1953 starting point), and likewise, a bit faster than the decline in *TGFI* indexes for computer systems.

One does not, however, continue to employ ever larger and ever faster computers in the same manner—the ways of solving the problem, and the problem itself, are redesigned to take advantage of the computer's enhanced capability. In engineering—as in economics—in the early applications the problem had to be simplified by neglecting aspects of it that, though vital, made its solution unmanageable. With greater computational capability, more realistic solutions can be modeled that take account of more of the relations that impinge on the true aerodynamic flows. The right-hand panel in figure 4.2 shows cost reduction associated with two regimes of computer aerodynamic simulation. These combine with the left-hand side as vectors, indicating cost improvements for calculations that are substantial magnitudes greater than those from computers alone, or that are shown by computer price indexes in this survey.

The calculation in figure 4.2 is a kind of "benchmark," differing from most benchmarks carried out in the computer's history in the complexity of the problem, in its allowing for expansion in the problem, and for the complementarity it admits between physical and human capital. Data on costs of computing other problems could no doubt be assembled from engineering sources and from computer users. Such data, used with the "quality-adjusted" price indexes reviewed in this survey, would permit forming a better picture of the impact of the computer as a productive input.

Notes

1. The Pollak (1975) and Blackorby and Russell (1978) definitions are equivalent only for special cases, which are implicitly assumed here to avoid expositional complexity.

2. Notations such as "cost of $q*(\,\cdot\,)$," and "cost of $q_1(\,\cdot\,)$" and so forth are elliptical, but are employed in order to conserve space.

3. These problems have been discussed in both the economics literature on hedonic functions and in parallel engineering literature on measuring technical change. See for example, Ohta and Griliches (1976), Martino (1985), and Dodson (1985).

4. Cale, Gremillion, and McKenney (1979, p. 230) remark, "Add-time, or multiply-time, or the like, is altogether too simplistic a measure of processor power to be useful. Many other aspects of computer architecture (parallel processing, for example) dominate the effect of single instruction timing." Flamm (1987, p. 22), citing sources in the computer literature, notes, "The relative productivity of [a computer] varies considerably by the job." See also the discussion of figure 4.1, above.

5. There are a number of alternative definitions of this variable, and it is not always clear whether the alternatives represent linguistic variation in describing the same measure, or slight differences in the way the variable is measured. The definition in the text corresponds to that in Sippl (1985, p. 110). Rosenberg (1984, p. 116) gives a definition similar to that of Phister (1979, p. 60), who defines memory cycle time as the "average time between two successive accesses to random words," which appears equivalent to the variable used by Chow (1967). A closely related variable is the "memory data transfer rate," the amount of time that it takes to transfer a certain amount of data; the transfer rate is constructed from the size of the unit in which the information is stored (the word length or the memory width size, typically measured in bits), divided by the memory cycle time as defined above. On

this definition, the cycle time measure reported for the Schneidewind and Scattum studies (see below) should probably have been termed the "memory data transfer rate." See also on this topic Ralston and Reilly (1983).

6. Though the Gibson mix is well-known within the industry its published documentation has only appeared in Ishida (1972), and has never been translated from Japanese. An unpublished documentation is Gibson (1970).

7. Knight (1966, p. 41) says that the logic category "combines a large number of branch, shift, logic and load-register instructions"; the weight attached to the "logic" category approaches 75% (see Knight, 1966, p. 42, or 1985, p. 117). What appear to be similar categories are presented in the Gibson mix, according to Serlin (1986) and Ishida (1972); the categories load/store, test/branch, shift, logical, and indexing receive 71.8% of the weight, quite comparable to Knight's figure, though the categories may not match exactly. In Knight's case, times for certain other operations, such as add time, were arbitrarily chosen to represent those of logic instructions. This represents a defect of Knight's speed measure, a potentially serious one in view of the weight attached to the categories that are measured by proxies—though in Serlin's data (see section 4.2.1.2.b), cycles per instruction for the "add/subtract" category was close to the average for the "logic" instructions listed above.

8. Idle time was estimated for the "most typical configuration" (processor plus peripherals) when the machine was first introduced. Writing recently, Knight (1985, p. 121) notes that his model was developed in 1963, and "since then, many of the parameters originally involved in differentiating between machines have become so standard they are now constraints." Presumably, the I-O idle time computation comes under that heading. Cale, Gremillion, and McKenney (1979), who considered using a version of Knight's method, note (at p. 229), "Knight's method of measuring I/O time would yield a zero value for most large modern computers, which employ satellite subprocessors to control input/output."

9. The form and the notation used in table 4.1 to present Knight's formula are modified substantially from the original, for clarity and compactness.

10. The Block and Galage (1978) formula is the most comprehensive:

$$(MIPS)^{-1} \approx (C/i)\, T_c + r\, (M/i) T_m,$$

where

C/i = (average) cycles per instruction,

M/i = (average) memory accesses per instruction,

T_c = machine cycle time,

T_m = memory access time,

r = a ratio reflecting the efficiency of the cache memory.

The ratios C/i and M/i are computed from a mix of instructions and from the number of machine cycles or memory accesses required for execution of particular instructions. A number of published sources (for example, Lias, 1980) have designated "IBM job mix number 5" as the source for MIPS or KOPS instruction mixes, but also suggest that documentation of the mix, or details of the measurement for particular machines, is not available.

11. On the other hand, the restriction to IBM and "plug-compatible" machines introduces a sampling bias. Dulberger's argument thus implies a sampling model in which there is negative covariance between sampling and measurement biases, and a judgment that minimizing mean square error occurs with a nonrandom sample (that is, the measurement bias is larger than the sampling bias).

12. Suppose the computer center "sells" instructions executed at market prices, and produces instructions executed from the processor's characteristics (assumed for simplicity to be the center's only inputs) according to the production transformation relation:

$$\gamma(I, c) = 0,$$

where I is a k-element vector of instructions and c is a $k + 1$ vector of processor characteristics (the k speeds plus memory size). The technology is fixed coefficients between each c_j $(j \neq k + 1)$ and the associated I_j (because each speed corresponds to an instruction); "weighting" each c_j by I_j therefore results in a count of the number of "units" of each speed actually used in production. MIPS is then a k-element quantity sub-index of the $k + 1$ inputs (or in the more general case where we acknowledge other computer center inputs, of the $k + m$ inputs) used by the computer center.

13. One reason is the prominence in the computer literature of Grosch's law, which states that the cost of a computer center (often interpreted as the cost of a computer processor) rises with the square root of its computing power. This proposition is particularly easy to test with the double-log form.

14. Although the economic issues inherent in determining hedonic functional form have not been treated adequately in any published source, they cannot be presented in full in the present chapter. Section 4.2.2.2 is based partly on my unpublished paper presented at the 1980 Allied Social Science meetings in Denver. An expanded treatment will appear in a methodological work on hedonic functions, in progress.

15. For example, the translog functional form of Christensen, Jorgenson, and Lau (1973) or the Box-Cox.

16. Note that convexity is required in *characteristics space*, not in goods space, since the inputs in $q(\cdot)$ and the outputs in $t(\cdot)$ are characteristics. Nothing in the foregoing should be construed as ruling out a linear hedonic contour— which would arise, for example, in a semilog hedonic function. If the linear hedonic contour cannot be rejected statistically, it means that one rejects *both* the special cases, since with normal convexity of production sets nonlinearity is a necessary, though not sufficient, condition for identification.

17. It should be acknowledged that researchers on computers have followed the regrettably inadequate proposals that have appeared in published literature on hedonic functional forms, none of which have considered forms

suggested in (6b). An article by Halvorsen and Pollakowski (1981) on functional forms for hedonic functions proposes that the well-known Box-Cox transformations be used to discriminate among hedonic functional forms, an appropriate suggestion, but one already made by Griliches (1971) many years before; their list of functional form choices includes none that can stand as transformation functions for the t-identification case. Horsley and Swann (1983) usefully consider various frontier-fitting econometric proposals, but despite noting Rosen's (1974) envelope results, do not consider functional forms that admit hedonic contours of the shape of those in figure 4.1.

18. *Wall Street Journal*, April 3, 1986, p. 6. The article also noted that "on the street" prices for the older models would probably adjust to reflect at least part of the value of their lower performance.

19. Because the number of computer introductions in the 1950s was small, Chow actually treated machines introduced in either of two adjacent years as "new" (Chow, 1967, p. 1121). Gordon (1987), in replications of Chow's work, excluded some of these paired-year observations; Chow's results were not affected.

20. Recall that Knight's purpose was to estimate technological change in computers, and not a price index, so his index is only biased as it has been used in the present survey, and not for his original research objective.

21. When price changes are small, the coefficient will approximate its antilog, so the error is small, but for larger percentage changes the error is substantial.

22. Some required assumptions are seldom explicitly stated in empirical work. Obviously, if the specification being imputed does not lie within the range of observed data points, one is assuming the function can be extrapolated outside those points. Less obviously, if the machine being imputed does not actually exist in the imputation period, one is assuming that the appearance of a machine of the imputed specification would have no impact on the supply and demand for characteristics, and thus that the hedonic function would have been unchanged had the imputation point been in fact occupied.

23. An anomaly of Chow's procedure is that in general $I_{rr} \neq 1$, because $\sum (P_{ir}/\hat{P}_{ir}) w_i \neq 1$ where w_i is some set of weights, and the regression includes observations for several periods. See, for example, the index value for 1960 in Chow (1967, table 2, p. 1124).

24. Dulberger's procedure attenuates the anomaly noted in note 23.

25. To amplify this point, an imputation for new models can be thought of as answering the question: What is the price, in the characteristics price regime of period 0, of a "new model" observed in period t, but not in period 0? Weights for new models are obviously available only for the period for which they are actually sold, so an imputation for new models has a positive weight in period t, but zero weight in period 0. Conversely, an index using beginning period weights implies imputations for *discontinued* models, and not for new models, since the new models have zero weight in the beginning period. Dulberger's indexes employ the fixed year 1982 (benchmark year for the

National Income and Product Accounts), so her imputation occurs for models that were in production in 1982, but were "new models" with respect to (some) earlier years and "discontinued models" for (some) subsequent years. A superlative index form (Diewert, 1976) or some other cross weight or mixed weight form could use imputations from both periods.

26. In practice, this freedom has seldom been utilized by the investigator, who typically has chosen to estimate a single hedonic function across a pair or group of years, either for convenience or because the null hypothesis of coefficient equality across years could not be rejected.

27. I base this statement on my own experience in estimating hedonic functions for a number of products and also on conversations with the several investigators in the IBM study of computer equipment (Cole et al., 1986).

28. Omitted from Table 4.4A, as well as from subsequent tables, are results of Gordon's study included in the present volume, which was received in February 1988, well after the completion of this survey in September 1987. Gordon's 1988 paper differs in method, content, and conclusions from his 1987 version, circulated as National Bureau of Economic Research Working Paper 2227. In particular, none of the price indexes in NBER Working Paper 2227 appears in his study in this volume.

It was not practical to rewrite this survey to take account of Gordon's new paper, so a compromise was adopted: The tables and accompanying text have been substantially unchanged, and so record Gordon's price indexes on Phister (1979) and *Computerworld* data that were circulated in NBER Working Paper 2227. In appropriate places, notes have been added to alert readers to major changes between the results reported in NBER Working Paper 2227 and the study published in this volume. Comments on those topics in NBER Working Paper 2227 that do *not* appear in Gordon's paper in this volume have been deleted from the present survey.

29. Chow's data were perhaps more nearly relevant to scientific computers than to business applications.

30. Knight's published coefficients for the 1950s frequently have been misinterpreted as annual rates of change, instead of two-year changes. Knight (1966) contains the coefficients, as does Knight (1970); the latter is particularly clear on the coding of the time dummy variables—the time dummy for, e.g., 1955–1956 records machines newly introduced in either of those two years, so the (antilog of the sign-reversed) coefficient of the time dummy for 1955–1956, multiplied by 100, shows an index number for (average) 1955–1956, relative to 1962, the omitted year in the regression. In table 4.4A these indexes were linked with post-1962 indexes and rebased to 1965 = 100. It is not clear why Knight's coefficients have been so often misinterpreted, but it is not always easy to understand the details of his study without assembling all the pieces in which it has been published over the years.

31. Gordon's chapter in this volume achieves a smoothly falling price index from the Phister data base by discarding outliers and averaging together two

hedonic indexes. Compare his "final price index" (Gordon, this volume, table 7) with his earlier indexes reproduced in table 4.4A. See also note 28.

32. See note 28.

33. In the Archibald and Reece (1979) regressions, asking retail prices of *used* IBM computer systems (processors plus specified peripheral equipment) served as the dependent variable. If one is willing to assume close substitution chains between new machines embodying the latest technology on the one hand and used machines of an earlier year of manufacture on the other, then prices in the used machine market should reflect quality-adjusted price change in the new machine market. That this "equilibrium" assumption is debatable, and has been challenged (Fisher, McGowan, and Greenwood, 1983), does not preclude our examining Archibald and Reece's indexes for what information they may yield on the estimates made by other researchers. However, because the relation between used second-generation (transistor) computers and the third-generation machines being produced in the late 1960s is especially tenuous, table 4.5B reports only the indexes Archibald and Reece constructed for third-generation computers, omitting their second-generation and combined sample results. I have also ignored the fact that Archibald and Reece's data pertained to systems, not just to processors.

34. The introduction of the third-generation computer with its associated technical change brought into question some of the parameter values that appear in Knight's "computing power" variable. Knight published (Knight, 1970) a kind of prediction test, or technological forecast, that seemed to do moderately well. However, the period covered by this test extended only through 1966; the work was then set aside for 10 years or so until it was updated for another purpose.

35. In addition to the research listed in table 4.5A, and Fisher, McGowan, and Greenwood (1983), cited above, an enlightening chart appears in Phister (1979, p. 101). This chart shows that the various models of the third-generation IBM series 360 occupied the same price range as the 1401 series they replaced, but were 5–50 times more powerful, depending on the model. A price index lacks plausibility that suggests, as does Gordon's, little or no market impact from the tremendous technological innovations incorporated in the IBM 360, CDC 6600, and similar machines. See, however, footnote 32, and also note 28.

36. A number of other studies of computer prices that were carried out in the 1970s used data for part or all of the period 1965–1972. However, during the 1970s the focus of hedonic studies for computers shifted to the question, "Does IBM charge more?" That is, researchers were interested in making comparisons across companies at the same point in time, rather than in price index comparisons that extended through time. Examples are Ratchford and Ford (1976, 1979), Michaels (1979), and Fisher, McGowan, and Greenwood (1983). Information can be gleaned from these studies that is useful for evaluating computer hedonic functions, but they do not develop usable price indexes.

37. See the explanation in note 30.

38. As an example of the calculation, the ratio of Knight's "scientific" index for 1955–1956 (1202.1) to 1953–54 (1657.5) is .725 (giving –27.5 as the two-year percentage change tabulated in table 4.4B). The square root of .725 is .851, and –14.9 is thus the average annual percentage change over the 1953–1954 to 1955–1956 interval. This –14.9 value was used (with the analogous calculation from Knight's "commercial" index) to chain an index for 1953 from the calculated value of 1954, and used as well (in combination with changes from Chow's study) to obtain the 1954 index from the 1955 value. Indexes for subsequent years to 1959 were calculated analogously.

39. With respect to Gordon's results in this volume, refer to note 28.

40. For part of the *Computerworld* sample, Gordon imputed a value for MIPS from a regression on machine cycle time. Ein-Dor (1985), using the same *Computerworld* data source, reports the R^2 between MIPS and "cycle time" is only –0.09. See also note 10 on the relation between MIPS and machine cycle time. In contrast, Dulberger uses "equivalent" MIPS—see her study. See also note 28.

41. See also note 28.

42. Recall that the logarithmic model bias (section 4.3.1) affects the intercept term and coefficients of dummy variables. Adding a correction equal to $(1/2)V(a_t)$ and using Dulberger's estimate of the standard error of a_t (from her appendix equations), the terminal value of the dummy variable method of column (3) is raised by less than 0.1 index point. This correction appears too small to affect the conclusions. The imputation index is also biased, but presumably by a similar magnitude (estimating the bias of the imputation index requires recalculation of the index, which was not practical for this survey).

43. This same "competitive equilibrium" argument has also been advanced as a rationale for preferring traditional "matched-model" methods (as used in the BLS Producer Price Index, for example) over hedonic methods. In array (11), the first g models are common to both r and s and could be used to construct a "matched-model" price index, ignoring both new and discontinued models. Dulberger computed a matched-model index from her data base; from 1972 to 1984, the matched-model index fell only 66%, compared with the 90% and more in her three hedonic indexes. Comparable results appear for peripheral equipment in Cole et al. (1986). That the matched-model index lags so far behind the hedonic could be taken as evidence against the "competitive equilibrium" argument, at least for price index purposes. Note also that the BLS export and import price index program contains matched-model price indexes for computer equipment: These indexes show very little decline in recent years, far less than the price decreases recorded by hedonic indexes.

44. I should make clear that I am not necessarily rejecting Dulberger's own explanation for the economic interpretation of her technology variables, only suggesting that there may be alternative explanations, and that at least one of those alternatives supports her handling of the technology measures in the price indexes.

45. The earlier version of this survey contained at this point a critique of the "final price index" from Gordon (1987). Because that index has been replaced by another "final price index" different both in construction and in movement (Gordon, this volume), the critique has been deleted from this survey. Also deleted is discussion of a section in Gordon (1987) pertaining to the deflation of the "Office, Computing and Accounting Machinery" component of the National Income and Product Accounts, because this topic does not appear in Gordon (this volume).

46. Flamm's index is, of course, a component of the best-practice index after 1965, but again it falls more rapidly than other studies, particularly from 1968 to 1972.

47. Much information on computer center costs other than equipment costs is contained in Phister (1979). Baumol et al. (1985) also present information on nonequipment (especially programming) costs.

48. I do not argue that this string of assumptions is entirely plausible or realistic. The way the vectors $c_1, \ldots, c_r$ (computer equipment characteristics) are entered into (4b) and (16) implies that the computer center's use (i.e., marginal products) of processor speed and memory size, for example, is independent of its employment of auxiliary storage characteristics, which is highly doubtful. Relaxing this assumption means constructing the computer systems price index out of time series of *characteristics* prices; though feasible in principle, this is beyond the scope of the present chapter. Moreover, if the output of the computer center is appropriately described as a vector, J, then we have

$$r(q_1(c_1), q_2(c_2), \ldots, q_r(c_r), Z, J) = 0,$$

where r is a set of transformation relations and all the arguments are vectors. This a model of a multi-output production process. Caves, Christensen, and Diewert (1981) discuss price and other measures for such cases. Again, exploring such a model is beyond the scope of the present chapter.

49. In the 1950s the stock of computer equipment was small enough, and the growth rate of new production large enough, that stock weights and new shipments weights may not differ greatly. Census data on shipments by type of computer equipment begin in 1971.

50. The 1982 fixed weight computer price index in table 4.14 is not exactly the same as the corresponding component of the published BEA fixed weight price indexes, owing to corrections made subsequent to the last benchmark revision.

51. However, the tape drive index in the historical NIPA files (and incorporated into table 4.14) is not a hedonic index. It has been discontinued. I experimented with substituting a tape drive index based on the Flamm (1972–1975) and Randolph (1975–1983) studies—see table 4.12—which index declines more slowly in the early 1970s, but otherwise approximates the discontinued NIPA tape drives index. The substitution yields the following *TGFI* (selected years):

	1972	1977	1982	1983 (last year)
Substitute *TGFI*	100.0	52.9	21.3	16.8
Table 4.14 *TGFI*	100.0	51.4	20.4	16.4

52. The 1977–1984 *TGIF* was calculated from fixed weight indexes for which 1977 = 100—that is, rebased versions of columns (2) and (3) of table 14, rather than the 1972=100 indexes shown in the table. The resulting *TGFI* (1977 = 100) was then itself rebased by linking it on to the 1977 value (51.4) of the 1972–1977 *TGFI*, in order to generate a time series for the entire 1972–1984 interval.

53. Figure 4.2 is a rearrangement of a similar figure in Peterson (1984); see also Ballhaus (1984) for a slightly different presentation of the same information.

References

Archibald, Robert B., and Reece, William S. (1979). "Partial Subindexes of Input Prices: The Case of Computer Services." *Southern Economic Journal*, 46 (October): 528–540.

Ballhaus, W. F., Jr. (1984). "Computational Aerodynamics and Supercomputers." Institute of Electrical and Electronics Engineers, Digest of Papers, Twenty-Eighth IEEE Computer Society International Conference, Spring.

Bard, Yonathan, and Sauer, Charles H. (1981). "IBM Contributions to Computer Performance Modeling." *IBM Journal of Research and Development*, 25: 562–570.

Baumol, William J., Blackman, Sue Anne Batey, and Wolff, Edward N. (1985). "Unbalanced Growth Revisited: Asymptotic Stagnancy and New Evidence." *American Economic Review*, 75 (September): 806–817.

Bell, C. Gordon (1986). "RISC: Back to the Future?" *Datamation* 32 (June): 96–108.

Blackorby, Charles, and Russell, R. Robert (1978). "Indexes and Subindexes of Cost of Living and Standard of Living." *International Economic Review*, 19 (February): 229–240.

Bloch, Erich, and Galage, Dom (1978). "Component Progress: Its Effect on High-Speed Computer Architecture and Machine Organization." *Computer*, 11 (April): 64–75.

Cale, E. G., Gremillion, L. L., and McKenney, J. L. (1979). "Price/Performance Patterns of U.S. Computer Systems." *Communications of the Association for Computing Machinery (ACM)*, 22 (April): 225–233.

Cartwright, David W. (1986). "Improved Deflation of Purchases of Computers." *Survey of Current Business*, 66 (March): 7–9.

Cartwright, David W., Donahoe, Gerald F., and Parker, Robert P. (1985). "Improved Deflation of Computers in the Gross National Product of the United States." Bureau of Economic Analysis Working Paper 4. Washington, D.C.: U.S. Department of Commerce, December.

Caves, Douglas W., Christensen, Laurits R., and Diewert, W. Erwin (1981). "A New Approach to Index Number Theory and the Measurement of Input, Output, and Productivity." Social Systems Research Institute Workshop Series, Paper 8112. Madison, Wisconsin: University of Wisconsin.

Chow, Gregory C. (1967). "Technological Change and the Demand for Computers." *American Economic Review*, 57 (December): 1117–1130.

Christensen, Laurits R., Jorgenson, Dale W., and Lau, Lawrence J. (1973). "Transcendental Logarithmic Production Frontiers." *Review of Economics and Statistics*, 55 (February): 207–224.

Cole, Rosanne, Chen, Y. C., Barquin-Stolleman, Joan A., Dulberger, Ellen, Helvacian, Nurhan, and Hodge, James H. (1986). "Quality-Adjusted Price Indexes for Computer Processors and Selected Peripheral Equipment." *Survey of Current Business*, 66 (January): 41–50.

Diewert, W. E. (1976). "Exact and Superlative Index Numbers." *Journal of Econometrics*, 4: 115–45.

Dodson, E. W. (1985). "Measurement of State of the Art and Technological Advance." *Technological Forecasting and Social Change*, 27 (May): 129–146.

Dulberger, Ellen R. (1988). "The Application of an Hedonic Model to a Quality Adjusted Price Index for Computer Processors." This volume (chapter 2).

Early, Barro, and Margolis, (1963). RAND RM-3072–PR (May), cited in Sharpe (1969, p. 351).

Ein-Dor, Phillip (1985). "Grosch's Law Re-revisited: CPU Power and the Cost of Computation." *Communications of the ACM [Association for Computing Machinery]*, 28 (February): 142–151.

Fisher, Franklin M., and Shell, Karl (1972). *The Economic Theory of Price Indices: Two Essays on the Effects of Taste, Quality, and Technological Change.* New York: Academic Press.

Fisher, Franklin M., McGowan, John J., and Greenwood, Joen E. (1983). *Folded, Spindled and Mutilated: Economic Analysis and U.S. v. IBM.* Cambridge, MA: MIT Press.

Flamm, Kenneth (1987). *Targeting the Computer.* Washington, D.C.: The Brookings Institution.

Gibson, Jack C. (1970). "The Gibson Mix." IBM Poughkeepsie Lab. Technical Report, TR 00.2043 (June 18).

Goldberger, Arthur S. (1968). "The Interpretation and Estimation of Cobb-Douglas Functions." *Econometrica*, 35 (September): 464–472.

Gordon, Robert J. (1987). "The Postwar Evolution of Computer Prices." National Bureau of Economic Research Working Paper 2227 (April).

_____ (1988). "The Postwar Evolution of Computer Prices." This volume (chapter 3).

Griliches, Zvi (1964). "Notes on the Measurement of Price and Quality Changes." In: Conference on Research Income and Wealth. *Models of Income Determination. Studies in Income and Wealth*, vol. 28. Princeton: Princeton University Press for the National Bureau of Economic Research, pp. 381–418.

_____, ed. (1971). *Price Indexes and Quality Change: Studies in New Methods of Measurement.* Cambridge, MA: Harvard University Press.

Halvorsen, Robert, and Pollakowski, Henry O. (1981). "Choice of Functional Form for Hedonic Price Equations." *Journal of Urban Economics*, 10: 37–49.

Horsley, A. and Swann, G. M. P. (1983). "A Time Series of Computer Price Functions." *Oxford Bulletin of Economics and Statistics*, 45 (November): 339–356.

Ishida, Haruhisa (1972). "On the Origin of the Gibson Mix." *Journal of the Information Processing Society of Japan*, 13 (May): 333–334 (in Japanese).

Jacob, Nancy (1969). Unpublished study summarized in Sharp (1969).

Kelejian, Harry H., and Nicoletti, Robert V. (c. 1971). "The Rental Price of Computers: An Attribute Approach," unpublished paper, New York University (no date).

Knight, Kenneth E. (1966). "Changes in Computer Performance: A Historical View." *Datamation* (September): 40–54.

_____ (1970). "Application of Technological Forecasting to the Computer Industry." In: James R. Bright and Milton E. F. Schoeman. *A Guide to Practical Technological Forecasting.* Englewood Cliffs, NJ: Prentice-Hall.

_____ (1985). "A Functional and Structural Measurement of Technology." *Technological Forecasting and Social Change*, 27 (May): 107–127.

Levy, David, and Welzer, Steve (1985). "An Unintended Consequence of Antitrust Policy: The Effect of the IBM Suit on Pricing Policy." Unpublished Paper, Rutgers University Department of Economics, December.

Lias, Edward (1980). "Tacking the Elusive KOPS." *Datamation* (November): 99–118.

Martino, Joseph (1980). "Measurement of Technology Using Tradeoff Surfaces." *Technological Forecasting and Social Change*, 27 (May): 147–160.

Michaels, Robert (1979). "Hedonic Prices and the Structure of the Digital Computer Industry." *The Journal of Industrial Economics*, 27 (March): 263–275.

Ohta, Makota, and Griliches, Zvi (1976). "Automobile Prices Revisited: Extensions of the Hedonic Hypothesis." In: Nestor E. Terleckyj, ed., *Household Production and Consumption. Conference on Research in Income and Wealth: Studies in Income and Wealth*, vol. 40. New York: National Bureau of Economic Research, pp. 325–390.

Patrick, James M. (1969). "Computer Cost/Effectiveness." Unpublished paper summarized in Sharpe (1969, p. 352).

Peterson, Victor L. (1984). "Impact of Computers on Aerodynamic Research and Development." *Proceedings of the IEEE (Institute of Electrical and Electronics Engineers)*, 72 (January): 68–79.

Phister, Montgomery Jr. (1979). *Data Processing Technology and Economics*, 2nd ed. Bedford, MA: Santa Monica Publishing Company and Digital Press.

Pollak, Robert A. (1975). "Subindexes of the Cost of Living." *International Economic Review*, 16: 135–50.

———— (1983). "The Theory of the Cost-of-Living Index." In: W. E. Diewert and Claude Montmarquette, eds., *Price Level Measurement: Proceedings from a Conference Sponsored by Statistics Canada.* Ottawa, Canada: Minister of Supply and Services.

Ralston, Anthony, and Reilly, Edwin D. Jr., eds. (1983). *Encyclopedia of Computer Science and Engineering*, 2nd ed. New York: Van Nostrand Reinhold.

Randolph, William C. (1985). "Price Measurement When Designs Are Changed: Estimation Theory with Applications to Computers." Washington, D.C., unpublished Bureau of Labor Statistics Paper, November.

Ratchford, Brian T., and Ford, Gary T. (1976). "A Study of Prices and Market Shares in the Computer Mainframe Industry." *The Journal of Business*, 49: 194–218.

———— (1979). "Reply." *The Journal of Business*, 52: 125–134.

Rosen, Sherwin (1974). "Hedonic Prices and Implicit Markets: Product Differentiation in Pure Competition." *Journal of Political Economy*, 92: 34–55.

Rosenberg, Jerry M. (1984). *Dictionary of Computers, Data Processing and Telecommunications.* New York: John Wiley and Sons.

Schneidewind, Norman F. (1969). "Analytic Models for the Design and Selection of Electronic Digital Computing Systems." Unpublished Ph.D. dissertation, summarized in Sharpe (1969, pp. 328–329).

Serlin, Omri (1986). "MIPS, Dhrystones, and Other Tales." *Datamation*, 32 (June 1): 112–118.

Sharpe, William F. (1969). *The Economics of the Computer.* New York and London: Columbia University Press.

Sippl, Charles J. (1985). *Computer Dictionary*, 4th ed. Indianapolis, IN: Howard W. Sams and Company, a subsidiary of Macmillan.

Skattum, Stein (1969). "Changes in Performance of Components for Computer Systems." Unpublished paper summarized in Sharpe (1969, p. 330).

Stoneman, Paul (1976). *Technological Diffusion and the Computer Revolution: The U.K. Experience.* Cambridge: Cambridge University Press.

———— (1978). "Merger and Technological Progressiveness: The Case of the British Computer Industry." *Applied Economics*, 10: 125–140. Reprinted as chapter 9 in: Keith Cowling, Paul Stoneman, John Cubbin, John Cable,

Graham Hall, Simon Domberger, and Patricia Dutton, *Mergers and Economic Performance*. Cambridge: Cambridge University Press (1980).

Teekens, R., and Koerts, J. (1972). "Some Implications of the Log Transformation of Multiplicative Models." *Econometrica*, 40 (September): 793–819

Triplett, Jack E. (1969). "Automobiles and Hedonic Quality Measurement." *Journal of Political Economy*, 77: 408–17.

_____ (1983). "Concepts of Quality in Input and Output Price Measures: A Resolution of the User Value-Resource Cost Debate." In: Murray F. Foss, ed., *The U.S. National Income and Product Accounts: Selected Topics*. Conference on Research in Income and Wealth, Studies in Income and Wealth, vol. 47. University of Chicago Press for the National Bureau of Economic Research, pp. 296–311.

_____ (1987). "Hedonic Functions and Hedonic Indexes." In John Eatwell, Murray Milgate, and Peter Newman, eds., *The New Palgrave: A Dictionary of Economics*. New York: Stockton Press, Volume 2:630–634.

Wallace, William E. (1985). "Industrial Policies and the Computer Industry." The Futures Group Working Paper #007. Glastonbury, CT: The Futures Group (March).

Zieschang, Kimberly D. (1985). "Output Price Measurement When Output Characteristics are Endogenous." Washington, D.C.: Bureau of Labor Statistics (unpublished paper).

Comments on
Chapter 3 (Gordon)

Rosanne Cole,
Ellen R. Dulberger,
and Jack E. Triplett

Gordon's new (February 1988) study is better than the one it replaces.[1] The new study is critical of earlier research, including Dulberger (chapter 2, this volume) and Triplett (chapter 4, this volume). In these comments, we respond to the most important points.

1   First- and Second-Generation Computers (1954–1965)

For this period, Gordon relies on data taken from Phister (1979). After discarding outliers and averaging together the price indexes from two hedonic regressions, Gordon achieves a "final price index" (table 3.7, column 9), which follows fairly closely the "best-practice" index in Triplett—this volume, table 4.6A. For example, with 1965 = 100, 1960 values for the two are 476 and 435, and their 1954 values are 1,136 and 1,139. Thus, the 20-year-old research by Chow and by Knight (incorporated into the "best-practice" index) stands up to replication on a new data base. Though there are research issues that have never been explored for this period of computer history, there is at present no disagreement about the empirical findings.

2   The 1965–1972 Period

This period is a problematic one that deserves some additional price index research. Earlier studies found that the introduction in 1965–1966 of "third-generation" computers made a very large impact on the computer market. Quality-corrected prices fell by nearly 75% from 1965 to 1967, according to best available estimates, and there was probably an additional "announcement effect" in 1964. That is, *third*-generation computers cost around one-fourth of the *second*-generation machines they replaced.[2]

Table A
Comparison of estimates, computer price index changes,
1972–1977

	Percent
Dulberger (this volume, table 2.6)	
Imputation index	−43.2
Characteristics price index	−35.8
Dummy variable index	−49.5
Gordon's "final price index" (this volume, table 3.7)	−42
Gordon's calculations with "new only" portion of Dulberger's data (this volume, table 3.9)	
Index A	−43
Index B	−66

Table B
Alternative comparisons of two IBM computers

1. Specifications and prices (Gordon, table 3.8)				
Year	Model	MIPS	Memory	Price
1972	IBM 370–155	0.55	1152	1553
1977	IBM 370–148	0.42	1000	687

2. Ratios of quality and quality-adjusted price
(1977/1972, or 370–148 / 370–155)

	Gordon			Dulberger[a]
	Phister	"Index A"	"Index B"	
"Quality ratio"	0.58	0.69	2.56	0.79
Quality-adjusted price index	83	70	19	56

a. Coefficients from Dulberger—this volume, equation (2′)—and prices and characteristics quantities in panel 1.

Gordon attempts to challenge previous research findings by comparing two *third*-generation families, the IBM 360 and 370 (". . . the price history of 1965–1972 boils down to a single question: How much did the quality-corrected price of [IBM] 370s decline relative to 360s?"). This seems a misunderstanding of the computer market in the mid-1960s. The price/performance level of the 1965 System 360 exerted downward pressure during 1964–1967 on prices of other computers that embodied earlier technology; one cannot measure that downward pressure by the 370–360 comparison. Gordon provides no new insights over, and no challenge to, previous research.

3   The 1972–1977 Interval

For this period, Gordon's "final price index" shows a total decline that is in the middle of the range of the three estimates (corresponding to alternative calculation methods) presented by Dulberger—see the first four lines of our table A. Estimates by other researchers lie in the same range.

It is thus astonishing to read Gordon's extraordinary passage in which Dulberger's name is repeatedly coupled with the word "implausible." Gordon makes a great to-do about the implausibility of the 2.56 "quality ratio" labeled "index B" in his text, and reproduced in our table B. It is true that the 1977 370 model 148 contained smaller quantities of characteristics than did the earlier 370 model 155, and we agree that a 2.56 ratio is implausible. However, though Dulberger's name is attached, the calculations are, once again, not hers. Coefficients from Dulberger's equation (2'), applied to the characteristics quantities and prices presented in Gordon's table 3.8 (reproduced in our table B), produce a "quality ratio" of 0.79, and a quality-adjusted price index of 56 (lower right-hand panel of table B).[3]

The "index B" calculations are indeed implausible; they are also irrelevant, as they do not represent Dulberger's work.[4] Gordon has produced no criticism of Dulberger's study, and in fact his "final price index"—if anything—confirms it.

4   The 1977–1984 Period

Gordon notes, "Overall . . . there is no conflict between the rate of change of [Gordon's] *Computerworld* and Dulberger's price indexes." We agree.

Gordon argues that the timing of the price decline is an issue over this period, and asserts that "... the Dulberger data set *for new models* ... contains only two new models for 1979 ... [and] an index based on these two models is misleading ..." (emphasis added). His small sample problems are solely attributable to his restricting Dulberger's data set to newly introduced models only. Gordon's discussion of 1977–1979 and 1979–1984 price movements should be understood not as criticism of Dulberger's research (to which it does not apply) but as an illustration of the shortcomings of his own "newly introduced models only" method.

5   Concluding Remarks

Hedonic indexes have been used for two different purposes. One is to trace out movements in the technological frontier; another is to deflate purchases.

When prices adjust instantaneously and fully to the introduction of new technology, an index that follows the technological frontier will be the same as an index that covers all models that are sold.[5] During periods of disequilibrium, however, these two indexes may differ.

In the case of computer processors, newly introduced models may not all lie on the technological frontier. Conversely, manufacturers often change the technology embodied in a processor without changing the model name, so the technological frontier may be extended by a model that does not appear to be "new."[6] Thus, the "newly introduced models only" method may not estimate the technological frontier. Even when newly introduced models trace out the frontier, they produce a biased measure for deflating purchases, because price changes in existing models are omitted.[7]

The above research problem, originally posed by Fisher, McGowan, and Greenwood (1983, pp. 148–149) in the context of frontier estimation, is discussed in the price index context by Dulberger (this volume, pp. 42ff.) and Triplett (this volume, pp. 158–161). Gordon's chapter represents the application of an older research methodology for frontier estimation ("newly introduced models only") to a data set (Phister, 1979) that has been neglected. The exercise in itself is useful. But its contribution to knowledge lies more in demonstrating the limitations of both the method and the data set than in illuminating the history of computer prices.

Notes

1. As the author himself has noted in correspondence, "Literally nothing in this paper resembles its previous versions"—the first presented at the November 1985 conference, and the second circulated in 1987 as National Bureau of Economic Research Working Paper No. 2227.

2. Most problematic is the pattern of price change after 1967 as the following tabulation illustrates:

Period	Knight	Flamm	Cartwright, Donahoe, and Parker	Gordon, this volume
1965–1967	−72	−75	—	−46
1967–1970	−77	−32	+8	−33
1970–1972	—	−53	−28	+3

3. Using data from Gordon's table 3.8 for the sake of comparability only, the "quality ratio" is given by

$$\frac{\text{MIPS}_{148}^{.78} \times \text{MEM}_{148}^{.22}}{\text{MIPS}_{155}^{.78} \times \text{MEM}_{155}^{.22}} = \frac{.42^{.78} \times 1000^{.22}}{.55^{.78} \times 1152^{.22}} = .79.$$

Dividing the ratio of Gordon's prices, 687/1,553 from his table 3.8, by the "quality ratio" produces a quality-adjusted price ratio of .56.

4. Gordon's parallel passage discussing Gregory Chow's sample and results has similar flaws. We judge Chow's old paper better both in method and in careful data review than Gordon's.

5. Indeed, the two indexes will be identical as well to a price index of matched models, so hedonic methods might not even be necessary.

6. Examples of both occur in the Dulberger data set, particularly (but not exclusively) with respect to the IBM 370 family of processors, which were first shipped in 1971.

7. Gordon's statement that Fisher, McGowan, and Greenwood (1983, p. 149) "argue forcefully" for a newly introduced models method ignores their subsequent analysis on the same page, and also that their context was the estimation of the technological frontier, not a price index covering the purchases of computers.

Comment on
Chapter 4 (Triplett)
and Rejoinder to the
Cole-Dulberger-Triplett
Comments

Robert J. Gordon

Not a single number or a single remark contained in Jack Triplett's survey (chapter 4 of this volume) that refers to my research on computer prices corresponds to chapter 3. Instead the Triplett survey refers to an earlier version of my chapter that was completely superseded on the basis of intensive further study of my basic data sources. The reader is urged to disregard every one of the 18 columns of tables in Triplett's chapter labeled "Gordon," since all refer to the obsolete version, and to all of his text remarks on that version as well. I regret that the reader of this volume is faced with the confusing prospect of two totally different versions of my work, the correct final version as printed in chapter 3, and the obsolete results reported by Triplett.[1] The purpose of the note is to flag for the purpose of clarification several remarks contained in Triplett's chapter that no longer accurately describe my results, and to provide a brief evaluation of differences between the price indexes for computer processors reported in chapters 3 and 4.

Conflicts between the Published Version and That Reported by Triplett

Triplett is highly critical of jumps in the annual rate of change registered by several price indexes developed in the obsolete version of my chapter. Since the primary issue of interest in the development of computer price indexes is the secular rate of change over periods of a half-decade or more, there seems to be little justification for focussing on year-to-year rates of change, as in his tables 4.4B, 4.5B, and 4.8B. In chapter 3, most of the jumps to which Triplett objects have disappeared. As explained in my text, this was achieved by minor editing of the Phister sample to exclude 8 out of 97 models having actual prices from two to seven times the price imputed by the regression equation. This is a much more conservative editing criterion than that applied by Knight, on whom Triplett relies as one of the three sources of his "best-practice" processor index for 1953–1966, and who excluded almost half of his models.

Also criticized in the obsolete version of chapter 3 is the development of regression indexes from an "augmented" data set that adds observations for old models still in production by assuming that their sales prices remain unchanged over their production run. This was an attempt to bridge the inconsistency problem discussed below and that still plagues Triplett's results — that all available data prior to the late 1960s include only new models, while the best data set from 1972 to 1984 (Dulberger's) contains both new models and old models still in production. Responding to Triplett's criticism of the augmented data, I switched in the version published here to the opposite solution to the inconsistency problem, and that is to include only new models both before and after 1972.

A further criticism contained in Triplett's chapter is that I estimated regression equations based on data for pairs of adjacent years, leading to very small sample sizes in some year-pairs. This comment also does not apply to chapter 3, in which the optimal sample interval was determined statistically by beginning with groups of three adjacent years and successively pooling further years until the pooling test failed. Finally, Triplett reports my indexes as showing a larger price drop during 1968–1972 than 1965–1968. This was indeed an incorrect result due to the unjustified pooling of observations for mini and mainframe models; in chapter 3 the price decline is substantially faster for 1965–1968 than 1968–1972.

Triplett's "Best-Practice" Index: A Critique

Triplett regards the Phister data used by myself and by Flamm as inferior to that used by Chow and Knight for the early period, 1954–1965. The Chow and Knight samples have the advantage that they are larger, and thus it is easier to obtain smooth price indexes than with the Phister data (although in Knight's case his price index was obtained only after heavy editing of his data set). The smaller size of the Phister data set has the countervailing advantage, however, that in contrast to Chow's data it contains many fewer minicomputers (which had a negligible market share before 1965) and a substantially larger share of market-dominant IBM models. Thus it is closer to the desired but usually unattainable market-share-weighted index.

There is no disagreement between my results and Triplett's best-practice index for the period 1954–1965. Indeed, the geometric annual rates of change are absolutely identical, respectively, –22.1% and –22.1%. Within this period my index declines more slowly before 1960 and more rapidly thereafter, a timing sequence that seems to accord more closely with the behavior of the imputed price index for IBM models displayed in my table 3.8. Nor is there any major difference for the period 1972–1984, when my index registers an annual rate of change of –20.0% and the Dulberger index preferred by Triplett a change of –21.3%.

Instead, the real disagreement occurs during the period 1965–1972, when my index changes at an annual rate of just –14.0%, much less than Triplett's best-practice index of –27.3%. According to Triplett, the 1965–1972 period witnessed the most rapid price declines of the postwar period, whereas according to my results this period witnessed the slowest decline. Who is correct? Cole, Dulberger, and Triplett in their comments dispute the statement in my chapter 3 that the issue boils down to a comparison of the price and performance of the IBM 370 introduced in 1972 versus the IBM 360 introduced in 1964–1965, but they do not support their position with any solid arguments. My comparison of 360s and 370s was made explicitly in the context of the high market share of IBM, and in the context of my research, which treats new models only and excludes all old models.

The basic reason that Triplett finds such a rapid rate of price decline after 1965 (concentrated in 1965–1967), is that in his "best-practice index" he has stumbled into the pitfall of mixing together inconsistent data sources. His estimate of 1964–1965 price change is based on the results of Chow and Knight, who cover new models only and include all of the price decrease achieved in the introduction of the IBM third-generation 360 family of models. Cole, Dulberger, and Triplett claim that "quality-corrected prices fell by nearly 75% from 1965 to 1967, according to the best available estimates." What they overlook is that Triplett switches sources at 1965 from the Chow and Knight indexes that include only new models to a partial dependence on Flamm's results for 1966, which primarily reflect price changes of old models and thus count the decline achieved by the 360 family *again*.[2] A price index that consistently included both new and old models before and after 1965 might indeed find that more of the price decline occurred in 1965–1967 and less in 1964–1965, but Triplett's chapter cannot address that point, since it mixes price changes for 1963–1965 based entirely on new models with a price change for 1965–1966 that is heavily based on old models.

The mystery of the true rate of price change between the 360 and 370 generations is solved in my table 3.8, which displays a consistent imputation index for the major models of newly introduced IBM mainframes over the whole period between 1954 and 1984. It avoids the inconsistency in other research of (a) shifting from sources based on new-only models to new-and-old models and (b) shifting from research that underrepresents the market share of IBM (as do all studies including my regression results before 1972) to research that properly reflects the share of IBM (Dulberger's results in chapter 2, which begin only in 1972). The crucial issue is consistency and the avoidance of double counting. This is the justification for my use throughout the 1954–1984 period of a data set that excludes old models, and my final index is the only one that can be used to assess changes in the pace of technological progress over the full postwar period. However, if we are interested only in the period after 1972, when Dulberger's data allow the inclusion of both newly introduced models and older vintages still in production, then for purposes of deflation it is clearly better to use Dulberger's results than mine.

Notes

1. Triplett's survey was completed in September 1987, and my final version was completed in February 1988.

2. In addition, the sharp decline in price for 1965–1966 in the Knight results, as in our index for mainframes, is heavily influenced by the underpriced IBM model 360-44, which, as Frank Fisher has observed, lies off the price surface and should be excluded from hedonic regression studies (see note 31 in my chapter 3).

5   Energy, Obsolescence, and the Productivity Slowdown

Charles R. Hulten,
James W. Robertson, and
Frank C. Wykoff

5.1   Introduction

Output per worker in the U.S. business sector grew at an average annual rate of 3.0% from 1948 to 1973. From 1973 to 1984, however, this annual rate plunged to 1.1%. This is the widely publicized "productivity slowdown" that has attracted so much attention from economic researchers.[1]

Some analysts see the slowdown as a consequence of the changing structure of the U.S. economy—the increased importance of international trade, the shift in economic activity toward the service sector, and the changing demography of the labor force; others see the problem resulting from policy inflicted wounds such as increased tax burdens on income from capital and increased regulatory requirements; still others see the problem as due to macroeconomic trends in inflation and recession. Some even hold the view that the slowdown is an artifact of the data and really did not occur at all.[2]

A prime suspect, however, is the rapid and unexpected rise in energy prices imposed by the OPEC cartel in 1973 and again in 1979. While there is still a debate over when the productivity slowdown started, few doubt that the sharpest decline occurred after 1973. The coincidence of this decline with the energy crisis is an obvious clue, and many analysts have suggested mechanisms through which higher energy prices cause economic growth to slow.

We gratefully acknowledge the financial support by the Bureau of Labor Statistics, U.S. Department of Labor. The findings and opinions presented in this chapter are strictly those of the authors and should not be attributed to BLS. We wish to thank Jerome Mark and William Waldorf of the Bureau of Labor Statistics, M. Wolfson of the Machinery Dealers National Association, Lloyd Sommers, and Victor Wykoff of Caterpillar Tractor Co. for their support of encouragement, and Ernst Berndt, Michael Harper, Dale Jorgenson, and Reza Ragozar for their comments and help.

In this chapter we examine one of the leading energy-related hypotheses. This hypothesis, advanced by Martin N. Baily (1981), holds that the rise in energy prices accelerated the rate of obsolescence of the U.S. stock of physical capital. Since conventional measures of the capital stock do not capture changes in the rate of obsolescence, conventional analyses of growth fail to identify this effect. Instead, they suppress it into a time trend or residual estimate of productivity change. Baily shows that this energy-induced obsolescence effect may have been large enough to account for most of the productivity slowdown.

If correct, the obsolescence hypothesis offers a sufficient explanation of the productivity slowdown. Baily's evidence is, however, based on the correlation between the rise in energy prices and the decline in Tobin's average q, and is subject to the criticism that the q ratio could have fallen during the 1970s for reasons unrelated to the energy crisis (e.g., the rise in effective income tax rates).[3] A more direct test is needed to establish the extent to which the energy price increases induced obsolescence in the stock of capital.

The model of this chapter provides such a test. If there is a significant link between energy and obsolescence, it should be revealed in the price of old capital: If rising energy costs did in fact render older, energy-inefficient capital obsolete, prospective buyers would have reduced the price that they were willing to pay for that capital (a decline in asset value is, indeed, the definition of obsolescence).[4] An examination of the market price of used capital before and after the energy price shocks should thus reveal the magnitude of the Baily effect.

We have carried out this examination for four types of used machine tools and five types of construction equipment. Our principal conclusion is that data for these assets do not support the obsolescence hypothesis. There is no systematic downward shift in used asset prices after 1973, and for construction equipment. The shifts tend to be upward, not downward.[5]

The chapter is organized as follows: In sections 5.2 and 5.3 we review the recent literature on the role of energy in the productivity slowdown. In the subsequent two sections we set out our model of used asset prices and relate it to the obsolescence hypothesis. We then describe our.data and present the empirical findings in sections 5.6 and 5.7.

5.2   Energy and Economic Growth

Energy can be directly related to economic growth via a production function in which gross output, Q, is assumed to depend on the quantities of capital, K, labor, L, energy, E, and material inputs, M:[6]

$$Q = AF(K,L,E,M). \tag{1}$$

In the production function (1), all variables are implicit functions of time and the variable A is included separately to allow for Hicks-neutral shifts in the function over time, i.e., to allow for changes in Q not captured by changes in the input quantities. The term A is thus a surrogate for technical change, but also includes the effects of such factors as managerial efficiency and worker effort.

The fundamental equation of growth analysis can be derived from the production function under the assumption that each input is paid the value of its marginal product. Logarithmic differentiation of F yields[7]

$$\hat{Q} = S_K\hat{K} + S_L\hat{L} + S_E\hat{E} + S_M\hat{M} + \hat{A}. \tag{2}$$

Hats over variables indicate rates of growth, and S's represent the shares of total cost allocated to each input; S_L, for example, represents labor's share of total costs; the variable $\hat{A}$ represents the rate at which the technology shifts over time (and is called the rate of change total factor productivity). All variables in (2) except $\hat{A}$ can be measured directly or imputed, so $\hat{A}$ can be measured as a residual.

If one assumes constant returns to scale, then the cost shares sum to one and (2) can be written as

$$\hat{Q}-\hat{L} = S_K(\hat{K}-\hat{L}) + S_E(\hat{E}-\hat{L}) + S_M(\hat{M}-\hat{L}) + \hat{A}. \tag{3}$$

The left-hand side of equation (3) is the growth rate of output per labor-hour—"labor productivity." Equation (3) states that labor productivity equals the sum of the growth rate of the capital-labor ratio, weighted by capital's share of total cost, the growth rates of energy and materials per labor-hour, weighted by their cost shares, and the growth rate of total factor productivity.

Equation (3) provides a framework for analyzing the slowdown in labor productivity. Any change in $\hat{Q}-\hat{L}$ after 1973 must be associated with changes in the variables on the right-hand side of (3). In particular, the impact of the energy costs on Q/L can be linked directly to changes in the energy intensity of production, E/L. This link suggests the following explanation for the productivity slowdown: The rise in the price of energy relative to other input prices caused the demand for energy to fall and this reduced the growth rate of $\hat{E}-\hat{L}$, which caused $\hat{Q}-\hat{L}$ to slow.

This explanation for the slowdown was among the first considered.[8] However, the problem with this explanation is that energy's cost share (S_E) is very small, about 2% for U.S. manufacturing, so that even large changes in $\hat{E}-\hat{L}$ will have a small impact on $\hat{Q}-\hat{L}$. An even more important problem is that, for U.S. manufacturing industries, the decline in E after 1973 was largely offset by a concomitant decline in L. Thus, according to data from the Bureau of Labor Statistics, covering the period 1948–1981, almost no change in $\hat{E}-\hat{L}$ occurred after 1973. This data—shown in table 5.1—leads to the conclusion, expressed in a similar study by Berndt (1980), that "energy price or quantity variations since 1973 do not appear to have played a significant direct or indirect role in the slowdown of labor productivity in U.S. manufacturing" (p. 72).

Another possible link between energy and economic growth was advanced by Hudson and Jorgenson (1978) and Berndt and Wood (1979). If energy and capital are complements in production, an increase in the price of energy should reduce the demand for capital and trigger a substitution of other inputs for capital. The impact of higher energy costs would then appear as a reduction in the growth rate K/L, as well as in the E/L term of (3). Unfortunately, the data of table 5.1 do not support this hypothesis either: The decline in E/L is small and explains only 5% of the decline in the growth of Q/L, while the growth rate of the capital-labor ratio actually increased after 1973.

According to the estimates of table 5.1, the slowdown in labor productivity is entirely related to a decline in the growth rate of total factor productivity. This would appear to exonerate the energy crisis as the primary cause of the productivity slowdown, and to shift attention to the residual variable A that some call "a measure of our ignorance." This conclusion, however, presumes that the price of energy and the growth rate of total factor productivity are not linked. In fact, two such links have been established.

First, Jorgenson and Fraumeni (1981) and Jorgenson (1984) argued that total factor productivity depends on the price of energy through a bias in technical change. They start with a model in which technical change occurs by augmenting particular factors of production. In our framework, this may be expressed with the following production function:

Table 5.1
The productivity slowdown in U.S. manufacturing

	1949–1981	1949–1973	1973–1981
Average annual weighted growth rates (percentage points)			
Output/labor	2.20	2.57	1.07
Capital/labor[a]	0.52	0.47	0.67
Energy/labor[a]	0.05	0.07	−0.01
Material/labor[a]	0.40	0.41	0.38
Service/labor[a]	0.29	0.27	0.34
TFP	0.92	1.34	−0.31
Unweighted average annual growth rates of inputs (percentage points)			
Capital	3.92	3.86	4.11
Labor	1.05	1.49	−0.25
Energy	3.67	5.05	−0.43
Materials	2.70	3.18	1.28
Services	4.95	5.44	3.49
Cost shares (percent)			
Capital	0.18	0.19	0.14
Labor	0.50	0.50	0.50
Energy	0.02	0.02	0.05
Material	0.23	0.23	0.23
Services	0.07	0.06	0.08
	1.00	1.00	1.00

Source: Bureau of Labor Statistics (1983).
a. Weighted by cost shares.

$$Q = F(A_K K, A_L L, A_E E, A_M M),$$ (4)

where A_i is the factor augmentation parameter for the ith type of input; total factor productivity change is then given by

$$\hat{A} = S_K \hat{A}_K + S_L \hat{A}_L + S_E \hat{A}_E + S_M \hat{A}_M.$$ (5)

The average rate of productivity change is thus the share-weighted average of the rates of factor augmentation.

Jorgenson and Fraumeni show that a change in the price of energy can change the average rate $\hat{A}$, even though the individual $\hat{A}_i$ are not affected. This occurs when the price of energy rises and when the relative bias with respect to energy, $\hat{A}_E - \hat{A}$, is positive, i.e., technical change is energy-using. The average rate falls, in this case, because the energy price increase causes production to become less energy intensive (other things being equal). This means that technical progress augments that input whose quantity is falling relative to other inputs.

Jorgenson and Fraumeni find that the bias in technical change was energy augmenting in a majority of U.S. industries, and thus have a potential explanation for the productivity slowdown. However, they do not offer an overall appraisal of the extent to which their energy price effect contributed to the productivity slowdown.

5.3   The Baily Hypothesis

The second link between energy costs and total factor productivity was developed by Martin N. Baily (1981). Baily noted that conventional measures of capital stock do not allow for changes in the rate of utilization or variations in the rate of depreciation of capital. Instead, the capital stocks are typically measured using a perpetual inventory method—that is, by cumulating investment during year t and subtracting the depreciation and retirement of the existing stock. Depreciation and retirement are assumed to be stationary processes that do not change with economic events.

According to Baily, this method of estimating capital is inadequate for measuring the contribution of capital to the growth of output, since the sharp rise in energy costs may have caused firms to utilize their old energy-inefficient capital less intensively and to retire it earlier. A trucking company, for example, may have had the incentive to operate its relatively energy-efficient trucks more frequently, and reserve its less efficient vehicles for peak load capacity. In this case, the rise in energy costs causes the trucking firm to some use of its capital less intensively. Yet perpetual inventory measures of capital, by their very nature, cannot capture this effect.

An important conclusion follows from this line of analysis: If utilization effects are present, they will be suppressed into the residual estimate of total factor productivity and thus misstate the impact of energy prices on capital. To illustrate this mismeasurement problem formally, let K^* denote the true growth rate of capital input (i.e. the rate adjusted for utilization) and A^* the true rate of total productivity growth; equation (3) then becomes

$$\hat{Q}-\hat{L} = S_K(\hat{K}^*-\hat{L}) + S_E(\hat{E}-\hat{L}) + S_M(\hat{M}-\hat{L}) + \hat{A}^*. \tag{6}$$

Comparing (3) and (6), we find that

$$\hat{A} = \hat{A}^* + S_K(\hat{K}^*-\hat{K}). \tag{7}$$

If $\hat{K}$ overstates $\hat{K}^*$ because utilization is ignored, then $\hat{A}$ will be biased downward by an amount equal to the change in utilization $(\hat{K}^*-\hat{K})$ multiplied by capital's share in total cost. It follows immediately that the sharp decline in the conventionally measured growth rate of total factor productivity after 1973, evident in the estimates of table 5.1 (which are based on perpetual inventory calculations of $\hat{K}$), may have been caused instead by an energy-induced decline in the rate of utilization of old capital.[9]

Any test of the Baily hypothesis must deal with the difficult problem of measuring the unobserved variable K^*. Baily provides an ingenious solution to this problem: He assumes a "putty-putty" Cobb-Douglas technology in which input substitution can occur both ex post and ex ante; he then derives a production function in which output depends on the value of the capital stock rather than on the quantity of capital. In our framework, this implies that the production function has the form

$$Q = F(K^*,L,E,M,A^*) = F(VK,L,E,M,A^*), \tag{8}$$

with the value of the stock (VK) substituted for the quantity of capital K^*. In this model, variations in the value of the capital stock act as a surrogate for variations in the utilization of this stock, given K.

The VK in (8) nominally refers to the present value of the income associated with the stock of capital. VK is therefore equal to the amount that rational investors would be willing to pay for the capital, and should thus be equal to the financial value of the firm (less "goodwill"). A financial measure of VK could thus be used as a surrogate for K^*.

Baily, however, uses a slightly different approach based on Tobin's q theory of investment decision. Tobin's average q as is defined as

$$q = VK/P_I K \tag{9}$$

(where P_I is the price of a new unit of capital stock, and $P_I K$ is the replacement cost of the capital stock). In view of (9) we can write VK as $qP_I K$ and substitute the result into the production function. Since K is measured in physical units and P_I is the price of new investment goods, an obsolescence induced decline in VK is reflected in q.

According to Summers (1981), Tobin's q fell during the 1970s (from 1.029 in 1973 to 0.747 in 1977), and Baily concludes that the movement in q is more than sufficient to explain the productivity slowdown. The obsolescence hypothesis thus provides a complete explanation of the productivity puzzle.

There are, however, at least two difficulties with this explanation. First, the decline in Tobin's q could be due to any number of factors, not just energy price shocks. Summers, for example, writing in the same volume as Baily, attributes the decline in q to perverse tax policy. Indeed, Baily himself is careful to note that the decline in effective capital stock may have been caused by structural changes in the U.S. economy due to such factors as increased foreign trade. The use of Tobin's q to explain the total factor productivity residual may simply substitute one "measure of ignorance" for another.

The second problem with using q theory arises because changes in the value of the capital stock due to obsolescence do not necessarily imply changes in the effectiveness of capital used in production. In Solow's vintage model, for example, the introduction of superior new capital reduces the net income accruing to old capital, but this capital continues to be operated so long as the net income of the vintage is positive. And, as we shall see below, it is even possible that older capital is operated more intensively for a period of time after the energy price shock renders old capital obsolete. This can occur if there is substantial uncertainty about the nature and speed of introduction of new energy-saving technology.

The studies by Berndt and Wood (1984) and Berndt et al. (1985) provides a more direct approach that avoids asset valuation problems associated with Tobin's q. They develop a putty-clay model in which each vintage of capital is built with a particular energy intensity based on the relative energy-capital prices prevailing at the date the capital was placed in service. Each vintage can be operated at a different intensity by switching labor from one vintage to another. Since energy and capital are "bundled," a rise in the cost of energy will cause those vintages designed under the assumption of lower energy prices to be operated less intensively.

In this framework, utilization is defined as $B_\tau = K^*_\tau / K_\tau$, where K^*_τ again denotes effective capital input and K the stock of capital. It is then shown that

$$\frac{\partial \ln B_\tau}{\partial \ln P^*_{EK,\tau}} = -\sigma, \tag{10}$$

where $P^*_{EK,\tau}$ is the expected relative price of capital services and energy at σ is the ex ante elasticity of substitution between capital and energy. From (7), it is evident that changes in B_τ introduce biases in the measurement of total factor productivity. Indeed, (7) can be rewritten as

$$\hat{A} = \hat{A}^* + S_K \hat{B}_\tau. \tag{7'}$$

This expression, in conjunction with (10), ties the mismeasurement of total factor productivity growth directly to changes in the expected price of energy.

Berndt and Wood (1984) report an average reduction in B_τ of 29% between 1973 and 1974, and a net change of 5% between 1973 and 1978. The second energy price shock reduced B_τ by 7% between 1979 and 1980, and by 3% between 1979 and 1981. This pattern suggests that the Berndt-Wood correction is primarily cyclical and that the secular change in B_τ over the 1970s was much more modest. Indeed, the average annual growth rate of B_τ, i.e., B_τ was 2.1% over the period 1973–1981. Since, capital's share of income was .14 for this period (according to Table 1), (7') implies a correction of 0.3% per year in $\hat{A}$. Since measured total factor productivity grew at an average annual rate of 1.34% over the period 1949–1973, and then declined to −0.31% over the period 1973–1981, the Berndt-Wood correction is not large enough to explain the decline in $\hat{A}$ as measured error.[10]

This finding is repeated in Berndt et al. (1985), who relate (10) to the sources of growth model (2), using a somewhat different rationale for (10). They find that, even when large values of σ are assumed, the implied utilization correction explains almost none of the productivity slowdown in U.S. manufacturing. In sum, the results of Berndt et al. do not appear to support the hypothesis that the energy crises was the primary cause of the productivity slowdown.

5.4 The Vintage Price Approach

We adopt in this study a variant of Baily's willingness-to-pay approach that avoids Tobin's q theory. Instead of inferring the value of capital stock (VK) from financial data that values the entire firm, we estimate capital value directly from market data on used equipment prices. This is possible because, at any time τ, the aggregate value of the capital stock is the sum of the values of the separate vintages:

$$VK = \sum_{s=0}^{T_{max}} P_{I,s} K_s. \tag{11}$$

This equation indicates that, in principle, VK could be measured by valuing the separate components of physical capital assets.[11]

We assume that the $P_{I,s}$ in (11) are equal to the amount an investor would be willing to pay for a piece of capital. This, in turn, is assumed to be equal to the present value of the expected net income stream generated by the asset. For an s-year-old asset, this present value is given by

$$P_{I,s} = \sum_{\tau=0}^{T_s} \frac{P_{K,s+\tau}}{(1+r)^{\tau+1}}, \tag{12}$$

where T_s is the optimal retirement age of an s-year-old asset, r is the expected discount rate, and $P_{K,s+\tau}$ is the expected net income flow accruing to the asset of age $s+\tau$ years in the future. Under constant returns to scale,

$$P_{K,s} = P_Q \left[\frac{Q_s}{K_s} \right] - P_L \left[\frac{L_s}{K_s} \right] - P_E \left[\frac{E_s}{K_s} \right] - P_M \left[\frac{M_s}{K_s} \right], \tag{13}$$

since the value of the output produced by a unit of capital just equals the cost of all the inputs. In a putty-clay model, the quantity ratios are fixed and a rise in P_E (other things being equal) will cause $P_{K,s}$ to fall. The lower net yield to energy-using capital is reflected in $P_{K,s}$ and is "capitalized" in price of used capital via (12). Furthermore, the percentage decline in price will tend to increase with age and the optimal time to retirement will be shortened. These capitalization effects occur without variation in utilization. They will be reinforced if assets of vintage-s are utilized less intensively, as Baily and Berndt et al. postulate.

The geometric interpretation of this model is given in figure 5.1. The curve AA is the locus of prices $P_{I,s}$ plotted against age, s, for a given year t. The curve AA is depicted with a negative slope, reflecting the fact that the value $P_{I,s}$ falls with increasing age because (1) the date of retirement is drawing closer (i.e., because T_s is smaller) and (2) older assets may generate less income because of increased maintenance expenses or decreased productivity (i.e., because $P_{K,s}$ is smaller). While we have drawn this "age-price" profile as convex, following the findings of Hulten and Wykoff (1981a, b), the profile could, in principle, be linear, concave, or irregular.

The capitalization effects discussed above are illustrated in figure 5.1 by a downward shift in the age-price profile from AA to $A'A'$. As $P_{K,s}$ falls because of an increase in P_E, and possibly because utilization decreases, $P_{I,s}$ falls for each age s. A new age-price is thus established at $A'A'$ immediately after the energy price shock. In subsequent years, the introduction of new energy-efficient assets may cause a portion of $A'A'$ to shift upward, in which case the age-price profile has a discontinuity at the age, s, corresponding to the time of the energy price shock.

This simple geometric framework suggests the following measurement procedure: Assume that the age-price profiles of a given set of assets are similar and collect data on the resale value of assets of different vintages; then, fit separate curves for the years before and after the energy crisis. The impact of the energy crisis should then be revealed by the magnitude of the downward shift in the postenergy shock age-price profiles.

The appearance of a downward shift in the age-price profile must, however, be interpreted with care. The shift may be the result of factors not related to energy prices. Similarly, the failure to detect a shift may be due to other factors offsetting the energy effect. However, if this is the case, the impact of the energy price shock is neutralized and the energy crises is not a plausible explanation of the productivity slowdown.

Second, a shift might signal the capitalization of higher energy costs without any change in output, as $P_{I,s}$ falls because P_E has risen, but $F(K,L,E,M)$ remains constant. In this case, there is no utilization effect and no explanation of the productivity slowdown. Thus, a downward shift in the age-profile does not necessarily imply confirmation of Baily's obsolescence hypothesis.

On the other hand, a significant decline in the rate of utilization of an asset that does not lead to a reduction in the asset's inflation-corrected value is hard to imagine. If firms plan to use a given vintage of capital less intensively after an energy price shock, it is unlikely that

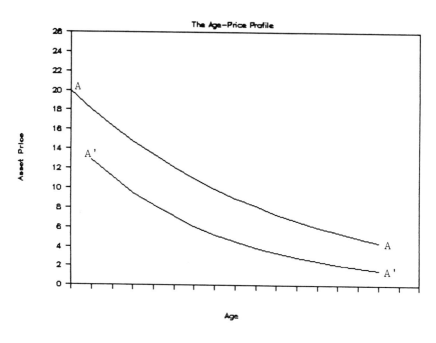

Figure 5.1

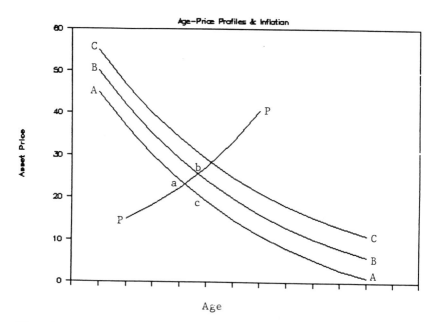

Figure 5.2

other firms would be willing to pay more for capital of that vintage after the price shock than before. A failure to detect a downward shift in the age-price profile thus constitutes evidence against the importance of the energy-induced obsolescence effect and the lower utilization of capital effect. It would also imply that the model of equations (11)–(13) is of limited relevance, since it means that an increase in P_E does not lead to a decline in $P_{I,s}$.

5.5   The Econometric Model

The framework implied by figure 5.1 requires further development in order to serve as an econometric model. First, and most important, inflation must be taken into account. Then, a functional form that is highly flexible for estimating the age-price profile must be developed so that apparent shifts in the function are not the result of functional form misspecification.

General inflation and market-specific factors will cause the asset value of all vintages to change over time. This causes the age-price profile to shift over time, from AA to BB to CC in figure 5.2. As an asset ages, the change in its price is the sum of two effects: a movement along the age-price profile from a to c (aging and obsolescence) and a movement from c on one profile to a point b on the next (revaluation). The observed path of the asset's price with respect to time is the curve PP.

Accurate measurement of the revaluation effect is crucial for the analysis, because an overcorrection for inflation will result in an excessive shift in the profile. Suppose, for example, the actual inflation rate causes a 10% vertical shift in the profile, AA to BB in figure 5.2. An accurate correction for inflation would be conceptually equivalent to shifting the curve BB downward until it is collinear with AA. An inaccurate correction, on the other hand, will create the appearance of a shift in the inflation-corrected BB relative to AA, even though none has occurred. Suppose, for example, that inflation is erroneously thought to be 15% when it is really 10%. The inflation correction to BB will cause the new curve to be below AA, giving the appearance that some event has caused the real age-price profile to shift downward.

Revaluation can be dealt with in two ways—by use of an existing index or by direct estimation. If revaluation is mainly caused by a general inflation, the deflation of used asset prices by a general price index is an appropriate device for capturing the shift of the profiles. If revaluation has more asset specific causes, however, then deflation by an asset specific price index for new equipment may be necessary. This course of action is, however, potentially dangerous. If new assets do not embody energy-saving technology, the energy price shock may also affect the price of new assets. If this is the case, deflation of used asset price by an index of new asset prices will tend to eliminate the downward shift in the age-price profile, which has actually occurred.

One way out of this bind is to assume that the supply of new capital is highly elastic. In this case, a change in energy prices will not greatly affect the equilibrium price of new assets. On the other hand, the supply of used assets is inelastic, so that capitalization via (12) can take place. Deflation of used asset prices using new asset prices is then appropriate.

In addition to deflation, the inclusion of a time trend in the econometric model may also be useful, because no single index will capture all intertemporal shocks to asset values. Furthermore, since the rate of revaluation cannot be assumed to follow a smooth trend (witness the history of the general rate of inflation in the 1970s), the functional form selected for the regression analysis must be highly flexible. Our general procedure for estimating revaluation has been to assume a flexible functional form in the time trend and perform all tests both on undeflated prices and on prices deflated by a machinery and equipment price index.

The functional form must be flexible for other reasons as well. The basic objective of the analysis is to approximate the age-price profiles of figure 5.2 and to detect any shifts occurring after 1973 not associated with revaluation. In so doing, one cannot assume, a priori, that the shapes of the age-price profiles themselves are convex, as shown in figures 5.1 and 5.2. There is considerable controversy over this point, as noted in Hulten and Wykoff (1981a, b), and while the balance of the evidence favors the convex form, the shape of the age-price profile is an empirical issue that should be resolved by data analysis, not by the assumption of a restrictive form.

The functional form should therefore be able to discriminate among a wide range of possible age-price profiles: "one-hoss shay" (concave), straight-line (linear), geometric (convex) depreciation, and others as well. Even apart from inflation effects, failure to allow for sufficient flexibility can result in false shifts in the estimated age-price profiles. This can occur because of cohort effects in the underlying data: If assets are constructed in "binges," the sample data will not be distributed uniformly over the age-price profile. If the underlying age-price profiles are convex, but linear functions are used in the regression analysis, then the profiles may appear to shift downward after 1973 when, in fact, no shift has occurred.

These considerations led us to adopt the Box-Cox power transformation model used in the earlier depreciation studies of Hulten and Wykoff.[12] The Box-Cox model has the following form:

$$\frac{P_i^{\theta_0} - 1}{\theta_0} = \alpha + \beta \frac{S_i^{\theta_1} - 1}{\theta_1} + \gamma \frac{T_i^{\theta_2} - 1}{\theta_2} + \varepsilon_i, \tag{14}$$

where P_i is the observed price of the used asset—corresponding to $P_{l,s}$ in equation (11)—S_i is the age of the asset at the time of sale, T_i is the year that the transaction took place, and ε_i is a random disturbance term. The coefficients α, β, and γ are conventional slope and intercept parameters; θ_0, θ_1, and θ_2 are power transformation parameters that fix the form of the function. When $\theta = (1,1,1)$, the form is linear; when $\theta = (1,0,0)$, it is geometric; and $\theta = (0,0,0)$ yields the log-log firm.

This model can be estimated under the assumption that ε_i is independently normally distributed. Since (14) is highly nonlinear, maximum likelihood methods, combined with grid searches, may be used to estimate the various parameters. The analysis can be carried out with real (i.e., inflation-corrected) P_i and with nominal (i.e., uncorrected) P_i.

The model (14) does not by itself provide a direct estimate of any shift in the age-price profile. To remedy this, we adjust (14) to include a dummy variable d equal to zero before 1973 and one thereafter:

$$\frac{P_i^{\theta_0} - 1}{\theta_0} = \alpha + \beta \frac{S_i^{\theta_1} - 1}{\theta_0} + \frac{T_i^{\theta_2} - 1}{\theta_2} + \phi d \frac{S_i^{\theta_1} - 1}{\theta_1} + \psi d + \varepsilon_i, \tag{15}$$

The theory of the preceding section suggest that ϕ and ψ should be negative if the age-price profile shifted downward after 1973.

5.6   The Data

These econometric models were fitted using data on two general classes of assets: heavy duty construction equipment, which includes five assets—D9 tractors, D6 tractors, motor graders, rubber tire loaders, and back hoes; and machine tools, which covers four general types of assets—turret lathes, milling machines, presses, and grinders. These assets were selected partly because of availability of data sources and partly because they represent one group of energy-intensive assets (construction equipment) and one group of non-energy-intensive assets widely used in the manufacturing industry. Direct energy cost increases should reduce the net return to the former more than to the latter, but energy cost increases may indirectly lower the capital values of the latter, to the extent that higher energy costs reduced demand for energy-using products made by machine tools and thereby lowered quasi rents.

The construction equipment data come from annual issues of International Equipment Exchange and cover the years 1968 to 1982. Each observation corresponds to a single transaction and contains information covering the auction price and individual asset characteristics, such as serial number, age, condition, ancillary equipment (tractor blade, canopy, air conditioners), and model number. In some instances, the prices may not reflect actual transactions but rather sub rosa agreements in which the owner agrees to buy back his asset if the auction price does not exceed his reservation price. However, the extent of this "buy-back" activity is impossible to document, and we have no way of knowing which transactions represent buy-backs.

The machine tool data were collected from auction reports compiled by the Machine Dealers National Association (MDNA). These reports cover the period between 1954 and 1983 and, for the most part, were issued monthly.[13] Each observation typically includes the auction price, the general condition of the asset, the serial number, and the configuration of that particular asset (i.e., whether it includes special equipment, the size of the chuck, etc.). If the age of the asset was not noted in the auction report, we were able to determine the age of the asset from the serial number.[14]

The available data for the construction equipment were sufficiently detailed to permit us to adjust prices to reflect differences in asset configuration. In other words, the adjusted prices for these assets reflect only the basic asset and not different asset add-ons, (e.g. the type of engine, blade attachments, and general conditions, etc.).

While some of the data for machine tools contains information on asset configuration, the coverage is too sparse to permit the estimation of the effects of different asset options on prices.[15] In order to achieve sufficient sample sizes, the minimum requirements for inclusion were that each observation have the price and either the age or a serial number, which would permit us to determine the age.

In the case of machine tools, we attempted to limit the variance in prices due to differences in makes and models by restricting the sample and through the use of dummy variables. For turret lathes, we restricted the sample to lathes manufactured by Warner and Swasey, one of the largest producers. Dummy variables were used to distinguish between different models. The milling machine sample was restricted to machines manufactured by Bridgeport, one of the most widely used machine tool brands in the world. The press sample consisted mainly of machines manufactured by Bliss Mfg. Co. and a few others. Obtaining a sample of sufficient size was more difficult for grinders; therefore observations for grinders produced by five different manufacturers were used; but the sample was dominated by machines produced by two firms.

Despite potential shortcomings, we assembled substantial samples of used asset auction prices. A summary of the sample characteristics is presented in table 5.2. Sample sizes range between 370 observations for back hoes to 1,241 observations for D9 tractors. Several general characteristics of the two major asset classes emerge from these data. Construction equipment assets are typically more expensive and shorter lived than machine tools. The rather high average ages for machine tools, greater than 20 years old for three classes, are noteworthy.

Average prices by age interval are shown in figure 5.3 for all nine assets. Prices were first adjusted for inflation using the Bureau of Labor Statistics deflators for metal-cutting machine tools and for construction equipment. Average prices were then calculated by age for the pre- and postenergy crisis eras. The resulting curves are actual age-price profiles corresponding to the age-price profiles depicted in figures 5.1 and 5.2. Inspection of figure 5.3 reveals the characteristic downward form of the age-price profile. Assets tend to lose value as they age, and, tend to lose relatively more value in the earlier years of life. This is consistent with most other studies of used asset prices.

Figure 5.3 also sheds some light on the capitalization of higher energy costs into capital values issue, at least for construction equipment. The age-price profiles of these assets appear to shift upward in three cases and might shift upward in one other case. The picture for machine tools is much less clear. Given the much greater variance in the machine tool prices within each class, this lack of clarity is not surprising. Recall that the machine tool data were not standardized for different add-ons, as were the construction equipment data. Thus, the post-1973 age-price profiles overlap the pre-1973 profiles, leaving some ambiguity regarding the price decline issue. These ambiguities will be addressed in the formal econometric analysis of the following section.

Table 5.2
Summary statistics of project date

Asset class	Number of observations	Maximum age	Sample years	Mean values		Price
				Age	Year	
Construction equipment						
D9 tractors	1241	27	1968–1982	10	1976	31235
D6 tractors	1063	38	1968–1982	11	1976	19454
Motor graders	1050	38	1968–1982	14	1975	18691
Rubber tire loaders	554	19	1968–1982	8	1979	40776
Backhoes	370	19	1968–1982	7	1978	6832
Machine tools						
Turret lathes	963	64	1954–1983	26	1965	4611
Milling machines	1027	42	1954–1983	12	1971	2232
Grinders	783	59	1954–1983	20	1970	4765
Presses	430	60	1954–1983	23	1967	7059

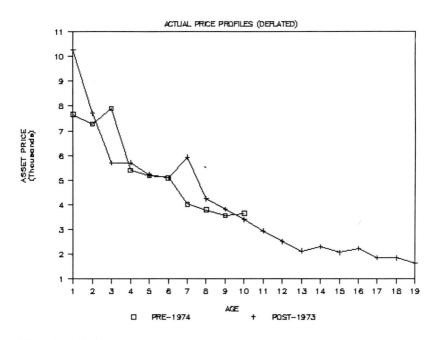

Figure 5.3   Backhoes.

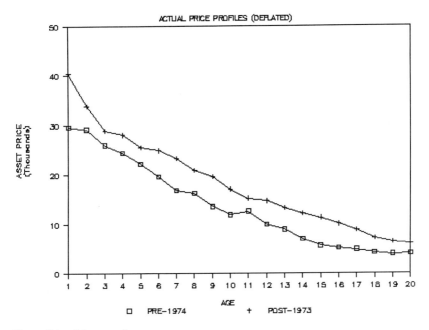

Figure 5.3   Motor graders.

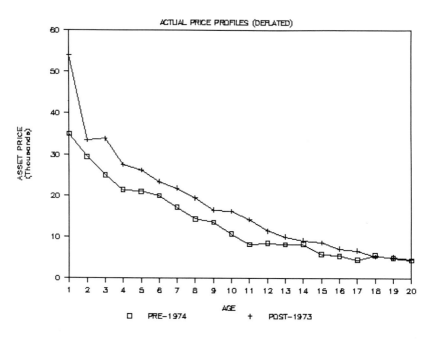

Figure 5.3   D6 tractors.

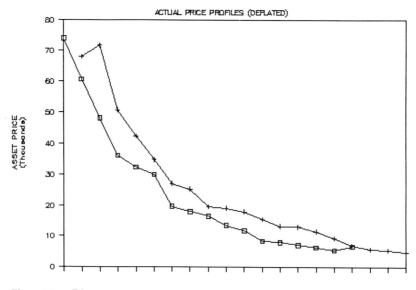

Figure 5.3   D9 tractors.

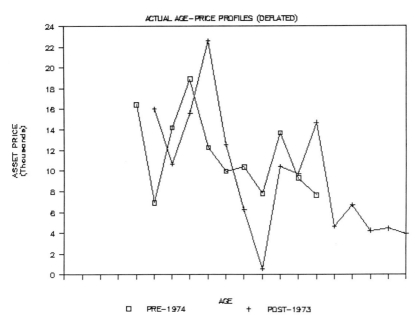

Figure 5.3   Turret lathes.

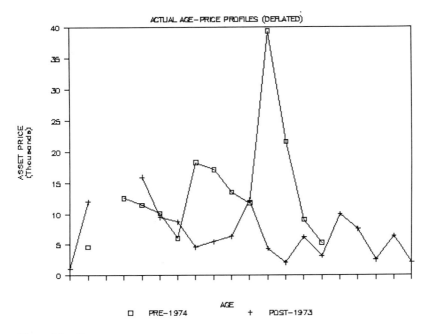

Figure 5.3   Presses.

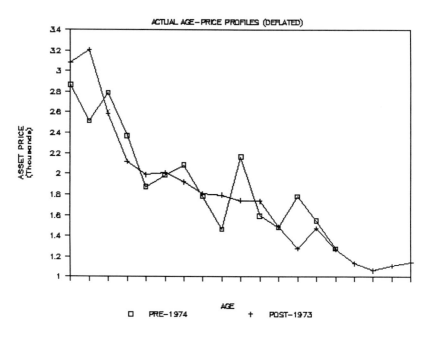

Figure 5.3   Milling machines.

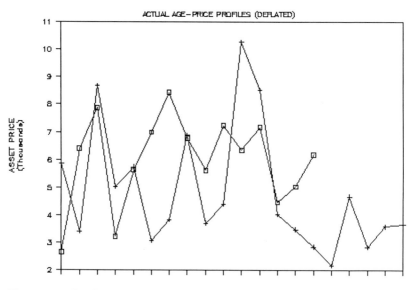

Figure 5.3   Grinders.

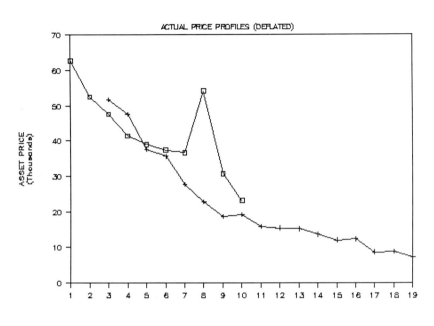

Figure 5.3   Rubber tire loaders.

5.7   Econometric Results

The parameters of (15) were estimated using maximum likelihood techniques, with deflated asset prices used as the dependent variable. The results are presented in table 5.3. The estimated coefficients of the age variable are uniformly negative, as expected, and statistically significant at conventional levels. The coefficients of time are significant in less than half the nine cases and the signs of the significant coefficients are divided between positive and negative. Since the time variable is introduced in addition to the deflation procedure as a correction for inflation, this last result suggests that the deflation procedure did not systematically over- or underestimate inflation.

The estimated coefficients of the intercept dummy variable, ψ, were significant and positive for four of the five construction equipment classes. This indicates, other things being equal, an upward shift in the age-price profile. The fifth class, back hoes, yielded a negative, but statistically insignificant, estimate. The machine tool classes on the other hand, yielded significantly negative estimates of the intercept dummy variable in three of the four asset classes. The fourth class, milling machines, yielded a statistically insignificant but positive estimate.

Table 5.3
Box-Cox dummy variable model estimates

Asset class	α (constant)	β (age)	λ (time)	ψ (intercept) (dummy)	φ (age) (dummy)	θ₀	θ₁	θ₂
Machine tools								
Turret lathe	18.546 (1.633)	-1.922 (.544)	.000 (.000)	-1.617 (.588)	.517 (.185)	.084 (.013)	.063 (.093)	8.308 (.043)
Milling machines	1.826 (.001)	-.003 (.000)	.000 (.000)	.001 (.001)	.000 (.000)	-.541 (.000)	.451 (.022)	2.162 (.066)
Presses	7.960 (.820)	-.003 (.004)	1.600 (1.705)	-.641 (.201)	.008 (.002)	-.021 (.024)	1.429 (.140)	-3.509 (2.352)
Grinders	6.445 (.284)	-.052 (.000)	.000 (.000)	-.268 (.057)	.004 (.000)	-.073 (.011)	1.698 (.069)	6.545 (.060)
Construction equipment								
D6 tractors	27.30 (.580)	-1.216 (.107)	1.011 (.294)	.990 (.240)	-.053 (.079)	.165 (.003)	.623 (.035)	-.430 (.229)
D9 tractors	66.03 (2.280)	-6.984 (.785)	-.011 (.003)	2.97 (.870)	1.374 (.232)	.254 (.039)	.399 (.053)	2.874 (.979)
Motor graders	72.73 (2.240)	-3.981 (.337)	1.597 (.461)	2.18 (.770)	.174 (.089)	.302 (.004)	.664 (.030)	.181 (.183)
Rubber tire loaders	10.58 (.100)	-.140 (.044)	-.006 (.000)	.640 (.140)	-.162 (.074)	-.007 (.001)	.377 (.145)	2.175 (.026)
Backhoes	6.37 (.990)	-.119 (.022)	3.993 (3.075)	-.140 (.090)	.007 (.140)	-.016 (.002)	.896 (.111)	-1.793 (.689)

a. Standard errors in parentheses.

Estimates of the intercept dummy variable are not sufficient to determine the overall shift in the age-price profile. The slope dummy variable, ϕ, indicates the degree to which the slope of the profile "twists" over time. The postenergy crisis age-price profile can thus intersect the precrisis profile and the overall result can therefore be ambiguous. To check this possibility visually, we have plotted the pre- and post-1973 profile in figure 5.4. These plots confirm that crossing does occur in the milling machine and rubber tire loader classes. The remaining construction equipment classes show an upward shift in the age-price profile and the remaining machine tool classes show a downward shift.

Maximum likelihood estimates of the parameters in (15) were also obtained using the unflated used assets prices. The results were much the same as in the deflated case, except that the coefficient of time tends to be statistically significant in more cases and the sign is uniformly positive, as might be expected. The estimates of the intercept dummy variable were uniformly significant, but the dichotomy between the two general classes is still evident.

These results suggest that the post-1973 shift in the age-price profile is highly asset specific. This pattern does not lend support to the obsolescence hypothesis since the more energy-intensive class of assets, construction equipment, apparently become more valuable after the energy crisis, not less valuable as predicted by the obsolescence hypothesis.[16]

If there is any pattern evident in figure 5.4, it is consistent with the hypothesis that energy costs were not a significant factor in used asset valuation. In this case, one would predict upward or downward shifts according to market-specific forces not related to energy. A study of two general types of assets might then yield a random distribution of shifts, possibly like those observed in figure 5.4. Further research with additional asset categories would be useful in sorting out the competing hypotheses.[17]

Another possible explanation for the upward shifts is that the model of section 5.3 fails to capture the full complexity of the problem. It may be that the price shock created uncertainty about the appropriate technology and about relative prices in the new post-energy price shock period. An implication of the Solow vintage capital model is that, under uncertainty, expected changes in future technology are relevant for deciding whether to adopt the most recent innovation.[18] This uncertainty might therefore have led to a wait-and-see strategy in which new capital investment was deferred. If this

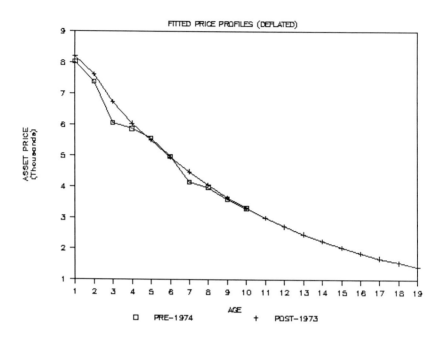

Figure 5.4 Backhoes.

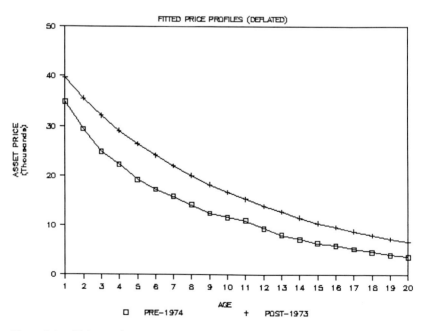

Figure 5.4 Motor graders.

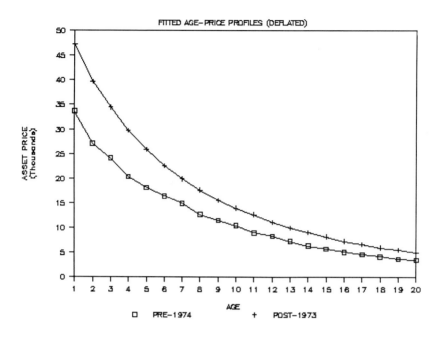

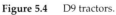

Figure 5.4   D6 tractors.

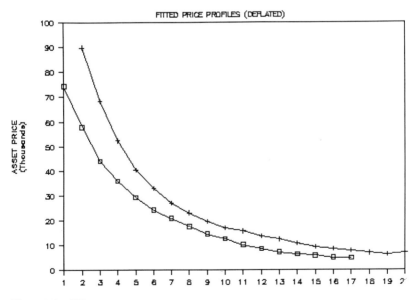

Figure 5.4   D9 tractors.

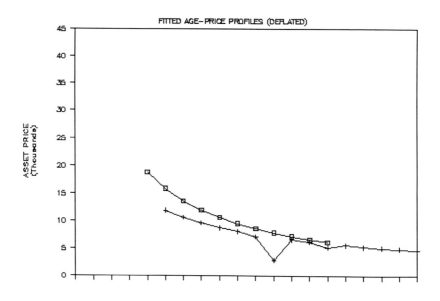

Figure 5.4 Turret lathes.

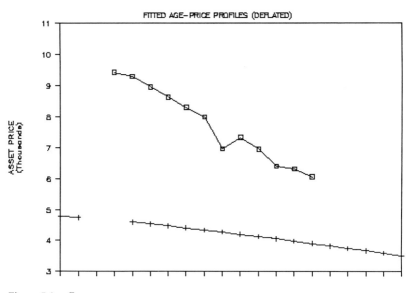

Figure 5.4 Presses.

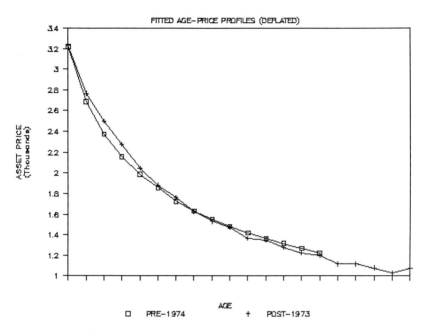

Figure 5.4 Milling machines.

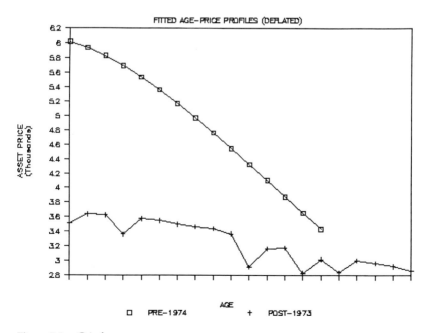

Figure 5.4 Grinders.

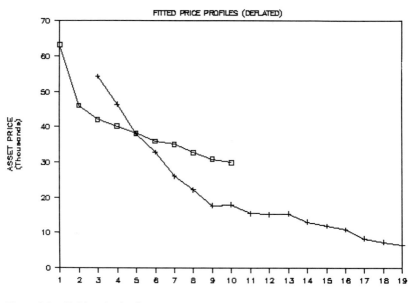

Figure 5.4   Rubber tire loaders.

occurred, then older assets would have been used more intensively than before and would be relatively more valuable. It is not clear, however, why this effect should apply to one type of asset but not another.[19]

In conclusion, it should be stressed that since our model does not allow for the influence of other factors, we cannot completely rule out energy price effects. The energy shocks of the 1970s may have had a partial effect that was offset by other factors. However, even if this were the case, it is not appropriate to conclude that the energy shock caused the productivity slowdown.

5.8   Summary

The recent collapse in energy prices gives renewed significance to the link between energy costs and industrial economic growth. If the 1970s energy price increase shocks retarded growth, then the subsequent fall in the mid-1980s may harbinger more rapid future growth. Unfortunately, this link has been hard to establish, and the results of the sample of assets studied in this chapter do not encourage the view that such a link exists.

Our results are, however, encouraging from another point of view. Estimates of economic depreciation are widely used in the imputation of the cost of capital services, P_K, and in perpetual inventory estimates of capital stocks. As noted above, it is generally assumed that depreciation follows a stationary process, so that the same pattern of depreciation can be applied over time. The findings of this chapter support this approach. While depreciation almost certainly varies form year to year in response to a variety of factors, we have found that a major event like the energy crises, which had the potential of significantly increasing the rate of obsolescence, did not in fact result in a systematic change in age-price profiles. This lends confidence to procedures that assume stationarity in order to achieve a major degree of simplification (and because non-stationarity is so difficult to deal with empirically). Or, put simply, the use of a single number to characterize the process of economic depreciation (of a given type of capital asset) seems justified in light of the results of this chapter.

Notes

1. These estimates are obtained from the BLS publication *Trends in Multifactor Productivity, 1948–81*, and subsequent press releases.

2. Denison (1979a, b) provides a detailed survey of the various theories of the productivity slowdown. See also Nordhaus (1980).

3. Tobin's average q is the financial value of a firm divided by the replacement cost of the firm's capital. If that capital becomes obsolete, the value of the firm is reduced and the q ratio declines. This effect is described in greater detail below.

4. Obsolescence, as conventionally defined, refers to the loss in the value of existing capital because it is no longer technologically suited to economic conditions or because technically superior alternatives become available. Obsolescence, in sense of the Baily hypothesis, refers to a loss in output. As we shall see later, the two definitions are not equivalent: The second definition implies the first but not vice versa.

5. It should be stressed, here, that the focus of this research is the relationship between energy and economic growth. While the methods used in this chapter are almost identical to those developed in earlier studies of economic depreciation (Hulten and Wykoff, 1981a,b), it is not our intention to offer new estimates of economic depreciation or to test the stability of our previous estimates in light of the energy crisis. This latter course would have required (1) data on a more extensive list of assets than was available for the pre- and post-energy crisis years; (2) estimates of how the energy crisis affected retirements of assets from service; and (3) a precise definition of stability, since the period-to-period change in the depreciation rate of a particular asset may be statistically significant, but the change so small that it is of little consequence for the measure of capital (see Bureau of Labor Statistics, 1983, for a detailed analysis of this point).

6. In discussions of aggregate growth, Q is interpreted as real value added and the input list is restricted to capital and labor.

7. See Solow (1957) or Jorgenson and Griliches (1967) for the derivation of equation like (2).

8. For a more complete survey of the literature on the relationship between energy prices and productivity growth, see Berndt and Wood (1985).

9. The assumption, here, is that the rise in energy prices causes a net decline in the utilization of capital stock. Recalling the example of the trucking firm, some capital is used more intensively and other capital less intensively as energy prices change. The direction of the utilization effect is an empirical issue; the theoretical point is that utilization effects should not be ignored.

10. This is, if the true growth rate of the total factor productivity residual, A, remained at the pre-energy crisis growth rate of measured TFP, A, the correction $S_K B$ would equal 1.65% or five times the observed value of this variable. It is worth noting that Berndt and Wood do find a large implied impact of energy prices on the value of used capital. The relationship between energy prices and used capital prices is studied in detail in subsequent sections of this paper.

11. The VK in (8) is the present value of the expected flow of net income accruing to capital. Equation (11) indicates that this flow can be disaggregated by the vintage of the capital generating that income.

12. In earlier work with age-price profiles, Hulten and Wykoff (1981a, 1981b) corrected for censored sample bias by deflating asset prices by the probability of retirement. We did not make this adjustment in this study because we do not have data on the change in retirement after 1973, and because deflation by the same retirement function would not change the pre- and post-1973 comparison by age-price profiles.

13. The MDNA is a professional organization of dealers in used machine tools. These reports consist of data on auction transactions for a wide range of machine tools submitted by MDNA members. The coverage of these reports obviously varies over time. There were no reports compiled during the years 1971 and 1972 and for some periods the number of observations greatly exceed those reported in other periods.

14. The relationship between serial numbers and the year of manufacture is published for most types and makes of machine tools in The Serial Number Reference Book for Metal Working Machinery, (9th edition) [1983]. In some cases, it was necessary to obtain data for later years directly from the manufacturers.

15. Attempts were made using dummy variables to correct for differences in asset configuration. Except in the few cases noted below, this approach did not yield statistically significant results.

16. Our results also bear on the simulated age-price profiles reported by Berndt and Wood (1985). Our findings suggest that potentially large effects noted by Berndt and Wood did not occur for the assets studied in this paper.

It must, however, be noted that Berndt and Wood were concerned with *ceteris paribus* effects; i.e., the change in the age-price profile due to a change in energy price, holding other factors constant, while the estimates of this paper refer to *mutatis mutandi* shifts in the age-price profile.

17. Evidence from other studies does tend to support the conclusions of this paper. In a study of several categories of industrial equipment, Shriver (1986) finds that the ratio of the value of seven-year-old equipment to new equipment did not decline appreciably after 1973. For all classes of assets, he reports that the ratio was .33 in 1973, .32 in 1976, and .34 in 1980. While this study was not specifically intended as an analysis of energy-induced obsolescence, it is nonetheless noteworthy because of the comprehensiveness of the asset categories studied.

18. In a putty-clay vintage model, the adoption of a new energy efficient technology immediately after an energy price shock may be unprofitable if an even more energy efficient technology is on the horizon. In this case, the newly adopted technology might be rendered obsolete itself and a firm would have an incentive to defer investment and prolong its use of existing equipment. Alternatively, uncertainty about the permanence of the energy price shock might also lead to an optimal strategy of utilizing old equipment more intensively than originally planned.

19. A further complication arises because the energy price shocks may have affected the market for used assets on the *demand* side. For example, to the extent that construction equipment were used to increase coal production, the energy crisis may have increased utilization of construction equipment rather than a reduction. If there is any mismeasurement of capital, it would work in the opposite direction of the Baily hypothesis.

References

Ackerlof, George (1970), "The Market for Lemons" *Quarterly Journal of Economics*, 3, August, 488–500.

Baily, Martin N. (1981), "Productivity and the Services of Capital and Labor," *Brookings Papers on Economic Activity*, 1, 1–50.

Berndt, Ernst R. (1980), "Energy Price Increases and the Productivity Slowdown in U.S. Manufacturing," The Decline in Productivity Growth, Federal Reserve Bank of Boston, Conference Series No. 22, Boston, 60–89.

Berndt, Ernst R., and David O. Wood (1979), "Engineering and Econometric Interpretations of Energy Capital Complementary," *American Economic Review*, 69, June, 342–354.

——— (1984), "Energy Price Changes and the Induced Revaluation of Durable Capital in U.S. Manufacturing during the OPEC Decade," MIT Energy Lab Report No. 84–003.

Berndt, Ernst R., Shunseke Mori, Takamitsu Sawa, and David O. Wood (1985), "Energy Price Shocks and Productivity Growth in Japan and U.S. Manufacturing Industry," paper presented at the Conference on Productivity Growth in Japan and the United States, Conference on Research in Income and Wealth, Cambridge, MA, August 26–28.

(U.S. Department of Labor) Bureau of Labor Statistics (1983), *Trends in Multifactor Productivity, 1948–81*, Bulletin 2178, U.S.G.P.O., Washington, D.C., September.

Denison, Edward F. (1979a), "Explanations of Declining Productivity Growth," *Survey of Current Business*, 59, August, 1–24.

_____ (1979b), *Accounting for Slower Economic Growth: The United States in the 1970s*, Brookings Institution, Washington, D.C.

Hudson, Edward A., and Dale W. Jorgenson (1978), "Energy Prices and the U.S. Economy, 1972–1976," *Natural Resources Journal*, 18, October, 877–897.

Hulten, Charles R., and Frank C. Wykoff (1981a), "The Estimation of Economic Depreciation Using Vintage Asset Prices," *Journal of Econometrics*, 15, April, 367–396.

_____ (1981b), "The Measurement of Economic Depreciation," in Charles R. Hulten, ed., *Depreciation, Inflation, and the Taxation of Income from Capital*, The Urban Institute Press, Washington, D.C.

Jorgenson, Dale W. (1984), "The Role of Energy in Productivity Growth," in John W. Kendrick, ed., *International Comparisons of Productivity and the Causes of the Slowdown*, Ballinger, Cambridge, MA, 279–323.

Jorgenson, Dale W., and Barbara M. Fraumeni (1981), "Relative Prices and Technical Change," in Ernest R. Berndt and Barry Field, eds., *Modeling and Measuring Natural Resource Substitution*, MIT Press, Cambridge, MA, 17–47.

Jorgenson, Dale W., and Zvi Griliches (1967), "The Explanation of Productivity Change," *Review of Economic Studies*, 34, August, 249–283.

Nordhaus, William D. (1980), "Policy Responses to the Productivity Slowdown," The Decline in Productivity Growth, Federal Reserve Bank of Boston, Conference Series No. 22, Boston, 147–172.

Rasche, Robert H., and John A. Tatom (1977a), "The Effects of the New Energy Price Regime on Economic Capacity, Production, and Prices," *Federal Reserve Bank of St. Louis Review*, 59, May, 2–12.

_____ (1977b), "Energy Resources and Potential GNP," *Federal Reserve Bank of St. Louis Review*, 59, June, 10–24.

Solow, Robert M. (1957), "Technical Change and the Aggregate Production Function," *Review of Economics and Statistics*, 39, August, 312–320.

_____ (1970), *Growth Theory: An Exposition*, Oxford University Press, New York and Oxford.

Summers, Lawrence H. (1981), "Taxation and Corporate Investment: A q-Theory Approach," *Brookings Papers on Economic Activity*, 1, 67–127.

6

Economic Depreciation and the User Cost of Business-Leased Automobiles

Frank C. Wykoff

6.1 Introduction

This chapter has two objectives—to estimate economic depreciation of business-leased automobiles and to evaluate the user-cost-of-capital and by implication the productive efficiency of business automobiles from 1978 to 1987. This period covers a major recession and a significant expansion as well as three different tax regimes including the Tax Reform Act of 1986.

The econometric estimates of depreciation are based on a 40,000 observation subsample drawn from a pool of 148,000 observations on market transaction prices of used automobiles sold by a major national leasing company from 1982 to 1986. Economic depreciation patterns are estimated for 4 automobile models from both new and used asset prices using the Box-Cox power transformation model.[1]

After estimating economic depreciation patterns for the 4 automobile models, we aggregate the rates into a single pattern for the class of business automobiles. Using existing estimates of interest rates and inflation, we construct user cost equations for debt and equity financed new and used automobiles from 1978 to 1987. Then, exploiting the price-quantity duality relation between marginal rates of substitution and user-costs, we construct efficiency patterns in each year. This gives us an index of efficiency over the time period for both new and used business-leased automobiles.

The data for this study provide a unique opportunity to estimate depreciation on business-leased automobiles. First, no research has been published on business-use cars. These cars are driven far more

I wish to thank David Hoekman for computer assistance. I alone am responsible for the contents of this chapter.

than household-use cars—about 1.7 times the mileage of household-use cars in the first few years—and thus their depreciation rates are probably larger. Second, the breadth of coverage of this data across cars, ages, and years, the completeness of each record on dates, condition, and price, and the actual market basis for prices recorded from legal documents are unique.

Our basic empirical result is that economic depreciation on business-leased automobiles is more rapid than a constant geometric rate pattern. First-year depreciation ranges from 35% to 40%. Second-year depreciation is about 20% and depreciation is approximately constant thereafter. Though we can only speculate about the cause of rapid depreciation on new business-use cars, relative to that of household-use cars, we suspect that it reflects the intense use of business cars.

User costs of new cars were quite volatile over the period 1978 to 1987, with the largest cost increases resulting from interest rate increases and acquisition price increases. Car prices fell, relative to the consumer price index, in 1979, 1980, 1981, and 1985 during periods of general inflation. Although the 1981 tax cuts substantially reduced costs, they were overwhelmed by interest rate and price effects. The new Alternative Minimum Tax (AMT) of 1986 could have a major impact on capital costs. Since these taxes fall on business cars, they raise the cost of capital well above the cost to household users, and this lowers the productive efficiency of the business automobile stock.

Sections 6.2 and 6.3 contain an analysis of problems encountered in measuring depreciation from new and used asset prices, the econometric model and methodology used to resolve these problems, and a description of the data. Section 6.4 contains the estimates of the unknown coefficients of the model and the patterns of economic depreciation. These results are compared to existing evidence on automobile depreciation. Section 6.5 contains the cost of capital measures and comments on asset efficiency.

6.2 Measurement and the Econometric Model

6.2.1 Deterioration, Obsolescence, and Revaluation

Estimation of depreciation is complex because several distinct forces operate on asset prices simultaneously.[2] To illustrate this, we present a model relating asset prices to the stream of user costs. Let $P_{I,s}$ represent the present value of the future stream of expected net user costs (or implicit rentals) on an asset. For an s-year-old car, this present value is given by

$$P_{I,\,s} = \sum_{x=0}^{A_s} \frac{C_{K,\,s+x}}{(1+r)^{x+1}}, \tag{1}$$

where A_s is the expected retirement age of an s-year-old car, r is the expected discount rate, and $C_{K,\,s}$ is the net user cost (or rental price) of the service flow provided by the asset at age s. We ignore taxes as this point, so that equation (1) does not include any tax terms. For simplicity, we also assume that the rates of inflation and discount are expected to remain constant.

As an asset ages, its inflation-corrected value falls. This reflects three forces. First, the date of retirement is drawing closer, so that the asset has fewer years of productive life (i.e., A_s is smaller). Second, old assets suffer input-decay because of increased maintenance expenses and down time (i.e., $C_{K,\,s}$ is smaller). Third, old assets suffer output-decay, because they slow down, wear out, and generally suffer physical decrepitation. We call the combination of these three forces, which are strictly related to aging, *deterioration*.

A given car usually loses value as it ages for an entirely different reason based on technological change and vintage. As a car ages, new vintages of cars come on line that are typically superior since they embody new technologies that make them faster, more efficient, durable, lighter, comfortable, and so forth. To the extent that one cannot retrofit old cars with new features, old cars become worth less than newer ones. This process, called *obsolescence*, is a vintage specific effect coinciding with the actual aging process of a given stock of assets—an entire "cohort." The combined effects of deterioration and obsolescence imply that a plot of vintage prices against age will normally exhibit a downward trend. We depict this downward trend by the curve AA, as an age-price profile, in figure 6.1.

Curve AA does not reflect the entire historical experience of an asset class if we allow for inflation and other changes in supply and demand that occur over time and that effect the prices of cars from one period to the next. We call these combined inter-temporal effects *revaluation*. General inflation and market-specific price effects will cause the asset value of all vintages to change over time. This causes the age-price profile to shift. This revaluation effect is illustrated as the shift from AA to BB to CC in figure 6.1. As the asset ages, the change in its price is the sum of two effects: a movement along the age-price profile from a to a' (aging and obsolescence) and a movement from a' on one profile to b on the next (revaluation). The observed path of the asset's price with respect to time is the curve PP.

Accurate measurement of the depreciation and revaluation effects is important, because errors in either can lead to measurement errors in the other. Revaluation can be dealt with in two ways—by use of an existing index or by direct estimation. Our general strategy for estimating revaluation is to assume a flexible functional form in the time trend and perform tests both on undeflated prices and on prices deflated by a Bureau of Economic Analysis automobile and parts price index taken from *The Survey of Current Business*.

6.2.2   The Box-Cox Power Transformation

We use the Box-Cox power transformation model, as described in Hulten and Wykoff (1981a), which has the following form:

$$P_i^* = a_0 + a_1 S_i^* + a_2 T_i^* + u_i, \qquad (2)$$

where

$$P_i^* = \begin{cases} \dfrac{P_i^{g_0} - 1}{g_0} & \text{if } g_0 \neq 0 \\ \ln P_i & \text{if } g_0 = 0, \end{cases} \qquad S_i^* = \begin{cases} \dfrac{S_i^{g_1} - 1}{g_1} & \text{if } g_1 \neq 0 \\ \ln S_i & \text{if } g_1 = 0, \end{cases}$$

$$T_i^* = \begin{cases} \dfrac{T_i^{g_2} - 1}{g_2} & \text{if } g_2 \neq 0 \\ \ln T_i & \text{if } g_2 = 0, \end{cases}$$

where P_i is the observed price of the used asset corresponding to $P_{I,s}$ in equation (1), S_i is the age of the asset at the time of sale, T_i is the year that the transaction took place—s in equation (1) is $T_i - S_i$—and u_i is a random disturbance term. The coefficients a_0, a_1, and a_2 are conventional slope and intercept parameters; g_0, g_1, and g_2 are power transformation parameters that fix the form of the function. When $g = (1,1,1)$, the form is linear; when $g = (1,0,0)$, it is geometric, and $g = (0,0,0)$ yields the log-log form.[3]

6.2.3   Cohort Heterogeneity and Retirement

One tends to think of age-price profiles on individual assets, but in fact, virtually all investment models aggregate capital, all tax laws classify assets in groups, and most firms use many assets of the same

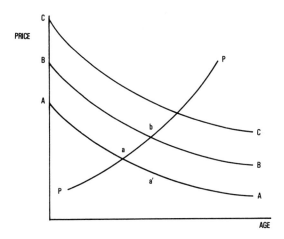

Figure 6.1   Age-price profiles and inflation effects.

type. Thus our principal interest is in depreciation of an entire depreciable cohort. We must consider two features of a cohort of depreciable assets that are not apparent when thinking in terms of individual units. Virtually every cohort of assets is heterogeneous in that each class includes different types of units. Even business-leased autos vary quite a bit within the class—some are smaller, some faster, some better equipped. This characterization leads to the *heterogeneity problem*.

Generally, the price-age profile, corrected for inflation, of a heterogeneous class of assets will be convex in that early years' depreciation will be greater than that in subsequent years. This means that asset class depreciation is "accelerated"; i.e., more depreciation occurs in earlier years.[4] This is because in early years average depreciation on the cohort depends on depreciation of the most rapidly depreciating assets as well as on all other assets in the class. Once the fastest depreciating assets have been retired, the next fastest depreciating assets are drawn down. After they, in turn, are retired, only slower depreciating assets are included from the original cohort. This means that even if depreciation on individual units in the cohort depreciate according to a flat pattern, such as one-hoss-shay or straight line, the entire cohort will depreciate according to a convex, or accelerated, pattern.

We illustrate the heterogeneity problem with a hypothetical example of an asset class containing 4 types of assets. For simplicity assume that each class has a different life—5, 10, 15, and 20 years—but that each asset type depreciates along a straight line pattern. These

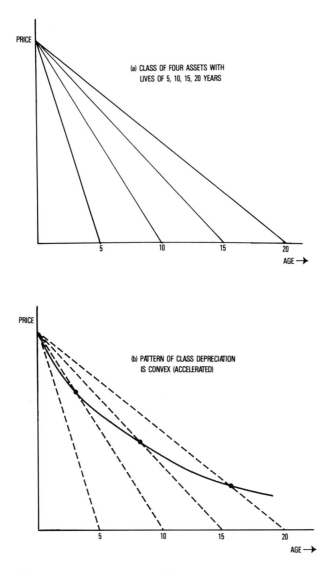

Figure 6.2 Heterogeneity problem.

are illustrated in panel (a) of figure 6.2. The pattern of depreciation for the class is convex or accelerated.

The cohort will depreciate greatest over the first 5-year interval, because depreciation in the first 5 years is the average of that of 5-, 10-, 15-, and 20-year assets. If asset holdings are equally distributed across types, then the average rate from age 0 to 5 is .10425. Depreciation, on average, of the cohort over years 5 to 10 will be the average of 10-, 15-, and 20-year assets, since the 5-year assets are now gone. The average depreciation rate over this second interval is .072. Average depreciation from years 10 to 15 is .058 and from years 15 to 20 is .05. Panel (b) depicts the pattern of cohort depreciation: .104, .072 .058, .050. Thus, cohort depreciation results in a price-age profile that is convex , regardless of the depreciation of individual units. Even a cohort of light bulbs, or one-hoss shays, will, due to heterogeneity, typically depreciate in a convex, or accelerated, pattern.

A second difficulty in dealing with cohorts is the retirement problem. To estimate depreciation from used prices, one must allow for retirement of assets in the original cohort, nonsurvivors, as well as the loss of value of those assets still in service—survivors. Otherwise, only assets still in service enter into calculation of depreciation of the entire original cohort. This biases depreciation estimates upward.[5]

In order to depreciate the original cohort, we estimate the prices of assets in service adjusted for retirements. To adjust for retirements, we construct a retirement distribution. This is done in two stages. First, we select a retirement curve that can be fitted to a specific asset based on the average life time of the asset. Second, we determine the average lifetime of automobiles to which the retirement curve will be fitted. We discuss construction of the retirement distribution in section 6.3.

One minus the probability of retirement distribution is the probability of survival—the probability of assets surviving to any given age. We adjust for retirement by deflating the prices of survivors at each age by the probability of survival. This is equivalent to adding back into the sample pool the nonsurvivors at zero price. Thus, the price at each age is an average of the prices of survivors and nonsurvivors and this corrects for sample selection bias due to retirement.

6.2.4   Adjustment for the Investment Tax Credit

Until now we have ignored taxes. In fact business buyers of new cars pay taxes on the stream of income from the product and may receive investment tax credits (ITC) and depreciation deductions. These tax policies effect new car prices. When the car is resold, the eventual new owner, typically a household user, will pay no business income tax and will receive no tax credits or deductions. Thus, the asset price will apparently have changed. If we want to measure economic depreciation on assets in the absence of tax policy, then we may wish to adjust market prices for tax policy.

Tax policy may cause new car prices to be too high or too low relative to what they would be without taxation. Lessors pay taxes and receive investment tax credits and accelerated depreciation deductions that are not passed on to subsequent buyers, though may be passed on to the lessee. One may argue that a new asset is a composite consisting of the asset itself and a set of tax policy terms that result in an after-tax price determined by the tax rate and the subsidy aspects of the ITC and accelerated depreciation. This suggests that we raise the price by the tax and reduce the new car price by the amount of the ITC-accelerated depreciation subsidy, then calculate economic depreciation on the residual alone.[6] This could be done by estimating the effective tax rate and correcting the new car price by this rate.

The above argument, however, is too simple because it does not allow for two complexities of the automobile market. First, new car demand is the sum of business and household demand, and, since households that use autos do not earn income from the product, do not pay income taxes on it, and do not receive the ITC, no change in household demand for cars would result from these business tax policies. This means that the total demand curve for cars will shift only by a fraction of the tax or subsidy—the fraction of new car demand represented by business demand.

Second, under constant returns to scale in auto production a shift in demand will not change price at all, and in general any change in demand for business-use cars will change price by only a fraction of the increase in demand. The net change in price will be therefore only a small fraction of the effective tax rate, both because producers sell to household-use buyers, which dissipates the producers' desire or ability to alter price, and because of competitive supply conditions. To measure economic depreciation, then, the appropriate treatment of tax policy depends on the shift in demand and on the incidence of the credit between auto producers, lessors, and lessees, which, in turn, depends on a complex of unknown supply and demand elasticities.

Our strategy is to estimate depreciation under two sets of assumptions: First, we assume that no tax policy effects accrue to lessors, so that prices are uncorrected for tax policy. Second, we assume that the lessor enjoys benefits from the ITC. We ignore accelerated depreciation, because this is unknown until depreciation is known. To adjust for the ITC, we reduce each new car price by the amount of the ITC allowed on that asset.

6.3   The Nature of the Data

The data consist of transaction prices of cars, purchased when new from automobile dealers by a large national leasing company based in the Midwest, leased to business users (often very large companies), and then resold to wholesale dealers at the end of the lease. The entire fleet of the lessor's cars are included. The sample period runs from the beginning of the 1982 model year to July 1986.

The data were drawn from invoices used by the lessor for its internal accounting and for official tax records. The data cover both cars being actively leased and those sold after the lease period. Each record reports make and model, initial price and purchase date by month, the resale date by month after the lease period, the price at resale, the mileage driven, and an estimate of reconditioning costs at that date.

The market is unique and the coverage of market transactions is comprehensive. First, the prices of the cars sold represent actual individual transactions, rather than guides to actual prices that are used in studies based on *Blue Book*, *Red Book* and the like. Actual transaction prices are valuable, since in an unfettered market, prices reflect the market valuation of the present value of the future flow of productive services of the asset. Thus, depreciation estimates based on these prices should reflect loss in value according to the market, not according to an accounting approximation or to some outside observer's opinion of value.

Second, the characteristics of the participants in the business-leased auto market lend credence to depreciation estimates based on the prices of used cars. The seller is an automobile-leasing company and the buyers are wholesale dealers. Thus, both participants are knowledgeable, experienced, market participants. Neither is likely to lack fundamental information about the quality of assets being exchanged.[7] In short, we do not appear to have lemon-type self-selection bias.

Third, in addition to detailed information about the costs, sale prices, and dates, we have detailed codes for various makes and models. This means that we can compile arrays of reasonably homogeneous asset classes, and can estimate depreciation without concern about heterogeneous characteristics within these classes.

Fourth, the data include miles driven by each car when sold and estimated costs of refurbishing the car. The average car in the sample is driven about 26,000–27,000 miles during each of the first two years. In contrast, household-use cars, according to Government statistics, are driven, on average, 14,000–15,000 miles each of the first several years.[8]

6.3.1 Selection of Sample Subset

The original sample consists of 148,112 cars, of which 39,311 are still actively leased, so that 108,801 cars in the sample have been sold. However, we cannot use all of these data, because sales are of three types, and two are not useful for our purposes. Although most sales occur in a competitive market, a third were sold directly to the driver after the lease period. These sales, according to industry sources, evidently reflect lessee company policies to sell used cars, at discount, to their drivers as part of personnel incentive programs. These policies are not related to the lease contracts and the prices do not reflect market value of cars, so we exclude them from analysis. In addition, some cars were wrecked and sold at virtually zero price. These too were excluded when estimating depreciation—*ordinary* wear, tear, and obsolescence.

From the entire sample, we next select only models that were sufficiently frequent to allow detailed estimation.[9] We selected 4 models designated in 1986—Chevrolet Celebrity, Buick Century, Oldsmobile Cutlass, and Oldsmobile Delta 88. Table 6.1 indicates the distribution of observations in the sub-sample of 4 models we chose to study. These 4 models are representative of the entire sample. Most cars in the original sample ranged from $8,000 to $12,000 when new. The Celebrity and Cutlass are moderate priced intermediate-range

Table 6.1
Distribution of sales by year makes and models to be studied

Make	Model	1982	1983	1984	1985	1986	Active
Chevrolet	Celebrity	458	1118	3333	5264	1432	11798
Buick	Century	324	625	813	1387	331	3000
Oldsmobile	Cutlass	552	1297	3187	2300	484	3976
Oldsmobile	Delta 88	133	176	410	406	105	1122

cars, costing about $9,000 when new. The Buick Century is a higher-scale intermediate-range car, costing about $10,000 when new. These three models represent about 60% of the sample. The Delta 88, a more expensive car, represents about 20% of the sample. This leaves out inexpensive compacts and light trucks, which are about 15% of the data and luxury cars, about 5% of the data.

6.3.2   Price Tableaux and Age-Price Profiles

Before the econometric analysis, we illustrate the prices of the cars by age and date to indicate the decline in prices from the data themselves. We illustrate below the distribution, by model year and age, of the average deflated price of each of the 4 models. These average prices are shown in a rectangular tableau in table 6.2. Nearly all cars in the entire sample were sold before the sixth year, as can be seen from the retirement distribution, so we present prices only for the first 5 years.

Reading down a column of a price tableau corresponds to tracing the depreciated values in any given year. The last column in each tableau is the average price across the rows. It is quite clear from these tableaux that prices fall rapidly in year 1—the Chevrolet Celebrity average price falls, for example, from $9,482 to $4,838; the price of the Oldsmobile Cutlass falls from $9,989 to $5,171. After the shock of the decline in price over the first two years, the cars' prices drop off at a slower steady rate.

The patterns of price decline can also be seen by visual inspection of the age-price profiles. The average prices by age, shown as the row averages in the tableaux of table 6.2, are plotted in figure 6.3.[10] The age-price profiles, averages of deflated prices, show that the rate of price decline is very rapid early on compared with later in the asset life. This pattern persists across all 4 models and is consistent with the findings of Hulten and Wykoff for other classes of assets.[11]

6.3.3   Adjustment for the ITC

Since our strategy for dealing with potential tax policy effects on asset prices is to estimate depreciation once with new car prices adjusted for the ITC and once with unadjusted prices, we must specify the ITC rules over the entire life of the study. The ITC adjustment depends on the vintage of the car, because different laws applied to different vintages.

Table 6.2
Average price by year and age

Chevrolet Celebrity

Age (years)	Year sold					Row average
	1982	1983	1984	1985	1986	
0	9538	8785	9407	9684	9997	9482
1	4181	4273	4802	5289	5646	4838
2	4475	4283	4791	4326	4122	4399
3	3431	3446	3685	3428	3299	3458
4	2648	2653	2680	2328	2341	2530
5	0	2035	1907	1562	1346	1713
6	0	0	1882	889	718	1163
7	0	0	0	659	550	605

Buick Century

Age (years)	Year sold					Row average
	1982	1983	1984	1985	1986	
0	9827	10959	9773	10418	10665	10328
1	5965	4854	4821	6361	0	5500
2	5246	4833	5444	4962	4503	4998
3	4124	4434	4564	4068	3895	4217
4	0	3460	3876	3214	2942	3373
5	0	0	2954	2936	0	2945
6	0	0	0	0	1200	1200

Oldsmobile Cutlass Supreme

Age (years)	Year sold					Row average
	1982	1983	1984	1985	1986	
0	9678	10402	9359	10162	10341	9989
1	6004	4780	4365	6014	4690	5171
2	5153	4841	5088	4729	4527	4868
3	4452	4334	3973	3955	3824	4108
4	3203	3769	3696	3124	2851	3329
5	0	0	2746	2291	1952	2330
6	0	0	0	1694	1763	1729

Table 6.2 (continued)

Oldsmobile Delta 88

Age (years)	Year sold					Row average
	1982	1983	1984	1985	1986	
0	11128	10976	12093	13228	9303	11346
1	0	3074	4805	5731	4402	4503
2	4663	4939	5948	5789	5756	5419
3	4081	4083	4737	4408	4129	4288
4	2475	3478	3741	3521	3176	3278
5	0	0	2891	2815	2250	2652
6	0	0	0	1027	1388	1208
7	0	0	0	0	749	749

In particular, over the sample period, the law changed from the Asset Depreciation Range System (ADR) to the Accelerated Cost Recovery System (ACRS). Under ADR a 10% credit was allowed, but was recaptured entirely for assets sold within 3 years, and a scale of recapture was applied up to 7 years and only then was the entire 10% retained. Under ACRS a 6% credit was allowed for three year assets under ACRS, with actual retention again depending on the holding period by the original owner. Table 6.3 shows the ITC-adjustment factors.

We adjusted new car prices for the ITC based on holding periods. The average new car price over the sample was reduced 3.6%. This is quite small, and our arguments, in section 6.2, on the impact of this credit on new car prices, suggest that prices increased even less.

6.3.4   The Retirement Distribution

As noted earlier, to measure economic depreciation on a cohort of assets, one must adjust used prices for retirement. We adopt the method used by the Bureau of Economic Analysis (BEA) for machinery and equipment, even though BEA did not use this method to construct automobile retirements.[12] We use a predetermined retirement distribution, the Winfrey S-3 curve. This curve is used by BEA for all machinery and equipment except automobiles. To implement the distribution, one needs to determine an average class life for the center of the distribution. We select the average life of

Table 6.3
New car price adjustment for ITC

Post-1980 vintages (ACRS)

Adjustment factor	Ages (in months)	
1.00	0	12
.98	12	24
.96	24	36
.94	36	120

Pre-1981 vintages (ADR)

Adjustment factor	Ages (in months)	
1.00	0	36
.98	36	48
.96	48	60
.94	60	72
.93	72	84
.90	84	120

passenger cars on the road during 1986—7.5 years—and center the Winfrey S-3 distribution on 7.5.

The actual distribution is then adapted from household-use cars to business-use cars by reference to relative mileage figures. Briefly, we determine a "household-use-equivalent" life for business-use cars from comparative mileage driven figures for business-leased automobiles and household-use cars.

To determine the average life of business-use automobiles, we begin with the fact that they are driven more intensely than household-use cars. Our data indicate that the leased cars average 26,000–27,000 miles per year. Household-use car mileage is considerably less, 15,000 miles. Since retirement due to wear and tear depends on miles driven, business-use automobiles actually experience shorter calendar lives than do household-use cars. Just as dog-years take less time than human-years, business-use cars accumulate household-use-year equivalents in much shorter spans of

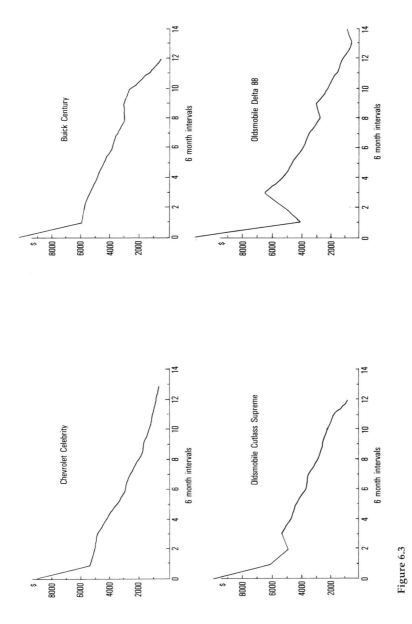

Figure 6.3

calendar years. Based on comparative mileage figures, business cars driven for 12 months have driven the equivalent mileage of a 2.3–year-old household-use car; in 24 months, of a 3.6–year-old car; in 36 months, 6 years; and in 42 months 7.5 years.

In the next table, we match the months a business car is driven with the equivalent in household car years based on accumulated mileage. We match these "household-use-year" equivalents to the Winfrey S-3 distribution, centered at a household-use car life of 7.5 years (see Gorman et al., 1984 for details). BEA assumes a 10-year average life for automobiles. This seems to be a conservative estimate, since average car on the road figures from Wards varies from 6.0 to 7.5. We selected 7.5 as the average life.[13]

Business car to household-use car conversion based on mileage driven figures

Business cars (age in months)	Household-use-year equivalents	% retired[a]
06	1.8	0.0
12	2.3	0.0
18	3.0	0.0
24	3.4	1.2
30	4.7	9.7
36	6.0	24.6
42	7.5	53.9
48	9.0	81.3
52	10.0	93.5

a. This percentage only applies to cars while in use as business cars. Once sold they are assumed to retire at the rate of household-use cars.

The effect of retirement on depreciation estimates of an original cohort in principle can be substantial in terms of form and rate. To illustrate this, consider the depreciation patterns used by BEA, whose procedures are based on the work of Young and Musgrave (1980). Young and Musgrave, who defend straight line depreciation, in fact, use a convex pattern over most of the asset life, because of the retirement distribution. The Young and Musgrave pattern of depreciation is depicted in figure 6.4.

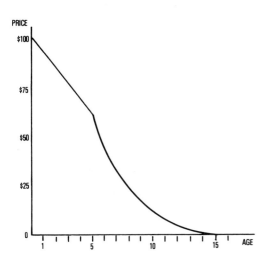

Figure 6.4   Young and Musgrave BEA depreciation.

6.4   Econometric Estimates of Depreciation Patterns and Rates

6.4.1   Parameter Estimates and Fit of Equations

In this section we report estimates of the unknown parameters of equation (2). Since the model is highly nonlinear in the unknowns and cannot be estimated using ordinary least squares, we use maximum likelihood estimation.[14]

We must estimate seven unknowns simultaneously—the three Box-Cox power coefficients, g_0, g_1, and g_2, the three "slope" coefficients, a_0, a_1, and a_2, of equation (2), and the variance of the random disturbance term u. Variations in the power coefficients allow the form to adopt different shapes as it attempts to approximate the age-price profile.

We considered 4 permutations of the data: (1) unadjusted prices, (2) ITC-adjusted prices, (3) retirement-adjusted prices and, (4) prices adjusted both for the ITC and for retirement. To conserve space table 6.4 contains a statistical summary of our estimates of the unknowns and the fit of the equations for the unadjusted prices case only. The discussion, however, focuses on the results from all four models.

The g_0-coefficients tend to be in the range of 0.75–1.5, while the g_1-coefficients are small, about 0.2–0.6. The slope coefficients, especially the age coefficient a_1, appear to be highly significant, judging from the standard errors that appear beneath each coefficient.[15] The negative

Table 6.4
Box-Cox regression results, unadjusted prices

Make and model	(a) Estimated coefficients					
	g_0	g_1	g_2	a_0 [a]	a_1	a_2
Chevrolet Celebrity	1.140	0.443	1.938	24766	−3711	−0.4544
	(0.002)	(0.010)	(0.126)	(483)	(5)	(0.2861)
Buick Century	1.438	0.195	3.936	272182	−48398	−0.0003
	(0.001)	(0.015)	(0.006)	(480)	(406)	(0.0000)
Oldsmobile Cutlass	1.344	0.189	2.781	130402	−20245	−0.0556
	(0.002)	(0.019)	(0.066)	(342)	(601)	(0.0186)
Oldsmobile Delta	0.966	0.394	−0.659	24320	−960	−12458
	(0.003)	(0.027)	(0.020)	(560)	(19)	(605)

Make and model	(b) Equation statistics				
	Degrees of freedom	Log-likelihood	Standard error (SE)	R^2	F-ratio
Chevrolet Celebrity	4997	−40270	2442	.7864	9196
Buick Century	3720	−30539	36738	.7692	6198
Oldsmobile Cutlass	2997	−25137	19100	.7016	3523
Oldsmobile Delta	1289	−11085	960	.5950	947

a. Standard errors beneath coefficients were calculated from the inverse of the information matrix.

signs of the date coefficients suggest that the standard deflators may overadjust for inflation.[16]

The fit of the equation to the data is not unreasonable. The R^2 statistics range from .54 to .78. Considering that we are dealing with very large samples, originally over 8000 observations in most cases and that the samples lump together different car styles, such as 2-doors, wagons, and 4-doors, and considering that no allowance is made for differences in condition, these goodness-of-fit statistics suggest a fairly accurate model.

One can visualize the fit of the Box-Cox models for unadjusted prices by observing figure 6.5, in which the Box-Cox fit is plotted against the average prices in the age-price profiles. These figures indicate that the Box-Cox model explains the price decline patterns,

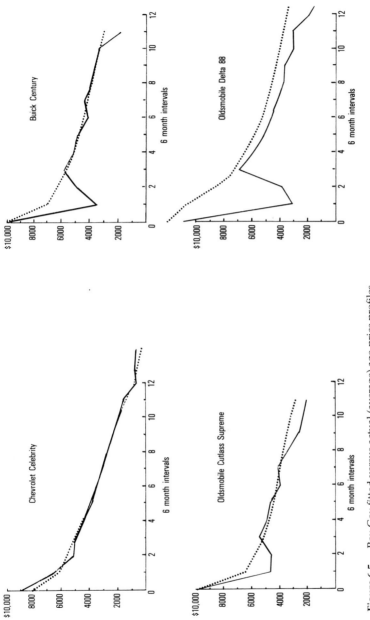

Figure 6.5 Box-Cox fitted versus actual (average) age-price profiles.

Table 6.5A
Average annual depreciation rates from Box-Cox model:
unadjusted prices

Age	Chevrolet Celebrity	Buick Century	Oldsmobile Cutlass	Oldsmobile Delta 88
1	.2795	.3698	.4080	.7619
2	.1963	.1497	.1420	.2451
3	.2015	.1224	.1090	.1732
4	.2287	.1121	.0947	.1403
5	.2839	.1087	.0871	.1214
6	.4009	.0000	.0000	.0000

Table 6.5B
Average annual depreciation rates from Box-Cox model:
maximum ITC-adjustment

Age	Chevrolet Celebrity	Buick Century	Oldsmobile Cutlass	Oldsmobile Delta 88
1	.3240	.3486	.3652	.3242
2	.2099	.1513	.1480	.1896
3	.2082	.1259	.1198	.1740
4	.2286	.1167	.1083	.1740
5	.2719	.1142	.1035	.1830
6	.0000	.0000	.0000	.0000

Table 6.5C
Average annual depreciation rates from Box-Cox model:
retirement-adjusted

Age	Chevrolet Celebrity	Buick Century	Oldsmobile Cutlass	Oldsmobile Delta 88
1	.3302	.3566	.3611	.3284
2	.2259	.1644	.1417	.2139
3	.2267	.1420	.1130	.2006
4	.2498	.1368	.1007	.2026
5	.2967	.1399	.0949	.2133
6	.3865	.1499	.1352	.2321

Table 6.5D
Average annual depreciation rates from Box-Cox model:
retirement and maximum ITC-adjustment

Age	Chevrolet Celebrity	Buick Century	Oldsmobile Cutlass	Oldsmobile Delta 88
1	.3187	.3505	.3429	.3032
2	.2210	.1650	.1637	.2073
3	.2249	.1436	.1415	.1985
4	.2525	.1392	.1357	.2040
5	.3085	.1434	.1375	.2187
6	.4228	.1548	.1451	.2430

over all, for three classes—Chevrolet Celebrity, Buick Century, and Oldsmobile Cutlass—rather well. The Oldsmobile Delta class does not fit as well. While the fit of the Box-Cox is reasonably accurate from the point of view of the age-price profiles, the model does not hit the end points of the data. This poor fit at the end points reflects the sharp plunge in new car prices over one or two months and a subsequent recovery. This leads to some peculiarities when estimating monthly depreciation rates. However, when annualizing these rates the anomalies disappear.

6.4.2   Economic Depreciation Rates

From the Box-Cox model above we measured the average annual rates of economic depreciation as $[P(s + 1) - P(s)]/P(s)$, where $P(s)$ is the price at age s, given the year. This gives us the percent rate of decline over each age interval. These average annual rates of depreciation are presented for all four cases, with and without the ITC and retirement adjustments, in tables 6.5A–6.5D.

Tables 6.5A–6.5D give the average annual depreciation rates on the four automobile models studied in detail according to the Box-Cox model. These rates apply to the revalued remaining bases of the assets, so that the original price of the car is depreciated in each period and then revalued in each period for inflation. The next period's depreciation is calculated on the remaining basis revalued from the previous period.

The rate of depreciation appropriate in each period is the Box-Cox rate presented in tables 6.5A–6.5D. During the first year, from age 0 to 1, the rates are typically higher then for subsequent ages. For unadjusted prices, the first year rates jump around—28%, 37%, 41%, and 76%. Taken individually these are not always reasonable. Obviously the 76% figure is too large and the 28% figure is too low. The Box-Cox cannot fit the early months of these two profiles very well. Taken as a whole, however, these results make sense—in the first year business-leased automobiles lose value at rates in the neighborhood of about 40–45%.[17] The adjusted price series produced more stable rates, usually in the range of 30–36% for new cars.

After year 1 the depreciation rate is slower, 14–25% of remaining revalued basis. Thereafter the rates slow down and level off. We calculated a best geometric approximation for the rates of decline after the first 2 years, and they ran in a range from 15% to 28% of remaining revalued basis. However, the increasingly significant impact of retirements on cohort value becomes apparent after 5 years and depreciation rates then tend to rise considerably. On average, then, depreciation in the years subsequent to years 1 and 2 are at a minimum about 15–17% but probably higher as retirements begin to dominate cohort depreciation.

Capital stock studies and tax laws, by necessity, deal with heterogeneous cohorts of assets, not with individual cars. Thus, a summary of economic depreciation on business-use cars is needed to make use of these estimates for cohort efficiency analysis purposes. This process of "data reduction" is naturally somewhat judgmental. We begin with table 6.6, which contains composite economic depreciation rates for all four automobile models for each of the 4 sets of potential adjustments to new prices.

It is evident that the economic depreciation pattern is accelerated relative to geometric depreciation. First-year depreciation appears to be between 35% and 45%. We select 40%. Second-year depreciation is close to 20%. In subsequent years, the Box-Cox estimates on unretired data suggest rates of 15–20%. Retirements, however, become increasingly important as assets are removed from service by all users at rates of 50% every two months after 4 calendar years; thus we conclude that rates of 30–35% would probably be appropriate for older business-use cars.

6.4.3   Comparison with Existing Studies

Table 6.7 contains summary statistics of existing research on automobile depreciation. It presents averages taken at the midpoints of each of the studies, which are portrayed as constant geometric

Table 6.6
Average annual depreciation rates composite for all 4 car-models by economic model

Age	Unadjusted prices	ITC-adjusted prices	Retirement-adjusted prices	Retirement and ITC-adjusted prices
1	.4548	.3405	.3444	.3288
2	.1833	.1747	.1865	.1893
3	.1515	.1570	.1706	.1771
4	.1440	.1569	.1725	.1829
5	.1503	.1682	.2259	.2020

Table 6.7
Comparison with existing research

Study (date)	Rate (%)	Present value
This study (1988)	40–20–35	.894
Hulten-Wykoff (1981a, b)	33.3	.893
Ohta-Griliches (1976)	29.0	.879
Ackerman (1973)	31.2	.886
Cagan (1973)	25.5	.864
Ramm (1970)	27.5	.873
Wykoff (1970)[a]	22.0	.846
Chow (1957, 1960)	24.5	.860

a. Calculated after first year.

rates. While these are all crude approximations of extensive research, they will serve as a basis for comparison. We also computed the present discounted value of a $1.00 asset that declined in value according to each economic depreciation pattern. These present discounted values appear in column (2) of table 6.7.

The most notable distinction of this study is that depreciation is more rapid in the first year than subsequently. This reflects both the heavy use of business-leased cars and the effects of first-year obsolescence. A similar pattern was detected by Hulten and Wykoff (1981a,b) for cars driven by federal government employees and by Wykoff (1970) in a study of household-use cars.

The only other research to use flexible functional forms were the Hulten-Wykoff studies and the Wykoff study, and thus others could not obtain higher rates in early years either by virtue of model restriction or sample selection; i.e., some exclude new car prices from their sample. Wykoff (1970) reported rates based on individual ages, using a user cost of capital approach, and also found higher rates for the first year compared to subsequent years. This study confirms that result—economic depreciation of cars is accelerated relative to a geometric pattern.[18]

One question observers may raise about these rapid early depreciation rates is the possibility that they reflect an inaccurate initial price. In addition to the ITC argument noted above, it is argued that new prices reflect sticker values, rather than actual transaction prices, and thus overstate new car prices by list price bias. The result would be excessive first-year depreciation. This argument does not apply to our study, since our new prices are the actual cost outlays by the buyer, the leasing company, for purchase of individual cars, and since the results hold up for ITC-corrected data.

Can the rapid early depreciation be justified by behavior of drivers of new cars? Two sources of information suggest so. First, as noted earlier, drivers of business-leased autos average about 26,000–27,000 miles per year in the first two years. Household-use car drivers average from 15,000 to 16,000 miles per year in new cars. The Department of Transportation statistics suggest that new cars are driven more, even by households, than used cars. These mileage figures may explain the accelerated (relative to geometric) patterns of depreciation detected by Wykoff (1970), Hulten and Wykoff (1981a, b), and by this research.

The rates of this study are somewhat larger than the average of earlier studies based mainly on household-use cars. This is seen if we compare the present discounted value of each stream at the same interest rate. Table 6.7 contains these present value results. At a 4% discount rate, the present value of household-use cars on $1.00 averages .872. The Hulten-Wykoff study, 33.3% average annual depreciation, implies a present value .893. The present value on our depreciation pattern is .894. (Inflation is irrelevant since economic depreciation is always applied to the remaining price corrected for inflation.) Thus, this chapter seems to confirm the overall lifetime average experience of the Hulten-Wykoff studies. However, here the pattern is accelerated.

6.5   The User Cost of Capital and Asset Efficiency

We are now prepared to use our new depreciation estimates in combination with measures of tax policy, interest rates, asset prices, inflation, and the price level to estimate the user cost of new and used cars from 1978 to 1987. We shall then analyze asset efficiency based on these user cost measures. Equation (3) represents the user cost of capital on an age-s asset, in year-t, of vintage-v:

$$C_{t, s, v} = \{[1-U_t T_{t, s, v}]/[1-U_t]\} \{DR_t + DEP_s\} Q_{t, s}, \tag{3}$$

where $T_{t, s, v} = Z_v + (K_{v, s}/U_t)$ and where

U_t = statutory tax rate in year t,

Z_v = present value of depreciation deductions for vintage-v assets,

$K_{v, s}$ = investment tax credit for vintage-v assets,

DR_t = period-t after-tax discount rate, [see equation (4)],

DEP_s = depreciation rate on age-s cars,

$Q_{t, s}$ = price index on new and used cars in year-t.

This user cost formula is well-known—the gross before tax cost of capital, C, depends on the tax treatment of capital that is captured by the terms U, Z, and K, on the real discount rate on capital, DR, which is described below, on the economic depreciation rate, DEP, and on the acquisition cost of capital, Q. The various terms are indexed by year, age, or vintage to indicate that their values are specific to either the current period, t, the age of the asset, s, or the vintage of the asset v.

The appropriate formula for the discount rate in (3) as well as the rate used to calculate Z depends on the financial policy of the firm. If capital is financed by debt issue, then we measure DR_t as

$$DR_t = .06 + (1-U_t)R_t - INF_t, \tag{4}$$

where R is the prime commercial paper rate and INF is the contemporaneous rate of inflation in period-t. This formula follows Auerbach and Hines (1986).

6.5.1   Measuring Automobile User-Cost

Table 6.8 contains the interest rate, price, and inflation data required to construct the user cost.[19] The last column of the table is the discount rate, equation (4). The discount rate is used both as the opportunity

Table 6.8
Interest rate, inflation and price data 1978–1987

Year	Prime rate	Inflation rate	New car price	Used car price	Producer price index	Discount rate
1978	7.99	7.30	153.8	186.5	195.9	3.0146
1979	10.90	8.90	166.0	201.0	217.7	2.9860
1980	12.29	9.00	179.3	208.1	247.0	3.6366
1981	14.76	9.70	190.2	256.9	269.8	4.2704
1982	11.89	6.40	197.6	296.4	280.7	6.0206
1983	8.89	3.90	202.6	329.7	285.2	6.9006
1984	10.16	3.80	208.5	375.7	291.1	7.6864
1985	8.01	3.30	210.0	380.0	293.7	7.0254
1986	6.45	2.65	220.0	385.0	289.3	6.8330
1987	6.45	2.65	230.0	390.0	287.8	7.7360

cost of capital in equation (3) and as the rate at which tax depreciation deductions are discounted in the computation of Z.

Construction of the before-tax cost of capital C requires measures for the relevant statutory tax rate, U_t, in each year, for the investment tax credit pertaining to each asset $K_{v,\,s}$, applicable to new cars only and based on vintage, and for the present discounted value of the stream of tax depreciation deductions allowed on the asset.

We make the following simplifying assumptions about tax treatment of these assets. First, we ignore state license fees and other state taxes. Second, we assume that the top marginal corporate tax rate applies, 46% from 1978 to 1986 and 32% in 1987. Third, we assume that the average holding period on cars is 32 months, so that the investment tax credit is 2% from 1978 to 1981, 6% from 1981 to 1986, and zero in 1986 and 1987 as a result of the new tax law.

The tax depreciation patterns we assume are based on the tax-liability-minimizing pattern subject to the limitations on the investment tax credit under each set of tax laws. Under the Asset Depreciation Range System (ADR) cars could be depreciated at a double declining balance pattern over a 5-year life, and if the car were sold after 32 months, one still retained a 2% investment tax credit. Cars were typically held at least 32 months. Under the Accelerated Cost Recovery System (ACRS), cars were assigned a 3-year life and allowed an ITC of 6%.

Under the Tax Reform Act of 1986 (TRA), the ITC was dropped and cars could be depreciated over a 3-year life, at a 33% rate, unless the

Table 6.9
User-costs of automobiles 1978–1987

Year	Nominal	Real	Indexed	% change
1978	67.1	.343	100.0	—
1979	72.4	.332	97.0	−2.98
1980	80.2	.325	94.7	−2.37
1981	81.2	.301	87.9	−7.23
1982	90.0	.321	93.6	6.49
1983	95.2	.334	97.4	4.10
1984	100.6	.346	100.9	3.59
1985	99.1	.337	98.5	−2.41
1986	118.5	.410	119.6	21.42
1987	119.9	.417	121.6	1.72

company's tax liability was below 20% when calculated under the Alternative Minimum Tax (AMT). Under the AMT cars can be depreciated only using the straight line method over a 5-year life. We calculated tax liability according to both ordinary corporate tax rules and the AMT.[20]

The only distinction we make between debt and equity finance is that the rate of interest in equation (4) is multiplied by $(1-U_t)$ to allow for interest deductibility of debt finance. The effect on equity cost of capital in this model is represented by the term $T_{t,\,s,\,v}$. Under equity finance, taxes effect the cost of capital only through the terms T and the term U. *Ceteris paribus*, the larger T the smaller the effective tax rate on capital.

Hulten and Wykoff (1981a, b) show that in a simple geometric model, if $T_{t,\,s,\,v}$ equals the present value of economic depreciation, then the effective tax rate will equal the statutory rate. If T exceeds this value, then the asset holder enjoys a subsidy. If T is less than this value, then the asset holder suffers a surcharge. For new business cars, economic depreciation equals .924, assuming a discount rate of 6%.

The initial impact of ACRS was to increase T from .97 in 1980 to 1.05 in 1981. T reached its peak in 1981–1982, during the recession, at values of 1.05 and 1.01. but this effect was eventually offset by large real discount rates, so that T was .986 by 1984. T is less than .924 only in 1986 and 1987. With the elimination of the ITC and the imposition of straight line depreciation, T is .82 and .80 in 1986 and 1987.

Table 6.10
Relative asset efficiencies 1978–1987

Age	1978	1979	1980	1981	1982	1983	1984	1985	1986	1987
0	1.000	1.000	1.000	1.000	1.000	1.000	1.000	1.000	1.000	1.000
1	.621	.621	.620	.637	.634	.633	.632	.633	.522	.490
2	.270	.270	.273	.300	.308	.311	.314	.312	.239	.214
3	.253	.253	.256	.298	.305	.308	.311	.309	.223	.188
4	.232	.232	.234	.254	.259	.262	.264	.262	.208	.166

Table 6.11
Quasi-efficiencies of new automobiles 1978–1987

Age	1978	1979	1980	1981	1982	1983	1984	1985	1986	1987
0	1.000	0.970	0.947	0.879	0.936	0.974	1.009	0.985	1.196	1.216

The combined effects on the user cost of automobiles during the interval from 1978 to 1987 resulting from the various tax measures, nominal interest rates, inflation, and automobile purchase prices can be seen in table 6.9.

As the last column of table 6.9 indicates, the cost of capital, taking into account all factors, fell from 1978 to 1981, the biggest drop occurring in 1981 as a result of ACRS, but the increases in real rates of interest and automobile prices offset the fall in user costs by 1982. As the real rates of discount continued to rise, due mainly to falling inflation rates, after 1982, the cost of capital continued to increase until 1985. Then the cost of capital fell with falling nominal interest rates. This temporary fall in automobile user costs was offset in 1986 and 1987 by the elimination of the ITC and the return to straight line depreciation in the Alternative Minimum Tax.

6.5.2 Relative Asset Efficiency

At a competitive equilibrium, producers equate the marginal rate of substitution between two inputs to the ratios of their prices. In the case of in-use capital goods this condition amounts to equating the marginal rate of substitution to the ratio of user costs, since these are the appropriate relative prices that effect producer decisions at the margin. In symbols, we have

$$MRS_{s,0,t} = C_{s,t}/C_{0,t}, \tag{5}$$

where $MRS_{s, 0, t}$ refers to the marginal rate of substitution between new and age-s capital in year-t and $C_{s, t}$ refers to the user cost of age-s capital at time-t.

Jorgenson (1973) suggests exploiting this relationship in order to infer from user costs the relative productive efficiency of various vintages of capital. Jorgenson shows that the ratio of user costs yields a sequence of values, which he calls the efficiency function of capital, that indicates the relative contribution to output of various types of capital. This efficiency sequence forms the basis for construction of consistent capital aggregates.

Table 6.10 contains the relative efficiencies of new and used assets in each year from 1978 to 1987. Note that these efficiency functions are relative efficiencies normalized, in each year, on the user cost of new capital.

Assets can be exchanged across time in a Debrue-Arrow world. In this spirit we construct relative asset efficiencies over time periods by equating the marginal rate of substitution between two new assets over two different time periods to their respective user costs, corrected for inflation:

$$MRS_{0, t} = C_{0, t} / C_{0, t0}. \tag{6}$$

Equation (6) suggests that the relative efficiency of new automobiles over time may be inferred from the ratio of their user costs, appropriately corrected for inflation. Thus, we construct a quasi-efficiency function over time, similar in spirit to Jorgenson's efficiency function constructed at a point in time. If capital, at equilibrium, can cover larger gross capital costs, then it can be said to be more efficient. These results appear in table 6.11.

Notes

1. See Hulten and Wykoff (1981a, b).

2. A more detailed discussion of these forces may be found in the chapter by Hulten, Robertson, and Wykoff in this volume.

3. This model was estimated under the assumption that u is independently normally distributed. Since (2) is highly nonlinear, maximum likelihood methods, combined with grid searches, were used to estimate the various parameters. Steepest gradient techniques require calculation of first and second derivatives and these are intractable for the Box-Cox model with 7 unknowns. The analysis was carried out with both real (i.e., inflation-corrected) P_i and nominal (i.e., uncorrected) P_i.

4. The phrase "accelerated pattern" is used to refer to a pattern of price decline that follows a constant geometric or exponential path. This phrase is from tax parlance—accelerated tax depreciation means that tax deductions are allowed earlier than under a straight line pattern; thus the deductions are accelerated relative to straight lines.

5. It is important, in the case of leased cars, to emphasize that retirement is distinct from disposition of cars by sale after the holding period by the original lessee. Retirement refers to the complete loss of assets from the productive capital stock. Disposition refers to sale by the lessor of cars after the lease period has elapsed.

6. For example, DeLeeuw (1981) makes this argument.

7. This, in turn, means that the basis of self-selection models that imply that "lemons" are overrepresented by used market transaction prices are inapplicable. The lemons argument (Ackerlof, 1970) depends on the relative ignorance of buyers in comparison to sellers. Since buyers in this market are dealers who buy and sell cars on a national scale, they are not ignorant of the nature of used cars.

8. U.S. Department of Transportation (1984).

9. Cars were coded by make and model—there were over 450 different codes. This reflects the many different makes (Chevrolet, Buick, Oldsmobile, Ford, Chrysler, and some foreign cars over a 5-year period), and since we include used cars, this means over 10 years of models. Each of these makes includes many different models and styles. It is obvious that we had to select a representative subsample. It was also necessary to match model names across years, since American auto producers change terminology of given designs from year to year and often change designs without changing model names. We sorted these complexities by talking with experts in the field and studying Wards Automotive Year Book to determine the appropriate model names for each type we decided to study.

10. Note that the age-price profiles are plotted for 6-month intervals, not years. Thus, the interval from 0 to 2 on the horizontal axis is two 6-month intervals or 1 year, and so on.

11. An anomaly of the age-price profiles of figure 6.3 requires explanation. The Oldsmobile Delta 88 profile falls, then rises. This reflects the fact that the data for very early sales, in the first 6 months, is rather thin, and this bump may be a result of averaging in some few cars in very bad condition.

Two points about deflating the prices and selecting only those prices from the sample that reflect market sales for the 4 models must be made. First, how much differences does deflating make to the profiles? Second, how did the nonmarketed car prices hold up in comparison to the market prices? Both of these questions were addressed for the Chevrolet Celebrity. We compared the age-price profiles of Chevrolets with and without deflation. It was evident from the figures that deflation does not change the age-price profiles noticeably. We also compared undeflated and deflated age-price profiles for nonmarketed assets. These cars, sold by the lessee to his driver rather than through a market to a wholesale dealer, decline much faster. As noted we dropped these prices from our analysis, and this removed about a third of the data.

12. See *The Survey of Current Business* September, 1985) and Hulten and Wykoff (1981a, b). BEA calculates automobile retirements from state-by-state registration figures, but these figures contain anomalies, and, in our judgment, are inaccurate.

13. If new automobile sales rise steadily over time, then the average life of cars on the road will be less than the average age of cars, but sales have fluctuated over the period in which the 7.5-year average life was reported.

14. The function is highly nonlinear so that calculations of analytical expressions for the first and second derivatives, required by steepest gradient techniques, are intractable. Thus, we developed a technique that combines grid searches and steepest gradient ascent techniques to determine the peak of the likelihood function. Crude grid search is used to locate the region about the peak of the likelihood surface. The surface area about the peak is then fitted by least squares to a cubic polynomial in the 3–unknown form parameters, g_0, g_1, and g_2. Including interaction terms this polynomial has 20 terms. A 4th-degree polynomial would require 45 terms. We then use a Newton-Ralphson steepest gradient technique with Greenstadt modification to locate the exact peak of the polynomial surface. We also inspect the fit of the polynomial surface to the true maximum likelihood surface. In practice this procedure is quite accurate—certainly in comparison to ordinary sampling error.

15. Note that the standard errors are the square roots of the principal diagonal elements of the inverse of the information matrix as suggested by Kmenta (1986, p. 161).

16. The large absolute values of the coefficients reflect the scaling of age and date variables. These values are simply counters starting at some arbitrary point. The age usually starts with a value of 1 for a 1-month asset and rises by an increment of 1 per month. The year variables start with 1954 set equal to 100 and rise incrementally by 1 per year. The very large coefficient on date for the Oldsmobile Delta class matches the negative power coefficient, so that the combined effects are not unlike those of the other asset classes.

17. This is the type of result reported for all cars by Wykoff (1970), though those results were based on published price guidelines not actual transaction prices.

18. Though the 1970 study was based on Blue Book Prices and may have suffered list price bias, new used car prices were also employed.

19. These data come from the *Survey of Current Business*.

20. This table contains the tax depreciation patterns by asset life that we assume applied under each tax regime, ADR, ACRS, the TRA and according to our assumption about economic depreciation.

Tax and economic depreciation patterns 1978–1987

Asset age	ADR 1978–1980	ACRS 1981–1985	TRA 1986–1987	Economic rates
1	0.40	0.33	0.20	0.40
2	0.24	0.33	0.20	0.30
3	0.20	0.33	0.20	0.15
4	0.16	0.00	0.20	0.15
5	0.00	0.00	0.20	0.00

References

Ackerlof, George (1970). "The Market for Lemons," *Quarterly Journal of Economics* 84, No. 3, August, 488–500.

Ackerman, Susan Rose (1973). "Used Cars as a Depreciating Asset," *Western Economic Journal* 11, December, 463–474.

Auerbach, Alan J. (1979). "The Optional Taxation of Heterogeneous Capital," *The Quarterly Journal of Economics* 93, No. 4, November, 589–612.

Auerbach, Alan J., and James R. Hines, Jr. (1986). "Anticipated Tax Changes and the Timing of Investment," N.B.E.R. Working paper No. 1886.

Auerbach, Alan J., and Dale W. Jorgenson (1980). "Inflation-Proof Depreciation of Assets," *Harvard Business Review*, September–October, 113–118.

Box, G. E. P., and D. R. Cox (1964). "An Analysis of Transformations," *Journal of the Royal Statistical Society*, Series B, 26, No. 2, 211–243.

Cagan, Philip (1973). "Measuring Quality Changes and the Purchasing Power of Money: An Exploratory Study of Automobiles," in Zvi Griliches (ed.), *Price Indexes and Quality Change* (Cambridge, MA).

Chow, Gregory C. (1957). *The Demand for Automobiles in the United States* (Amsterdam: North Holland).

_____ (1960). "Statistical Demand Functions for Automobiles and Their Use for Forecasting," in Arnold Harberger (ed.), *The Demand for Durable Goods* (Chicago: University of Chicago Press).

DeLeeuw, Frank (1981). "Discussion of Charles R. Hulten and Frank C. Wykoff, 'The Measurement of Economic Depreciation,'" in Charles R. Hulten (ed.), *Depreciation, Inflation and the Taxation of Income from Capital* (Washington, DC: The Urban Institute Press).

DeLeeuw, Frank, Jerry Green, and Eytan Sheshinski (1978). "Inflation and Taxes in a Growing Economy with Debt and Equity Finance," *Journal of Political Economy* 86, No. 2, Pt. 2, April, S53–S70.

Gorman, John A., John C. Musgrave, Gerald Silverstein, and Kathy A. Comins (1984). "Fixed Private Capital in the United States," *Survey of Current Business*, April, 36–47.

Hall, Robert (1968). "Technical Change and Capital from the Point of View of the Dual," *Review of Economic Studies* 35, January, 35–46.

_____ (1973). "The Measurement of Quality Change from Vintage Price Data," in Zvi Griliches (ed.), *Price Indexes and Quality Change* (Cambridge, MA).

Hall, Robert, and Dale W. Jorgenson (1967). "Tax Policy and Investment Behavior," *American Economic Review* 57, June, 391–414.

Hotelling, Harold S. (1925). "A General Mathematical Theory of Depreciation," *Journal of the American Statistical Society* 20, September, 340–353.

Hulten, Charles R., and Frank C. Wykoff (1978). "On the Feasibility of Equating Tax to Economic Depreciation," in U.S. Department of Treasury, Office of Tax Analysis, *1978 Compendium on Tax Research*, 89–120.

_____ (1979). "Economic Depreciation of the U.S. Capital Stock," report submitted to U.S. Department of Treasury, Office of Tax Analysis (Washington, DC).

_____ (1980). "Economic Depreciation and the Taxation of Structures in U.S. Manufacturing Industries: An Empirical Analysis," *National Bureau of Economic Research 1976 Conference on the Measurement of Capital*, 23–119.

_____ (1981a). "The Estimation of Economic Depreciation Using Vintage Asset Prices: An Application of the Box-Cox Power Transformation," *Journal of Econometrics* 15(3), April, 367–396.

_____ (1981b). "The Measurement of Economic Depreciation," in Charles R. Hulten, (ed.), *Depreciation, Inflation and the Taxation of Income from Capital* (Washington, DC: The Urban Institute Press).

Jorgenson, Dale W. (1973). "The Economic Theory of Replacement and Depreciation," in W. Sellykaerts (ed.), *Essays in Honor of Jan Tinbergen*.

Kmema, Jan (1986). *Elements of Econometrics*, 2nd ed., Macmillan, New York.

Marston, Anson, Robley Winfrey, and Jean C. Hempstead (1953). *Engineering Valuation and Depreciation* (New York: McGraw-Hill).

Musgrave, John C. (1976). "Fixed Nonresidential Business and Residential Capital in the United States, 1925–27," *Survey of Current Business* 56, August, 45–52.

Ohta, Makoto, and Zvi Griliches (1976). "Automobile Prices Revisited: Extensions of the Hedonic Price Hypothesis," *National Bureau of Economic Research, Studies in Income and Wealth*, 40, 325–390.

President of the United States (1985). *The President's Tax Proposals to the Congress for Fairness, Growth, and Simplicity*, May (Washington, DC: U.S. Government Printing Office).

Ramm, Wolfhard (1970). "Measuring the Services of Household Durables: The Case of Automobiles," in *Proceedings of the Business and Economics Statistics Section of the American Statistical Association* (Washington, DC), 149–158.

Stiglitz, Joseph E. (1973). "Taxation, Corporate Financial Policy, and the Cost of Capital," *Journal of Public Economics*, 2.

_____ (1976). "The Corporation Tax," *Journal of Public Economics* 5, Nos. 3–4, April-May, 303–311.

U.S. Department of Commerce, Bureau of Economic Analysis. *Survey of Current Business*, selected issues (Washington, DC).

U.S. Department of the Treasury, Bureau of Internal Revenue (1942). *Income Tax Depreciation and Obsolescence Estimated Useful Lives and Depreciation Rates*, Bulletin F, January (revised).

U.S. Department of the Treasury, Internal Revenue Service (1964). *Depreciation Guidelines and Rules, Revenue Procedure 62–21* (revised).

_____ (1977). *Blueprints for Basic Tax Reform*, January 17 (Washington, DC: U.S. Government Printing Office).

_____, Report to the President (1984). *Tax Reform for Fairness, Simplicity, and Economic Growth*, November.

U.S. Department of Transportation, Federal Highway Administration (1984). *Highway Statistics 1984* (Washington, DC: U.S. Government Printing Office).

Winfrey, R. (1935). "Statistical Analyses of Industrial Property Retirements," *Iowa Engineering Experiment Station Bulletin* 125.

Wykoff, Frank C. (1970). "Capital Depreciation in the Postwar Period: Automobiles," *Review of Economics and Statistics* 52, May, 168–172.

_____ (1973). "A User Cost Approach to New Automobile Purchases," *Review of Economic Studies* 40, July, 377–390.

Young, Allan H. and John C. Musgrave (1980). "Estimation of Capital Stock in the United States," in Dan Usher (ed.), *The Measurement of Capital*, Vol. 45 (Chicago: National Bureau of Economic Research, Studies in Income and Wealth), 23–82.

7

Construction Price Statistics Revisited

Paul Pieper

The deflation of structures has long been one of the most problematic areas of national income accounting. The area first received widespread attention in 1961 with the publication of the report of the NBER's Price Statistics Review Committee. The report heavily criticized the Department of Commerce structures deflators, calling them "defective in almost every possible way."[1] Main criticisms were that the indexes measured input costs rather than output prices, had antiquated bases and inaccurate weights, relied on list prices rather than transaction prices, and were often compiled by private companies that kept source materials secret. Subsequent work by Dacy (1964, 1965) and Gordon (1967, 1968b) focused on the development of output based deflators. These studies along with work by Musgrave (1969) led to a major revision in structures deflation by the Bureau of Economic Analysis (BEA) in 1974, with changes made retroactively to 1947. Very little research has been conducted in the area since then.

Twenty-five years after the release of the NBER's report, this chapter will reexamine the BEA construction deflators. Does the lack of recent research indicate that the deflation problems uncovered by the NBER have been solved? Or, after an initial surge of interest, do the problems still remain, largely forgotten and ignored by the profession?

Far from being a subject of interest only to national income accountants, the deflation of structures is of major importance to a wide range of issues. Two issues in particular deserve mention here. First, accurate structures deflation is necessary for the measurement of construction productivity. The productivity performance of the construction industry has been perhaps the most puzzling of all industries. After increasing at a 2.5% annual rate between 1947 and 1963, construction productivity began abruptly falling in 1963, with rates of decline equal to 0.7% per year between 1963 and 1972 and 2.5% per year between 1972 and 1981. Thus, while the aggregate productivity slowdown was marked by a decline in the productivity growth rate, the construction industry productivity decline was marked by a precipitous decline in the productivity level. Yet given the quality of the structures deflators, it is uncertain how much of the construction productivity decline is real and how much is due to mismeasurement. An overdeflation of structures would result in an underestimate of construction output and hence productivity.

Second, accurate structures deflation is crucial for proper measurement of real investment. New structures account for over half of gross private investment and two-thirds of net private investment. In addition, nearly all public nonmilitary investment is in the form of structures. Apparently low rates of investment in the seventies caused widespread concern, leading to the enactment of measures intended to stimulate investment. However, given the large proportion of structures in total investment, it is again unclear how much of the investment slowdown was real and how much was due to mismeasurement. An overdeflation of structures would result in an underestimate of real investment.

This chapter is organized as follows. The next section will review the methodology of the present BEA structures deflators, summarizing their strengths and weaknesses. The second section examines the accuracy of the deflators, focusing on the two most important indexes, the Census Single Family Homes index and the Federal Highway Administration index. The section examines whether the present indexes have overdeflated construction output and the implications for construction productivity and capital formation. The third section compares the present structures deflators with those used at the time of the NBER's report and assesses the amount of progress made during the past 25 years. The fourth section offers some suggestions for improving the deflators. Concluding remarks are presented in the fifth section.

7.1 Department of Commerce Structures Deflators

The problem of construction deflation stems from the extreme heterogeneity of construction output. Whereas most goods have a limited number of brands or styles, most structures are unique. Very few structures are built with the same specifications, not only over time but even at a point in time. Thus it is difficult to identify a unit of structures output from which to determine price changes. Because of heterogeneity, construction deflators do not usually measure the price of final output. Instead, inputs or intermediate units of output are deflated.

Present structures deflators may be grouped into three categories. The simplest type, termed input-cost, is an average of wage rates and materials costs, with some indexes also making an allowance for profit margins and overhead costs. The major disadvantage of input-cost indexes is that they assume the same relationship of output to inputs over time, thereby assuming constant productivity. If productivity is actually increasing, an input-cost index will be biased upward.

A second method of deflation, termed input-productivity, also deflates inputs but attempts to make an adjustment for productivity. However, it is impossible to state how output per unit of input changes without first measuring output. In practice, the productivity adjustment may be based on a few of the more homogeneous tasks, such as bricklaying, or may be simply an arbitrary estimate. The unscientific and incomplete method of adjustment severely limits the usefulness of this approach.

The third deflation method is closer to a true price index. It assumes that while the final structures project is heterogeneous, it is made up of a number of homogeneous components. These are then priced, yielding a "component-price" deflator. Components may refer to a certain quantity of materials put in place, such as cubic yards of structural concrete, or to some physical attribute of a structure, such as square feet of floor space. Although a major improvement over input-based deflators, component-price deflation is far from problem free. Its success depends crucially on the homogeneity of the components. A broad definition will permit a large amount of quality change to occur within categories, thus potentially yielding an inaccurate price index.

Presently the BEA uses nine primary indexes to deflate construction output. The indexes are shown in table 7.1 by their method of deflation. Two of the indexes are hybrids, using both input-cost and component-price methods. Column (3) shows the weight of each index in the composite structures deflator in 1972. Since each index is applied to a certain type of construction, the weights will vary with the composition of expenditures. Six of the nine indexes used by the BEA are based at least partly on inputs rather than output.[2] However, the input-based indexes have a relatively small weight in the composite deflator. Thus the common impression that structures are

Table 7.1
Primary indexes used to deflate construction output

Index	(1) Expenditures deflated	(2) 1972 weight
Input-Cost		7.51
1. EPA Sewer	Water and sewer	2.00
2. Handy-Whitman	Electric utilities	5.51
a. Power Plants		4.96
b. Buildings		0.55
Input-Productivity		13.83
1. Bell System Telephone	Telephone and telegraph	2.55
a. Outside Plant		2.04
b. Buildings		0.51
2. Turner Construction Co.	Nonresidential buildings[a]	11.28
Input-Cost—Component-Price		5.04
1. Bureau of Reclamation	Conservation and development	3.12
2. FERC Pipeline	Gas and petroleum pipelines	1.92
Component-Price		73.63
1. BEA-DOD Military	Military construction	0.90
2. Census Single-Family Homes, excluding land	Residential, nonresidential buildings	54.83
3. Federal Highway Administration		17.90
a. Composite	Highways, railroads and other	9.62
b. Structures	nonresidential buildings	8.28

a. Private nonresidential buildings are deflated by an unweighted average of the Turner, Census, and FHWA structures indexes, but public nonresidential use varying weights of the three indexes, depending on the type of structure. Thus the weights for the Turner and FHWA structures indexes listed above are not identical.

deflated primarily by cost indexes is incorrect. Altogether, about 75% of all structures are deflated by component-price indexes.

The predominance of the component-price method is due to the large weight of two indexes, the Census Single Family Homes (hereafter termed Census) and the Federal Highway Administration (FHWA). The two indexes together deflate 70% of all structures, with the Census alone deflating over half. The large weight of these indexes is due partly to their use in deflating expenditures other than what they are based on. For instance, both indexes have a one-third weight in the nonresidential building deflator, while the Census is also used to deflate multiunit residential and residential additions and alterations.

The expenditures deflated by the individual indexes are shown in column (2) of table 7.1. The BEA's deflation methodology can be summarized by dividing new contruction into three roughly equal categories: residential, nonresidential buildings, and nonresidential nonbuilding.[3] The first category is deflated almost entirely by the Census index.[4] Nonresidential buildings are deflated by an average of the Census index, the FWHA structures index and the Turner Construction Company index.[5] Of the three, only the Turner even attempts to measure building prices, The Census and FHWA measure prices of houses and highways, respectively, but are used as proxies for buiildings. About one-third of the nonbuilding category is deflated by the FHWA index. Small parts of the category, including military construction and conservation and development, are deflated by indexes that are based at least partly on output measures. However, most of the sector is deflated by cost indexes.

Of the five indexes that use component-price methods, three measure prices of federal construction and one measures private residential construction. Only the FERC, which is only partly output based and covers a tiny segment of construction, measures prices of private nonresidential construction. Thus the price statistics are weakest for private nonresidential construction, which because it comprises a large part of investment, is paradoxically one of the most closely scrutinized areas.

A brief description of the indexes is given below. Information for each index is based on direct contact with its publishers. Published information, where available, is often vague and at times inaccurate.

7.1.1 Input-Cost Indexes

1. Environmental Protection Agency

The EPA index is a typical input-cost index. Intended to measure the cost of sewer construction, the index is an average of prices of 13 types of materials and 6 types of labor. Weights for labor and materials are based on a study of sewer projects undertaken between 1956 and 1962. The EPA, along with several other indexes, uses the *Engineering News-Record*, a construction trade journal, as its data source. Privately compiled data sources such as the *Engineering News-Record* are often of questionable reliability. Unlike government statistical agencies, thay have no system of compulsory reporting and are not required to meet any uniform statistical standards.[6]

The EPA compiles separate indexes for 20 cities. The national index is a simple unweighted average of the city indexes, with no attempt made to reflect the actual geographic composition of expenditures. The 20 cities used by the EPA (which in turn are those used by the *Engineering News-Record*) are disproportionately weighted toward the Northeast and Midwest. The South and West are represented by 9 cities, or 45% of the total, but accounted for 58% of all sewer and water construction in 1982.[7] The EPA index is used to deflate all sewer construction and one-half of water construction.

2. Handy-Whitman

The Handy-Whitman index is an input-cost index published by a Baltimore-based consulting firm. One difficulty with privately compiled indexes such as the Handy-Whitman is that detailed source materials are not available to the public. At best, a general outline of the index's methodology is made public.

Handy-Whitman publishes separate indexes for buildings and for a steam-powered electric utility plant. The building index is an average of the cost of five types of materials and seven types of labor. The plant index measures the cost of labor and the price of forty types of materials. Both indexes use union contractual wage rates, including fringes, to measure labor costs. A variety of sources are used to measure materials costs, including the *Engineering News-Record*, manufacturers list prices, and surveys of builders. Neither index makes an explicit productivity or profit adjustment.

Six regional cost indexes are developed for both the building and plant indexes. The national index is again not based on the actual geographic composition of expenditures but is instead an unweighted average of the regional indexes. The BEA deflator for electric utility construction is derived by applying a 10% weight to the building index and a 90% weight to the plant index.

7.1.2   Input-Productivity

1.   Bell System Telephone Plant Indexes

The Bell indexes were compiled by AT&T to measure the cost of telephone-related construction. Separate indexes for buildings and outside plant (cables, lines, etc.) were published. The indexes were discontinued in 1983 after the breakup of AT&T. The Bell indexes are one of the few privately compiled indexes that publish a detailed description of their methodology.

a. *Buildings.*   The building cost index was compiled for AT&T by the American Appraisal Company, a Milwaukee-based consulting firm. Building construction is divided into 16 components, each of which is an average of materials and labor costs. The primary data source is a survey of builders. The American Appraisal Company went out of its way to avoid using transaction prices, asking respondents instead to report "normal" or "average" prices. Some BLS producer price indexes are also used as sources. The base year of the weights vary by component but are generally outdated. Nine of the 16 components have base year weights of 1946.[8]

An index for each component is developed for 32 different cities. For the 1946–1969 period, the national index is an unweighted average of the city indexes. After 1969, the cities are weighted by the amount of Bell construction in their surrounding region. The total building index is calculated by averaging the 16 components using fixed 1946 weights.

The American Appraisal Company states that the index is adjusted for productivity but is very vague about how this is done. The Bell Systems cost manual states only that the adjustment is based on "interviews with contractors and unions and searches of literature on the subject." A profit adjustment is also based on interviews with contractors.

b. *Outside Plant.* The outside plant index measures the cost of nonbuilding construction, such as laying cable and installing telephone lines. Materials costs are based on Western Electric—published prices for six different items, while labor costs are based on the Bell annual employee census. Labor costs are adjusted for years of experience and for fringe costs, such as social security and pension costs. An overhead and profit adjustment is calculated simply as the ratio of administrative costs to direct labor costs.

The outside plant index is a prime example of the arbitrariness of productivity adjustments in input-based indexes. AT&T "adjusted" labor costs for productivity simply by assuming labor productivity growth of 1% per year in the 1946–1966 period and 2% per year thereafter.

Due to the breakup of AT&T, the Bell indexes were discontinued after 1982. Since that time, the BEA deflator for telephone construction has been derived by trending the Bell index by the *Engineering News-Record* construction index. This index exemplifies some of the worst attributes of construction cost indexes. The index measures just four factors: list prices of steel, cement, and lumber and union wage rates for common labor. These four factors are averaged using ancient 1913 weights, which in any case were never intended to represent telephone construction. The national index is simply an unweighted average of the indexes for twenty cities.

2. Turner Construction Company

Published by a New York-based construction company, the Turner index has the most imprecise methodology and the poorest documentation of any of the BEA construction deflators. In the final analysis, the index is based simply on a judgment by an official of the Turner Construction Company. A Turner Company analyst considers factors such as wages and material costs , but the index is based on his own subjective evaluation rather than a statstical average of these costs.[9] Although classified here as an input-productivity index, the only productivity adjustment made is that which is implicit in the analyst's judgment. For an index with such a flimsy basis, the Turner index has a large weight, deflating over 10% of new construction.

7.1.3   Input-Cost — Component-Price

1.   Bureau of Reclamation

Published by a division of the Department of the Interior, the Bureau of Reclamation index is intended to measure the price of Western water projects. The index is composed of 12 main subindexes representing the cost of different types of projects, such as dams, canals, and concrete pipelines. Most of the subindexes are calculated as averages of labor, materials, and equipment costs. The major sources are union wage rates from the *Engineering News-Record* and materials and construction equipment price indexes from the Bureau of Labor Statistics (BLS).

Some of the subindexes, however, use component-price measures. Contractors bidding on reclamation projects bid separately on each item or component of construction specified in the contract. The bids refer to the price in place of a particular item and thus reflect not only materials costs but all construction costs. The Bureau of Reclamation uses these bids to develop price indexes for two important construction components, excavation and structural concrete. Both components are priced on a cubic yard basis and are classified by type of project: dams, canals, laterals, concrete pipes, and tunnels. Because the Bureau of Reclamation awards only a small number of contracts each year, the indexes are not a statistical average of the bids but are more akin to a smoothed trend line.

The Bureau of Reclamation index is therefore a hybrid of the input-cost and component-price methods. The composite deflator has weights of 24% for labor, 30% for materials, 14% for equipment, and 32% for bid price components. Besides deflating conservation and development expenditures, the Bureau of Reclamation is given some weight in the deflators for railroads and other private and public construction.

2.   Federal Energy Regulatory Commission Pipeline

The FERC index is an average of over 60 subindexes intended to measure all phases of petroleum pipeline construction. The two most important subindexes are for line pipe and pipeline construction, which had weights of 33% and 42%, respectively, in 1978. The subindexes use a variety of deflation methods, including input-cost, component-price, and reliance on judgment. Some of the subindexes measure only materials costs. These include the subindexes for line pipe, which is based on actual transaction prices, including discounts, and the subindex for pumping equipment, which is based on the producer price index.

One of the most important subindexes measures the cost of pipeline contruction. Typically pipeline companies are responsible for providing pipe to the construction firm, which is then in charge of its installation. The pipeline construction subindex thus measures the cost of laying pipe, digging the trench, welding, etc., but not the cost of the pipe itself. Three sources are used to develop this subindex. The first is the cost per linear foot of pipelines laid, as reported by pipeline companies to the FERC. This is not an entirely homogeneous measure since costs vary according to terrain, number of road and river crossings, and other construction specifications. The FERC attempts to adjust the index for the effect of any unusual operations, such as rock blasting, whose costs are reported separately. Unfortunately there are frequently years during which few or no major pipelines (over 100 miles in length) are constructed. During these periods the FERC relies heavily on two other sources to trend the index. The first is a simple index of construction union wages, as reported in the *Engineering News-Record*. Since 1972 the FERC has also collected courtesy bids from three construction companies, who estimate the cost of constructing a hypothetical pipeline of fixed specifications. The final subindex number is a judgmental evaluation based on all three sources. The weight given to the actual costs per linear foot varies from about 25% to 75%, depending upon the amount of construction.

Only the subindex for oil tanks is strictly a component-price measure. The index is based on actual bid prices of constructing oil tanks, categorized by size. The oil tank subindex has about a 6% weight in the total pipeline index.

Weights for the various components are based on actual construction expenditures, as reported to the FERC, and are updated every four or five years. Besides deflating petroleum pipeline construction, the FERC index is used to deflate gas construction and half of water construction. Because of deregulation and budget pressures, the FERC index is scheduled for discontinuance after 1985.

Table 7.2 provides a summary of the input-based deflators. The indexes share several common problems. First, very few of the indexes use actual transaction prices to measure either labor or materials costs. With few exceptions, the indexes use list prices of materials and

Table 7.2
Summary of input based structures deflators[a]

Index	Transaction prices		Current geographic weights	Profit adjustment	Base year of weights
	Materials	Labor			
1. EPA	No	No	No	Yes	1957–1962
2. Handy-Whitman	No	No	No	No	1980
3. AT&T Buildings	No	No	Yes	Yes	Primarily 1946
4. AT&T Plant	No	Yes	Yes	Yes	1965–1975
5. *Engineering News-Record*	No	No	No	No	1913
6. Bureau of Reclamation	No	No	No	No	1930–1946
7. FERC	Yes	No	Yes	No	1978

a. The Turner index has been omitted from the table due to its lack of any formal methodology.

union contractual wage rates to measure input costs. As a result, the indexes may understate the extent of cyclical fluctuations in construction prices. Most of the indexes fail to measure discounts on materials purchases or wage concessions, both of which are commonplace during slack periods. The absence of an adjustment for profit margins will also lead to a cyclically insensitive measure, since profit margins are highly procyclical.

A second recurring feature of the indexes is their outdated weights. Three of the indexes have base year weights of 1946 or earlier. Finally, several of the indexes have fixed geographic weights that do not reflect the geographic composition of current expenditures. The AT&T plant and FERC index meet most of the above criteria but there is little in the remaining indexes to commend.

7.1.4   Component-Price

1.   BEA-DOD Military

The deflator for military constuction is compiled by the BEA on the basis of Department of Defense (DOD) data. The DOD classifies its construction purchases into about 850 detailed categories. Each category has its own "performance specifications" that set minimum construction standards, such as noise transmission levels and the number of bathrooms for residential construction. Assuming the categories are relatively homogeneous, a deflator can be calculated as the price per physical unit, which in most cases is taken to be square feet. The BEA calculates deflators for about 180 of the 850 categories used by DOD. The categories are aggregated using current weights, yeilding an implicit deflator for military construction. The BEA-DOD deflator has been in existence only since 1972. Prior to 1972, the BEA used a weighted average of the FHWA composite, the Census index, and the Turner index to deflate military construction.

Many of the individual component price indexes exhibit drastic year-to-year changes. For example, the index for army troop housing increased by 58.1% in a single year. The index for military maintenance shops fell by 26.5% between 1976 and 1978, only to increase by 58.7% in the following two years. The price variability may be due partly to regional shifts, which are likely to be severe due to the small number of observations in a given year for most components. A more disquieting possibility is that the extreme annual price changes are due to heterogeneity, which could bias the index.

2. Bureau of the Census Single Family Homes Index

The Census index uses the hedonic method of deflation, whereby the price of quantifiable characteristics is estimated from a cross-section regression. It is thus a type of component-price deflation, where the independent variables are the components and the regression coefficients their estimated prices. The Census collects information on the sales price, estimated lot value, and ten house characteristics from a sample of approximately 9,000 new speculatively built single-family homes. The sales price less the estimated lot value is regressed against the ten house characteristics. The price index is then calculated as

$$P_t = \frac{\sum_i b_{i,t} q_{i,b}}{\sum_i b_{i,b} \, q_{i,b}}, \tag{1}$$

where

P_t = Census price index,

$b_{i,t}$ = regression coefficient of variable i in year t,

$q_{i,b}$ = mean of the independent variables in the base year.

The ten independent variables are square feet of floor area, lot size, number of stories and bathrooms, presence or absence of a basement, garage, fireplace, and central air conditioning, and metropolitan and geographic location. The floor area and lot size variables are quantitative, but the other variables enter as dummies. Prior to 1974, lot size and fireplaces were not included in the regression and floor area entered as a dummy variable.

3. Federal Highway Administration Price Index

The FHWA index measures the price in place of six major items of highway construction. As with reclamation projects, construction firms bidding on federal highway contracts must submit bids for each of the items specified in the contract. The bids refer to the price per unit of an item in place and thus reflect all construction costs. The FHWA index covers all federally financed primary highway construction in the United States with contract values greater than $500,000.

The FHWA calculates the average bid price simply by dividing total bid value by total bid quantities for each of the six items. No adjustments or editing of any kind is performed.

The six component items are excavation, portland cement, bituminous concrete, reinforcing steel, structural steel, and structural concrete. The latter three items are combined to form a price index for highway structures, which consist mainly of bridges and overpasses but also include concrete structures such as retaining walls. A price index for highway surfacing is calculated as a weighted average of the price per square yard of portland cement and the price per ton of bituminous concrete. The composite index is a weighted average of the excavation, surfacing, and structures indexes using 1977 quantity weights. At 1977 prices, the weights were 43% for structures, 36% for surfacing, and 21% for excavation.

The FHWA is one of the longest continuous construction price series available, dating back to 1921. Presently the composite index is used to deflate highways and half of railroads and other private and public construction. The structures index has a one-third weight in the deflator for nonresidential buildings.

7.2   Has the BEA Overdeflated Construction Output?

The dearth of component-price indexes has lead several researchers to question the accuracy of the BEA's composite construction deflator. Baily (1981) and Allen (1985) have suggested that an overdeflation of construction output is at least partly responsible for the construction productivity decline. The coincidence of the construction productivity decline and a rapid increase in structures prices offers superficial support for this position. Table 7.3 shows the rate of increase of price indexes for construction and GNP exclusive of structures. The 1947–1981 period is divided into three periods, using the benchmark years of 1963 and 1972 as end points.[10] Structures prices increased somewhat less than prices of other components of GNP in the 1947–1963 period but have risen considerably faster since then. The difference between the annual increase in the composite structures deflator and the GNP deflator exclusive of structures was 1.2% in the 1963–72 period and 2.5% in the 1972–81 period. This corresponds to a period of an accelerating fall in construction productivity.

On the other hand, neither Baily nor Allen has been able to provide much hard evidence in support of an overdeflation. In addition,

Table 7.3
Annual percentage rates of growth of construction price indexes, 1947–1981

Index and type	1947–1963	1963–1981	1963–1972	1972–1981
1. EPA	NA	7.45	5.57	9.37
2. Handy-Whitman				
a. Buildings	4.43	7.44	5.47	9.45
b. Plant	4.23	7.32	4.71	9.99
3. Bell Telephone				
a. Buildings	3.22	7.52	5.87	9.19
b. Plant	2.01	6.54	4.92	8.19
4. Turner	3.04	7.08	6.33	7.84
5. Bureau of Reclamation	2.57	7.00	4.79	9.26
6. FERC	3.56	6.46	2.75	10.30
7. BEA-DOD	NA	NA	NA	9.06
8. Census	NA	7.03	3.96	10.18
9. FHWA				
a. Composite	1.40	7.88	5.40	10.42
b. Structures	1.65	8.09	6.35	9.85
10. Commerce composite construction deflator[a]	2.05	7.40	4.81	10.06
11. Composite less FHWA and residential indexes	3.05	7.07	5.33	8.85
12. GNP minus structures	2.38	5.59	3.65	7.58

a. Calculated as implicit deflator for total construction.

Stokes (1981) dismisses claims of an overdeflation, noting the high percentage of output deflated by the Census index, a component-price measure.

The following section examines the deflation dispute, focusing almost exclusively on the Census and FHWA indexes. Because of their large weight in the composite deflator, a significant overdeflation is not possible without some bias in these two indexes. Moreover, the FHWA and Census indexes are responsible for most of the large relative increase in the price of structures. The two indexes had the highest rate of increase of all structures deflators in the 1972–1981 period, while the FHWA had a very low rate of increase during the 1947–1963 period. The remaining price indexes show only a modest acceleration of structures prices after 1963. The commerce composite exclusive of the FHWA and residential price indexes increases 0.7%

more per year than the GNP deflator during the 1947–1963 period, versus 1.5% in the 1963–1981 period.

7.2.1   Census Single Family Homes Index

Stokes's rejection of a possible overdeflation is based on the presumed accuracy of the Census index. Noting that the Census index has been in use only since 1963, he argues that "the shift to a more correct price index should have resulted in an increase in productivity growth."[11] However, it is an open question whether the Census index is indeed "more correct" than other deflators. The index has two potentially large problems: adjusting for geographic shifts and accounting for ommitted quality characteristics.

1.   *Fixed versus Current Geographic Weights*

The Census uses twelve geographic regions and a metropolitan area dummy to describe house location. The index is calculated by applying fixed base year weights to the coefficients of the location variables. Location variables are thus assumed to represent a quality characteristic, since they enter the price index in exactly the same manner as square feet or other housing quality variables. As a result, any regional shift that alters average prices is measured as a quality change rather than a price change. For example, a shift from a low priced region to a high-priced region would be measured as a quality increase.[12]

More realistically, the regional dummies are measuring price differences between regions rather than quality differences.[13] In this case an index with geographic weights of the current year is appropriate. Letting j denote the regional and metropolitan area dummies and i denote the nonlocation variables, the index would take the following form:

$$P_t = \frac{\sum_i b_{i,t}\, q_{i,t} + \sum_j b_{j,t} q_{j,t}}{\sum_i b_{i,b}\, q_{i,b} + \sum_j b_{j,b}\, q_{j,b}}. \tag{2}$$

As defined before, the b's represent the regression coefficients and the q's represent the means of the independent variables. The above result is analogous to deflating each region separately and developing an implicit deflator for the total.

A simple example may clarify the problem of fixed weights. Assume that the same number of identical houses is built in years one

Table 7.4
Census index with current regional weights and excluding houses over
2,400 square feet

	Annual rates of growth		
	(1) 1963–1981	(2) 1963–1972	(3) 1972–1981
1. Census index including land	7.3	4.1	10.7
2. Census index with current regional weights	7.1	4.0	10.2
3. Census index excluding houses over 2,400 square feet and with current regional weights	6.9	4.2	9.7

and two and that prices remain the same within regions. If a higher
percentage of houses is built in the high-priced region in year two,
average prices and thus nominal investment will rise. The fixed
weight regional price index will ignore this shift and register no
increase in prices. Thus real investment will rise even though the
same number of identical houses was built in both years. A current
regional weight index will measure the shift to a high-priced region as
a price increase and therefore show no change in real investment.

If regional shifts were small or if regional prices varied little, there
would be little difference between the current and fixed weight
indexes. As shown in table 7.4, this was the case for the 1963–1972
period. But since 1972 neither of these conditions has been met. There
has been a large shift toward the South, where prices are below
average. The Census index recalculated with current regional weights
increases 0.4% less per year than the fixed weight index between 1972
and 1981.

2.   Omitted Quality Characteristics

With the exception of fireplaces and central air conditioning, all of the
independent variables in the Census index are size related. Size,
however, is only one facet of housing quality. The Census index does
not include variables such as materials quality; nor does it include
design and amenities, such as closet space, kitchen fixtures, and
patios. The absence of these variables means that the Census
regression coefficients measure the price of the independent variable
plus the value of any omitted quality characteristics correlated with it.

Therefore the price index will be upward biased if omitted quality features have risen relative to included variables. Available information suggests that this is indeed the case. For example, houses have become more energy efficient and are more likely to include "extras," such as appliances.[14]

The problem of omitted quality characteristics is not easily solved because many housing characteristics are not easily quantified. The problem, however, can at least be mitigated by focusing on a more homogeneous category of homes. Large houses are by far the most amenity intensive and thus the least suitable for hedonic deflation. This can be seen in the coefficients of the dummy size categories, which were used by the Census prior to 1974. The marginal cost per square foot is roughly constant for homes less than 2,400 square feet but increases tremendously for homes above that size. For instance, in 1973 the marginal cost of floor space was about $12 per square foot for homes smaller than 2,400 square feet but $36 per square foot for homes above that size.[15] Since the regression coefficients hold constant the effect of other included variables, this difference reflects a far higher concentration of omitted quality characteristics in large homes. The omitted quality problem is greatest for this category of houses.

The average sales price of houses larger than 2,400 square feet has increased far more rapidly than average since 1972. Between 1972 and 1981, average prices of houses larger than 2,400 square feet increased 191%, compared with only 143% for houses below that size. This difference cannot be explained by an increase in the measured quality among large houses. Since 1974 there has been a large increase in the square foot coefficient and a downward shift in the constant, the expected response from a relative increase in the price of large homes. Between 1974 and 1981 the square foot coefficient increased 188% compared with only 113% for the entire index. The constant, including a weighted average of the regional dummies, declined from $4,997 to –$2,677. It thus appears that there were large unmeasured quality increases in the large house category.[16]

The preceding suggests that restricting the sample to houses less than 2400 square feet will yield a more accurate measure of the price of new homes. This would increase the sample's homogeneity and lessen the problem of unmeasured quality. Although houses larger than 2,400 square feet are only 14% of the sample, they have a large effect on the price index.[17] Line 3 of table 7.4 shows that the price index for houses less than 2,400 square feet increases 0.9% less per year than the Census index between 1972 and 1981. About half this difference is attributable to the use of current regional weights and half is due to the exclusion of large homes.

3.   Comparison with the pre-1963 Residential Deflator

Stokes argues that the Census index has a lower rate of increase than the residential deflator it replaced, thus making an overdeflation unlikely after 1963. This contention can be tested by comparing the pre- and post-1963 deflators. Contrary to Stokes's assertions, the early BEA deflator is not a cost index but is based on output measures. The BEA uses an average of two indexes, both based on Federal Housing Administration (FHA) data, to deflate residential construction in the 1947–1963 period. The first is an index of the price per square foot (PPSF) of new FHA-insured homes. The second, termed the FHA 70 cities index, is based on builder's estimates of constructing a house with fixed specifications.[18] Since the house specifications were very detailed, the 70 cities index in principle fully adjusts for quality change.

Because the FHA 70 cities index was discontinued in 1968, only the FHA PPSF index can be updated to 1981. As shown in table 7.5, it rises slightly more than the Census index in the 1963–1972 period but 0.4% less per year in the 1972–1981 period. Furthermore, the FHA PPSF index rose considerably faster than the 70 cities index during the 1947–1963 period. Thus an average of these two FHA indices would have likely risen significantly less than the Census index.

Since both components of the early BEA residential deflator cannot be updated to 1981, a proxy was constructed by dividing an index of sales prices less estimated lot costs of new FHA homes by a quality index. The quality index, $Q(t)$, takes the form

$$Q_t = \frac{\sum_i q_{i,t} \, b_{i,\,1963}}{\sum_i q_{i,\,1963} b_{i,\,1963}}, \tag{3}$$

where as before q denotes housing quality characteristics and b the Census regression coefficients. The quality characteristics inluded in the index are floor area, number of bathrooms and stories, presence of a garage, basement, air conditioning, and fireplace. The resulting index, shown in line 5 of table 7.5, nearly matches both the early BEA deflator and the Census index in the 1963–1972 period. However, the Census index once again has a significantly higher rate of increase after 1972, amounting to 0.7% per year.

Table 7.5
Annual percentage rates of increase of residential price indexes, 1950–1981

Index	(1) 1950–1963	(2) 1963–1981	(3) 1963–1972	(4) 1972–1981
1. FHA PPSF	2.0	6.9	4.2	9.8
2. FHA 70 cities	0.8	NA	NA	NA
3. Pre-1963 BEA deflator	1.4	NA	NA	NA
4. Census index excluding land	NA	7.0	4.0	10.2
5. FHA 7 characteristics[a]	1.4	6.7	3.9	9.4
6. FHA 7 characteristics, regional adjustment	1.3	6.4	4.1	8.8
7. FHA PPSF, regional adjustment	1.7	6.6	4.5	9.1
8. Adjusted Census index[b]	NA	6.8	4.2	9.3

a. Price index for FHA homes based on 7 characteristics: square feet, bathrooms, garage, basements, stories, air conditioning, and, after 1972, fireplaces.

b. Census index excluding land with current regional weights and excluding houses over 2,400 square feet.

One potential problem with FHA data is that the geographic distribution of FHA homes is unrepresentative of new homes. To control for regional differences, an adjustment factor was calculated using regional price indexes and regional weights for Census and FHA homes.[19] The adjustment estimates what the price of FHA homes would be if they had the same regional distribution as Census homes. The regional adjustment is considerable during the 1972–1981 period. FHA homes are disproportionately located in the Southwest and West, two areas with above average housing inflation. A price index for FHA homes based on equation (3) and adjusted for the regional composition increases 1.4% less per year than the Census index. After controlling for the regional composition, even a simple price per square foot index of FHA homes rises 1% less per year than the Census index.

In conclusion, all of the residential price indexes are in general agreement during the 1963–1972 period, showing rates of inflation of close to 4%. However, price indexes based on FHA data consistently increase less than the Census index during the 1972–1981 period. Had the pre-1963 BEA residential deflator been in use during the 1972–1981 period, it would likely have risen about 1% less per year than the

Census index. Thus the switch to the Census index in 1963 did not raise construction productivity growth, as stated by Stokes, but instead lowered it. Finally, FHA data provide support for the earlier adjustments made to the Census index. FHA homes are smaller than average and contain practically none of the large homes that have contributed to a bias in the Census index. The FHA index based on seven house characteristics differs only slightly from the Census index with current regional weights and excluding large homes.

7.2.2 Federal Highway Administration Index

The harsh criticisms of the construction price statistics by the NBER and others led to a search for alternative deflators in the early sixties. With few component-price indexes to choose from, researchers naturally focused on the FHWA index. Almost without exception, the FHWA was judged to be an exemplary index. The GNP data improvement report states that the FHWA index "conform[s] to the desired concept of output price indexes," while Dacy, summarizing the professional consensus, states that the index is "the most reliable of the available construction price indexes."[20] In addition, the FHWA index was accorded a major role in the work of Dacy (1964), Jorgenson and Griliches (1967), and Gordon (1968b).

The high regard for the FHWA index is due to its component-price methodology and the apparent homogeneity of its components. Yet the highway component's homogeneity was never closely examined but was instead simply assumed. The variation of prices in a cross-section will give some indication of the component's homogeneity. If the FHWA components are relatively homogeneous, prices should vary only modestly, reflecting only area cost differences. However, if the components are not well defined, unmeasured quality differences will provide an additional source of price variation.

The mean, standard deviation, and range of average bid prices by state in 1981 are shown in table 7.6. All six highway components show a tremendous amount of price variation. For example, average excavation prices range anywhere from 78¢ per cubic yard to $15.71. Price variation, as measured by the standard deviation of the state means, is lowest for the bituminous concrete and reinforcing steel components, at 20% of their respective means. This ratio rises to 39% for structural steel and an incredible 96% for common excavation. As a comparison, the standard deviation of state construction costs is about 10% of the state means, with the highest cost state roughly 50%

Table 7.6
Variation of state highway bid price means in 1981[a]

				Range		
Component	(1) Mean	(2) Standard deviation	(3) SD/ mean	(4) Low	(5) High	(6) High/ low
1. Excavation (cubic yard)	2.26	2.17	0.96	0.78	15.71	20.14
2. Portland cement concrete (square yard)	18.19	11.45	0.63	8.24	70.50	8.56
3. Bituminous concrete (ton)	26.26	5.12	0.19	17.04	40.60	2.38
4. Reinforcing steel (pound)	0.45	0.09	0.20	0.30	0.72	2.39
5. Structural steel (pound)	0.85	0.28	0.33	0.58	1.99	3.43
6. Structural concrete (cubic yard)	234.15	90.18	0.39	153.40	676.41	4.41

a. The table lists the mean and standard deviation of the state bid price means, calculated by giving each state equal weight. The sample consists of the lower 48 states and the District of Columbia, except for portland cement concrete, where data is unavailable for 11 states. The data source is the Federal Highway Administration, "Price Trends for Federal-Aid Highway Construction."

costlier than the lowest cost state.[21] Thus the FHWA components vary far more in price than can be attributed to regional cost differences. Instead, the large price variations reflect a very imprecise measure of output.

Furthermore, prices differ drastically even between neighboring states, suggesting that regional cost differences are not responsible. For example, in 1981 the price per cubic yard of structural concrete averaged $208 in Virginia but $676 in West Virginia. The erratic movements of the index from quarter to quarter, attributed by some to competitive conditions, may also be the result of heterogeneity. For example, between the second and third quarters of 1980, average contract prices of structural steel decreased by 22.5% while the average price of structural concrete increased by 21.6%. These changes can hardly be attributed to demand pressures if prices were moving in opposite directions.

Cross-sectional component heterogeneity is important because it leads to the possibility of heterogeneity over time, and thus bias in the price index. The FHWA index will be unbiased only if the quality characteristics accounting for cross-sectional price differences remain constant over time. However, this seems unlikely because the character of highway construction has changed markedly in the post-war period. First, there have been sharp swings in interstate highway construction. The interstate percentage of total FHWA contract value rose from near zero in 1952 to a peak of 70 in 1968 and then fell to slightly less than half in 1981.[22] A related trend is a large decline in average project size. Average contract size declined by over half in real terms from 1968 to 1981.[23] This reflects both the decline in large interstate projects and a shift from new construction to alterations of existing highways, such as resurfacing projects.

The possible effect of these shifts is estimated from a 1981 cross-sectional regression. The dependent variable is the log of the average state price, which is in turn an average of the six component prices. Independent variables include regional dummies, the urban-rural composition, and the log of average project size. The regressions were estimated by weighted least squares, using the number of highway contracts per state as weights. The results, shown in table 7.7, indicate a significant negative effect of project size on costs. A 10% increase in project size is associated with a 2% decrease in the composite price index. On the other hand, the coefficient of the interstate variable is positive but insignificant. Thus interstate projects do not have any measurable effect on prices after controlling for their above average size. These results are also confirmed in regressions using individual component prices as the dependent variable. Project size appears to have the greatest negative influence on excavation costs, but the variable is also significant at the 90% level for surfacing and structures costs. As a final note, urban excavation costs are an estimated 80% greater than rural costs, which is in general agreement with FHWA data.[24]

The regressions are evidence that the shift toward smaller reconstruction projects beginning in the late sixties significantly increased per unit costs, leading to an upward bias in the FHWA index. A corrected price index can be estimated by holding average project size constant. The measured price index, P_t, is equal to the "true" price index, P_t^*, plus the effect of changing contract size:

Table 7.7
Coefficients and standard errors of 1981 cross-sectional highway regressions[a]

Independent variables	Dependent variable			
	(1) Composite	(2) Excavation	(3) Surfacing	(4) Structures
1. Constant	9.575 (0.696)	2.984 (1.308)	8.031 (0.565)	7.998 (0.709)
2. North Central	−0.318 (0.086)	−0.574 (0.162)	−0.315 (0.070)	−0.133 (0.088)
3. South	−0.077 (0.096)	−0.181 (0.181)	−0.059 (0.078)	−0.053 (0.098)
4. West	−0.111 (0.098)	−0.249 (0.184)	−0.220 (0.079)	0.080 (0.100)
5. Percentage interstate	0.096 (0.181)	0.265 (0.339)	0.088 (0.147)	−0.18 (0.184)
6. Log (average real contract size)	−0.217 (0.092)	−0.316 (0.173)	−0.144 (0.075)	−0.129 (0.084)
7. Percentage urban	0.304 (0.154)	0.826 (0.289)	0.088 (0.125)	0.158 (0.157)
R^2	0.995	0.545	0.996	0.994
SE (standard error)	1.24	2.34	1.01	1.27
N	49	49	49	49

a. Dependent variable is the log of the average state price. The composite regression is a weighted average of the component prices. The sample consists of the continental 48 states and the District of Columbia. Regressions were estimated by weighted least squares, using number of contracts as weights. Data sources are "Price Trends for Federal-aid Highway Construction" and "Bid Opening Report."

$$\ln P_t = \ln P_t^* + b \ln S_t, \tag{4}$$

where S is an index of average real project size. Using the estimated regression coefficient of $-.2$ for b, a corrected index, P^*, may be calculated. Since average contract size was nearly the same in 1972 as in 1963, the two indexes move at the same rate during those years. However, the 60% drop in average contract size between 1972 and 1981 implies a 1.7% annual overstatement of the FHWA index.

The accuracy of this correction may be tested by comparing the FHWA index with the Bureau of Reclamation index. Both of these indexes price excavation and structural concrete in place. Table 7.8 compares price indexes for these two identical components. In both

Table 7.8
Annual percentage change in Bureau of Reclamation and Federal Highway Administration component prices, 1963–1981

Component	(1) 1963–1972	(2) 1972–1981	(3) 1963–1981
1. Excavation			
Bureau of Reclamation			
Dams	3.65	8.55	6.07
Canals	4.28	9.07	6.65
Laterals	4.98	8.45	6.70
Tunnels	2.96	9.50	6.18
Pipelines	NA	7.05	NA
All projects[a]	3.91	8.63	6.24
FHWA	5.47	10.43	7.92
2. Structural concrete			
Bureau of Reclamation			
Canals	2.44	9.82	6.07
Laterals	2.29	8.89	5.53
Tunnels	2.31	10.48	6.32
Pipelines	NA	7.85	NA
All projects[a]	2.36	9.32	5.78
FHWA	6.41	9.76	8.07

a. Calculated using Bureau of Reclamation weights. For excavation the weights are 8/19 for dams, 5/19 for canals, and 2/19 for laterals, tunnels, and pipelines. The weights for structural concrete projects are 3/8 for canals and laterals and 1/8 for tunnels and pipelines. Source: U.S. Department of Transportation, Federal Highway Administration (1984) and unpublished data from the Bureau of Reclamation.

cases, the Bureau of Reclamation index increases significantly less than its FHWA counterpart. The Bureau of Reclamation measure of excavation prices increased 1.7% less per year than the FHWA measure over the 1963–1981 period. The difference between the two indexes is even larger for structural concrete, averaging over 2% per year. The Bureau of Reclamation index therefore supports the conclusion that the FHWA index is upward biased. The FHWA index adjusted for contract size shows about a 1.7% annual bias in the 1972–1981 period. However, unlike the Bureau of Reclamation index, it shows no bias in the 1963–1972 period.

7.2.3   Nonresidential Buildings

The largest remaining question concerns the price of nonresidential buildings. The BEA deflator is an unweighted average of the Census, FHWA structures, and Turner indexes. The first two indexes measure prices of other sectors, namely, houses and highways, and in any case have been shown to be upward biased. The Turner index, while at least nominally based on nonresidental buildings, is a cost index with a large amount of subjectivity. As a result, the BEA deflator conveys almost no useful information on nonresidential building prices.

Indexes of costs per square foot will provide at least a rough measure of building costs. If anything, this will probably overstate true building costs since building codes have become stricter over time and building electrical and heating systems have become more sophisticated. The most homogeneous building category, as measured by the cross-sectional variation of square footage costs, is commercial buildings.[25] A price per square foot index for office buildings is shown in line 2b of table 7.9.[26] Costs per square foot increased 1.4% less per year than the BEA deflator in the 1963–1972 period and 1.0% less per year in the 1972–1981 period.

7.2.4   Summary and Implications

A close examination of the Census, FHWA, and nonresidential building price indexes leaves little doubt that the BEA has overdeflated construction output. The overdeflation stems from a lack of a homogeneous output measure in both the Census and FHWA indexes and the lack of any type of price measure for nonresidential buildings. Estimates of the extent of the bias in the BEA deflator are presented in table 7.9. The revised residential deflator is the Census

Table 7.9
Annual percentage change of official and revised structures deflators, 1963–1981

Category	(1) 1963–1981	(2) 1963–1972	(3) 1972–1981
1. Residential			
a. BEA	7.0	4.0	10.2
b. Revised	6.8	4.2	9.3
c. Difference	0.3	−0.1	0.9
2. Nonresidential building			
a. BEA	7.3	5.4	9.3
b. Revised	6.1	3.9	8.3
c. Difference	1.2	1.4	1.0
3. Nonresidential nonbuilding			
a. BEA	7.2	4.7	9.8
b. Revised	6.5	4.4	8.6
c. Difference	0.7	0.3	1.2
4. Total structures			
a. BEA	7.2	4.7	9.7
b. Revised	6.4	4.2	8.7
c. Difference	0.8	0.5	1.0

index with current regional weights and excluding houses over 2,400 square feet, while the nonresidential building deflator is based on the cost per square foot of commercial buildings. The nonresidential nonbuilding deflator is an unweighted average of the FHWA index adjusted for contract size and the bid price components of the Bureau of Reclamation index. The revised composite deflator shows a modest 0.6% annual bias in the BEA deflator during the 1963–1972 period, all of it occurring in the nonresidential sector. However, the overdeflation is much more significant in the 1972–1981 period. The BEA deflator has an upward bias of approximately 1% per year, with a large bias occurring in all three construction sectors.

A few implications of the revised price index for new construction will be briefly discussed. First, an understatement of real construction output will result in an understatement of real construction value added and productivity. Real construction value added is estimated by the double deflation method as the difference between deflated output and deflated inputs. Thus an overdeflation of output would understate construction value added and output by the same absolute amount but result in a proportionally greater understatement of value added. A 1% annual overdeflation of construction output would result in an approximately 2% understatement of construction productivity growth.[27] Thus instead of falling by 2.5% per year between 1972 and 1981, construction productivity falls by only 0.5% per year using the revised indexes. This explains most, although not all, of the construction productivity decline.

The deflation revisions will also increase measures of real investment. This effect can be considered cumulative: The understatement of investment will be small during the first years of the overdeflation, but will steadily increase as the gap between the actual and "true" price indexes grows. The revised structures deflator increases about 10% less than the BEA deflator during the entire 1972–1981 period. Thus 1981 real gross investment in structures would be about 10% higher under the revised deflator, an amount equal to about 0.8% of GNP.

It should be noted that the deflation revisions will affect both nominal and real net investment. Nominal net investment is affected because the deflator is used to revalue historical depreciation to current prices. Thus an overstatement of structures prices will overstate nominal depreciation and understate net investment. Again a rough estimate of the magnitude of this effect may be attempted. A 10% overestimate of structures prices in 1981 would result in approximately a 10% overestimate of nominal depreciation. Since depreciation charges for structures are about 5% of GNP, nominal net investment would be understated by about 0.5% of GNP. Real net investment would of course be understated twice, once due to the overstatement of nominal depreciation and a second time due to deflation. Since net structures investment was about 3% of GNP in 1981, the latter understatement would amount to 0.3% of GNP in that year. The total understatement of real net investment is thus about 0.8% of GNP, or about 20% of total measured net investment in 1981. Thus the deflation revisions can potentially have a very large effect on net investment.

7.3   Comparison with the 1961 Commerce Construction Deflators

Table 7.10 shows the construction deflators in use at the time of the NBER's Price Statistics Review Committee. The 1961 deflators were entirely worthy of the committee's description as "defective in almost every possible way." Only 13% of constuction output was deflated by

Table 7.10
1961 commerce construction deflators

Index	(1) Expenditures deflated	(2) 1959 weight
Input-Cost		64.89
1. E. H. Boeckh	Residential	45.33
2. George Fuller Co.	Office buildings	4.15
3. U.S. Department of Agriculture	Farm buildings	2.25
4. Handy-Whitman	Electric Utilities, gas and pipelines	7.76
5. Associated General Contractors	½ sewer and water, Conservation and development	2.70
6. *Engineering News-Record*	Same as (5)	2.70
Input-Productivity		21.68
1. Turner Construction Co.	Industrial buildings	5.07
2. American Appraisal Co.	Other nonresidential buildings	16.61
Component-Price		13.44
1. Bureau of Public Roads	Highways	11.21
2. Interstate Commerce Commission		2.23
a. Railroads	Railroads	0.53
b. Communications	Telephone and telegraph	1.70

Source: National Bureau of Economic Research (1961).

component-price indexes. Moreover, the cost indexes used extraordinarily poor methodology. The indexes generally priced only a few inputs, which were not always representative of the expenditures that they were used to deflate. The indexes combined the inputs using ancient weights, whose accuracy even in the base period was questionable. No fewer than six of the indexes had weights based on the 1910–1914 period, while the Boeckh and Turner indexes had comparatively recent weights of 1926–1929 and 1939.

Compounding these difficulties was a lack of available source materials for the privately compiled indexes. Several companies regarded their indexes as trade secrets and jealously guarded the release of detailed information. As a result, the exact methodology of the indexes was seldom known. The input-productivity indexes were particularly vague as to how the indexes were "adjusted" for productivity.

Compared to the low standards of the 1961 deflators, the 1985 deflators are undeniably an improvement. Only three of the 1961 deflators are still in use: the FHWA (then Bureau of Public Roads), Turner, and Handy-Whitman indexes. Over 75% of construction output is currently deflated by component-price measures versus 13% in 1961. Input-cost indexes still in use are generally more representative of the expenditures they deflate than their 1961 counterparts. Fewer indexes are compiled by private companies.

The construction price statistics have therefore improved since 1961 but this does not necessarily mean that they have reached an acceptable level of quality. One method of evaluating the current price statistics is to review the present applicability of the original NBER criticisms.

1. *Indexes measure input costs rather than output prices.* Given the high percentage of construction deflated by component-price indexes, the BEA has on the surface made great strides in solving this problem. However, much of this increase is the result of applying existing component-price deflators to sectors that they are not intended to measure rather than developing new indexes. The composite structures deflator is heavily dependent on two deflators, one of which was in existence in 1960.

The major improvement over the past 25 years is the development of the Census index. However, the only component-price deflator developed since the midsixties is the deflator for military construction, while one index, the ICC railroad, has been discontinued, and a second, the FERC, is scheduled to be discontinued. Furthermore, closer analysis of the Census and FHWA indexes reveals that component-price deflators are not always unbiased. The output measure must also be homogeneous, a criterion that is lacking in the FHWA index and in the case of large homes, in the Census index as well.

2. *Indexes are compiled mostly by private companies and source materials are unavailable to the public.* Three of the nine current construction deflators are privately compiled, compared with seven out of ten in 1961. Privately compiled indexes have roughly a 19% weight in the current composite deflator compared with 84% in 1961. Source materials for the privately compiled indexes still in use are still very difficult to obtain, particularly for the Handy-Whitman and Turner indexes.

3. *Indexes are not prepared in order to provide appropriate coverage for the categories of construction that they are used to deflate.* Very little progress has been made in this area. The main sectors lacking their own deflators are nonresidential buildings and multifamily residential. Altogether about 55% of new construction is deflated by indexes derived from other sectors.[28]

4. A number of the NBER's criticisms pertain primarily to input-based indexes:

• The bill of materials priced is incomplete.

• Weights are based on periods of the remote past.

• Wage rates and materials prices used do not represent actual transaction prices.

The first criticism is not presently a major problem. Most of the cost indexes cover a fairly broad spectrum of materials. The only exceptions are the Handy-Whitman building index and *Engineering News-Record* index used for telephone construction after 1982. As covered in section 7.1, the remaining two criticisms are still relevant. Generally, list prices of materials and contractual union wage rates are used. Three of the indexes have base periods of 1946 or earlier.

5. *The geographic coverage and weighting of the indexes is rarely suitable.* The problem of geographic weighting is nearly as acute today as it was in 1960. The Census index has appropriate geographic coverage, but its use of fixed weights has resulted in a significant overstatement of prices after 1972. Several of the cost indexes, including the EPA and Handy-Whitman, do not use geographic weights based on current expenditures but instead use simple averages of city or regional prices. In addition, applying indexes to other sectors, such as the FHWA and Census to nonresidential buildings, is only appropriate if the geographic composition of the sectors is similar. One notable example of an index that conforms to the desired standard is the FHWA index, which is nationwide in coverage and reflects the current geographic composition of highway expenditures.

6. *The timing of the indexes is not appropriate for the deflation of construction activity estimates.* This criticism applies mostly to the FHWA and Bureau of Reclamation indexes. Both are based on new contracts issued but deflate current work in progress. Prices of current and future work may differ considerably in times of major price shocks, such as those in 1973 and 1979–1980. Because of the relatively short time lag between the construction and sale of houses, this criticism applies with much less force to the Census index.

7.4 Improving the Construction Deflators

While the primary focus of this chapter has been on evaluating the present structures deflators, a few comments on how to improve the deflators are in order. The most pressing need is of course the development of additional price indexes. There appear to be three major approaches to achieving this end: hedonic price indexes, unit price indexes estimation, and indexes based on contractor cost estimates.

7.4.1   Hedonic Price Indexes

The successful development of the Census index led to the hope that the construction deflation problem could be solved through the widespread use of the hedonic technique. These hopes, however, have remained unfulfilled. There are two main requirements for a hedonic price index: the ability to quantify construction characteristics and a relatively large number of observations. Single-family home construction meets both of these requirements but most other types of construction do not. For example, the Census Bureau has experimented with a hedonic price index for multiunit residential construction (see Pollock, 1984). The experiments have been largely unsuccessful, in part because only three characteristics have been quantified (region, square feet, and number of bathrooms.) A further difficulty was a small number of available observations, especially for quarterly periods.

Perhaps the most promising area for hedonic pricing is highway construction. As shown earlier in this chapter, a number of highway characteristics may be quantified. In addition, the FHWA awards a large number of highway contracts each year.[29] But widespread use of hedonic price indexes does not appear possible, because either the sectors are too small or too heterogeneous.

7.4.2   Unit Price Deflators

A unit price deflator measures the price per physical unit, which is usually taken as either floor area or as a specified quantity of materials in place. The present FHWA and BEA-DOD deflators are of this type. The weakness of this type of deflation is that it does not control for other quality characteristics. As seen with the FHWA index, this may lead to bias over time. However, if the construction types can be narrowly defined, as in the BEA-DOD index, the heterogeneity problem will be much less severe. The most likely candidate for unit price deflation is nonresidential buildings, which, if segmented into narrow categories, may be adequately priced by a square foot-based index. Materials-in-place deflators may be possible for some types of nonbuilding construction, such as water and sewer or telephone construction.

7.4.3   Contractor Cost Estimates

This method of deflation relies on cost estimates from contractors or on other types of "informed judgment." For example, firms may be surveyed and asked to estimate the cost of a hypothetical project with fixed specifications. This method of deflation was used by the FHA-70 cities index, which formed half of the BEA's residential deflator from 1947 to 1963. Courtesy bids from construction firms are also given a small weight in the FERC subindex for pipeline construction.

The advantage of this method of deflation is that there is no problem of heterogeneity since the construction specifications are fixed over time. The primary disadvantage is that the index is based on hypothetical bids rather than market transactions. Contractors submitting hypothetical bids know that they will not be required to construct the project and therefore may bid differently from what they would in actual practice. This may be especially a problem over the short run. FHWA and Bureau of Reclamation cost estimates are insensitive to current market conditions, and their relationship to actual bid prices varies with the business cycle.[30] Therefore contractor estimates should probably be used only for the most heterogeneous types of construction that cannot be deflated by more traditional means. Examples might include institutional buildings or electric utilities.

Cost indexes should be used for deflation only as a last resort. When used, they should meet certain minimum standards that are generally lacking from the present indexes. For example, the input-output tables can be used for developing recent and relatively accurate input weights. Public rather than private data sources should be used and detailed source materials should be available.

In conclusion, the problem of construction deflation is difficult but not insoluble. The major need is a commitment of government resources, which will be forthcoming only if there is a greater demand for better statistics from the statistics users.

7.5   Conclusion

Construction price statistics continue to be an area in need of major improvement. The BEA has made progress since the issuance of the NBER report, particularly with the development of the Census index. However, major gaps still remain, especially for private nonresidential structures. Furthermore, very little research has been conducted in the area since the late sixties. Indeed, with the discontinuance of the AT&T and FERC indexes, it is arguable that the statistics are retrogressing.

This chapter has presented evidence that the rate of growth of structures prices has been overestimated since 1963, with a consequent underestimate of real investment and construction productivity. This is the price of having subpar statistics. The responsibility for the current state of affairs does not rest entirely with the BEA but is in large measure the result of indifference by the profession. The quality of construction price statistics is certainly not proportional to the importance attached by many to measures of real investment. More research is needed in order to restore a proper balance.

Acknowledgment

I wish to thank Robert J. Gordon for first suggesting the topic of construction deflation to me and giving me very valuable comments.

Notes

1. National Bureau of Economic Research (1961, p. 87).

2. The phrase "based on output" is used here to refer to a component-price index, i.e., an index that measures output prices rather than input costs.

3. All information in this chapter is based on the BEA's methodology as of November 1985. Some changes in the weighting of the indexes were made in December 1985 as part of the BEA's benchmark revisions.

4. A minor exception is residential additions and alterations, which since 1978 have been deflated by an average of the Census index and the CPI index for maintenance and repair. Prior to 1978 it was deflated solely by the Census index.

5. Private nonresidential buildings are deflated by an unweighted average of the three indexes. The three indexes are used in varying proportions, depending on the type of building, to deflate public buildings.

6. A perusal of the *Engineering News-Record* price quotations shows several questionable entries. Prices between neighboring cities often differ

drastically. For instance, in July 1977 the price for a hundred pounds of reinforcing steel was listed as $9.50 in San Francisco and $18.00 in Seattle. Common brick prices were listed as $79.00 in Chicago and $145.00 in Minneapolis.

7. *Census of Construction Industries*, 1982 U.S. summary, table 12.

8. Of the seven remaining components, two have 1960 weights, one each has weights of 1965, 1967, and 1978, and two are taken directly from the BLS producer price index.

9. In addition, the Turner index is heavily weighted toward costs in Eastern cities.

10. The 1981 end point was chosen because it marks the end of both high structures inflation and the decline in construction productivity.

11. Stokes (1981, p. 496).

12. A quality index may be calculated implicitly as an index of sales prices divided by a price index. A shift to a high-price region would increase sales prices but have no effect on a fixed regional weight price index, thus increasing quality.

13. An alternative possibility is that the regional coefficients are measuring omitted quality characteristics that are regionally correlated. However, cost differences of 40% or more are too large to be explained by omitted quality differences. Furthermore, Pieper (1984, chapter 3) found no significant differences in omitted quality characteristics between regions.

14. For example, the percentage of new homes with double-glazed windows increased from 25% in 1974 to 54% in 1982. Eighty-four percent of all new houses built after 1975 have wall insulation, compared with 54% of those built between 1950 and 1969. As for appliances, the percentage of new homes including a dishwasher in the sales price increased from 26% in 1963 to 82% in 1981.

15. This calculation assumes an average size of 2,800 square feet in the category of 2,400 square feet and above.

16. Alternatively one could argue that the relative price increase of large homes was real. However, it seems unlikely that prices of such closely related types of construction could diverge so greatly. Furthermore, quality improvements in large homes would have likely taken the form of increased amenities and would have thus gone unmeasured by the Census.

17. The least squares regression technique will tend to give a large weight to large homes, since the residuals will generally be large in absolute terms.

18. The index is termed the 70 cities index because the FHA surveyed builders in 70 different cities. Further information about the index can be found in Gordon (1968a) and U.S. Department of Commerce, Bureau of Economic Analysis (1974).

19. More formally, the FHA price index is multiplied by the following regional adjustment factor, R:

$$R_t = \frac{\sum_j n^c_{j,t} P_{j,t}}{\sum_j n^f_{j,t} P_{j,t}},$$

where $P_{j,t}$ is a price index for region j in year t and $n_{j,t}$ is the percentage of homes in region j in year t. The superscript c refers to census homes and f to FHA homes.

20. *Gross National Product Improvement Report*, p. 146, and Dacy (1964, p. 476).

21. State construction costs (averages of materials and labor costs) are from Moselle (1983).

22. Unpublished data provided by Tom Pettit of the Federal Highway Administration.

23. Average contract size is from the Federal Highway Administration, *Bid Opening Report*. The FHWA composite was used to convert nominal values into real values.

24. The only breakdown of prices provided by the FHWA is for the urban-rural composition. Urban excavation prices were 60% higher than rural prices in 1981, which is insignificantly different from the regression estimate.

25. Otelsberg (1972) reports that the standard deviation of costs per square foot of commercial buildings was 13.1% of the mean in a 1971 cross-section. In contrast, this ratio varied between 50% and 83% for hospitals and public, educational, and religious buildings.

26. The cost per square foot index is based on F. W. Dodge data, as published in Otelsberg (1972) and the *Architectural Record*. The indexes estimate the price of construction put in place by taking an average of previous new contract prices, using progress patterns as weights. Detailed methodology will be furnished by the author on request.

27. With the double deflation method, an index of construction output, C', can be written as an average of an index of inputs, M', and value added, V':

$$C' = (1 - a)M' + aV',$$

where the above variables refer to real quantities, a is the value added share of output, and the prime refers to an index number. Thus a 1% underestimate of real construction output would result in a $1/a$ underestimate of value added. Value added is roughly 40% of construction output and new construction is about 80% of total construction. Therefore a 1% underestimate of new construction due to deflation would result in an approximately 2% (.8/.4) underestimate of value added.

28. Construction sectors with their own deflators are telephone and telegraph, electric light and power, petroleum pipelines, single-unit residential, highways, military, conservation and development and sewers.

29. For example, in 1981 the FHWA awarded 2,126 contracts with a contract value of $500,000 or more.

30. FHWA and the Bureau of Reclamation estimate the cost of their projects before bids are placed. These estimates can be thus taken as measures of "informed judgment." The ratio of actual bid prices to the engineer's estimate is generally around one at business cycle peaks but may fall to .9 or lower in a major downturn. See Pieper (1985) for further details.

References

Allen, Steven G. (1985). "Why Construction Productivity Is Declining," *Review of Economics and Statistics* 67 (November), 661–669.

Baily, Martin N. (1981). "Productivity and the Services of Capital and Labor," *Brookings Papers on Economic Activity*, 1–65.

Dacy, Douglas (1964). "A Price and Productivity Index for a Nonhomogeneous Product," *Journal of the American Statistical Association* 59 (June), 469–485.

_____ (1965). "Productivity and Price Trends in Constructon since 1947," *Review of Economics and Statistics* 47 (November), 406–411.

Gordon, Robert J. (1967). "Problems in the Measurement of Real Investment in the U.S. Private Economy," unpublished Ph.D. dissertation, M.I.T.

_____ (1968a). "An Evaluation of Alternative Approaches to Construction Price Deflation," mimeo, August.

_____ (1968b). "A New View of Real Investment in Structures, 1919–1960," *Review of Economics and Statistics* 50 (November), 417–428.

Jorgenson, Dale, and Griliches, Zvi (1967). "The Explanation of Productivity Change," *The Review of Economic Studies* 34 (July), 249–284.

Moselle, Gary, ed. (1983). *Building Cost Manual* (Carlsbad, CA: Craftsman Book Co.).

Musgrave, John C. (1969). "New Bureau of the Census Construction Price Indexes," *Journal of the American Statistical Association* 64 (September), 771–786.

National Bureau of Economic Research (1961). *The Price Statistics of the Federal Government* (New York: National Bureau of Economic Research).

Otelsberg, Jonah (1972). "Trends in Valuation per Square Foot of Building Floor Area, 1947–71," *Construction Review* 18 (August), 4–11.

Pieper, Paul (1984). "The Measurement of Real Investment in Structures and the Construction Productivity Decline," unpublished Ph.D. dissertation, Northwestern University.

_____ (1985). "Alternative Approaches to Nonresidential Building Deflation," mimeo, November.

Pollock, Jesse (1984). "Research into a Cost Index for Multiunit Residential Construction," Bureau of the Census mimeo, April.

Stokes, H. Kemble (1981). "An Examination of the Productivity Decline in the Construction Industry," *Review of Economics and Statistics* 63 (November), 495–502.

U.S. Department of Commerce, Bureau of the Census (1980). *Value of New Construction Put in Place*, Construction Reports Series C30, supplement.

——— (1982). *Census of Constuction Industries*.

U.S. Department of Commerce, Bureau of Economic Analysis (1974). "Revised Deflators for New Construction, 1947–73," *Survey of Current Business* 54 (August), 18–27.

U.S. Department of Commerce, Office of Federal Statistical Policy and Standards (1977). *Gross National Product Improvement Project Report*, (Washington, DC: U.S.G.P.O.).

U.S. Department of Transportation, Federal Highway Administration (1981). "Price Trends for Federal-Aid Highway Construction."

——— (1982). "Bid Opening Report."

8

Rates of Return and Capital Aggregation Using Alternative Rental Prices

Michael J. Harper,
Ernst R. Berndt, and
David O. Wood

8.1 Introduction

The publication by the U.S. Bureau of Labor Statistics (BLS) of multifactor productivity growth estimates for major U.S. sectors and industries (BLS, 1983) reflects an important research theme in the modern theory and measurement of economic cost and production. Until then, the BLS productivity program had focused almost exclusively on labor productivity—units of output per unit of labor. Increasingly, however, productivity researchers have been concerned with developing more comprehensive measures that reflect changes in output versus changes in all inputs—units of output per unit of aggregate input. While BLS has contributed to and monitored these research efforts, in the late 1970s an independent review of productivity research was provided by a National Academy of Sciences Panel (1979), which then recommended that BLS undertake to develop and publish multifactor productivity measures for the United States. BLS (1983) is, therefore, the first result of an expanded BLS productivity measurement program, including both labor and multifactor productivity statistics.

The opinions expressed herein are those of the authors, and are not necessarily those of the institutions with which they are affiliated

This research has been sponsored by the BLS as part of its ongoing program in assessing methodological issues underlying productivity measurement. Special thanks to former BLS staff members William Waldorf and Charles R. Hulten, who offered valuable advice and suggestions during the formative stages of this project. The detailed comments of Edwin Dean, W. Erwin Diewert and an anonymous referee are also gratefully acknowledged.

A first version of this chapter was given at the John F. Kennedy School of Government, Harvard University, Program for Technology and Economic Policy Conference, 8 November 1985.

The conceptual framework for a measure of multifactor productivity (MFP) is due to Jan Tinbergen (1942) and Robert Solow (1957). In their formulation, MFP growth is related to outward shifts in the aggregate production function, and—under certain conditions—can be computed as growth in aggregate output minus growth in aggregate input, where growth rates in aggregate output and input are computed as the cost share-weighted growth rates in the components of output and input. The key assumptions required to compute the MFP measure directly from observable data are (i) that production technology is characterized by constant returns to scale, (ii) that output prices equal marginal production costs, (iii) that inputs are purchased in competitive markets, and (iv) that input quantities adjust instantaneously to their long-run equilibrium levels. Significant violation of any of these assumptions implies that more complicated models of production are required, and that econometric methods must be employed in obtaining MFP measures.

The above discussion dramatizes the difficult task that economic theorists have set for economic statisticians, namely, how to measure and/or impute the price and quantity components of outputs and inputs required to compute the cost share weights used in calculating aggregate output and input. The history of both conceptual and empirical research on MFP measurement since Solow (1957) is almost entirely taken up with this task. And of all the difficult problems, perhaps the most troublesome—and the subject of the present chapter—has been the measurement of capital input service prices.

The basic issue in measuring capital input service prices is that capital goods are durable, and since rental markets for most durable inputs are not sufficiently widespread, it is usually not possible to observe the appropriate service price as the result of a market transaction. Under these conditions, the economic statistician must appeal to the theorist for assistance in deriving a rental price formula sufficient to impute rental prices for capital assets from observable data. These imputed rental prices can then be combined with estimates of capital input service flows to calculate the rental cost share weights required to compute the aggregate capital services.

While economic theory has provided important guidance in the specification of rental price formulas, it as yet has not been able to resolve completely all the empirical questions that the economic statistician must answer. Most important, two critical components of the asset-specific rental prices are (i) the expected rate of return and (ii) the expected capital gains terms. Empirical implementation of these expected rates of return and capital gains components typically requires making certain choices about which economic theory offers little guidance. For example, are expectations on capital gains myopic, are they perfectly anticipated, or are they a weighted average of recent asset-specific capital gains experiences? Whatever choice is made in the empirical implementation, it is clear that the resulting measures of aggregate capital input growth, and, therefore, MFP growth, will be affected.

The empirical effects of alternative capital rental price formulas have been investigated elsewhere in the economic literature. For example, Dale Jorgenson and Calvin Siebert (1968a, b) have considered alternative rental price formulations in explaining investment behavior for individual firms in the 1950s and 1960s. Ernst Berndt (1976) has shown that much of the apparent disparity in studies of capital-labor substitution elasticities in the 1960s and early 1970s could be reconciled by recognizing that different capital rental price measures were being employed. Michael Hazilla and Raymond Kopp (1984) have explored the effects of alternative capital rental price measures on econometric, parametric productivity growth measures for two-digit manufacturing industries, 1958–1977.

Capital rental price measurement was also a prominent issue in the famous "productivity growth measurement debate" between Edward Denison, and Dale Jorgenson and Zvi Griliches. In their classic article, Jorgenson and Griliches (1967) employed an annual adjustment for asset appreciation—capital gains due to inflation effects—in their measure of the capital service price. Denison (1969, p. 45) argued that incorporating long-term averages of capital gains "might be appropriate," but that use of annual capital gains calculations was dubious, "since capital gains are highly erratic from year to year."[1] In responding, Jorgenson and Griliches (1972, p. 70) noted that the capital gains adjustment was logically implied by their use of the perpetual inventory method for measuring net capital stock, leaving open the empirical possibility of incorporating capital gains by means other than annual adjustments, e.g., some variant of Denison's idea of "long term averages of capital gains."

In this chapter we continue empirical research on evaluating alternative capital rental price formulas in the context of MFP measurement. We first review the guidance provided by economic theory in discriminating among alternative rental price formulas employed in the empirical literature. This results in identifying a set of five possible rental price measures that we then evaluate in the context of a nonparametric, noneconometric MFP growth accounting framework. The empirical evaluation procedure is based on a comparison of the five alternative rental price estimates using a common data set covering 21 two-digit U.S. manufacturing industries over the 1948–1981 time period, where each industry has from 10 to 20 distinct types of capital assets.

The outline of the chapter is as follows. In section 8.2 we review the economic theory underlying productivity growth accounting, capital rental price measurement, and capital service flow aggregation. In section 8.3 we motivate five alternative rental price formulations, each of which has an historical precedent in the investment, factor demand, and/or productivity literature. In section 8.4 we discuss the data set underlying this study, motivate three quantitative measures we propose to employ in comparing the alternative rental prices, and then present empirical results. Finally, in section 8.5 we summarize, present concluding remarks, and offer suggestions for further research.

8.2   Theoretical Foundations

Since the purpose of this chapter is to identify and evaluate the effects of plausible alternative capital service price measures on estimates of multifactor productivity (MFP) growth, in this section we first briefly review the derivation of the MFP growth accounting equation, then summarize the derivation of rental price measures as estimates of the (usually) unobservable capital service prices, and finally discuss economic procedures for employing rental price estimates of capital service prices in aggregating capital services. This sets the stage in section 8.3 for specifying the five alternative rental price estimates of capital service prices that span the range of possibilities suggested by economic theory and empirical practice in the investment and productivity liturature.

8.2.1   Multifactor Productivity Growth Accounting

Economic growth analysts have typically specified multifactor productivity as

$$MFP \equiv Y/X, \tag{1}$$

where $Y(X)$ is aggregate output (input). Assuming a single output.

one can measure growth in aggregate input as the cost share-weighted aggregate of the growth in each of the inputs, so that (1) may be expressed in terms of growth rates as

$$MFP = \dot{Y} - \sum \frac{P_i X_i}{C} \dot{X}_i , \tag{2}$$

where P_i is the price of input X_i, C is total cost ($\equiv \sum P_i X_i$), and where the dot notation refers to the time derivative.

The multifactor productivity (MFP) growth-accounting equation (2) may also be derived from the theory of cost and production. Assume that production technology is described by a twice-differentiable production function relating a single output to several inputs. Thus,

$$Y = F (X_1, \ldots, X_n, t). \tag{3}$$

The total differential of (3) with respect to time is

$$\frac{dY}{dt} = \sum \frac{\partial F}{\partial X_i} \frac{dX_i}{dt} + \frac{\partial F}{\partial t} . \tag{4}$$

Dividing both sides of (4) by Y, noting that

$$\frac{dX_i}{Ydt} = \frac{X_i}{Y} \dot{X}_i , \qquad \text{defining technical change as} \qquad \dot{A} \equiv \frac{1}{Y} \frac{\partial F}{\partial t} , \tag{5}$$

and rearranging we have

$$\dot{A} = \dot{Y} - \sum \frac{\partial /F}{\partial X_i} \frac{X_i}{Y} \dot{X}_i . \tag{6}$$

Comparing (6) with (2), we see that the condition necessary for technical change and MFP growth rate measures to be equivalent is that

$$\dot{X} = \sum \frac{P_i X_i}{C} \dot{X}_i .$$

Note that the first-order conditions for cost minimization imply that

$$\frac{\partial F}{\partial X_i} = \frac{P_i}{\partial C / \partial Y}, \qquad \text{where } \partial C / \partial Y \text{ is marginal cost,} \tag{7}$$

and that returns to scale of production may be measured as the reciprocal of the cost-output elasticity,

$$\varepsilon_{CY} = \frac{\partial C}{\partial Y} \frac{Y}{C} \Rightarrow \frac{\partial C}{\partial Y} = \varepsilon_{CY} \frac{C}{Y} . \tag{8}$$

Substituting (7) and (8) into (6), and rearranging yields

$$\dot{A} = \dot{Y} \sum \varepsilon_{CY}^{-1} \frac{P_i X_i}{C} \dot{X}_i .$$
(9)

Equations (2) and (9) are equal provided that production is characterized by constant returns to scale, i.e.,

$$\varepsilon_{CY}^{-1} = 1.$$

In this case, technical change and MFP growth are equivalent. Note that MFP growth may be calculated directly employing data on output growth and on prices and quantities of inputs including, for example, prices and quantities of capital service inputs.[2]

8.2.2   Derivation of Capital Rental Price Formulas

Productivity analysts, at least since the work of Jorgenson and Griliches (1967), have noted that the aggregation of capital stocks is quite different from the aggregation of flows of capital services. Since the economic theory underlying multifactor productivity measurement is based on a production function relating flows of outputs to flows of inputs, the distinction between aggregation of capital stocks and the aggregation of capital service flows is an important one. On the dual side, it is correspondingly important to distinguish the purchase or asset prices of capital goods from their user costs or rental prices.[3]

While rental prices can be observed for some durable goods, in most cases rental market data are not sufficiently broad in coverage, and thus one must instead infer implicit rental prices based on the assumed correspondence between the purchase price of an asset and the discounted value of all future capital services derived from that asset.

There are a number of ways in which the rental price formula can be derived. Assume that as capital ages, physical deterioration and obsolescence cause it to depreciate relative to new goods, at the rate $\delta(\alpha)$, where α is the age of the asset. Denote the rental price of capital services at time t as $p(t)$. Continuous time derivations relating $p(t)$ to the asset price have been presented by, among others, Jorgenson (1967) and Hall (1968). For example, with geometric deterioration,[4] $\delta(\alpha) = \delta$, and the flow of capital services over the time interval dt beginning at t from a unit of capital goods acquired at time s is

$$e^{-\delta(t-s)} dt.$$
(10)

Since $p(t)$ is the anticipated rental price of capital services at time t, the expected discounted value of capital services is $e^{-rt}p(t)$, so that the value of the expected stream of capital services over the time interval dt is

$$e^{-rt}p(t) \cdot e^{-\delta(t-s)}dt. \tag{11}$$

Now let $q(s)$ be the expected asset price of capital goods at time s. Then at time $t = 0$, the anticipated value of a unit of capital goods to be acquired at time s is

$$e^{-rs}q(s). \tag{12}$$

In equilibrium, however, the expected value of capital goods acquired at time s must equal the expected discounted value of all future capital services derived from these capital goods, i.e.,

$$e^{-rs}q(s) = \int_s^\infty e^{-rt}p(t) \cdot e^{-\delta(t-s)}\,dt = e^{\delta s}\int_s^\infty e^{-(r+\delta)t}p(t)\,dt. \tag{13}$$

Equation (13) can be solved for the expected asset price of capital goods, yielding

$$q(s) = \int_s^\infty e^{-(r+\delta)(t-s)}p(t)\,dt. \tag{14}$$

Following Jorgenson (1967, p. 144), one can obtain the rental price of capital implicit in this equation by differentiating the expected asset value $q(s)$ with respect to time,

$$\dot{q}(s) = [r(s) + \delta]q(s) - p(s), \tag{15}$$

which can be rewritten as

$$p = q(r+\delta) - \dot{q}. \tag{16}$$

Notice in particular that the rental price depends on the expected change in the asset price—the expected capital gains term. This capital gains term will play a prominent role in the empirical analysis of this chapter. It might also be noted that continuous time derivations of the rental price of capital that incorporate in addition expected corporate tax factors can be found in, among others, Hall and Jorgenson (1967).

A discrete time derivation for the rental price of capital is presented in Christensen and Jorgenson (1969). The expected asset price is related to expected rental prices in discrete time form via the equality

$$q_t = \sum_{\gamma=t}^{\omega} \prod_{s=t+1}^{\gamma+1} \left[\frac{1}{1+r_s} \right] p_{\gamma+1}(1 - \delta)^{\gamma-t}, \tag{17}$$

where the quantity of capital services at time $\gamma+1$ from one unit of investment in capital goods at time t is $(1-\delta)^{\gamma-t}$. Christensen and Jorgenson rewrite (17) in the form

$$q_t = \left[\frac{1}{1+r_{t+1}} \right] \cdot [\, p_{t+1} + (1-\delta)q_{t+1}], \tag{18}$$

and then solve for the capital rental price, obtaining

$$p_t = r_t q_{t-1} + \delta q_t - \left[q_t - q_{t-1} \right]. \tag{19}$$

Equation (19) may be interpreted as corresponding to the notional case where an asset is purchased at the very end of the previous period (virtually the beginning of the current time period), the rental lease p_t is received at the end of the current time period, and the unknown but expected asset price at the end of the current time is $q_{t,t}^*$. Notice therefore that in the Christensen-Jorgenson discrete specification underlying (19), the capital revaluation term is

$$\text{expected capital gains} \equiv q_{t,t}^* - q_{t-1}. \tag{20}$$

An alternative derivation of the discrete rental price of capital services is due to Diewert (1980, pp. 470–473). Diewert assumes that capital is instantaneously adjustable and that during each time period firms lease all their capital goods at the rental price $p(t)$ from a competitive leasing firm. The pressures of competition require that the leasing firm earn only the "prevailing" rate of return $r(t)$ on its leasing activities. This implies the following equality at time period t:

$$\left[q_t - p_t \right] \left[1+r_t \right] = (1-\delta)q_{t,t+1}^*, \tag{21}$$

i.e., the purchase cost of one unit of capital q_t minus the rental p_t received, all multiplied by the opportunity cost of holding these funds $1+r_t$, must equal the expected depreciated value of the capital good next period, this latter term being the product of the survival rate $(1-\delta)$ and the expected purchase price at time t for capital goods purchased in time period $t + 1$, denoted $q^*_{t, t+1}$. When (21) is solved for p_t, one obtains

$$p_t = \frac{r_t q_t + \delta q^*_{t, t+1} - \left[q^*_{t, t+1} - q_t \right]}{1+r_t}. \tag{22}$$

It should be emphasized that in (22), the expected capital gains term,

$$\text{expected capital gains} \equiv q^*_{t, t+1} - q_t, \tag{23}$$

plays a prominent role. Note from (22) that this expected capital gains term at time t is "forward looking," i.e., the rental price at time t depends on the expected asset price in period $t + 1$. Finally, equations (21) and (22) can easily be modified to incorporate provisions of the tax code; see, for example, Diewert (1980, pp. 470–479).

It is informative to compare the Diewert and Christensen-Jorgenson discrete time formulas.[5] Rearranging (19) provides the Christensen-Jorgenson analog to (21):

$$q_{t-1} \left[1+r_t \right] - p_t = (1-\delta)q^*_{t, t}. \tag{24}$$

Equation (24) differs from (21) in several ways. While in Diewert's framework the opportunity cost of capital $(1+r_t)$ multiplies the difference $(q_t - p_t)$, in the Christensen-Jorgenson specification $(1 + r_t)$ multiplies only q_{t-1}. Further, while the variables are identical (r, p, and q), the time subscripts differ. In Diewert's formulation, (21), the expected capital gains term affecting the rental price at time t is forward looking $(q_{t+1} - q_t)$, while in the Christensen-Jorgenson formulation, (24), the capital gains term is retrospective, i.e., $q_t - q_{t-1}$ affects p_t. The difference stems, of course, from the discrete time choices made by Christensen-Jorgenson in specifying the time subscripts of (18) and (19).[6]

It is clear then, that while time subscripts differ, in both the Diewert and the Christensen-Jorgenson discrete time theoretical specifications, expected capital gains play a very prominent role. An issue facing empirical researchers, therefore, is how to measure the expected capital gains term. On this, practice has varied among researchers and over time, due to the obvious fact that theory provides little guidance, and that how expectations are formed is to a major extent an empirical issue.

In Jorgenson (1963, 1965) and in Hall and Jorgenson (1967), the expected capital gains term is set equal to zero since "... we assume all capital gains are regarded as 'transitory'" (Jorgenson, 1963, p. 249). By contrast, in Jorgenson and Siebert (1968a, b) two models are compared empirically, one with perfectly anticipated capital gains where $q^*_{t,t} = q_t$ (this empirical alternative is called Neoclassical I), and the other where expectations are myopic and expected capital gains are zero, i.e., $q^*_{t,t} = q_{t-1}$ (this is called Neoclassical II). Empirical results reported by Jorgenson-Siebert indicate a modest preference for Neoclassical I (perfectly anticipated capital gains) over Neoclassical II (no expected capital gains) in explaining the investment behavior of fifteen firms. It is perhaps in part for this reason that since the late 1960s, Jorgenson and his associates have only used Neoclassical I in their empirical work on investment and productivity; see, for example, Jorgenson and Griliches (1967), Fraumeni and Jorgenson (1980), Jorgenson and Sullivan (1981) and Jorgenson and Fraumeni (1981).

At this point it is worth recalling that when Jorgenson and Griliches (1967) originally introduced capital gains into the rental price calculations underlying their MFP measures, they were sharply criticized by Edward Denison (1969, p. 45), who argued that incorporating long-term averages of capital gains "... might be appropriate," but that use of annual capital gains calculations was dubious "... since capital gains are highly erratic from year to year." Moreover, Denison noted that the relative capital gains of various types of capital goods are of course unknown. This suggests that alternatives other than the two neoclassical cases considered by Jorgenson-Siebert may merit empirical examination; one obvious possibility is to employ as an estimate of $q^*_{t,t}$ a moving average of previous asset prices, as has been done by Epstein (1977) and Gillingham (1980). We shall return to this point of alternative capital gains specifications in the next Section.

What is clear from this brief review of the theoretical literature, however, is that there are compelling reasons why the expected capital gains term should be included in the rental price formulas; how these expectations are measured and implemented empirically, however, is not as clear. Diewert (1980, p. 476) summarizes this as follows: "... from our rather narrow viewpoint, which concentrates on the measurement of capital in the context of production function estimation and the measurement of total factor productivity, it seems clear that the capital gains term belongs in the rental price formula—what is not as clear is the validity of the Jorgenson-Griliches perfect anticipations assumption."

The above discussion has focused on the capital gains term in the rental price formula. It is of course the case that other variables are also very important, e.g., expected (marginal) tax terms, depreciation rates and the discount rate or rate of return r. Diewert (1980, pp. 476–477) comments on this as follows: "Which r should be used? If the firm is a net borrower, then r should be the marginal cost of borrowing an additional dollar for one period, while if the firm is a net lender, then r should be the one-period interest rate it receives on its last loan. In practice, r is taken to be either (a) an exogenous bond rate that may or may not apply to the firm under consideration, or (b) an internal rate of return. I tend to use the first alternative, while . . . Jorgenson and his co-workers use the second. As usual, neither alternative appears to be correct from a theoretical a priori point of view; so again, reasonable analysts could differ on which r to use in order to construct a capital aggregate."

A principal focus of this chapter is to examine empirically not only these two alternative measures of r but also others that have appeared in the capital rental price and capital aggregation literature. Before pursuing these alternative r measures, however, we briefly review the literature concerning the aggregation of capital services.

8.2.3   Capital Aggregation Theory and Procedures

In the next few paragraphs we provide a brief overview of procedures for aggregating over diverse capital services. Recall that since the analysis underlying MFP measurement is based on the economic theory of cost and production relating flows of inputs to flows of outputs, empirical implementation with durable goods requires obtaining measures of the aggregate flows of capital services, not aggregate stocks. Although it is relatively straightforward to obtain measures of the one-period value of capital services, it is more difficult to decompose this value into price and quantity components. In the previous paragraphs we have outlined how rental prices can be formed for different capital assets; details concerning tax factors affecting these rental prices will be discussed later.

With respect to quantities of service flows, we follow tradition here and make the assumption that capital services for each type of asset (e.g., producers' durable equipment, nonresidential structures, inventories, and land) are a constant proportion of capital stocks; this factor of proportionality can, however, vary among the diverse types of capital assets. In order to estimate service flows for each asset type, it is therefore only necessary to develop corresponding capital stock estimates. We employ the perpetual inventory method (PIM) to perform vintage aggregation for each asset. When deterioration is geometric, the PIM for capital type i is

$$K_{i,\,t} = \left[\, 1{-}\delta_i \right] K_{i,\,t-1} {+} I_{i,\,t-1}, \tag{25}$$

where δ_i is the rate of deterioration for capital type i, $K_{i,\,t}$ is the beginning-of-year constant dollar capital stock, and $I_{i,\,t-1}$ is constant dollar gross investment in capital type i during time period $t{-}1$ that is assumed to be installed by the beginning of time period t. Repeated substitution into (25) yields an expression relating $K_{i,\,t}$ to the history of vintage-specific gross investments, each weighted by its relative efficiency. When deterioration patterns other than geometric are employed, the $1{-}\delta_i$ factor for each vintage reflects the assumed deterioration pattern of the asset based on a fixed schedule of remaining efficiency as a function of age. Notice that the PIM is applied separately to each of the various capital assets.

Once these rental price and capital service quantity flows are separately measured, they must be aggregated. Here we assume that capital is instantaneously adjustable and employ the familiar Tornqvist discrete approximation to the continuous Divisia index. The Tornqvist approximation to the Divisia index has attractive properties, for as has been shown by Diewert (1976), it can be viewed as an exact index corresponding to a second-order approximation in logarithms to an arbitrary production or cost function.[7] In particular, this index places no prior restrictions on the substitution elasticities among the goods being aggregated. With the Tornqvist approximation, the change in aggregate capital service flow is a weighted sum of the changes in the n asset-specific capital stocks, where the weights are the relative cost shares:

$$\ln\!\left[\, K_t / K_{t-1} \right] = \sum_{i=1}^{n} \bar{s}_{i,\,t} \ln\!\left[\, K_{i,\,t} / K_{i,\,t-1} \right], \tag{26}$$

where

$$\bar{s}_{i,\,t} \equiv \left[\, s_{i,\,t} + s_{i,\,t-1} \right] / 2,$$

$$s_{i,\,t} \equiv p_{i,\,t} K_{i,\,t} / \left[\, P_{K,\,t} K_t \right],$$

and where the aggregate value of capital services $P_{K,\,t} K_t$ sums over all n asset values,

$$P_{K,t} \, K_t \equiv \sum_{i=1}^{n} p_{i,t} \, K_{i,t}, \tag{27}$$

where i refers to the ith type of capital asset and p_i is its rental price.[8] Equations (26) and (27) demonstrate the important role of the rental price in capital service aggregation, and in decomposing the aggregated value of capital service flows into price and quantity components.

This Divisia aggregation of capital services weights each type of capital by its relative cost share, and should be distinguished from the direct summation or aggregation of capital,

$$\tilde{K}_t \equiv \sum_{i=1}^{n} K_{i,t}. \tag{28}$$

An important feature of aggregate capital growth, emphasized by Jorgenson and Griliches (1967), is that Divisia aggregation (26) can generate very different growth rate results from the direct aggregation (28). For example, suppose that the composition of capital changes because investment is growing faster for shorter-lived equipment than for longer-lived structures. As a result, since δ_e for equipment is larger than δ_s for structures (equipment has a shorter life span and thus a larger deterioration rate), from (16), (18), and (22) it is clear that, *ceteris paribus*, the rental price of equipment p_e will be larger than the rental price of structures p_s. This implies that the growth of equipment investment will be weighted more highly than growth in structures in the Divisia aggregation (26), and aggregate capital computed using this Divisia index will grow at a larger rate than aggregate capital calculated using direct aggregation (28). The economic intuition underlying this is that because of the shorter life of equipment, the investor needs to require more services per year from a given dollar of investment in equipment than in structures, i.e., a dollar's worth of investment in equipment has higher "quality" (in terms of service flow per dollar) than a dollar's worth of investment in structures.

The empirical importance of employing correct capital aggregation procedures may be illustrated using data for the U.S. Private Business Sector. We denote the difference between the growth rates of the rental price-weighted Divisia index and a directly aggregated capital stock as the *capital composition effect*. In the post-World War II U.S. economy, this effect has been strongly positive, due to the steady shift in the investment mix toward shorter-lived equipment assets and away from structures and land.

Table 8.1
Measures related to multifactor productivity growth, U.S. private business
sector, percent change at a compound annual rate

Time span	Multi-factor produc-tivity	Output	Capital produc-tivity	Capital input	Capital stock	Composi-tion effect
1948–1984	1.5	3.4	0.0	3.4	2.6	0.8
1848–1973	2.0	3.7	0.2	3.6	2.6	0.9
1973–1981	0.1	2.2	−1.1	3.4	2.8	0.6
1981–1984	1.8	3.5	1.2	2.3	2.1	0.2

Source: Bureau of Labor Statistics (1985).

As is seen in table 8.1, for the 1948–1984 time period in the U.S. Private Business Sector, capital input (using the Divisia aggregation) grew 3.4% per year, while capital stock (using direct aggregation) grew only 2.6% per year; this implies a 0.8% capital composition effect. One underlying reason for this is that equipment grew 4.9% per year while nonresidential structures grew 2.8%, inventories grew at 3.3%, and land at only 2.0%. The resulting MFP measure increased at a 1.5% rate; had the unweighted direct aggregation been employed to aggregate capital stock instead of capital services, the measured MFP growth would have grown at 1.8% per year. Average capital productivity (growth in output minus growth in capital input) is 0.0% using Divisia aggregation, and is 0.8% if defined instead in terms of growth in output per unit of capital stock. The long-run constancy of the capital-output ratio, incidentally, is consistent with an economy experiencing long-run balanced growth, and is an empirical finding that would be overlooked were the rental price approach to capital measurement not employed. Finally, note that the importance of the capital composition effect has declined considerably over time; from 1948 to 1973 it averaged 0.9% per year, while from 1973 to 1981 it fell slightly to 0.6% per year, and over the most recent 1981–1984 time period it dropped to 0.2% per year.

This concludes our discussion of the theory and interpretation of rental price formulas, as well as their role in the aggregation of capital services. An important conclusion of the above discussion is that while capital gains and rates of return should enter into the calculation of capital rental prices, economic theory alone cannot tell us how they should be measured empirically. In the next section, therefore, we outline five alternative rental price measurement procedures, and then in section 8.4 we compare them empirically using a common data set.

8.3   Alternative Specifications of the Rental Price Model

Earlier it was noted that the capital rental price formulas can easily be modified to incorporate effects of corporate tax provisions in the United States. For example, the Christensen-Jorgenson formula (22) for the ith capital asset type now becomes

$$p_{i,t} = T_{i,t}\left[q_{i,t-1}r_t + \delta_{i,t}q_{i,t} - \left[q_{i,t}^* - q_{i,t-1}\right]\right] + b_{i,t},\tag{29}$$

where $b_{i,t}$ is the effective rate of property taxes (nominal valued taxes assessed on the real stock of capital type i), and $T_{i,t}$ is the effective rate of taxation on capital income, given by

$$T_{i,t} \equiv \frac{1 - u_t z_{i,t} - k_{i,t}}{1 - u_t},\tag{30}$$

where u_t is the maximum statutory corporate income tax rate,[9] $z_{i,t}$ is the present value of depreciation deductions for tax purposes on a dollar's investment in capital type i over the lifetime of the investment, and $k_{i,t}$ is the effective rate of the investment tax credit. Note that each of the variables in (29) and (30) is estimated for different asset type categories, thereby generating distinct estimates of the rental prices of the various capital types.

BLS researchers have implemented estimation of (29) and (30) for various asset types and sectors of the economy; such calculations underlie the figures presented in table 8.1 above. In almost all cases, procedures developed by Christensen and Jorgenson (1969), as modified slightly in Fraumeni and Jorgenson (1980), have been followed. In particular, the $q_{i,t}$ are capital asset-specific investment goods deflators, while the $\delta_{i,t}$ are inferred from the assumed deterioration function by making use of the duality between the service flow and price of an asset as it ages. This relationship has been derived by Hall (1968) in continuous time terms, and by Jorgenson (1974) in discrete time. Discussion of the tax variable computations is found in Christensen-Jorgenson (1969) and in Harper (1982).

As was noted in the previous section, empirical practice has varied concerning choice of the rate of return r_t and the specification of capital gains $(q_{it,t}^* - q_{i,t})$. We now discuss five alternative empirical implementations of (29), comment briefly on their salient empirical features, and then in the next section compare them empirically in more detail.

8.3.1 Internal Nominal Rate of Return Specification

We begin with the internal nominal rate of return specification, developed in detail by Christensen and Jorgenson (1969), discussed in further detail by Fraumeni and Jorgenson (1980), and applied to aggregate sectors by the BLS (1983). Define property income in year t as I_t ($\equiv P_{K,t}K_t$), where I_t consists of pretax profits, capital consumption allowances, net interest, transfer payments, business subsidies, indirect taxes, and the portion of proprietor's income attributable to capital, all taken from the National Income and Product Accounts. Assuming that the rate of return is the same for all assets, one can solve for the internal nominal rate of return r_n as

$$r_{n,t} \equiv \left[I_t + \sum_{i=1}^{n}\left(-\delta_{i,t}T_{i,t}q_{i,t}K_{i,t} \right. \right.$$
$$\left. \left. + q_{i,t}T_{i,t}K_{i,t} - b_{i,t}K_{i,t} \right) \right] / \sum_{i=1}^{n} q_{i,t-1}T_{i,t}K_{i,t}, \tag{31}$$

where I is property income as defined above and $\Delta q_{i,t} = q^*_{i,t} - q_{i,t-1}$. Note that with this internal nominal rate of return procedure the aggregate capital gains term $\sum \Delta q_{i,t}T_{i,t}K_{i,t}$ enters with a positive sign so as to augment capital income reported in the National Income and Product Accounts, and thereby increases r. However, as seen in (29), asset-specific inflation reduces p_i. This suggests that when asset-specific inflation coincides with the aggregate rate of capital inflation, p_i calculated using (31) will be unaffected; we discuss the importance of nonneutral inflation further in the next subsection. It is also important to recognize that when the internal nominal rate of return procedure (31) is employed, expected capital gains are replaced with realized capital gains, which implies that in this procedure capital gains are assumed to be perfectly anticipated.

We refer to this rate of return as an after-tax "nominal internal" rate because it is derived in terms of property income for the specific industry (thereby, internal) and because it includes perfectly anticipated capital gains (hence, nominal).[10] This procedure corresponds with what Jorgenson and Siebert (1968a, b) have called their "Neoclassical I" model. Hereafter we denote the rental prices of capital for the ith capital type based on this internal nominal rate of return $p_{i,n}$.

We now examine movement in $p_{i,n}$ and its components empirically. It will be useful to divide the rental price (29) into four components: (i) rate of return, $T_{i,t}q_{i,t-1}r_t$; (ii) depreciation, $T_{i,t}\delta_{i,t}q_{i,t}$; (iii) capital gains, $T_{i,t}\Delta q_{i,t-1}r_t$; and (iv) indirect taxes, $b_{i,t}$. A striking feature of the $p_{i,n}$ time series we have observed is its volatility; note that volatility in $p_{i,n}$ generally results in comparable volatility in the cost share weights used to aggregate capital—see (26). We illustrate this feature in table 8.2 with the metal working machinery asset in the miscellaneous manufacturing industries sector. The data underlying these results are described in section 8.4.1. Shown for the period 1971–1981 are the shares of this asset in this industry's total capital income—equation (27)—the rental price $p_{i,n}$ based on the internal nominal rate of return—equations (29) and (30)—the four components of the rental price listed above, and finally, the internal nominal rate of return derived for this industry—see (31).

Empirical results for this asset and this industry are representative of those obtained for other assets and industries with $p_{i,n}$. Substantial fluctuations occur for the income share, with particularly large drops experienced in 1975 and 1981. The rental price shows similar sharp decreases, moderated to some extent by the strong inflationary trend.

Table 8.2
Miscellaneous manufacturing industries—asset: metalworking machinery—internal nominal rate of return used

| Year | Share | Rental price | Additive contributions to rental price | | | | Nominal rate of return |
			Rate of return	Depreci- ation	Capital gains	Indirect taxes	
1971	0.1301	0.2622	0.1529	0.1386	−0.0350	0.0056	0.1160
1972	0.1290	0.2856	0.1723	0.1395	−0.0331	0.0068	0.1281
1973	0.1608	0.3180	0.2095	0.1426	−0.0413	0.0071	0.1502
1974	0.2475	0.3332	0.3010	0.1608	−0.1362	0.0075	0.1921
1975	0.0799	0.2065	0.3089	0.1989	−0.3117	0.0104	0.1636
1976	0.1273	0.3118	0.2051	0.2024	−0.1084	0.0127	0.1035
1977	0.1265	0.3449	0.2947	0.2237	−0.1872	0.0138	0.1371
1978	0.1840	0.4204	0.3437	0.2493	−0.1883	0.0156	0.1463
1979	0.2318	0.5169	0.4697	0.2776	−0.2484	0.0180	0.1799
1980	0.2390	0.5827	0.5730	0.3296	−0.3436	0.0238	0.1876
1981	0.0838	0.3589	0.2950	0.3370	−0.3065	0.0334	0.0970
Mean	0.1582	0.3583	0.3024	0.2182	−0.1763	0.0141	0.1456
Standard deviation	0.0571	0.1051	0.1208	0.0696	0.1102	0.0081	0.0314

The depreciation component increases steadily, buoyed by inflation; steady increases also occur for the indirect tax component.

An examination of the rate of return and capital gains components reveals that these two terms are the source of most of the fluctuations around trend in $p_{i,n}$; note that standard deviations for the rate of return and capital gains components are substantially larger (especially relative to their means) than those for the depreciation and property tax components. For example, in 1975 the sharp drop in rental price can be linked to a substantial increase in capital gains, indicating that the investment goods deflator for this asset advanced rapidly between 1974 and 1975. By contrast, in 1981 the drop in rental price occurs primarily due to the sharp drop in the rate of return; this decrease in the nominal internal rate of return was in turn due in large part to the decreased rate of inflation for all other asset types, which enters of course into the r_n calculation (31). Note that capital gains for this particular asset increase considerably (in absolute value) from 1976 to 1980, but these asset-specific capital gains are roughly offset by increased contributions from the rate of return term, contributions which in turn are influenced by the general inflation in capital asset prices.[11]

8.3.2   Internal Own Rate of Return Specification

The second alternative rental price specification we consider is very closely related to the "Neoclassical II" model examined by Jorgenson and Siebert (1968a, b); interestingly, this alternative is also discussed by Jorgenson and Griliches (1967, p. 256, footnote 2), who attribute it to an earlier paper by Domar (1961). This specification, which we call the internal own rate of return, seems to exclude capital gains from the rental price formula and therefore apparently incorporates the assumption of zero expected capital gains, or myopic expectations. If this were true, then this alternative would be subject to Jorgenson and Diewert's theoretical criticism that capital gains should be included in the rental price formula. As we shall see, however, this is not quite the case.

Suppose we exclude the capital gains term from (20),

$$p_{i,o} = T_{i,t}\left[q_{i,t-1}r_{o,t} + \delta_{i,t}q_{i,t} \right] + b_{i,t}, \tag{32}$$

and, correspondingly, simultaneously solve for an "own" rate of return, denoted r_o, which excludes from (31) the aggregate capital gains term $\Sigma T_i q_i K_i$, as

$$r_{o,t} \equiv \left[I_t - \sum_{i=1}^{n} \left(\delta_{i,t} T_{i,t} q_{i,t} K_{i,t} + b_{i,} K_{i,t} \right) \right] / \sum_{i=1}^{n} q_{i,t-1} K_{i,t} T_{i,t}. \tag{33}$$

We denote the rental price measure based on r_o, the internal own rate of return, as $p_{i,o}$, and equations (32) and (33) as the "internal own rate of return" model.

When this alternative set of computations is performed with our same sample data for the metalworking machinery asset in SIC 39, we find that fluctuations (as measured by the standard deviation) in the rate of return contribution and in the income share are greatly reduced. This is demonstrated in table 8.3. One other interesting feature of this table is that while r_o has only one-third as large a standard deviation as r_n from table 8.2, due to the very large rental price $p_{i,o}$ in 1981 in table 8.3, the standard deviations of the rental prices $p_{i,n}$ and $p_{i,o}$ are approximately equal.

The above discussion would seem to suggest that this internal own rate of return model suffers from Jorgenson and Diewert's theoretical

Table 8.3
Miscellaneous manufacturing industries—asset: metalworking machinery—internal own rate of return used

| Year | Share | Rental price | Additive contributions to rental price | | | | Nominal rate of return |
			Rate of return	Depreciation	Capital gains	Indirect taxes	
1971	0.1256	0.2532	0.1090	0.1386	0.0000	0.0056	0.0826
1972	0.1227	0.2717	0.1254	0.1395	0.0000	0.0068	0.0932
1973	0.1283	0.2536	0.1039	0.1426	0.0000	0.0071	0.0745
1974	0.1579	0.2127	0.0443	0.1608	0.0000	0.0075	0.0283
1975	0.1401	0.3622	0.1529	0.1989	0.0000	0.0104	0.0810
1976	0.1494	0.3659	0.1508	0.2024	0.0000	0.0127	0.0761
1977	0.1535	0.4184	0.1810	0.2237	0.0000	0.0138	0.0842
1978	0.1707	0.3899	0.1249	0.2493	0.0000	0.0156	0.0532
1979	0.1800	0.4013	0.1057	0.2776	0.0000	0.0180	0.0405
1980	0.1895	0.4619	0.1085	0.3296	0.0000	0.0238	0.0355
1981	0.1535	0.6571	0.2866	0.3370	0.0000	0.0334	0.0943
Mean	0.1519	0.3678	0.1357	0.2182	0.0000	0.0141	0.0676
Standard deviation	0.0210	0.1192	0.0582	0.0696	0.0000	0.0081	0.0227

criticism that capital gains should be included in the rental price formula. We now demonstrate that this is not the case. A comparison of (31) and (33) reveals that the internal nominal and internal own rate of return notions are related as follows:

$$r_{n,t} = r_{o,t} + \left[\sum_{i=1}^{n} \Delta q_{i,t} T_{i,t} K_{i,t} \Big/ \sum_{i=1}^{n} q_{i,t-1} T_{i,t} K_{i,t} \right]$$

$$= r_{o,t} + \left[\Delta \bar{q}_t / \bar{q}_{t-1} \right] = r_{o,t} + \text{average capital gains,} \tag{34}$$

where

$$\Delta \bar{q}_t \equiv \sum_{i=1}^{n} \Delta q_{i,t} T_{i,t} K_{i,t} \quad \text{and} \quad \bar{q}_{t-1} \equiv \sum_{i=1}^{n} q_{i,t-1} T_{i,t} K_{i,t}. \tag{35}$$

Incidentally, Fraumeni and Jorgenson (1980) have defined the difference between r_n and average capital gains—see (34)—as the "own rate of return."

Let us define a new rental price formula where average rather than own capital gains appear, and denote this rental price with average capital gains as $p_{i,a}$:

$$p_{i,a} = T_{i,t} \left[q_{i,t-1} r_{a,t} + \delta_{i,t} q_{i,t} - q_{i,t-1} \left[\Delta \bar{q}_t / \bar{q}_{t-1} \right] \right] + b_{i,t}, \tag{36}$$

where $r_{a,t}$ is calculated as

$$r_{a,t} \equiv \left[I_t + \sum_{i=1}^{n} \left[-\delta_{i,t} T_{i,t} q_{i,t} K_{i,t} \right. \right.$$
$$\left. \left. + q_{i,t-1} \left[\Delta q / \bar{q}_{t-1} \right] T_{i,t} K_{i,t} - b_{i,t} K_{i,t} \right] \right] \Big/ \sum_{i=1}^{n} q_{i,t-1} K_{i,t} T_{i,t}$$
$$= \left\{ \left[I_t - \sum_{i=1}^{n} \left[\delta_{i,t} T_{i,t} q_{i,t} K_{i,t} \right. \right. \right.$$
$$\left. \left. \left. + b_{i,t} K_{i,t} \right] \right] \Big/ \sum_{i=1}^{n} q_{i,t-1} K_{i,t} T_{i,t} \right\} + \left[\Delta \bar{q}_t / \bar{q}_{t-1} \right]. \tag{37}$$

By substituting into (33), the second part of (37) can be rewritten as

$$r_{a,t} = r_{o,t} + \Delta \bar{q}_t / \bar{q}_{t-1}. \tag{38}$$

Now if (38) is substituted into (36), the average capital gains terms weighted by $q_{i,t-1}$ cancel out, and, comparing the result with (32), yields $p_{i,a} = p_{i,o}$. This implies the following very important result:

Use of the internal own rate of return model (with apparently no capital gains) yields the same rental prices and thus cost shares as would the nominal internal rate of return model provided average capital gains were employed in the nominal rental price equations (29) and (31) instead of the asset-specific capital gains rates.

Hence, the internal own rate of return model preserves the important theoretical requirement that some account of capital gains be made in the rental price expression.

One other result is worth emphasizing. Together (34) and (38) imply that $r_a = r_n$, i.e., aggregate internal rates of return based on nominal asset-specific and average capital gains are equal. However, for specific assets, $p_{i,o}$ $(=p_{i,a})$ differs from $p_{i,n}$ by the difference between the average and asset-specific capital gains rates. Hence instability of rental prices $p_{i,n}$ relative to $p_{i,o}$ can be attributed to unequal movements in *relative* asset prices.

8.3.3   Internal Nominal Rate of Return with Smoothed Capital Gains

Earlier we noted that in his survey of capital aggregation, Diewert (1980) suggested that researchers may wish to follow the lead of Epstein (1977) and use time series techniques to obtain asset-specific expected capital gains measures; such a "smoothed" capital gain term could provide a useful alternative to the polar assumptions of zero and perfectly anticipated capital gains.

The issue of asset-specific capital gains was raised earlier by Denison (1969), who in his discussion of the Jorgenson and Griliches (1967) productivity analysis provided a numerical example in which asset-specific price changes affected both cost share weights and the measure of aggregate capital, albeit in a moderate manner. Denison conceded that asset-specific price changes should theoretically affect firms' decisions, yet also noted that firms do not know in advance how relative prices will move. Thus the empirical researcher must attempt to model the relative price expectations process.

As we demonstrated above, it is only the relative movements in asset prices that affect rental prices and aggregation. While a full econometric model of price determination and price expectations may be desirable in this context, a much simpler procedure would be to employ time series or autoregressive integrated moving average (ARIMA) techniques in measuring *ex ante* relative price expectations, where relative price is defined as the ratio of each asset's price to the overall average of all investment goods prices.

Such a moving average of previous relative asset prices has been employed by Gillingham (1980), in conjunction with his study of restructuring the BLS Consumer Price Index housing component. After finding an "unacceptable" amount of volatility emerging from the traditionally computed capital gains term (sometimes resulting even in negative rental prices), Gillingham experimented with using moving averages of from two to five years, reasoning that in forming their expectations firms and individuals may examine recent trends particularly closely. Unfortunately, Gillingham found that whether the moving average notion was applied only to capital gains, only to the rate of return, or to both, the result was still the same in that very large variations still occurred. This led Gillingham to suggest that for this component of the CPI it would be preferable to use market rental prices of equivalent rental housing rather than rental prices computed using the above methods.

In this chapter, we propose to examine empirically the behavior of a special case of the ARIMA model, namely, a three-year moving average with equal weights applied to each lag. We therefore measure both capital gains and rates of return with the three-year moving average replacing $\Delta q_{i,\,t}$ in (29) and (31).

8.3.4   External Nominal Rate of Return Specification

A number of studies of investment behavior and costs of capital have employed as a measure of the expected or *ex ante* discount rate some bond yield in external markets. The most common are Moody rates for Aaa- or Baa-rated bonds, or long-term U.S. government bond yields. Aaa yields, for example, have been employed by Coen (1968), Evans (1967), Grunfeld (1960), and Miller and Modigliani (1966), while Baa yields were used by Holland and Myers (1979); Eisner (1969) reports results of experiments with the U.S. government long-term bond rate as reported in the *Survey of Current Business*.

As an empirical alternative, therefore, we replace r_n in (29) with r_b, where r_b is the Moody Baa bond rate; given the implied rental prices $p_{i,\,b}$, we recompute costs of capital for each asset as $p_{i,\,b}K_i$, and then use (27) to obtain new cost shares. Note that if this measure is used as an *ex ante* measure of the cost of capital, unrealized expectations could result in a divergence between *ex ante* and *ex post* capital costs. As a measure of the implied "surprise," we take the ratio of actual income to the implied *ex ante* capital income, $I / \left[\sum p_{ib}K_i \right]$. This ratio can also be interpreted as the adjustment necessary to use the $p_{i,b}$ to apportion actual current income. To see this, note that the above ratio is a stock-weighted average of the ratio of *ex post* rental prices to *ex ante* rental prices, due to the relationship (31) between income and the *ex post* internal rate of return. We refer to this specification as the external nominal rate of return model.

Using the same asset category and industry as in tables 8.2 and 8.3, in table 8.4 we present results based on rental price and rate of return calculations with r_b. The additional final column in table 8.4 is the "surprise" ratio defined in the previous paragraph. Note that this ratio is very large, varying from –2.47 to 6.34, implying considerable magnitude in the "surprise" element. Moreover, for some years capital income is computed as being negative, since a negative rental price results from using r_b. It is also worth noting, incidentally, that the results in table 8.4 are representative of employing the r_b method for other assets and industries.

8.3.5   Constant External Own Rate

When property income becomes negative, none of the above four methods is capable of generating reasonable capital rental prices. In particular, the implied shadow price of capital is in such cases negative, implying that the firm could reduce variable costs by discarding its capital plant and equipment. While such a situation may be possible in theory, one would not expect to observe this in practice, for firms do have the option of shutting down in the short run if revenues do not cover variable costs. On the other hand, one could argue that if one obtained negative capital income measures, that would indicate problems with the data or the measurement method employed. We shall discuss negative capital income issues further in the next section.

One way of obtaining "reasonable" rental price measures in such cases is to remove from the underlying calculations the elements causing the large fluctuations. As has been pointed out earlier, these elements in most cases are the capital gains term and the linking of the rate of return to capital or property income. Possibilities here include employing a before-tax constant nominal rate of return, such as 14% (Hall and Jorgenson, 1968), 20% (Hall and Jorgenson, 1969), or 10% (Coen, 1975). More recently, Fraumeni and Jorgenson (1980) have calculated that the difference between nominal discount rates and inflation rates appears to be approximately 3–4% for most industries.

Table 8.4
Miscellaneous manufacturing industries—asset: metalworking machinery—
external nominal rate of return (Moody's Baa bond yield) model

Year	Share	Rental price	Rate of return	Depreci-ation	Capital gains	Rate of indirect taxes	Moody Baa	Ratio ex post to ex ante income
				Additive contributions to rental price				
1971	0.1487	0.2997	0.1523	0.1870	−0.0472	0.0076	0.0856	1.3492
1972	0.1589	0.3518	0.1732	0.2201	−0.0522	0.0107	0.0816	1.5772
1973	0.2799	0.5535	0.2848	0.3534	−0.1024	0.0176	0.0824	2.4780
1974	−0.3322	−0.4473	−0.3678	−0.3973	0.3363	−0.0185	0.0950	−2.4700
1975	0.0734	0.1898	0.3884	0.3856	−0.6042	0.0201	0.1061	1.9389
1976	0.1399	0.3425	0.2206	0.2312	−0.1238	0.0145	0.0975	1.1424
1977	0.1469	0.4006	0.3178	0.3687	−0.3086	0.0227	0.0897	1.6483
1978	0.2756	0.6294	0.4684	0.5237	−0.3955	0.0328	0.0949	2.1004
1979	0.9271	2.0676	1.7686	1.7591	−1.5744	0.1143	0.1069	6.3375
1980	0.5222	1.2731	1.2441	0.9818	−1.0238	0.0709	0.1367	2.9791
1981	0.0952	0.4075	0.3603	0.2490	−0.2265	0.0247	0.1604	0.7389
Mean	0.2214	0.5517	0.4555	0.4420	−0.3748	0.0288	0.1034	1.8018
Standard deviation	0.2955	0.6138	0.5488	0.5178	0.5040	0.0338	0.0233	1.9683

This suggests our final empirical alternative, namely, a model in which the the real rate of return (r_n minus capital gains) is set to a constant 3.5%; we denote this as r_c. In this alternative we therefore substitute r_c for r_o in (32), calculate the corresponding $p_{i,o}$ (which are now always strictly positive), compute the capital costs as $p_{i,o}K_i$, and then calculate shares using (27). It is worth noting, incidentally, that this 3.5% constant real rate of return has been employed by the BLS (1983) in its MFP calculations for the agriculture sector, a sector in which traditional property income measures occasionally become negative.

8.3.6   Summary

We propose to compare and evaluate the five alternative capital rental price formulas discussed in sections 8.3.1–8.3.5. The sources and characteristics of these formulae are summarized in table 8.5. The important features include:

Table 8.5
Summary of alternative capital rental price characteristics

Model	Description	Capital gains	Rate of return
M1	Internal nominal rate of return (Jorgenson-Siebert [1968a,b], Christensen-Jorgenson [1969], Fraumeni-Jorgenson [1980], BLS [1983, except agriculture]	Asset specific appreciation, perfectly realized	From capital income identity
M2	Internal own rate of return (Jorgenson-Siebert [1968a,b]	Average asset appreciation, perfectly realized	From capital income identity
M3	Constant external own rate (Hall-Jorgenson [1968], Hall-Jorgenson [1969], Coen [1975], BLS [1983, agriculture])	Average asset appreciation, perfectly realized	Constant nominal rate (= 3.5%)
M4	Internal nominal rate of return with smoothed capital gains (similar in concept to Epstein [1977], Gillingham [1980])	Asset specific appreciation, expected	From capital income identity
M5	External nominal rate of return (Coen [1968], Eisner [1969], Evans [1967], Grunfeld [1960], Holland-Myers [1979], Miller-Modigliani [1966]	Asset specific appreciation, perfectly realized	External rate, Moody Baa bond rate

i. All five capital rental price estimates reflect capital appreciation, and so are consistent with the theoretical conditions of Jorgenson and Diewert.

ii. Formulae M1, M2, and M4 ensure that NIPA capital income estimates equal the "payments" to specific assets, while formulae M3 and M5 do not impose this constraint. Hence in calculating MFP growth—see equation (9)—M1, M2 and M4 leave the aggregate capital share unaffected and differ only in their estimate of aggregate capital service growth rates due to differences in specific asset rental value shares. For M3 and M5, both rental cost shares and service flow growth rates are affected.

iii. Formulas M1 and M2 are closely related, differing only in the contribution of nonneutral changes in relative asset prices to average capital appreciation.

It should be recalled that the M1–M5 formulas are all motivated either by conceptual arguments or their use in the literature. Given the assumptions underlying the multifactor productivity growth equation (9), however, we prefer the standard internal nominal rate of return (M1), the internal own rate of return (M2), and the internal nominal rate of return with smoothed capital gains (M4) models. Theoretical arguments cannot discriminate further among these formulas, and so final choices must depend on empirical evaluation.[12]

8.4   Empirical Results

We now turn to a comparative evaluation of the five capital rental price formulas described above. At the outset, it is useful to note that there are two possible outcomes from such comparisons. First, perhaps there is not much empirical difference among the various measures, or at least among the measures for the preferred rental price estimates (M1, M2, and M4). This would be good news for productivity growth analysts since then they would not need to be too concerned about the lack of theoretical help in choosing a specific rental price formula—at least for U.S. manufacturing industries. Alternatively, of course, there may be considerable empirical variation in the estimated rental price formulas, leaving productivity growth analysts with the difficult task of choosing and justifying a particular formula.

The comparative quantitative measures we employ to evaluate the effects of alternative rental price specifications focus on (i) the overall capital measure, (ii) the variability of the rental prices, and (iii) the consistency of the measures with the requirements of basic economic theory. Recall from equation (9) that the capital rental prices influence MFP growth estimates via effects on (i) the aggregate capital service flows as estimated by equation (26)—a quantity effect—and on (ii) the value of aggregate capital services calculated by identity (27)—a price effect. We evaluate the quantity effect by calculating the ratio of the price weighted aggregate capital service flow to the unweighted, or physical, aggregate capital service flow from equation (28). As noted in section 8.2.3, we call the growth rate of this measure the capital composition effect (our first comparative measure).

The price effect may be evaluated by focusing on the variability of the asset rental prices. As noted, aggregate rental prices may be computed using Tornqvist-Divisia indexes of capital service flows (26) and the capital income identity (27). By inspection of (26) and (27), it is seen that asset rental price variability contributes to variability of aggregate service prices directly, and indirectly via the relative size of the asset value shares used in capital service aggregation. We focus on the net effect of component rental price variability by calculating as our second comparative measure the average year-to-year percentage changes in absolute values of aggregate rental price estimates, a measure we call the volatility statistic.[13]

Finally, recall that the assumptions underlying the derivation of the multifactor productivity growth equation (9) require that input flow prices be positive. Nothing in the procedures for calculating any of the five capital rental prices considered in this study imposes the restriction that the resulting estimates are positive. Accordingly, we tabulate first by industry, and then for total U.S. manufacturing, the number of negative outcomes, expressing the result as a percentage of the total observations for all assets and years. We call this characteristic the percentage negative statistic.

Table 8.6 presents values of the composition effect and the volatility and percent negative statistics for each of the 21 two-digit U.S. manufacturing industries over the 1948–1981 time period. Several results should be noted. First, composition effects and especially the volatility statistics are very large and questionable for the external nominal rate of return model (M5). This suggests that the problem illustrated in table 8.4 concerning the large required reallocation of property income due to differences between *ex post* and *ex ante* incomes is significant in the industries considered in this study. The relatively large percentage of negative rental prices and the general breakdown of other statistics stems from the fact that the *ex post* capital gains term frequently dominates the *ex ante* rate of return as measured by the Moody Baa bond yield. Because of these adverse results, we exclude the external nominal rate of return model (M5) yield from further analysis.

Second, notice that for three of the remaining four rental price alternatives (M1, M2, M4), the composition effect is extremely large for NIPA 16 (transportation equipment excluding motor vehicles). This occurs because in these internal rate of return calculations, property income occasionally becomes negative, especially in 1980 and 1981. Note also that for this same industry, the percent negative values are higher than for any other industry. The other industry with atypical statistics is NIPA 15 (motor vehicles and equipment), closely

Table 8.6
A comparison of methods of computing rental prices for two-digit manufacturing industries 1948–1981

NIPA industry	Internal nominal rate of return model (M1)			Internal own rate of return model (M2)		
	Composition effect	Volatility statistic	Percent negative	Composition effect	Volatility statistic	Percent negative
8–Lumber & Wood	0.032	0.291	0.0	0.001	0.185	0.0
9–Furniture & Fixt.	−0.016	0.267	0.2	0.002	0.150	0.0
10–Stone Clay Glass	−0.001	0.236	2.2	−0.024	0.138	0.9
11–Primary Metals	0.152	0.424	2.7	0.106	0.185	0.0
12–Fabr. Metal Prod.	0.142	0.277	0.6	0.160	0.121	0.0
13–Mach. Except El.	0.455	0.170	0.0	0.221	0.111	0.0
14–Electrical Mach.	0.083	0.223	0.4	0.070	0.161	0.0
15–Motor Vehicles	0.393	0.472	2.8	0.393	0.484	2.4
16–Other Transp Eqp.	+10.871	−0.054	7.3	−11.091	−0.199	4.0
17–Instruments	0.069	0.441	0.2	−0.131	0.131	0.0
18–Miscellaneous Mfg	0.464	0.410	0.9	0.265	0.173	0.0
19–Food	0.112	0.194	0.5	−0.028	0.073	0.0,
20–Tobacco	0.433	0.062	0.0	0.435	0.056	0.0
21–Textile	0.128	0.459	5.3	0.011	0.189	3.0
22–Apparel	−0.255	0.328	0.7	−0.189	0.173	0.0
23–Paper	−0.145	0.231	0.2	−0.104	0.111	0.0
24–Printing	−0.008	0.169	0.0	−0.030	0.100	0.0
25–Chemicals	0.204	0.174	1.2	0.067	0.094	0.0
26–Petroleum	−0.074	0.371	4.2	−0.096	0.181	1.3
27–Rubber	−0.044	0.459	3.0	0.007	0.151	1.9
28–Leather	0.329	0.664	2.8	−0.001	0.372	0.0

NIPA industry	External own rate of return model (constant 3.5%) (M3)			Internal nominal rate calculated with smoothed capital gains (M4)			External nominal rate return model using Moody's Baa bond rate (M5)		
	Composition effect	Volatility statistic	Percent negative	Composition effect	Volatility statistic	Percent negative	Composition effect	Volatility statistic	Percent negative
8–Lumber & Wood	0.187	0.184	0.0	0.015	0.204	0.6	3.671	1.045	5.0
9–Furniture & Fixt.	-0.161	0.147	0.0	0.097	0.179	0.5	-0.168	0.728	3.0
10–Stone Clay Glass	-0.085	0.138	0.0	0.024	0.151	1.7	0.051	183.114	3.5
11–Primary Metals	0.006	0.178	0.0	0.120	0.230	2.0	0.895	6.799	6.2
12–Fabr. Metal Prod.	0.137	0.119	0.0	0.217	0.140	0.4	-17.626	9.004	3.7
13–Mach. Except El.	0.252	0.110	0.0	0.417	0.118	0.2	0.743	3.610	3.9
14–Electrical Mach.	-0.153	0.161	0.0	0.138	0.168	0.4	-0.248	0.326	1.2
15–Motor Vehicles	0.206	0.623	0.0	0.419	0.477	2.8	0.221	0.730	1.1
16–Other Transp Eqp.	-0.109	0.237	12.1	-11.093	-0.236	6.5	1.069	0.868	16.2
17–Instruments	-0.164	0.130	0.0	-0.008	0.138	0.5	-0.190	0.650	2.8
18–Miscellaneous Mfg	0.106	0.166	0.0	0.562	0.596	0.5	-1.638	59.861	5.6
19–Food	-0.078	0.070	0.0	0.097	0.104	0.2	0.060	0.276	0.5
20–Tobacco	-0.051	0.052	0.0	0.427	0.056	0.0	-0.054	0.052	0.0
21–Textile	0.002	0.167	0.0	0.283	0.192	3.3	-12.856	0.576	3.5
22–Apparel	-0.179	0.166	0.0	-0.152	0.185	0.5	0.115	487.091	2.6
23–Paper	-0.112	0.110	0.0	-0.078	0.135	0.6	18.466	0.744	3.8
24–Printing	-0.057	0.095	0.0	0.112	0.129	0.3	-0.273	61.024	3.8
25–Chemicals	0.022	0.091	0.0	0.220	0.121	0.4	0.124	0.773	3.9
26–Petroleum	-0.148	0.179	0.0	-0.127	0.222	3.4	-0.076	0.405	2.4
27–Rubber	-0.065	0.151	0.0	0.033	0.163	3.3	-0.197	0.529	1.9
28–Leather	-0.017	0.339	0.0	0.227	0.420	0.8	-7.474	NA	5.8

related to NIPA 16. The atypical behavior of these two sectors suggests that they be eliminated from further consideration until questions about the underlying data can be resolved.

In table 8.7, we present simple averages of the composition, volatility, and percent negative statistics for 19 of the 21 two-digit industries (excluding NIPA 15 and 16), separately for the 1948–1965, 1966–1973 and 1974–1981 time periods, for the four remaining rental price specifications (M1–M4). Several points should be noted.

First, a striking result from table 8.7 is that the ranking of the four alternatives is essentially the same for all three measures, with M1 and M4 having the two highest values, then M2, and finally M3. This relative ranking holds for all subperiods, with the absolute differences among the four alternatives being largest during the relatively turbulent 1974–1981 time period. This average ranking pattern is also approximately the same for individual industries, as can be seen from table 8.6.

Second, the composition effect (the ratio of economic and physical aggregate capital services) is positive and largest for the two internal nominal alternatives (M1, M4 of table 8.7), is positive but much smaller for the internal own (M2), and is slightly negative for the external own (M3). Moreover, while the entries in the composition effect panel of table 8.7 might appear small, in fact the differences among the four alternatives are substantial, especially for the 1974–1981 time period, when they range from −0.037 to 0.315; such magnitudes are as large as some of the other major factors typically examined in studies of the sources of the post-1973 productivity growth slowdown, and clearly indicate that measurement procedures do matter.

Third, the capital composition effect reflects a systematic trend in the relative prices of the different asset types. Recall that for the two nominal internal models (M1, M4), asset-specific capital gains are incorporated, while with the internal own (M2) and external own (M3) they are omitted. Significantly, M1 and M4 have the largest capital composition effects, while M2 and M3 have much smaller composition statistics. This result is due to (i) the long-term historical shift toward equipment and away from structures (which directly increases the capital composition effect) and (ii) the long-term tendency for the prices of new structures to rise more rapidly than those for equipment, causing the capital gains term subtracted in the structures rental price to be larger than that subtracted in the equipment rental price. This latter effect accentuates the existing

Table 8.7
Summary of models used to compute capital rental prices: simple averages of statistics over 19 of 21 two-digit U.S. manufacturing industries

Time period	Rate of return used in model			
	Internal nominal (M1)	Internal own (M2)	External own (3.5%) (M3)	Internal nominal smoothed (M4)
	Composition effect			
1948–1981	0.108	0.039	−0.029	0.138
1948–1965	0.016	−0.033	−0.071	0.065
1966–1973	0.149	0.105	0.067	0.116
1974–1981	0.266	0.128	−0.037	0.315
	Volatility statistic			
1948–1981	0.308	0.150	0.145	0.192
1948–1965	0.282	0.149	0.144	0.162
1966–1973	0.174	0.122	0.116	0.135
1974–1981	0.498	0.180	0.175	0.314
	Percent of rental prices negative			
1948–1981	1.3	0.4	0.0	1.0
1948–1965	0.5	0.2	0.0	0.8
1966–1973	0.6	0.0	0.0	1.0
1974–1981	3.9	1.0	0.0	2.3

difference between equipment and structures rental prices occurring due to the higher economic depreciation of equipment, and thereby results in a larger rental price and cost share weight for the more rapidly growing equipment services component. The more investors take these differential asset-specific capital gains into consideration, therefore, the larger should be the composition effect.

Fourth, the standard internal nominal rate of return specification (M1) yields the largest percent of negative rental prices; for the 1948–1973 time period, this percent negative is rather small at 0.5%, increasing to 3.9% in the 1974–1981 period. By comparison, the percent negative figures for M4 for the 1974–1981 period is 2.3%, and for M2, 1.0%. For M3, the percent negative is of course zero for all time periods. What the bottom horizontal panel of table 8.7 suggests, therefore, is that most of the negative rental price occurrences correspond with the use of asset-specific capital gains (the largest percent negative values are with internal nominal and internal nominal smoothed); when average capital gains or no capital gains at all are employed (M2, M3), the percent negative occurrences for the rental price fall sharply.

While direct inspection of tables 8.6 and 8.7 is instructive, we are still left with the question, how statistically significant are differences among alternative rental price formulae in explaining variations in the three characteristics—composition, volatility, and percent negative? To address that question, we have analyzed each of the three characteristics using regression models in which the dependent variables are the composition effect, the volatility statistic, and the percent negative. In one case the right-hand variables are dummy variables for M2, M3, and M4, and time dummy variables for the 1966–1973 and 1974–1981 time periods. In the second case, we include interaction terms between each model and each dummy time period defined as $M(I) * D(K)$ ($I = 2,3,4$, and $K = 1966–1973, 1974–1981$). For both models, the constant term is therefore interpreted as the mean difference from the standard internal nominal rate of return model (M1) for the 1948–1965 time period. These six regressions are run using the data set consisting of the 19 industries, 4 models and 3 time periods, yielding a total of 228 observations. Results from this set of regressions are presented in table 8.8.

We begin with a discussion of the composition effect. As shown in the first column of table 8.8, of the model dummy variables only the M3 (constant external own at 3.5%) coefficient is statistically significant, and it is negative, indicating a statistically significant smaller composition effect with the M3 model than with the standard M1 specification (internal nominal own). Since the 1966–1973 and 1974–1981 time dummies are both positive and statistically significant, we conclude that for all models the composition effect is larger in the more recent time periods than in 1948–1965. Inspection of column (ii) of the composition effect indicates that, as judged by their implied t-statistics, at most one of the interaction terms (M3: 1974–1981) is statistically significant (and this is marginal). A joint test of the null hypothesis that simultaneously all interaction term coefficients are zero cannot be rejected; the F-test statistic is 1.51, while the .95 (.99) critical value is 2.10 (2.80).

Table 8.8
Summary of effects of alternative capital rental price measures: ordinary least squares regression with data from three time periods, 4 models and 19 of 21 two-digit U.S. manufacturing industries (estimated standard error in parentheses)

Dependent variable	Composition effect		Volatility effect		Percent negative	
	(i)	(ii)	(i)	(ii)	(i)	(ii)
Constant[a]	0.047	0.016	0.298	0.282	0.012	0.005
	(0.040)	(0.057)	(0.028)	(0.038)	(0.003)	(0.004)
M2 dummy	−0.077	−0.049	−0.167	−0.133	−0.012	−0.002
	(0.047)	(0.080)	(0.032)	(0.054)	(0.004)	(0.006)
M3 dummy	0.022	0.050	−0.114	−0.120	−0.006	0.036
	(0.047)	(0.080)	(0.032)	(.054)	(0.004)	(0.004)
M4 dummy	−0.157	−0.087	−0.173	−0.138	−0.17	−0.005
	(0.047)	(0.80)	(0.028)	(0.054)	(0.003)	(0.006)
1966–1973 dummy	0.115	0.133	−0.047	−0.107	−0.002	0.002
	(0.040)	(0.080)	(0.028)	(0.054)	(0.003)	(0.006)
1974–1981 dummy	0.174	0.250	0.108	0.216	0.014	0.034
	(0.040)	(0.080)	(0.028)	(0.054)	(0.003)	(0.006)
Interaction Terms						
M2* 1966–1973 dummy		0.005		0.081		−0.004
		(0.113)		(0.076)		(0.009)
M3* 1966–1973 dummy		−0.083		0.081		−0.009
		(0.113)		(0.076)		(0.009)
M4* 1966–1973 dummy		0.005		0.079		−0.002
		(0.113)		(0.076)		(0.009)
M2* 1974–1981 dummy		−0.089		−0.184		−0.026
		(0.113)		(0.076)		(0.009)
M3* 1974–1981 dummy		0.000		−0.064		−0.019
		(0.113)		(0.076)		(0.009)
M4* 1974–1981 dummy		−0.215		−0.185		−0.034
		(0.113)		(0.076)		(0.009)
Mean of dependent variable	0.090	0.090	0.204	0.204	0.008	0.008
Standard error of regression	0.249	0.248	0.170	0.166	0.020	0.019

a. The constant term is interpreted as the mean for the standard internal nominal rate of return model over the 1948–1965 time period.

The second set of regressions reported in table 8.8 employs the volatility characteristic statistic as the dependent variable. As seen in the middle two columns of table 8.8, each of the model coefficients is statistically significant (and negative). In the specification with no interactions, this indicates that the volatility of the M1 base case (internal nominal rate of return) model is statistically significantly larger than that of the other three models, while in the interaction specification this statistically significant difference holds in both the 1948–1965 base case and even more so in the 1974–1981 time period. The coefficient of .216 for the 1974–1981 time dummy in the interaction specification implies that for the standard internal nominal own rate of return model (M1), volatility is statistically significantly larger in the turbulent 1974–1981 time period than in 1948–1965. Here a joint test of the null hypothesis that all interaction terms in the volatility equation are simultaneously equal to zero is rejected; the F-test statistic is 2.99, while the .05 (.01) critical value is 2.10 (2.80).

Regression results for the "percent negative" measures are presented in the final two columns of table 8.8. In the model with no interactions, as implied by their t-statistics, the M2 (internal own) and M3 (external own) model coefficients are negative and statistically significant, while the 1974–1981 time period coefficient is positive and statistically significant. This leads us to conclude that while the M1 base case (internal nominal own rate of return) model has statistically significantly more occurrences of negative rental prices than both the M2 (internal own) and M3 (external own 3.5%) models in the 1948–1965 time period, this difference is increased further during the 1974–1981 epoch; differences between the M2 and M3 models are, however, statistically insignificant. These conclusions are amended slightly when one examines the interaction model. Now the model-specific coefficients are negative and statistically significant primarily only in the 1974–1981 time period, suggesting that during this time span the M1 base case (internal nominal own rate of return) model experienced significantly more occurrences of negative rental prices. Finally, the test of the null hypothesis that all six interaction term coefficients are simultaneously equal to zero is again rejected; the F-test statistic is 3.56, while the .05 (.01) critical value is 2.10 (2.80).

8.5   Summary and Concluding Remarks

The U.S. Bureau of Labor Statistics has recently begun to estimate and publish measures of multifactor productivity (BLS, 1983). An important issue in constructing these estimates is the measurement of (typically) unobservable capital service prices. In this chapter, we (i) review the economic theory underlying the derivation of rental price estimates of unobservable capital service prices, (ii) formulate five alternative rental price formulas based on economic theory and on previous empirical applications in the economic literature, and (iii) empirically analyze these five alternatives.

The review of the underlying theory and the motivation of the five alternative capital rental price formulas emphasizes the importance of incorporating information on economic depreciation, expected rate of return, expected tax rates, and expected capital asset appreciation— the so-called capital gains. One contribution of this chapter is to show that while the nominal internal own rate of return specification (M2) appears to exclude capital gains, in fact it is numerically equivalent to a rental price formula in which asset-specific capital gains are replaced with the average capital gain over all assets. Hence this alternative is consistent with the strong theoretical result that capital gains should be reflected in the rental price estimate of capital service prices.

The empirical analysis of the alternative rental price estimates of capital service prices employs a common data set covering 21 two-digit U.S. manufacturing industries over the 1948–1981 period, where each industry purchases from 10 to 20 distinct types of capital assets. Our approach is to calculate the aggregate capital rental prices for each formula described in table 8.5, and to compare the results based on three characteristics including the ratio of economic and physical aggregate capital services (composition effect), average year-to-year variability in aggregate capital rental prices (volatility), and percentage of aggregate rental prices with negative estimated values (percent negative).

The most important conclusion from this empirical analysis is that there are significant differences in the three measures we employ in analyzing the five alternative capital rental price formulae. Taking the internal nominal rate of return model (M1) as the benchmark (and eliminating one formula, M5, and two industries, NIPA 15 and 16, for atypical performance), we find that for each of the three measures— composition effect, volatility, and percent negative—one or more of the remaining formulas (M2–M4) is statistically significantly different, even after accounting for "time period" effects for the 1965–1973 and 1974–1981 epochs. Evidently, not only must analysts of U.S. manufacturing industry MFP growth choose among at least four alternative capital rental price formulas with little additional help from economic theorists, but at least for U.S. manufacturing, the choice will matter.

Given this conclusion, we offer a number of suggestions for further research. First, for those capital assets that are both purchased and rented (leased) in existing markets, it may be instructive to examine historically the relationship between asset and rental prices, and in particular to determine whether any of the expectations representations are clearly inconsistent with the data. In this way, certain seemingly plausible rental price specifications could be eliminated, and thus the choice of particular specifications in calculating MFP growth rates could be further restricted based on empirical evidence.

Second, the occasional negative property income values for NIPA 15 and 16 (motor vehicles, and transportation equipment excluding motor vehicles) are puzzling, and further analysis needs to be done to interpret and/or revise the underlying data.

Third, our findings suggest that at least three viable alternatives to the standard nominal internal rate of return specification (M1) are available—nominal internal smoothed (M4), nominal internal own (M2), and possibly in special cases, the constant external real (M3). Because it accounts for asset-specific capital gains, we have a subjective preference for the nominal internal smoothed alternative, but believe further comparative empirical work may be fruitful. In particular, specifications other than the simple three-year moving average procedure merit examination; an obvious possibility is the estimation and implementation of ARIMA models for the expected capital gains component of each of the 20 types of capital plant and equipment.

Fourth, if one wishes to maintain the instantaneous capital adjustment assumption underlying the rental price formulations considered here, we do not understand why separate nominal rates of return are computed for each industry; a priori, instantaneous adjustment could be argued to generate equality in these rates of return. Hence, in future empirical research it might be useful to determine whether equality in industry rates of return changes the capital composition, volatility, and percent negative results in any systematic manner.[14]

Fifth and finally, we believe the research presented here highlights conceptual and empirical difficulties encountered when one equates ex ante with ex post rates of return in a model with instantaneous adjustment of capital. Following recent analytical developments by

Berndt and Fuss, Hulten, and Morrison in specifying models for productivity measurement that distinguish temporary from full equilibrium, we believe future empirical research comparing, among other attributes, the composition, volatility, and percent negative characteristics of alternative instantaneous adjustment, short-run, and long-run productivity measurement models would be particularly informative and useful.

Data Appendix

The data used in this study are part of a BLS project to develop multifactor productivity growth measures for two-digit manufacturing industries. A description of this effort is provided in Gullickson and Harper (1987). In general, capital income data are taken from the U.S. Department of Commerce National Income and Product Accounts (NIPA), while capital stock data are based on estimates of investment and service lives of various capital types by two-digit industry as reported by Gorman et al. (1985) and Musgrave (1986). We are grateful to these authors for making this detailed data available. Capital stocks have been constructed using the perpetual inventory method and age-efficiency functions, which imply that services decline slowly during the early years of the life of an asset. The hyperbolic efficiency functions employed are identical to those specified in appendix C of BLS (1983).

Estimates of capital income are based on NIPA. Capital income is equal to industry current dollar gross product originating except for labor compensation (wages, salaries, supplementary compensation, and a portion of proprietors' income). Hence capital income consists of before-tax corporate profits, net interest payments, capital consumption allowances, subsidies, indirect taxes, transfers, and the portion of proprietors' income not attributed to labor.

The remaining elements of the rental price formula are determined as follows. Given the hyperbolic efficiency function, the rate of economic depreciation is derived based on the duality between the efficiency of an asset and its price, as discussed in Harper (1982). Deflators for new investment goods by asset type are calculated as the ratio of investment in current dollars to investment in constant dollars, as reported in NIPA. Tax rate parameters are formulated based on estimated marginal incentives rather than effective average rates. In particular, following Jorgenson and Sullivan (1981) and Hulten and Robertson (1981), we employ the maximum statutory corporate tax rate as the estimate of the marginal tax rate; further discussion on this tax issue is also found in Bradford and Fullerton (1981). As estimates of the present value of one dollar's worth of depreciation allowances, and for the effective rate of the investment tax credit, we employed values computed for the published BLS (1983) major sector measures. Finally, for the rate of indirect taxation, we divided NIPA estimates of indirect taxes by the estimated capital stock.

Notes

1. In fact, the effect of a capital gains adjustment may actually cause rental price estimates to be negative in periods of rapid inflation, such as those experienced in the U.S. during 1974–1981. This question of negative rental price estimates is an important feature in our evaluation of alternative rental price formulas.

2. The importance for MFP growth analysis of properly measuring capital service input prices and quantities is suggested by the fact that for the post-World War II period, capital value share in aggregate U.S. manufacturing averaged 15–20% of value added output, and 4–8% of gross output.

3. Hereafter we employ the term rental price of capital, for at least since Keynes (see the appendix to his *General Theory*, chapter 6) the user cost notion has also incorporated effects of variations in utilization or intensity of use. While such utilization issues are important, they are not addressed in this chapter.

4. The assumption of geometric decay, while maintained in the brief derivations shown in this section, need not be maintained to derive the rental price formula and is not maintained in the empirical section of this chapter (see data appendix). Derivations of the rental price formula with a general (monotonically declining) efficiency decay schedule appear in Hall (1968) (in continuous terms) and in Jorgenson (1974) (in discrete terms). Hall (pp. 39–40) shows that the depreciation rate, δ, in the rental price formula is in general the initial depreciation rate for a new asset.

5. See Hulten and Wykoff (1980) for yet another alternative discrete time formulation that yields a rental price formula very similar to that of Diewert.

6. As is noted in Diewert (1980, footnote 57), in the limiting case of a nondurable good when $\delta = 1$, the Diewert formulation has the attractive property that $q_t = p_t$ (the rental price and asset price are equal), whereas the Christensen-Jorgenson specification yields $p_t = (1+r_t) \cdot q_{t-1}$. The latter relationship follows from the Christensen-Jorgenson representation of events in discrete time; that is, services and rents are first delivered in the period after purchase.

7. See Caves, Christensen, and Diewert (1982) for further discussion.

8. When the capital aggregate quantity index is computed using (26), the implicit aggregate capital rental price can be computed using (27).

9. Following Jorgenson and Sullivan (1981) and Hulten and Robertson (1984), we use the maximum statutory corporate tax rate as most representative of the effective marginal tax rate.

10. Note that using this r_n measure in the rental price formula is appropriate only if, among other assumption, capital is instantaneously adjustable. But if capital is adjustable, then its after-tax rate of return should be equal for all sectors of the economy. To the best of our knowledge, this constraint is rarely imposed in the empirical literature.

11. The sample correlation coefficient between the rate of return and capital gains components of $p_{i,n}$ is $-.0796$, while that between the capital gain component and the nominal rate of return (the last column of table 8.2) is -0.331.

12. More general models relating to productivity measurement are, of course, possible. See Berndt and Fuss (1986) for a model in which the full equilibrium assumptions underlying equation (9) are relaxed.

13. While useful for comparative purposes, it is impossible within our present framework to state whether particular values of the volatility statistic are reasonable, excessive, or insufficient. The difficulty arises due to the full equilibrium assumptions underlying equation (9), which require that the rental price of capital equal the value of its marginal product. If capital is not sufficiently adjustable (due to its durability and to adjustment costs), then the underlying data will incorporate these disequilibrium effects. For discussions of capital and multifactor productivity measurement that distinguish partial from full equilibrium see Berndt and Fuss (1986), Hulten (1986), and Morrison (1986).

14. One possibility here is to define capital income as net of capital gains, compute aggregate rates of return as equal across all industries, and then allow industry-specific capital gains income and capital gains components in the rental price formula.

References

Berndt, Ernst R. (1976), "Reconciling Alternative Estimates of the Elasticity of Substitution," *Review of Economics and Statistics*, Vol. 58, No. 1, February, pp. 59–68.

Berndt, Ernst R., and Melvyn A. Fuss (1986), "Productivity Measurement with Adjustments for Variations in Capacity Utilization and Other Forms of Temporary Equilibrium," *Journal of Econometrics*, Vol. 33, No. 1/2, October/November, pp. 7–29.

Bradford, David F., and Don Fullerton (1981), "Pitfalls in the Construction and Use of Effective Tax Rates," in Charles R. Hulten, ed., *Depreciation, Inflation, and the Taxation of Income from Capital*, Washington, D.C.: The Urban Institute Press, pp. 251–278.

Bureau of Labor Statistics, United States Department of Labor (1983), *Trends in Multifactor Productivity, 1948–81*, Bulletin 2178, Washington, D.C.: U.S. Government Printing Office.

Bureau of Labor Statistics, United States Department of Labor (1985), "Multifactor Productivity Measures," News Release USDL 85–405, October.

Caves, Douglas W., Laurits R. Christensen, and W. Erwin Diewert (1982), "The Economic Theory of Index Numbers and the Measurement of Input, Output, and Productivity," *Econometrica*, Vol. 50, No. 6, pp. 1393–1414.

Christensen, Laurits R., and Dale W. Jorgenson (1969), "The Measurement of U.S. Real Capital Input, 1919–67," *Review of Income and Wealth*, Series 15, No. 4, December, pp. 293–320.

Coen, Robert M. (1968), "Effects of Tax Policy on Investment in Manufacturing," *American Economic Review*, Vol. 58, No. 2, May, pp. 200–211.

Coen, Robert M. (1975), "Investment Behavior, the Measurement of Depreciation, and Tax Policy," *American Economic Review*, Vol. 65, No. 1, pp. 59–74.

Denison, Edward F. (1969), "Some Major Issues in Productivity Analysis: An Examination of Estimates by Jorgenson and Griliches," *Survey of Current Business*, Part II, May 1969, pp. 1–27. Reprinted in "The Measurement of Productivity," *Survey of Current Business*, Vol. 52, No. 5, Part II, pp. 37–63.

Diewert, W. Erwin (1976), "Exact and Superlative Index Numbers," *Journal of Econometrics*, Vol. 4, No. 4, pp. 115–145.

Diewert, W. Erwin (1980), "Aggregation Problems in the Measurement of Capital," chapter 8 in Dan Usher, ed., *The Measurement of Capital*, Chicago: University of Chicago Press for National Bureau of Economic Research, pp. 433–528.

Domar, Evsey D. (1961), "On the Measurement of Technological Change," *Economic Journal*, Vol. 71, No. 284, December, pp. 709–729.

Eisner, Robert (1969), "Tax Policy and Investment Behavior: Comment," *American Economic Review*, Vol. 59, No. 3, June, pp. 379–388.

Epstein, Larry E. (1977), "Essays in the Economics of Uncertainty," unpublished Ph.D. dissertation, University of British Columbia, Department of Economics.

Evans, Michael K. (1967), "A Study of Industry Investment Decisions," *Review of Economics and Statistics*, Vol. 49, No. 2, May, pp. 151–164.

Fraumeni, Barbara M., and Dale W. Jorgenson (1980), "The Role of Capital in U.S. Economic Growth, 1948–76," in George M. von Furstenberg, ed., *Capital, Efficiency and Growth*, Cambridge, MA.: Ballinger Publishing Company, pp. 9–250.

Gillingham, Robert (1980), "Estimating the User Cost of Owner-Occupied Housing," *Monthly Labor Review*, Vol. 103, No. 2, February, pp. 31–35.

Gorman, John A., John C. Musgrave, Gerald Silverstein, and Kathy Comins (1985), "Fixed Private Capital in the United States," *Survey of Current Business*, Vol. 65, No. 7, July, pp. 36–55.

Grunfeld, Yehuda (1960), "The Determinants of Corporate Investment," in Arnold C. Harberger, ed., *The Demand for Durable Goods*, Chicago: University of Chicago Press.

Gullickson, William, and Michael J. Harper (1986), "Multifactor Productivity Measurement in U.S. Manufacturing," *Monthly Labor Review*, vol. 110, No. 10, October, pp. 18–28.

Hall, Robert E. (1968), "Technical Change and Capital from the Point of View of the Dual," *Review of Economic Studies*, Vol. 35 (6), January, pp. 35–46.

Hall, Robert E., and Dale W. Jorgenson (1967), "Tax Policy and Investment Behavior," *American Economic Review*, Vol. 57, No. 3, June, pp. 391–414.

Harper, Michael J. (1982), "The Measurement of Productive Capital Stock, Capital Wealth, and Capital Services," Washington, D.C.: U.S. Bureau of Labor Statistics, Working Paper No. 128.

Hazilla, Michael, and Raymond J. Kopp (1984), "The Measurement of Sectoral Productivity: A Comparative Evaluation of Alternative Approaches," Washington, D.C.: Resources for the Future, unpublished.

Holland, Daniel M., and Stewart C. Myers (1979), "Trends in Corporate Profitability and Capital Costs," in Robert Lindsay, ed., *The Nation's Capital Needs: Three Studies*, New York: Committee for Economic Development, pp. 103–188.

Hulten, Charles R. (1986), "Productivity Change, Capacity Utilization, and the Sources of Efficiency Growth," *Journal of Econometrics*, Vol. 33, No. 1/2, October/November, pp. 31–50.

Hulten, Charles R., and James W. Robertson (1984), "The Taxation of High Technology Industries," *National Tax Journal*, pp. 327–345.

Hulten, Charles R., and Frank C. Wykoff (1980), "Economic Depreciation and the Taxation of Structures in United States Manufacturing Industries: An Empirical Analysis," chapter 2 in Dan Usher, ed., *The Measurement of Capital*, Chicago: University of Chicago Press for National Bureau of Economic Research, pp. 83–109.

Jorgenson, Dale W. (1963), "Capital Theory and Investment Behavior," *American Economic Review*, Vol. 53, No. 2, May, pp. 247–259.

Jorgenson, Dale W. (1965), "Anticipations and Investment Behavior," *The Brookings Quarterly Econometric Model of the United States*, Chicago: Rand McNally and Company, pp. 35–92.

Jorgenson, Dale W. (1967), "The Theory of Investment Behavior," in R. Ferber, ed., *Determinants of Investment Behavior*, New York: National Bureau of Economic Research, pp. 129–155.

Jorgenson, Dale W. (1974), "The Economic Theory of Replacement and Depreciation," in Willy Sellekaerts, ed., *Econometrics and Economic Theory*, White Plains, N.Y.: International Arts and Science Press, Inc., pp. 189–221.

Jorgenson, Dale W., and Barbara Fraumeni (1981), "Substitution and Technical Change in Production," in Ernst R. Berndt and Barry C. Field, eds., *Modeling and Measuring Natural Resource Substitution*, Cambridge, MA: MIT Press, pp. 17–47.

Jorgenson, Dale W., and Zvi Griliches (1967), "The Explanation of Productivity Change," *Review of Economic Studies*, Vol. 34 (3), No. 99, July, pp. 249–282. Reprinted in "The Measurement of Productivity," *Survey of Current Business*, Vol. 52, No. 5, Part II, pp. 3–36.

Jorgenson, Dale W., and Zvi Griliches (1972), "Issues in Growth Accounting: A Reply to Edward F. Denison," *Survey of Current Business*, Special Issue on the Measurement of Productivity, Vol. 52, No. 5, Part II, pp. 65–94.

Jorgenson, Dale W., and Calvin D. Siebert (1968a), "A Comparison of Alternative Theories of Corporate Investment Behavior," *American Economic Review*, Vol. 58, No. 4, September, pp. 681–712.

Jorgenson, Dale W., and Calvin D. Siebert (1968b), "Optimal Capital Accumulation and Corporate Investment Behavior," *Journal of Political Economy*, Vol. 76, No. 6, November/December, pp. 1123–1151.

Jorgenson, Dale W., and Martin A. Sullivan (1981), "Inflation and Corporate Capital Recovery," in Charles R. Hulten, ed., *Depreciation, Inflation, and the Taxation of Income from Capital*, Washington, D.C.: The Urban Institute Press, pp. 171–237.

Miller, Merton H., and Franco Modigliani (1966), "Some Estimates of the Cost of Capital to the Electric Utility Industry, 1954–57," *American Economic Review*, Vol. 56, No. 3, June, pp. 333–391.

Morrison, Catherine J. (1986), "Productivity Measurement with Nonstatic Expectations and Varying Capacity Utilization: An Integrated Approach," *Journal of Econometrics*, Vol. 33, No. 1/2, October/November, pp. 51–74.

Musgrave, John C. (1986), "Fixed Reproducible Tangible Wealth in the United States: Revised Estimates," *Survey of Current Business*, Vol. 66, No. 1, January, pp. 51–75.

National Academy of Sciences (1979), *The Measurement and Interpretation of Productivity*. Washington, D.C.: National Academy of Sciences.

Solow, Robert M. (1957), "Technical Change and the Aggregate Production Function," *Review of Economics and Statistics*, Vol. 39, No. 3, pp. 312–320.

Tinbergen, Jan (1942), "Zur theorie der langristigen wirtschaftsentwicklung," *Weltwirtschaftliches Archiv.*, Band 55:1, pp. 511–549. English translation, "On the Theory of Trend Movements," in L. H. Klassen, L. M. Koyck, and H. J. Witteveen, eds., *Jan Tinbergen, Selected Papers*, Amsterdam: North Holland, 1959.

9   The Market Valuation
of Credit Market Debt

John S. Strong

In recent years, there has been a resurgence of interest in the measurement and analysis of both public and private debt. At the macroeconomic level, much of the discussion has been concerned with the effects of federal debt management on private financing and capital formation. At the micro level, rising debt levels and the use of debt to finance merger-related activity has created renewed interest in corporate debt policy. Recent work on capital structure theory has also contributed to this growing literature, since leverage is an important variable in issues concerning the risk of a firm and its securities. Indeed, the measurement of corporate income, the valuation of corporate assets, and the correct rate-setting mechanism in regulatory proceedings all depend to at least some extent on the measurement and valuation of financial claims.

The financial theory underlying the study of leverage, valuation, and risk is relatively unambiguous, dating from the original Miller and Modigliani paper (1958) on capital structure. Regardless of whether tax shields and other factors are considered, the market value, not the book value, of a firm's debt and equity are required to estimate correctly the leverage position and the required rate of return. Similarly, as Eisner and Pieper (1984) point out, market values of public debt are also required to interpret the effects of federal debt and government deficits on the economy.

Unfortunately, and by contrast, most of the empirical work on capital structure, debt policy, and financial macroeconomics has used book-value (accounting) measures. Although the reported results of these studies have been widely disseminated, there have been few attempts to evaluate the effects of using these book-value measurements as surrogates for market value. This chapter attempts to fill some of this void by providing direct empirical evidence on the comparability of book-value and market-value measures of debt.

The chapter is divided into two sections. The first section develops annual estimates of the holding gains on various classes of long-term financial liabilities for nonfinancial corporations for 1945–1983. The relationships between par and market values are examined to assess the validity of par values as proxies for market measures in macroeconomic reporting and analysis. Estimates of market-valued capital structures for the nonfinancial corporate sector are constructed. These estimates are used to evaluate the contention that U.S. firms are becoming more highly leveraged, with concomitant effects on the nation's financial stability.

Eisner and Pieper (1984) recently have published estimates of the market value of the liabilities of the federal government. The second section of this chapter extends their work by estimating the market value of credit market liabilities for each of the seven major nonfinancial sectors of the economy. Market-to-par indexes for a variety of debt instruments are constructed and then used to restate sectoral liabilities to market value. Thus, the methodology incorporates both the different classes of securities as well as their sectoral distribution.

9.1   The Market Value of Nonfinancial Corporate Liabilities

As part of its flow-of-funds data, the Federal Reserve System constructs balance sheet accounts for each of the major sectors of the economy. Table 9.1 presents the liabilities of nonfinancial corporations for the postwar period. The percentage distribution is shown in table 9.2. The tables clearly indicate the rising share of short-term liabilities commensurate with the growth of the commercial paper market beginning in the late 1960s. The continuing importance of bank lending to nonfinancial corporations is also evident. For long-term debt, there are four main classes: bank loans, corporate bonds, tax-exempt bonds, and mortgages.

The process of marking securities to market is likely to result in greater revisions in the value of longer-term instruments, for several reasons. First, a large portion of the financial assets and short-term debt have floating rate provisions. Second, to the extent that inflation was correctly anticipated, there is no gain or loss from being a short-term debtor or creditor. However, to the degree that movements in the price level were unanticipated by creditors in the design of short-term debt contracts, nonfinancial corporations were likely to have experienced some measure of debt revaluation. Estimates of these

Table 9.1
Outstanding liabilities, nonfinancial corporations, 1945–1983 (at par value; $ billions)

Year	Short-term financial liabilities	Trade debt	Bank loans	Corporate bonds	Tax-exempt bonds	Mortgages	Deferred taxes	Foreign direct investment	Total liabilities
1945	2.1	14.2	9.4	23.5	0.0	8.6	10.8	2.5	71.3
1946	2.0	20.0	12.8	24.4	0.0	10.2	8.8	2.5	80.8
1947	2.0	23.3	15.9	27.2	0.0	11.7	11.3	2.6	93.9
1948	2.0	24.9	16.4	31.4	0.0	13.1	12.1	2.8	102.7
1949	2.0	24.6	14.6	34.2	0.0	13.9	9.7	2.9	101.8
1950	2.0	32.9	18.3	35.7	0.0	15.1	17.3	3.4	124.8
1951	2.5	33.8	22.1	38.9	0.0	16.2	21.9	3.7	139.0
1952	3.0	35.5	23.0	43.6	0.0	17.2	18.7	3.0	144.8
1953	3.6	35.2	22.4	47.0	0.0	18.1	19.3	4.3	149.7
1954	3.8	37.6	21.8	50.4	0.0	19.7	16.0	4.6	154.0
1955	3.8	46.3	25.6	53.3	0.0	21.6	20.1	5.1	175.6
1956	3.9	50.6	30.7	56.9	0.0	23.2	18.1	5.4	188.9
1957	4.5	52.1	31.9	63.2	0.0	24.9	16.0	5.7	198.4
1958	4.9	55.8	31.6	68.9	0.0	27.7	13.4	6.1	208.4
1959	5.4	61.1	35.5	71.0	0.0	30.8	15.8	6.6	227.0
1960	7.7	64.1	37.9	75.3	0.0	33.4	13.6	6.9	238.9
1961	8.3	67.9	39.3	80.0	0.0	37.4	15.0	7.4	255.3
1962	8.3	71.1	42.6	84.5	0.0	41.9	15.9	7.6	272.1
1963	8.8	78.8	46.1	88.4	0.0	46.8	17.5	7.9	294.5
1964	9.9	86.0	51.3	92.4	0.0	49.4	18.0	8.4	315.3
1965	10.5	98.2	61.6	97.8	0.0	51.6	20.2	8.8	348.7
1966	11.6	108.8	69.8	108.0	0.0	54.5	20.4	9.1	382.3
1967	13.1	116.2	77.1	122.7	0.0	56.6	15.6	9.9	411.2

Table 9.1 (continued)

Year	Short-term financial liabilities	Trade debt	Bank loans	Corporate bonds	Tax-exempt bonds	Mortgages	Deferred taxes	Foreign direct investment	Total liabilities
1968	15.7	133.4	86.5	135.6	0.0	58.8	18.5	10.8	459.2
1969	21.6	154.2	98.3	147.6	0.0	58.0	15.2	11.8	506.7
1970	24.7	161.7	104.2	167.3	0.0	58.9	11.5	13.3	541.5
1971	24.2	174.0	108.3	186.1	0.1	61.3	13.3	13.9	581.4
1972	28.8	196.2	120.6	198.3	0.6	64.1	13.3	14.9	636.9
1973	35.2	235.1	150.3	207.5	2.4	65.9	15.6	20.6	732.6
1974	47.9	174.1	181.5	227.1	4.1	66.8	16.7	25.1	743.4
1975	49.2	180.5	172.4	254.3	6.7	65.9	14.3	27.7	770.9
1976	60.5	190.7	176.3	277.2	9.2	68.3	21.8	30.8	834.7
1977	76.3	212.8	197.0	300.0	17.4	71.9	20.3	34.6	930.3
1978	91.5	263.9	227.4	321.2	25.0	76.1	24.6	42.5	1072.0
1979	112.8	318.1	272.6	338.5	35.0	77.5	27.1	54.5	1236.1
1980	121.8	358.9	299.2	365.1	45.9	80.0	25.3	68.4	1364.6
1981	148.6	386.7	341.9	387.2	59.3	73.7	18.5	90.4	1506.4
1982	146.1	376.5	383.0	406.0	74.5	76.7	2.4	101.8	1567.1
1983	158.7	425.7	400.1	421.0	83.8	79.7	5.2	110.5	1684.7

Source: Federal Reserve Board, *Balance Sheets for the U.S. Economy*.

Table 9.2
Percentage distribution, nonfinancial corporate liabilities

Year	Short-term financial liabilities	Trade debt	Bank loans	Corporate bonds	Tax-exempt bonds	Mortgages	Deferred taxes	Foreign direct investment	Total liabilities
1945	0.03	0.20	0.13	0.33	0.00	0.12	0.15	0.04	1.00
1946	0.02	0.25	0.16	0.30	0.00	0.13	0.11	0.03	1.00
1947	0.02	0.25	0.17	0.29	0.00	0.12	0.12	0.03	1.00
1948	0.02	0.24	0.16	0.31	0.00	0.13	0.12	0.03	1.00
1949	0.02	0.24	0.14	0.34	0.00	0.14	0.10	0.03	1.00
1950	0.02	0.26	0.15	0.29	0.00	0.12	0.14	0.03	1.00
1951	0.02	0.24	0.16	0.28	0.00	0.12	0.16	0.03	1.00
1952	0.02	0.25	0.16	0.30	0.00	0.12	0.13	0.03	1.00
1953	0.02	0.24	0.15	0.31	0.00	0.12	0.13	0.03	1.00
1954	0.02	0.24	0.14	0.33	0.00	0.13	0.10	0.03	1.00
1955	0.02	0.26	0.15	0.30	0.00	0.12	0.11	0.03	1.00
1956	0.02	0.27	0.16	0.30	0.00	0.12	0.10	0.03	1.00
1957	0.02	0.26	0.16	0.32	0.00	0.13	0.08	0.03	1.00
1958	0.02	0.27	0.15	0.33	0.00	0.13	0.06	0.03	1.00
1959	0.02	0.27	0.16	0.32	0.00	0.14	0.07	0.03	1.00
1960	0.03	0.27	0.16	0.32	0.00	0.14	0.06	0.03	1.00
1961	0.03	0.27	0.15	0.31	0.00	0.15	0.06	0.03	1.00
1962	0.03	0.26	0.16	0.31	0.00	0.15	0.06	0.03	1.00
1963	0.03	0.27	0.16	0.30	0.00	0.16	0.06	0.03	1.00
1964	0.03	0.27	0.16	0.29	0.00	0.16	0.06	0.03	1.00
1965	0.03	0.28	0.18	0.28	0.00	0.15	0.06	0.03	1.00
1966	0.03	0.28	0.18	0.28	0.00	0.14	0.05	0.02	1.00
1967	0.03	0.28	0.19	0.30	0.00	0.14	0.04	0.02	1.00
1968	0.03	0.29	0.19	0.30	0.00	0.13	0.04	0.02	1.00
1969	0.04	0.30	0.19	0.29	0.00	0.11	0.03	0.02	1.00
1970	0.05	0.30	0.19	0.31	0.00	0.11	0.02	0.02	1.00
1971	0.04	0.30	0.19	0.32	0.00	0.11	0.02	0.02	1.00
1972	0.05	0.31	0.19	0.31	0.00	0.10	0.02	0.02	1.00
1973	0.05	0.32	0.21	0.28	0.00	0.09	0.02	0.03	1.00
1974	0.06	0.23	0.24	0.31	0.01	0.09	0.02	0.03	1.00
1975	0.06	0.23	0.22	0.33	0.01	0.09	0.02	0.04	1.00
1976	0.07	0.23	0.21	0.33	0.01	0.08	0.03	0.04	1.00
1977	0.08	0.23	0.21	0.32	0.02	0.08	0.02	0.04	1.00
1978	0.09	0.25	0.21	0.30	0.02	0.07	0.02	0.04	1.00
1979	0.09	0.26	0.22	0.27	0.03	0.06	0.02	0.04	1.00
1980	0.09	0.26	0.22	0.27	0.03	0.06	0.02	0.05	1.00
1981	0.10	0.26	0.23	0.26	0.04	0.05	0.01	0.06	1.00
1982	0.09	0.24	0.24	0.26	0.05	0.05	0.00	0.06	1.00
1983	0.09	0.25	0.24	0.25	0.05	0.05	0.00	0.07	1.00

Table 9.3
Holding gains and losses on short-term financial instruments ($ billions)

Year	Short-term financial assets	Short-term financial liabilities	Net Short-term financial liabilities	Inflationary gain on net short-term liabilities
1945	61.8	36.7	−25.1	−0.6
1946	60.2	43.7	−16.5	−2.6
1947	67.8	52.4	−15.4	−2.0
1948	72.1	55.4	−16.7	−1.2
1949	74.9	50.8	−24.1	0.2
1950	90.6	70.6	−20.0	−0.4
1951	97.5	80.2	−17.3	−1.1
1952	101.3	80.1	−21.2	−0.3
1953	102.8	80.3	−22.5	−0.4
1954	107.0	79.3	−27.7	−0.3
1955	122.7	95.6	−27.1	−0.6
1956	124.7	103.4	−21.3	−0.7
1957	126.5	104.6	−21.9	−0.7
1958	136.1	105.7	−30.4	−0.5
1959	148.9	117.7	−31.2	−0.7
1960	149.8	123.3	−26.5	−0.4
1961	159.9	130.5	−29.4	−0.3
1962	169.3	138.1	−31.2	−0.6
1963	181.5	151.4	−30.1	−0.5
1964	192.6	165.1	−27.5	−0.4
1965	209.5	190.5	−19.0	−0.4
1966	221.3	210.7	−10.6	−0.3
1967	233.4	222.0	−11.4	−0.3
1968	260.7	254.0	−6.7	−0.3
1969	287.4	289.3	1.9	0.1
1970	299.3	302.0	2.7	0.1
1971	329.6	320.0	−9.6	−0.5
1972	374.0	359.0	−15.0	−0.6
1973	434.3	436.2	1.9	0.1
1974	416.3	420.3	4.0	0.4
1975	443.5	416.3	−27.2	−2.5
1976	485.3	449.2	−36.1	−1.9
1977	536.3	506.4	−29.9	−1.7
1978	612.6	607.2	−5.4	−0.4
1979	713.4	730.6	17.2	1.5

Table 9.3 (continued)

Year	Short-term financial assets	Short-term financial liabilities	Net Short-term financial liabilities	Inflationary gain on net short-term liabilities
1980	790.3	805.2	14.9	1.4
1981	840.3	895.8	55.5	5.2
1982	854.1	908.1	54.0	3.2
1983	966.7	989.7	23.0	1.0

holding gains or losses on short-term instruments are presented in table 9.3. Column 1 is the sum of the year-end outstandings of open market paper, demand deposits, short-term time deposits, repurchase agreements, and government securities. Column 2 is a parallel construct for financial liabilities, consisting mainly of commercial paper, acceptances, finance company loans, and short-term bank credit. The net position is presented in column 3. For most of the postwar period, nonfinancial corporations were net creditors; not until 1979 did holdings of current financial liabilities exceed financial assets to any substantial degree. The final column in table 9.3 presents one estimate of inflationary gain on net short-term liability position. Following Shoven and Bulow (1976), this estimate was calculated by assuming that the net liability position was accumulated evenly throughout the year, so that the inflationary gain or loss could be calculated by multiplying the net position by the change in the GNP deflator over the second half of the year.

The estimates show that throughout the postwar period, holding losses and gains have been small. It should be noted that these estimates are almost certainly upper bound estimates of inflationary gains, since they do not incorporate any rolling over of instruments, do not contain allowances for floating rates, and assume that inflation is completely unanticipated by creditors. If it were possible to incorporate such information, the inflationary gains and losses on short-term financial assets and liabilities might be reduced by as much as 75%.

The principal differences between par and market values are likely to arise in the long-term accounts. Tables 9.4–9.6 report calculations of accrued but unrealized holding gains on long-term debt experienced by nonfinancial corporations during the postwar period.[1] The esti-

Table 9.4
Market and par values of corporate bonds ($ billions)

Year	Par value of outstanding bonds	Average end-of-year price	Market value of outstanding bonds	Cumulative holding gain	Change from previous year
1945	23.5	101.25	23.8	−0.3	—
1946	24.4	95.13	23.2	1.2	1.5
1947	27.2	89.53	24.4	2.8	1.7
1948	31.4	93.22	29.3	2.1	−0.7
1949	34.2	97.08	33.2	1.0	−1.1
1950	35.7	99.50	35.5	0.2	−0.8
1951	38.9	93.16	36.2	2.7	2.5
1952	43.6	96.20	41.9	1.7	−1.0
1953	47.0	95.21	44.7	2.3	0.6
1954	50.4	99.50	50.1	0.3	−2.0
1955	53.3	97.76	52.1	1.2	0.9
1956	56.9	87.40	49.7	7.2	6.0
1957	63.2	88.09	55.7	7.5	0.4
1958	68.9	89.06	61.4	7.5	0.0
1959	71.9	83.77	60.2	11.7	4.1
1960	75.3	86.41	65.1	10.2	−1.4
1961	80.0	88.13	70.5	9.5	−0.7
1962	84.5	90.22	76.2	8.3	−1.2
1963	88.4	90.45	80.0	8.4	0.2
1964	92.4	92.31	85.3	7.1	−1.3
1965	97.8	91.32	89.3	8.5	1.4
1966	108.0	84.40	91.2	16.8	8.4
1967	122.7	82.07	100.7	22.0	5.2
1968	135.6	82.25	111.5	24.1	2.1
1969	147.6	72.12	106.4	41.2	17.1
1970	167.3	80.78	135.1	32.2	−9.0
1971	186.1	89.93	167.4	18.7	−13.4
1972	198.3	91.48	181.4	16.9	−1.8
1973	207.5	85.71	177.8	29.7	12.8
1974	227.1	76.35	173.4	53.7	24.1
1975	254.3	84.13	213.9	40.4	−13.4
1976	277.2	97.03	269.0	8.2	−32.1
1977	300.0	93.13	279.4	20.6	12.4
1978	321.2	86.43	277.6	43.6	23.0
1979	338.5	79.76	270.0	68.5	24.9

Table 9.4 (continued)

Year	Par value of outstanding bonds	Average end-of-year price	Market value of outstanding bonds	Cumulative holding gain	Change from previous year
1980	365.1	74.04	270.3	94.8	26.3
1981	387.2	70.12	271.5	115.7	20.9
1982	406.0	83.46	338.8	67.2	−48.5
1983	421.0	83.27	350.6	70.4	3.3

mates present macro time series data on changes in the market value of bonds, mortgages, and tax-exempt industrial securities (principally industrial revenue and pollution control bonds). The character of each of these securities is sufficiently different that construction of separate market-to-par indices is warranted, although previous research has not done so.

Table 9.4 reports market values and holding gains on corporate bonds. Par values represent the dollar volume of bonds outstanding at year end, as reported in the flow of funds accounts. The second column is the average end-of-year price as measured by the New York Stock Exchange Bond Index for all listed U.S. companies.[2] The index indicates that at the end of 1983, the average bond was selling at 83.27% of its par value.[3] The index is then used to calculate estimates of market value, presented in column 3. At the end of 1983, the total value of outstanding bonds was $350.6 billion, or $70.4 billion less than their par value. This number (shown in column 4) represents the cumulative accrued gain of firms (and the symmetric loss of bondholders). Because this number would tend toward zero with stable interest rates, it is intriguing that cumulative holding gains have remained positive for the entire 1946–1983 period. At no time was the average price of bonds above par. An interesting sidelight to this analysis is that interest rate movements alone fail to account for more than about two-thirds of the debt depreciation reported here. While other factors are difficult to evaluate at the aggregate level, a companion paper dealing with individual firms suggests that between one-fourth and one-half of the decline in the market value of corporate liabilities can be ascribed to increased credit risk.[4]

The final column of table 9.4 presents year-to-year changes in holding gains, calculated as the change in cumulative gains from the prior year. This column thus represents the annual gains and losses experienced by nonfinancial corporations due to changes in the value of their bond liabilities.[5] The holding gains from the credit crunches of 1966, 1969, and 1973–1974 are apparent, as is the ongoing pattern of gains during 1977–1981. In contrast, firms experienced annual holding losses on bonds in 1975–1976 and in 1982.

Table 9.5 presents similar calculations of the gains experienced by nonfinancial corporations on their mortgage liabilities.[6] Construction of a separate par-to-market index was required, since there exists no widely traded market for mortgages owed by nonfinancial corporations. Although previous research has used the NYSE bond index to discount mortgage liabilities as well, this approach was rejected because the longer average maturity of mortgages makes them more susceptible to interest rate movements. It has been argued that the longer maturities are largely offset since principal is paid off over the term of the mortgage (see Shoven and Bulow, 1976). However, the common use of sinking fund provisions suggests that principal repayments over the term also characterize a substantial percentage of bonds, so that the maturity problem remains.

To value mortgage liabilities explicitly, an index was constructed by assuming a fifteen-year life, monthly interest payments, and an interest rate as given in the Federal Reserve's survey of the terms of lending for long-term commercial and industrial loans. The annual flows into the mortgage market were estimated by taking new issues for each year and estimating cash flow requirements over the assumed fifteen-year life.[7] Market values were calculated as the sum of interest and principal payments, discounted by the interest rate on new long-term commercial and industrial loans.[8] Thus, the estimated market-to-par index reflects both interest rate and volume changes.

The calculations are presented in table 9.5. At the end of 1983, the present value of mortgages held by nonfinancial corporations was $64.2 billion, or $15.5 billion less than par value. As was the case with bonds, the market-to-par discount has persisted throughout the postwar period.

The third major component of long-term liabilities is tax-exempt bonds. These securities are issued by firms with the imprimatur of a state or local government entity, which confers tax-exempt status under current tax law. These instruments became important in the early 1970s, originally being used to finance pollution control equipment. The bonds quickly outgrew their original application, however, with an increasing volume being dedicated to industrial expansion. By 1983, the par value of tax-exempts held by corporations

Table 9.5
Market and par values of mortgage liabilities, nonfinancial corporations
($ billions)

1945	8.6	103.81	8.9	−0.3	—
1946	10.2	104.79	10.7	−0.5	−0.2
1947	11.7	103.32	12.1	−0.4	0.1
1948	13.1	99.36	13.0	0.1	0.5
1949	13.9	99.61	13.8	0.1	0.0
1950	15.1	101.81	15.4	−0.3	−0.3
1951	16.2	97.90	15.9	0.3	0.6
1952	17.2	98.51	16.9	0.3	−0.1
1953	18.1	99.78	18.1	0.0	−0.2
1954	19.7	98.34	19.4	0.3	0.3
1955	21.6	95.87	20.7	0.9	0.6
1956	23.2	91.86	21.3	1.9	1.0
1957	24.9	87.36	21.8	3.1	1.3
1958	27.7	92.57	25.6	2.1	−1.1
1959	30.8	87.88	27.1	3.7	1.7
1960	33.4	87.31	29.2	4.2	0.5
1961	37.4	90.82	34.0	3.4	−0.8
1962	41.9	92.81	38.9	3.0	−0.4
1963	46.8	93.13	43.6	3.2	0.2
1964	49.4	90.92	44.9	4.5	1.3
1965	51.6	92.18	47.6	4.0	−0.5
1966	54.5	89.03	48.5	6.0	1.9
1967	56.6	92.46	52.3	4.3	−1.7
1968	58.8	84.33	49.6	9.2	4.9
1969	58.0	83.14	48.2	9.8	0.6
1970	58.9	78.62	46.3	12.6	2.8
1971	61.3	82.86	50.8	10.5	−2.1
1972	64.1	82.77	53.1	11.0	0.5
1973	65.9	80.59	53.1	12.8	1.7
1974	66.8	76.21	50.9	15.9	3.1
1975	65.9	75.75	49.9	16.0	0.1
1976	68.3	83.28	56.9	11.4	−4.6
1977	71.9	86.84	62.4	9.5	−2.0
1978	76.1	88.21	67.1	9.0	−0.5
1979	77.5	88.52	68.6	8.9	−0.1
1980	80.0	83.41	66.7	13.3	4.4
1981	73.7	70.23	51.8	21.9	8.7
1982	76.7	72.10	55.3	21.4	−0.5
1983	79.7	80.54	64.2	15.5	−5.9

totaled $83.8 billion, or roughly one-fifth of the outstanding volume of corporate bonds. The amount of corporate liabilities represented by tax-exempt securities now exceeds that of nonfinancial corporate mortgage liabilities.

Previous research on market revaluation has not explicitly considered tax-exempt instruments. The methodology used here is similar to that used above for mortgage liabilities. It was assumed that the bonds have liabilities of ten years,[9] biannual interest payments, and coupon rates equal to the yield on private purpose tax-exempt offerings as reported in *Barron's* for the years they were issued. The volume of new issues was taken from the Department of Commerce *Business Statistics* and from the Flow of Funds data. Market values were calculated as the sum of interest and principal commitments, discounted by the current annual yield on private-purpose tax-exempt bonds.

The calculations are presented in table 9.6. As might be expected, the market values of tax-exempt bonds are much closer to par than bonds or mortgages. However, nonfinancial corporations did experience a cumulative holding gain on tax-exempts of over $6 billion by the end of 1983. Most of this gain was the result of interest rate increases in 1980–1981. It should be noted that despite the rising

Table 9.6
Par and market values of tax-exempt bonds held by nonfinancial corporations ($ billions)

Year	Par value tax-exempt bonds (IRBs)	Average end-of-year price	Market value tax-exempt bonds	Cumulative holding gain	Change from previous year
1971	0.1	100.00	0.1	0.0	—
1972	0.6	100.05	0.6	0.0	0.0
1973	2.4	99.57	2.4	0.0	0.0
1974	4.1	95.49	3.9	0.2	0.2
1975	6.7	95.43	6.4	0.3	0.1
1976	9.2	100.45	9.2	0.0	−0.3
1977	17.4	102.66	17.9	−0.5	−0.4
1978	25.0	99.07	24.8	0.2	0.7
1979	35.0	97.58	34.2	0.8	0.6
1980	45.9	91.96	42.2	3.7	2.8
1981	59.3	84.38	50.0	9.3	5.6
1982	74.5	88.67	66.1	8.4	−0.8
1983	83.8	92.77	77.7	6.1	−2.4

rates, volume increased almost $25 billion over the period. This continuing issuance means that this class of corporate securities will continue to be important in measuring debt liabilities.

The aggregate holding gains on long-term liabilities for nonfinancial corporations can be estimated by combining the three components above. In addition, it is necessary to add the share of bank loans that are long term. To estimate this component, the Federal Reserve's survey of the terms of lending by commercial banks was reviewed.[10] Over the entire period, roughly 40% of bank loans had maturities exceeding one year, although this share has decreased in recent years. The 40% estimate is also used by the Fed in its own estimates of long-term bank loans to corporations. No separate revaluation was undertaken for bank loans, for two reasons. First, a majority of loans carried floating rates, usually linked to the prime. Second, the average maturity of these term loans was between three and four years. At any given time, half of the bank loans made under fixed rates were issued either in the current or in the immediately preceding year. Thus, it was assumed that the book value of bank loans approximated market. This omission does result in a biased estimate of market values of corporate debt. To determine the direction of this bias, changes in the prime lending rate were examined. While changes were both positive and negative from year to year, the size of the resulting market discount or premium was small (averaging just over one percent, and never exceeding four percent of total long-term bank loans). With the growth of below-prime lending in recent years, measurement errors from assuming the equivalence of par and market values for bank loans appear to be smaller than errors introduced by calculating present values based on the prime. In addition, bank requirements for compensating balances and commitment fees also reduce the accuracy of strict interest rate revaluations.[11]

Table 9.7 combines the bank lending component with the valuations of tables 9.4–9.6 to provide summary estimates of holding gains on long-term credit market instruments. At the end of 1983, the market value of long-term debt was $92 billion less than par value (representing a discount of 12.4%). Cumulative holding gains have been positive every year since 1950, although year-to-year changes have been much more volatile (as shown in the last column). The average market-to-par discount was 90.8%, with a standard deviation of 5.8%. Since 1970, however, market values have averaged only 87% of par, reaching a low of 77.6% in 1981. This divergence is presented

Table 9.7
Market and par values of total long-term debt, nonfinancial corporations
($ billions)

Year	Par value debt	Market: par index	Market value debt	Cumulative holding gain	Change from previous year
1945	35.9	1.017	36.5	−0.6	—
1946	39.7	0.982	39.0	0.7	1.3
1947	45.3	0.947	42.9	2.4	1.7
1948	51.1	0.957	48.9	2.2	−0.2
1949	53.9	0.980	52.8	1.1	−1.1
1950	58.2	1.002	58.3	−0.1	−1.2
1951	63.9	0.953	60.9	3.0	3.1
1952	70.0	0.971	68.0	2.0	−1.0
1953	74.1	0.969	71.8	2.3	0.3
1954	78.8	0.992	78.2	0.6	−1.7
1955	85.2	0.975	83.1	2.1	1.5
1956	92.4	0.902	83.3	9.1	7.0
1957	100.9	0.895	90.3	10.6	1.5
1958	109.3	0.912	99.7	9.6	−1.0
1959	116.9	0.868	101.5	15.4	5.8
1960	123.9	0.884	109.5	14.4	−1.0
1961	133.1	0.903	120.2	12.9	−1.5
1962	143.4	0.921	132.1	11.3	−1.6
1963	153.7	0.925	142.1	11.6	0.3
1964	162.3	0.929	150.7	11.6	0.0
1965	174.0	0.928	161.5	12.5	0.9
1966	190.4	0.880	167.6	22.8	10.3
1967	210.1	0.875	183.8	26.3	3.5
1968	229.0	0.855	195.7	33.3	7.0
1969	244.9	0.792	193.9	51.0	17.7
1970	267.9	0.833	223.1	44.8	−6.2
1971	290.8	0.900	261.6	29.2	−15.6
1972	311.2	0.910	283.3	27.9	−1.3
1973	335.9	0.873	293.4	42.5	14.6
1974	370.6	0.812	300.8	69.8	27.3
1975	395.9	0.857	339.2	56.7	−13.1
1976	425.2	0.954	405.6	19.6	−37.1
1977	468.1	0.952	445.4	22.7	3.1
1978	513.3	0.897	460.5	52.8	30.1
1979	560.0	0.860	481.8	78.2	25.4

Table 9.7 (continued)

Year	Par value debt	Market: par index	Market value debt	Cumulative holding gain	Change from previous year
1980	610.7	0.817	498.9	111.8	33.6
1981	657.0	0.776	510.1	146.9	35.1
1982	710.4	0.863	613.4	97.0	−49.9
1983	744.5	0.876	652.5	92.0	−5.0

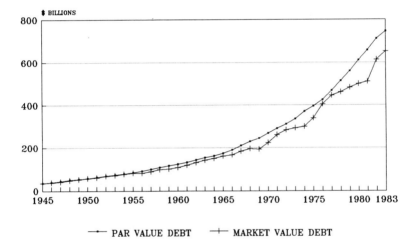

Figure 9.1

graphically in figure 9.1. The widening gap beginning in the late 1960s is clearly evident.

Table 9.7 clearly indicates that nonfinancial corporations have experienced substantial gains on their liabilities. Under a Haig-Simons definition of income, gains on debt should be included in corporate profits, so that the last column of table 9.7 indicates the annual restatements that would be necessary to incorporate these gains. These revisions are quite substantial and would have increased or decreased reported profits, depending on the year chosen. Thus, while gains on debt have been experienced over the entire period, the annual influences on firm and equity values is less clear. However, the variability and uncertainty involved in such revaluations does not mean they should be ignored. While subject to measurement error, such estimates are almost surely better estimates of true value than par or issue price. Indeed, such factors should be explicitly considered in mergers, refundings, or recapitalizations.

9.1.1 The Stochastic and Temporal Structure of Market and Par Value

The estimates of the time series of the market value of corporate debt are primarily motivated by the usefulness of such series for a variety of empirical analyses. Since for many purposes market value is the correct measure of debt, studies using other measures fact potentially large misspecification problems. In this section, the univariate stochastic properties of the market value and par value series are compared. These calculations are done for both the summary series and for each of the component types of debt.

Over the long run, the two series move together quite closely. With the exception of the mortgage series, the data reflect steady growth over the past forty years. As a result, the correlations between market and par values are quite high: for bonds, .990; for mortgages, .987; for tax-exempts, .998; and for the aggregate series, .996.

While these correlations are extremely high, they do not imply that errors from using par values are inconsequential. Part of the correlation can be traced to common trends in the series. The correlations of both par and market values with a time trend are very high. The effect of this common trend can be eliminated by regressing each series on a time trend and then correlating the residuals. The regressions are presented in table 9.8, and the residual correlations in table 9.9. For simple OLS regressions, the correlations between

Table 9.8
Time trend regressions[a]

Dependent variable	Constant	Time trend coefficient	Coefficient of determination	F-statistic	Durbin-Watson
Par value bonds	−52.56	10.01 (0.62)	.875	258.7	0.035
Market value bonds	−36.26	8.06 (0.51)	.868	245.4	0.194
Par value mortgages	3.07	2.09 (0.05)	.978	652.9	0.266
Market value mortgages	6.66	1.58 (0.07)	.930	488.6	0.550
Par value tax-exempts	−21.89	7.13 (0.72)	.897	95.5	0.260
Market value tax-exempts	19.18	6.43 (0.62)	.907	108.1	0.324
Par value total debt	−90.45	16.70 (1.10)	.862	231.9	0.040
Market value total debt	−69.47	14.17 (0.93)	.862	232.0	0.097

a. Standard errors in parentheses.

Table 9.9
Residual correlations[a]

	Correlation between market and par values
Corporate bonds	.924
Mortgages	.860
Tax-exempt bonds	.982
Total long term debt	.972

a. Data calculated by regressing market and par values of each aggregate on a time trend, and then correlating the regression residuals.

Table 9.10
First difference correlations[a]

	Correlation between market and par values
Corporate bonds	.466
Mortgages	.837
Tax-exempt bonds	.917
Total long term debt	.621

a. Data estimated by correlating residuals from regressions of first differences of market and par values on a time trend variable.

Table 9.11
Long-term debt as percent of capitalization, 1945–1983

Year	Book value debt and equity	Book value debt, market value equity	Market value debt, market value equity
1945	0.418	0.290	0.294
1946	0.423	0.323	0.319
1947	0.415	0.348	0.335
1948	0.418	0.378	0.368
1949	0.407	0.369	0.364
1950	0.399	0.333	0.333
1951	0.396	0.316	0.306
1952	0.404	0.318	0.312
1953	0.398	0.338	0.331
1954	0.402	0.267	0.266
1955	0.403	0.240	0.236
1956	0.406	0.242	0.224
1957	0.418	0.294	0.271
1958	0.433	0.242	0.226
1959	0.436	0.244	0.219
1960	0.448	0.259	0.236
1961	0.461	0.237	0.219
1962	0.470	0.269	0.253
1963	0.481	0.252	0.238
1964	0.479	0.242	0.228
1965	0.480	0.239	0.226
1966	0.489	0.274	0.250

Table 9.11 (continued)

Year	Book value debt and equity	Book value debt, market value equity	Market value debt, market value equity
1967	0.504	0.244	0.220
1968	0.519	0.237	0.210
1969	0.513	0.275	0.231
1970	0.532	0.292	0.256
1971	0.539	0.277	0.256
1972	0.529	0.266	0.248
1973	0.516	0.330	0.301
1974	0.493	0.425	0.375
1975	0.482	0.365	0.330
1976	0.472	0.348	0.337
1977	0.479	0.382	0.370
1978	0.479	0.396	0.371
1979	0.467	0.373	0.338
1980	0.456	0.319	0.277
1981	0.460	0.349	0.294
1982	0.479	0.337	0.305
1983	0.461	0.311	0.283
Mean	0.458	0.304	0.283
Standard deviation	0.042	0.052	0.051

market and par values fall to .925 for bonds; to .860 for mortgages; to .982 for tax-exempts; and to .972 for the debt aggregate. When a further correction is made for first-order autoregressive residuals in the time trend regressions (table 9.10), the correlations fall dramtically: for bonds, to .466; for mortgages, to .838; for tax-exempts, to .917; and for the debt aggregate, .622.

Thus, correlations in levels substantially overstate the underlying comovement of the two series. Although the levels of the par value series explain (in the sense of squared correlation) over 99% of the level of the market value series, simple detrending reduces this explanatory power to less than 40%. Although this amount remains statistically·significant, it demonstrates the limitations of par value as a surrogate for market value. This has become a more severe problem in recent years as the increase in interest rate variability has caused a further decline in the relation between the market and par value series. Since 1973, the correlation between market and par values for total debt is .973, but the correlation between their first differences is only .170. It should also be noted that these estimated differences between market and par values are much larger than those estimated by Seater (1981) and Cox and Hirschhorn (1983) for Treasury securities. Two possible explanations for this are that corporate debt is more volatile than Treasuries, or that the economic events of the 1970s were particularly damaging to nonfinancial corporations, resulting in increased credit risk.

9.1.2   Market Values and Capital Structure

The resurgence of interest in financial markets by monetary and macroeconomists has emphasized the importance of leverage considerations in economic performance. Table 9.11 presents estimates of three alternative measures of long-term debt as a percentage of total capitalization (long-term debt plus preferred and common stock). The second column is calculated directly from par values of debt and book values of equity. Although there is little theoretical justification for their use, they are included for comparison. Column 2 incorporates market values of preferred and common stock, while the last column introduces the market-valued debt estimates calculated above. The table clearly illustrates the importance of using market values in measuring equity. While the choice between par and market values of debt is not as critical as that for equity values, the revisions are not trivial, changing the ratio by as much as 5% in some years. The correlation between the two series that use market value equity is .965.

Except for a notable increase during the late 1970s, capitalization ratios have not exhibited much trend during the postwar era. The standard deviations of the ratios are very small relative to their means, indicating relative stability.[12] Somewhat surprisingly, the correct market value ratio exhibits only slightly more variability than book values. This suggests that a common justification for not using market values, that of greater volatility, may be untenable. Measurement error does not appear to be substantially greater for market values than for book values.

9.2   The Market Value of Credit Market Debt: A Sectoral Approach

Recent work in financial macroeconomics has been concerned with the growth and magnitude of debt in the U.S. economy. The most noteworthy research has been done by Friedman (1981, 1983a, b, 1985), with related work by Pollin (1985) and Wojnilower (1983). However, none of these authors has attempted to evaluate the question of the nation's debt capacity from a market value perspective. Since market values of debt incorporate price, quantity, and timing considerations, they ought to be the starting point for an evaluation of the economy's debt capacity. This point has been recognized by Eisner and Pieper (1984) in their careful construction of a market-valued balance sheet for the federal government, but to date, no comprehensive restatement of credit market liabilities has been undertaken for the economy as a whole. This section extends Eisner and Pieper's government revaluations to a multisector framework in order to gain insights about the relation between market and par values for the economy as a whole.

Data on the par value of outstanding credit market debt is available from the Federal Reserve's *Balance Sheets for the U.S. Economy* for each of the seven major nonfinancial sectors of the economy. Foreign debt instruments were included because of their growing importance in U.S. capital markets. The estimation of market values requires construction of sectoral market-to-par indexes. In turn, each sectoral index requires consideration of the different types of debt instruments on the balance sheet. Conversions of values from par to market for each sector were accomplished as follows

Federal government. The data represent credit market liabilities for the federal government, federally sponsored credit agencies, and the monetary authority. No attempt was made to estimate and include retirement liabilities.[13] Indexes for 1946 through 1980 were kindly provided by Eisner and Pieper, based on the previous work of Cox and Hirschhorn (1983). Updated market-to-par indexes were calculated for 1981–1983. For Treasury bonds and notes, the *Treasury Bulletin* reports on a monthly basis the market price and par value of outstanding quantities. Market prices are converted to fractions of one dollar and then multiplied by outstanding par values to produce market value estimates. Market prices for bills are not reported, since they are sold at a discount. However, their market value can be estimated using the formula

$$MV = 100 \cdot (1 - (D/360)r),$$

where MV is the market value, D is the number of days until maturity, and r is the bid rate of interest. The 360-day year is a convention used in the capital markets. Calculated bill prices were then multiplied by the outstanding volume to obtain market value. A weighted average of the market-to-par indexes for Treasury bonds and notes were used for agency obligations.

State and local government. For short-term obligations, par was assumed to approximate market. Most of the credit market debt owed by state and local governments, though, consists of long-term bonds. To estimate market values, it was assumed bonds have maturities of ten years, biannual interest payments, and coupon rates equal to Standard and Poor's annual yields on long-term municipals in the years they were issued. The volume of new bond issues was taken from the *Federal Reserve Bulletin.* Market values were calculated as the sum of interest and principal requirements, discounted by the Standard and Poor's yield, of the bonds issued over the ten most recent years.

Nonfinancial corporations. Estimates of the market value of long-term debt were constructed in the initial section of this chapter. For short-term credit market instruments, par value was assumed to approximate market. The various indexes were then weighted by outstanding volumes to construct an aggregate sectoral market-to-par index.

Farm business: nonfinancial noncorporate business. Mortgages represent the principal long-term liability for these two sectors. Unfortunately, detailed information on rates, maturities, and terms on mortgage liabilities for these smaller sectors is unavailable. Since most of these mortgages appear to be written by farm banks and small commercial banks, it was assumed that the rates and terms on mortgages reported by the Federal Home Loan Bank Board (FHLBB) were reasonable proxies. A market-to-par index for mortgages was constructed by assuming a fifteen-year life and discounting by the FHLBB yield on new mortgages. Volumes were taken from the flow of funds accounts. The other credit market instruments reported by these two sectors were principally bank loans and "other loans" on which no information was available. Since most bank lending is of relatively short term and frequently at floating rates, par was assumed to approximate market. Sectoral market-to-par indexes were constructed by weighting the mortgage and nonmortgage liabilities by their respective volumes.

Table 9.12
Market-to-par ratios, various debt instruments

Year	Federal government securities	State and local bonds	Non-financial corporate bonds	Non-financial corporate mortgages	Non-financial corporate tax-exempt bonds	Mortgages
1946	103.58	100.30	95.13	104.79	NA	103.90
1947	101.27	98.20	89.53	103.32	NA	100.50
1948	101.54	99.20	93.22	99.36	NA	100.10
1949	103.46	100.00	97.08	99.61	NA	101.20
1950	101.09	102.00	99.50	101.81	NA	101.40
1951	98.67	99.80	93.16	97.90	NA	98.60
1952	98.70	98.20	96.20	98.51	NA	99.40
1953	99.77	98.20	95.21	99.78	NA	98.40
1954	100.38	99.90	99.50	98.34	NA	100.30
1955	97.90	98.20	97.76	95.87	NA	99.30
1956	94.65	95.20	87.40	91.86	NA	95.20
1957	98.01	96.40	88.09	87.36	NA	93.00
1958	83.78	95.70	89.06	92.57	NA	95.50
1959	91.73	96.00	83.77	87.88	NA	94.50
1960	98.01	99.60	86.41	87.31	NA	96.90
1961	97.03	99.70	88.13	90.82	NA	97.80
1962	98.44	101.40	90.22	92.81	NA	99.50
1963	97.05	100.30	90.45	93.13	NA	99.10
1964	97.51	101.10	92.31	90.92	NA	99.60
1965	95.52	99.00	91.32	92.18	NA	99.70
1966	96.22	98.20	84.40	89.03	NA	96.50
1967	93.66	95.70	82.07	92.46	NA	97.50
1968	93.31	94.80	82.25	84.33	NA	95.30
1969	89.23	88.20	72.12	83.14	NA	92.30
1970	96.43	95.70	80.78	78.62	NA	93.90
1971	99.03	97.20	89.95	82.86	100.00	97.70
1972	97.52	99.30	91.48	82.77	100.05	98.80
1973	95.92	101.20	85.71	80.59	99.57	95.50
1974	96.52	101.80	76.35	76.21	95.49	93.10
1975	98.78	94.80	84.13	75.75	95.43	96.10
1976	102.72	101.80	97.03	83.28	100.45	96.70
1977	98.43	102.30	93.13	86.84	102.66	97.60
1978	94.38	97.40	86.43	88.21	99.07	94.50
1979	93.38	95.40	79.76	88.52	97.58	89.80

Table 9.12 (continued)

Year	Federal govern-ment securities	State and local bonds	Non-financial corporate bonds	Non-financial corporate mortgages	Non-financial corporate tax-exempt bonds	Mortgages
1980	91.29	86.10	74.04	83.41	91.96	86.80
1981	91.39	80.14	70.12	70.23	84.38	82.74
1982	93.82	79.50	83.46	72.10	88.67	81.95
1983	97.60	83.98	83.27	80.54	92.77	89.60

Households. The two principal sources of household credit market liabilities are mortgages and consumer installment credit. The FHLBB index constructed above was used to estimate the market value of mortgages. Consumer installment credit was valued at par, as were other classes of debt (mainly short-term bank and finance company loans).

Foreign. These liabilities are principally foreign bonds held in the United States. These securities were converted to market value by using the New York Stock Exchange Bond Index. The small portion of remaining credit market debt was assumed to be at market value.

The estimated market-to-par indices for each of the major types of securities are shown in table 9.12. For each sector, the outstanding dollar value of each type of security was multiplied by its market-to-par index and weighted by its proportion of total sector liabilities to create a market valued sectoral portfolio. Sectoral market-to-par indices are presented in table 9.13. With the exception of the state and local government sector, market values have been below par throughout the last twenty-five years. While the size of the discounts may seem small, this is a result of the large amount of short-term debt in each sector. The market-to-par indices for long-term instruments in table 9.12 reflect the sizable discounting of these securities. It is interesting to note that the market-to-par ratios in table 9.13 fell substantially in the late 1970s and early 1980s despite the increasing use of short-term debt by all sectors. Estimates of the market values of credit market instruments are presented in table 9.14. For comparison, the equivalent par value data is shown in table 9.15. The difference

Table 9.13
Sectoral market-to-par indexes (weighted average of debt instruments)

Year	Total credit market debt	Federal government	State and local government	Non-financial corporations	Farm business	Non-financial non-corporate business	House-holds	Foreign
1946	1.024	1.036	1.003	0.984	1.027	1.021	1.024	0.982
1947	1.000	1.013	0.983	0.958	1.003	1.003	1.003	0.976
1948	1.002	1.015	0.992	0.966	1.001	1.001	1.001	0.985
1949	1.018	1.035	1.000	0.985	1.008	1.007	1.007	0.994
1950	1.008	1.011	1.019	0.999	1.009	1.008	1.008	0.999
1951	0.984	0.987	0.998	0.964	0.991	0.992	0.992	0.984
1952	0.988	0.987	0.983	0.978	0.996	0.997	0.996	0.991
1953	0.991	0.998	0.983	0.976	0.989	0.991	0.991	0.990
1954	1.001	1.004	0.999	0.993	1.002	1.002	1.002	0.999
1955	0.985	0.979	0.983	0.981	0.995	0.996	0.996	0.996
1956	0.951	0.947	0.954	0.921	0.968	0.973	0.970	0.975
1957	0.958	0.980	0.966	0.914	0.953	0.962	0.956	0.976
1958	0.950	0.938	0.959	0.929	0.971	0.975	0.971	0.975
1959	0.935	0.917	0.962	0.893	0.965	0.969	0.966	0.961
1960	0.966	0.980	0.996	0.906	0.980	0.983	0.980	0.966
1961	0.968	0.970	0.997	0.921	0.986	0.987	0.986	0.971
1962	0.981	0.984	1.013	0.935	0.997	0.997	0.997	0.975
1963	0.976	0.971	1.003	0.939	0.994	0.995	0.994	0.975
1964	0.981	0.975	1.011	0.943	0.997	0.998	0.997	0.981
1965	0.974	0.955	0.990	0.943	0.998	0.998	0.998	0.979
1966	0.958	0.962	0.983	0.906	0.977	0.979	0.978	0.961
1967	0.951	0.937	0.959	0.903	0.984	0.984	0.984	0.954
1968	0.941	0.933	0.950	0.888	0.969	0.969	0.971	0.953
1969	0.907	0.892	0.887	0.844	0.950	0.949	0.953	0.925
1970	0.941	0.964	0.959	0.874	0.961	0.957	0.963	0.946
1971	0.970	0.990	0.973	0.923	0.986	0.983	0.986	0.972
1972	0.975	0.975	0.993	0.932	0.992	0.991	0.993	0.978
1973	0.958	0.959	1.011	0.908	0.972	0.965	0.973	0.964
1974	0.941	0.965	1.017	0.868	0.957	0.945	0.958	0.943
1975	0.956	0.988	0.950	0.897	0.976	0.968	0.976	0.956
1976	0.989	1.027	1.017	0.967	0.980	0.973	0.979	0.991
1977	0.981	0.984	1.022	0.955	0.986	0.980	0.985	0.978
1978	0.953	0.944	0.975	0.929	0.968	0.954	0.965	0.964
1979	0.929	0.934	0.956	0.906	0.940	0.915	0.934	0.948

Table 9.13 (continued)

Year	Total credit market debt	Federal govern- ment	State and local govern- ment	Non- financial corpora- tions	Farm business	Non- financial non- corporate business	House- holds	Foreign
1980	0.902	0.913	0.867	0.877	0.922	0.892	0.913	0.941
1981	0.879	0.914	0.810	0.855	0.898	0.862	0.886	0.933
1982	0.895	0.938	0.804	0.911	0.894	0.858	0.881	0.956
1983	0.932	0.976	0.847	0.920	0.938	0.917	0.932	0.957

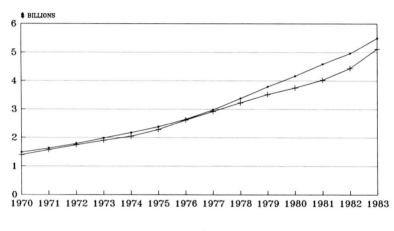

—•— PAR VALUE   —+— MARKET VALUE

Figure 9.2

between market and par values of total credit market debt for 1970 through 1983 is shown graphically in figure 9.2.

Table 9.16 presents estimates of the cumulative holding gains on credit market instruments experienced by each sector in the economy, calculated as the difference between par and market values. In total, cumulative gains on debt have been positive every year since 1955, although the year-to-year changes are quite variable in both directions. For instance, between 1977 and 1981, gains on debt amounted to almost $500 billion dollars; however, between 1981 and 1983 falling interest rates had reduced those gains by almost one-third, to $372 billion at the end of 1983. To put these numbers in perspective, the cumulative gains on debt represent more than 10% of 1983 nominal GNP.

The effects of the credit crunches of 1969 and 1974 are apparent in the large increases in holding gains. The effect of recession-induced declines in interest rates is also evident, with annual holding losses between 1953–1954, 1959–1961, 1969–1971, and 1974–1976. The rising interest rates that persisted through the 1980 recession did not result in an annual holding loss, though, and the legacy of high rates between 1979 and 1982 meant that, despite economic recovery, inflationary gains were reduced as interest rates fell during 1983.

The sectoral distribution of holding gains is also of interest. Throughout most of the period, gains on state and local debt were far less than for federal securities. In 1982 and 1983, however, the rising volume of municipal issues and the longer maturities of state and local instruments pushed the corresponding holding gains past those of the federal government for the first time. Rising interest rates on mortgages held by households have resulted in cumulative gains of over $100 billion since 1980. While the farm sector has also experienced holding gains on its mortgage liabilities, the size of the gains has been reduced by the persistence of farm borrowing throughout the last decade, despite continually rising rates. The results for nonfinancial corporations were discussed in detail in the previous section.

Table 9.14
Market value credit market instruments

Year	Fourth-quarter nominal GNP (SAAR)	Total credit market debt	Federal government	State and local government	Non-financial corporations	Farm business	Non-financial non-corporate business	House-holds	Foreign
1946	230.8	359.8	236.1	15.4	48.7	7.2	8.6	36.0	7.8
1947	259.6	367.3	223.5	16.5	54.3	7.4	9.6	43.8	12.1
1948	286.8	380.8	217.5	18.9	60.7	8.1	10.4	51.9	13.3
1949	273.2	404.5	225.2	21.5	63.6	8.6	11.1	60.6	13.8
1950	323.6	425.3	218.9	25.4	71.2	9.6	13.1	73.2	14.0
1951	356.8	437.4	213.2	27.3	76.7	10.7	14.1	80.8	14.5
1952	380.8	469.4	218.5	30.9	84.9	11.6	15.2	93.4	15.0
1953	384.8	499.9	227.9	34.7	88.8	11.4	15.8	105.3	16.1
1954	396.0	530.9	231.7	41.0	95.1	12.3	16.7	117.5	16.6
1955	432.8	558.0	225.2	45.5	102.2	13.6	18.3	136.6	16.5
1956	429.5	564.5	212.2	47.7	105.6	14.1	19.0	148.9	17.0
1957	441.5	595.8	217.6	52.5	113.8	14.9	19.7	159.0	18.3
1958	464.4	629.0	216.9	57.6	123.5	16.5	21.3	172.8	20.3
1959	490.5	666.8	218.6	64.0	128.2	18.2	23.6	193.7	20.6
1960	503.3	724.8	231.6	71.7	139.8	19.6	25.5	214.0	22.5
1961	537.7	770.8	236.2	77.1	152.1	21.3	27.8	231.6	24.8
1962	572.0	835.5	246.6	84.3	166.0	23.8	31.3	256.2	27.3
1963	605.8	889.4	246.9	89.4	178.6	26.2	35.7	282.2	30.4
1964	645.1	960.4	254.2	96.4	191.4	28.9	42.1	312.6	34.7
1965	708.4	1023.3	250.6	102.1	209.0	32.2	49.6	342.8	37.0
1966	762.1	1071.8	256.0	107.4	221.1	34.7	55.6	359.3	37.7

Year									
1967	815.9	1141.9	261.4	112.5	243.2	38.2	63.1	382.5	41.1
1968	890.2	1221.3	273.0	120.9	263.3	40.3	71.0	409.2	43.6
1969	948.9	1259.2	257.9	122.3	274.6	42.4	82.3	434.6	45.2
1970	988.4	1394.9	290.1	143.1	310.4	45.1	95.1	463.3	47.9
1971	1078.1	1576.2	322.5	162.4	350.8	50.7	117.6	518.9	53.3
1972	1199.2	1746.3	332.3	180.2	384.5	56.8	146.6	586.7	59.2
1973	1337.5	1902.9	334.9	195.9	418.7	65.0	171.4	652.3	64.6
1974	1430.9	2046.0	348.2	212.8	457.6	71.5	186.8	693.7	75.3
1975	1588.2	2275.7	440.9	211.8	492.2	81.2	205.1	757.3	87.2
1976	1755.4	2615.0	529.8	242.3	572.1	91.5	221.1	848.5	109.6
1977	1988.9	2920.4	563.5	259.2	633.0	104.1	250.5	988.9	121.2
1978	2281.6	3221.4	591.0	265.9	688.4	116.4	272.9	1130.7	156.1
1979	2502.9	3517.5	619.7	280.0	758.1	133.2	293.3	1260.2	173.0
1980	2739.4	3753.6	678.1	277.6	800.3	143.9	315.6	1341.1	197.2
1981	3027.9	4027.4	758.6	277.3	863.8	154.7	339.0	1412.8	221.2
1982	3109.6	4435.2	930.1	303.7	989.3	162.0	357.9	1475.7	216.5
1983	3431.7	5116.2	1149.6	355.0	1051.3	172.4	445.8	1707.5	234.5

Table 9.15
Par value credit market instruments

Year	Fourth-quarter nominal GNP (SAAR)	Total credit market debt	Federal government	State and local government	Non-financial corporations	Farm business	Non-financial non-corporate business	Households	Foreign
1946	230.8	351.3	227.9	15.4	49.5	7.0	8.4	35.2	7.9
1947	259.6	367.3	220.7	16.8	56.7	7.4	9.6	43.7	12.4
1948	286.8	379.9	214.2	19.0	62.8	8.1	10.4	51.9	13.5
1949	273.2	397.4	217.7	21.5	64.6	8.5	11.0	60.2	13.9
1950	323.6	421.8	216.5	24.9	71.3	9.5	13.0	72.6	14.0
1951	356.8	444.3	216.1	27.4	79.6	10.8	14.2	81.5	14.7
1952	380.8	475.3	221.4	31.4	86.8	11.6	15.3	93.7	15.1
1953	384.8	504.7	228.4	35.3	91.0	11.5	15.9	106.3	16.3
1954	396.0	530.5	230.8	41.0	95.8	12.3	16.7	117.3	16.6
1955	432.8	566.4	230.0	46.3	104.2	13.7	18.4	137.2	16.6
1956	429.5	593.8	224.2	50.0	114.7	14.6	19.5	153.4	17.4
1957	441.5	622.0	222.0	54.4	124.5	15.6	20.5	166.2	18.8
1958	464.4	662.0	231.3	60.1	133.0	17.0	21.9	177.9	30.8
1959	490.5	713.5	238.3	66.5	143.5	18.9	24.3	200.6	21.4
1960	503.3	750.1	236.3	72.0	154.3	20.0	25.9	218.3	23.3
1961	537.7	796.0	243.4	77.3	165.1	21.6	28.2	234.9	25.5
1962	572.0	851.5	250.5	83.2	177.5	23.9	31.4	257.0	28.0
1963	605.8	911.0	254.4	89.1	190.2	26.4	35.9	283.8	31.2
1964	645.1	979.1	260.7	95.4	203.0	29.0	42.2	313.4	35.4
1965	708.4	1050.3	262.4	103.1	221.6	32.3	49.7	343.4	37.8
1966	762.1	1118.3	266.1	109.3	244.1	35.5	56.8	367.3	39.2

Year									
1967	815.9	1200.4	279.1	117.3	269.5	38.8	64.1	388.5	43.1
1968	890.2	1298.2	292.6	127.2	296.5	41.6	73.2	421.3	45.8
1969	948.9	1388.5	289.0	137.9	325.5	44.6	86.7	455.9	48.9
1970	988.4	1482.9	300.8	149.2	355.0	46.9	99.4	481.0	50.6
1971	1078.1	1624.7	325.7	166.9	380.1	51.4	119.6	526.2	54.8
1972	1199.2	1791.5	340.8	181.4	412.5	57.2	148.0	591.0	60.6
1973	1337.5	1986.2	349.1	193.7	461.3	66.9	177.7	670.5	67.0
1974	1430.9	2173.9	360.8	209.2	527.4	74.7	197.8	724.2	79.8
1975	1588.2	2380.1	446.3	222.9	548.5	83.2	211.9	776.1	91.2
1976	1755.4	2643.3	515.8	238.2	591.5	93.4	227.3	866.5	110.6
1977	1988.9	2977.9	572.5	253.6	662.6	105.6	255.6	1004.1	123.9
1978	2281.6	3380.0	626.2	272.7	741.1	120.3	286.0	1171.8	161.9
1979	2502.9	3786.4	663.6	292.9	836.5	141.6	320.4	1348.9	182.5
1980	2739.4	4163.1	742.8	320.2	912.0	156.0	353.7	1468.8	209.6
1981	3027.9	4580.2	830.1	342.5	1010.8	172.3	393.2	1594.2	237.1
1982	3109.6	4954.9	991.4	377.9	1086.4	181.3	417.1	1674.4	226.4
1983	3431.7	5488.0	1177.9	419.4	1143.3	183.8	486.2	1832.2	245.2

Table 9.16
Holding gains and losses on credit market instruments, by sector

Year	Total credit market debt	Federal government	State and local government	Non-financial corporations	Farm business	Non-financial non-corporate business	House-holds	Foreign
1946	-8.5	-8.2	0.0	0.8	-0.2	-0.2	-0.8	0.1
1947	0.0	02.8	0.3	2.4	0.0	0.0	-0.1	0.3
1948	-0.9	-3.3	0.1	2.1	0.0	0.0	0.0	0.2
1949	-7.1	-7.5	0.0	1.0	-0.1	-0.1	-0.4	0.1
1950	-3.5	-2.4	-0.5	0.1	-0.1	-0.1	-0.6	0.0
1951	6.9	2.9	0.1	2.9	0.1	0.1	0.7	0.2
1952	5.9	2.9	0.5	1.9	0.0	0.1	0.3	0.1
1953	4.8	0.5	0.6	2.2	0.1	0.1	1.0	0.2
1954	-0.4	-0.9	0.0	0.7	0.0	0.0	-0.2	0.0
1955	8.4	4.8	0.8	2.0	0.1	0.1	0.6	0.1
1956	29.3	12.0	2.3	9.1	0.5	0.5	4.5	0.4
1957	26.2	4.4	1.9	10.7	0.7	0.8	7.2	0.5
1958	33.0	14.4	2.5	9.5	0.5	0.6	5.1	0.5
1959	46.7	19.7	2.5	15.3	0.7	0.7	6.9	0.8
1960	25.3	4.7	0.3	14.5	0.4	0.4	4.3	0.8
1961	25.2	7.2	0.2	13.0	0.3	0.4	3.3	0.7
1962	16.0	3.9	-1.1	11.5	0.1	0.1	0.8	0.7
1963	21.6	7.5	-0.3	11.6	0.2	0.2	1.6	0.8
1964	18.7	6.5	-1.0	11.6	0.1	0.1	0.8	0.7
1965	27.0	11.8	1.0	12.6	0.1	0.1	0.6	0.8
1966	46.5	10.1	1.9	23.0	0.8	1.2	8.0	1.5

1967	58.5	17.7	4.8	26.3	0.6	1.0	6.0	2.0
1968	76.9	19.6	6.3	33.2	1.3	2.2	12.1	2.2
1969	129.3	31.1	15.6	50.9	2.2	4.4	21.3	3.7
1970	88.0	10.7	6.1	44.6	1.8	4.3	17.7	2.7
1971	48.5	3.2	4.5	29.3	0.7	2.0	7.3	1.5
1972	45.2	8.5	1.2	28.0	0.4	1.4	4.3	1.4
1973	83.3	14.2	-2.2	42.6	1.9	6.3	18.2	2.4
1974	127.9	12.6	-3.6	69.8	3.2	11.0	30.5	4.5
1975	104.4	5.4	11.1	56.3	2.0	6.8	18.8	4.0
1976	28.3	-14.0	-4.1	19.4	1.9	6.2	18.0	1.0
1977	57.5	9.0	-5.6	29.6	1.5	5.1	15.2	2.7
1978	158.6	35.2	6.8	52.7	3.9	13.1	41.1	5.8
1979	268.9	43.9	12.9	78.4	8.4	27.1	88.7	9.5
1980	409.5	64.7	42.6	111.7	12.1	38.1	127.7	12.4
1981	552.8	71.5	65.2	147.0	17.6	54.2	181.4	15.9
1982	519.7	61.3	74.2	97.1	19.3	59.2	198.7	9.9
1983	371.8	28.3	64.4	92.0	11.4	40.4	124.7	10.7

Notes

1. The basic conceptual approach and discussion in this section draws heavily from Shoven and Bulow (1976). Much of the empirical work represents an updating and revision of their pioneering work.

2. Because the bond index is an average of all traded bonds, it incorporates both new issues and retirements.

3. The reported discount is from par value, not issue price or book value. The number of securities issued at a discount has risen in recent years, especially with the advent of zero coupon bonds.

4. See John S. Strong, "Debt Revaluations at the Firm Level," unpublished manuscript, 1985.

5. This is not exactly true, since the NYSE index is likely to understate actual depreciation. The quality of bonds traded on the New York Bond Exchange is higher than that for all outstanding bonds.

6. The mortgage liabilities reported here is substantially different from that used by Shoven and Bulow and other researchers. The revised Flow of Funds accounts published in 1982 made a large downward revision in the mortgage liabilities of nonfinancial corporations. The effect was to reduce the liability account by almost half, from $131 billion in 1974 to a revised $66.8 billion. The distribution of liabilities was shifted so that most of the growth in debt over the 1970s appears as net borrowing by the noncorporate sector. This revision was based on IRS real estate industry data through 1979, which shows that virtually all of the growth in the industry's assets and debts during the 1970s occurred in partnerships and virtually none in corporations. This would appear to provide additional support to those analysts concerned with a depressed rate of corporate investment in physical plant.

7. The average effective maturity has ranged from thirteen to eighteen years over the period.

8. Although the Federal Loan Bank Board publishes a series on new home mortgage yields, the different nature and segmentation of residential lending markets made this index seem inappropriate. In general, the discount on corporate mortgages is greater for two reasons. First, there was virtually no net growth in corporate mortgages in the 1970s, so most of the outstanding liabilities are at older, low rates. Second, the tendency for residential mortgage volume to decrease sharply during "credit crunches" means that fewer residential mortgages were made at high rates.

9. The selection of a ten-year maturity presents problems. Through the later 1970s, most corporate tax-exempt offerings were used to finance pollution control equipment, so the ten-year horizon appears reasonable. In recent years, though, the expansion of tax-exempt financing for industrial expansion has resulted in a large volume of long-term bonds. Because data on the outstanding mix are not available, the ten-year assumption was maintained. The effect is to reduce the degree of discount and thus overstate the market values of these securities.

10. This information is based on a weekly survey of reporting banks. The survey provides data on volume, rates, maturity, and sectoral classification. For more details, see Federal Reserve Board Statistical Release E.2 (416).

11. While additional requirements such as bond covenants sometimes exist for other corporate liabilities, secondary markets for these instruments make it more likely that these provisions are reflected in security prices.

12. To the extent that short-term financing has supplanted long-term instruments for firms, aggregate leverage may not be measured here. However, little empirical work on trends in maturity structure has been done. Mitchell (1984) presented evidence that firms increasingly have issued bonds with intermediate maturities, but found little evidence of a persistent increase in short-term debt. See Karlyn Mitchell, "The Relevance of Corporate Debt Maturity Structure: An Empirical Investigation," Research Working Paper 84–11, Federal Reserve Bank of Kansas City, 1984.

13. In addition to its explicit accounting liabilities valued here, the federal government and its agencies have substantial other contractual obligations. Eisner and Pieper (1984) estimate that these "contingent" liabilities amount to over $8.5 trillion, far in excess of direct liabilities and net debt. While these obligations may have a substantial impact on the economy, they are clearly different in character and implications than the formal current debt. The magnitude of such contingent debt varies greatly with assumptions as to future government policy and as to public perceptions and expectations, as has been shown by Leimer and Lesnoy (1982). It was decided that construction of relevant measures of such contingent liabilities was beyond the range of this chapter. Any estimate would also require estimates of contingent assets, such as possible higher tax receipts, which may eventually be generated to meet these commitments.

References

Balance Sheets for the U.S. Economy, 1945–1983, (1984), Washington: Board of Governors of the Federal Reserve System.

Butkiewicz, James L. (1983), "The Market Value of Outstanding Government Debt," Journal of Monetary Economics, 11, pp. 373–379.

Cox, W. Michael, and Hirschhorn, Eric (1983), "The Market Value of U.S. Government Debt: Monthly, 1942–1980," Journal of Monetary Economics, 11, pp. 261–272.

Economic Report of the President, February 1984 (1984), Washington: Government Printing Office.

Eisner, Robert, and Pieper, Paul J. (1984), "A New View of the Federal Debt and Budget Deficits," American Economic Review, March, 74, pp. 11–29.

Flow of Funds Accounts, 1949–1978: Annual Total Flows and Year-End Assets and Liabilities (1979), Washington: Board of Governors of the Federal Reserve System.

Friedman, Benjamin M. (1981), "Financing Capital Formation in the 1980s: Issues for Public Policy," in Michael L. Wachter and Susan M. Wachter, eds., *Toward a New U.S. Industrial Policy*, Philadelphia: University of Pennsylvania Press, pp. 95–126.

Friedman, Benjamin M. (1983a), "Implications of the Government Deficit for U.S. Capital Formation," in *The Economics of Large Government Deficits*, Federal Reserve Bank of Boston Conference Series No. 27, pp. 73–95.

Friedman, Benjamin M. (1983b), "Managing the U.S. Government Deficit in the 1980s," *Harvard Institute of Economic Research Discussion Paper 1021*, November.

Friedman, Benjamin M. (1985), "Portfolio Choice and the Debt-to-Income Relationship," *American Economic Review*, May, 75, pp. 338–343.

Haig, Robert M. (1921), *The Federal Income Tax*. New York: Columbia University Press.

Leimer, Dean, and Lesnoy, Selig (1982), "Social Security and Private Saving: New Time-Series Evidence," *Journal of Political Economy*, June, 90, pp. 606–629.

Mitchell, Karlyn (1984), "The Relevance of Corporate Debt Maturity Structure: An Empirical Investigation," Federal Reserve Bank of Kansas City Research Working Paper 84–11.

Modigliani, Franco, and Miller, Merton (1958), "The Cost of Capital, Corporation Finance and the Theory of Investment," *American Economic Review*, June, 48, pp. 261–297.

Pollin, Robert (1985), "Stability and Instability in the Debt-Income Relationship," *American Economic Review*, May, 75, pp. 344–350.

Seater, John (1981), "The Market Value of Outstanding Government Debt, 1919–1975," *Journal of Monetary Economics*, July, 8, pp. 85–101.

Shoven, John B., and Bulow, Jeremy I. (1976), "Inflation Accounting and Nonfinancial Corporate Profits: Financial Assets and Liabilities," *Brookings Papers on Economic Activity*, 1, pp. 15–58 (with comments and discussion on pp. 59–67).

Shoven, John B., and Bulow, Jeremy I. (1975), "Inflation Accounting and Nonfinancial Corporate Profits: Physical Assets," *Brookings Papers on Economic Activity*, 3, pp. 557–598.

Simons, Henry C. (1938), *Personal Income Taxation*, Chicago: University of Chicago Press.

Wojnilower, Albert M. (1983), "Implications of the Government Deficit for U.S. Capital Formation: Discussion," in *The Economics of Large Government Deficits*, Federal Reserve Bank of Boston Conference Series No. 27, pp. 99–111.

10

Capital in the U.S. Postal Service

Dianne C. Christensen,
Laurits R. Christensen,
Carl G. Degen, and
Philip E. Schoech

The purpose of this chapter is to describe our development of a complete system of capital accounts for the U.S. Postal Service (USPS). We and our coworkers previously developed capital accounts at the national level for the United States and eight of her major trading partners.[1] We and our coworkers have also developed capital accounts for numerous firms and industries in the U.S. economy.[2] Our current work draws heavily on the methods that we developed in our previous studies.

To our knowledge the current study represents the most detailed and extensive attempt to measure capital for a U.S. government enterprise. We have used detailed accounting records for the Postal Service as the building blocks for our study. The principal challenge was to develop accounting records, which were not intended to be used for measurement of economic variables, into a form suitable to implement the procedures for measuring capital stock and capital input. We believe that the resulting measures provide knowledge about the USPS that could not be obtained by any other means.

We have measured capital input for seven types of capital goods employed by the USPS: land, buildings, vehicles, customer service equipment, postal support equipment, mail-processing equipment, and automated-processing equipment. Capital goods that are leased or rented are recorded, in addition to capital goods owned by the USPS. It is essential to include nonowned capital because it comprises a substantial portion of the capital goods used by the Postal Service.

We have found to be true the popular perception that the Postal Service has been becoming more capital intensive. Its capital input has grown nearly four times as fast as its output, 4.2% per year versus 1.2% per year over the 1963–1985 period. The two fastest-growing asset categories have been postal support equipment (much of which is computers) and mail-processing equipment. Thus capital input now accounts for nearly twice the share of total input cost as it did in

1963. In spite of this, the Postal Service remains one of the least capital intensive sectors of the U.S. economy, with capital input accounting for only 5% of the total cost of production.

Completion of this set of capital accounts will permit improved measurement of total factor productivity (TFP) for the USPS. However, given the relatively small role of capital in provision of postal services, it is clear that TFP measurement for the Postal Service is not highly sensitive to errors in capital measurement. Furthermore, unless the growth of postal inputs other than capital and labor have grown at a substantially different rate, total factor productivity growth for the USPS has not differed greatly from its growth of labor productivity.

10.1   The Measurement of Capital

For capital items that are rented or leased, the value of rent and lease payments equals the value of capital input. However, many of the capital goods employed by the Postal Service are owned rather than leased. For these items, the value of capital input must be inferred by constructing the annualized cost of owning the various types of capital. We follow the methodology developed by Christensen and Jorgenson (1969) in constructing these accounts.

The flow of capital services from each type of asset is assumed to be proportional to the stock of the asset at the end of the previous period (the beginning of the current period). Denoting these factors of proportionality by Q_{Ki}, the service flows from capital assets may be written as

$$K_{it} = Q_{Ki} K_{i,t-1}^{A},$$

where $K_{i,t-1}^{A}$ is the stock of the ith asset type. Using the Tornqvist (1936) aggregation procedure, aggregate capital input is defined as

$$\Delta \ln K_t = \sum_{i=1}^{p} \bar{S}_{Kit} \, \Delta \ln K_{i,t-1}^{A},$$

where the $\bar{S}_{Kit}$ are the capital service cost shares averaged over two years. This shows that the rate of growth of aggregate capital services is a weighted average of the rates of growth of the various types of capital stock. It is incorrect, however, to interpret this as the rate of growth of aggregate capital stock, because the weights are relative value shares in the total service flow rather than relative shares in the value of capital stock. Aggregate capital stock can be expressed as a Tornqvist index of its components

$$\Delta \ln K_t^A = \sum_{i=1}^{p} \bar{S}_{Ait} \, \Delta \ln K_{i,t}^A,$$

where $\bar{S}_{Ai}$ is the relative asset share of the ith asset class, averaged over two years.

While the capital service flow from each type of asset is proportional to the corresponding stock at the end of the prior period, the analogous relationship is not true for aggregate capital services. The ratio of aggregate capital services to aggregate capital stock depends on the composition of the aggregate stock. Therefore, it is incorrect to use the aggregate capital stock to represent aggregate capital services. Denote the ratio of capital services to capital stock by Q_{Kt}. This ratio is potentially different for each time period. The flow of services from the aggregate capital stock can be written as

$$K_t = Q_{Kt} K_{t-1}^A.$$

Since Q_{Kt} can be written as K_t / K_{t-1}^A, we see that it indicates the flow of capital services per unit of aggregate capital stock, which is also referred to as the "composition index of capital."

10.2   Perpetual Inventory Method

Over the past decade, there have been a number of attempts to measure the owned capital stocks of the USPS. The Bureau of Economic Analysis (BEA) has created USPS buildings and equipment stocks using the change in asset value as investment. These investment data are net of retirements and thus understate the growth in the capital stock. BEA uses a buildings deflator to deflate investment in buildings and a general producer price index to deflate equipment investment. Stevenson (1973) has constructed a capital stock for buildings from measures of physical space for structures and a capital stock for equipment from recorded book value. These estimates provide crude measures of capital stock.

In this study the computation of capital stocks is based on the perpetual inventory equation. If K_t^A is the real end of year stock, I_t is the real investment, and δ the depreciation rate, the perpetual inventory equation can be represented as

$$K_t^A = I_t + (1 - \delta) K_{t-1}^A.$$

For each asset class, a real stock can be generated from current dollar investment, a price index for the asset class, a depreciation rate, and an initial value (or benchmenk) of the capital stock.

Real investment, I, includes not only investment in new goods but also net transfers of assets from other government agencies. These net transfers are recorded in the USPS accounts at book value. To obtain an estimate of the quantity of net transfers, we assume that the vintage distribution of the assets transferred is no different from the stock at the beginning of the period. Then the perpetual inventory equation becomes

$$K_t^A = N_t + (1 - \delta)K_{t-1}^A + T_t(K_{t-1}^A / B_{t-1}),$$

where N_t is the quantity of new goods, T_t is the book value of net transfers, and B_t is the book value of all assets at end of year.

The number of asset classes, or the level of aggregation used in constructing the stocks, is determined on the basis of four factors: (1) differences in price indexes, (2) differences in depreciation rates, (3) different roles in the production process, and (4) different USPS locations. In practice, the lack of data makes it infeasible to make as many distinctions as would be theoretically desirable. In these cases, a level of disaggregation is chosen that comes as close as possible to the above objectives, subject to the constraint of data availability. For the USPS, we distinguish seven different classes of owned capital assets: land, buildings, vehicles, mail-processing equipment net of new optical character readers and bar code sorters (MPE), customer service equipment (CSE), postal support equipment (PSE), and automated-processing equipment, consisting of new optical character readers and bar code sorters (OCR).

The data used in constructing capital stocks are obtained from a number of USPS reporting systems and documents: the *Annual Report of the Postmaster General*, the National Consolidated Trial Balance, the Personal Property Accounting System, the Vehicles Management Asset System Subsidiary Ledger, and the Facilities Management System.

10.3   Investment

The construction of investment series for the seven asset classes presents several basic problems. First, a number of different financial and accounting reports were needed to construct a consistent time series of investment back to 1962. Due to late book entries, some of these reports are not as accurate as others; in such cases, additional documents were used to calculate the values of these late entries. In addition, the General Classification of Accounts (GCA) has undergone a number of changes since 1962, necessitating the development of a set of mappings linking old accounts to new accounts. Finally, the recent introduction of a new technology to mail processing, the use of optical character readers and bar code sorters, is so important that investment in this area was distinguished, even though including it necessitated the use of additional data sources.

Total investment in capital includes not only purchases and transfers from work in progress but also transfers from other government agencies. While purchases and transfers from work in progress are recorded at current market value, transfers from other agencies are recorded at book value, and must be adjusted to market value. The GCA has separate accounts for transfers from other government agencies and for purchases and transfers from work in progress, allowing for the adjustment described in the previous section.

For the 1971–1985 period, the basic source for investment data is the National Consolidated Trial Balance (NCTB). The NCTB is the complete listing of the balances of all accounts. While the NCTB is the most detailed report, it does not include late bookings and audited changes. These changes are entered in journal voucher adjustments, which must be added to NCTB totals to obtain actual expenditures for the year. For the years 1976–1985, the journal voucher adjustments were available from the USPS archives, but prior to 1976 the voucher adjustments must be estimated. The NCTB has separate accounts for each of the asset classes described above, except for MPE and OCR, which are consolidated.

In earlier years the NCTB is unavailable, but the *Annual Report of the Postmaster General* (ARPMG) in those years contains enough detailed financial information that it can be used to develop investment series for the 1963–1970 period. Futhermore, the ARPMG has the advantage that all late bookings and audited changes are included in its figures. No journal voucher adjustments must be estimated. Because all postal service accounts are on a fiscal year basis, the capital accounts developed in this chapter are also for fiscal years.

Investment in OCR and MPE equipment is determined by referring to a third reporting system, the Personal Property Accounting System (PPAS). The PPAS is an inventory system of all nonvehicular equipment owned by the USPS. The PPAS indicates the date of purchase and cost of each item of equipment. From this, the ratio of OCR to MPE equipment can be determined and applied to the relevant NCTB accounts to arrive at OCR and MPE investment.

To link the ARPMG and NCTB accounts over time, a number of changes to the General Classification of Accounts must be addressed. The first occurred in 1966 when "Platform, Yard, and Miscellaneous Equipment" and "Automatic Mail Equipment, Undistributed Freight and Discount," were merged into a single account, "Other Equipment." A second change took place in 1969 when three accounts were created from two of the 1968 accounts. Robert Hayes and Richard McWilliams of the USPS Accounting Division helped construct a mapping between the 1968 end-of-year balances and 1969 beginning-of-year account balances. It is assumed that the mapping of investment between the two sets of accounts has the same percentage distribution as the mapping of balances between the accounts.[3]

The mapping between the 1970 ARPMG and the 1971 NCTB is complicated by the fact that the accounting system underlying the NCTB also changed in that year. To accomplish the necessary linking, the 1970 ARPMG is mapped into the 1970 NCTB, and then the 1970 NCTB is mapped into the 1971 NCTB. Figure 10.1 indicates the mapping of these accounts. It is assumed that the mapping of investment between the two sets of accounts has the same percentage distribution as the mapping of the balances between the accounts. If no percentage is indicated, the entire account is transferred to the new account.

During 1976, the fiscal year of the USPS was changed to end September 30, rather than June 30. The period July 1, 1976, to September 30, 1976, is generally referred to as the transition quarter. Between the 1976 fiscal year and the 1976 transition quarter there was another major accounting change in the NCTB. A "crosswalk" between the old and new accounting systems was employed to link accounts. Investment in the transition quarter is added to investment during the 1976 fiscal year to obtain total investment for 1976. This investment corresponds to a period fifteen months in length.

An additional accounting change occurs in the treatment of Class D assets. These assets include minor equipment, such as lock boxes, distribution cases and tables, carrier/folding nose carts, collection and relay boxes, mail bags, and locks. Prior to 1972, Class D items were capitalized under the GCA; beginning in 1972 they were expensed. Because these expenditures cannot be identified during the period they are expensed, Class D purchases are excluded from investment in all years to maintain consistency. From 1967 to 1971, Class D expenditures can be identified from the ARPMG tables. Prior to 1967, the expenditures are estimated based upon their 1967 expenditure shares.

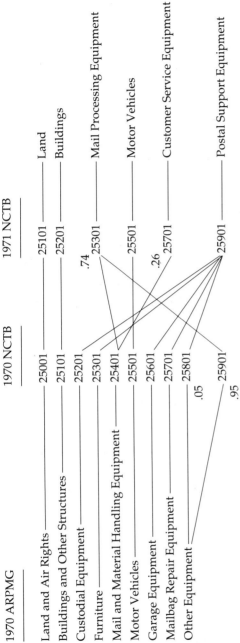

Figure 10.1   Mapping of 1970 ARPMG Accounts to 1971 NCTB Accounts.

Finally, as mentioned above, journal voucher adjustments must be estimated for the years 1971–1975. In most instances, they are estimated as the difference between the end-of-year balance and the subsequent year's beginning-of-year balance for the relevant property accounts in the NCTB. However, in a few cases, additional estimates are necessary.

The 1974 end-of-year balance for mail processing equipment is divided between two 1975 beginning-of-year equipment balances: account 25301 ("In Service") and account 25331 ("Unidentified Fixed"). The second account includes assets actually in service, but without an identification number. For purposes of estimating the 1974 voucher adjustment, the end-of-year 1974 balance should be compared to the sum of accounts 25301 and 25331 for 1975. For purposes of computing the 1975 implied voucher adjustment, the end-of-year 1975 balance should include 25331 for comparison with 1976.

For postal support equipment, the large journal voucher adjustment estimated for 1974 was offset by negative purchases of a similar magnitude in 1975. To correct for this, the 1974 estimated voucher adjustment is added to 1975 purchases for this category. Estimated investment by asset type is presented in table 10.1.

10.4 Price Indexes

Price indexes are used to deflate investment to real terms before implementing the perpetual inventory algorithm. In deflating USPS investment, it must be recognized that the annual price indexes available from government sources are for the calendar year, not the government fiscal year. The timing problem that is introduced can only be addressed fully by building up a fiscal year deflator from the quarterly or monthly deflators. Prior to 1982, this was not feasible; hence a small measurement error may have been introduced in those years. Beginning in 1982, quarterly or monthly price deflators are used for all assets, except land, to build up a fiscal year deflator.

The methods used to construct the land accounts require a price index extending back to 1886. We construct such an index by merging two data sources. The land deflator for the years 1945 to the present is based on data from the Federal Reserve Board's "Balance Sheets for the U.S. Economy" (table 701, line 29). The price of land is assumed to grow at the same rate as the FRB estimate for the market value of non-farm, nonfinancial, corporate land. For the years prior to 1946, the

Table 10.1
Investment by asset class (millions of dollars)[a]

Year	Land	Buildings	Vehicles	Customer service equipment	Postal support equipment	Mail-processing equipment	Automated-processing equipment
1963	.2	8.0	9.2	1.5	5.0	7.8	
1964	.2	10.6	15.4	1.3	7.3	22.2	
1965	.7	14.7	19.7	1.7	5.3	8.9	
1966	.7	16.4	24.6	1.9	4.9	4.4	
1967	-.5	38.5	22.9	2.4	11.8	22.1	
1968	1.6	22.4	38.5	2.2	26.4	14.7	
1969	1.4	32.3	27.3	2.5	25.4	24.9	
1970	45.3	200.9	63.2	3.6	24.7	24.4	
1971	42.7	102.6	54.1	3.0	31.9	66.3	
1972	22.6	116.7	55.7	2.2	9.6	25.6	
1973	14.3	122.8	21.9	4.8	13.7	32.8	
1974	8.2	148.9	44.7	2.6	26.9	37.9	
1975	27.8	183.6	55.5	2.2	37.6	256.0	
1976[b]	69.9	761.0	87.9	2.8	24.3	291.2	
1977	53.5	385.8	59.3	1.4	16.0	43.3	
1978	44.4	264.7	35.9	3.8	26.6	63.4	
1979	42.0	218.9	66.1	2.6	28.9	47.5	
1980	43.1	283.7	40.9	3.5	28.2	78.8	
1981	22.4	201.9	33.2	6.9	30.4	42.0	
1982	36.2	220.4	54.9	11.4	43.4	36.7	
1983	43.2	280.2	89.3	9.6	52.8	67.0	79.4

Table 10.1 (continued)

Year	Land	Buildings	Vehicles	Customer service equipment	Postal support equipment	Mail-processing equipment	Automated-processing equipment
1984	59.3	199.0	127.9	11.6	76.1	41.6	63.1
1985	46.9	332.8	102.3	10.8	168.0	36.9	34.0
Average annual growth rates (percent)							
1963–1971	57.3	31.9	22.1	8.2	23.1	26.7	
1971–1985	.7	8.4	4.6	9.2	11.9	-4.2	
1963–1985	21.3	17.0	10.9	8.9	15.9	7.0	
1983–1985							-42.4

a. All numbers are reported on a fiscal year basis.
b. The 1976 values include the transition quarter.

land price index is based on Goldsmith's (table A-41, p. 188, column 6) price index for corporate land. Goldsmith's deflator is not available for every year. Missing years are estimated by linear interpolation. The price of land is assumed to be constant from 1886 to 1900.

Through 1981, the price index used for buildings is taken from the *National Income and Product Accounts*, table 7.19, "Government Structures—New Industrial, Educational, Hospital, and Other." Beginning in 1982, a quarterly price index is developed from the three price indexes underlying the NIPA index: the Turner Construction Company Index, the Department of Transportation Structures Index, and the Bureau of the Census Price Index of New One-Family Houses excluding lots. The Turner Index and DOT Structures Index are smoothed using a three-period moving average to account for lags between price negotiations and project completion. The three indexes are combined using weights of 50%, 25%, and 25%, approximately the weights used in development of the NIPA index. The resulting quarterly price index of buildings is converted to a fiscal year price index by averaging the values in the four quarters of the fiscal year.

Price indexes for motor vehicles, customer service equipment, and postal support equipment are based totally on output price indexes for three- and four-digit SIC industries. Price indexes for mail-processing equipment and automated-processing equipment are based in part on price indexes for SIC industries, and in part on price indexes specific to USPS equipment. Through 1981 annual price indexes are obtained from the Bureau of Economic Analysis; beginning in 1982 monthly Producer Price Indexes are used. The PPI are adjusted for lags between orders and deliveries, using techniques proposed by Rottenberg and Donahoe (1975), then averaged over the fiscal year.

For vehicles, one SIC industry is used in developing a price index: industry 3711. For the other equipment classes, a number of SIC industries are used with weights assigned to each. Tables 10.2–10.5 show the SIC industries used for each of the four remaining equipment classes, along with the weights assigned them in 1984.

For the years 1982–1985, the weights to be used in aggregating the price indexes are constructed using the annual transactions tapes of the PPAS system. New purchases are identified on the transactions tape, and the costs of these purchases are used in developing the weights. Prior to 1982, annual weights are based on the 1981 Personal Property Asset Master. The Asset Master records the vintage and original cost of each asset in place at the end of 1981. The original cost

Table 10.2
SIC price indexes used to construct
customer service equipment price
index

SIC industry	1984 weight
252	.187
3574	.000
3579	.012
3576	.388
357	.000
3581	.413

Table 10.3
SIC price indexes used to construct postal support equipment
price index

SIC industry	1984 weight	SIC industry	1984 weight
252	.014	3572	.016
3499	.027	3573	.563
354	.023	3574	.002
356	.017	3579	.011
357	.066	3585	.011
3531	.002	3589	.027
3537	.009	364	.000
3546	.001	3651	.033
3549	.058	382	.035
3563	.004	3841	.002
3564	.002	3861	.050

Table 10.4

Price indexes used to construct mail-processing equipment price index[a]

Price index (SIC sector)	1984 weight	Price index (SIC sector)	1984 weight
CAN	.001	3535	.178
PEF	.013	3536	.102
LSM	.067	3537	.061
OCR	.001	3569	.057
PSM	.033	3579	.415
2394	.000	3621	.001
2451	.010	3629	.002
252	.005	3662	.005
2542	.002	3692	.008
3448	.069	3751	.000
3462	.000	3823	.000
		3953	.000

a. USPS specific assets: CAN, cancellers; PEF, edger/feeders; LSM, letter sorting machines; OCR, older vintage optical character readers; PSM, parcel sorting machines.

Table 10.5

Price indexes used to construct OCR price index[a]

Price index	1984 weight
OCRC	.862
BSCR	.138

a. OCRC, new vintage optical character readers; BSRC, small bar code sorters.

of assets remaining in 1981 is used in lieu of new purchases in obtaining weights for these earlier years.[4]

Mail-processing equipment and automated-processing equipment consist of machines to handle, cancel, and sort the mail. Some of the equipment is similar to equipment widely used in industry. Other types of machines are unique to the USPS. To adequately capture the price changes of MPE and OCR over time, price indexes specific to USPS are combined with SIC deflators in obtaining equipment price indexes.

Price deflators for equipment specific to the USPS were based on data recorded in the Personal Property Accounting System. The PPAS lists each item in the inventory by its detailed Property Code Number (PCN), the date purchased, and average unit cost. Attention was focused on PCNs of significant size and where purchases were recorded in a number of years. A total of seven PCNs, accounting for almost half of all mail-processing equipment and automated-processing equipment, were used. Average unit costs were used to construct price series, with missing years interpolated. The price indexes for these seven PCNs are presented in table 10.6.

For each of the equipment classes, the SIC industry and USPS specific price deflators are aggregated in a Tornqvist index, using the weights described above. The price indexes for the five equipment categories are presented in table 10.7, while the price indexes for buildings and land are presented in table 10.8.

10.5   Rates of Replacement

Numerous econometric studies have been conducted on rates of replacement for buildings and motor vehicles.[5] No comparable studies were found that have been done for mail-processing equipment, automated-processing equipment, customer service equipment, or postal support equipment. An initial objective was to use investment data and data on assets presently in service to construct rates of replacement for the five depreciable asset classes. An attempt was made to estimate retirement functions for each asset class based on the historical time series of investment and the vintage distribution of assets presently in service. The latter information is available in the Personal Property Accounting System, the Vehicle Accounting System, and the Facilities Management System. For USPS assets, this approach has been successful only for motor vehicles. For mail-processing equipment, postal support equipment, and customer

Table 10.6
Asset classes for which the price index incorporates USPS specific data (shares in percent)

PCN	Description	Average share
990301	12 position LSM	24.6
440101	Optical character reader	1.9
452301	Mark II canceller/facer	5.0
990604	BMC parcel sorting machine	4.5
469106	Edger/feeder	1.3
994001	New optical character readers	6.0
994002	Small bar code readers	1.0
	Total	44.3

USPS specific price deflators

Year	452301 Cancellers	469106 Edger feeders	990301 Letter-sorting machines	440101 Old OCRs	990604 Parcel-sorting machines	994001 New OCRs	994002 Bar code reader
1963	.740	.809	1.018	.874	.809		
1964	.749	.819	1.018	.874	.819		
1965	.771	.843	1.018	.874	.843		
1966	.790	.864	1.018	.874	.864		
1967	.815	.891	1.018	.874	.891		
1968	.832	.910	1.018	.874	.910		
1969	.846	.925	1.018	.874	.925		
1970	1.010	.957	.966	.874	.957		
1971	.978	.976	1.005	1.000	.976		

Table 10.6 (continued)

USPS specific price deflators

Year	452301 Cancellers	469106 Edger feeders	990301 Letter-sorting machines	440101 Old OCRs	990604 Parcel-sorting machines	994001 New OCRs	994002 Bar code reader
1972	1.000	1.000	1.000	1.000	1.000		
1973	.922	1.091	.943	1.000	1.023		
1974	.844	1.283	.886	.948	1.106		
1975	1.553	1.520	1.105	.896	1.192		
1976	1.501	1.757	1.325	.849	1.294		
1977	1.315	1.645	1.545	1.049	1.331		
1978	1.385	1.608	1.654	1.120	1.402		
1979	1.467	1.713	1.764	1.109	1.486		
1980	1.602	1.818	1.873	1.109	1.622		
1981	1.642	1.923	2.151	1.109	1.662		
1982	1.682	1.923	1.779	1.109	1.662		
1983	1.722	1.923	2.249	1.109	1.622	1.000	1.000
1984	1.764	1.923	2.249	1.109	1.662	1.000	.766
1985	2.056	1.871	2.249	1.109	1.662	1.000	.607
Mean values							
1963–1971	.837	.888	1.011	.888	.888		
1971–1985	1.429	1.598	1.585	1.042	1.383		
1963–1985	1.217	1.347	1.386	.983	1.207		
1983–1985						1.000	.791

Table 10.7
Equipment price indexes (1972 = 1)

Year	Vehicles	Customer service equipment	Postal support equipment	Mail-processing equipment	Automated-processing equipment
1963	.802	.808	.882	.831	
1964	.813	.816	.898	.836	
1965	.820	.821	.899	.846	
1966	.827	.843	.904	.865	
1967	.837	.868	.917	.881	
1968	.866	.875	.925	.896	
1969	.883	.919	.936	.915	
1970	.916	.965	.961	.944	
1971	.969	.987	.987	.992	
1972	1.000	1.000	1.000	1.000	
1973	1.008	1.012	1.014	.987	
1974	1.082	1.098	1.081	1.053	
1975	1.179	1.185	1.144	1.221	
1976	1.255	1.238	1.171	1.316	
1977	1.338	1.294	1.202	1.431	
1978	1.436	1.392	1.233	1.528	
1979	1.552	1.505	1.265	1.647	
1980	1.675	1.625	1.337	1.795	
1981	1.830	1.726	1.380	1.962	
1982	1.926	1.807	1.395	1.897	
1983	1.978	1.868	1.399	1.964	1.000
1984	2.026	1.892	1.401	1.973	.946
1985	2.063	1.921	1.409	1.985	.931

	Average annual growth rates (percent)				
1963–1971	2.4	2.5	1.4	2.2	
1971–1985	5.4	4.8	2.5	5.0	
1963–1985	4.3	3.9	2.1	4.0	
1983–1985					−3.6

Table 10.8
Land and building price indexes (1972 = 1)

Year	Land	Buildings
1963	.773	.628
1964	.798	.639
1965	.824	.655
1966	.854	.680
1967	.856	.706
1968	.856	.730
1969	.886	.795
1970	.907	.856
1971	.932	.933
1972	1.000	1.000
1973	1.101	1.077
1974	1.287	1.214
1975	1.337	1.325
1976	1.450	1.362
1977	1.634	1.452
1978	1.910	1.595
1979	2.171	1.809
1980	2.583	2.026
1981	3.074	2.166
1982	3.434	2.243
1983	3.815	2.295
1984	4.200	2.379
1985	4.509	2.491

	Average annual growth rates (percent)	
1963–1971	2.3	4.9
1971–1985	11.3	7.0
1963–1985	8.0	6.3

service equipment, it appears that no significant number of assets purchased since 1969 have been retired. Since these are the only years for which the vintages of personal property assets are available, no useful rate of replacement can be estimated.

Useful service lives for these three asset classes are based on the accounting lives used by the USPS in calculating depreciation. Using the 1981 Personal Property Asset Master, each asset's accounting life is weighted by its cost, and average lives for mail-processing equipment, automated-processing equipment, customer service equipment, and postal support equipment are calculated. These average lives are 18 years, 18 years, 14 years, and 13 years, respectively. The 1.5 declining balance rates of replacement are .083 for MPE and OCR, .107 for CSE, and .115 for PSE.

Constructing a retirement function for buildings from the Facility Management System is impossible because of the many capital improvements that have been made to older buildings over time. Consequently, the Hulten-Wykoff rate of replacement for buildings (.0233) is used.

A retirement function for vehicles is estimated using the Vehicles Accounting System. From this retirement function the useful service life of nine years is obtained. A double declining balance rate, .222, is computed using this service life.

10.6   Benchmarks

Initial investigations in this area focused on asset records contained in the Personal Property Accounting System, the Vehicle Accounting System, and the Facility Management System. Except for land, these records appear to be inadequate to construct benchmarks. The Facilities Management System can be used with other accounting reports to construct a land benchmark as described below. This section describes the methods used to successfully construct benchmarks for the other six asset classes.

Motor vehicles have high rates of replacement. Because of this, the best stock estimates for vehicles can be obtained by taking a benchmark as early as possible, provided an investment series is available from that date forward. Records on dollar investment in vehicles are unavailable prior to 1963. Records do exist in the *Annual Report of the Postmaster General* (table 502) on the number of vehicles purchased by the USPS prior to that year. Though the number of vehicles purchased is an imperfect measure of real investment (due to quality changes and the shift toward the purchase of smaller vehicles), a comparison of the vehicles purchased series and real investment after 1962 provides convincing evidence that the former series can be used in constructing a reasonably accurate stock estimate for 1962. Hence, the series for the number of vehicles purchased from 1949 to 1963 is linked to real investment for 1963. Since motor vehicles purchased before 1949 play a very minor role in the real stock in 1963, those purchases can be ignored. Starting with a zero level of stock in 1948, purchases are cumulated between 1949 and 1962 using the perpetual inventory method. Before 1958 most vehicles purchased were large vehicles (semitractors, trailers, etc.). Investment occurring in these early years have a rate of replacement of .167, which is three-fourths of the rate used for investment occurring after that date.

Benchmarks for all other asset classes are based on the 1962 net book value of these assets. Real capital stock differs from net book value in two respects. First, net book value is equal to the gross book value less accumulated depreciation. Accumulated depreciation is based on accounting rules, with straight line depreciations methods generally the norm. Real capital stock adjusts the gross stock for declines in economic efficiency, which is measured through the rate of replacement. These rates of replacement generally differ from the accounting depreciation rates used in the construction of net book value. Second, net book value expresses the capital stock at historical cost while the real capital stock expresses it in constant dollars. Therefore the 1962 net book value must be adjusted by estimated real stock to net book value ratios to obtain benchmarks.

The estimate of the real stock to net book value ratio for mail-processing equipment, postal support equipment, and customer service equipment is based on the same ratio as calculated for producer durable equipment in the U.S. nonmanufacturing sector. Estimates of the real stock and net book value for nonmaunfacturing producer durable equipment are taken from the BLS publication, *Capital Stock Estimates for Input-Output Industries: Methods and Data* (chapter 5, tables 12 and 13). The ratio of the real stock to net book value for buildings is based on the real stock and net book value for buildings in the U.S. nonmanufacturing sector, also obtained from this BLS publication.

Using the Facilities Management System records for the year 1982, a real stock to net book value ratio is constructed for land parcels acquired before 1963. For each parcel acquired before 1963, the recorded book value of the asset is divided by the land price index for the year in which the land parcel was acquired. This yields an estimate of the real capital stock embodied in that parcel of land. The real values of these parcels are added, and then divided by the total book value of these parcels. This real capital stock to net book value ratio is then applied to the book value of land recorded in 1962.

10.7   Capital Stock

Real investment is obtained by deflating current dollar investment by the corresponding price index. Real investment by asset type is shown in table 10.9. By far the largest share of real investment has gone to buildings. This particularly holds true since reorganization. The large investment in buildings occurring in 1970 is in part due to the transfer of ownership of some buildings from the GSA to the USPS, corresponding to the establishment of the Postal Service as a government enterprise. In the succeeding years, real investment in buildings was at a higher level than in the 1960s, particularly in 1975 and 1977. Much of the investment in these years was related to the modernization of facilities and the centralized processing of bulk and regular mail.

There was a surge of real investment in mail-processing equipment in 1975 and 1976. But in 1977 investment in mail-processing equipment fell back to, and has remained at, previous levels. However, since 1983 there has been substantial investment in automated-processing equipment. Other asset categories have had pronounced cycles in investment, but none saw the massive spurt of investment that took place in buildings and mail-processing equipment.

The estimated capital stocks appear in table 10.10. The largest growth occurred in the buildings asset class, which grew at an average annual rate of 8.8% between 1963 and 1985. Much of that growth occurred in those periods in which large investment occurred. Between 1969 and 1973, and again between 1973 and 1978, the stock of buildings doubled. The stock of mail-processing equipment also grew rapidly, at an average annual rate of 7.9%. During the 1974–1976 period, the stock increased nearly 250%, but has been declining since then. In recent years, the stock of automated-processing equipment has grown rapidly.

The stock of vehicles grew at a rapid rate of 14.4% per year up to the time of reorganization, and continued its growth up to 1976, but it has been below the 1976 level ever since. In fact by 1982 it had fallen by 30%, before resuming growth in 1983. Postal support equipment and customer service equipment have had steady growth, though the

Table 10.9
Real investment by asset class (millions of 1972 dollars)

Year	Land	Buildings	Vehicles	Customer service equipment	Postal support equipment	Mail-processing Equipment	Automated-processing Equipment
1963	.2	12.7	11.5	1.9	5.7	9.4	
1964	.2	16.6	19.0	1.5	8.1	26.6	
1965	.9	22.5	24.0	2.1	5.9	10.5	
1966	.8	24.1	29.8	2.3	5.4	5.1	
1967	-.6	54.6	27.4	2.8	12.8	25.1	
1968	1.9	30.7	44.5	2.6	28.6	16.4	
1969	1.6	40.6	30.9	2.7	27.2	27.2	
1970	49.9	234.6	69.0	3.8	25.7	25.9	
1971	45.9	109.5	55.8	3.0	32.3	66.9	
1972	22.6	116.7	55.7	2.2	9.6	25.6	
1973	12.9	114.0	21.7	4.8	13.6	33.2	
1974	6.3	122.6	41.3	2.4	24.9	35.9	
1975	20.8	138.6	47.1	1.8	32.9	209.6	
1976[a]	48.2	558.7	70.0	2.3	20.8	221.4	
1977	32.7	265.7	44.3	1.1	13.4	30.3	
1978	23.2	166.0	25.0	2.7	21.6	41.5	
1979	19.3	121.0	42.6	1.7	22.8	28.8	

Year							
1980	16.7	140.0	24.4	2.2	21.1	43.9	
1981	7.3	93.2	18.1	4.0	22.1	21.4	
1982	10.5	98.2	28.5	6.3	31.1	19.3	
1983	11.3	122.1	45.2	5.2	37.8	34.1	79.4
1984	14.1	83.6	63.1	6.2	54.3	21.1	66.7
1985	10.4	133.6	49.6	5.6	119.2	18.6	36.5

a. The 1976 values include the transition quarter. The numbers reported are on a fiscal year basis.

Table 10.10
Estimated end-of-year real stocks and asset prices by type of asset (millions of 1972 dollars)

Year	Land		Buildings		Vehicles	
	Real stock	Asset price	Real stock	Asset price	Real stock	Asset price
1963	431.5	.773	359.8	.628	59.4	.802
1964	431.8	.798	368.0	.639	67.4	.813
1965	432.6	.824	381.9	.655	78.3	.820
1966	433.4	.854	397.2	.680	92.2	.827
1967	432.8	.856	442.5	.706	100.4	.837
1968	434.7	.856	462.9	.730	123.6	.866
1969	436.3	.886	492.7	.795	128.0	.883
1970	486.2	.907	715.9	.856	169.3	.916
1971	532.1	.932	809.1	.933	188.1	.969
1972	554.7	1.000	907.0	1.000	202.5	1.000
1973	567.6	1.101	999.8	1.077	179.6	1.008
1974	574.0	1.287	1099.2	1.214	181.4	1.082
1975	594.8	1.337	1212.2	1.325	188.4	1.179
1976	643.0	1.450	1735.6	1.362	206.4	1.255
1977	675.7	1.634	1960.9	1.452	205.1	1.338
1978	698.9	1.910	2081.2	1.595	184.7	1.436
1979	718.3	2.171	2153.7	1.809	186.4	1.552
1980	735.0	2.583	2243.6	2.026	169.5	1.675
1981	742.2	3.074	2284.5	2.166	150.0	1.830
1982	752.8	3.434	2329.5	2.243	145.3	1.926
1983	764.1	3.815	2397.3	2.295	158.2	1.978
1984	778.2	4.200	2425.1	2.379	186.3	2.026
1985	788.6	4.509	2502.2	2.491	194.5	2.063

Average annual growth rates (percent)						
1963–1971	2.6	2.3	10.1	4.9	14.4	2.4
1971–1985	2.8	11.3	8.1	7.0	0.2	5.4
1963–1985	2.7	8.0	8.8	6.3	5.4	4.3

Table 10.10 (continued)

Estimated end-of-year real stocks and asset prices by type of asset (millions of 1972 dollars)

Year	Customer service equipment		Postal support equipment		Mail-processing equipment		Automated-processing equipment	
	Real stock	Asset price	Real stock	Asset price	Real stock	Asset price	Real stock	Asset price
1963	14.7	.808	63.6	.882	80.4	.831		
1964	14.6	.816	64.4	.898	100.3	.836		
1965	15.2	.821	62.9	.899	102.4	.846		
1966	15.8	.843	61.1	.904	99.0	.865		
1967	16.9	.868	66.8	.917	115.9	.881		
1968	17.7	.875	87.7	.925	122.7	.896		
1969	18.5	.919	104.7	.936	139.6	.915		
1970	20.3	.965	118.3	.961	153.8	.944		
1971	21.1	.987	137.0	.987	207.9	.992		
1972	21.1	1.000	130.8	1.000	216.1	1.000		
1973	23.6	1.012	129.3	1.014	231.3	.987		
1974	23.5	1.098	139.2	1.081	248.0	1.053		
1975	22.8	1.185	156.0	1.144	436.9	1.221		
1976	22.0	1.238	154.3	1.171	612.8	1.316		
1977	20.7	1.294	149.9	1.202	592.0	1.431		
1978	21.3	1.392	154.2	1.233	584.1	1.528		
1979	20.7	1.505	159.2	1.265	564.3	1.647		
1980	20.7	1.625	161.9	1.337	561.2	1.795		
1981	22.4	1.726	165.3	1.380	535.8	1.962		
1982	26.3	1.807	177.3	1.395	510.5	1.897		
1983	28.7	1.868	194.6	1.399	502.1	1.964	79.4	1.000
1984	31.7	1.892	226.5	1.401	481.3	1.973	139.5	.946
1985	34.0	1.921	319.6	1.409	459.8	1.985	164.4	.931

Average annual growth rates (percent)								
1963–1971	4.5	2.5	9.6	1.4	11.9	2.2		
1971–1985	3.4	4.8	6.0	2.5	5.7	5.0		
1963–1985	3.8	3.9	7.3	2.1	7.9	4.0		
1983–1985							36.4	−3.6

rate of growth has been somewhat slower since reorganization. The growth in the land stock has been quite slow.

Aggregate capital stock estimates are presented in table 10.11. Both the aggregate stock and asset price nearly quadrupled between 1963 and 1985. As with the stocks of buildings and equipment, we see large increases in the 1970–1971 period, corresponding with reorganization, and in 1975–1977, corresponding with modernization.

10.8 Capital Stock Transferred from GSA to USPS after Reorganization

As part of the reorganization effort, GSA transferred $126 million in buildings to the USPS in 1970 and $92 million in 1971 (book value). These were largely buildings constructed prior to 1963, which had not previously been entered into the Post Office ledgers. However, prior to 1971, the Post Office was the major occupant in these buildings. For this reason, these buildings must be included as part of USPS capital input prior to 1971 as well as after 1971. Since all indications are that these buildings were constructed prior to 1963, the calculations are relatively simple. The perpetual inventory equation with the rate of replacement for buildings, zero investment, and the 1971 constant dollar value of these transfers are used to produce the stock series. The methods used to obtain this constant dollar value are the same as those described above for book value entries. This provides the value of this stock for the years 1963–1970. The current and constant dollar values of the stock are presented in table 10.12. This stock can be added to owned buildings before owned capital input is measured.

10.9 Capital Input from Owned Capital

In order to construct a quantity index of capital input, relative shares are assigned to the asset classes based on capital service flows. The estimates of capital service flows for USPS-owned assets are based on the methodology developed by Christensen and Jorgenson (1969). As a government corporation, the USPS does not pay any income taxes or property taxes. In the absence of taxation, the value of capital services for a particular asset is the sum of the cost of capital and depreciation, less revaluation:

$$p_{kt}K_t = [p_{A,t-1}\, r_t + p_{A,t}\, \delta - (p_{A,t} - p_{A,t-1})]\, K_{t-1}.$$

Given the quantity of each type of asset held (K_{t-1}), the acquisition

Table 10.11
Aggregate USPS end-of-year real stock and asset price
(millions of 1972 dollars)

Year	Real stock	Asset price
1963	1015.7	.730
1964	1055.1	.747
1965	1080.9	.765
1966	1104.4	.788
1967	1178.1	.802
1968	1254.9	.816
1969	1326.5	.855
1970	1662.8	.895
1971	1896.0	.947
1972	2032.2	1.000
1973	2132.1	1.063
1974	2265.4	1.195
1975	2599.1	1.295
1976	3361.6	1.361
1977	3595.0	1.470
1978	3718.2	1.624
1979	3799.2	1.820
1980	3893.5	2.053
1981	3908.5	2.259
1982	3951.3	2.369
1983	4079.5	2.483
1984	4176.3	2.607
1985	4313.6	2.731

	Average annual growth rates (percent)	
1963–1971	7.8	3.2
1971–1985	5.9	7.6
1963–1985	6.6	6.0

Table 10.12
Value and quantity of
transferred GSA building stock
(quantities in millions of 1972
dollars)

Year	Current dollar value	Constant dollar value
1963	184.3	293.5
1964	183.2	286.6
1965	183.4	280.0
1966	185.9	273.4
1967	188.5	267.1
1968	190.4	260.8
1969	202.5	254.8
1970	78.6	91.8

price ($p_{A,t}$), and the rate of replacement (δ), only the cost of capital (r_t) is required to compute capital services for each type of asset. In recent years, the USPS has used a cost of capital in its budget planning. This would, in theory, be the preferred measure of the cost of capital. Unfortunately, this rate has not been adjusted frequently for changing market conditions and is only available for the most recent years. For those years in which it is available, it follows the same general trends as Moody's composite of average yields on corporate bonds. Thus we have used Moody's composite rate as the Postal Services cost of capital in the analysis (see table 10.13). Because capital gains are large in isolated years for land and buildings, the service flows calculated in those years are negative. To adjust for this problem, the current year's asset price in the equation defining the value of capital services is replaced by a fitted asset price ($\tilde{p}_{A,t}$). The fitted price is obtained by extrapolating a five-year average of the capital gains rate for buildings and a ten-year average for land. Algebraically, the fitted value is

$$\tilde{p}_{A,t} = \exp\left[\ln\left(p_{A,t-1}/p_{A,t-1-N}\right)/N\right] p_{A,t-1},$$

where N is the length of time over which the average is computed. Even after these adjustments, the calculated service flow for land is negative for some years; it is set to zero in those years.

The implicit annualized cost of owned capital input for the six asset classes is presented in table 10.14. Real capital input for each asset is proportional to the real stock in place at the beginning of the year.

Table 10.13
Cost of capital
(percent)

Year	Cost of capital
1963	4.50
1964	4.57
1965	4.64
1966	5.34
1967	5.82
1968	6.51
1969	7.36
1970	8.51
1971	7.94
1972	7.63
1973	7.80
1974	9.03
1975	9.57
1976	9.01
1977	8.43
1978	9.07
1979	10.12
1980	12.75
1981	15.06
1982	15.53
1983	12.85
1984	13.48
1985	12.48

Table 10.14
Implicit annalized cost of owned capital input (millions of dollars)

Year	Land	Buildings	Vehicles	Customer service equipment	Postal support equipment	Mail-processing equipment	Automated processing equipment
1963	0.0	23.3	12.9	1.7	9.2	8.2	
1964	0.0	21.3	12.3	1.7	8.1	8.3	
1965	0.0	18.9	14.3	1.8	9.3	9.9	
1966	0.0	17.1	17.3	1.7	9.3	10.1	
1967	4.9	25.6	20.7	1.8	8.9	10.7	
1968	11.1	29.3	21.9	2.4	10.6	13.6	
1969	15.9	28.2	30.0	2.1	14.5	15.1	
1970	22.5	32.5	31.4	2.5	17.3	17.8	
1971	24.8	26.9	39.8	3.3	19.4	16.9	
1972	23.8	22.0	49.9	3.6	24.4	31.4	
1973	23.3	20.2	59.5	3.7	23.7	37.5	
1974	25.8	29.4	46.2	2.9	19.2	25.5	
1975	34.1	39.8	48.7	3.4	24.1	8.6	
1976	28.4	58.8	58.3	4.2	32.9	54.9	
1977	16.3	75.6	66.1	4.1	32.0	70.2	
1978	7.9	97.4	70.2	3.5	33.0	94.8	
1979	9.9	144.0	69.1	4.0	36.7	100.8	
1980	26.8	250.2	83.3	5.1	38.8	119.6	
1981	45.2	358.8	85.4	6.8	51.5	149.7	
1982	54.8	444.8	92.5	8.5	59.5	282.9	
1983	0.0	408.0	92.2	9.8	59.8	174.0	
1984	26.8	566.7	105.8	12.3	67.7	210.8	21.2
1985	0.0	617.1	125.5	13.1	74.5	192.4	29.5

Average annual growth rates (percent)

1963–1971	40.5[a]	1.8	14.0	7.8	9.4	9.1	
1971–1985	0.6[b]	22.4	8.2	9.9	9.6	17.4	
1963–1985	10.0[c]	14.9	10.3	9.2	9.5	14.4	
1984–1985							32.9

a. 1967–1971.
b. 1971–1984.
c. 1967–1984.

The price and quantity indexes of owned capital input are presented in table 10.15.

10.10   Rented Capital

Rented capital can be separated by asset type into privately owned buildings, government owned buildings, and postal support equipment. The input these values represent is included as part of capital input.

In the case of postal support equipment there are no separate data prior to 1969. The rental of postal support equipment is fairly minor in 1969, and it appears that rents prior to 1969 are very small. Thus it is possible to ignore pre-1969 rents without biasing the estimates of postal support equipment rental capital. Postal support equipment rents for 1969–1985 are included as part of capital input.

Building rents are a significant portion of capital input. Rents are paid to three types of owners: private, General Services Administration,[6] and other government agencies. Rents paid to private owners are assumed to be at market rates, since they are subject to the competition of the market place. The value of privately rented buildings input is the rent paid plus the property taxes paid by the USPS as part of the lease. Both rents and property taxes paid are reported in the NCTB and ARPMG. Rents to the two government groups are believed to be below market rates, not reflecting the true opportunity cost of the resources involved. Square footage figures are available for USPS-owned buildings, and also for buildings occupied by the USPS but owned by government agencies. To estimate the true value of the government-owned building input, the estimated service flow for USPS-owned buildings and owned square footage figures are compared to produce a service flow per square foot. This flow per square foot is applied to government leased building square footage. Table 10.16 contains the series involved in this calculation. The sixth column of table 10.16 shows government rents as reported in the NCTB. Rents to government agencies are not available prior to 1969 because they do not appear in the ARPMG. A comparison of the estimated market rents and acutal rents shows that the greatest divergence occurs in the last few years of the sample. This should be expected since the cost of capital rose significantly in these years. It is likely that government agencies lagged in incorporating these higher capital costs into their rents.

Table 10.15
Quantity of owned capital input (millions of 1972 dollars)

Year	Land	Buildings	Vehicles	Customer service equipment	Postal support equipment	Mail-processing equipment	Automated-processing equipment
1963	19.3	17.9	15.4	2.4	11.6	11.7	
1964	19.3	17.8	15.7	2.5	11.3	12.1	
1965	19.3	17.8	17.9	2.5	11.4	15.1	
1966	19.4	18.0	20.8	2.6	11.2	15.5	
1967	19.4	18.3	24.4	2.7	10.9	14.9	
1968	19.4	19.3	26.6	2.9	11.9	17.5	
1969	19.5	19.7	32.8	3.0	15.6	18.5	
1970	19.5	20.3	33.9	3.1	18.6	21.1	
1971	21.8	22.0	44.9	3.4	21.0	23.2	
1972	23.8	22.0	49.9	3.6	24.4	31.4	
1973	24.8	24.7	53.7	3.6	23.3	32.6	
1974	25.4	27.2	47.6	4.0	23.0	34.9	
1975	25.7	29.9	48.1	4.0	24.7	37.4	
1976	26.6	33.0	50.0	3.8	27.7	65.9	
1977	28.8	47.2	54.7	3.7	27.4	92.4	
1978	30.2	53.4	54.4	3.5	26.6	89.3	
1979	31.3	56.6	49.0	3.6	27.4	88.1	

1980	32.1	58.6	49.4	3.5	28.3	85.1	
1981	32.9	61.1	44.9	3.5	28.8	84.7	
1982	33.2	62.2	39.8	3.8	29.4	80.8	
1983	33.7	63.4	38.5	4.4	31.5	77.0	
1984	34.2	65.2	42.0	4.8	34.6	75.7	21.2
1985	34.8	66.0	49.4	5.4	40.3	72.6	37.3
Average annual growth rates (percent)							
1963–1971	1.5	2.6	13.4	4.4	7.4	8.6	
1971–1985	3.4	7.9	.7	3.2	4.6	8.1	
1963–1985	2.7	5.9	5.3	3.6	5.6	8.3	
1984–1985							56.3

Table 10.15 (continued)

Price of owned capital input (1972=1)

Year	Land	Buildings	Vehicles	Customer service equipment	Postal support equipment	Mail-processing equipment	Automated-processing equipment
1963	.000	1.307	.840	.720	.788	.699	
1964	.000	1.197	.778	.687	.715	.681	
1965	.000	1.062	.803	.719	.813	.654	
1966	.000	.949	.832	.664	.830	.651	
1967	.255	1.402	.845	.689	.819	.718	
1968	.576	1.519	.822	.852	.891	.777	
1969	.818	1.429	.916	.704	.931	.816	
1970	1.151	1.598	.927	.801	.932	.843	
1971	1.141	1.224	.887	.950	.922	.729	
1972	1.000	1.000	1.000	1.000	1.000	1.000	
1973	.938	.819	1.109	1.033	1.021	1.149	
1974	1.017	1.080	.971	.728	.835	.732	
1975	1.328	1.330	1.013	.857	.975	.229	
1976	1.067	1.783	1.166	1.101	1.185	.832	
1977	.566	1.600	1.207	1.107	1.165	.760	
1978	.261	1.824	1.292	1.000	1.238	1.062	
1979	.317	2.543	1.411	1.121	1.339	1.144	
1980	.835	4.269	1.686	1.456	1.372	1.405	
1981	1.375	5.876	1.900	1.946	1.788	1.768	
1982	1.651	7.153	2.324	2.253	2.027	3.500	

1983	.000	6.436	2.395	2.194	1.897	2.259	1.000
1984	.785	8.686	2.523	2.548	1.956	2.783	.791
1985	.000	9.349	2.542	2.446	1.851	2.650	

Average annual growth rates (percent)

1963–1971	37.5[a]	-.8	.7	3.5	2.0	.5
1971–1985	-2.9[b]	14.5	7.5	6.8	5.0	9.2
1963–1985	6.6[c]	8.9	5.0	5.6	3.9	6.1
1984–1985							-23.4

a. 1967–1971.
b. 1971–1984.
c. 1967–1984.

Table 10.16
Estimation of market value of building rents paid to government agencies
(quantities in millions)

Year	Estimated owned service flow	USPS-operated square feet	Ratio of flow to square feet	Rented square feet from government agencies	Implied market rent	Actual rents paid
1963	23.3	49.7	.470	6.7	3.1	
1964	21.3	49.6	.429	8.0	3.4	
1965	18.9	51.5	.367	7.0	2.6	
1966	17.1	51.5	.332	7.1	2.3	
1967	25.6	50.4	.508	7.4	3.8	
1968	29.3	50.6	.580	6.9	4.0	
1969	28.2	53.9	.523	8.3	4.4	2.1
1970	32.5	53.1	.612	9.6	5.9	2.5
1971	26.9	58.8	.458	9.1	4.2	1.7
1972	22.0	64.4	.342	8.6	2.9	3.2
1973	20.2	70.1	.289	8.1	2.3	3.7
1974	29.4	75.8	.388	7.6	2.9	6.6
1975	39.8	81.4	.489	7.1	3.5	1.3
1976	58.8	87.1	.675	6.6	5.5	4.5
1977	75.6	92.8	.814	6.1	4.9	3.5
1978	97.4	96.0	1.015	6.2	6.3	3.1
1979	144.0	99.8	1.444	5.4	7.7	1.7
1980	250.2	103.6	2.414	5.4	12.9	2.6
1981	358.8	106.2	3.378	4.8	16.4	3.6
1982	444.8	108.0	4.117	4.7	19.4	3.2
1983	408.0	109.8	3.716	4.7	17.6	5.4
1984	566.7	111.3	5.090	5.0	25.7	7.8
1985	617.1	114.0	5.414	5.0	27.0	14.1

Because government-owned rented buildings are valued based on the service flow of USPS-owned buildings, the service price of USPS-owned buildings is used to deflate rents from government-owned buildings. The rents from privately owned buildings are deflated by the Consumer Price Index for rents. Real rented buildings (private plus government owned) is a Tornqvist index of these two categories with the price of rented buildings residually determined. Value, price, and quanitity for rented buildings and rented postal support equipment appear in table 10.17. Prior to reorganization the quantity of rental buildings was growing at a rate of 6.0% per year. However, by 1973, the quantity peaked, and has been lower ever since. Comparing table 10.17 with table 10.14, one sees that rented buildings input was much larger in 1963 than owned buildings input, but by 1985 it was much smaller. The quantity of rented Postal Support Equipment input has grown very rapidly since 1969, and by 1985 its value was 74% as large as the value of owned postal support equipment input.

10.11   Total Capital Input

The total value of capital input for each asset class is the sum of the service flow of the owned assets and rents, if there are any. Real capital input for each asset class is obtained by aggregating owned and rented capital input. Real total capital input is computed by aggregating over the seven asset classes. The price and quantity indexes of total capital input are reported in table 10.18.

Over the 1963–1985 period, the price of capital input grew 6.6% per year while the quantity of capital input grew 4.2%. The price of capital input showed a lower rate of increase prior to reorganization. Since 1971, the rate of increase has been much higher, with a considerable jump in prices occurring in 1979 with the onset of high real interest rates.

The quantity of capital input grew very rapidly during the period of reorganization. This trend continued through 1977 with the modernization that was taking place. Since 1977, the level of real capital input has stagnated, and not until 1985 did real capital input exceed its 1977 level. Real capital input in 1985 was higher than in any year, except for 1976, which included the transition quarter. When allowance is made for the 15-month length of fiscal 1978, USPS real capital input is at an all time high.

Table 10.17
Value, price and quantity of rented capital stock (quantities in millions of 1972 dollars)

Year	Buildings			Postal support equipment		
	Value	Price	Quantity	Value	Price	Quantity
1963	80.3	.809	99.3			
1964	88.5	.813	108.9			
1965	93.8	.818	114.6			
1966	103.1	.827	124.7			
1967	111.9	.851	131.5			
1968	127.2	.873	145.7			
1969	128.3	.898	142.8	1.8	.931	1.9
1970	142.2	.938	151.6	1.9	.932	2.0
1971	155.5	.971	160.0	2.4	.922	2.6
1972	168.7	1.000	168.7	7.0	1.000	7.0
1973	216.2	1.039	208.0	7.9	1.021	7.7
1974	210.1	1.095	191.9	9.8	.835	11.8
1975	218.2	1.154	189.1	11.7	.975	12.0
1976	229.4	1.221	187.8	17.5	1.185	14.8
1977	232.7	1.291	180.2	17.9	1.165	15.4
1978	234.9	1.382	170.0	16.0	1.238	12.9
1979	234.7	1.494	157.1	15.3	1.339	11.5
1980	245.6	1.657	148.3	18.0	1.372	13.1
1981	259.1	1.825	142.0	19.7	1.788	11.0
1982	280.8	1.980	141.9	27.3	2.027	13.5
1983	304.9	2.068	147.4	39.5	1.897	20.8
1984	331.7	2.206	150.4	55.9	1.956	28.6
1985	359.3	2.339	153.6	55.5	1.851	30.0

Average annual growth rates (percent)

1963–1971	8.3	2.3	6.0			
1971–1985	6.0	6.3	−.3			
1963–1985	6.8	4.8	2.0			
1969–1985				21.5	4.3	17.2

Table 10.18
Value, price, and quantity of total capital input
(quantities in millions of 1972 dollars)

Year	Current dollar value	Price	Quantity
1963	135.7	.772	175.8
1964	140.1	.752	186.4
1965	148.0	.749	197.7
1966	158.5	.746	212.4
1967	184.6	.826	223.4
1968	216.2	.882	245.1
1969	235.9	.923	255.6
1970	268.1	.987	271.6
1971	288.9	.963	299.9
1972	330.8	1.000	330.8
1973	391.9	1.036	378.2
1974	369.1	1.014	364.1
1975	388.6	1.056	367.8
1976	605.5	1.231	491.8
1977	514.9	1.200	428.9
1978	557.6	1.324	421.1
1979	614.6	1.512	406.5
1980	787.6	1.956	402.6
1981	976.2	2.450	398.4
1982	1251.1	3.159	396.0
1983	1088.2	2.686	405.2
1984	1399.0	3.271	427.7
1985	1466.9	3.303	444.2

	Average annual growth rates (percent)		
1963–1971	9.4	2.8	6.7
1971–1985	11.6	8.8	2.8
1963–1985	10.8	6.6	4.2

Notes

1. See Christensen and Jorgenson (1969, 1970, 1973a, b), Christensen, Cummings, and Jorgenson (1978, 1980, 1981), and Christensen and Cummings (1981).

2. See Berndt and Christensen (1973), Caves, Christensen, and Swanson (1980), Caves and Christensen (1980), Caves, Christensen, and Tretheway (1981, 1983), and Christensen, Cummings, and Schoech (1983).

3. For example, 1% of the end-of-year asset appearing in "Mailbags and Mailbag Equipment" in 1968 appears in "Mailbag Repair Equipment" in 1969. This factor of 1% is used to link investment appearing in "Mailbags and Mailbag Equipment" with "Mailbag Repair Equipment."

4. Assets purchased before 1969 are reported as being of 1968 vintage. Therefore 1969 weights are used for the 1963–1968 period also.

5. See Hulten and Wykoff (1981) for a survey of the literature as well as their recent econometric studies in this area.

6. This is net of the stock that was transferred to USPS ownership in 1970 and 1971.

References

Berndt, E. R., and L. R. Christensen (1973), "The Translog Function and the Substitution of Equipment, Structures, and Labor in U.S. Manufacturing 1929–1968," *Journal of Econometrics*, March, pp. 81–113.

Bureau of Economic Analysis, U.S. Department of Commerce (1981), *The National Income and Product Accounts of the United States, 1929–1976 Statistical Tables*, September. A supplement to the *Survey of Current Business*. U.S. Government Printing Office, Washington, D.C.

Bureau of Economic Analysis, U.S. Department of Commerce (1983), "National Income and Product Accounts Tables," *Survey of Current Business*, October, Volume 63, Number 10, U.S. Government Printing Office, Washington, D.C.

Bureau of Labor Statistics, U.S. Department of Labor, *BLS Handbook of Methods*.

Bureau of Labor Statistics, U.S. Department of Labor, *Monthly Labor Review*.

Bureau of Labor Statistics, U.S. Department of Labor (1978), *Time Series Data for Input-Output Industries: Output, Price, and Employment*, October, Bulletin #2002, U.S. Government Printing Office, Washington, D.C.

Bureau of Labor Statistics, U.S. Department of Labor (1979), *Capital Stock Estimates for Input-Output Industries: Methods and Data*, September, Bulletin #2034, U.S. Government Printing Office, Washington, D.C.

Caves, D. W., and L. R. Christensen (1980), "The Relative Efficiency of Public and Private Firms in a Competitive Environment: The Case of Canadian Railroads," *Journal of Political Economy*, October.

Caves, D. W., L. R. Christensen, and J. A. Swanson (1980), "Productivity in U.S. Railroads, 1951–1974," *Bell Journal of Economics*, Vol. 11, No. 1, Spring, pp. 166–181.

Caves, D. W., L. R. Christensen, and M. W. Tretheway (1981), "U.S. Trunk Air Carriers, 1972–1977: A Multilateral Comparison of Total Factor Productivity," in Cowing and Stevenson, eds., *Productivity Measurement in Regulated Industries*, Academic Press, New York

Caves, D. W., L. R. Christensen, and M. W. Tretheway (1983), "Productivity Performance of U.S. Trunk and Local Service Airlines in the Era of Deregulation," *Economic Inquiry*, Vol. XXI, No. 3, July.

Christensen, L. R., and D. Cummings (1981), "Real Product, Real Factor Input, and Productivity in the Republic of Korea, 1960–1973," *Journal of Development Economics*, Vol. 18, pp. 285–302.

Christensen, L. R., and D. W. Jorgenson (1969), "Measurement of U.S. Real Capital Input, 1929–1967," *Review of Income and Wealth*, Series 15, No. 4, December, pp. 293–320.

Christensen, L. R., and D. W. Jorgenson (1970), "U.S. Real Product and Real Factor Input, 1929–1967," *Review of Income and Wealth*, Series 16, No. 1, March, pp. 19–50.

Christensen, L. R., and D. W. Jorgenson (1973a), "Measuring Economic Performance in the Private Sector," in M. Moss ed., *The Measurement of Economic and Social Performance*, National Bureau of Economic Research, New York, pp. 233–351.

Christensen, L. R., and D. W. Jorgenson (1973b), "U.S. Income, Savings and Wealth, 1929–1969," *Review of Income and Wealth*, Series 19, No. 4, December, pp. 329–362.

Christensen, L. R., D. Cummings, and D. W. Jorgenson (1978), "Productivity Growth, 1947–1973: An International Comparison," in W. Dewald, ed., *The Impact of International Trade and Investment on Employment*, U.S. Department of Labor, Washington, D.C.

Christensen, L. R., D. Cummings, and D. W. Jorgenson (1980), "Economic Growth, 1947–1973: An International Comparison," in J. Kendrick and B. Vaccara, eds., *New Developments in Productivity Measurement and Analysis*, University of Chicago Press for the National Bureau of Economic Research, Chicago.

Christensen, L. R., D. Cummings, and D. W. Jorgenson (1981), "Relative Productivity Levels, 1947–1973: An International Comparison," *European Economic Review*, Vol. 16, No. 1, May.

Christensen, L. R., D. Cummings, and P. E. Schoech (1983), "Econometric Estimation of Scale Economies in Telecommunications," in L. Courville, A. R.

Dobell, and A. de Fontenay, eds., *Economic Analysis of Telecommunications: Theory and Applications,* Vol. 1, North-Holland Publishing Company, Amsterdam.

Goldsmith, R. W. (1963), *Studies in the National Balance Sheet in the United States,* Princeton University Press, Princeton.

Hulten, C. R., and F. C. Wykoff (1981), "The Measurement of Economic Depreciation," in C. Hulten, ed., *Depreciation, Inflation, and the Taxation of Income from Capital,* Urban Institute Press, Washington.

Rottenberg, I. and G. Donahoe (1975), "Improved Deflation of Producers' Durable Equipment," *Survey of Current Business,* United States Department of Commerce, Bureau of Economic Analysis, Vol. 65, No. 8, July.

Stevenson, R. (1973), "A Study of the Nature of Scale Economies in the United States Postal Service," discussion paper prepared for Postal Rate Commision Seminar on Economies of Scale, September 18.

Tornqvist, L. (1936), "The Bank of Finland's Consumption Price Index," *Bank of Finland Monthly Bulletin,* No. 10, pp. 1–8.

11

New Estimates of Federal Government Tangible Capital and Net Investment

Michael J. Boskin, Marc S. Robinson, and John M. Roberts

11.1 Introduction

In all countries, the public sector, as well as the private sector, owns substantial amounts of capital, makes investment as well as consumption-type expenditures and transfer payments, and experiences depreciation in the value of its tangible capital. Most advanced economies incorporate this in their formal budget documents, generating separate capital and current services accounts. The United States is the most conspicuous exception. Fortunately, the Bureau of Economic Analysis (BEA) of the Commerce Department has generated substantial information on federal, and state and local, government investment, depreciation, and capital stocks in the United States for the past 60 years. While one of the purposes of this chapter is to generate alternative estimates, and these differ somewhat from those of the BEA, it is clear from even a cursory examination of the data that government capital formation is substantial. The sum of the federal, state, and local government capital stocks is more than half as large as private nonresidential capital in the United States. In many other countries it is a still larger fraction of the total national capital stock.

Government capital formation raises a number of issues important to national economic well-being. For example, government net capital

This chapter is part of Professor Boskin's larger project on more comprehensive and comprehensible federal government accounts. We are indebted to Stanford University's Center for Economic Policy Research for support of this research, to Terrance O'Reilly for advice and assistance, to participants at the Kennedy School Conference on Technology and Capital Formation for helpful comments, to Jessica Primoff and Matt Cameron for valuable research assistance, and to John Musgrave for kindly providing us with unpublished data. This research was undertaken while Robinson was a John M. Olin Postdoctoral Research Fellow and Roberts was a John M. Olin Graduate Research Fellow at Stanford.

formation can be a major component of net national saving. Also, it may be more appropriate to finance government capital formation than government consumption by borrowing rather than taxing. Obviously, some types of government capital formation are complementary to private activity and enhance productivity. But government capital formation does not have to meet the same kind of market test as private investment, and we do not have an analog to the stock market to value it. Thus, measures of government capital and investment may be particularly useful information that cannot be inferred from other data. Measures of the productivity of the government investment are hard to come by. Further, because taxes are distortionary, the cost of these distortions must be included in proper social cost-benefit analyses, and therefore the optimal public sector investment must have a larger marginal product than that in the private sector.

It may well be the case that government investment expenditures have different impacts on the economy than transfer payments or government consumption expenditures, which add the same amounts to traditionally measured deficits. Further, it is unclear that the deficit on current account is the sole information one would want to use, for example, in short-run macroeconomic analyses. Do we really believe that shifting a dollar from government consumption to government investment, thereby reducing the current services deficit by a dollar, has the same macroeconomic impact as a dollar decrease in spending and/or a dollar increase in taxes? Still, separating out capital and current expenditures, and generating sensible measures of depreciation and net investment, can be important inputs into various kinds of economic analyses, some examples of which are presented below.

First, such an endeavor would enable us to have a more accurate picture of how the government is really using the funds it raises. Second, it could help us get better measures of the productivity of this capital, by component or in the aggregate. Third, it is a necessary input into comprehensive measures of national wealth. Fourth, it may be valuable in establishing alternative budget procedures and/or in better understanding and implementing various fiscal policies. Fifth, it is also a necessary input in measures of net national saving, and indeed, the United Nations system of national income accounts, implemented in most OECD countries, expressly incorporates net government saving in the measure of net national saving. Sixth, it can improve our understanding of fiscal history and help highlight emerging fiscal issues, such as the deterioration of the infrastructure or, alternatively, a rapid government investment buildup (as appears to be happening in Japan at the moment).

The purpose of this chapter is to provide alternative estimates of federal government net investment and net capital stocks as potential inputs into such studies. It also tests the sensitivity of alternative approaches to depreciation in terms of their potential impact on aggregate measures of net capital stock and investment in the federal government sector of the United States, as we compare our numbers with those of the BEA. We estimate a federal government net non-residential capital stock 18% higher than that estimated by the BEA's method, and, hence, correspondingly higher government consumption, national income, and, when the changes in net capital stock differ, net national saving. The results systematically differ with respect to structures but are quite comparable with respect to equipment. A similar result was found using the same methodology for the private capital stock by Hulten and Wykoff (1981). It is likely that their pattern will be found for the state and local sector when we present those results in a sequel to this chapter.

The chapter is organized as follows. In section 11.2, we briefly review other attempts to create government investment and capital stock estimates. These include the Bureau of Economic Analysis (BEA) (and several studies based on the BEA numbers), Goldsmith (1962), and Kendrick (1976), as well as special studies of the Office of Management and Budget and the special analyses of the Budget of the United States. We describe each briefly, together with what we consider to be the strengths and weaknesses of each study.

In section 11.3, we present the methodology employed in this study for measuring investment, depreciation, and net capital stocks. We discuss various reasons why our approach to depreciation is likely to lead to somewhat different results in the time pattern of accumulation and depreciation, and also various strengths and weaknesses of the methodology we employ—which follows the approximation to a used asset price approach suggested by Hulten and Wykoff (1981)—relative to that of the BEA or other options.

Section 11.4 presents our principal results. Data are presented for gross and net investment, depreciation, and net capital stocks annually from 1927 to 1984 for all federal government capital using the BEA method, our depreciation method, and also, for the sake of comparison, double-declining balance. In aggregate we estimate a net capital stock nearly 20% larger than the BEA's estimate, almost $800 billion of tangible capital compared with their $675 billion in 1984.

Various tables decompose the aggregate numbers into their components by type of capital and nature of its use. The focus is primarily on the distinction between military and nonmilitary capital, and between equipment and structures. Interestingly, the bulk of the difference is in the treatment of nonresidential structures, as our estimates are quite similar to the BEA's for equipment in recent years.

Section 11.5 presents a series of interpretations and implications of our results. We analyze the potential importance of these results for measuring the net national saving rate, national wealth, the trend in government capital formation relative to private capital formation, the relationship of net investment and traditionally measured government deficits, etc. It is evident that for a wide range of issues, improved measures of the government net capital stock, gross investment, depreciation, and net investment can be quite important.

We conclude with some caveats, directions for future research, and the hope that by presenting our estimates, and comparing them to those of the BEA, we shall stimulate further work on this potentially important set of topics.

11.2   Literature Review

The most noted early contributions to the estimation of the capital stock of the government were made by Raymond Goldsmith. As part of his project estimating national wealth for the period 1946–1958, Goldsmith (1962) creates series for the military and civilian capital stock and net investment by type of asset and level of government. The basic methodology was the perpetual inventory method, cumulating gross investment and subtracting estimated depreciation. For military capital, a 1946 benchmark for the stock from Reeve (1950) was used and depreciation was assumed to be geometric for the various components.[1] For federal civilian capital, Goldsmith took gross investment figures dating back to the nineteenth century from his earlier (1955) study and assumed straight-line depreciation over different service lives to obtain a net capital stock series.[2]

Kendrick (1976) also estimated the tangible capital assets of the government, though this was not the primary focus of his study. He also used the perpetual inventory method, with Goldsmith's estimates as benchmarks for the various components. Kendrick used different investment series and depreciation assumptions[3] but does not report separate series for the federal government.

Table 11.1
Comparison of Goldsmith, BEA, and OMB estimates, selected years

| Year | Net federal nonresidential capital stock (billions of current dollars) | |
	Goldsmith	BEA
1946	92.3	108.4
1958	126.0	123.7

| Year | Gross federal nonresidential investment (billions of current dollars) | |
	OMB[a]	BEA
1970	33.2	13.8
1983	88.6	71.3

Sources: BEA (1982, tables A19 and B12), Goldsmith (1962, tables B-150, B-155, and B-172), OMB (1985, table D-2).

a. Fiscal years; investment would be even higher on a calendar-year basis.

The Bureau of Economic Analysis (1982), using improved estimates of current- and constant-dollar gross investment series in revisions of the NIPAs, also developed estimates of government capital using the perpetual inventory method. Gross investment figures for the various components prior to 1929 were taken from Goldsmith, in order to obtain the capital stock in 1925 and to estimate depreciation in later years. The service lives and depreciation assumptions made by the BEA are discussed in detail below. Goldsmith (1982) and Eisner and Pieper (1984) use the BEA estimates of net government fixed capital stock in their studies. A comparison between the net federal non-residential capital stock estimates of Goldsmith (1962) and the BEA is given in table 11.1.

The Office of Management and Budget (OMB) has begun to include estimates of federal investment in the Special Analyses section of the Budget, as required by an act of Congress. These gross investment figures are much larger than those of the BEA, as shown in table 11.1.[4] In addition, the OMB also estimates investment based on a more comprehensive measure, such as including loan programs, research and development, and human capital investment.

These differences demonstrate a fundamental underlying dilemma: defining capital, and therefore estimating gross investment, raises conceptual difficulties. We use the BEA figures though others might prefer a more inclusive series. Further, the federal government finances substantial investment that is owned by others, particularly state and local governments. The BEA treats this as state and local investment and capital, which is fine, but this must be distinguished from budget documents reporting the amount of investment financed by the federal government.

Since we differ from the BEA in our estimates of the depreciation of government capital, a brief review of depreciation theory is in order. The definition preferred by most economists, including ourselves, is that economic depreciation is the decline in the value of an asset through time.[5] In equilibrium, the value of an asset is the discounted value of the services it is expected to provide, net of maintenance and repair plus its expected scrappage value.

Replacement, as defined by Christensen and Jorgenson (1973), is based on productive efficiency rather than economic value. It is the level of investment necessary to maintain the productive efficiency of the capital stock. If an asset provides equal services, net of maintenance and repair, over its life—like a light bulb or one-hoss shay—replacement is zero until retirement, when it is equal to the cost of the asset.

An example may clarify these concepts. Consider a one-hoss shay costing $100 that will become totally obsolete in two years, though its physical life is three years, and suppose the real interest rate is 5%. Since the one-hoss shay must be producing services worth $51.22 each year in order to sell for $100, depreciation is $49.78 in the first year and $51.22 in the second.[6] Replacement is zero in the first year and $100 at the end of the second.

The appropriate definition of the capital stock depends on the use of the measure, as emphasized by Christensen and Jorgenson (1973). For questions of productivity and factor inputs, the appropriate capital stock is cumulative investment less cumulative replacement, since that gives the productive efficiency of the stock at any particular date. For measuring national wealth, the capital stock should be measured as cumulative investment less cumulative economic depreciation, since that gives the remaining market value of capital.

Replacement is equal to depreciation only when productive efficiency declines geometrically as the asset ages.[7] The two measures—value and productive efficiency—of the capital stock are equal in magnitude only when depreciation takes the form of a declining balance.

The BEA, in its estimates of government capital stock, assumes straight-line depreciation over the estimated economic service life of the asset. This would be an accurate measure of economic depreciation if the asset had no decline in productive efficiency as it aged (one-hoss shay) and the discount rate were zero.[8] The one-hoss shay assumption would mean that discards (retirements) measured by the BEA would equal replacement.

The BEA defines the gross capital stock as cumulative investment less discards, while the net stock subtracts depreciation from investment. The BEA gross stock would be, therefore, the relevant measure for productivity calculations under the one-hoss shay assumption. Under the unrealistic additional assumption of a zero real discount rate, the BEA net stock is the correct measure for national wealth calculations.

Hulten and Wykoff (1981) have found that the declining-balance assumption for depreciation, in addition to being more convenient, is a more accurate approximation to the decline in value of some private-sector assets than the straight-line assumption. In the next section, we discuss their methodology and our application of their estimates to develop an alternative measure of the depreciation and replacement of the fixed capital stock of the federal government.

11.3   Methodology

Our new estimates of the net federal capital stock are in the spirit of a used asset price approach. They are based, however, on BEA estimates of gross investment and economic service lives. We begin with a discussion of the treatment of service lives. We then turn to our use of the information obtained by analyzing used asset prices.

The BEA takes two approaches to estimating economic service lives for the federal sector. For some categories, mostly structures, the approach is the same as that used in the private sector. The BEA applies the bell-shaped "Winfrey" distribution to the investment, assigning service lives varying from 45% to 155% of the central value to various fractions of the investment for a given year. A variety of sources is used for the central service lives, including agency data and comparisons with the private sector.[9]

For some categories, including all military equipment and much of nonmilitary equipment, discards can be inferred from accounting records, and so detailed service life estimates are available. These vary across years, and can vary within a single year. For example, the service lives of most types of military equipment are shortened during wartime. Since any variation in service life is captured, a Winfrey distribution is not used. We are able to reproduce military equipment estimates exactly in recent years from detailed service life data kindly provided by John Musgrave.

To adjust for intersectoral transfers and for other possible statistical discrepancies,[10] we added the difference between the BEA's estimate of the net stock of a component and our attempt to reproduce them to our estimates. The discrepancy peaks at $3 billion 1984 dollars in 1965 and drops to about $1.2 billion in 1984. The results described in section 11.4 use the actual BEA estimates, and our figures are adjusted for the discrepancy.

We attempt to use the best available technique for estimating economic depreciation, and apply it to the federal government. Young and Musgrave (1980) argue that the BEA approach may be a good approximation to the economic approach. It is our view, however, that the used asset price approach is preferable, because it attempts to take into account market data. The most well-known and, we believe, thorough attempt to implement the used asset price approach in the private sector is that of Hulten and Wykoff (1981). While not perfect, we feel that the Hulten-Wykoff approach is the best available, and it forms the basis for our estimates of the federal capital stock.

An important facet of the implementation of a used asset price approach is the treatment of assets for which market information is not available. Since we do not attempt to utilize new market information in this study, we review the method of Hulten and Wykoff.

The use of market data to arrive at estimates of economic depreciation involves a number of econometric problems. Two problems that Hulten and Wykoff address directly are those of functional form and the censored sample problem. As mentioned above, the question of the "shape" of the depreciation path is a critical one, which can only be settled empirically. In order to allow their market data sufficient freedom to determine the shape of the depreciation path, they used a Box-Cox transformation, which nests the major functional forms. They found that all of the major forms, such as geometric or one-hoss shay, are rejected by the data. By visual inspection, however, they conclude that for each case the fit is "nearly" geometric and proceed accordingly.

The censored sample problem is an upward bias to used asset values based on observed prices, since only the prices of "survivors" are available. To correct for this bias, the prices are adjusted to take into explicit account the censoring problem by weighing the observed price by the survival probability. These probabilities are based on the BEA estimates of economic service lives and the Winfrey distribution, which were discussed earlier.

There are a number of additional potential problems with the used asset price approach. Some critics of the used asset price approach argue that most used asset markets will be dominated by lemons, biasing the observed price downward. Hulten and Wykoff (1981) defend their approach against the lemons critique by pointing out that the lemons problem arises out of asymmetric information and that in the market for business assets that they study, most of the participants are specialists, minimizing misinformation.

A "shopping mall" problem can introduce a downward bias to depreciation through an upward bias in the prices of structures. If it is difficult to disentangle the value of land from the value of the structures on the land, the value of a structure earmarked for demolition, which may be zero, will be ascribed a positive value. This is true even if a structure of the same vintage on another piece of land still has many years of useful life in it.[11] By ignoring this source of bias, we are implicitly putting great confidence in the ability to separate the value of land from that of structures.

The existence of an investment tax credit can introduce an upward bias to depreciation rates to the extent that new investment goods are treated more favorably than old ones. New goods will sell at a premium, so that prices drop not because of a drop in productive efficiency, but because actual costs to users are in post-tax prices. DeLeeuw (1981) suggests adjusting new asset prices for the tax advantages as a correction.

Yet another concern of Hulten and Wykoff is that as real interest rates and tax regimes vary, the pattern of used asset prices for a good with a fixed pattern of services might vary. They find, however, that for office buildings, time paths of prices do not vary significantly over subsamples, suggesting that a single geometric rate is appropriate, regardless of the prevailing tax regime or real interest rate. DeLeeuw (1981) points out that this is rather more distressing than consoling, since we would expect market participants to take such information into account. One factor in the stability that Hulten and Wykoff find may have been the constancy of real interest rates over their sample. This suggests that their stability result may be sample-specific. On the other hand, since the assets we are concerned with are governmental, tax considerations are unimportant. Lacking a systematic guide for deviating from them, we shall accept Hulten and Wykoff's constant rates, with the caveats here mentioned.

Having concluded that used asset price behavior can be described by a single geometric depreciation rate, Hulten and Wykoff turned to the problem of what geometric depreciation rates are appropriate for assets for which no resale data exists. They find the number R such that the ratio of R to the BEA service life equals the depreciation rates reflected in used asset prices (for the components for which they did not have data) and use the average value of R to find depreciation rates for the other categories. For four categories of equipment, they found an average R of 1.65; for two types of buildings, the average is 0.91.

We have adopted this distillation of the relation between market depreciation and BEA services lives in our calculations rather than attempting to relate the categories for which market depreciation rates exist to various government categories. We have used this approach chiefly because private and government assets may differ in their pattern of service flow, even when private-sector counterparts to government assets appear to exist. This is suggested by the differences in BEA service lives for various assets, depending on whether they are held by the federal government or the private sector, as shown in table 11.2. Rather than attempting to second-guess these comparisons, we have followed the approach of Hulten and Wykoff and accepted the BEA assessments of the appropriate service lives for various items and used these lives to infer depreciation rates. The depreciation rates we use are those consistent with Hulten and Wykoff's approach for their nonmarket data cases, namely, 1.65/BEA service life for equipment and 0.91/BEA service life for structures. The service lives that Hulten and Wykoff use for the private sector are the "central" ones, so that no Winfrey retirement pattern is used. For those assets for which detailed service lives are available, however, we have utilized this detail. This allows our estimates, like those of the BEA, to account properly for the rapid "depreciation" of military equipment in wartime and its aftermath.[12] These problems and approximations suggest that our results should be interpreted with some caution; they are a first step, not definitive.

Table 11.2
Service lives used by the BEA, selected assets

	Private	Federal government
Aircraft	16	12[a]
Ships	22	30[a]
Vehicles	8–10[b]	20[a]
General industrial equipment	14	19
Industrial buildings	27	32
Electric and gas facilities	30	50
Hospitals	48	50

Source: BEA (1982, table B, T-17 to T-19).
a. Service life varies over time.
b. Autos, 10; trucks and buses, 9; tractors, 8.

Table 11.3
Estimates of net federal nonresidential capital stock (billions of 1984 dollars)

	Net stock			Net investment			Gross investment
Year	BEA	BRR	DDB[a]	BEA	BRR	DDB	
1939	101.3	115.5	87.7	5.1	6.0	4.7	9.3
1942	387.3	316.0	248.5	193.4	130.8	104.6	224.9
1945	991.0	794.1	646.9	65.5	58.8	50.4	321.0
1948	469.1	476.8	353.5	−109.3	−61.4	−52.5	14.6
1951	374.1	410.1	302.0	1.6	2.0	4.4	47.0
1954	478.8	503.6	388.5	23.0	20.2	17.1	70.7
1957	485.6	516.8	393.5	−3.9	−0.5	−3.1	41.5
1960	492.7	536.1	404.7	6.1	10.1	7.2	48.1
1963	530.0	581.2	439.2	12.8	14.9	11.2	53.5
1966	556.6	614.7	460.7	8.8	11.6	7.7	51.3
1969	555.9	627.7	462.1	−2.8	2.1	−1.6	41.4
1972	549.4	637.1	461.1	1.8	6.6	3.3	46.0
1975	548.4	649.4	463.8	2.7	6.8	3.8	46.3
1978	565.3	678.3	483.2	10.7	14.3	11.1	55.2
1981	606.5	726.4	520.3	10.2	12.2	8.5	57.4
1984	675.0	795.6	576.1	19.6	19.7	15.2	72.6

a. BEA—BEA estimates using straight-line depreciation. Source: BEA (1982) and updates from BEA. BRR—"Boskin-Robinson-Roberts," using declining balance depreciation rates based on used-asset-prices. Source: Authors' calculations (see text). DDB—double declining balance depreciation. Source: Authors' calculations (see text).

Table 11.4
Total federal nonresidential capital stock (millions of 1984 dollars)

Year	Net stock BEA	Net stock BRR	Net investment BEA	Net investment BRR	Depreciation BEA	Depreciation BRR	Gross investment
1927	68808	73601	−1649	−1128	2812	2290	1163
1928	67296	72726	−1480	−847	2797	2164	1317
1929	66202	72345	−1065	−365	2780	2081	1716
1930	65664	72556	−514	223	2785	2048	2270
1931	66626	74278	960	1711	2801	2050	3761
1932	68974	77407	2318	3083	2854	2089	5173
1933	72581	81790	3585	4345	2936	2177	6521
1934	77511	87449	4904	5619	3119	2405	8023
1935	82730	93480	5199	5999	3307	2507	8506
1936	87540	99144	4792	5621	3509	2680	8301
1937	91410	103906	3855	4736	3699	2818	7554
1938	96108	109489	4667	5530	3930	3067	8597
1939	101270	115514	5109	5959	4240	3390	9350
1940	109619	124144	8236	8510	4959	4685	13195
1941	181951	178360	68550	51874	14493	31170	83044
1942	387342	315959	193391	130756	54512	94175	224931
1943	691098	515901	283953	187834	136833	187008	374842
1944	920686	720145	213537	190450	215139	215253	405704
1945	990996	794120	65541	68837	255431	252134	320972
1946	761813	645098	−212707	−137937	233418	158649	20712
1947	587323	543135	−161276	−94267	173420	106410	12143
1948	469094	476794	−109324	−61449	123935	76060	14611
1949	405267	436142	−59070	−37506	80597	59033	21527
1950	372937	408430	−29698	−25388	53516	49207	23819
1951	374122	410094	1634	1956	45360	45039	46995
1952	416660	448757	40320	36717	47126	50730	87446
1953	454321	482376	35809	32079	48325	52056	84135
1954	478781	503560	23026	20170	47710	50566	70736
1955	485786	511601	6854	7967	47892	46779	54747
1956	489591	517398	3390	5474	47351	45267	50741
1957	485610	516806	−3916	−533	45437	42054	41521
1958	484324	519346	−1244	2547	43671	39881	42428
1959	486291	525555	1977	6108	42637	38506	44614
1960	492667	536112	6053	10095	42054	38012	48107
1961	503821	550518	10652	13836	41400	38216	52052
1962	516503	565690	12013	14496	40857	38374	52870
1963	529976	581163	12824	14856	40707	38676	53532
1964	540833	593825	10295	12182	40969	39081	51264
1965	547555	602821	6713	9010	41646	39348	48359
1966	556565	614668	8809	11612	42496	39693	51305

Table 11.4 (continued)

Year	Net stock BEA	Net stock BRR	Net investment BEA	Net investment BRR	Depreciation BEA	Depreciation BRR	Gross invest-ment
1967	558101	620199	1729	5566	43395	39557	45123
1968	558991	625725	1042	5458	43968	39552	45010
1969	555948	627726	−2754	2053	44183	39376	41429
1970	551723	628862	−3928	1181	44239	39130	40311
1971	547277	630042	−4055	1298	44304	38951	40249
1972	549424	637124	1814	6582	44203	39436	46018
1973	548253	640586	−1125	3379	43887	39384	42763
1974	545763	642525	−2395	1924	43580	39261	41185
1975	548440	649400	2734	6825	43560	39469	46294
1976	551912	657021	3347	7394	43935	39889	47283
1977	554449	663841	2342	6523	44270	40093	46612
1978	565263	678289	10699	14255	44451	40896	55151
1979	581383	697016	15744	18336	45031	42439	60775
1980	595770	713647	13932	16175	46183	43939	60115
1981	606522	726391	10175	12181	47268	45263	57443
1982	628508	749117	20808	21646	48403	47564	69210
1983	654477	775086	24585	24717	51363	51231	75948
1984	674956	795604	19581	19743	53036	52874	72617

The Hulten-Wykoff depreciation rates are consistent with observations of Young and Musgrave (1980) and of Hulten and Wykoff (1981) in summarizing earlier studies: Equipment depreciates faster than straight-line in the early years, and structures depreciate more slowly. These depreciation rates are certainly significant topics for future research. We feel that they are the best depreciation estimates available that are consistent with the spirit of the asset-price approach.

11.4   Results

Our estimates of the net investment and net stock of federal non-residential capital in constant 1984 dollars are reported in tables 11.3 and 11.4, which also include those of the BEA. Appendix table 11A shows the same results in current dollars.

We estimate that the net federal capital stock is at an all-time high of nearly $800 billion after growing steadily since 1950. The broad trends in our estimates are roughly consistent with those of the BEA—with a sharp peak during World War II and growth after

Billions of 1984 $

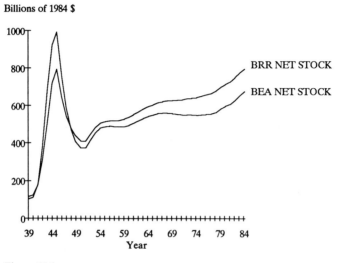

Figure 11.1

Billions of 1984 $

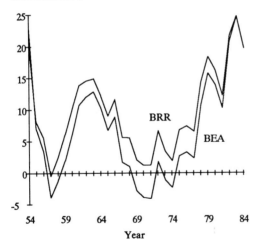

Figure 11.2

1950—which is not surprising given our use of BEA figures for gross investment and service lives. Nevertheless, as shown in figure 11.1, we obtain a strikingly different level and pattern for the net federal capital stock. Whereas our value is more than 17% below that of the BEA at the end of World War II, our estimate is currently 18% higher. The net stock of the federal government in 1984 is above the World War II peak according to our estimates, while the BEA's 1984 figure is still far below its 1945 value.

We also estimated the net federal capital stock using a frequently used alternative to straight-line depreciation, double-declining balance. This series is also shown in table 11.3. The double-declining balance assumption yields a net stock that is always below the estimates of the BEA, by as much as a third in 1945, but 15–20% for most of the postwar period. Clearly, it is not only the form— declining-balance or straight-line—of depreciation that matters, but also the rate.

Since we start with a much lower net stock but end substantially higher, our estimates of net federal non-residential investment are, of course, larger than the BEA's over the postwar period. As shown in figure 11.2, however, the two series track quite closely over the last thirty years. Note that the BEA estimates that net investment was negative in seven years in that period, while, according to our estimates, there was net disinvestment only in 1957.

Disaggregated net capital stock and investment series for military and civilian equipment and structures are presented in 1984 dollars in tables 11.5–11.8. Our estimate of the net stock of structures is always above that of the BEA, as shown in figure 11.3. Straight-line depreciation is always greater than 0.91-declining-balance depreciation. The difference between our aggregate net stock estimates and those of the BEA in recent years is almost completely the result of differences in the stock of structures. This can be seen in figure 11.4, which compares the two estimates of the net stock of equipment. The two series are quite close after 1950. The more rapid early depreciation of 1.65–declining balance relative to a straight line is approximately balanced by its thicker tail. The more rapid early depreciation of equipment during World War II more than outweighs, however, the slower depreciation of structures. Equipment, which had fallen to about 40% of the net stock during the mid-1970s after being two-thirds in 1945, is now about half of the net stock.

Figure 11.5 pictures the division of the aggregate federal capital stock between military and nonmilitary. It is interesting that, until the

Table 11.5
Nonmilitary equipment (millions of 1984 dollars)

Year	Net stock BEA	Net stock BRR	Net investment BEA	Net investment BRR	Depreciation BEA	Depreciation BRR	Gross investment
1927	2176	1942	−289	−131	409	250	119
1928	1940	1852	−234	−87	379	232	145
1929	1852	1877	−87	25	333	221	246
1930	1924	2023	71	142	303	232	374
1931	2132	2257	207	234	280	253	487
1932	2240	2358	108	101	250	257	358
1933	2666	2726	423	365	239	296	662
1934	4028	3942	1353	1208	306	450	1659
1935	4370	4180	340	237	377	480	717
1936	5251	4922	875	737	439	577	1314
1937	6120	5646	864	719	521	666	1385
1938	7220	6578	1093	926	618	786	1711
1939	7329	6545	108	−32	737	878	845
1940	8436	7075	1100	526	1050	1624	2150
1941	13266	10150	4799	3055	2332	4075	7131
1942	34650	23848	21247	13613	7326	−8013	5601
1943	66706	44122	31851	20142	16944	−17291	2851
1944	75852	46046	9088	1911	26078	10282	12194
1945	64396	41154	−11383	−4861	32253	25731	20870
1946	42455	33714	−21800	−7392	25097	10689	3296
1947	31832	28579	−10556	−5102	12141	6687	1585
1948	26428	25245	−5369	−3315	7142	5088	1773
1949	23425	23069	−2984	−2162	4921	4098	1937
1950	21946	22487	−1470	−577	4466	3572	2996
1951	22045	23330	99	838	4119	3379	4218
1952	26246	27584	4174	4227	3705	3653	7879
1953	30999	31698	4723	4087	3313	3949	8036
1954	34123	33977	3104	2265	3062	3901	6166
1955	36980	35984	2839	1994	3046	3891	5885
1956	37466	35806	482	−177	3092	3751	3574
1957	36745	34643	−717	−1158	3120	3561	2403
1958	35910	33573	−829	−1061	3170	3402	2341
1959	35353	32941	−554	−629	3225	3301	2672
1960	36143	33700	786	753	3306	3338	4091
1961	36481	34095	335	393	3391	3333	3726
1962	36890	34557	407	459	3466	3414	3873
1963	38118	35845	1220	1280	3613	3554	4833
1964	39517	37323	1390	1468	3820	3742	5210
1965	42099	39900	2566	2561	4045	4050	6611
1966	45163	42883	3044	2966	4287	4365	7330
1967	46298	44014	1128	1121	4498	4505	5626

Table 11.5 (continued)

Year	Net stock BEA	Net stock BRR	Net investment BEA	Net investment BRR	Depreciation BEA	Depreciation BRR	Gross investment
1968	46686	44439	386	423	4622	4585	5008
1969	46090	43983	−593	−453	4702	4562	4110
1970	45306	43445	−779	−535	4732	4489	3953
1971	44839	43262	−464	−184	4735	4454	4270
1972	42661	41565	−2164	−1684	4746	4266	2582
1973	41450	40939	−1204	−623	4744	4163	3540
1974	39762	39838	−1677	−1093	4762	4179	3085
1975	38455	39313	−1298	−519	4751	3972	3453
1976	36925	38661	−1521	−648	4645	3772	3124
1977	37124	39579	198	910	4457	3744	4654
1978	39729	42643	2589	3044	4420	3965	7009
1979	45479	48453	5713	5773	4553	4493	10266
1980	49881	52649	4374	4169	4739	4944	9113
1981	49333	51981	−544	−664	4868	4987	4323
1982	48642	51167	−687	−809	4872	4994	4185
1983	48811	51107	168	−62	4902	5132	5070
1984	49229	51306	416	198	4971	5189	5387

Table 11.6
Military equipment (millions of 1984 dollars)

Year	Net stock BEA	Net stock BRR	Net investment BEA	Net investment BRR	Depreciation BEA	Depreciation BRR	Gross investment
1927	13284	11698	−768	−849	890	970	122
1928	12529	10969	−740	−714	895	869	155
1929	11811	10365	−704	−592	903	792	199
1930	11204	9937	−595	−419	911	735	316
1931	10732	9697	−463	−238	926	701	463
1932	10212	9449	−510	−241	942	673	432
1933	9718	9258	−484	−189	949	655	466
1934	9282	9145	−427	−111	960	644	533
1935	8720	8926	−551	−212	965	626	414
1936	8055	8630	−652	−292	973	613	321
1937	7445	8403	−598	−220	975	598	378
1938	7453	8773	8	362	1004	649	1012
1939	8348	9958	877	1162	1076	792	1953
1940	9126	10993	763	1014	1182	931	1945
1941	47450	33221	35180	20500	7772	22453	42953
1942	183916	109731	125691	70827	39193	94057	164884

Table 11.6 (continued)

Year	Net stock BEA	Net stock BRR	Net investment BEA	Net investment BRR	Depreciation BEA	Depreciation BRR	Gross investment
1943	430225	261543	227248	140427	109101	195921	336349
1944	644156	453747	198083	178648	177391	196826	375475
1945	725643	527989	76640	69166	211135	218609	287775
1946	526080	389989	−183428	−127069	197060	140701	13632
1947	367693	295696	−145397	−86723	151555	92880	6157
1948	257988	233800	−100945	−57094	108324	64473	7378
1949	197922	194640	−55393	−36071	68028	48706	12635
1950	166228	165448	−29108	−26892	41801	39585	12693
1951	161265	159024	−4420	−6015	33979	35574	29559
1952	188952	181423	25703	20705	35979	40977	61682
1953	212031	199462	21453	16747	37077	41783	58530
1954	226453	209522	13145	9228	36345	40262	49490
1955	226977	209900	445	408	36462	36499	36907
1956	227904	211490	534	1315	35919	35138	36453
1957	222399	207702	−5432	−3685	33876	32130	28444
1958	218965	206049	−3376	−1592	31888	30104	28512
1959	217866	206861	−1063	779	30649	28807	29585
1960	219412	210127	1263	2894	29870	28239	31133
1961	225286	216738	5420	6132	29067	28355	34487
1962	232412	223865	6505	6537	28368	28337	34874
1963	239154	230095	6158	5721	27966	28403	34124
1964	243720	233883	4062	3407	27890	28545	31952
1965	243193	233034	−478	−730	28188	28440	27710
1966	244917	235008	1569	1827	28685	28427	30253
1967	243359	234736	−1367	−189	29230	28053	27864
1968	242511	235699	−700	934	29559	27924	28859
1969	240676	235921	−1587	285	29646	27774	28059
1970	238688	236145	−1757	249	29680	27673	27923
1971	234717	234621	−3617	−1388	29700	27471	26083
1972	238814	240217	3719	5098	29544	28165	33263
1973	238046	240525	−749	246	29223	28228	28474
1974	236679	239997	−1305	−527	28878	28100	27573
1975	239839	243601	3198	3589	28886	28495	32084
1976	244014	248109	4026	4308	29382	29099	33407
1977	244989	249742	784	1388	29892	29291	30676
1978	250880	255921	5808	6067	30082	29823	35890
1979	260295	265017	9056	8763	30498	30791	39554
1980	269126	273469	8398	8053	31354	31699	39752
1981	279040	282657	9342	8673	32191	32859	41533
1982	301151	302785	20920	19070	33571	35421	54491
1983	326761	325783	24230	21787	35711	38155	59942
1984	346363	342797	18709	16281	37744	40171	56453

Table 11.7
Nonmilitary, nonresidential structures (millions of 1984 dollars)

Year	Net stock BEA	Net stock BRR	Net investment BEA	Net investment BRR	Depreciation BEA	Depreciation BRR	Gross investment
1927	19583	23550	250	426	571	395	821
1928	19889	24038	307	487	578	397	885
1929	20392	24731	502	689	600	412	1101
1930	21076	25607	682	872	621	431	1304
1931	22838	27557	1742	1932	641	451	2383
1932	26127	31035	3239	3424	702	517	3941
1933	30338	35441	4173	4365	780	588	4953
1934	34818	40128	4445	4650	877	672	5322
1935	40849	46376	5991	6206	984	769	6975
1936	46142	51922	5252	5498	1110	864	6362
1937	50393	56451	4218	4495	1209	932	5427
1938	54374	60740	3950	4249	1311	1012	5261
1939	58305	64994	3900	4224	1413	1090	5313
1940	63834	70732	5457	5668	1689	1477	7146
1941	79594	85922	15410	14858	3189	3740	18598
1942	109914	115767	29562	29106	6446	6902	36008
1943	119723	127639	9571	11588	8866	6849	18437
1944	122479	133441	2683	5659	9516	6539	12199
1945	120167	134869	−2258	1396	9788	6134	7530
1946	113687	131819	−6302	−2954	8958	5610	2656
1947	109545	129937	−4010	−1802	7405	5197	3395
1948	108076	129770	−1391	−111	6147	4868	4757
1949	109046	131461	1002	1715	5332	4619	6333
1950	111373	134270	2336	2812	4937	4460	7273
1951	116127	139487	4686	5144	4923	4464	9609
1952	123653	147638	7378	8000	5017	4396	12396
1953	130773	155634	6977	7841	5415	4551	12393
1954	136089	162082	5208	6325	5709	4592	10917
1955	136985	164194	896	2089	5715	4522	6611
1956	136904	165258	−54	1076	5582	4452	5528
1957	137235	166827	355	1574	5593	4374	5948
1958	137981	168961	768	2131	5683	4321	6451
1959	139191	171660	1227	2693	5750	4285	6977
1960	141204	175209	2017	3522	5785	4280	7802
1961	144189	179668	2977	4425	5770	4323	8748
1962	147949	184849	3740	5144	5765	4361	9505
1963	152531	190846	4543	5934	5804	4413	10347
1964	157563	197312	4980	6398	5899	4481	10879
1965	162759	204014	5144	6625	6030	4548	11174

Table 11.7 (continued)

Year	Net stock BEA	Net stock BRR	Net investment BEA	Net investment BRR	Depreciation BEA	Depreciation BRR	Gross invest-ment
1966	167994	210807	5189	6724	6126	4591	11315
1967	171174	215587	3166	4739	6247	4674	9413
1968	173514	219601	2328	3977	6359	4709	8686
1969	173866	221669	370	2061	6401	4710	6771
1970	174004	223564	167	1902	6394	4660	6562
1971	175280	226583	1287	3001	6434	4720	7720
1972	176490	229602	1222	3005	6464	4682	7686
1973	178295	233229	1805	3607	6466	4665	8272
1974	180198	236979	1900	3723	6489	4666	8389
1975	182098	240691	1891	3673	6479	4697	8370
1976	183733	244105	1634	3391	6457	4700	8091
1977	186349	248476	2589	4325	6465	4729	9054
1978	189776	253650	3391	5112	6505	4784	9896
1979	192109	257708	2327	4034	6549	4841	8875
1980	194270	261561	2148	3827	6675	4996	8823
1981	197002	266007	2698	4389	6804	5113	9501
1982	198485	269239	1474	3206	6560	4828	8034
1983	199141	271657	644	2390	7364	5618	8008
1984	200068	274363	916	2676	6947	5187	7863

Table 11.8
Military structures (millions of 1984 dollars)

Year	Net stock BEA	Net stock BRR	Net investment BEA	Net investment BRR	Depreciation BEA	Depreciation BRR	Gross invest-ment
1927	33765	36412	−842	−574	942	675	101
1928	32937	35866	−812	−533	945	666	133
1929	32147	35372	−775	−487	945	656	169
1930	31461	34989	−672	−373	949	650	277
1931	30925	34768	−526	−217	954	645	428
1932	30395	34565	−519	−210	961	643	441
1933	29859	34364	−526	−197	968	638	441
1934	29383	34234	−467	−128	977	638	510
1935	28791	33998	−581	−231	981	631	400
1936	28094	33669	−684	−323	988	627	304
1937	27452	33406	−629	−258	993	622	364
1938	27061	33399	−384	−7	997	620	613
1939	27289	34017	224	606	1013	631	1237
1940	28222	35344	915	1301	1038	652	1953
1941	41640	49068	13161	13461	1201	901	14362

Table 11.8 (continued)

	Net stock		Net investment		Depreciation		Gross invest-
Year	BEA	BRR	BEA	BRR	BEA	BRR	ment
1942	58862	66614	16892	17210	1546	1228	18438
1943	74444	82597	15284	15677	1921	1528	17205
1944	78199	86911	3683	4232	2155	1606	5837
1945	80790	90108	2541	3136	2255	1661	4796
1946	79591	89577	−1176	−522	2303	1649	1128
1947	78253	88924	−1313	−640	2319	1647	1006
1948	76602	87979	−1619	−929	2322	1631	702
1949	74874	86972	−1695	−988	2317	1610	622
1950	73390	86226	−1455	−732	2312	1590	858
1951	74685	88252	1269	1988	2340	1622	3609
1952	77810	92112	3065	3785	2425	1704	5490
1953	80517	95582	2656	3404	2521	1773	5176
1954	82117	979979	1569	2351	2594	1812	4163
1955	84843	101524	2674	3477	2669	1866	5343
1956	87317	104844	2427	3259	2758	1926	5185
1957	89232	107633	1878	2736	2848	1990	4726
1958	91468	110763	2194	3070	2930	2054	5124
1959	93882	114093	2367	3266	3012	2113	5380
1960	95908	117076	1988	2925	3092	2155	5080
1961	97865	120016	1919	2887	3172	2205	5092
1962	99252	122418	1361	2356	3257	2262	4618
1963	100173	124377	903	1921	3323	2306	4227
1964	100033	125308	−137	910	3360	2312	3223
1965	99504	125872	−519	554	3383	2310	2864
1966	98492	125970	−993	96	3399	2310	2406
1967	97270	125863	−1199	−105	3420	2326	2221
1968	96279	125986	−972	124	3429	2333	2457
1969	95316	126152	−945	160	3433	2328	2489
1970	93725	125709	−1560	−435	3433	2308	1873
1971	92440	125576	−1260	−130	3436	2306	2175
1972	91459	125739	−963	162	3449	2324	2486
1973	90463	125893	−977	149	3454	2328	2477
1974	89124	125711	−1313	−178	3452	2317	2139
1975	88047	125795	−1057	82	3445	2306	2388
1976	87240	126145	−791	343	3452	2317	2660
1977	85988	126045	−1228	−101	3456	2328	2228
1978	84878	126075	−1089	32	3445	2324	2356
1979	83500	125839	−1352	−233	3431	2312	2079
1980	82492	125968	−988	126	3415	2301	2427
1981	81147	125746	−1320	−217	3406	2303	2086
1982	80230	125926	−899	178	3399	2322	2500
1983	79764	126539	−457	602	3385	2326	2928
1984	79295	127138	−460	588	3374	2326	2914

Billions of 1984 $

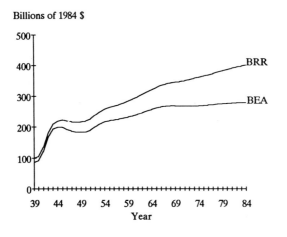

Figure 11.3

Billions of 1984 $

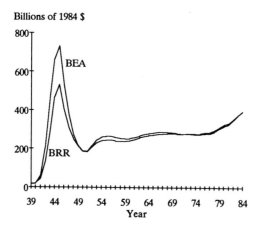

Figure 11.4

Billions of 1984 $

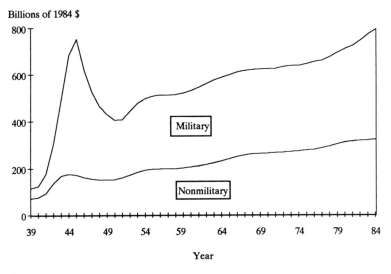

Figure 11.5

1980s, most of the postwar surges in the net stock of military capital have corresponded to similar increases in civilian capital. We estimate military capital comprised 59% of the net federal nonresidential capital stock in 1984.

11.5   Interpretations and Implications

The results reported above amply document an important fact of life in the U.S. economy: the federal government's capital is large and growing, and federal government investment is an important part of national capital formation. While the investment and capital stock series exhibit interesting trends and movements of their own, the facts that the federal capital stock is large and net investment quantitatively important, irrespective of depreciation methods, are the most important findings of this chapter. In order to highlight the importance of improved measures of federal government investment, net capital formation, and depreciation, let us try to put these estimates in perspective.

First, figure 11.6 compares our estimate of federal government net investment with the federal government budget deficit. Obviously, the federal government fiscal deficits currently swamp both gross and net investment. In more normal budgetary times, however, failure to separate capital and current expenditure accounts not only can cause a misstatement of the deficit but in fact can reverse its sign. A cursory

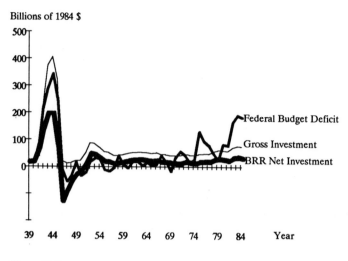

Figure 11.6

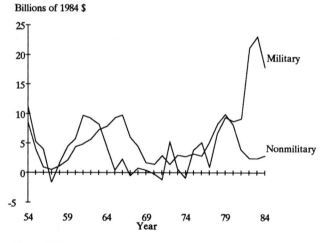

Figure 11.7

examination of figure 11.6 reveals that for the bulk of the postwar period through 1970, with an occasional exception, federal government net investment exceeded the size of the federal government budget deficit, implying that a federal government current expenditures budget would actually have been in surplus. Numerous other adjustments need to be made to make sense of federal government budget deficit figures, such as adjusting for the decline in the real value of the federal government's previously issued debt, and inclusion of a variety of items left out of the official budget figures.[13] Thus, we do not propose merely to subtract federal government net investment expenditures from total outlays in order to arrive at a final current expenditures budget deficit figure, but it is one important component to more comprehensive and accurate budget reporting.

Second, various historical episodes are of interest in the composition of federal government net investment. These are displayed pictorially in figure 11.7. Of particular interest is the substantial rate of military investment in the late 1950s and early 1960s, followed by a reduction in military net investment to virtually zero (with an occasional two- and three-year exception) until the Jimmy Carter and Ronald Reagan years. Beginning in 1977, net military investment increased substantially and really took off in 1981. Nonmilitary investment grew from the late 1950s to a peak in 1966, and then began a substantial decline until a trough at a trivial level from the late 1960s through 1976. Net nonmilitary investment then grew substantially until 1980 but has since declined.

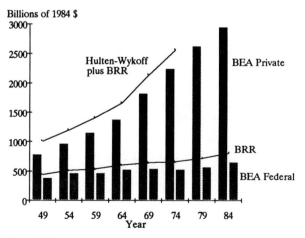

Figure 11.8

Next, consider measures of national wealth. While it is not our purpose here to discuss various measures of the private capital stock, we report in figure 11.8 the BEA estimates of federal and private tangible nonresidential capital, together with our estimates of federal capital along with the Hulten-Wykoff (1981) estimates of private capital through 1974, the last year for which their data are available. Whether one takes the BEA estimates or ours combined with Hulten/Wykoff, it is clear that federal government capital is a substantial fraction, approximately one-quarter, of private tangible capital. If we unified accounts for all levels of government, including state and local governments, which have much larger capital stocks in the aggregate than does the federal government, the government share of total tangible capital in the United States would be substantially larger. Thus, our national wealth is seriously understated if we ignore federal capital, and estimates of the growth of this tangible capital can also be misleading when growth rates differ between government and private capital, as appears to have been the case from a cursory examination of figure 11.8. Note that, by either measure, the federal capital stock has been growing less rapidly than the private. While this trend is noteworthy, we draw no normative conclusions.

A comparison of gross and net federal investment with federal expenditures on goods and services is given in table 11.9. Gross investment has returned to the level of the early 1950s—more than 20% of federal expenditures—after falling below 15% in the late 1960s. It is interesting that the current share is approximately the same as is gross private domestic investment in the private domestic product.

Finally, we note in table 11.10 a comparison of net federal government investment to the traditional NIPA net national saving figures as a share of NNP. On average, from 1951 to 1980, total net national saving averaged between 6% and 7% of NNP. That figure has plummeted in the 1980s, falling below 2% in 1982 and 1983. Thus, in these years when the net investment of the federal government was 0.7% of NNP, the net national saving rate could be underestimated by more than a third by excluding net investment in federal government tangible capital. As mentioned earlier, most of the net federal investment in the 1980s has been military. On average, net federal investment ran about 10% of NIPA net saving. Of course, there are other problems with the NIPA measures of net saving. We prefer to include consumer durables as saving, and the rental flow from them as consumption; and we would also impute services to the tangible

Table 11.9
Federal nonresidential investment as
a percentage of federal expenditures
on goods and services, selected years

Year	Gross	Net
1939	16.9	10.7
1944	50.7	24.3
1949	16.6	−25.2
1954	26.7	7.9
1959	18.3	3.0
1964	19.3	4.8
1969	12.7	0.7
1974	15.9	0.8
1979	22.7	7.1
1984	22.0	6.0

Sources: Federal expenditures on
goods and services, *The National
Income and Product Accounts
1929–1974*, tables 3.2 and 3.7, and
Economic Report of the President, 1985,
tables B-76 and B-3; gross and net
federal nonresidential investment,
table 11.4.

Table 11.10
Contribution of net federal nonresidential investment to net national saving

Year	Percent of NNP		
	NIPA net national saving	Net federal nonresidential investment	Net federal civilian nonresidential investment
1951–1960	7.6	.9	.4
1961–1970	8.2	.4	.3
1971–1980	6.8	.2	.1
1981	5.9	.3	.1
1982	1.8	.7	.1
1983	2.0	.7	.1
1984	4.5	.5	.1

Sources: NNP—*Economic Report of the President, 1985*, tables B–19 and B–3; net
federal nonresidential investment—tables 11.4, 11.5, and 11.7.

capital of state and local governments as consumption, while adding net investment of this sector as part of net saving.

While federal government net investment is a relatively modest share of NNP, it is a substantial share of our very low traditionally measured net national saving rate. It has also been growing during this period of substantial nominal budget deficits on combined current and capital accounts.

Finally, ignoring net federal government investment and tangible capital, failing to impute a service flow to the consumption from the large net capital stock, etc., lead to mismeasurements of net national product, consumption, and net saving and investment. For example, a federal government capital stock of $800 billion would imply a consumption out of that capital stock at current real interest rates of 1% of net national income and therefore a 1.5% understatement of consumption.[14]

It is clear that for a variety of purposes, from properly measuring net national income, consumption, saving, and national wealth to understanding the uses of government funds, improved estimates of government investment, depreciation, and capital stocks are potentially valuable information. We hope in this chapter that we have helped to elevate the discussion of these issues to a position of greater prominence and have begun to provide some very preliminary answers to these important questions.

Appendix

Table 11A
Total federal nonresidential capital stock (millions of current dollars)

	Net stock		Net investment		Depreciation		Gross invest-
Year	BEA	BRR	BEA	BRR	BEA	BRR	ment
1927	7485	7989	−189	−123	322	256	133
1928	7169	7743	−160	−85	311	236	151
1929	6849	7484	−108	−28	305	225	197
1930	6337	6994	−35	42	289	212	254
1931	5670	6298	101	170	265	196	366
1932	5570	6227	165	224	233	174	398
1933	6510	7311	358	418	248	188	606
1934	7480	8393	572	634	299	237	871
1935	8203	9203	605	677	318	246	923
1936	9225	10370	560	638	345	267	905

Table 11A (continued)

Year	Net stock BEA	Net stock BRR	Net investment BEA	Net investment BRR	Depreciation BEA	Depreciation BRR	Gross investment
1937	10040	11319	486	575	394	305	880
1938	10512	11877	564	652	422	334	986
1939	11201	12660	589	678	445	356	1034
1940	12785	14305	917	936	548	529	1465
1941	21261	21241	6968	5391	1550	3128	8519
1942	44659	38076	20874	14487	5789	8784	23272
1943	77154	60166	30621	20668	14486	17929	38597
1944	100898	80914	22669	20222	23007	22229	42450
1945	117239	96129	6764	7307	27896	27353	34660
1946	108411	94801	−26761	−17089	29662	19990	2901
1947	95275	91050	−23207	−13493	25373	15659	2166
1948	83553	86438	−16790	−9465	19519	12194	2729
1949	74437	80549	−9289	−5813	13286	9810	3997
1950	73535	80763	−4709	−3964	9178	8433	4469
1951	79535	87408	902	916	8759	8745	9661
1952	90360	97584	8720	7956	9239	10003	17959
1953	100163	106274	8260	7403	9871	10728	18132
1954	105768	111066	5168	4608	10072	10633	15240
1955	112860	118591	2404	2622	10584	10365	12988
1956	121667	128385	623	1231	11437	10829	12060
1957	123488	131242	−1272	−284	11607	10619	10335
1958	123688	132452	−474	615	11323	10234	10849
1959	124608	134505	524	1661	11213	10075	11737
1960	126438	137408	1569	2662	11118	10025	12687
1961	130844	142775	2917	3776	10970	10111	13887
1962	136151	148916	3207	3889	11054	10372	14261
1963	141589	155137	3611	4165	11282	10728	14893
1964	146389	160815	2792	3342	11382	10833	14174
1965	152034	167637	2176	2827	11797	11145	13972
1966	159832	176875	2831	3612	12320	11539	15151
1967	166588	185521	541	1659	13015	11897	13556
1968	174889	196461	281	1633	13627	12275	13908
1969	183952	208935	−932	652	14362	12778	13430
1970	195511	224460	−1433	387	15272	13453	13839
1971	204563	237741	−1328	681	16124	14115	14796
1972	215251	252846	371	2316	16631	14686	17002
1973	231378	275313	−437	1525	17229	15267	16792
1974	255295	306589	−1170	964	18198	16065	17029
1975	278903	335891	1062	3345	20177	17894	21239
1976	297236	359827	1570	3933	21815	19452	23385
1977	325772	396004	1142	3732	23878	21290	25020

Table 11A (continued)

Year	Net stock BEA	Net stock BRR	Net investment BEA	Net investment BRR	Depreciation BEA	Depreciation BRR	Gross investment
1978	358842	437111	7124	9605	26109	23628	33233
1979	414345	506647	10998	13088	29373	27284	40371
1980	470619	572241	10606	12637	33561	31531	44167
1981	522605	633083	8062	10064	37920	35919	45983
1982	567370	679648	18287	19272	42637	41652	60924
1983	619405	735149	23243	23453	48042	47831	71284
1984	674956	795604	19581	19743	53036	52874	72617

Notes

1. Goldsmith (1962, tables B–169, B–175). Depreciation rates were assumed to be 45% for aircraft, 15% for ships, 22.5% for other equipment, and 7.5% for structures. With these rates, depreciation is several times more rapid in the early years than that assumed by the BEA (see table 11.2).

2. Goldsmith (1962, tables B–158, B–159, B–161). Service lives used were 30 years for highways and streets, 50 years for buildings, 80 years for conservation and development structures, and 12 years for most civilian equipment.

3. See Kendrick (1976, B1–20 to B1–29) for a detailed description of his methodology.

4. Most of the discrepancy arises because the BEA does not include grants-in-aid to state and local governments in investment, except for a fraction of highway and street expenditures. This is only partially offset by OMB's lower estimates for civilian equipment, which are possibly due to OMB's restriction to acquisition of major equipment. In addition, OMB's estimate for military investment in 1970 is more than $10 billion larger than the BEA's. See OMB (1985), particularly table D–2.

5. A competing definition of depreciation is advanced by Young and Musgrave (1980). They state that depreciation as defined by the BEA in both its capital stock estimates and in the NIPA is based on the concept of productive efficiency. "NIPA depreciation" is the cost of the asset allocated over the service life in proportion to the services net of maintenance and repair provided in a given year. Obsolescence is reflected by a one-time charge when the asset is retired prior to the end of its physical life, rather than spread over the economic life of the asset.

There are two important distinctions between economic depreciation (the definition used in the text) and "NIPA depreciation": the use of discounting and the treatment of obsolescence. Under economic depreciation, potential services from an asset after its retirement are irrelevant, since they are worthless. Obsolescence affects the value of the asset over its entire economic life, so there is no need for a special charge. This tends to increase (while the use of discounting reduces) economic depreciation in the early years of asset life relative to the NIPA definition.

6. "NIPA depreciation" is $33.33 in the first year and $66.67 in the second year, since the lost services of the third year are charged off at the end of the second year.

7. See Jorgenson (1973) for a proof of this.

8. If, in addition to the one-hoss shay assumption, the physical service life was equal to the economic service life, the BEA measure would equal "NIPA depreciation." Since "NIPA depreciation" is appropriate for neither production nor valuation measures of the capital stock, we shall not consider it further.

9. For some categories, we were able to reproduce the depreciation and capital stock estimates of the BEA from the gross investment figures. Other categories, though, were slightly overestimated relative to the BEA. John Musgrave of the BEA alerted us to the presence of "intersectoral transfers" that occur when federal buildings are sold to the private sector. Since the categories we reproduce exactly include highways and dams, and those we overestimate include industrial and office buildings, this seems a plausible explanation, and an adjustment, described in the text, was made to our estimates to compensate.

10. We were not able to reproduce BEA's estimates for nonmilitary equipment exactly, possibly because more detailed service life information was needed for these categories also.

11. DeLeeuw (1981) argues that the shopping mall problem introduces an upward bias to depreciation, because still "useful" buildings are counted as having no value. However, obsolete buildings, like obsolete equipment, have no value, net of scrappage.

12. One drawback of any geometric approach is that some of the investment of any year is always present in the capital stock. For some items, this may not be plausible. Following World War II, there was a large overhang of federal capital, mostly in military categories. Much of the stock of federal military structures of 1945, with a service life of 50 years, is still remaining: 48%, comprising 6% of the total 1984 federal nonresidential capital stock. By the BEA's measure, investment from the early 1940s retains less than 20% of its value, contributing only about 1.4% to the 1984 total. The equipment of that era, though, has long ceased to make a significant contribution to the total. Aircraft of that era had service lives as short as 3 years, and these have depreciated to less than one-billionth of their original value. Some equipment, though, has been more long-lived, particularly ships (e.g., the *New Jersey*), so that World War II era equipment constitutes about 0.3% of the total 1984 federal nonresidential capital stock.

13. See Boskin (1982, 1986).

14. Ideally, national product accounts would include an income imputation to all forms of capital not currently counted, including consumer durables and state and local government capital, as well as federal capital. Since we do not present comparable estimates of the stock of state and local capital or consumer durables, we do not attempt to make a partial adjustment here.

Bibliography

Boskin, M. J. (1982), "Federal Government Deficits: Myths and Realities," *American Economic Review*, May, 72:296–303.

Boskin, M. J. (1986), *The Real Federal Budget*, Cambridge, MA: Harvard University Press.

Bureau of Economic Analysis, U.S. Department of Commerce (1982), *Fixed Reproducible Tangible Wealth in the United States, 1925–79* (Washington, D.C.: GPO).

Christensen, L. R., and D. W. Jorgenson (1973), "Measuring Economic Performance in the Private Sector," in M. Moss, ed., *Measurement of Economic and Social Performance* (New York: National Bureau of Economic Research), 233–337.

DeLeeuw, F. (1981), "Discussion," in C. Hulten, ed., *Depreciation, Inflation, and the Taxation of Income from Capital* (Washington, D.C.: Urban Institute), 126–129.

Eisner, R., and P. Pieper (1984), "A New View of Federal Debt and Budget Deficits," *American Economic Review*, March, 74:11–29.

Goldsmith, R. (1955), *A Study of Saving in the United States*, 3 vol. (Princeton: Princeton University Press).

Goldsmith, R. (1962), *The National Wealth of the United States in the Postwar Period* (Princeton: Princeton University Press).

Goldsmith, R. (1982), *The National Balance Sheet of the United States, 1953–1980* (Chicago: University of Chicago Press).

Hulten, C. R. and F. C. Wykoff (1981), "The Measurement of Economic Depreciation," in C. Hulten, ed., *Depreciation, Inflation, and the Taxation of Income from Capital* (Washington, D.C.: Urban Institute), 81–125.

Jorgenson, D. W. (1973), "The Economic Theory of Replacement and Depreciation," in W. Sellekaerts, ed., *Econometrics and Economic Theory* (New York: Macmillan).

Kendrick, J. W. (1976), *The Formation and Stocks of Total Capital* (New York: NBER).

Office of Management and Budget (OMB), Executive Office of the President (1985), "Special Analysis D: Federal Investment and Operating Outlays," in *Special Analyses, Budget of the United States Government, FY1986* (Washington, D.C.: GPO).

Reeve, J. E., et al. (1950), "Government Component in the National Wealth," in *Studies in Income and Wealth*, vol. 12 (New York: NBER).

Taubman, P. (1981), "Discussion," in C. Hulten, ed., *Depreciation, Inflation, and the Taxation of Income from Capital* (Washington, D.C.: Urban Institute), 129–133.

Young, A. H., and J. C. Musgrave (1980), "Estimation of Capital Stock in the United States," in D. Usher, ed., *The Measurement of Capital* (Chicago: University of Chicago Press), 23–82.

12   Technology and Capital Formation

Ralph Landau

During the course of the conference on which this book is based, various discussions took place about capital formation and, at various other times, and sometimes simultaneously, the discussion of technology and its relation thereto. The chapters in this book reflect such concerns. This chapter summarizes such discussions as well as a round-table specifically devoted to this topic. Industrial spokesmen, such as Robert O'Connell, James Baker, and Norman Hochgraf, made it very clear in an earlier presentation that in the industrial sector the technological innovation process (or simply technology) is the driving force for productivity improvement and is very strongly related to capital investment. This leads inevitably to some fundamental questions, such as *what are the factors that contribute to economic growth? And how critical is the capital investment factor in economic growth? Is there a relationship between capital and technology and what is this relationship?*

Michael Boskin[1] has recently summarized these issues and their relation to economic growth as follows:

Policies designed to alter the rate of economic growth directly tend to focus on enhancing technological advances, the quality of the labor force, and the level or rate of growth of capital per worker.... Loosely, the rate of technical change is affected by R&D expenditures, and the rate of improvement of the quality of the labor force is affected by investment in human capital, such as education and training. A policy that can lead to higher levels of income and a temporarily higher growth rate is one that increases the capital-labor ratio (for example, by increasing the rate of investment and net capital formation). But such a policy will lead only temporarily to a higher growth rate, although it will lead permanently to a higher level of income. This is not just semantics. The situation is described in Figure 1 [figure 12.1], in which we see the economy's original growth path (labeled 1), given its presumed (for the moment exogenous) constant rate of technical change. Real per capita income grows at the rate of technical change and labor-quality improvement, given the capital-labor ratio. Now along comes a policy, perhaps tax policy, that increases the desired capital stock of firms (or perhaps more accurately, the

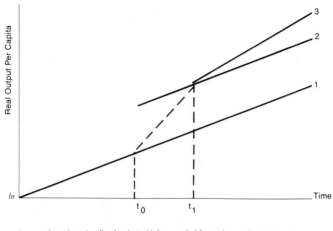

t_0: proinvestment policy leads to higher capital formation and transition to higher level of income.

t_1: economy resumes long-run growth rate or, through interaction of investment and technical change, moves to more rapid growth path.

Figure 12.1

desired wealth of the population, relative to levels of income). This leads to an investment boom for a span of years, which will cause a spurt in the short-run growth rate along the dotted path in Figure 1 until we get to the new long-run growth path (labeled 2). Note that the level of per capita income is permanently higher along (2) than on growth path (1), but that once the transition to the new growth path is complete, the rate of economic growth (given by the slope of the output curve) returns to the original rate given by the underlying factors of the rate of technical change and improvement in labor-force quality. . . .

Boskin also says that, since it is conjectured in the economic literature that the rate of investment affects the rate of technical change in a positive manner (i.e., the rate of technical advance may in fact also depend to a considerable degree on the level of investment and the reverse), it is possible that a change in the capital:labor ratio may lead to at least a longer-term increase in the rate of growth in productivity, which is predominantly due to technical advances. James Brian Quinn[2] shows such a relationship for a number of countries in figure 12.2, based on data from John Kendrick. In this case, we move along Growth Path 3 in figure 12.1.

In the anecdotal versions presented by the industrial speakers at the conference, and certainly from many of the industrial people, it seems

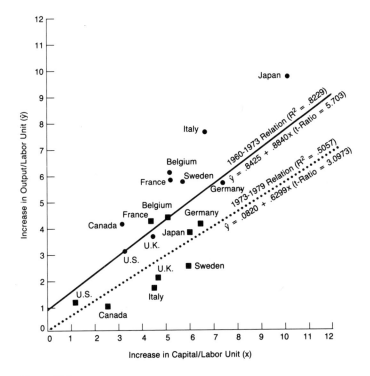

Figure 12.2

that there *is* such an interaction between technology and capital formation. For example, Norman Hochgraf described the situation in the polyethylene industry, where it took a new technological innovation to shut down some old plants and put up new ones. Clearly technological change was an important factor in encouraging both retirement of old capacity and installation of new. In addition, the point made by John Kendrick and others must be considered, namely, that in much of this subject of productivity one does not have a good handle on the matter of quality. From my own experience in the chemical industry, and from those described for the automobile industry and in the General Electric products mix, the changing quality of the products that are made, which are simply measured in units or tons, is a very important factor in assessing the performance of the American economy. It is equally important, but by its absence, in the Soviet economy. In the ultimate analysis, it is the growth of our economy and of that of other countries that are really the important factors in keeping our civilization stable, and here the central issue is technology and its relation to capital formation.

First, let us consider the important findings of Charles Hulten, who spoke at the conference essentially as follows:

I have been studying the interactions of investment and technology for some time now, and have reached the conclusion that the conventional story told by growth accountants is somewhat misleading. In the conventional view, the growth in output is attributed to three independent factors: capital formation, the growth in labor input, and progress in technology. The possibility that technology is carried (or embodied) by capital, so that the rate of investment is a determinant of the rate of productivity change, as discussed by Boskin, is not explicitly taken into account. Neither is the reverse effect: that the rate of a productivity increase is a determinant of the rate of capital formation. My remarks will focus on the implications of this second effort.

In the formal sources of the growth model developed by Solow, Denison, Kendrick, Jorgenson, and Griliches, the growth rate of output is equal to the growth rate of capital times capital share of total income, plus the growth rate of labor times labor share of income, plus the residual output not directly attributable to the growth rate of capital and labor. This last term is termed "total factor" or "multifactor" productivity. It is a surrogate for technical and organizational change.

The growth rate of output per unit of labor ("labor productivity") is measured using a similar procedure. The growth rate of labor productivity is equal to the growth rate of the ratio of capital to labor, weighted by capital's share, plus the growth rate of multifactor productivity.

The sources of U.S. economic growth have been calculated in a number of studies. The Bureau of Labor Statistics has recently initiated an ongoing study of U.S. growth that will be updated annually. The most recent BLS estimates indicate that the output of the U.S. private business sector grew at an average annual rate of 3.2% over the period 1948–1985. Capital, weighted by its income share, grew at an average annual rate of 1.2% over this period, and the share-weighted growth rate of labor input was 0.6%. The growth rate of multifactor productivity was thus 1.4% per year. Taken at face value, these numbers suggest that multi-factor productivity accounted for 43% of the growth in output over the period 1948–1985. This inferential leap, however, is not correct, even though the BLS numbers are accurate. The problem lies with the feedback effect between multifactor productivity and capital formation. When this feedback effect is taken into account, as in some of my earlier work,[3] multifactor productivity is found to account for almost *all* of the growth in output (or, put differently, multifactor productivity accounts for almost all of the growth rate of labor productivity). Capital accumulation is found to have almost no independent role in determining economic growth.

The intuition behind this remarkable result is provided by Figure 3 [figure 12.3]. Let us assume that there is a production function that relates capital per unit labor to output per unit labor. And let us assume that the economy is at some point A where labor force "growth" is static and investment is just enough to keep the capital stock intact (i.e., that the economy stays at A period after period). Suppose that a new technology is introduced that causes the production function to shift. The multifactor productivity residual will now show a positive growth rate, as measured by BLS and others.

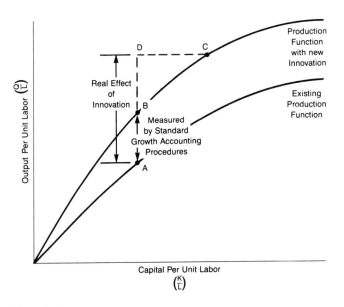

Figure 12.3

Under the standard growth accounting story, we would measure the importance of multifactor productivity as a source of economic growth by the shift in the production function A to B. But we should also notice that this shift results in additional output per person and that the additional output will result in extra savings (except in the unlikely event that the marginal propensity to save is zero). The extra saving will result in more capital per worker, so the economy moves along the production function. This extra capital generates still more saving and capital, which generates still more output, etc. The economy will come to rest at some point C at which depreciation of the larger capital stock just equals the additional saving.

The contribution of the initial shift in the production function is therefore *not* the distance A to B; it is *really* the vertical distance between A and C (the segment AD in Figure 3). That is, *all* of the economic growth that occurs as the economy moves from A to C is due to technical change, qua shift in the production function. The conventional growth accounting story, on the other hand, would erroneously say that BD/AD percent of the total change in output per worker is due to capital, and AB/AD is due to technical change.*

The primacy of technical progress in the process of economic growth may strike some as counterintuitive. If this is so, one should ask, what is the main reason that per capital output in eighteenth-century America was lower than

---

* It should be emphasized, however, that the conventional growth accounting story does provide conceptually correct estimates of the *magnitude* of the shift AB. My quarrel is with the interpretation of this shift as an indicator of the importance of technical change.

the per capital output of modern America? Is it because modern Americans save more? Work harder? Make more efficient use of resources? No, it is clearly the difference in technical knowledge that explains the difference. The other factors are "endogenous" to the growth process in the long run. In the long run, technical change permits more capital formation. Technology working through the mechanism I have described is a far more important motive force in growth than is commonly believed.

Putting the above discussion into more mathematical terms, the basic growh equation can be written

$$G_Q = G_T + s_K G_K + s_L G_L,$$

where G_Q = the growth rate of output, G_K = the growth rate of capital input, G_L = the growth rate of labor input, G_T = the rate of productivity growth, s_K = the share of capital, and s_L = the share of labor. In the national income accounts, of course, output is allocated among labor and capital as the two essential resources, weighted according to price. Therefore, the shares of the two primary factors of production, capital and labor, must add to one, so that the share of capital s_K is one minus the share of labor s_L.

A sustainable growth path is one in which all growth rates are constant. We take the rate of productivity growth G_T and the rate of growth of labor input G_L to be given exogenously and as required for sustainable growth; we assume that the growth rates of output G_Q and capital input G_K are *constant*. The following will demonstrate that these two rates must be the same:

The definition of the share of capital s_K is the following:

$$s_K = \frac{P_k K}{P_Q Q},$$

where P_K and P_Q are the prices of capital and output, respectively, and K and Q are the corresponding quantities. We take the price ratio P_K/P_Q to be given exogenously.

Now suppose we consider a sustainable growth path with $G_K > G_Q$. Then $s_K \cdot G_K$ will grow indefinitely, eventually reducing the share of labor s_L to a negative number, which is absurd. Similarly, a path with $G_K < G_Q$ must eventually raise the share of labor to a number greater than one, which is equally absurd. We conclude that $G_K = G_Q$, which is the only remaining possibility.

Accordingly, we can rewrite the equation for a sustainable path by substituting G_Q for G_K, and $1-s_K$ for s_L in the basic growth equation, yielding

$$G_Q = \frac{1}{1-s_K} G_T + G_L.$$

Since the best findings to date indicate that the share of capital S_K is about 0.4, this version of the growth equation reduces to

$$G_Q = 1.67 G_T + G_L.$$

It gives much greater weight to the rate of productivity growth G_T than has previously been recognized. Either form of the growth equation has the implication that a permanent increase in the growth rate requires an increase in G_T. The growth rate of labor G_L is comprised of two components—the growth of hours worked and the increase in labor quality. An increase in labor quality requires more investment in human capital per worker. For any given proportion of the national product devoted to investment in human capital, labor quality will reach an upper limit. Something like this has actually occurred in the United States in recent years.

A second implication of this framework is that an increase in the proportion of the national product devoted to investment in nonhuman capital can increase the growth rate in the short and intermediate runs. This is the story behind Japanese economic growth in the 1960s and early 1970s.[4] However, the capital formation proportion has an upper bound, so that the increase in the growth rate cannot continue in the long run. This is an important component of the explanation of the dramatic slowdown in Japanese economic growth after 1973.

The conclusion from this line of reasoning is that productivity growth is the central focus for long-term growth policy. This is the key to a positive-sum strategy. The problem is that the microeconomics of innovation, diffusion, and technical change are poorly and incompletely understood. A more complete understanding will require the combined efforts of economists, technologists, and scientists. Some of these participated in the conference upon which this book is based, and a similar effort was made at the Stanford Conference, which produced "The Positive Sum Strategy: Harnessing Technology for Economic Growth." (See note 1.)

A recent review in the *Journal of Economic Literature*[5] refers to the work by Brunner in confirming Hulten's ideas. These are the key sections:

Lawrence Brunner seeks to reexamine Hulten's (1975) thesis that traditional methods of growth accounting underestimate the contribution of technologial change by ignoring its feedback effect on the growth of capital. In this book, developed out of a Ph.D. dissertation, the author uses a general equilibrium model with six sectors of the economy, three types of labor, two types of capital and explicit consideration of intermediate goods. A modified version of the Scarf algorithm is used to simulate alternative growth paths of the U.S. economy from 1947 to 1974 under various assumptions about productivity growth. The author shows ingenuity in using a methodology developed to study the welfare implications of tax changes to gain insight into the distributional effects of technological change.

Hulten's argument can be easily summarized for the Hicks-neutral case. Suppose the economy is in a steady-state where gross investment just equals the depreciation of existing capital. Assume now that the production function makes a once and for all shift upward due to Hicks-neutral technical change. Output increases at a given level of capital, generating higher savings (investment), and the capital stock grows (since investment now exceeds the depreciation of existing capital). This in turn generates higher output and investment. The process continues until the depreciation of the higher stock of capital equals the new investment level. Hulten's point is that the traditional Solow index measures the proportionate increase in the height of the production function at the new equilibrium level of capital but ignores the growth in output from a movement along the production function, due to the increased capital created by the process described above.

Boskin's diagram and conjectures now fit into this picture more clearly. The interrelationship of capital and technology and the two combined are the central causes of long-term economic growth, and the policy implications need to be very carefully drawn.

At the same time, it must be recognized that many economists and policymakers do not recognize these issues, and it has been difficult to find quantitative confirmation of the feedback effects and endogeneities discussed herein. Economists still prefer hard data to anecdotal accounts, but slowly more such data are appearing. An excellent confirmation of the embodiment conjecture was recently published by the National Bureau of Economic Research, based on extensive and rich data from the Bell Telephone system.[6] One of the economists from the AT&T Bell Laboratories, Kenneth Laitinen, also participated in the panel discussion, and gave a micro view of the real complexities of the factors brought about by technical change. Essentially, he said:

The way I'm going to approach this is to worm my way in from the bottom instead of talking about whole plants. I am not going to talk about AT&T now; I'm going to talk about the old Bell System, no longer with us. You've had experience with this actually, so you know that the basic accounting system that the telephone companies have been landed with for one reason or another has about half a dozen major categories. Land and buildings are perhaps the smallest and least interesting of those. There are four types of technical equipment: switching equipment—material that sits in central offices and is used to move calls around; interoffice transmission, which is essentially getting calls from one central office to another; local distribution type plant, which is the equipment that takes it from your house to the central office; and something that really isn't there anymore but used to be, which is terminal equipment, the telephone instrument itself and a group of related items of business content. There's also a not historically terribly large but growing area, which is "other" or miscellaneous, that has several components. One of those is vehicles, which is all the telephone repair trucks, and the other one is computers, billing equipment and equipment that keeps track of calls, and so on. All of those categories have very different types of material in them. They are very complex, meaning that there are at a minimum hundreds of different types and quantities of items that go into each one of these categories. What I would like to do is focus on one of those: switching equipment. It has the advantage of being the simplest of the categories in all probability, with the exception of land and buildings. Now there is an interesting technology question in connection with switching equipment. In the last century there have been roughly six generations of technology change, going back to manual equipment, which was put in largely in the nineteenth century. That was the "hello central" type, that is, the operator pushing the tape, plugging the boards, etc. Panel equipment, step-by-step equipment, cross bar equipment—these are three more that came in successively, and those are all sort of electromechanical in one form or another, meaning that they involve relays and similar items. They're clumsy, big, hard to operate, and so on. Then more recently there have been two versions of electronic switches that have come into existence. One of them is analog electronic, the other is digital electronic. The major difference among these has to do with the question of whether the poles that are being switched are in analog form, which is the type that you see on the radio generally, or whether they've been digitized. To get into that detail I would have to start discussing the transmission side of things and that's a great deal more complicated. What may not be obvious, and I think is not obvious to most economists, is the fact that each one of the seven operating companies that was recently divested from AT&T has at least five of those technologies *still in place.* That is to say, although now all manual equipment is gone, it wasn't very long ago, however, that it wasn't. It was as recently as the seventies that there was still money being spent in the capital accounts for that kind of equipment, with a technology that is roughly a century old. The other five categories include items that go back to the early twenties in terms of when they were introduced; money is still being spent on them, capital is still being invested. The reason for that is because these essential offices exist and they have specific equipment in them. In particular, there are central offices where they are still using panel equipment or step-by-step equipment. You don't just throw that away, not in general. What you do, is do a little bit of replacement with incremental things in place, very much like the kind of thing that takes place in process plants like aluminum. And that process goes on. So the result is that, say in 1980, any one of the operating companies was in fact investing money simultaneously in five of these technologies, including technologies which were way out of date. There are a couple of other connections associated with that. The reasons for these new technologies by and large have been because of labor savings that they offered. The obvious advantage of getting away from manual equipment is that you've got operators that are actually making connections manually, so you automate that. You can automate it more and more efficiently as you go through these technologies. And, in fact, if you sit down and look at statistics about the Bell System from say 1950–1980 which is where I've seen it, for example, employment went up from on the order of perhaps a factor of two to on the order of maybe a factor of eight or ten. Those are very rough numbers and I won't be held accountable for them. But it's the right relationship roughly. Now more recently there's been something a little more interesting going on, and that probably has been going on for a while, actually. That's the fact that most of the original labor saving was in people like operators. More recently, systems hooking up the outside line to your house to the switch have been automated more and more. That is more of a flexibility kind of installation; it may or may not eliminate labor. Recently, though, one of the interesting things about the electronic switching is that it eliminates an enormous amount of maintenance. Roughly, this is strictly, I have to add, anecdotal because I don't and have not been able to verify this, but the stories that I hear are for cross bar equipment that is the last and best version of the electromechanical stuff. Basically, they needed something like twelve people, full-time, to keep one of those switches up and running, whereas they need a half-person to keep an electronics switch of the same general nature up and running. Now it's not clear for a lot of reasons that they are actually saving that labor; what they're really doing is redeploying it, and the reason for that is the fact that these workers who maintain the switches are heavily trained; there's a lot of investment in human capital that goes into these people. The anecdotal word is that it takes two to three years on the job before people are really productive enough to be terribly useful in those jobs. Therefore there is no great desire to do some things like pull the plug on the labor force. All that you're really doing is throwing a different kind of capital down the drain. Actually, that leads to an interesting question, which I'm not sure I fully understand, namely, the fact that capital goods aren't used in isolation—they really are used as part of a production process. Now this is obvious to all of you I'm sure. It's not so obvious maybe that the types of labor that are combined with it may be of several kinds. There are people like the operator type of labor input, which is really directed toward a direct production of the services we've got. There are also the sort of co-use types of things where you've got to have a certain amount of labor to do the maintenance to keep the switch running. And that one seems to be a little bit different, but I'm not quite sure how it's different. I suspect that it's got something to do with a couple of other things that have been touched on here that have to do with, for example, questions like depreciation rates. I have never been terribly happy with the geometric declining method of dealing with depreciation. It may work very well in aggregated situations, but it clearly doesn't work well when you're talking about very disaggregated capital. At times, capital just dies—the one-horse shay model. There comes a time when you retire it or throw it away; junk it. The fact of the matter is that most of this equipment, until the point when it actually dies, is just as good as it was before. What makes it die, eventually, is the fact that it costs too much to maintain. It's too expensive to keep in place. And, therefore, this whole question of depreciation rates, maintenance, and so on fits together in some fashion or other. I don't think that anyone in the profession really understands it very well at this point.

Laitinen has illuminated one of the essential problems of growth accounting—that technological obsolescence may be brought about by various causes, such as excessive maintenance, as well as by superior economics or efficiencies in other ways, and that the assumptions economists have often made in the past about economic depreciations fail to take adequately into account the destructive side of technology. Jorgenson deals with depreciation and obsolescence in his chapter, entitled "Capital as a Factor of Production." Schumpeter called it creative destruction, but it is difficult to measure it, in view of the many different actual cases, and therefore the interaction of technical change and capital formation is likewise complex. And what about quality and variety of the product offered? How about the effect on human capital that Laitinen identifies?

Another micro view of the real world came from Robert Hornbeck, speaking about Alcoa's experience in aluminum essentially as follows:

It has been my observation that certain technologies and training must be developed and applied if we are to retain semi-manufacturing and possibly the manufacturing industry in the United States. The funds must be made available to make that effort possible. It is also my observation that there comes a time when an industry or a company will run a factory and its people to destruction and move out because it cannot compete in the new worldwide marketplace.

The U.S. mineral base process industry is in that position and is in its final throes.

Let me describe by a few examples why I make that observation and how we, Alcoa, view technology and capital.

First, let me provide you with some financial, capital and noncapital, expense information for reference. Alcoa sales are approximately $6 billion per year with assets of $6 billion. Our repair and maintenance "expense" on our facilities is $450 million per year. We spend an additional $350 million per year in "capital" dollars on capital projects designed to sustain the businesses and keep them competitive. These businesses vie for an additional $150 million in capital for modernization, advanced technology, manufacturing automation systems, designed to improve the businesses so they can be "number one" in our product line. We also spend $125 million in research and development to support these businesses, and we do R&D in engineered materials manufacturing. That is the capital and facilities expense data base we are working with.

I'll give you five examples or anecdotes that range from "history" (life is over) to the "future" (world-class facilities) with reference to the relationships of capital and technology.

1. Let's look at a 1940 vintage bauxite refinery. The replacement cost of this facility was estimated at $300–500 million. After a number of years of capital starvation, it was apparent that we either had to abandon the facility or provide fresh capital input. We refurbished the facility with one $80 million "infusion" to regain its former effectiveness, including substantial cost improvements, but without technology improvements. The worldwide aluminum market has deteriorated, the location and the raw material supply were not economic, and the expenditure was inappropriate. Life was over. It's shut down; it's torn down.

2. We have another refinery, also a bauxite refinery, making white powder, a 1972 vintage, with the same replacement cost of $300–500 million. It was sustained at a capital input equivalent to depreciation or a portion of that $350 million I mentioned above. Coupling research from the laboratories, operational technical improvements at the facilities, plus one additional year's sustaining capital spent over two years, we were able to increase capacities 80%, decrease energy consumption 25%, reduce the cost of the product 30%, and improve the quality of the products.

Essentially, technology, some capital, and people created an effective operation. We're still alive.

3. The primary aluminum business is a major segment of our company with $1 billion of the company's $6 billion in assets. The management has operated for years on a philosophy of continual technological and capital input, which was 10–20% over sustaining capital dollars—or, in this case, 10–20% over depreciation. The continual modernization for the most part is in technology that we developed on-site, bringing most of our smelters to better computer control of the existing process and increasing the size of pots and anodes. It was an evolutionary process of "line-balancing" or what we called "debottlenecking," maximizing throughput and minimizing crewing. It worked marvelously well for a while, but the existing technology is approaching its thermodynamic limits. This means that there is nothing technically in this process that will make a significant economic difference. Energy and material cost have become the dominant cost factors. U.S. primary aluminum production is contracting and will continue to contract because of increasing Third World and developing countries' government participation and U.S. noncompetitive energy rates, plus the technical problem mentioned above. We are "still alive" and can compete in metal production where we own the power facilities and can keep our energy costs under control. Technology probably won't save the U.S. primary aluminum business from "intrusion" by offshore metal.

4. One of our large aluminum scrap-processing and ingot-manufacturing facilities is another example of technology and capital as quality components. The melting, processing, casting, and handling equipment has a value of more than $100 million and requires a minimum sustaining capital of $10 million per year. A complete modernization program was put into place utilizing the

latest technology developed inside and outside of the company. The modernization is scheduled in phases over 6–8 years and will cost slightly less than the current sustaining (maintenance) capital mentioned above. The technology and systems utilized allow a complete modernization of the process on-site. Our emphasis is on customized ingot integrated from order entry to the customer's dock with significantly lower costs, superior quality, and flexible manufacturing.

5. Let me take one more example. We have an extensive modernization program underway in our flat rolled/packaging products division. This is where the bulk of the company is, the aluminum products portion of the company. Pick a number—it's a $3 billion business. The business is characterized as changing; it is highly competitive, dimensional dynamic, quality critical, price-cost demanding, and supply-oriented. We are spending over $500 million to implement change. In this case, the capital required is more than twice the sustaining capital value and a major part of the machinery and technology was purchased offshore and coupled with our process and information systems technology to capture the step beyond the "state-of-the-art." The success of the project hinges not only on continuing input of technology in a fast-changing but fruitful arena and all the usual commercial factors, but, additionally, on the tax situation which is critical in our capital intensive industry. This example is not a "history"—this is the "future."

Let me say in conclusion that to be successful in the United States in the manufacturing market sector I'm talking about will require a large input of technology and training and must be largely paid for by lower inventories, higher productivity, high throughput, better quality, and better service. The technology and training I refer to is that characterized by many buzzwords, but it involves integrated systems, sensors, models, software, hardware, flexible manufacturing, computer-integrated manufacturing, and more. There has to be a level of profitability to support that activity, and it's going to be in the hands of private enterprise with appropriate government support, not the least of which is an internationally competitive system of tax incentives for these capital intensive, basic industries. I also believe we may be launched on the next big wave of the industrial revolution, avoiding the demise of basic manufacturing.

Hornbeck's examples from a technologically aware heavy manufacturing company illustrate the complexity of the interrelationships between technology and capital formation. He brings out the point that gross investment that includes depreciation often fails to recognize that the depreciation or maintenance capital carries a large component of new technology, in addition to the net capital additions that are almost always related to new technology. He also refers to the "one-horse shay" depreciation, in which life is suddenly over for an investment in place, even if its economic depreciation has still not been used up. In short, he too illustrates a basic aspect of the subject matter of this book: *Capital and technology must be viewed as interchangeable complements, not as separate discrete components of growth.*

Policies that aid one must necessarily be accompanied by policies that favor the other.

Finally, the panel discussion was concluded by Dale Jorgenson, who put the whole subject of accounting for growth into perspective. Here is a summary of his remarks:

I would like to begin with a few observations to the technologists. One thing that inevitably results from a discussion of the topics we have reviewed is the feeling that economists cannot agree. I would like to try to explain, at least from my perspective, one reason why you find so many different points of view on technology and capital formation.

In economics as well as in other fields of study there are differences in emphasis at different points of time. For the last 15 years or so the most important macroeconomic phenomenon has been the slowdown that has characterized growth in the United States and in other countries. However, most of the people who do "macroeconomics" have been focusing on inflation and unemployment. The last time that macroeconomists paid attention to economic growth was around 1960. As a consequence, we have difficulty in dealing with various vintages of information.

The initial insight that led to the development of the theory of economic growth was the idea that savings and investment had to be brought into balance. The simplest way to do this was within a framework in which the capital-output ratio was fixed and in which the saving ratio was a constant. These ideas were developed by Harrod and Domar in the late 1930s and 1940s and became the subject of a great deal of discussion.

In the middle 1950s a very radical shift occurred. This led to a neoclassical paradigm, which is based on a completely different idea. This is the idea that Hulten has put before you here, based on the aggregate production function. The production function was combined with a constant saving ratio. In the aggregate production function shifts result from changes in technology. Associated with these shifts there are changes in the capital-labor ratio that are the consequences of saving.

From the Harrod/Domar point of view the growth rate was simply the ratio of the saving rate to the capital-output ratio. Therefore, the growth rate is proportional to the saving rate. By contrast, in the story that Hulten has outlined for us, the growth rate of the economy, at least in the long run, is completely independent of the saving rate. Growth depends, as Hulten says, only on the rate of productivity growth.

The initial studies of the movement from A to B in Figure 1 [figure 12.1] by Solow and by Denison and Kendrick led to a conclusion that is still widely quoted. This is that productivity growth is the most prominent source of economic growth, accounting for 80% or 90% of growth. All the other factors, including capital accumulation, are relatively unimportant. That was how things stood as of roughly 1960.

All economists were exposed to the views developed by Solow and others and the profession moved on to other things. Much of the research that we have been discussing here has not reached anywhere near the visibility within

Table 12.1
Growth in aggregate output and its sources, 1948–1979

Variable	Average annual rates of growth							
	1948– 1979	1948– 1953	1953– 1957	1957– 1960	1960– 1966	1966– 1969	1969– 1973	1973– 1979
Value added	.0364	.0511	.0309	.0277	.0449	.0323	.0324	.0310
Contribution of capital input	.0153	.0187	.0153	.0105	.0144	.0190	.0156	.0144
Contribution of labor input	.0113	.0204	.0036	.0078	.0142	.0130	.0090	.0101
Rate of techno-logical change	.0097	.0120	.0120	.0093	.0163	.0003	.0078	.0064

the economics profession that this early work did. The subject that we are here to discuss has become an intellectual backwater.

Even knowledgeable economists continue to quote the findings I have mentioned, based on information that was current as of 1959 or 1960, or even as early as 1957. This is not paradoxical, but reflects different vintages of learning. Until the subject of growth again occupies a prominent place in professional discussions—and I don't think that it is yet on the horizon—we can anticipate that there will continue to be an echo that reflects this earlier understanding.

I would like to give you some idea as to how misleading it can be if you listen to the echo and not to the current signal from the research that we are discussing. First of all, focus on Table 1[7] [table 12.1] and look in the first column there, 1948–1979. This describes the movement from A to B in Figure 1. This deals with the allocation of the total growth picture among the various growth sources.

You can see that the growth rate of the economy from 1948 to 1979 was about 3.4% per year. That does not differ from numbers that other people produce, including BLS, BEA, and so on. If you look at the allocation, however, among the different sources, what you find is that capital accounts for 1.56% of the growth rate, labor for 1.05%, and productivity for .81%.

By contrast with the picture held over from 1960 that productivity accounts for most of economic growth, productivity accounts for only 23.7% of the total, capital in this reckoning accounts for 45.6%, and labor accounts for 30.7%.

I would like you to turn to the last column for the period 1973–1979. This has been the subject of discussion at conferences that have dealt with the slowdown. There has been a slowdown that certainly goes back as far as 1966. Focusing on 1973–1979, the growth rate of the economy has been 2.83%. The contribution of capital input is hanging in there at 1.44%. The contribution of labor is about 1.05%. The slowdown is accounted for, at least 80% of it, by the decline in the rate of productivity growth to .34%.

Productivity during the last period of this study, 1973–1979, accounts for 12% of the growth of output, labor 37.1%, and capital 50.9%. If there is an explanation for the slowdown, it is surely in terms of productivity growth. If we simply look at the difference between 1973–1979 on the one hand, and the average of the postwar period 1948–1979 on the other, we see that there has been a slowdown as I said of approximately .6% in the growth rate. Of that capital accounts for 20% and the slowdown of productivity accounts for 80%. So in a way that is an indirect line of support for the basic tack that Hulten took in his remarks, which is that technology is extremely important, that it is the predominant explanation of the slowdown and really has to be the main focus of any attempt to think about what to do next.

I have described the point of view that prevailed in 1960 and I have, perhaps, caricatured it slightly. I would like to make a few remarks about how we got from there to here. In other words, what happened in the intervening period that led us to these conclusions? If you refer to Table 2 [table 12.2], I would like to draw a few additional facts to your attention.

First of all, the contribution of labor can be divided between two parts, the growth of hours and the growth of labor quality. Think of quality as the upgrading of the labor force. This is an important contribution to economic growth, as you can see. For the postwar period as a whole it accounts for about a third, or maybe a little bit more, of the growth of labor input.

A measure of labor input based on hours worked ignores the contribution of labor quality. An unweighted hours measure fails to reflect the relative productivity of different parts of the labor force. If you would like to learn more about this, my version of the story is in a paper with Frank Gollop[8] and is published in a volume edited by Jack Triplett from the University of Chicago Press.

I would like to focus my remaining remarks on the contribution of capital. That is also broken down into two parts, the contribution of capital quality and the contribution of capital stock. During the slowdown the contribution of capital quality has tailed off a little bit. It has declined from about .4% a year to about .3%. By contrast the contribution of capital stock is essentially unchanged. In terms of the postwar averages, there was no slowdown in capital formation at all. There was only a slight tailing off in the contribution of capital quality.

I would like to focus on the role of capital. It is important to think about how these numbers compare with the ones that were conventional back in 1960, the last time that most economists were focusing on these issues. First, there is a question of how to measure the input of capital. There has been a very, very modest infusion of the methodology of hedonic indexes. I think that hedonic methods provide a promising methodology for solving the key problem of heterogeneity in the technologies that are being applied.

It is not as if computers had recently arrived on the scene. They have been around for a while, and they have not been accounted for in a satisfactory way. The same problems arise for structures and other kinds of equipment. We are now on the horizon of opportunities to make major improvements in our prices of capital.

However, improvements in the price deflators of capital will result in an increase in the measured growth of output as well as the measured growth of

Table 12.2
Aggregate output, inputs, and productivity: rates of growth, 1948–1979

Variable	Average annual rates of growth							
	1948– 1979	1948– 1953	1953– 1957	1957– 1960	1960– 1966	1966– 1969	1969– 1973	1973– 1979
Value added	.0364	.0511	.0309	.0277	.0449	.0323	.0324	.0310
Capital input	.0397	.0492	.0389	.0269	.0366	.0488	.0414	.0378
Labor input	.0186	.0329	.0061	.0130	.0235	.0213	.0146	.0166
Contribution of capital input	.0153	.0187	.0153	.0105	.0144	.0190	.0156	.0144
Contribution of labor input	.0113	.0204	.0036	.0078	.0142	.0130	.0090	.0101
Rate of techno-logical change	.0097	.0120	.0120	.0093	.0163	.0003	.0078	.0064
Contribution of capital quality	.0040	.0069	.0042	.0016	.0050	.0039	.0028	.0028
Contribution of capital stock	.0114	.0118	.0112	.0089	.0095	.0151	.0128	.0116
Contribution of labor quality	.0038	.0081	.0036	.0082	.0040	.0030	.0013	.0006
Contribution of hours worked	.0076	.0122	−.0000	−.0004	.0102	.0100	.0077	.0095
Rates of sectoral technological change	.0091	.0200	.0161	.0124	.0169	.0017	.0050	−.0061
Reallocation of value added	−.0005	−.0090	−.0047	−.0022	−.0024	−.0025	.0020	.0101
Reallocation of capital input	.0011	−.0000	.0020	.0015	.0019	.0013	.0012	.0001
Reallocation of labor input	.0001	.0009	−.0014	−.0024	−.0001	−.0001	−.0004	.0024

capital input. The investment goods will be counted, and the contribution to capital stock that is contributed by those investment goods will be counted. Roughly speaking, those balance out. After we have done all the appropriate accounting, we may arrive at a higher growth rate of output, but we shall probably find that the allocation of growth among the various sources is very similar.

It is very worthwhile to improve the investment goods price deflators. As you go from the aggregate level to the industry level and from the industry level to the firm level, heterogeneities in capital goods become more and more significant. Nonetheless, there is a possibility of progress there, as Paul Pieper has pointed out and as Ellen Dulberger and Robert Gordon have demonstrated in this volume. These opportunities are largely unexploited.

The second change dealing with capital is more fundamental. This is the use of new methodology to get at a problem that was essentially intractable 25 years ago, namely, the problem of measuring economic depreciation. If we examine the price of capital services, we can see that it is a weighted sum of a rate of return and the depreciation rate. The depreciation rate differs among assets. If it turns out that we are dealing with the problem of heterogeneity, it is important to get the weights right.

A major thrust in measuring depreciation is associated with the work of Hulten and Wykoff. They have succeeded in estimating age-price profiles for a wide range of assets and brought the measurement of economic depreciation at least up to the same level as price deflation of assets. We now have much more satisfactory numbers than we did 25 years ago. The depreciation rates themselves are quite different from the ones that were current 25 years ago and are still used by BEA in much of its work.

Hulten, Robertson, and Wykoff have now validated the original methodology by showing that the results are unaffected by the energy crisis. This is a very important forward step, and it has increased the growth rate of capital for any given level of capital formation. It did change the numbers that I have published elsewhere, say, in my article with Frank Gollop back in 1980,[9] where the Hulten/Wykoff findings were not used. Second, we have a much better fix on the issue of capital quality.

The remaining problem is the one that Berndt, Harper, and Wood have attempted to deal with in this volume. This problem is going to be with us for some time, namely, how to measure the rate of return. My own preference would be to use some kind of market-based estimate of the inflation rate. Unfortunately, the people who work on that kind of thing, the financial economists, have yet to come up with a story that we can use.

We also need to incorporate features of the tax structure. Martin Sullivan and I[10] have developed a historical record on the depreciation actually claimed by various taxpayers. Our estimates are based on their records and on what the Treasury would allow at each point of time. We combine the historical experience ex post and the tax laws ex ante to produce a much better picture of depreciation actually claimed.

At the same time, people have begun to realize that economists look at the investment tax credit in a different way from tax lawyers. A tax lawyer's view is that there is something called equipment to which the investment tax credit can be applied. An economist has learned that some things we think of as structures are eligible for the investment tax credit. By bits and pieces we have managed to obtain good estimates of what the investment tax credits are for individual types of assets. By now we have a clear picture of the determinants of the prices of individual types of capital. The frontier right now is in studies that are relevant to applying the results implementing Hulten's ideas.

The rate of return is a weighted average of returns to equity and to debt. The weight is the debt/asset ratio. It is precisely this ratio that John Strong has measured in terms of market prices. We now have a much better and different measure of these debt/asset ratios available for this kind of analysis. Second, we have to separate the debt part from the equity part. We require an effective tax rate on capital gains and an estimate of the tax liability for corporate dividends at the individual level. Finally, we have to deal with the tax deductibility of interest.

The conclusion, it seems to me, is that we have made a lot of progress even though it has not been highly visible. Just to sum up what we have found: It is possible to strengthen the empirical underpinnings of each of the measurements that go into our analysis of growth. When we do that we find a completely, and I emphasize completely, different picture from the ones that most economists learned back in the 1960s. Progress strengthens the underpinnings for the analysis of the implications of these findings for economic policy.

The issues that have to be resolved in this kind of measurement are precisely those that are needed in order to analyze the process that results from any kind of change in technology. This is the process of capital formation that is induced by changes in technology. This is the subject of a great deal of public discussion and will continue to be for the indefinite future.

What are the lessons that can be drawn from this panel discussion and this book? While, as Dale Jorgenson says, better measurements will produce better insights into the causes of long-term economic growth, one also needs new paradigms and further development of Hulten's neoclassical growth analysis to get out of the rut in which growth accounting has been in recent years. It is important to comprehend where technical change comes from—it is not at all purely exogenous, but mostly endogenous. As Hulten points out, his growth equation does not provide for the endogeneities. Thus these feedback effects make it more difficult, in fact, to separate causes and effects. Technical change itself is largely determined by capital investment (human and physical) as well as by R&D. Thus, for true longer-term improvement in the growth rate of the economy, attention must be paid to all of these factors, which can lead to higher productivity growth and hence a higher standard of living. It is the endogeneity of technical change that moves the production function of figure 12.3 continuously upward, and offers the possibility of much longer-term increases in the growth rate of the economy.

As mentioned earlier, the quality of the resources used by the economy needs better quantifications. Furthermore, technical change is not the only component of productivity growth. Many social, psychological, legal, and cultural factors also influence productivity improvement—technical advance is not the whole of the measured "residual" although it is probably its principal component.

What is clearly needed as a very minimum is a better understanding of the interrelationship of capital formation and technological change. Technologists, such as those at the conference, unhesitatingly acknowledge such a close linkage. In the real world, they say, capital investment is seldom made just to repeat the past; improvements and new technologies *are* incorporated in new investment, even if only for maintenance. It is important to strengthen this understanding at the micro level, and to impress upon policymakers the intimate association between capital formation and technological change. That this link is still poorly understood is exemplified in the Tax Reform Bill of 1986, which continues to give incentives for R&D, but strangely discontinues incentives for capital formation, such as ACRS (Accelerated Cost Recovery System) and ITC (Investment Tax Credit). A fuller understanding would lead to more consistent policies, and the possibility of a *longer-run* higher growth rate, which would be very desirable indeed for the sake of a more harmonious and secure country. The country is beginning to pay more serious attention to the role of productivity growth in American competitiveness and growth.[11]

Notes

1. Boskin, M., *The Positive Sum Strategy* by R. Landau and N. Rosenberg, National Academy Press, Washington, 1986, pp. 33–55; see also Griliches, Z., in NBER Reporter, Spring, 1986, pp. 1–4; Boskin, M., in F. G. Adams and S. Wachter, *Savings and Capital Formation: The Policy Options*, Lexington Books, Lexington, MA., 1986, pp. 11–43; Summers, L. H., *J. Econ. Lit.*, Dec. 1985, pp. 1799–1800; Boskin, M., in *Carnegie-Rochester Conference Series on Public Policy*, 1981, pp. 201–217; Mirrlees, J. A. M., *Rev. Econ. Studies*, 1967, pp. 95–124; Phelps, E. S., *Quart. J. Econ.*, 1962, pp. 548–567; Arrow, K., *Rev. Econ. Studies*, 1961–1962, pp. 155–173.

2. Quinn, J. B., *The Positive Sum Strategy* by R. Landau and N. Rosenberg, National Academy Press, Washington, 1986, pp. 357–371.

3. Hulten, C. R., *Am. Econ. Rev.*, March 1979, pp. 126–136; *Am. Econ. Rev.*, Dec., 1975, pp. 956–964.

4. Jorgenson, D. W., with M. Kuroda and M. Nishimizu, "Japan-U.S. Industry Level Comparisons 1960–1979," *Journal of the Japanese International Economies*, Vol. 1, No. 1, Mar. 1987, pp. 1–30.

5. Brunner, L. P., *U.S. Productivity Growth: Who Benefitted?* reviewed by R. Ramachandran, *J. Econ. Lit.*, Vol. 23, June, 1985, pp. 633–634.

6. Gordon, R. H., Schankerman, M., and Spady, R. H., "Estimating the Effects of R&D on Bell System Productivity: A Model of Embodied Technical Change," National Bureau Econ. Res. Working Paper No. 1607, April 1985.

7. Jorgenson, D. W., "Microeconomics and Productivity" in R. Landau and N. Rosenberg, *The Positive Sum Strategy*, National Academy Press, 1986.

8. Gollop, F. M. and Jorgenson, D. W., "Sectoral Measures of Labor Cost for the United States, 1948–1978," in J. E. Triplett (ed.), *The Measurement of Labor Cost, Studies in Income and Wealth*, Vol. 44, Chicago, University of Chicago Press, 1983, pp. 185–235, 503–520.

9. Gollop, F. M. and Jorgenson, D. W., "U.S. Productivity Growth by Industry, 1947–73," in J. W. Kendrick and B. Vaccara (eds.), *New Developments in Productivity Measurement and Analysis, Studies in Income and Wealth*, Vol. 41, Chicago, University of Chicago Press, 1980, pp. 17–136.

10. Jorgenson, D. W. and Sullivan, M. A., "Inflation and Corporate Capital Recovery," in C. R. Hulten (ed.), *Depreciation, Inflation, and the Taxation of Income from Capital*, Washington, The Urban Institute Press, 1981, pp. 171–238, 311–313.

11. *Wall St. J.*, Nov. 7, 1986, p. 70.

List of Contributors

Ernst R. Berndt
Sloan School of Management
Massachusetts Institute of Technology
Cambridge, Massachusetts

Michael J. Boskin
Department of Economics
Stanford University
Stanford, California

Dianne C. Christensen
L. R. Christensen Associates
Madison, Wisconsin

Laurits R. Christensen
L. R. Christensen Associates
Madison, Wisconsin

Carl G. Degen
L. R. Christensen Associates
Madison, Wisconsin

Ellen R. Dulberger
International Business Machines Corporation
Armonk, New York

Robert J. Gordon
Department of Economics
Northwestern University
Evanston, Illinois

Michael J. Harper
Bureau of Labor Statistics
Washington, D.C.

Charles R. Hulten
Department of Economics
University of Maryland
College Park, Maryland

Dale W. Jorgenson
Kennedy School of Government
Harvard University
Cambridge, Massachusetts

Ralph Landau
Department of Economics
Stanford University
Stanford, California
and
Kennedy School of Government
Harvard University
Cambridge, Massachusetts

Paul Pieper
Department of Economics
University of Illinois at Chicago
Chicago, Illinois

John M. Roberts
Board of Governors
Federal Reserve System
Washington, D.C.

James W. Robertson
Bureau of Labor Statistics
Washington, D.C.

Marc S. Robinson
General Motors Corporation
Warren, Michigan

Philip E. Schoech
L. R. Christensen Associates
Madison, Wisconsin

John S. Strong
School of Business Administration
College of William and Mary
Williamsburg, Virginia

Jack E. Triplett
Bureau of Economic Analysis
Washington, D.C.

David O. Wood
Sloan School of Management
Massachusetts Institute of Technology
Cambridge, Massachusetts

Frank C. Wykoff
Department of Economics
Pomona College
Pomona, California

Author Index

Page numbers in **boldface** indicate tables.

Ackerman, Susan Rose, 20, 281
Allen, Steven G., 306
Archibald, Robert B., 134, **140**, 150, 151, **152**, 173, **173**, 175, **180**, 182
Auerbach, Alan J., 283

Baily, Martin N., 226, 230, 234, 306
Barquin-Stolleman, J. A., 17
Barro, **138**, **152**, **154**
Beidleman, C. R., 20
Bell, C. Gordon, 146, 149
Berndt, Ernst R., 228, 232, 233, 234, 333, 367
Blackorby, Charles, 132
Bloch, Erich, 146, 148
Bradford, David F., 368
Bulow, Jeremy I., 379, 382
Bureau of Economic Analysis (BEA), 42, 453, **455**, 455
Bureau of Labor Statistics (BLS), 21, 22, 23, 28, **229**, 331, 354, **355**, 364, 368

Cagan, P., 20
Cale, E. G., **141**, **152**, **180**
Cartwright, David W., 127, **142**, 148, 151, **153**, **154**, **172**, 173, **173**, 174, **177**, 178, **180**, 182, **183**, 185, **186**, 187, 198
Chen, Y. C., 17
Chinloy, P., 20
Chow, Gregory C., 20, 78, 85, 86, 87–88, 89, 90, 95–97, 118, 119, **139**, 145, 150, **152**, 158, 161–162, **167**, **168**, 169, 170, 171, 175, **177**, 215, 222, 223, 281
Christensen, Laurits R., 28, 29, 338, 339, 345, 346, **355**, 410, 434, 456
Coen, Robert M., 20, 352, 353, **355**
Cogan, Philip, 281
Cole, Roseanne, 17, 82, 86, 90, 127, 151, 155, 162, 164, 189, **191**, 198, 223
Cox, W. Michael, 392, 393

Dacy, Douglas, 293, 313
DeLeeuw, F., 459
Denison, Edward F., 21–22, 22, 25, 26–27, 28, 29, 340, 351
Diewert, W. Erwin, 193, 338, 340, 341, 342, 349–350, 351, 355
Domar, Evsey D., 348
Donahoe, Gerald F., **142**, 148, 151, **153**, **154**, **172**, 173, **173**, 174, **177**, 178, **180**, 182, **183**, 187, 419
Dulberger, Ellen R., 17, 50, 78, 85–86, 86, 87, 88, 89, 97, 102, **109**, 114, 118, 119, 127, 137, **142**, 148, 149, **153**, **154**, 157, 158, 159, 162, 164, **180** 182, **183**, 184–185, **186**, 187, 189, 198, 199, 200, 215, **216**, 217, 218, 223, 224, 502

Early, **138**, **152**, **154**
Ein-Dor, Phillip, **143**, **153**, 199
Einstein, Marcus E., 80
Eisner, Robert, 20, 352, **355**, 373, 374, 393, 455
Epstein, Larry E., 340, 351, **355**
Evans, Michael K., 352, **355**

Federal Reserve Board (FRB), **375**
Feldstein, M. S., 20
Fisher, Franklin M., 41, 89, 91, 132, 133, 136, 137, **141**, 145, 157, 158, 172, 185, 187, 218
Fisher, Irving, 1, 193
Flamm, Kenneth, 78, 90, 137, **143**, 148, **153**, 155, 156, 164, **167**, **168**, 169, 170, 171, **172**, 173, **173**, 174, **177**, **180**, 182, 183, 189, **190**, **191**, 192, **194**, 195, 196, 197, 198, 199, 222
Foot, D. K., 20
Ford, Gary T., **140**, 145, 150, **152**
Franklin, James, **80**
Fraumeni, Barbara M., 21, 22, 28, 29, 228, 230, 340, 345, 346, 350, 353, **355**

Friedman, Benjamin M., 393
Fullerton, Don, 368
Fuss, Melvyn A., 367

Galage, Dom, 146, 148
Gillingham, Robert, 340, 352, **355**
Goldberger, Arthur S., 160
Goldsmith, Raymond, 453, 454, **455**, 455
Gollop, F. M., 21, 22, 28, 500, 502
Gordon, Robert J., **142**, **153**, **154**, **167**, **168**, 169, 170, 171, **172**, 173, 174, **180**, 182, **183**, 184, 215, **216**, 217, 221, 293, 313, 502
Gorman, John A., 274, 367
Greenwood, Joen E., 41, 89, 136, 137, **141**, 145, 157, 158, 172, 185, 187, 218
Gremillion, L. L., **141**, **152**, **180**, 182
Griliches, Zvi, 16, 17, 20, 27, 131, 154, 163, 281, 336, 340, 343, 348, 351
Grossman, E. S., 22, 26
Grunfeld, Yehuda, 352, **355**
Gullickson, William, 367

Hall, Robert E., 15, 16, 20, 336, 337, 339, 345, 353, **355**
Harper, Michael J., 345, 367
Hazilla, Michael, 333
Helvacian, N., 17
Hicks, J. R., 1
Hines, James R., 283
Hirschhorn, Eric, 392, 393
Hodge, J. H., 17
Holland, Daniel M., 352, **355**
Horsley, A., **153**, 159
Hudson, Edward A., 228
Hulten, C. R., 15, 17, 18, **18**, **19**, 20, 22, 23, 28, 235, 238, 239, 262, 269, 281, **281**, 282, 285, 367, 453, 457, 458, 459, 463, 476, 491, 502

Jacob, Nancy, **138**, **152**
Jorgenson, Dale W., 16, 21, 22, 27, 28, 29, 228, 230, 287, 336, 337, 338, 339, 340, 341, 343, 345, 346, 348, 349–350, 350, 351, 353, 355, **355**, 367, 410, 343, 456, 495, 498

Kelejian, Harry H., **143**, **153**
Kendrick, J. W., 21, 22, 25, 26, 28, 29, 453, 454
Knight, Kenneth E., 83, 93, 118, **139**, 147–148, **152**, 158–159, 160, **167**, **168**, 170, 171, **172**, 173, **173**, 174, 175, **177**, **180**, 215, 222, 223
Koerts, J., 160, 161
Kopp, Raymond, 333
Kuh, E., 20

Lee, B. S., 20
Levy, David, **143**, 148, **153**, **154**, **180**, 182

Lias, Edward, 148, 149
Lindahl, E., 1

Malinvaud, E., 1
Malpezzi, S. L., 20
Margolis, **138**, **152**, **154**
McGowan, John J., 41, 89, 136, 137, **141**, 145, 157, 158, 172, 185, 187, 218
McKenney, J. L., **141**, **152**, **180**, 182
Meyer, J., 20
Michaels, Robert, 42, **140**, 145, **152**, 154, **154**
Miller, Merton H., 352, **355**, 373
Modigliani, Franco, 352, **355**, 373
Morrison, Catherine J., 367
Musgrave, John C., 27, 28, 274, 293, 367, 458, 463
Myers, Stewart C., 352, **355**

National Academy of Sciences (NAS), 331
Nicoletti, Robert V., **143**, **153**

Office of Management and Budget (OMB), 453, 455, **455**
Ohta, Makoto, 20, 281, **281**
Ozanne, L., 20

Parker, Robert P., **142**, 148, 151, **153**, **154**, 173, **173**, 174, **177**, 178, **180**, 182, **183**, 187
Patrick, James M., **138**, 145, 150, **152**
Peterson, Victor L., 199
Phister, Montgomery, Jr., 78, 79, **80**, 85, 86–87, 88, 89, 90, 92, **109**, 120, 137, **142**, **143**, 147, 151, 164, 169, 170, 174, **180**, 189, 197, 215, 218, 221
Pieper, Paul J., 373, 374, 393, 455, 502
Pollak, Robert A., 131, 132
Pollin, Robert, 393
Pollock, Jesse, 324
Pugh, Emerson W., **47**

Ramm, Wolfhard, 20, 281
Randolph, William C., 155, 189, **191**
Rasche, R., 20
Ratchford, Brian T., **140**, 145, 150, **152**
Reece, William S., 134, **140**, 150, 151, **152**, 173, **173**, 175, **180**, 182
Reeve, J. E., 454
Robertson, James W., 367, 502
Rosen, Sherwin, 88, 129, 130, 133, 155
Rottenberg, I., 419
Russell, R. Robert, 132

Schneidewind, Norman F., **138**, **152**, **171**, 188, **188**
Seater, John, 392
Serlin, Omri, 145, 146, 147, 148, 149
Sharpe, William F., 137, 145, 146, 148,

171, 189
Shell, Karl, 132, 133
Shoven, John B., 379, 382
Siebert, Calvin D., 333, 340, 346, 348, **355**
Sippi, Charles J., 145
Skattum, Stein, **138**, **152**, **171**, **188**,
    188–189
Solow, Robert M., 16, 232, 332
Stevenson, R., 411
Stokes, H. Kemble, 307, 311
Stoneman, Paul, **141**, 150, **152**, **154**, 178,
    179
Stoneman, Peter, 41
Sullivan, Martin A., 340, 367, 502
Summers, Lawrence H., 232
Swann, G. M. P., **153**, 159

Taubman, P., 20
Teekens, R., 160, 161
Terborgh, G., 20
Thibodeau, T., 20
Tinbergen, Jan, 332
Triplett, Jack E., 79, 81, 83, 87, 91, 107,
    114, 115, 129, 130, 131, 132, 133, 178,
    192, 215, 218, 221, 500

Wall Street Journal, 149
Wallace, William E., **142**, 148, **153**, 154,
    154, 157
Welzer, Steve, **143**, 148, **153**, **154**, **180**, 182
Wojnilower, Albert M., 393
Wood, David O., 228, 232, 233
Wykoff, Frank C., 15, 17, 18, **18**, **19**, 20,
    22, 23, 28, 281, 235, 238, 239, 262, 269,
    281, 282, 285, 453, 457, 458, 459, 463,
    476, 502

Young, Allan H., 27, 28, 274, 458, 463

Zieschang, Kimberly, 131

Subject Index

Page numbers in **boldface** indicate tables; those in *italics* indicate figures.

Accelerated Cost Recovery System (ACRS), 271, 284
Accounting for Slower Economic Growth (Denison), 21, 23
Accounting for United States Economic Growth, 1929–1969 (Denison), 21, 23
Accounting system
of Bell System, 492–494
for capital inputs, 5
ADR (Asset Depreciation Range System), 271, 284
Aerodynamic problem, costs of solving equations for, 199–201
Age-price profiles, 261
in automobile depreciation study, 269, **270–271**, *273*
for construction equipment, 240, **242**, *243–245*, 247, **248**, *250–252*
and energy crises, 255
Hulten-Wykoff estimation of, 502
and inflation effects, **263**
for machine tools, 240–241, **242**, *245–247*, 247, **248**, *252–254*
and revaluation, 261–262
and vintage price approach, 234–239
Alcoa, technology and capital at, 495–497
Alternative Minimum Tax (AMT), 260, 284–285
American Appraisal company, 299
Announcement effect, 215
ARIMA (autoregressive integrated moving average), 351–352, 366
Asset Depreciation Range System (ADR), 271, 284
Asset efficiency. *See* Relative efficiency
Assets
present value for, 260–261, 267
short-term financial, **378–379**
Assets, age-price data on. *See* Age-price profiles
AT&T Structures Indexes, 296, 299–300,

303, **307**, 326
Auerbach Computer Technology Reports, 86
Automobiles, business-leased, depreciation study on, 259–260. *See also* Depreciation study
Automobiles, business-use, 259–260, 266, 272, 274
Autoregressive integrated moving average (ARIMA). *See* ARIMA

Baily hypothesis. *See* Obsolescence hypothesis
Baker, James, 485
Bank loans, 374, **375–376**, 385
BEA-DOD military index, 304–305, **307**, 324
Bell System, accounting system of, 492–494
Bell System Telephone Plant Indexes, **296**, 299–300, **303**, **307**, 326
Benchmark(s), computer performance, 40, 146–147
aerodynamic calculation as, 201
synthetic, 149
Benchmarks in USPS study, 427–429
Best-practice index, 215, 222–224
BLS. *See* Bureau of Labor Statistics
Bonds, corporate, 374, **375–376**
market and par values of, **380–381**, 381–382, **389**, **390**, 391
time-trend regressions for, **389**
Bonds, foreign, 396
Bonds, tax-exempt, 374, **375–376**
market and par values of, **389**, **390**, 391
time-trend regressions for, **389**
Boskin, Michael, 485–486, 488, 492
Box-Cox power transformation model and rates
and constant rate, 18
and depreciation study, 259, 262, 275–280

Box-Cox (cont.)
  and hedonic model application, 44, 55
  and obsolescence-hypothesis test, 239,
    248
Brunner, Lawrence, 491–492
Buildings. *See also* Structures deflators
    problem
  USPS investment in, 429, 434
  USPS price index for, 419, **426**
Bureau of the Census Price index of New
    One-Family Houses, 419
Bureau of the Census Single Family
    Homes Index, 305, 307, **307**, 308–313,
    318–319, **321**
Bureau of Economic Analysis (BEA), 451
  capital stock estimates by, 21
  computer deflator by, 78, 81
  and computer price indexes, 81
  construction deflators of, 293, 295–297
  methodology of, 457
  overdeflation by, 306–320, 326
  and study on federal government, 451,
    456 (*see also* Federal government
    capital/investment study)
  and USPS capital stock, 411
Bureau of Labor Statistics (BLS)
  capital stock estimates by, 21
  growth study by, 488
  indexes from, 81–82, 82–83, 301
  multifactor productivity measures by,
    364–365
Bureau of Reclamation index, **296**, 301,
    303, **307**, 317–318, 323
Business-leased automobiles, deprecia-
    tion study on, 259–260. *See also*
    Depreciation study
Buy-back activity, 240

Capital, 1
  cost of (USPS), 436, **437**, 439
  economic theory of, 29
  efficiency function of, 287
  growth of, 488
  instantaneous adjustment of, 366–367
  measurement of, 410–411
  rented (USPS), 439, **444**, 445, **446**
  shadow price of, 353
  user cost of, 283–286, 287
  vintages of, 1, 2, 232–233 (*see also* Vin-
    tage price approach)
Capital accounts, of Bell System, 492–494
Capital assets, rental prices for. *See* Ren-
    tal prices for capital assets
Capital composition effect, 343, **344**, 356,
    357, 362, **363**, 365
  in manufacturing industries, **358**, **359**,
    360–361
Capital costs, and AMT, 260
Capital formation
  and productivity, 488

  and tax incentives, 504
Capital formation, government, 451–452.
    See also Federal government
    capital/investment study
Capital gains
  in productivity growth measurement
    debate, 333
  and rate of return specification, 346–348
  and rental price formula, 332–333, 337,
    339–340, 344, 360–361, 362, 365
Capital goods
  acquisition price of, 9–11
  vs. capital services, 134
  labor combined with, 494
  price for acquisition of, 16
  and USPS study, 409, 410
Capital input
  in economic growth, 499, **499**, 500, **501**
  improvement in price deflators of, 500
  measurement of, 8, 11–13, 21–29
  percent changes in 1948–1984, **344**
  price index for, 192–193
  price of, 9–11
  and USPS study, 409, 410, 434, 436–439,
    440–443, 445, **447**
Capital productivity, percent changes in
    1948–1984, **344**
Capital service price, 12–13, 14
  index for, 132
  and multifactor productivity estimates,
    365
  problem in measurement of, 332
Capital services, 2, 3
  aggregation of, 341–344
  vs. capital goods, 134
  and USPS study, 410–411, 434
Capital stock
  in economic growth, 500
  energy-induced obsolescence of, 226,
    230–231 (*see also* Obsolescence
    hypothesis)
  estimating, 13–14, 21–22
  federal government, 453, **461**, **462–463**,
    463, 464, 465, **466–471**, 472, 473,
    478–480
  federal government (literature review),
    454–457
  federal vs. private, 476
  governmental, 451
  measurement of (Baily), 230–232
  percent changes in, **344**
  and USPS study, 409, 410–412, 429–435,
    435, **436**
Capital structure
  and debt measurement, 373
  and par vs. market values, 373, 392
Capital value, vintage price approach to,
    234
Capital-labor ratio, 485, 486, 498

Capital-technology relation, 485
  Alcoa view of, 495–497
  and economic growth, 485–490, 492, 497–498
  need for understanding of, 504
Card punchers, price indexes for, **188, 190**
Card readers, price indexes for, **188, 190**
Cars, business-use, 259–260, 266, 272, 274. *See also* Depreciation study
CEC (central electronic complex), 45
Censored sample problem, 17–18, 20, 458–459
Census Single Family Homes index, **296**, 297, 307, **307**, 308–313, 318, 318–319, **321**, 323, 324
Characteristics in hedonic model (computer), 37–38, 40, 129, 136
  and adjacent-year regressions, 84
  combined interaction among, 135
  and hedonic function, 128
  memory capacity as, 40, 57, **58**, 137
  and price, 55, 57, **58**
  resource cost of, 133
  and sample, 44
  speed as, 40–41, 46, 57, **58**, 137–150
  substitution possibilities among, 199
  vs. technology variables (computer price study), 116
Characteristics price index or method, 61, 129, 132, 163–164, 164
  for 1972–1984 period, **180**, 184
Circularity, 193
Cohort, 261
Cohort effects, 238
Cohort heterogeneity, 262–265. *See also* Heterogeneity problem
Cohort retirement, 265
Commerce Department
  BEA of (*see* Bureau of Economic Analysis)
  structures deflators of 1961, 293, 320–323 (*see also* Structures deflators problem)
Commodity boundaries, and computer price study, 85
"Competitive equilibrium" argument, 207n.43
Component-price structures indexes, 295
  BEA-DOD Military, 304–305, **307**, 324
  Bureau of the Census Single Family Homes, 305, 307, **307**, 308–313, 318–319, **321**
  Federal Highway Administration, **296**, 297, 305–306, 307, P318, 321, 323, 324
Composite price index, 60
Composition effect (capital composition effect), 343, **344**, 356, 357, 362, **363**, 365

in manufacturing industries, **358, 359**, 360–361
Composition index of capital, 411
Computational costs, for aerodynamic problem, 199–201
Computer history
  first epoch of (1953–1965), 166–172, 215
  second epoch of (1965–1972), **172**, 172–175, 215, 217
  third epoch of (1972–1984), **180–181**, 182–188, **216**, 217–218
Computer industry
  auto industry contrasted with, 77
  components as basic in, 39–40
  postwar development of, 79–81
  and quality change, 37
Computer memory. *See* Memory, computer
Computer price index. *See* Price indexes for computers
Computer prices, viii, x-xi, 127
  alternative estimates for (1953–1965), **168**
  alternative estimates for (1965–1972), **173**
  fall in unacknowledged, 77–78
  for new-only vs. new-plus-old models, 88–89, 118, 158, 218
  1953–1972 decrease in, 176
  1972–1984 decrease in, 184
  in United Kingdom, 178, **179**
Computer prices, hedonic method for. *See* Hedonic model
Computer prices study, 78–79, 118
  Chow data in, 86, 87–88, 95–97, 111, **112**, 119
  Chow vs. Phister indexes in, 114, 222
  Cole/Dulberger/Triplett on, 215–218
  component indexes linked in, 103–107
  Computerworld data in, 78, 85, 86, 87, 88, 89, 89–90, 100, **101**, 102–103, 106–107, 111, **112**113, 117
  data sources for, 78, 85–88, 120
  Dulberger data in, 86, 87–88, 89, 97, 99, 102, 103, 111, 114, 116, 117–118, 119
  final index by, 103–107, 118–119, 217
  and future research, 119–120
  and hedonic regression model, 81–85, 88
  and IBM mainframe performance, 107–111, **113**
  market shares weighting in, 89–90
  and new-only vs. all-model index, 88–89, 118, 218, 223–224
  obsolete vs. final version of, 221–222
  peripherals in, 90–91
  Phister data in, 78, 79, 83, 85, 86–87, 88, 92–102, 106–107, 111, **112, 113**, 116, 117, 120, 215

Computer prices study (cont.)
  reconciliation of discrepancies in,
    111–118, 119
  regression results from, 92–103
  rental rates vs. purchase prices in, 90
  sample period for, 83–84
  software in, 91–92
Computer processors. *See* Processors,
  computer
Computer system, 192
  performance improvement in interfaces
    of, 91, 134–136
  price indexes for, 192–201
  processor in, 39
Computers, IBM. *See* IBM computers
Computers, U.S. domestic purchases of,
  80
Computerworld magazine, in computer
  price studies, 44, 78, 85, 86, 87, 88, 89,
  89–90, 100, **101**, 102–103, 106–107, 111,
  112–113, 117, **142**, **143**, 180, 182, 217
Constant external own rate of return,
  353–354, **355**, **359**, **361**
Constant quality price indexes, 128, 132
Construction deflators. *See* Structures
  deflators problem
Construction equipment, for
  obsolescence-hypothesis test,
  239–240, 241, **242**, 243–245
Consumer Price Index (CPI), vs. hedonic
  price indexes, 82
Consumer tolerance, and multiple-price
  regimes, 54, 56–57, 63
Contractor cost estimates, as structures
  deflator, 325
Corporate liabilities, nonfinancial. *See*
  Liabilities, nonfinancial corporate
Corporate profits, gains on debt in, 388
CPU (central processing unit), 39
Credit risk, 381
Cycle speed, machine, as measure, 146
Cycle speed, memory, as measure,
  145–146

Data source effects, and price-index
  dispersion, 165–166
Data sources, privately compiled, 298
Datamation, data from, 44, **142**
Debt, credit market, x
  importance of measuring, 373
  nonfinancial corporate liabilities, 374,
    375–376 (*see also* Liabilities,
    nonfinancial corporate)
  par and market-value of, 373–374
  sectoral approach to, 393–394, **395–396**,
    396, **397–398**, *398*, 399, **400–405**
Declining balance pattern, 3
Deficits, government
  and federal government investment,

473–475
  and government investment vs. other
    expenditures, 452
Deflators. *See* Price indexes
Denison, Edward, 488, 498
Department of Commerce. *See* Commerce Department
Department of Transportation Structures
  index, 419
Depreciation, 5–6, 260–262, 456,
  480–481n.5
  acceleration of, 263
  and age-price profile study, 255
  for assets in National Income and Pro-
    duct Accounts, 18–20
  and Baily hypothesis, 230
  best geometric average (BGA) rates of,
    17–18, 22, 28
  capital input method of, 27, 28, 29
  and capital input price, 10, 11
  and capital stock/relative efficiency,
    24–28
  and capital-stock measurement, 25–28
  for commercial and industrial build-
    ings, 17–18
  constant and Box-Cox rates of, 18
  discounted value definition of, 27–28,
    29
  and federal government capital stock,
    456–457, 460, **462–463**, 465, **466–471**,
    478–480
  geometric, 13, 14, 20, 28, 238, 336–337,
    460, 481n.12, 494
  and market data, 458–460, 463
  measuring, 502
  and rental prices, 20, 29
  and replacement investment, 20–21
  single parameter approach to, 18
  and structures deflation, 320
  in USPS study, 428
  and vintage price functions, 11–12, 20
Depreciation study, 259–260
  and Box-Cox transformation model,
    262, 275–280
  and cohort heterogeneity, 262–265
  and cohort retirement, 265
  in comparison with existing research,
    280–282
  data for, 267–274
  economic depreciation rates for,
    278–279, 279–280, **281**
  and investment tax credit, 265–267, 269,
    271, **272**, 282
  and measurement, 260–261
  parameter estimates and fit of equation
    for, 275–276, **277**
  and relative asset efficiency, **286**,
    286–287
  user cost in, 283–286

Deterioration, 261
"Dhrystone" measure, 149
Discount rate, for 1978–1987 period, **284**
Discounted value definition of depreciation, 27–28
Discounting, of older computers, 46, 157–158, 185
Disequilibrium, technologically induced. *See* Technologically induced disequilibrium
Disk drives, price indexes for, 189, **190, 191**, 192
Dispersion, price index, 165–166
Domar, Evsey D., 498
Double deflation method, 319–320, 328n.27
Duality, 4–5
Dummy variable method, 83, 160–161, 164–165
 and hedonic equation, 42–43
 vs. imputation method (computer price study), 111, 115
 for 1972–1984 period, **180**, 184, 185, **186**
Durable equipment, producers', ix
Durable goods
 depreciation of, 5–6
 replacement of, 5–6
Durable goods model of production, 2–3, 4, 14

Econometric model(s) and modeling, 14–16
 for depreciation study, 260–267
 illustration of, 17–21
 for vintage price approach, 237–239
Economic growth. *See* Growth
Economic theory of price indexes, 131
EDP Industry Report, 85
Efficiency, productive, and depreciation, 480–481n.5
Efficiency, relative, 2–3
 decline in, 20–21
 geometric decline in, 13–14
Efficiency(ies) of capital goods, vii
Efficiency function of capital, 287
Energy and energy prices
 and Baily obsolescence hypothesis, 226, 230–232, 249, 254
 and economic growth, 227–230, 254
 and productivity slowdown, 225–226, 235
 and revaluation, 238
 and vintage of capital, 232–233, 235, 237
Energy price shocks and crises of 1970s, viii, 233, 502
Engineering News-Record, as data source, 298, 301, 302

Engineering News-Record construction index, 300, 303, 323
ENIAC computer, 79, 111, 122n.12
Environmental Protection Agency index, **296**, 298, **303, 307**
Equivalent quality price index, 132
External nominal rate of return specification, 352–353, **354, 355**, 364
 for manufacturing industries, 357, **359**
External own rate of return specification, 353–354, **355, 361**
 for manufacturing industries, **359**

Farm business, market-to-par ratios for, 394, **397–398, 400–405**
Federal Energy Regulatory Commission (FERC) Pipeline index, **296**, 297, 301–302, **303**, 304, **307**, 322, 325, 326
Federal government, contingent liabilities of, 407n.13
Federal government capital/investment study, 452–453
 findings of, 473–478
 literature review for, 454–457
 methodology of, 457–463
 on military, 460, **467–468, 470–471**, 473, 473, 474, 475
 results of **461, 462–463**, 463, 464, 465–473
Federal government credit market liabilities, market-to-par ratios for, 393–394, **395–396, 397–389, 400–405 307**, 313
Federal Highway Administration (FHWA) index, **296**, 297, 305–306, 307, **307**, 313–318, 321, 323, 324
Federal Housing Administration (FHA) indexes, 311–313, **321**, 325
Financial markets, debt claims in, x. *See also* Debt, credit market
Fisher Ideal index, 193
Floor space, as hedonic function variable, 150–151, 178
Foreign securities, market-to-par ratios for, 396, **397–398, 400–405**
Frontier, technological, 89, 158, 218
Frontier-regression problem, and technological leapfrogging, 158–159
Functional form, and hedonic functions, **152–154**, 154–159

General Classification of Accounts (GCA), 413, 414
Geometric depreciation, 336–337, 460, 481n.12, 494
 and age-price profile, 238
 in Coen study, 20–21
 and discounted value definition, 28
 as efficiency decline, 13, 14
Gibson mix, 147

Government capital formation, 451–452. *See also* Federal government capital/investment study, 452–453

Griliches, Z., 488

Grosch's law, 203n.13

Growth. *See also* Productivity growth
capital in, 499, **499**, 500, **501**
of computer equipment purchases, 38
and energy, 227–230, 254
labor in, 499, **499**, 500, **501**
measurement of, 503
in microcomputer sales, 119
multifactor productivity as, 334–336
and productivity, 490–492, 498–500
sources of (1948–1979), 499, **499**, **501**
sustainable path of, 490–491
and technology-capital relation, 485–490, 492, 497–498
in value of computing equipment, 62

Handy-Whitman index, **296**, 298–299, **303**, **307**, 321, 322, 323

Harrod, 498

Hayes, Robert, 414

Hedonic contour, 155–156

Hedonic equation, 42–43

Hedonic functions, 128
and characteristics cost or revenues, 133
choice of functional form for, **152–154**, 154–159
choice of variables for, 136–151
and dispersion, 165–166
and hedonic indexes, 132
theory of, 129–131

Hedonic hypothesis, 128, 129–130

Hedonic literature for computers, 137

Hedonic method, 82–84

Hedonic model, 37–38, 63–64, 81–85
application of, 134–136, 144
characteristics prices in, 55, 57, **58** (*see also* Characteristics in hedonic model)
and component interactions, 40, 91, 134–136
empirical framework for, 42–44
empirical results for, 46–54, **69–70**
equation (1) values for, **64** (appendix)
equation (2) values for, **65–68** (appendix)
and functional form, 55
issues to be addressed in, 38
and linear homogeneity, 55
memory size rule in, 55–56, **68**
plausibility of findings from, 56–57
pooling of cross-sections in, 54–55
sample for, 44–46
and technologically associated coefficient bias, 56
and technologically induced

disequilibrium, 38, 41–42, 46–47, 54, 56, 63

Hedonic price indexes, **58**, 59–62, 127, 129, 159, 218. *See also* Computer prices study; Price indexes
computational procedures for, 160–165
for computer systems, 192–201
for construction, 310, 324
dispersion among, 165–166
and heterogeneity, 500
and matched model, 59–60, 81–82, 207n.43
for new and new-plus-old computers, 88–89, 158, 218
for peripherals, **188**, 188–192, 197
processor "best-practice," 175, **176**, 189, 197, 215, 222–223
from processor studies for first epoch (1953–1965), 166–172
from processor studies for second epoch (1965–1972), **172**, 172–175
from processor studies for third epoch (1972–1984), **180–181**, 182–188
and resource-cost vs. user-value criteria, 133
theory of, 131–133
and U.K. processor prices, 178, **179**

Hedonic regressions, 78
in computer price study (Dulberger sample), **99**
in computer price study (Phister sample), **94**, **98**, **99**
in computer price study (Phister vs. Chow), **96**
for *Computerworld* sample, **101**
of Dulberger, **46**, **48–49**, **69–70**
interpreting residuals in, 84–85

Hedonic technique, 17, 30n.9

Heterogeneity problem, 263–265, 502
and construction deflation, 294–295, 314–315, 324, 325
and hedonic indexes, 500

History, computer. *See* Computer history

Hochgraf, Norman, 485, 487

Hornbeck, Robert, 495–497

Hulten, Charles, 488–490, 498, 500, 503

IBM computers
360/370 series of, 79, 114, 115, **216**, 217, 223, 224
7000 series of, 79
in computer price study, 92, 97, 100, 103
mainframe dominance of, 118
mainframe price/performance history of, **113**, 107–111, 114–118, 224
and "make effect," 85, 92
market share of, 90

model *4341*, 117
in 1972–1984 price indexes, **186**, 187
and Phister vs. Chow data, 222
price policy/marketing for, 97, 117
reserach on as compared with competitors, 206
software provided with, 91
third generation introduced by, 174
ICI (input-cost index), 131–132, 133
Imputation method, 83, 93, 161–163,
164–165
and depreciation, 254–255
vs. dummy variable (computer price study), 111, 115
for 1972–1984 period, **180**, 184
Index computation methods, 184
characteristics price method, 61, 129,
132, 163–164, 165, **180**, 184
dummy variables method, 83, 111, 115,
160–161, 164–165, **180**, 184, 185, **186**
imputation method, 83, 93, 111, 115,
161–163, 164–165, **180**, 184, 254–255
Inflation
and age-price profile, 262, *263*
for 1978–1987 period, **284**
and productivity slowdown, 225
and rate of return specification, 346–348
revaluation from, 261
and short-term financial assets, 379
and vintage price approach, 237–238
Information on technology, and new-model offerings, 54
Input
capital as, 5 (*see also* Capital input)
computer as, 132, 201
Input vs. output price measures, and hedonic indexes, 134, 135–136
Input-cost index. *See* ICI
Input-cost structures indexes, 295
EPA, **296**, 298, **303**, **307**
Handy-Whitman, **296**, 298–299, **303**,
307, 321, 322, 323
Input-Cost–Component-Price structures indexes, 295
Bureau of Reclamation, **296**, 301, **303**,
307, 317–318, 323
FERC Pipeline, **296**, 297, 301–302, **303**,
304, **307**, 322, 325, 326
"Input-output devices," price indexes for, 189, **191**, 192
Input-productivity structures indexes, 295
Bell System Telephone Plant (AT&T),
296, 299–300, **303**, **307**, 326
Turner Construction Company, **296**,
300, **303**, **307**, 318, 321, 322, 419
Instantaneous adjustment of capital,
366–367

Instruction mix, and hedonic function,
145
Instruction mix measures, weighted,
147–149
Intensiveness, as hedonic function variable, 151
Interest rate, for 1978–1987 period, **284**
Internal nominal rate of return specification, 346–348, 350, 351, **355**, 356,
361, 364
for manufacturing industries, **358**, **361**
Internal nominal rate of return with smoothed capital gains, 351–352, **355**,
356, **359**, **361**, 366
Internal own rate of return specification,
348–351, **355**, 356, 365
for manufacturing industries, **358**, **361**
International Data Corporation (IDC), 85
International Equipment Exchange, construction equipment data from, 240
Intertemporal theory of production, 1
notation for, 3–4
Inventory approach. *See* Perpetual inventory approach or method
Investigator effects, and price-index dispersion, 166
Investment, 3
and depreciation, 20–21
federal government, 452, **461**, **462–463**,
465, **466–471**, 473–475, 476–478,
478–480
federal government (literature review),
454–457
and structures deflation, 320
and technical change, 486
and USPS study, 411–416, **417–418**, 429,
430–431
Investment goods
hedonic studies and computers as, 134
price deflators for, 502
Investment Tax Credit (ITC), 502–503
and depreciation rates, 459
and depreciation study, 265–267, 269,
271, **272**, 282, 284–285
and Tax Reform Bill, 504

Japanese economic growth, 491
Joint production, and hedonic hypothesis, 130
Jorgenson, Dale, 488, 503

Kendrick, John, 486, 487, 488, 498
Knight indexes (performance measures),
86–87, 123n.30, 147–148, 160–161, 170,
172, **173**, 174
and IBM computers, 114, 115
and range of indexes, 173
"seconds" variable in, 151, 161
two-year, 175

Labor
  capital-labor ratio, 485, 486, 498
  in economic growth, 499, **499**, 500, **501**
Labor productivity, 227
  and Bell System technology change,
    494
Laitinen, Kenneth, 492–495
Land
  USPS benchmark for, 428–429
  USPS price index for, 416, 419, **426**
"Laspeyres" version of imputation index,
    162–163, 193, 197
Leapfrogging, technological, 41, 157–159
Lemons problem, 267, 459
Leverage
  and debt measurement, 373
  and par vs. market values, 373, 392
Liabilities, nonfinancial corporate, 374,
    375–376
  corporate bonds par and market
    values, **380–381**, 381–382
  and credit risk, 381
  holding gains and losses on short-term,
    378–379, 379
  mortgage market and par values, 382,
    383
  par and market values of, **378–379**,
    379–388
  par and market values of (capital struc-
    ture), **390–391**, 392
  par and market values of (ratios), 393,
    395–396, **397–398**, **400–405**
  par and market values of (stochastic
    and temporal structure), 388–392
  percentage distribution of, 374, **377**
  tax-exempt bonds market and par
    values, 382, **384–385**
  and Treasury securities, 392
Linearly declining pattern of relative
    efficiency, 23–26, 27
"Linpack" measure, 149
Literature on computers, hedonic, 137
Loans, bank, 374, **375–376**, 385
Long-term debt, nonfinancial corpora-
    tions
  market and par values of, 385–388
  as percent of capitalization, **390–391**,
    392

Machine Dealers National Association
    (MDNA), machine tool data from,
    240, 256n.13
Machine tools, for obsolescence-
    hypothesis test, 239–241, **242**, *245–247*
Macroeconomics, 498
Mainframe computers
  decline in market share for, 81
  extra services from, 100
  hedonic regressions for (Phister), **99**

price definition of, 121n.10
  unit values for, 81
  U.S. domestic purchases of, **80**
"Make effects," 84–85
Manufacturing industries, rental price
    computations for, 357, **358–359**
Matched model method or price index,
    59–60, 81–82, 207n.43
McWilliams, Richard, 414
Memory, computer
  drum vs. core, 92
  magnetic core vs. semiconductor, 50–51
Memory cycle speed, as measure,
    145–146
Memory price, and mini-mainframe
    shift, 100
Memory size
  as characteristic, 40, 57, **58**, 137
  and hedonic model, 55–56, **68**
Mergers, and revaluations, 388
Metalworking machinery
  depreciation rate of, **19**
  external nominal rate of return for, **354**
  internal nominal rate of return for, **347**
  internal own rate of return for, **349**
Microcomputers
  and computer price decline, 119–120
  price definition of, 121n.10
  unit values for, 81
  U.S. domestic purchases of, **80**
Microeconomics, and growth policy, 491
Military
  BEA-DOD military index, 304–305, 307,
    324
  and federal government capital/invest-
    ment study, 460, 467–468, 470–471,
    473, 473, 474, 475
Mineral base process industry, 495, 496
Minicomputers
  hedonic regressions for (Phister), **99**
  vs. mainframes, 100
  and Phister vs. Chow data, 222
  price definition of, 121n.10
  unit values for, 81
  U.S. domestic purchases of, **80**
MIPS (millions of instruction executions
    per second), 40–41, 148–149,
    202–203n.10
  and computer manufacture, 130
  in hedonic function, **143**
  and 1972–1984 price indexes, 187
  ratings for, 44
  and weighting, 150
Modeling of computer, "systems" view
    for, 135
Mortality distribution
  of capital good, 6–7
  for linearly declining relative
    efficiency, 23–24

Mortgage liabilities, nonfinancial cor-
    porations, market and par values of,
    382, **383**
Mortgages, **375–376**
    market and par values of, **389**, **390**, 391,
    395–396, 396
    time-trend regressions for, **389**
Motor vehicles. *See* Business-leased
    automobiles; Vehicles
Multifactor productivity, 331–332,
    488–490
    assumptions in computing of, 332
    BLS measures of, 364–365
    and capital aggregation, 341
    and capital rental prices, 356
    and capital stocks vs. capital services,
        336
    growth accounting for, 334–336
    measures related to growth of, 344, **344**
    and rental price imputation, 332–334
    (*see also* Rental prices for capital
        assets)
Multiple price regimes
    and consumer tolerance, 54, 56–57, 63
    and discounting, 185 (*see also* Discount-
        ing)
    and hedonic model, 60
    and technological frontier, 158
    and technologically induced disequili-
        bria, 41, 60, 63, 184–185

National Consolidated Trial Balance
    (NCTB), 413, 439
Neoclassical I model, 340, 346
Neoclassical II model, 340, 348
Neoclassical paradigm, 498, 503
NIPA (national income and product
    accounts), 18, 78, 81, 127, 177–178,
    196, 346, **358–359**, 476, **476**
NIPA depreciation, 480–481n.5
Nominal internal rate of return
    specification, 346–348, 350, 351, **355**,
    356
Nonfinancial corporate liabilities. *See*
    Liabilities, nonfinancial corporate
Nonfinancial noncorporate business,
    market-to-par ratios for, 394, **397–398**,
    400–405

Obsolescence, 261
    definitions of, 255n.4
    varied causes of, 495
Obsolescence hypothesis (Baily
    hypothesis), 226, 230–232
    data for testing of, 239–241, **242**,
        243–246
    and definition of "obsolescence,"
        255n.4
    results from testing of, 247–254

and vintage price approach, 234–239
O'Connell, Robert, 485
One-hoss shay age-price profile, 238
One-hoss shay pattern of deprecia-
    tion/replacement, 456, 457, 494–495,
    497
One-hoss shay pattern of relative
    efficiency, 2, 20, 23, 24, 25, 26, 27
Output characteristics price index, 133
Output per worker, growth of, 225
Output price index, 132
Output vs. input price measures, and
    hedonic indexes, 134, 135–136
"Own rate of return," 350

"Paasche" form of price index, 38, 59,
    162–163, 193
PCs. *See* Microcomputers
Peripherals
    in computer price study, 90–91
    hedonic function variables in, 151
    price decline for, 127
    price indexes for, **188**, 188–192, 197
Perpetual inventory approach or
    method, vii, x
    and Baily hypothesis, 230–231
    capital gains adjustment in, 333
    and capital input, 8
    and capital services aggregation,
        341–342
    capital stock estimates from, 21
    and depreciation, 254–255
    in government capital stock studies,
        454
    problem in, vii
    and USPS study, 411–412, 416, 434
    and vintage accounts, 9, 10, 11
"Positive Sum Strategy: Harnessing
    Technology for Economic Growth,
    The," 491
Postal Service study. *See* U.S. Postal Ser-
    vice study
Present value, 260–261
    market valuation of, 267
Price(s). *See also* Age-price profiles
    of capital input, 9–11
    of capital services, 12–13, 14
    and characteristics, 55, 57, 58, 128
    discounting of, 46, 157–158, 185
    IBM policy on, 97
    multiple regimes of, 41, 54, 56–57, 63,
        184–185
    and technology, 41 (*see also* Technologi-
        cally induced disequilibrium)
Price, computer. *See* Computer prices
    study; Hedonic model; Hedonic price
    indexes
Price, rental. *See* Rental prices

Price, vintage. *See* Vintage price
   approach; Vintage price functions
Price function
   for producing unit, 4–5
   vintage, 11–21
Price indexes
   component-price, 295, **296**, 304–306 (*see
      also* Component-price structures
      indexes)
   economic theory of, 131
   input-cost, 131–132, 133, 295, **296**, 298,
      299 (*see also* Input-cost structures
      indexes)
   input-cost–component-price, 295, **296**,
      301–304 (*see also* Input-Cost–Compo-
      nent-Price structures indexes)
   input-productivity, 295, **296**, 299–300
      (*see also* Input-productivity structures
      indexes)
   Paasche-like, 38, 59, 162–163, 193
   in USPS study, 416, 419–422, **423–426**
Price indexes for computers. *See also*
   Hedonic price indexes
   characteristics price index, 61, 129, 132,
      163–164, 164, 180, 184
   composite price index, 60
   and computer output, 199–201
   constant quality, 128, 132
   output characteristics, 133
   quality-adjusted, 37–38
   of speed, 150
   by technology class, **52**
   as time series, 193
   and vintage price functions, 17
Prime rate, for 1978–1987 period, **284**
Printers, price indexes for, **188**, **190**, **191**,
   192
Processor, computer, 38–39
   hedonic model of, 38–49, 63–64 (*see also*
      Hedonic model)
Processors, computer
   "best-practice" research price index for,
      175, **176**, 189, 197, 222–223
   comparison of alternative indexes for,
      112–113
   hedonic price indexes for, 165–188, 197
   IBM (price and performance), **108–110**,
      224
   measuring speed of, 40
   price index for, **104–105**
   and technological frontier, 218
   technological improvements in, 41–42
Producers Price Index (PPI)
   vs. hedonic price indexes, 82
   for 1978–1987 period, **284**
   in USPS study, 419
Producers' durable equipment, ix
Production
   durable goods model of, 2–3, 4

   intertemporal theory of, 1, 3–4
Production function, under hedonic
   hypothesis, 129–130, 134, 135
Productive efficiency, and depreciation,
   480–481n.5
Productivity
   and capital formation, 488
   and capital input measurement, 21–29
   and capital : labor ratio, 486, 498
   and quality, 487
   total factor, TFP, 410, 488
Productivity, capital, **344**
Productivity, multifactor. *See* Multifactor productivity
Productivity growth
   and capital goods, viii–ix
   factors in, 504
   multifactor, 334–336, **344**, 357
   and sustainable growth path, 490–492,
      498–500
Productivity growth measurement
   debate, 333
Productivity measurement models,
   research suggestion for, 366–367
Productivity slowdown, 225, **229**,
   499–500
   Baily hypothesis on, 230–232
   and deflation of structures, 293–294,
      306, 320
   and energy price, 227–230, 233, 235, 254
   as macroeconomic phenomenon, 498
Profits, corporate, and debt, 388

q ratio and theory, 226, 232, 234
q-identification, 156
Quality, and productivity, 487
Quality change problems, 37–38
   and resource-cost vs. user-value cri-
      teria, 133
Quinn, James Brian, 486

R&D
   and Tax Reform Bill, 504
   and technical change, 485, 503
Rate of return (*r*), ix
   and capital rental prices, 341, 344
   measuring, 502–503
Rate of return specifications, 345–346,
   365–366
   constant external own rate of return,
      353–354, **355**, **359**, **361**
   data for study of, 367–368
   empirical results on, 356–364
   external nominal rate of return,
      352–353, **354**, **355**, 357, **359**, 364
   internal nominal rate of return,
      346–348, 350, 351, **355**, 356, **358**, 361,
      361, 364
   internal nominal rate of return with

smoothed capital gains, 351–352, **355**, 356, **359**, **361**, 366
internal own rate of return, 348–351, **355**, 356, **358**, **361**, 365
research suggestions on, 366–367
Recapitalizations, and revaluations, 388
Recession, and productivity slowdown, 225
Refundings, and revaluations, 388
Regression price index, 61–62. *See also* Hedonic price indexes
Regression-based price indexes, and BEA, 81
Relative efficiency, vii-viii, ix, 2–3
and automobile depreciation study, **286**, 286–287
and capital input measure, 22–28
linearly declining pattern of, 23–26, 27
and vintage price functions, 11, 16
Renewal equation, 7
Rental prices
of capital goods of different ages, 5
and capital services price, 26–27
and depreciation, 20, 29
in hedonic functions, **138–141**, **143**
in theory of hedonic functions, 129
Rental prices for capital assets, 332–334
alternative formulas for, 333
in computer price study, 90
data for study of, 367–368
derivation of formulas for, 336–341, 344
rate-of-return specifications for, 345–356, 365–366
rate-of-return specifications for (empirical results), 356–364
research suggestions on, 366–367
Rented capital, in USPS study, 439, **444**, 445, **446**
Replacement, 5–6, 456. *See also* Retirement
and capital input price, 10, 11
and depreciation, 456–457
and geometric efficiency decline, 13
and mortality distribution, 5–6
rate of, 7, 8–9
rates of (USPS study), 422, 427, 428
Replacement distribution, 7, 10–11
Resource-cost approach, 133
Retirement, 265. *See also* Replacement
and Baily hypothesis, 230
in USPS study, 422, 427
Retirement distribution, 265
for automobile depreciation study, 271–272, 274, 280, 288n.5
Revaluation, 261–262
and corporate profits, 388
and tax-exempt bonds, 384
and vintage price model, 237–238

Revaluation, debt. *See also* Debt, credit market
for bank loans, 385
by nonfinancial corporations, 374

Schumpeter, Joseph, 495
Semiconductor main memory, 45, 50–51
Service lives
BEA estimates of, 21–22, 460, **461**
and federal government capital/investment study, 460
Service price, capital, 12–13, 14
Shadow price of capital, and rate of return specifications, 353
Shopping mall problem, 459
Short-term financial instruments, holding gains and losses on, **378–379**, 379
Software
in computer price study, 91–92
manufacturers' supplying of, 91
and powerful hardware, 199
Solow, R. M., 488, 498
Sources of Economic Growth (Denison), 23
Speed of computer, as characteristic, 40–41, 46, 57, **58**, 137–150
Stanford Conference, 491
State and local government, federally financed capital of, 456
State and local government credit market liabilities, market-to-par ratios for, 394, **395–396**, **397–398**, 399, **400–405**
Stock, capital. *See* Capital stock
Straight-line age-price profile, 238
Straight-line pattern of relative efficiency, 3, 23, 24, 25, 27
Strong, John, 503
Structures deflators problems, 293–294, 326
and BEA indexes, 295–306
and categories of structures deflators, 295
and Commerce construction deflators, 293, 320–323
and heterogeneity of construction output, 294–295
improvement suggests for, 323–325
and overdeflation dispute, 306–320, 326
Superlative index number, 193, 199
Survey of Current Business, automobile data from, 262
Switching equipment (Bell System), 493–494

t-identification, 156, 157
Tape drives, price indexes for, **188**, 189, **190**, **191**, 191–192
Tax policy, and Tobin's q, 232
Tax Reform Act (TRA), (1986), 259, 284–285, 504

Tax-exempt bonds of nonfinancial corporations, market and par values of, 382, 384–485
Taxation
  Alternative Minimum Tax, 260, 284–285
  and depreciation, 502
  investment tax credit, 502–503 (*see also* Investment Tax Credit)
  and productivity slowdown, 225
Technical change
  determinants of, 503–504
  and economic growth, 485, 486, 489–490
  new models as information on, 54
  and productivity, 504
  and quality of capital goods, 16–17
Technological frontier, 89, 158–159, 218
Technological leapfrogging, 41, 157–159
Technologically induced disequilibrium
  and frontier- vs. all-models index, 218
  and hedonic model, 38, 41, 42, 46–47, 54, 56, 60, 63
  and 1972–1984 indexes, 184–185
Technology
  and Bell system changes, 493–494
  and computer processors, 41–42
  and growth slowdown, 500
  and hedonic equation, 43
  and hedonic function or index, 130–131, 132–133
  and mineral base process industry, 495, 496
  for U.S. Postal Service, 413
Technology, information on. *See* Information on technology
Technology variables, vs. quality characteristics (computer price study), 116
Technology-capital relation. *See* Capital-technology relation
Theory of hedonic functions, 129–131
Theory of hedonic price indexes, 131–133
Time series price index, 193
Time-Series Generalized Fisher Ideal (TGFI) index, 193, 195, 197–198, 199
Time-sharing capability, as hedonic function variable, 151
Tobin's average q, 226, 232, 234
Total factor productivity (TFP), 488
  measurement of for USPS, 410
Trends in American Economic Growth (Denison), 22, 23
Trucks, as vintage price function illustration, 16
Turner Construction Company index, **296**, 300, **303**, **307**, 318, 321, 322, 419

Unbundling, 72n.14
  and computer price study, 91–92

by IBM, 91
  and interpreting of price indexes, 175, 177–178
Unit price deflators, for construction, 324–325
United Kingdom, computer prices in, 178, 179
UNIVAC I, 79, 111
U.S. Postal Service study, 409–410
  and accounting changes, 414–416
  benchmarks in, 427–429
  and capital input from owned capital, 434, 436–439, **440–443**
  and capital stock, 429–434, **435**, **436**
  and investment, 411–416, **417–418**, 429, **430–431**
  and measurement of capital, 410–411
  perpetual inventory method in, 411–412, 416, 434
  price indexes in, 416, 419–422, **423–426**
  and rented capital, 439, **444**, 445, **446**
  on replacement rates, 422, 427, 428
  and total capital input, 445, **447**
Used asset prices
  and federal-government capital stock study, 457, 458–460
  and obsolescence hypothesis, 226 (*see also* Obsolescence hypothesis)
  vintage price approach to, 234–239 (*see also* Vintage price approach)
User cost of capital, and automobile depreciation study, 259, 283–286, 287. *See also* Depreciation study
"User friendly" attributes, 151
User-value approach, 133
Utilization
  and Baily hypothesis, 231
  and productivity slowdown, 233
  in vintage price approach, 234, 235, 237

Value of capital, vintage price approach to, 234
Variety of computer, 128
Vehicles. *See also* Business-leased automobiles
  truck illustration, 16
  USPS benchmark for, 427
  USPS price index for, 419, **425**
Vintage accounts, 9, 10
  and capital stock estimates, 23
  and geometric decline in efficiency, 13
Vintage aggregation of assets, 341–342
Vintage capital model (Solow), 249
Vintage distribution of assets, in USPS study, 422
Vintage of capital, 1
  and energy, 232–233
  and relative efficiency, 2–3

Vintage price approach, 234–237
  alternatives to, 20–21
  data for, 239–241, **242**, *243–246*
  econometric model for, 237–239
  results for, 247–254
Vintage price functions, 11–21
  for commercial and industrial build-
    ings, 17–18
  and depreciation, 20
  econometric model for, 14–16, 17
  estimation of, 18
  and geometric efficiency decline, 14
  and obsolescence, 261
Volatility effect or statistics, 356–357, **361**,
  362, **363**, 364, 365

Wealth, national, and federal govern-
  ment capital, 476
Weighted instruction mix measures,
  147–149
"Whetstone" measure, 149
Why Growth Rates Differ (Denison), 23
Winfrey distribution, in BEA estimates,
  457–458
Winfrey S-3 curve, 271, 274